# Contents

**Traveling exhibition** In New York, provocative works of art aren't restricted to museums.

**Edited and designed by Time Out New York Guides**
**627 Broadway, seventh floor**
**New York, NY 10012**
**Tel: 212-539-4444**
**Fax: 212-253-1174**
**E-mail: guides@timeoutny.com**
**www.timeout.com/newyork**

**Guides/Online Director** Shawn Dahl
**Guides Editor** Betsy Beckmann **Guides Designer** Caroline Jackson
**Associate Project Editors** Connell Barrett, Joanna Milter **Guides Copy Editor** Ann Lien
**Guides/Online Assistant Editor** Andrea Delbanco **Guides/Online Editorial Coordinator** Heather Tierney
**Copy Editor** Elizabeth Gall **Researchers** Jodi Lynn, Kirsten Matthew, Jessica Reed

**With Time Out New York**
**E-mail: letters@timeoutny.com**
**www.timeoutny.com**

**President/Editor-in-Chief** Cyndi Stivers
**Publisher** Alison Tocci
**Financial Director** Daniel P. Reilly

**Production Director** Jonathan Bruce **Technology Director** Daniel G. Hernandez
**Production Manager** Nestor Cervantes **Associate Production Manager** Jim Schuessler
**Advertising Production Manager** Tom Oesau
**Advertising Production Coordinator** Andrea Dunn **Advertising Designers** Ilan Altman, Jamie Dunst, Jay Guillermo

**Advertising Director** Anne Perton **Advertising Manager** Tony Monteleone
**Senior Account Managers** Dan Kenefick, Jim Lally, Ridwana Lloyd-Bey, Melissa Norberg
**Account Managers** Emily Kelton, Claudia Pedala, Paula Sarapin
**Assistant to the Publisher** Maggie Puddu

**Associate Publisher/Marketing** Marisa Guillen Fariña
**North American Guides Publicity and Marketing Associate** Rosella Albanese

**For Time Out Guides Ltd**
**Universal House**
**251 Tottenham Court Road**
**London W1T 7AB**
**Tel: +44 (0)20 7813 3000**
**Fax: +44 (0)20 7813 6001**
**E-mail: guides@timeout.com**
**www.timeout.com**

**Editorial Director** Peter Fiennes **Series Editor** Ruth Jarvis **Group Art Director** John Oakey **Art Director** Mandy Martin
**Deputy Series Editor** Jonathan Cox **Guides Coordinator** Anna Norman

**Group Commercial Director** Lesley Gill **Sales Director** Mark Phillips

**Chairman** Tony Elliott **Chief Operating Officer** Kevin Ellis **Managing Director** Mike Hardwick
**Chief Financial Officer** Richard Waterlow **Group Marketing Director** Christine Cort **Marketing Manager** Mandy Martinez
**Group General Manager** Nichola Coulthard **Guides Production Director** Mark Lamond

**Chapters in this guide were written or updated by:**
**History** Connell Barrett **Architecture** Howard Halle **The Sky's the Limit** Kevin Pratt **Fringe Scene** David Cote **Only in New York** Connell Barrett **Museums** Billie Cohen (nonart museums), Linda Yablonsky (art museums) **Downtown** Mia Sulpor **Midtown** Erica Kennedy **Uptown** Lesa Griffith **Brooklyn** Michael Gollust **Queens** Kate Papacosma **The Bronx** Joanna Milter **Staten Island** Joanna Milter **Tour New York** Guides staff **Accommodations** Andrea Delbanco **Bars** and **Restaurants** adapted from *Time Out New York Eating & Drinking 2003 Guide; Rosé-colored glasses* Randall Lane *Chain reaction* Maile Carpenter and Reed Tucker *The Upper crust* Connell Barrett **Shopping & Services** Sarah Breckenridge; *Southern comforts* Katherine Wheelock; *Butt, bath, and beyond* Kiki Barksdale; *Sugar shacks* Andrea Delbanco **By Season** Billie Cohen **Art Galleries** Linda Yablonsky; *Street art* Michelle Memran **Books & Poetry** Mimi Kriegsman **Cabaret & Comedy** Joe Grossman (comedy), H. Scott Jolley (cabaret) **Clubs** Bruce Tantum **Film & TV** Darron D'Addario **Gay & Lesbian** Les Simpson **Kids' Stuff** Barbara Aria **Music** Elisabeth Vincentelli, Jay Ruttenberg, Mike Wolf (pop, rock, etc), K. Leander Williams (jazz, world music), Margeaux Watson (hip-hop, R&B), Steve Smith (classical); *This is it* Elisabeth Vincentelli **Sports & Fitness** Brett Martin **Theater & Dance** Jason Zinoman (theater), Gia Kourlas (dance) **Trips Out of Town** Ann Lien; *Inn Coming!* Beth Greenfield.

**Photographs by** Jeremy Balderson

**Additional photographs courtesy of** Library of Congress, Prints and Photographs Division, 7–18; Mayor's Photo Unit, 19; Paul Warchol, 22; The Lower Manhattan Development Corporation, 30; Susana Bates, 34; John Bigelow Taylor, courtesy the Frick Gallery, 43; Brooklyn Museum of Art, 45; Garibaldi-Meucci Museum, 52; Seth Taras, courtesy the Museum of Sex, 53; Patrik Rytikangas, 63, 67, 68, 90, 273, 355, 389; Jodi Lynn, 73; Jessica Reed, 75; Anna Kirtiklis, 76, 100, 155, 157, 260, 294; Brooks Walker, courtesy the Metropolitan Museum of At, 93; Apollo Theater, 105; Elizabeth Felicella, 119; Nadaman Hakubai, 145; City Club, 146; Hudson, 149; W Times Square, 151; Weston Times Square, 153; Carlton Arms, 159; On the Ave, 162; Inbal Sivan, 172, 237; John Peters, 135, 175, 206; Aran Fedor, 177; Philip Friedman, 179, 185, 191, 197, 200, 201, 202; Ken Shung, 180, 183, 194; Michelle Mercurio, 188; James Leighton, 186, 192; Rod Morata, 193; Katherine Aguilar, 199; Andrea Delbanco, 205; Paul Kolnik, courtesy the New York City Ballet, 249, 345; Michael Toomey, courtesy of Bike New York, 250; Ethan Lercher, courtesy Bryant Park Restoration Corporation, 251; Nathan's Famous, 253; National Choral Council, 255; John Branch, 263; Robb Leigh Davis, 285; Kimberlee Hewitt courtesy the Brooklyn Museum of Art, 297; Shawn Ehlers, 306; DFA Records, 311; Robert Smith, 317; Don Perdue, 319; Carol Rosegg, 320; Laurie Lambrecht, 322; Steve Smith/Getty Images, courtesy the New Jersey MetroStars, 326; Robert Laberge/Getty Images, courtesy the USTA, 327; Joan Marcus, 335; Tom Power, courtesy Second Stage Theater, 339; Eric Hall, courtesy Danspace Project, 343; Piro Patton, courtesy Williamsburg Art neXus, 346; Historic Hudson Valley, 347; Nino Ruisi, 349; The Enclave Inn, 351; Mick Hales, courtesy Historic Hudson Valley, 353.
**Photo page 28** by Charlie Samuels (www.charliesamuels.com) and reprinted with the kind permission of Charlie Samuels and Creative Time. *Tribute in Light* initiative: John Bennett, Gustavo Bonevardi, Richard Nash Gould, Julian LaVerdiere, Paul Marantz, Paul Myoda. Produced by Creative Time and the Municipal Art Society with support from the Battery Park City Authority.

**Maps by** J.S. Graphics (john@jsgraphics.co.uk); maps on pages 408–411 reproduced by kind permission of the Metropolitan Transportation Authority.

# Introduction



When people think of New York, they think *big*. Big buildings, big Broadway shows, big ideas, big money, big attitude. But when visitors first explore Manhattan, the most famous of the city's five boroughs, many are surprised: It's tiny, relatively speaking. The slender sliver of an island comprises just 23 of New York's 309 square miles—that's half the space taken up by Peoria, Illinois.

Of course, there's a lot more to do here. The lack of real estate gives Manhattan a close-knit (if cramped) feeling that makes it superbly easy to navigate. Everything is a short walk, cab or subway ride away: countless chic (and cheap) restaurants, remarkable museums, bawdy burlesque shows, dazzling emporiums, brilliantly designed gardens and parks, and history at every turn.

Be sure to venture past the island's waterfront; tourists and locals alike tend to overlook New York's outer boroughs. *Big* mistake. You don't want to miss attractions such as the **Brooklyn Botanic Garden** *(see* **Seasons in the sun**, *page 112)*, the **Museum of Modern Art**, temporarily housed in Queens *(see* **Modern convenience**, *page 118)*, **Yankee Stadium** in the Bronx *(see page 324)* and the scenic jaunt to Staten Island on its eponymous—and free—ferry *(see page 132)*.

The city's most prized possession is its people. New Yorkers, like Americans everywhere, still feel the effects of the terrorist attack of September 11, 2001. Remarkably, the community spirit with which most citizens responded to that tragedy continues to cushion urban life. The public, both in New York and abroad, have been keeping tabs on the power brokers working to rebuild the World Trade Center site, to ensure that something worthy of New York rises again in lower Manhattan *(see* **The Sky's the Limit**, *page 28)*.

While certain aspects of the metropolis has changed dramatically in recent years—the dot-com boom bust, coupled with the city's multibillion-dollar deficits—much has not. New York remains the nation's cultural capital, and its artists, writers and performers (along with the institutions that bring their art to the public) have met a tough economy with scrappy inventiveness. What's more, America's largest city is still America's safest big city. Bucking national trends, violent crime in New York continued an 11-year free fall in 2002 and the murder rate fell to a 30-year low—despite higher unemployment and a police force focused on fighting terror as well as street crime.

If the big city is becoming somehow smaller, more neighborly in its approach to daily life, it continues to think big. Reinvention has long been the engine of New York, and this is a particularly splendid time to visit: a moment in which the city actively reimagines itself.

## ABOUT THE TIME OUT CITY GUIDES

The *Time Out New York Guide* is one of an expanding series of Time Out City Guides—now numbering more than 40—produced by the people behind London and New York's successful weekly listings magazines. All the guides are written and updated by resident experts who strive to provide the most current information you'll need to explore the city, whether you're a local or first-time visitor.

The staff of *Time Out New York* magazine worked on this 11th edition of the *Time Out New York Guide. TONY* has been "the obsessive guide to impulsive entertainment" for all inhabitants of the city (and a few passers-through) for seven years. Some chapters have been rewritten from scratch; all have been thoroughly revised, and offer new feature boxes.

## THE LOWDOWN ON THE LISTINGS

While navigating this guide and the city, there are a few facts you should know. All listings include addresses, telephone numbers, travel directions, opening times, admission prices and credit-card information. We've given up-to-date details on facilities, services and events, all checked and correct at press time. However, owners and managers can—and often do—change their policies. It's always best to call and check the when, where and how much.

▶ For an online version of this guide, including many suggested itineraries, check out **www.timeout.com/newyork**.

▶ Visit the website of *Time Out New York*, the weekly listings magazine, at **www.timeoutny.com**.

# Time Out

# New York

timeout.com/newyork

Penguin Books

PENGUIN BOOKS

Published by the Penguin Group
Penguin Books Ltd, 80 Strand, London WC2R ORL, England
Penguin Books USA Inc., 375 Hudson Street, New York, New York 10014, USA
Penguin Books Australia Ltd, 250 Camberwell Road, Camberwell, Victoria 3124, Australia
Penguin Books Canada Ltd, 10 Alcorn Avenue, Toronto, Ontario, Canada M4V 3B2
Penguin Books (NZ) Ltd, cnr Rosedale and Airborne Roads, Albany, Auckland, New Zealand

Penguin Books Ltd, Registered Offices: Harmondsworth, Middlesex, England

First published 1990
Second edition 1992
Third edition 1994
Fourth edition 1996
Fifth edition 1997
Sixth edition 1998
Seventh edition 1999
Eighth edition 2000
Ninth edition 2001
Tenth edition 2002

**11th edition 2003**

10 9 8 7 6 5 4 3 2 1



Printed and bound by Cayfosa-Quebecor, Ctra. de Caldes, Km 3, 08 130 Sta, Perpètua de Mogoda, Barcelona, Spain



**Manhattan transfer** Grand Central Terminal is an elegant portal to suburbia.

MetLife
GRAND CENTRAL
TERMINAL

Throughout the book, you'll find bold-faced items (sights or restaurants, for example) for which we give the detailed listings information within that chapter, or in one that is cross-referenced. For your convenience, we've included cross-reference boxes throughout (they're outlined in red, like the one on the previous page).

### PRICES AND PAYMENT

We have noted whether places such as shops, hotels and restaurants accept credit cards or not, but have only listed the major cards: American Express (**AmEx**), Diners Club (**DC**), Discover (**Disc**), MasterCard (**MC**) and Visa (**V**). Some businesses will also accept other cards. Virtually all venues will accept U.S.-dollar travelers' checks issued by a major financial institution (such as American Express).

The prices we've listed should be treated as guidelines, not gospel. Fluctuating exchange rates and inflation can cause prices—especially in stores and restaurants—to change overnight. While every effort has been made to ensure the accuracy of this guide, the publishers cannot accept responsibility for any errors it may contain. If you find things altered beyond recognition, ask why—and then write to let us know. Our goal is to furnish the most accurate information available, so we always want to know if you've been badly treated or overcharged.

### TELEPHONE NUMBERS

All telephone numbers in this guide are written as dialed within the United States. Manhattan's area codes are 212 and 646; the ones in Brooklyn, Queens, the Bronx and Staten Island are 718 and 347; generally (but not always), 917 is reserved for cellular phones and pagers. You must dial 1, then the area code and the seven-digit phone number (from abroad, dial 00 first as well), even if the place you're calling is in the same area code as the one you're calling from. Phone numbers beginning with 800, 877 and 888 are free of charge when called from anywhere in the U.S. When numbers are listed as letters for easy recall (e.g., 800-AIR-RIDE), dial the corresponding numbers on the telephone keypad.

### ESSENTIAL INFORMATION

Turn to the **Directory** chapter at the back of this guide for all the practical information you might need for visiting the city, including visa and customs procedures, access for people with disabilities, emergency telephone numbers, a list of helpful websites and how to use the subway system. The Directory starts on page 355.

**A policeman's best friend** A memorial in Union Square Park honors fallen K-9 officers.

**McMarquee** The Golden Arches get star billing at McDonald's Times Square.

### THE LAY OF THE LAND

We've included cross streets in all of our addresses, so you can find your way more easily. And there's a series of fully indexed **color street maps**, a map of the surrounding metropolitan area, and subway and bus maps at the back of the guide, starting on page 389. The very last page is **Key Sights**—a quick list of the famous places you've heard about; the directions are given so you can quickly get started on your sightseeing.

### LET US KNOW WHAT YOU THINK

We hope you enjoy the *Time Out New York Guide,* and we'd like to know what you think of it. We welcome tips on places that you believe we should include in future editions and appreciate your feedback of our choices. There's a reader's reply card at the back of this book. Or please e-mail us at guides@timeoutny.com.

## A note about our advertisers

We would like to emphasize that no establishment has been included in this guide because it has advertised in any of our publications, and no payment of any kind has influenced any review. The opinions given in this book are those of *Time Out* writers and are entirely independent.

# Perspective



## Feature boxes



**Railroaded** The original Penn Station, once a grand gateway to New York, was demolished in the 1960s.

# History

## How a Dutch trading post became the capital of the world

### THE PROSPECTORS

Before Manhattan ever lured visitors with its skyscrapers and street-corner spectacles—in fact, long before it was even called Manhattan—this once lush, forested region offered the finest natural harbor on the East Coast. The island was protected from the elements and strategically located along a vast river—in short, it was the greatest trading post Mother Nature ever created. New York became an attractive destination for immigrants seeking their fortunes, and at every stage in its history, the buzzword has been *commerce.*

The first European to get a glimpse of the island was Giovanni da Verrazano, a Florentine sailing under the French flag and searching for the fabled Northwest Passage to China. In 1524, he sought refuge from a storm in what is now called New York Harbor; later, he navigated a small boat into the Upper Bay, where he was greeted by the local Native Americans. Today, Verrazano is remembered by the majestic bridge that links Staten Island with Brooklyn and bears his name.

It would be 85 years before the next European arrived. Henry Hudson, who was backed by the Dutch East India Company, was also looking for the Northwest Passage. He instead found…Albany.

### LET'S MAKE A DEAL

Four years after Hudson reached the area, a trading post—the beginning of a Dutch settlement—was established and named Fort Orange (present-day Albany)in 1624. In 1621, Holland granted the Dutch West India Company a long-term trade and governing monopoly over New Netherlands (the area between the Connecticut and Delaware Rivers) and elsewhere. Soon, the first Dutch settlers, about 30 families, arrived in the area. By 1626, when the first director-general (governor), Peter Minuit, took power, about 300 Europeans lived on the southern tip of Manhattan.

In an exchange now regarded as the greatest real-estate swindle in history, Minuit gave a Munsee Indian chief a few trinkets and some blankets (which scholars have revalued from the famous $24 to a still bargain-basement $600)

**High society** By 1900, majestic Trinity Church was no longer the city's tallest structure.

and got him to sign an incomprehensible document. Minuit then assumed the deal was sealed; the Dutch had bought themselves the 13-mile-long island of Manhattan. Of course, like many real-estate deals that seem too good to be true, this one was a scam: The Native Americans had very different ideas about property and could not conceive of owning land, let alone in perpetuity.

It also turned out to be a shakedown. Once the Europeans had moved in, they wouldn't move out. The Dutch settlement tried to tax native hunters and prevent them from owning firearms, and enforced harsh penalties for petty crimes. It was only a matter of time before, in 1643, a bloody war broke out between the Dutch and the Native Americans, lasting two years. Guess who won?

Little trace of New York's original inhabitants remains, apart from various Munsee place-names, such as Canarsie ("grassy place"), Rockaway ("sandy place"), Maspeth ("bad water place") and Matinecock ("at the lookout point").

## PEG-LEG PETE

After the war, the colonists and Native Americans continued to engage in bloody confrontations: More than 100 Indians were massacred between 1643 and 1655. In 1647, the Dutch West India Company hired Peter Stuyvesant to keep the peace. Stuyvesant's right leg had been shattered by a cannonball—hence his nickname, Peg-Leg Pete. He ordered a defensive ditch and wall (today's Wall Street) to be built along the northern end of what was by then called New Amsterdam. A commercial infrastructure was built (banks, brokers' offices, wharves), and chandleries and taverns soon lined the waterfront. The city's capitalist culture was born.

And so was its first locally administered government. Stuyvesant founded a municipal assembly, and encouraged the education of the colony's children. In his 17 years as governor, the settlement doubled in size. The town grew more cosmopolitan, expanding to include English, French, Portuguese and Scandinavian settlers, and the area's first African slaves. Both English and Dutch were spoken.

But Peg-Leg was a little too authoritarian. His intolerance of Jewish refugees and Quaker leader John Bowne provoked scoldings from his bosses, who forced Stuyvesant to make the settlement a haven for religious freedom.

## THE BRITISH ARE COMING!

Perhaps the Dutch West India Company tried to expand its colony too quickly. By the 1660s, less than four decades after the Dutch had settled the area, New Amsterdam was nearly bankrupt. When four British warships sailed into the harbor one day in August 1664, the population abandoned the fortifications Stuyvesant had built and welcomed Captain Richard Nicolls and his crew. New Amsterdam was renamed after the British king's brother, the Duke of York.

By 1700, New York's population had reached about 20,000. The colony was a big money-maker for the British, but it was hardly what you would call a stable concern. In 1683, to cut administrative costs, the British tried to consolidate New York, New Jersey and New England into a single dominion. The colonies rebelled, and after nearly two years of battle, ten men were hanged for treason. In the 1730s, John Peter Zenger's *New-York Weekly Journal* provoked gasps by accusing British governor William Cosby's administration of corruption. Zenger's trial on libel charges resulted in a landmark decision: The newspaper publisher was acquitted because, as his lawyer argued, the truth cannot be libelous. The Zenger verdict set the stage for the First Amendment to the Constitution, which established the principle of freedom of the press. This was just the beginning of trouble for the British.

**Apples and oranges** Mulberry Street was once a mobile market of pushcarts.

## REVOLUTION—AND THE BATTLE FOR NEW YORK

In British-run outposts in Boston, Philadelphia and Virginia, progressive thinkers such as John Adams, Benjamin Franklin and Thomas Jefferson spread the ideals of democratic government, while merchants in those settlements chafed under ever-rising British taxes. New York, especially, felt the pinch as the British struggled to pay off debts accumulated in colonial wars against France. The colonies declared independence on July 4, 1776, but the British weren't about to give up New York—its economic value and strategic position on the Hudson River were too important. That summer, British commander Lord Howe led 200 ships into New York Harbor and occupied the town. New Yorkers vented their fury by toppling a gilded equestrian statue of George III that stood on Bowling Green.

The war's first major confrontation, the Battle of Long Island, actually took place in present-day Brooklyn. American General George Washington had garrisoned his troops along what is now Flatbush Avenue near Prospect Park. His army, outnumbered two to one, was routed, and they retreated to Manhattan. (Washington slept at what is now called the Morris-Jumel Mansion in Washington Heights; *see page 107.*) On September 11, 1776, Benjamin Franklin met Lord Howe in Staten Island's Billop Manor House, now known as the Conference House *(see page 130),* but he refused Howe's offer to make all colonists full-fledged British subjects. "America cannot return to the domination of Great Britain," Franklin said firmly.

Life in occupied New York was grim. The town teemed with British soldiers and loyalists fleeing the American army. Fires destroyed much of the city, and many people starved to death. When the Crown surrendered in 1783, bitter British troops in New York greased the city's flagpole, hoping to make it

# NYC 101

A look at pivotal moments in New York history

**1524** Giovanni da Verrazano is the first European to visit Manhattan.
**1609** Henry Hudson sails into New York Harbor.
**1624** The Dutch settle New Amsterdam.
**1626** First governor Peter Minuit arrives and "buys" Manhattan from the Indians. New Amsterdam's population: 300.
**1647** Peter Stuyvesant is made governor.
**1661** The Dutch colony nearly goes bankrupt.
**1662** Quaker John Bowne's struggle wins the right of religious freedom for the people of New Amsterdam.
**1664** The British invade; New Amsterdam is renamed New York.
**1733** John Peter Zenger's *New-York Weekly Journal* criticizes the British, sowing the seeds of free speech in America.
**1754** King's College (which will become Columbia University) is founded.
**1776** The Declaration of Independence is adopted. The Revolutionary War rages; the British occupy New York.
**1783** The defeated British army leaves New York.
**1785–90** New York serves as the new nation's capital.
**1811** The Commissioners' Plan creates the grid system for the city's future growth.
**1812–14** America fights another war with Britain. New York is isolated from international trade.
**1837** Financial panic ruins all but three city banks.
**1840s** Immigrants begin flooding into the city.
**1851** The *New York Daily Times,* which would later become the *The New York Times,* publishes its first issue.
**1857** Frederick Law Olmsted and Calvert Vaux lay out plans for Central Park.
**1859** Cooper Union, the first American school open to all—regardless of race, religion or gender—is established.
**1860** Abraham Lincoln is elected president.
**1861** The Civil War erupts.
**1863** Conscription causes riots in New York.
**1865** The Union wins, and slavery is abolished.
**1870** The Metropolitan Museum of Art is founded.
**1882** Thousands demanding an eight-hour work day march in Union Square.
**1883** The Brooklyn Bridge is completed.
**1886** The Statue of Liberty is dedicated.
**1890** Photojournalist Jacob A. Riis publishes *How the Other Half Lives,* spurring new housing regulations.
**1895** The New York Public Library is founded.

harder for the Revolutionaries to raise the banner of the new republic.

But the war was won. On December 4, Washington joined his officers for an emotional farewell dinner at Fraunces Tavern on Pearl Street (now the Fraunces Tavern Museum; *see page 51*), where the general announced his retirement. In 1785, New York became the nation's capital, so when Congress looked to Washington to lead the country, he returned to the city. On April 30, 1789, in the Old Federal Hall (on the same site as the present one, on Wall Street), he took the oath of office as the first president of the United States of America.

## THE FIRST U.S. CAPITAL

Before the Revolution, Alexander Hamilton, a young immigrant from the Caribbean island of Nevis, studied at King's College (now Columbia University) and hobnobbed with colonial high society; he married into a powerful merchant family after serving under Washington during the war. Hamilton, who helped create the Bank of New York in 1784, was appointed the first U.S. Treasury secretary in 1789. During his term, Hamilton initiated pro-business measures that nurtured New York's ascension as a financial center. In 1791, he established the nation's central banking system—much to the horror of Thomas Jefferson, who envisioned a simple agrarian economy.

The fledgling nation's capital was moved to Philadelphia in 1791, then in 1800, to a new city built on mosquito-infested swampland—Washington, D.C. By that time, with business booming and the port prospering, New York's financial clout was secured, and it has remained the country's capital of capitalism.

## CROWD CONTROL

By 1800, more than 60,000 people lived in what is now lower Manhattan. Rents were high, housing demands were great, and development had been scattershot. The local government

**1898** Manhattan, Brooklyn, Queens, Staten Island and the Bronx are incorporated into New York City, creating the world's second-largest city.
**1902** The world's first skyscraper—the Fuller Building (now called the Flatiron)—is built.
**1907** Metered taxicabs are introduced.
**1911** The Triangle Shirtwaist factory fire sparks the introduction of workplace-safety regulations.
**1917** America enters World War I.
**1920** Prohibition begins; speakeasies open throughout the city. Women win the right to vote.
**1929** The Wall Street stock-market crash on October 29 plunges the nation into the Great Depression. The Museum of Modern Art opens nine days after the crash.
**1931** The Empire State Building is completed.
**1932** Franklin D. Roosevelt is elected president; his New Deal funds massive public-works projects.
**1933** Prohibition ends.
**1939** World's Fair opens in Flushing Meadows-Corona Park, Queens.
**1941** America enters World War II.
**1945** The war ends. United Nations is formed and becomes based in New York within a year.
**1947** Brooklyn Dodger Jackie Robinson breaks baseball's color barrier.
**1962** Lincoln Center opens.
**1965** The entire city endures a 25-hour power blackout.
**1968** A student sit-in shuts down Columbia University.
**1973** The World Trade Center is completed.
**1975** A fiscal crisis puts the city on the verge of bankruptcy.
**1977** Another citywide blackout. More than 3,000 people are arrested for looting, rioting and arson.
**1978** Mayor Edward Koch presides over an economic turnaround.
**1987** Another Wall Street crash.
**1989** David Dinkins is elected the city's first black mayor.
**1993** Terrorists detonate a bomb in the basement of the World Trade Center. Rudolph Giuliani is elected the city's first Republican mayor in 28 years.
**1996** TWA Flight 800 crashes off the coast of Long Island, killing all 230 aboard.
**1997** The murder rate falls to a 30-year low. Disney arrives on 42nd Street.
**1998** New York City falls to 112th on a list of the most dangerous cities in America.
**1999** The Dow tops 10,000. The city mourns the death of John F. Kennedy Jr.
**2000** Hillary Rodham Clinton is elected as the state's junior senator to Washington.
**2001** On September 11, two hijacked jets fly into the Twin Towers, killing 2,801 and demolishing the World Trade Center. Mike Bloomberg is elected the city's 108th mayor.
**2002** Six initial proposals for rebuilding the World Trade Center site are rejected as dreary and unimaginative. Mayor Bloomberg announces budget cuts in response to a fiscal crisis. The Dow hits a five-year low of 7,528. New York City's population: 8 million.

decided that the city needed a more orderly way to sell and develop land. A group of city officials, called the Commissioners, came up with a solution: the famous "grid" street system of 1811. It ignored all the existing roads—with the exception of Broadway, which ran the length of Manhattan, following an old Indian trail—and organized the island into a rectangular grid with wide, numbered avenues running north to south and narrower streets running river to river.

When the 362-mile Erie Canal opened in 1825—linking New York to the Midwest via the Hudson River and the Great Lakes—the port city became even more vital to the young country. Along with the new railroads, this trade route facilitated the making of many fortunes, and New York's merchants and traders thrived.

## THE ABOLITIONISTS

Today, the African Burial Ground near City Hall in lower Manhattan preserves the chilling memory of a time when New York was second only to Charleston, South Carolina, as a slave-trade port. As late as the 1700s, such prominent local families as the Beekmans and Van Cortlandts increased their fortunes by trafficking in human beings.

But as Northern commercial cities became less reliant on manual labor, dependence on slavery waned—and the abolitionist movement bloomed. When New York State abolished slavery in 1827, the city celebrated with two days of fireworks and parades. While the South remained defiant, the antislavery movement flourished in the Northeast.

In New York, the cause was kept alive in the columns of Horace Greeley's *Tribune* newspaper and in the sermons of Henry Ward Beecher, pastor of the Plymouth Church of the Pilgrims on Orange Street in Brooklyn. (He was the brother of Harriet Beecher Stowe, who wrote *Uncle Tom's Cabin.*) Beecher once shocked his congregation by auctioning a slave from his pulpit and using the proceeds to buy her freedom.

## NEW YORK AND THE CIVIL WAR

Preservation of the Union was the hot issue of the 1860 presidential campaign. Abraham Lincoln wavered in his position on slavery—until one fateful trip to New York that year, when he addressed a meeting in the Great Hall of Cooper Union (the first American school open to all, regardless of race, religion or gender). In his speech, Lincoln declared, "Neither let us be slandered from our duty by false accusations against us, nor frightened from it by menaces of destruction to the government nor of dungeons to ourselves. Let us have faith that right makes might, and in that faith let us, to the end, dare to do our duty as we understand it."

The newly formed Republican Party moved to make Lincoln its presidential candidate. The Southern states promptly seceded from the Union and became the Confederate States of America. The Civil War had begun.

## WHITE RIOT

When Lincoln started a military draft in 1863, the streets of New York erupted in rioting. Although New York sided with the Union against the Confederacy, there was considerable sympathy for the South, particularly among poor Irish and German immigrants, who feared that they would lose jobs to freed slaves.

For three days, New York raged. African-Americans were assaulted in the streets; Horace Greeley's office was attacked twice; Brooks Brothers was looted. In all, between $1.5 and $2 million in property was destroyed and total casualties (predominantly blacks) are estimated to be as high as 1,000. The violence came to an end only when Union troops, returning from victory at Gettysburg, subdued the city. The Draft Riots remain the single worst civilian uprising in American history—bloodier than Watts, Crown Heights and the Los Angeles riots of 1992.

Apart from the riots, New York emerged from the Civil War unscathed. The city had not seen any actual fighting—and it had prospered as the

**Cry freedom** Born a slave, Sojourner Truth became a vocal abolitionist and preacher after she gained freedom and moved to NYC.

**Fountain of youth** Opened in 1859, the Bethesda Terrace fountain, *Angel of the Waters,* is just one of Central Park's many restorative attractions.

financial center of the North. As immigration soared, so did the wealth of New York's upper-class captains of industry.

## HIGH FINANCE

Jay Gould made enormous profits in the stock market during the Civil War by having the outcome of military engagements secretly cabled to him and trading on the results before they became public knowledge. Gould, together with another master swindler, Jim Fisk, seduced shipping magnate Cornelius Vanderbilt into buying vast quantities of Erie Railroad bonds before the bottom dropped out of the market. (Vanderbilt had the resources to sit out the crisis and the grace to call Gould "the smartest man in America.") Vanderbilt, industrialist Andrew Carnegie and banker J.P. Morgan consolidated their fortunes by controlling the railroads. John D. Rockefeller made his money in oil, at one point owning 95 percent of the refineries in the United States.

All of these men—each in his own way representing a blend of capitalist genius and robber baron—erected glorious mansions in New York (*see chapters* **Uptown**, **Museums** *and* **Music**). Their homes now house some of the city's finest art collections and their legacies are as apparent on Wall Street as they are along Fifth Avenue. Swindles, panics and frequent market collapses were cyclical events in the late 19th century, but New York's millionaires weathered the financial disasters, built major cultural institutions and virtually created high society.

The 1800s saw the birth of the Metropolitan Museum of Art, the Astor Library (now the Public Theater), the American Museum of Natural History, the New-York Historical Society and the Metropolitan Opera. Carnegie gave Carnegie Hall to New York, even though the devoted Pittsburgher rarely mingled in New York's social circles (his Fifth Avenue mansion is now the Cooper-Hewitt, National Design Museum; *see page 43*). Six years after the New York Public Library was created in 1895, Carnegie donated $5.2 million to establish branch libraries. The nucleus of the library consists of the combined collections of John Jacob Astor, Samuel Jones Tilden and James Lenox.

## MAJOR CAPITAL IMPROVEMENTS

As the rich moved uptown, so did innovation. By 1850, the mansions along Fifth Avenue had indoor plumbing, central heating and a reliable water supply—secured by the 1842 construction of the Croton Reservoir system. In 1859, Frederick Law Olmsted and Calvert Vaux welcomed crowds to Central Park *(see page 93),* the nation's first landscaped public green space. A daring combination of formal gardens and rolling hills, the park remains the city's great civilizing force, offsetting the oppressive grid and providing an oasis of sanity in the heart of Manhattan.

Nineteenth-century New York also witnessed many industrial marvels. In 1807, Robert Fulton started the world's first steamboat service on Cortlandt Street. Samuel Morse founded his

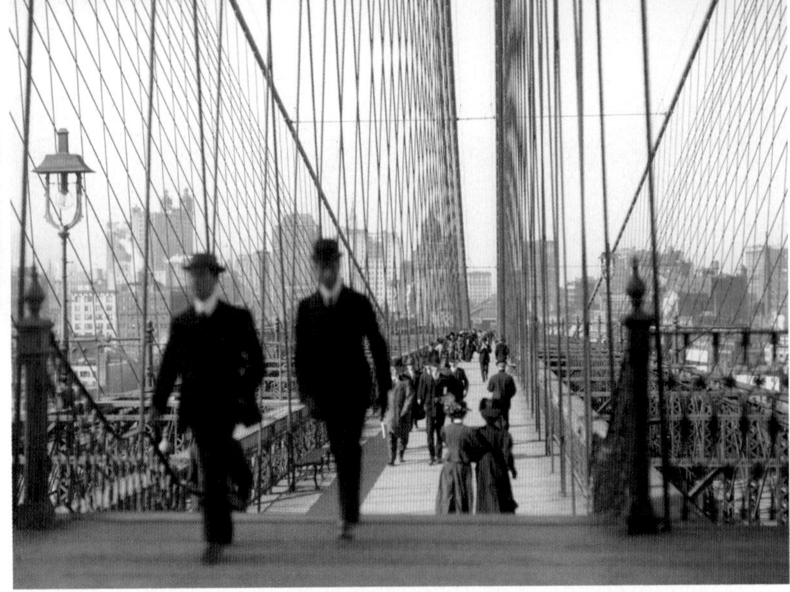

**Over the river** The Brooklyn Bridge is a stunning display of 19th-century engineering.

telegraph company in the 1840s. Twenty years later, Isaac Merritt Singer was producing 13,000 sewing machines a year. In the late 1800s, Thomas Edison formed the world's first electric company in New York; it still carries his name, Consolidated Edison. In 1882, 800 new electric street lamps turned New York into the city that never sleeps (it does, however, take an occasional nap).

Another extraordinary achievement of the era was the construction of the Brooklyn Bridge (1869–83), then the longest suspension bridge in the world and the first to use steel cable *(see page 109)*. Designed by John A. Roebling (who died in an on-site accident before construction began) and completed by his son, Washington, the bridge opened up the independent city of Brooklyn—and paved the way for its merger with New York.

## POLITICAL MACHINATIONS

The 1898 consolidation of all five boroughs into the City of New York assured New York's transformation into an international force: It became the world's second-largest city (London was biggest). But the merger happened only after several false starts. Local bosses wouldn't give up their power, and most of the metropolis had become mired in corruption. William M. "Boss" Tweed, the young leader of a Democratic Party faction called Tammany Hall (named after a famous Indian chief), had turned city government into a lucrative operation: As commissioner of public works, he collected large payoffs from companies receiving city contracts. The Tweed ring is estimated to have pilfered up to $200 million from various building projects, including the Tweed Courthouse at 52 Chambers Street *(see page 67)*. Although they distributed enough of that money in political bribes to keep a lot of influential mouths shut, they were finally exposed, thanks in large part to Thomas Nast's scathing cartoons in *Harper's Weekly* and reform lawyer Samuel J. Tilden.

The reform movement soon grew stronger, led by a young state assemblyman named Theodore Roosevelt. The future president drew his power not so much from his wealth and class as from the sheer force of his personality (and his ability to manipulate the media). In the 1880s, Roosevelt turned the town on its ear, accusing capitalist Jay Gould of bribing a judge. Although Gould was exonerated, Roosevelt earned a reputation as a fighter of corruption. (For information on the Theodore Roosevelt Birthplace museum, *see page 83*.)

## COMING TO AMERICA

"Give me your tired, your poor, your huddled masses yearning to breathe free," entreats Emma Lazarus's "The New Colossus," inscribed at the base of Frédéric-Auguste Bartholdi's Statue of Liberty—one of the first sights glimpsed by newcomers to the U.S. as they approached by sea.

The first great waves of immigrants landed in America well before the Civil War; the twin ports of welcome were Boston and New York. The Northeast's Irish population surged after the 1843 potato famine, and German liberals arrived after their failed 1848 revolution. The

1870s and '80s witnessed an influx of Southern Italians and large numbers of immigrants from the old Russian empire—Lithuanians, Poles, Romanians and Ukrainians, many of them Jews. Chinese laborers, who had been brought to America to do backbreaking work on the railroads in California, moved to New York in droves to escape a violent anti-Chinese movement on the West Coast.

From 1855 to 1890, the immigration center at Castle Clinton in Battery Park processed 8 million people. The Ellis Island center, built in 1892, served the same purpose for roughly the same length of time and handled more than twice as many until 1924 after the U.S. government restricted immigration. (For information on the Ellis Island Immigration Museum and the Statue of Liberty, *see chapters* **Downtown** and **Museums**).

### HOW THE OTHER HALF LIVES

New immigrants usually ended up in the grim, crowded tenements of the Lower East Side. By 1879, the first of a series of housing laws was passed to improve conditions for the poor. In 1890, writer and photographer Jacob A. Riis published *How the Other Half Lives,* an exposé of sweatshops and squalor in the ghetto; the uptown populace was horrified. The settlement-house movement and a temperance drive would preoccupy New York's philanthropic circles throughout the Great Depression (1929–39).

The frenetic growth of the city's industries created an appalling lack of health-and-safety conditions. Child labor was common. "Nearly any hour on the East Side of New York City, you can see them—pallid boy or spindling girl—their faces dulled, their backs bent under a heavy load of garments piled on head and shoulders, the muscles of the whole frame in a long strain," wrote poet Edwin Markham in 1907. In 1882, some 30,000 people marched in Union Square, demanding an eight-hour work day, and they won that right four years later.

It took the horror of the 1911 fire at the Triangle Shirtwaist factory *(23–29 Washington Pl)* in Greenwich Village to stir politicians to further action. The fire killed 146 women because the proprietors had locked the doors to the exits. The state legislature passed more than 50 health-and-safety measures within months of the tragedy.

### THE SUBWAY

If, while staring at a subway map, you wonder why there is no easy connection between depots such as Grand Central Terminal and Penn Station, it is because the two were at one time run by different private rail companies. The original names of the subway lines—the IRT (Interborough Rapid Transit), BMT (Brooklyn-Manhattan Transit Corporation) and IND (Independent Subway System)—are preserved in old signage. Many lifelong New Yorkers still use these names to refer to various routes.

The 685-mile subway system, an astounding network of civic arteries that currently serves at least 4.5 million passengers a day, became the 20th century's largest single factor in the growth of the city. The first of the three companies started underground excavation in 1900, but by the 1940s, the system was consolidated and hasn't changed much since.

The subway also holds a unique place in the city's imagination: It offers the perfect metaphor for New Yorkers' fast, crowded lives lived among strangers. Most famously, the Duke Ellington Orchestra's signature song, written by Ellington and Billy Strayhorn, implored its listeners to "Take the A Train," noting, "That's the quickest way to get to Harlem." Subway culture permeates New York life. Tin Pan Alley's songwriters composed such popular ditties as "Rapid Transit Gallop" and "The Subway Glide."

### NEW YORK STORIES

Since the 19th century, New York has consistently sprouted its own artistic and literary movements. Following the seminal figures of New York letters—writers such as satirist Washington Irving and Gothic storyteller Edgar Allan Poe—were Brooklyn poet Walt Whitman and novelist Samuel Clemens, a.k.a. Mark Twain. During his most prolific period, Twain spent significant time in New York (mostly Greenwich Village), writing *The Adventures of Tom Sawyer, Life on the Mississippi* and *Huckleberry Finn.*

By the early 1900s, a strain of social consciousness had cropped up in New York literature. Lincoln Steffens (the political muckraker), Stephen Crane *(Maggie: A Girl of the Streets),* Theodore Dreiser *(Sister Carrie)* and O. Henry ("The Gift of The Magi") all pricked the city's conscience with style and fervor.

### THE JAZZ AGE

New York benefited from wartime commerce, once World War I thrusted America onto center stage as a world power. The Roaring '20s brought "looser morals" (women voting and dancing the Charleston!), just as Prohibition provoked a bootleg-liquor culture. Speakeasies fueled the general jazz-age wildness and made many a gangster's fortune. Even Mayor Jimmy Walker went nightclubbing at a casino in Central Park.

At Harlem's Cotton Club *(see page 105),* Josephine Baker, Duke Ellington and Lena Horne played for white audiences enjoying what poet

Langston Hughes called "that Negro vogue." On Broadway, the Barrymore family—Ethel, John and Lionel (Drew's forebears)—were treading the boards between movie roles. Over at the New Amsterdam Theatre on West 42nd Street, Ziegfeld's high-kicking *Follies* dancers were opening for entertainers such as W.C. Fields, Fanny Brice and Marion Davies.

New York also saw the birth of the film industry: D.W. Griffith's early pictures were shot in Manhattan, and the Marx Brothers filmed in Astoria. In 1926, hundreds of thousands of New Yorkers flooded the streets to mourn the death of matinee idol Rudolph Valentino.

## RADIO DAYS

After the 1929 stock-market crash, when Americans stopped going out and instead turned to their radios for entertainment, New York became the airwaves' talent pool. Unemployed vaudeville players, such as George Burns and Gracie Allen, found stardom, as did Jack Benny and Fred Allen. The careers of artists as disparate as Bing Crosby and Arturo Toscanini were launched on New York radio, and Enrico Caruso went from Italian immigrant to worldwide recording star. The Art Deco masterpiece Radio City Music Hall became the industry's Great Depression–era show palace.

Since theatrical productions were tailored for the airwaves, some of the most acclaimed stage directors made their names in radio. In 1938, Orson Welles and John Houseman, who had already shaken up Broadway with an all–African-American stage version of *Macbeth,* terrified America with their radio adaptation of H.G. Wells's *War of the Worlds.*

## LA GUARDIA, FDR AND THE POWER BROKER

After the turn of the century, more and more skyscrapers (including the Woolworth Building) began pressing the heavens. The 1920s and '30s saw a boom in buildings, including the Chrysler and Empire State Buildings and Rockefeller Center; Art Deco design was the order of the day (*see chapter* **Architecture**).

In 1933, with the Depression in full swing, the city elected as mayor a stocky, short-tempered young congressman, Fiorello La Guardia. Boosted by former New York governor Franklin D. Roosevelt's presidential election, La Guardia imposed austerity programs that, surprisingly, won wide support. FDR's New Deal, meanwhile, reemployed the jobless on public-works programs and allocated federal funds to roads, housing and parks.

Enter Robert Moses, the city's master builder. As the head of a complex web of governmental authorities and commissions, Moses employed thousands of New Yorkers to build huge public parks (including Long Island's Jones Beach) and recreation centers; he also demolished entire neighborhoods to construct expressways and bridges (including the Verrazano-Narrows). No one since Dutch colonizer Peter Minuit had left a greater stamp on the city. Before his influence ebbed in the 1960s, Moses erected such indelible New York landmarks as Lincoln Center, Shea Stadium and the Flushing World's Fair grounds.

## BUILDING BETTER ARTISTS

Roosevelt's Federal Works Progress Administration (WPA) also made money available to New York's actors, writers, artists and musicians. As the Nazis terrorized Europe, the city became a favored refuge for the continent's fleeing intelligentsia. Composer Arnold Schoenberg and architects Ludwig Mies van der Rohe and Walter Gropius (the former director of the influential Bauhaus school of design) were among those who moved to New York from Germany, along with many visual artists.

Arshile Gorky, Piet Mondrian, Hans Hofmann and Willem de Kooning were among the immigrant painters welcomed by the fledgling Museum of Modern Art, founded in 1929 by three collectors. By the '50s, MoMA had fully embraced a generation of painters known as the New York School. Critics such as Clement Greenberg hailed Abstract Expressionism as the next step in painting. Willem and Elaine de Kooning, Jackson Pollock, Lee Krasner, Robert Motherwell and Mark Rothko became the stars of a gallery scene that, for the first time, decisively topped that of Paris.

In 1949, when a young man named Andrew Warhola decided to leave Pittsburgh to become an artist, he dropped the last letter of his name and headed for New York. Warhol used commercial silk-screening techniques to fuse the city's advertising culture and art world (who can forget those Campbells' soup cans?). At his peak, he was the king of Pop Art.

## MEDIA CENTRAL

Stepping back a bit to the Roaring Twenties literary scene: The monarchs were Ernest Hemingway and his friend F. Scott Fitzgerald, whose *The Great Gatsby* portrayed a dark side of the 1920s. They worked with editor Maxwell Perkins of the publishing house Charles Scribner's Sons, as did Thomas Wolfe, who constructed enormous semi-autobiographical mosaics of small-town life. Dorothy Parker, Robert Benchley, George S. Kaufman and Alexander Woollcott gathered regularly at the famous Round Table in the Algonquin hotel *(see page 151).* Royals of stage

**Up and away** From 1866 to 1902, elevated trains, like this one photographed sometime between 1910 and 1930 at Herald Square, kept New Yorkers mobile.

and screen, such as Tallulah Bankhead and various Marx Brothers, would show up to pay their respects. Much of the modern New York concept of sophistication and wit took shape in the caustic alcoholic banter of this glamorous clan.

Political discourse was equally scathing. By World War II, the city's socialists were divided over the support some showed for Stalin. The often stormy arguments spawned a generation of intellectuals spanning the political spectrum, including William F. Buckley Jr., Irving Howe, Norman Podhoretz, and Lionel and Diana Trilling. At the same time, a counterculture emerged: William Burroughs, Allen Ginsberg and Jack Kerouac met at Columbia in the 1940s, initiating the Beat movement of the '50s. Greenwich Village was the lab for alternative culture, from the Bolshevism of the '20s to the '50s New York School of poets (John Ashbery and Kenneth Koch among them).

## ENCORES AND HOME RUNS

In the theater, Irving Berlin, George and Ira Gershwin, Cole Porter, Richard Rodgers and Oscar Hammerstein II modified and codified the Broadway musical, adding plots and characters to the traditional follies format. Eugene O'Neill revolutionized American drama in the 1920s, only to have it revolutionized again by Tennessee Williams a generation later. By mid-century, the Group Theatre had fully imported Stanislavsky's Method acting techniques to America, launching the careers of Actors Studio founder Lee Strasberg, director Elia Kazan and actor Marlon Brando.

Theater, especially on Broadway, became big business. The Shubert brothers—Sam, Lee and J.J.—started a national 100-theater empire in the 1910s. Mid-century, David Merrick pushed modern musicals *(Gypsy, 42nd Street).* By the '60s, Joseph Papp's Public Theater was bringing Shakespeare to the masses with free shows in Central Park, a tradition that continues today.

The theater of the outer boroughs was baseball. Between 1921 and 1956, the New York Yankees played against either the Brooklyn Dodgers or the New York Giants in 13 World Series ("subway series," to New Yorkers). The mighty Yankees—whose mythic figures included Joe DiMaggio, Lou Gehrig, Mickey Mantle and Babe Ruth—provided as many thrills as any Broadway show. The Dodgers' Jackie Robinson broke major-league baseball's color barrier in 1947; when the team moved to Los Angeles a decade later, Brooklyn fans were devastated. The Giants left the same year.

## THE INTERNATIONAL CITY

The affluence of the 1950s allowed many families to head for the suburbs: Towns sprang up around new highways, and roughly a million children and grandchildren of European immigrants—mostly Irish, Italian and Jewish—moved to them. But the vacancies in the city were soon filled by a wave of newcomers—a million Puerto Ricans and African-Americans, most of the latter relocating from the South. Meanwhile, the United Nations, the international organization supporting global peace and security, established its headquarters overlooking the East River in Manhattan, on land donated by John D. Rockefeller Jr. *(see page 25).*

By the mid-1970s, poverty, prejudice and a huge rise in street crime had cast a shadow of fear across the city. Times Square was a drug-infested sleaze scene whose denizens hustled porn and prostitution—an economy that was supported in large part by the invisible hand of organized crime. Many white New Yorkers in working- and middle-class neighborhoods grew disenchanted with the city and its inability to provide safe streets or effective schools, so they fled to the suburbs in droves. To make matters worse, by 1975, the city was all but bankrupt, and the federal government refused to bail it out. The grim situation was immortalized in an infamous *Daily News* headline: FORD TO CITY—DROP DEAD. With a growing population on welfare and a declining tax base, Gotham resorted to heavy municipal borrowing.

Culturally, New York remained a hotbed of music and nightlife, Times Square notwithstanding. In the 1950s and '60s, Burt Bacharach, Neil Diamond and Carole King got their starts

**Buy me some peanuts and Cracker Jack...** Dodgers fans load up on snacks at Ebbets Field, circa 1920. The beloved team broke Brooklyn's heart when it left for L.A. in 1957.

in the Brill Building *(see page 87)*, and Bob Dylan rose to fame in the Village. In the mid-'70s, CBGB, on the grungy Bowery, launched Blondie, the Ramones and Talking Heads, while midtown's Studio 54 blended disco, drugs and celebrity glamour into a potent, if short-lived, cocktail.

## BOOM AND BUST

New York climbed out of its fiscal crisis under Mayor Edward Koch, a onetime liberal from Greenwich Village who wangled state and federal help to ride the 1980s boom in construction and finance. The 1980s and early '90s were the best and worst of times for New York: A new art scene and the booming Wall Street–takeover culture brought money back downtown, fueling the revitalization—some would say gentrification—of the East Village, Soho and Tribeca. But the AIDS and crack epidemics hit the city hard, as did racial strife. David Dinkins was elected New York's first African-American mayor in 1989. However, his tenure was marred by racial tension—incidents in Crown Heights, Brooklyn, and Washington Heights polarized the city, and he was not reelected.

Dinkins was succeeded in 1993 by former federal prosecutor Rudolph Giuliani. The tough-talking Italian-American cracked down on crime, and New York's reputation for being dangerous and unlivable softened. Although he was unpopular with minorities and liberals, mainly because of police brutality and housing issues, Giuliani won reelection in 1997.

## THE 21ST CENTURY

Fueled by the dot-com wave, New York's economy soared in the late 1990s, and tourists flocked to a city whose reputation changed from urban wasteland to urban Disneyland. One of Giuliani's major successes was transforming Times Square—once the domain of drug dealers and strip bars—into a family-friendly attraction, with a cornucopia of big-name restaurants and shops.

A city-budget surplus of more than $2 billion for the year 2000 led to tax cuts—including the elimination of sales tax on clothing items costing less than $110 (another major draw for out-of-towners). But due in large part to the recession and the attack on the World Trade Center, the budget surplus would become a projected $5 billion deficit by fall 2002.

As in 1800, real-estate prices have risen beyond affordability for many New Yorkers. Formerly dangerous neighborhoods, such as Harlem and Alphabet City, are now sought-after areas where one-bedroom rentals can go for $2,000 a month. The gentrification has led to a displaced class of working homeless, whose earning power can't keep up with real-estate values.

**Bloomberg's news** Mayor Mike says the city's money woes call for belt-tightening.

And of course, the events of September 11, 2001, put the city at risk of a longer downturn. But the terrorist attack also unified the city in a way no one alive had ever seen before, as citizens volunteered, donated money and generally put their in-your-face attitude on hold while the city regrouped and rebuilt.

To many, Giuliani became a hero for his calm leadership throughout the crisis, but he was unable to run for mayor in 2001 because of term-limit laws. His successor, billionaire businessman Michael Bloomberg, quickly reached out to the minority communities and labor groups Giuliani had spurned, showing his own liberal core. But "Mayor Mike" has also waged a Giuliani-like war on several quality-of-life fronts, including his proposed ban on smoking in all city bars and restaurants, and his plan to muffle the city's 24 noisiest neighborhoods.

More than a year after the World Trade Center attack, New York remains Ground Zero in more ways than one. The city's residents are forging into the 21st century with groundbreaking art, literature, music, film and fashion; meanwhile, city and state leaders are developing a rebuilding plan to restore grandeur to lower Manhattan's skyline and to honor those who died on 9/11. New Yorkers continue to show the world that they are tough, compassionate and not easily intimidated. While their city may not be the capital of the U.S., they like to think it remains the capital of the world.

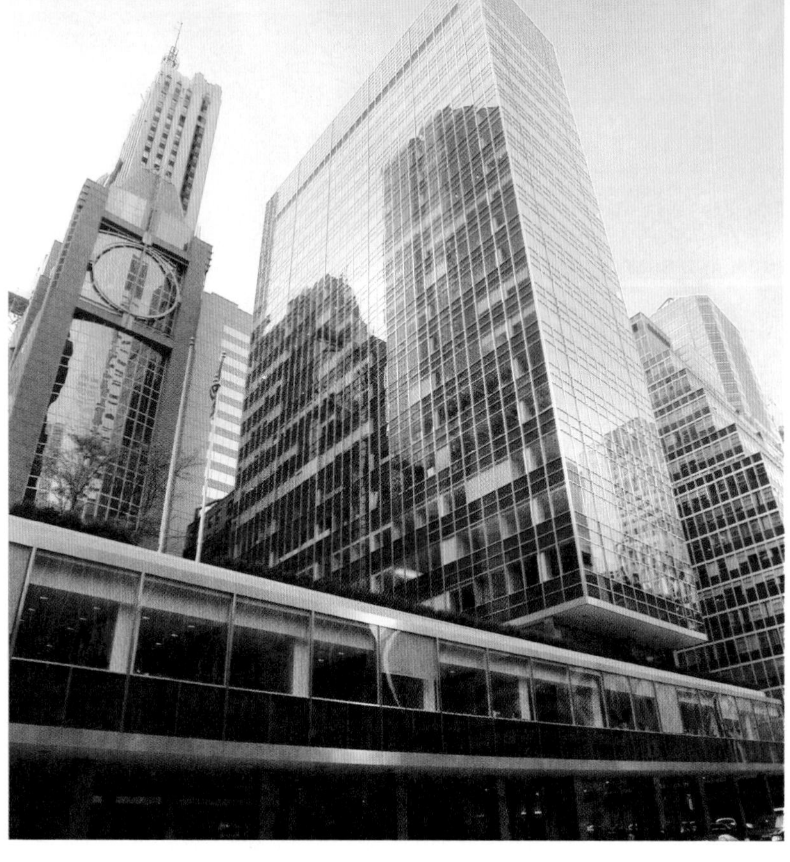

# Architecture

## Change is the only constant as the city's skyline rises and falls—and rises again

It's a grim irony, but one of the biggest architectural attractions in New York right now is something that isn't even around anymore. The 110-story Twin Towers of the World Trade Center were destroyed in 2001 by terrorists, but the area continues to draw visitors, if only to the footprint, which has undergone an agonizing transformation from burial mound to construction site. Grieving has given way to New York politics as usual, as various constituencies—among them commercial developers, City Hall, the victims' families and even the architect critic of *The New York Times*—duke it out to see who determines the next move. The public has already rejected one developer-driven round of proposals for rebuilding the area; the second round called on design teams that included such international "starchitects" as Peter Eisenman and Daniel Libeskind (for more info on the plans, *see* **The Sky's the Limit**, *page 28*). In the meantime, the towers themselves seem to linger on, in old

**Design Lever-age** The landmarked Lever House ignited the city's glass-box building boom of the 1950s and '60s.

postcards and on business signs that used them as logos, and in the mind's eye—an architectural equivalent of the "phantom limb" syndrome experienced by amputees.

As awful as the events of September 11, 2001, were, they were also reminders of some basic truths about the lives of buildings in New York. The most important of these is that New York architecture has always been vulnerable to the vicissitudes of a metropolis that, for better and worse, exists in a constant churn of reinvention. This city has seen a succession of not only immigrant waves, but also economic boom-and-bust cycles, each leaving distinctive marks on the urban topography.

The original Dutch colony, with its gabled farmhouses and low-ceilinged taverns, gave way to the Georgian elegance of the British trading city that supplanted it. In turn, the American Revolution brought with it the confident Yankee Neoclassicism of the Federal period, when New York was briefly the capital of the nascent republic. Later, a more restrained Greek Revival style characterized the booming "Empire City" of the early 19th century, as the Erie Canal extended New York's power as a trading center deep into the nation's heartland. The Civil War transformed the city yet again, turning it into the Union's armory, and bringing with it dazzling cast-iron buildings—and less-than-dazzling tenement blocks to house the immigrants who were also pouring in. The war's aftermath created the Gilded Age of rich industrial tycoons and a grand new Beaux Arts style that was a concrete testament to their substantial fortunes. That same expansive sensibility would, thanks to the invention of the elevator in the mid-19th century, reach upwards to create the first spurt of tall buildings colonizing the sky. Later, some of these structures would be cut down for a second growth of modern towers. Building in New York, which typically puts commerce above aesthetic considerations, often seems to take forever, but few structures last very long.

In this respect, the fate of the World Trade Center, which stood a mere 28 years from the time of its completion in 1973, is simply the latest, if deadliest, link in a long chain of memorable casualties that include the Singer Building, Ebbets Field and the original Pennsylvania Station. (Within the next few years, a new Penn Station with a soaring central atrium space is expected to rise on Eighth Avenue, across from the old location.) In fact, construction of the Twin Towers destroyed an entire commercial neighborhood: the old "Radio Row" of consumer electronics shops.

Like the Empire State Building, the Twin Towers and the complex surrounding them were begun at a time of unparalleled prosperity and completed during an economic depression. As originally conceived, they were meant to convey a new sense of permanence. The towers were a late expression of Corbusier's Radiant City plan, which envisioned an urban future of widely spaced towers separated by plazas, greenbelts and superhighways. This notion influenced urban planners such as Robert Moses for half a century. In his role as the city's Parks and Planning Commissioner, the famously tyrannical Moses acted on these ideas with a vengeance throughout the 1930s, '40s and '50s, tearing down whole sections of Brooklyn, Queens and the Bronx in the process.

Although Moses himself had nothing to do with the towers, the buildings—plunked down in the oldest section of Gotham—embodied the purest distillation of Moses's thinking. They were, in fact, a private and public consortium, hatched in the early 1960s by businessman David Rockefeller and his brother Nelson, then governor of New York.

A sleek, self-contained city-within-a-city isolated from the rest of the island, the World Trade Center stood as a structural rebuke to the urban messiness of lower Manhattan. The towers' scale was almost impossible to apprehend—except by car, zipping along one of the many expressways Moses had imperiously plowed through established New York neighborhoods. The WTC was never really meant to be a true part of the city; it was meant to symbolize New York's transformation from American conurbation to global megalopolis.

Predictably then, when the towers opened, architecture critics sneered: One described them as the boxes that the Empire State and Chrysler Buildings had come in, and an edition of the *AIA Guide to New York City* called them "banal." So how did this monstrosity become beloved? First, there's architect Minoru Yamasaki's understated—and underrated—design. Although boxy and huge, the Twin Towers shimmered in the light, thanks to a stainless-steel exterior corrugated by narrowly spaced columns, which resulted in shoulder-wide mullions. This relationship, between the width of the windows and the height of the towers, imbued them with an elongated grace that was as anthropomorphic as it was aspirational, like a pair of El Greco's saints.

► For an overview of the city's development and key influential figures, see chapter **History**.

► Other significant architectural sights are listed in the **Sightseeing** section.

Yamasaki also tasseled the fenestration along the top and bottom of each facade with bands of ogival tracery. The pointed archways along the base became hauntingly familiar as charred remnants at Ground Zero.

In their lifetime, the towers inspired dreamers if not critics, and two in particular put their stamp on the buildings in ways that would win them a place in the hearts of the public. In 1973, Frenchman Philippe Petit walked a tightrope between the edifices; four years later, an American named George Willig climbed one of the towers with the aid of special rigging that fit into an existing track for window-cleaning scaffolds. Paul Goldberger, architecture critic for *The New Yorker,* once suggested that such acts lent the WTC the romanticism that its original design lacked. But if that quality had really been missing, what inspired these daredevils in the first place? In spite of their detractors, the towers were undeniably compelling.

**In his element** Frank Gehry makes titanium soar in his interior for Issey Miyaki's store.

## RESHAPING THE SKYLINE

As much as the World Trade Center remains a presence in the hearts of New Yorkers, its demise could pave the way for an important new period of rebuilding in New York. Granted, the cost of cleanup and recovery will burden a city budget already threatened by blooming deficits; eagerly awaited amenities such as the Brooklyn Bridge Park could be deferred. And it's also true that even before September 11, an economic downturn precipitated by the great stock bust of 2000 was having a negative impact on new building. A windfall of federal-aid dollars should see New York through its greatest difficulties (though federal, state and local politicians have had to fight hard to get the promised money). In any case, a number of important architectural additions to the city that were under way before the attacks have recently been completed.

Although his planned downtown Guggenheim satellite has been scrapped, Frank Gehry has realized one small project that is currently open to the public: the Tribeca **Issey Miyake** boutique *(119 Hudson St between Franklin and North Moore Sts, 212-226-0100)*. The store's 15,000-square-foot interior is dominated by a tornado-like titanium sculpture—perhaps meant to encourage shoppers to buy up a storm? The Soho **Prada** store *(575 Broadway at Prince St, 212-234-8888),* designed by Rem Koolhaas as a combination retail-performance space, has been a must-see destination since it opened in January 2002.

Richard Meier, architect of the J. Paul Getty Center in Los Angeles, has recently added his imprimatur to the skyline. Two sleek apartment towers *(173 and 176 Perry St at West St),* hard by the West Side Highway, are his first major buildings in New York.

Also a first: Aldo Rossi's posthumous addition to Soho. The Italian architect died in 1997, but 2001 saw the completion of his design for the **Scholastic Books** headquarters *(557 Broadway between Prince and Spring Sts);* the neotraditional building stands out even as it blends in with its cast-iron environs.

More prominent along the skyline are two highly sculptural buildings in midtown that now join Christian de Portzamparc's equally striking **LVMH** tower *(19 E 57th St between Fifth and Madison Aves)*: Raimund Abraham's **Austrian Cultural Institute** *(11 E 52nd St between Fifth and Madison Aves)* and the **American Folk Art Museum** *(see* **New**

**Folk's home**, *page 26)* by Tod Williams and Billie Tsien. Abraham's creation, which was sandwiched between existing buildings, rises from its narrow site like a soaring Easter Island stone head. While the dark, slanting louvered facade has a masklike presence, the building as a whole suggests the spinal column of some enormous prehistoric vertebrate. The American Folk Art Museum, meanwhile, is clad in faceted panels of Tombasil, a white bronze alloy. Its delicately textured surface, which brilliantly captures light, has the look of stone and metal—reflecting the museum's mission of promoting handcrafted art while lending a touch of warmth to the block. The Folk Art's neighbor, the **Museum of Modern Art** *(see page 46)*, closed in June 2002 for three years of reconstruction, which will include Yoshio Taniguchi's seamless contemporary addition, built on the site of the old Dorset Hotel.

Columbus Circle, which was once dominated by the New York Coliseum convention center, is soon to be the home of a gleaming new complex across from Central Park: the **AOL Time Warner** headquarters *(1 Central Park at Broadway)*, a soaring mix of buildings that will include upscale apartments, a Mandarin Oriental hotel, high-end shops and media-conglomerate offices, plus a new venue for Jazz at Lincoln Center. The story behind its construction is indicative of the way things get done in New York. The original Coliseum, another Robert Moses behemoth, closed in 1986 while the city tried to find a private developer to buy it, raze it and rebuild on the property. Proposal after proposal, including one infamous Moshe Safdie plan that would have cast a giant shadow across Central Park, was scotched by various civic groups. The present design by David Childs, of Skidmore, Owings & Merrill, finally passed muster and construction began in early 2001. The building's twin-tower motif, which allows for more light in the park, has become as instant a fixture in this neighborhood as the Twin Towers were in theirs.

## BUILDINGS OF THEIR TIME

The World Trade Center, which lorded over the oldest part of Manhattan, reflected the city's infrastructure in a fascinating way. Given their height and surface design, the modernist towers were arguably a downtown model of the city's famous grid of streets that begins higher on the island. The Commissioner's Plan, which was envisioned by the State Legislature in 1811, laid down the crisscross streets that would eventually fill up with buildings (like a "thermometer," as Rem Koolhaas memorably put it in his book *Delirious New York*), to create the Gotham we know today. The history of the city's architecture can be followed south to north—plus or minus some detours, starting with the Dutch themselves.

All that's left of Dutch architectural influence in lower Manhattan is the distinctive warren of narrow lanes and streets that cover the lower part of the island (major arteries such as Broadway and the Bowery follow Native American trails).

For actual Dutch buildings, you'll have to make your way uptown or deep into Brooklyn. The **Dyckman Farmhouse Museum** *(see page 107)* was built in 1783, well after Dutch rule, but it retains the distinctive characteristics of the Dutch Colonial style, such as a gambrel roof and decorative brickwork. The **Pieter Claesen Wyckoff House Museum** *(5902 Clarendon Rd at Ralph Ave, East Flatbush, Brooklyn)* is the oldest house in New York City. It was built around 1652 by Wyckoff, who had arrived in America in 1637 as an illiterate indentured servant. He later became the wealthiest citizen of what was later called the town of Flatlands. This modest house, with shingled walls, pine floorboards and wide overhanging eaves, was typical of its time. The **Lefferts Homestead** *(Prospect Park, Flatbush Ave near Empire Blvd, Park Slope, Brooklyn)*, completed in 1783, combines Dutch Colonial architecture—the bell-shaped gambrel roof—with early Federal details, such as front and back porches set off by slender columns.

In Manhattan, early 19th-century New York buildings are easier to come by. The island's population grew rapidly, and the buildings were designed in the Georgian/Neoclassical styles of the English and Federal periods, starting with **St. Paul's Chapel and Churchyard** *(see page 65)*. Manhattan's only extant pre-Revolutionary structure, the church was begun in 1764 and enhanced with the addition of a steeple in 1796. It was almost lost in the World Trade Center attack: Although covered by debris from the collapsing towers, the columned and quoined chapel miraculously survived. The more familiar Episcopal landmark, **Trinity Church** *(Broadway at Wall St)*, is the third iteration at this site, completed in 1846. The original, consecrated in 1698, was destroyed by fire after the Revolutionary War. A second version, built in 1790, was eventually demolished because of structural problems. **Fraunces Tavern** *(see page 51)*, where George Washington held a victory celebration in 1783 after the British evacuation of New York, was built as a private residence in 1719 and renovated in the 20th century. The largest group of Federal-style houses in New York, dating from the 1820s, can be found in the **Charlton-King-Vandam Historic District** *(9–43, 20–42 Charlton St; 11–49, 16–54 King St; 9–29 Vandam St; and 43–51 MacDougal St)* along the southwestern edge of Greenwich Village. But perhaps the supreme expression of the Federal style, complete with some French Renaissance flourishes, is **City Hall** *(see page 67)*. Completed in 1812, this is the mayor's headquarters.

The Greek Revival style is best exemplified by the 1842 **Federal Hall National Memorial** *(see page 65)*, whose colonnaded facade, carved of Westchester marble, is modeled on the Parthenon (albeit sans sculptured frieze and pediment). George Washington took his oath of office at this site, when the old Federal Hall, originally built as the city hall in 1699, stood here. (A statue of Washington graces the spot where the oath was sworn.) **Colonnade Row** *(428–434 Lafayette St between Astor Pl and E 4th St)* is another fine example of the style, though only four of the nine elegant homes that Seth Geer built (between 1832 and 1833) still stand. A more complete concentration of Greek Revival housing can be found along **"the Row"** *(1–13 Washington Sq North between Fifth Ave and University Pl)* and its neighboring block to the west *(19–26 Washington Sq North between Fifth Ave and Washington Sq West)*, which were built in the 1830s. The former **13th Street Presbyterian Church** *(143 W 13th St between Sixth and Seventh Aves)* from 1847 was once the finest Greek Revival church in the city. Unfortunately, its interior was gutted to make way for apartments; the last visible vestige of its pedigree is the impressive, beautifully proportioned portico.

**William Van Alen's design for the Chrysler Building is the first pure expression of the skyscraper vernacular in that it owed little to previous historical styles. It is, instead, a paean to the automobile and the new age of the machine.**

The cast-iron buildings of the mid- to late 19th century were forerunners of the modern, curtain-wall method of construction: cheap, quick and meant to support large expanses of glass, resulting in structures that were remarkably airy, if not technically lightweight. Often, the cast-iron components—interior columns, exterior sashing and details—were catalog items that could be ordered and bolted together. The first cast-iron buildings were located below Canal Street, including the 1846 **A.T. Stewart Dry Goods Store** *(280 Broadway between Chamber and Reade Sts)*, but the Soho neighborhood between Canal and Houston Streets remains the city's preeminent cast-iron domain. There, some of the more remarkable examples include the Palladian-style **Haughwout Building** *(488–492 Broadway at Broome St)*, which had the distinction of including the first Otis elevator in New York when it was built in 1857; and the 1904 **"little Singer Building"** *(561 Broadway between Prince and Spring Sts)*, with its curly Art Nouveau archways, recessed glass and textured terra-cotta panels.

Chronologically, the cast-iron era overlapped with the grander expressions of the Beaux Arts revival, driven by robber barons who put some of their money (made mainly from rail and steel) to good use by building the city's greatest civic edifices. Supreme among these are **Carnegie Hall** *(see page 318)*, completed in 1891; the 1902 Fifth Avenue facade of the **Metropolitan Museum of Art** *(see page 44)*, built by the sure hand of architect Richard Morris Hunt; the Carrère & Hastings design for the **New York Public Library** *(see page 58)*, erected in 1911 next to what was once an Egyptian Revival–style reservoir (now Bryant Park); and the grandest of all, **Grand Central Terminal** *(see page 92)*. Originally completed in 1913, it ducked the wrecking ball a generation ago and was recently restored to its full glory.

The architectural firm synonymous with the Beaux Arts period is, of course, McKim, Mead & White. Collectively, they brought forth the 1913 **Municipal Building** *(see page 67)*, the 1917 **Morgan Library** *(see page 46)* and the old Pennsylvania Station, whose design lives on in its Eighth Avenue sister—the 1913 **General Post Office** *(see page 85)*. Another outstanding example of the Beaux Arts style is the **Alexander Hamilton Custom House** *(see* **National Museum of the American Indian**, *page 53)*, built between 1899 and 1907. Before the national income tax was imposed in 1913, custom duties were the principal means of financing the government. Thus, Cass Gilbert's Italianate design is suitably monumental—it's set off by the *Four Continents*, the group of allegorical sculptures by Daniel Chester French (who made the Lincoln Memorial in Washington, D.C.). The building also serves as a stylistic bridge to the next great period of New York architecture—the skyscraper era.

## REACHING NEW HEIGHTS

To erect skyscrapers, architects had to overcome the height limitations imposed by the use of load-bearing masonry walls; happily, the technologies developed in cast-iron building pointed the way. Elevators and steel-frame

**Pitched-perfect** A sloped roof gives the Citicorp building the shape of a giant whistle.

construction permitted buildings to rise higher, and Daniel Burnham took advantage of these new techniques when he designed the first skyscraper, the 20-story **Flatiron Building** *(see page 81),* which was completed in 1903. Still, aside from its height and narrow triangular footprint, the Flatiron's Renaissance palazzo facade and flat roof had more in common with the loft buildings of lower Broadway than it did with what we consider to be skyscrapers today. Gilbert's Gothic-inflected design for the **Woolworth Building** *(233 Broadway between Barclay St and Park Pl)* was a true tower: a sheer shaft soaring 792 feet over the city. When it was finished in 1913, this monument to wealth was the world's tallest building, a title it held until the completion in 1930 of its midtown rival, the **Chrysler Building** *(see page 91).*

William Van Alen's design for the Chrysler Building is the first pure expression of the skyscraper vernacular in that it owed little to previous historical styles. It is, instead, a paean to the automobile and the new age of the machine. Its 1,048 feet culminate in a spired stainless-steel crown, meant to represent a series of overlapping hubcaps that diminish in diameter as they climb into the sky. Begun at the height of the Roaring '20s speculative frenzy, the Chrysler Building held the title of world's tallest building for only a few months before being surpassed in 1931 by the 1,250-foot **Empire State Building** *(see page 88).*

The Empire State Building is New York's most storied, in both senses of the word. It has never diminished in stature, even while existing in the shadow of the World Trade Center. Rising 102 stories along a series of incremental setbacks that are capped by an enormous Art Deco lantern, its rapid construction during the aftershock of the 1929 stock market crash inspired the city much as the rescue effort at Ground Zero did after September 11. Like the WTC, the Empire State was also the scene of an aircraft disaster: In 1945, an errant bomber on a training mission slammed into the 80th floor, killing 14 people but causing no major permanent damage to the building. The ESB remained nearly vacant for many years after completion—the commercial development hoped for by its owners was scuttled by the Great Depression. It stood isolated against the skyline, "a lighthouse in the harbor of commerce," as architect Robert A.M. Stern once put it. Today, it stands once again as Gotham's tallest building.

Like all phases in New York, the romantic age of skyscrapers soon gave way to something new as economic depression and war slowed development, and refinements in curtain-wall construction permitted the purity of form embodied by the International Style. Many have harped on the so-called sterility of the glass boxes that sprang up in the years following the Second World War. But at their best, buildings such as **The United Nations Headquarters** *(First Ave at 46th St; see also page 92)* rival anything else in the skyline. Designed in 1947 by an A-team of modernist architects (including Corbusier, Oscar Niemeyer, Sven Markelius and Wallace K. Harrison), the UN's arrangement clearly flows from Corbusier's Radiant City concept, though the structure's details are largely by Harrison. The main building, housing the Secretariat, is a broad slab of glass, steel and stone 554 feet high, set perpendicularly between

East River frontage and the swooping, low-slung buildings of the library and conference hall below.

This play of horizontal and vertical lines was reprised in New York's first commercial modernist structure, **Lever House** *(390 Park Ave between 53rd and 54th Sts),* built in 1952. Designed by Gordon Bunshaft of Skidmore, Owings & Merrill, and recently restored, it was also the city's first building to be constructed entirely of steel and glass. The main part of the building—a slender rectangular slab set at a right angle to the street—cantilevers over a much lower building, which in turn floats above a ground floor that contains only a small lobby. The remaining ground-level space, a large plaza, is a pleasingly luxurious waste of air space—a Manhattan commodity that is just as valuable as real estate. It's an indulgence that wouldn't fit today's maximum-interior-space standards. The next major development in the glass-box form, Ludwig Mies van der Rohe's magnificent bronze-clad **Seagram Building** *(375 Park Ave between 52nd and 53rd Sts),* completed in 1958, is likewise given plenty of breathing room, courtesy of its sizable plaza. The work of another Bauhaus alum, Walter Gropius, is represented by the **MetLife Building**, formerly the Pan Am Building *(200 Park Ave at 45th St),* which towers dramatically over Grand Central Station. Since it was yet another slab, this time straddling Park Avenue, the building was roundly criticized for being too large and for blocking the straight-shot view up and down the street. Its precast concrete curtain wall, one of the first in New York, can seem, at turns, sinister or warm, depending on the light. The structure also served as a billboard for the Pan Am logo until the airline went bankrupt in 1991. In 1992, MetLife affixed its own name to the building— over the protests of those who wanted to landmark the original sign. In many respects, the Pan Am building came to symbolize the failure of modernism in New York.

The "stagflation" and fiscal crisis of the 1970s slowed building once again—with the notable exception of the pennywhistle-shaped **Citicorp Center** of 1978 *(Lexington Ave between 53rd and 54th Sts),* the last building to noticeably contribute to the city's skyline.

## New Folk's home

### A narrow building next door to MoMA grabs some of the design spotlight

The loudest buzz—both literal and figurative—on Manhattan's West 53rd Street emanates from the ongoing expansion of the **Museum of Modern Art**, which has temporarily transferred operations to Queens *(see* **Modern convenience**, *page 118).* But another crafty attraction on that busy block is generating noise of its own. The **American Folk Art Museum** *(see page 48)* opened a striking new home next door to MoMA headquarters in December 2001. Designed by local firm Tod Williams Billie Tsien & Associates, the building has garnered accolades from architecture buffs who consider it one of the most attractive places the town has seen in years.

"People were looking for something they could be positive about," says Billie Tsien, noting that the opening took place while the city was still reeling from September 11. "People were glad to know something was being built in New York. This is a building that's meant to stand the test of time. It's the opposite of anonymous; it's not a white box. It's a building with a very strong personality—and an interesting collection."

The eight-story structure, whose facade is clad from top to bottom in massive sheets of faceted metal, is the museum's first substantial home since its founding in 1961. (Most recently, it spent 12 years near Lincoln Center, in an imperfect ground-floor space that will continue to show limited-run exhibitions.) The new midtown edifice immediately gave the museum an A-list standing with both critics and visitors.

"I'm very happy that people who aren't architects, or who don't necessarily have an inclination to modern architecture, feel incredibly comfortable in this museum," says Tsien. "People like the connection to natural light, and they're also drawn to the different textures. We didn't realize that so many people would feel moved to touch what's around them. They're really noticing materials, like the concrete and the cherry railings."

Unfortunately, the museum's pretty face will be obscured until 2005, when MoMA's renovation is expected to be completed. City law stipulates that protective scaffolding extend 20 feet beyond the edge of a construction site, and since the slender Folk Art building is only 40 feet wide, that means half of it is now hidden by a maze of metal. For the best view (albeit a slightly obscured one), approach from the mid-block arcade that cuts through the south side of West 53rd Street.

## THE POSTMODERN '80S

The 1980s brought a booming stock market and a sense of exuberance harking back to the '20s, which manifested itself as a rejection of modern design. Postmodern architecture, with its mix of modern building methods and historicized details, has its detractors (quite rightly, since it spawned a lot of glass-and-stone dreck). But as the style recedes into history, it is predictably becoming burnished by nostalgia. Three build-ings that are getting a second evaluation (all completed in midtown in 1983) include the former **IBM Building** *(590 Madison Ave between 56th and 57th Sts);* Philip Johnson's **Sony Building** *(see page 92 and* **Sony Wonder Technology Lab**, *page 299),* which was originally AT&T's headquarters; and **Trump Tower** *(725 Fifth Ave at 56th St).* Together, they express the full emotional palette of postmodern design, from the relatively sober (Edward Barnes's black-granite prism for IBM) and past the kitschy signature (Johnson's Chippendale breakfront top at Sony) to the marvelously vulgar (Trump's gold-trimmed pink-granite lobby). Two other buildings, the 1983 futuro-Egyptian "**lipstick building**" *(885 Third Ave between 53rd and 54th Sts)* by John Burgee and Philip Johnson, and **750 Lexington Avenue** *(between 59th and 60th Sts),* likewise possess a grandeur that's both awe-inspiring and absurd, though the latter has the slight advantage of having a true New York tale behind it.

This cylindrical blue-glass tower, with a finial top, is built around a lone tenement brownstone, a survivor of the block torn down to make way for Helmut Jahn's structure in 1988. The story is that one woman, an occupant of the rent-controlled building, refused to move, despite being offered generous financial inducements to do so. By rights, she could stay, so she did—enduring a construction process that included tunneling under her top-floor apartment to create a side entrance for the main lobby. She never left her home, fearing it would be demolished in her absence. As the construction workers built around her, she flew a tiny American flag from her window.

Inside the museum, the architects make the most of an intimate 30,000-square-foot space. The structure is perforated by openings, overhangs, landings and a variety of glass skylights and vitrines, while a narrow atrium opens the building from floor to ceiling. Transparent surfaces and lookouts offer myriad opportunities to glance over, down and around. Two poured-concrete staircases are completely exposed.

"There's a constantly changing series of views," says Tsien. "You'll find that you're looking all the way through some spaces, because windows cut through from one side to the other. There's even a kind of surprise with the "secret" stairs from the fifth to the fourth floor; some people told us they didn't even notice the stairs until several visits in. We like the sense of being enveloped by objects, and things coming from unexpected places."

The permanent collection, displayed on a rotating basis amid temporary themed exhibits, is dominated by the holdings of Ralph Esmerian, president of the museum's board since 1977 and a collector since 1966. His renowned trove focuses on traditional folk art: more than 400 objects, from the late 17th to early 20th centuries, created by European immigrants (and their descendants) who settled in the eastern half of the country.

The growing public interest in folk and outsider art, along with the solid presence of the new building, makes Tsien confident that the museum will hold its own when the art-ogling hordes return to the block in search of MoMA fun. "[MoMA addition architect Yoshio] Taniguchi's work is extremely elegant and refined," she says. "The addition is huge but very quiet. We'll work well together."

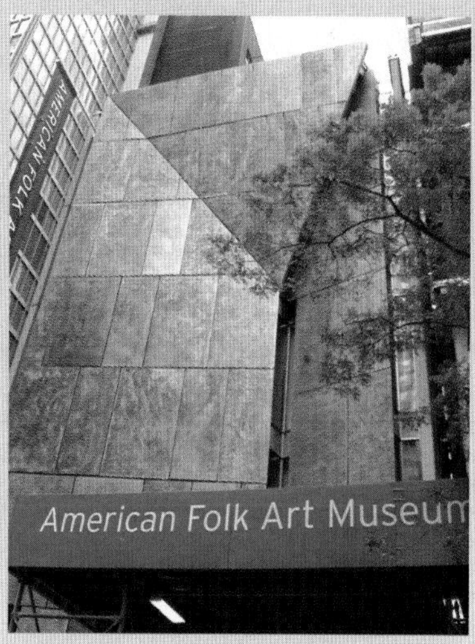


**Two's a crowd** The museum shares space with scaffolding from MoMA.

# The Sky's the Limit

## It will take both imagination and cooperation to restore grandeur to lower Manhattan

On the morning of May 30, 2002, the final remnant of the fallen World Trade Center—the 35-foot-tall steel beam that had survived the South Tower's collapse—was placed on a flatbed truck, shrouded in black cloth and hauled away. At that moment, Ground Zero officially made the transition from recovery site to construction site.

The 16-acre superblock has since become a bustling work zone. The mountain of twisted metal and pulverized concrete known as "the pile" has been replaced by shiny steel planks (the beginnings of a new PATH train terminal) and workers are busily inspecting the foundation for a resurrected 7 World Trade Center, to be completed by 2005.

But remaking lower Manhattan is no easy task—the tangled web of intragovernmental dealings, the opaque nature of the real-estate business and the hurly-burly of local politics make it difficult to predict downtown's destiny. It's an ongoing tug-of-war between conflicting interests that include the mayor, the governor, the agency overseeing design proposals, the Port Authority (which owns the land), developers, the victims' families and the public.

### WHO'S THE BOSS?

The Trade Center was owned by the Port Authority of New York and New Jersey. Created 82 years ago to manage ports in New York and New Jersey, the PA is a powerful body largely financed not by taxes but fees and tolls from the facilities it runs, including the Holland and Lincoln Tunnels and all three area airports. It can issue bonds to fund construction projects, enjoys exemption from many local laws and codes, and has the power of eminent domain—the authority to condemn private property and appropriate private lands for public use.

The consequence of the Port Authority's ownership is profound: New York City has little say over what will become of the site. The elected officials with real clout are the governors of New York and New Jersey—George Pataki and James McGreevey, respectively—who appoint the PA bosses.

Further complicating matters is the land deal reached in July 2001, when the PA leased the

**Afterglow** Twin beams of light marked the six-month anniversary of September 11, 2001, illuminating the sky for 32 nights.

World Trade Center to a group of developers led by Larry Silverstein. The terms of the $3.2 billion lease allow Silverstein a measure of control over the rebuilding, but exactly how much is debatable. He has backed away from initial statements asserting a "moral obligation" to rebuild the Twin Towers—thereby restoring 11 million square feet of lost office space—but the man who was the city's largest commercial landlord on September 10, 2001, will remain a force to be reckoned with.

Two months after the attack, Governor Pataki announced the creation of the Lower Manhattan Development Corporation, an entity charged with overseeing almost all facets of rebuilding Ground Zero. The LMDC is a conduit for most of the $20 billion dollars in emergency funds the federal government granted the city in the wake of September 11, and it continues to manage the reconstruction process. Although New York Mayor Michael Bloomberg was allowed to appoint a few of the agency's board members, it's Pataki who hand-picked its chairman, executive director and most influential officers. The governor also controls the Empire State Development Corporation, which has the power to build whatever it wishes, wherever it wishes, virtually anywhere in the state, and is immune to local zoning laws. While none of the power players involved in rebuilding Ground Zero holds all the cards, Pataki has a fistful of aces.

## "LOOKS LIKE ALBANY"

In early 2002, the LMDC hired Alexander Garvin, an urban-planning professor from Yale University, to lead its design efforts. He brought aboard two respected, but less-than-visionary, architectural firms—Beyer Blinder Belle and Parsons Brinkerhoff—thus eliciting groans from the design community. While Beyer Blinder Belle's Adirondack-style rest stops along the New York State Thruway are attractive enough, they hardly inspire awe.

Driven by fears that they would be shut out of the planning process, various September 11–related foundations started coming together in the spring of 2002, hoping to influence the LMDC as well as Pataki, who seemed particularly attuned to public opinion (he was running for a third term as governor). Chief among their priorities is assuring that the footprints of the towers be left for a memorial and that significant space remain free from commercial development.

"We don't want the site to be a cemetery," says Anthony Gardner, who founded the WTC United Family Group soon after his older brother, Harvey, died in the North Tower. "The more vibrant and more alive [the rebuilding] is, the more people will come downtown. But it's important to provide enough space to honor the victims. This is the final resting place of 3,000 people. It's sacred ground."

While these groups were organizing, the LMDC and the Port Authority were settling on six plans and a schedule: The public were to view the designs in July 2002; by December, one would be selected and incorporated into a master plan for lower Manhattan.

**None of the players working to rebuild holds all the cards, but Governor Pataki has a fistful of aces.**

About 5,000 people attended a public showing of the proposals, including nearly 1,000 relatives of the victims. Most onlookers were underwhelmed. The architects followed their instructions to cram the towers' original square footage of office space into each plan, and they did so in the form most palatable to the real-estate community—blocky office buildings, with minimal land devoted to a memorial. Experts and amateurs alike ripped the designs for lacking ambition. "Looks like Albany," scoffed one critic, comparing the models to the state's architecturally banal capital. In an editorial titled "The Downtown We Don't Want," *The New York Times* called the schemes "dreary, leaden." LMDC spokesman Matthew Higgins agreed: "They were unimaginative. [The designs] failed to communicate the extent to which the memorial would always be the centerpiece of whatever emerged in lower Manhattan."

## BACK TO THE DRAWING BOARD

The people had spoken—"Score one for grassroots democracy," trumpeted the New York *Daily News*—and they demanded a grand plan on par with the Eiffel Tower, the Brooklyn Bridge or the Empire State Building. To its credit, the LMDC showed agility: It quickly announced a design competition and summoned the kind of talent it had thus far avoided. More than 400 bids poured in, and six teams from around the world—as well as one local firm—were invited to reimagine lower Manhattan. Notable names included Richard Meier (Los Angeles' Getty Center) and Daniel Libeskind (Berlin's Jewish Museum, which resembles a silver lighting bolt).

The LMDC asked finalists to incorporate the following facets in their designs: a large transit hub linked to commuter rail lines and local airports (a sort of Grand Central South); a promenade connecting the site to Battery Park; and ample room for a memorial (the memorial will be chosen in another competition, with officials hoping to approve a design by September 11, 2003). A master plan for the redevelopment has been promised by early 2003.

The LMDC also opened the door to reducing the amount of office space to as little as 6 million square feet—a far cry from the 11 million first proposed, but still more than all of the office space in downtown St. Louis. This reduction should leave more room for the inclusion of a cultural institution, like a proposed Museum of Tolerance, or a new home for the City Opera, an idea that intrigues its director, Sherwin Goldman. "It's an opportunity to create another center of attraction [downtown]," he said on the first anniversary of the attacks. "You go to Nobu, you go to Bouley Bakery. Why wouldn't you go three more blocks to the opera?"

The new designs were unveiled in late December and were so daring, more than one critic called them "pies in the sky." But the creative efforts far surpassed the first batch. London's Sir Norman Foster envisioned "kissing" towers, a pair of twisting crystalline structures that touch in three places. Meier's team designed five 1,111-foot-tall buildings with interconnecting walkways—sort of a giant, futuristic tic-tac-toe board—as well as a park with 2,800 lights, one for each victim. Of the seven teams' nine proposals, four called for structures that would climb higher than the Twin Towers.

A final decision, planned for early 2003, had not been reached at press time, but one design decision is not in doubt: The first building to rise again will be the one that fell last. Seven World Trade Center collapsed late in the afternoon on September 11, after sustaining massive structural damage when the towers came down. Financed by Silverstein, the new 52-floor, glass-clad office tower will sit astride Greenwich Avenue, abutting a 15,000-square-foot park and pedestrian plaza. (Because the building will lie just north of the main site, Silverstein didn't have to wait for redevelopment plans to be completed.)

## ZERO HOUR

One of the planners' long-term goals is to turn lower Manhattan into something it has not been since the 19th century: a mixed-use community. Prior to the attack, the area emptied after the workday ended. While the idea of creating a vital new neighborhood is appealing, Battery Park City is ample proof that simply placing residents into a cluster of high-rise buildings hardly generates the kind of urban vigor that animates better-loved parts of the city. It will take more than people and office space; for starters, it will take new museums, schools, parks and small businesses, in addition to restoring streets that were taken off the map when the World Trade Center was built. While Mayor Bloomberg's influence at Ground Zero is marginal, in December 2002 he proposed a bold $10 billion redevelopment for the surrounding area that would include new institutions, new schools and a tree-lined promenade in the manner of the Champs-Elysées.

The political rivalries will make a consensus difficult. Pataki has remained involved, but he's not a master builder in the tradition of Robert Moses, Nelson A. Rockefeller or Franklin D. Roosevelt. A strong hand will be needed to guide the development process through the inevitable thicket of protesters, lawyers and naysayers that will work to disrupt it.

The planners are seeking to do what is perhaps impossible—restore grandeur to the scarred skyline, honor the dead, make downtown the world's capital of capitalism again and revive the city's sluggish economy. Can it be done? "Time will tell," said WTC United founder Gardner. "You have to trust the people involved. And you have to have faith."

Bloomberg was more emphatic. "Some doubt that we have the stamina required to get this done," he told the press in late 2002. "But if history teaches us anything, it's that you should never doubt New York. Never."

**United they stand** A proposal for the WTC site by Richard Meier & Partners Architects, Eisenman Architects, Gwathmey Siegel & Associates and Steven Holl Architects.

# Fringe Scene

## There's a burlesque and vaudeville renaissance in bars and cabaret spaces throughout the city. Just don't call it stripping.

We've got news for the bluenosed boosters of the new 42nd Street, those pooh-bahs of puritanism who claim to have cleaned the streets of strippers and peep-show parlors: New York is still Sin City. Granted, except for a few sex-shop holdouts *(see* **Times a-changin'**, *page 86)*, the most titillation you'll find in Times Square these days is a 50-foot-high billboard for Victoria's Secret, but that doesn't mean adult entertainment is dead. In fact, in the past few years, there's been an explosion of striptease acts, unofficially dubbed the new burlesque. Encompassing more than a dozen participating venues all over town and scores of practitioners, the "burly-q" renaissance signals the return of an old art form given a novel twist by dancers and performance artists.

Burlesque, a popular and slightly disreputable pastime that involved elaborate striptease and clowning to music, flourished in America roughly from the 1860s to the 1940s, reaching its apogee with striptease superstar Gypsy Rose Lee. In the 1950s and on, the elegant and comic art of striptease decayed into the hardcore strip routine that became associated with a degenerate Times Square. Forty years later, the burgeoning new burlesque movement includes a diverse array of performers whose acts may include elements from traditional burlesque, cabaret, old-time vaudeville and the circus. These shows have become a preferred pastime for a canny young crowd that wants to gets its rocks off and still respect itself in the morning.

What's the difference between burlesque and, say, Hooters? Or a sleazy strip club, for that matter? "It's very clear," says Kate Valentine, one of the movement's most successful impresarios. In her alter ego as the eye-patch–wearing German dominatrix Miss Astrid, Valentine hosts the weekly **Va Va Voom Room** *(www.vavavoomroom.com)* at Fez *(see page 309)*. "I've been to a strip club before, and there's a definite exchange of power between the stripper and the (usually male) client," Valentine explains. "I don't think strip has much to do with sex. Striptease, on the other hand…has something celebratory and fun about it." She laughs. "We're certainly not in it for the money. Strippers make much more."

**Fresh produce** Striptease artist Harvest reaps applause at the Va Va Voom Room.

In strip clubs, bored pseudomodels with implants gyrate on poles to tacky techno music. In burlesque, the nudity is never complete, the costumes are imaginative, and the dominant mood is jolly nostalgia. Music-wise, expect lots of hot jazz and swing. The dancers—who come in a dazzling variety of shapes and sizes—almost seem to be having more fun than the audience. They adopt colorful monikers like "Dirty Martini," "The World Famous Bob" or "Tigger." The strip portion of the act (which never goes beyond pasties and a G-string) is almost secondary to the concept. New burlesque fuses performance art, dance and comedy—and carries a pro-sex postfeminist sentiment that rejects both the cartoonish sex-doll images of Britney Spears and old-school feminism. Some of the dancers are in their late twenties, but most are in their thirties. This ain't your grandmother's burlesque, but it's also not your kid sister's.

Va Va Voom, which recently celebrated its fourth anniversary in New York, hosts a remarkable amalgam of acts. There's Red Diamond, a Cab Calloway impersonator in a glittering white suit leading the audience in a sing-along of "Minnie the Moocher." A puppet act follows, then traditional striptease from The World Famous Bob. Despite her cheeky name, Bob is a woman, who's quite zaftig, with a smile frozen on her Marilyn Monroe face. Accompanied by ironically cheesy lounge jazz, Bob strips to her bustier and garters. The climax of her act includes pouring gin into a shaker, shoving it deep within her cleavage and shimmying it to martini perfection—the cocktail is served to the lucky front row. "My audiences like the homemade quality of the acts," Valentine explains. "It's not exactly antitechnology, but it's charming because it's so low-tech and different from the slick, special effects–laden stuff on Broadway. And it's titillating, but not exploitative."

Boo Froebel, the artistic director of the Williamsburg bar and performance space **Galapagos** *(see page 309),* once invited a friend to see the club's Monday Evening Burlesque. "At first, she didn't want to come," Froebel said. "She had never seen strip or striptease, but she was surprised by how many women were in the audience hooting and hollering. That's how I gauge the success of the show, if I can get the women to enjoy it. The last thing I want to do is make anybody nervous. I certainly don't want to make it a sex show or peep show where guys come to ogle women."

Froebel sounds and looks like the mild-mannered girl next door, yet the weekly shows she schedules at Galapagos are anything but. One week in fall 2002, the lineup included a textbook example of classic burly-q by one of the scene's veterans—Dirty Martini, a Rubenesque blond who does a routine about a housewife undressing to just her garters and pasties. Another evening, the show will feature the burlesque equivalent of punk, with pieces by the naughty retro '60s Bombshell Girls, a troupe of svelte dancers who create variations on a theme, such as stripteases using umbrellas. One particularly inventive number involves a performer in male drag being terrorized by a blow-up doll that comes to life (played by another dancer in costume).

A number of new burlesque performers, like Va Va Voom Room regular Julie Atlas Muz, come from performance-art and dance backgrounds. Muz creates dances that blend political commentary, quirky humor and, occasionally, morbidity. One number involves a bloodied, disembodied hand manipulated by Muz, which travels over her semi-exposed body and ends up strangling her. The cherubic, strawberry-blond Muz straddles the border between silly and dangerous. She's also nicely candid about her craft. "I don't do it exclusively for money, but it is a job. There are times when I'm sighing 'Oh, God, I have to go-go for two hours and I have to put on the glitter and eyelashes!' "

**The climax of Bob's act includes pouring gin into a shaker, shoving it deep within her cleavage and shimmying it to martini perfection—the cocktail is served to the lucky front row.**

As for the sexual politics of striptease, Muz makes a distinction between private and public. "There's a time and a place for everything," she says. "When I walk down the street and I get 'Nice ass!' it drives me out of my mind. Over the years, I've tried different tactics to stop men from catcalling. But in a burlesque setting, that's totally appropriate, and if it doesn't happen, I'm a little disappointed."

Other major stops on the New York burlesque circuit include **The Slipper Room** *(167 Orchard St at Stanton St, 212-253-7246; www.slipperroom.com),* a cozy, red-curtained bar on the Lower East Side where, once a month, the owners throw the go-go dance party Daddy's Chicken. For more in-your-face shows, try **The Cutting Room** *(19 W 24th St between Broadway and Sixth Ave, 212-691-1900; www.thecuttingroomnyc.com)* in Chelsea. Each

**Fly girl** Fire Goddess swings through the air with the Bindlestiff Family Cirkus.

Saturday night at midnight, the intimate back room is commandeered by the ladies of Le Scandal *(www.lescandal.com)*. The tone is grittier and less innocent than Va Va Voom. Dancers go topless, for one thing. The act also includes fire-eating, sword swallowing and high-concept striptease, such as Twisted Sister Anne, who bumps and grinds to Nightranger's "Sister Christian" while slowly ditching her nun's habit for white socks and a wimple. On Friday nights at midnight, Miss Kitty's The Goddess Show presents a potpourri of comedy and magic; the producers describe it as a cross between *Sex and the City* and *Saturday Night Live*.

During the summer, head to Coney Island for **Burlesque at the Beach** *(see* **Coney Island USA**, *page 115)*, a tip of the hat to the neighborhood's past that features a new lineup every Friday night at 10pm. The talent includes Insectavora, a slim woman with a heavily pierced and tattooed face who eats live bugs and worms (no joke). She also performs an impressive fire dance, brandishing ten flaming minitorches attached to her fingers.

Some burlesque acts survive without permanent homes.These include: the Folies Bergère–inspired **Pontani Sisters** *(www.pontanisisters.com)*, the singing–and–trapeze-flying **Wau Wau Sisters** *(www.wauwausisters.com)* and the witty, plus-size women of **The Glamazons** *(www.glamazongirls.com)*. Keep track of where the troupes are playing each week by visiting their websites.

To witness a performance that defies categorization, buy a ticket to the **Bindlestiff Family Cirkus** *(877-246-3537; www.bindlestiff.org)*. The nine-year-old troupe presents a variety show that incorporates clown acts, magic, music, aerial daring and burlesque numbers that frequently include risqué fetish tricks. The company recently completed a four-month run at the experimental-theater venue **Chashama** *(125 W 42nd St between Sixth Ave and Broadway, 718-907-0819; www.chashama.org)*. Founders Keith Nelson and Stephanie Monseu spend about six months of the year on tour, bringing New York's premier variety acts to the rest of the country; Nelson performs rope tricks and some truly stomach-churning sword-swallowing feats. At a recent Bindlestiff show, Nelson summed up the variety aesthetic in his sly, lisping voice, "If you don't like what you see, wait five or six minutes for the next attraction!"

Why is there so much recent interest in these old-fashioned stage shows—even down to reproductions of classic fan dances and acts from the early part of the 20th century? "Every generation rebels against what came before," says Travis Stewart, a playwright, emcee and founder of the American Vaudeville Theatre. "It was like Sherman's march through Georgia in terms of what the '60s generation did to old-school popular culture; they killed off everything they thought was corny and old-timey." Says Stewart, whose history of vaudeville and burlesque will be published by Farrar, Straus and Giroux in the spring of 2004, "The new movement recaptures traditions that were lost and functions as a reaction to the previous generation's aesthetic."

Given the volume of shows and its devoted following, an argument could be made that burlesque—once a guilty pleasure—has already gone mainstream. There may not yet be a bona fide burlesque show on Broadway at the $80-ticket level, but you can bet some producer out there is raising the money. "If someone were to put together a lineup of new burlesque performers for a big theater extravaganza, I'd do it," says Muz. "I'd love to have a job on Broadway. And then do the crazy stuff late at night when the show's over."


▶ For a taste of old-school gay burlesque, see **Gaiety**, page 288.

▶ To locate venues that regularly schedule burlesque, see chapters **Cabaret & Comedy**, **Music** and **Theater & Dance**.

# Only in New York

## A loincloth-wearing "prayformer" and a bevy of Barbies are among the attractions that make Gotham a singular sensation

**THE LOIN KING**

Even hard-boiled, seen-it-all New Yorkers stop and ask, "Who is *that*?" His name: **Thoth**. His office: Central Park, near Bethesda Fountain. His job: playing original violin ditties (he calls them "soloperas") while whirling like the Tasmanian devil and warbling in a style that's part opera, part pagan chant. (Don't try to make out the words—it's all Thothspeak.) His attire: golden loincloth, ankle bells, stripes of yellow face paint and a red plume in his dreadlocked hair. The 48-year-old falsetto, a cross between King Tut and Tiny Tim, typically "prayforms" in the park from 3 to 5pm, Wednesday through Sunday, "but only if the temperature is above 44 degrees windchill," he says. Thoth isn't for everybody, but he is a skilled fiddler, has a vocal range of five octaves and *almost* makes gold lamé look good. (For more information, visit *www.skthoth.com*.)

**DYNAMIC DUO**

Two New York City delights dovetail at Sicilian eatery **Ferdinando's Focacceria** *(151 Union St between Columbia and Hicks Sts, Cobble Hill, Brooklyn, 718-855-1545)*. Finding an ice-cold bottle of **Manhattan Special**—that sudsy, send-you-flying espresso soda—is hard enough, but finding it on tap? Holy caffeinated cow, Batman! The family-owned restaurant, which dates back to 1906, will serve you a glass of the Brooklyn-brewed rocket fuel, an 1895 brand that predates the current crop of taurine-laced energy drinks by nearly a century. The brown bubbly goes great with the **city's best sardines**: Owner Francesco Buffa panfries them with onions, then adds wild fennel, raisins, pignoli nuts, saffron and a dot of tomato paste. Try them in the house specialty, pasta *con le sarde,* a fragrant dish of sardines over *bucatini.*

**AND...THEY'RE OFF!**

Evel Knievel? A wuss. The daredevils from *Jackass*? Pansies. They're pretenders compared to the fearless **New York City cabdrivers**

**Super freak** Central Park mainstay Thoth fiddles to his own beat.

who will risk life and limb (theirs and yours) to get you where you want to go. Here's our favorite move: Let's say your driver is eastbound on 42nd, a four-lane, two-way street. He wants to turn onto Sixth Avenue heading north (never mind the NO LEFT TURN sign), but he's stuck in the right lane as he approaches a green light. He creeps into the intersection and stops, provoking a blare of horns and epithets from behind. Suspense builds as green turns to yellow—the oncoming crosstown traffic rushes to make the light, while the three lanes of cars ready to race uptown inch forward, engines revving. Then, a nanosecond before the light changes, your man whips the wheel leftward, guns the gas and shoots through the intersection, leading the herd uptown, and leaving in his wake a parade of pissed-off drivers. It's a thing of vehicular beauty, a masterful, dexterous display that only a New York cabbie—or perhaps a NASCAR racer—could pull off.

**BABES IN TOYLAND**

True, Barbie's not a New York kind of girl—she's all California shallowness. But there's something alluringly anachronistic about the **Barbie Store in FAO Schwarz** *(see page 238)*. The lair of Her Blondness is tucked away in the back corner of the toy emporium's second floor, and encountering it after the wholesome barrage of teddy bears and train sets is like discovering your big brother's porn stash: Boxed busty dolls line the walls from floor to ceiling, with personas to entice every gentleman caller—Sorority Girl Barbie, Cheerleader Barbie, Lingerie Barbie, Princess of the Nile Barbie. There are many look-but-don't-touch collectors' editions kept behind glass, and you can even buy scary disembodied *talking* Barbie heads, if that's your thing. The hot-pink room often contains more wide-eyed dads than doll-obsessed kids, which prompts the question: How could something so wrong feel so right?

**LADY LOOK**

There are plenty of great spots to spy America's matriarch, but there's something special about the **view of the Statue of Liberty from the F train**. A gorgeous glimpse awaits those who remember to gaze westward at the right instant. As the train wends its way above the roofs of redbrick apartment buildings and the surrounding bristly treetops of Carroll Gardens, Brooklyn, you'll get a first-rate view of Lady Liberty that's so clear, you can distinguish the folds in her robe. Nowadays, her status as a symbol of strength and pride is more meaningful than ever. But stay alert: She's visible for only a short time between the Carroll Street and Smith–9th Streets stations.

**UNDERGROUND MUSIC**

Here are five sensations you can see in the subway:

- A member of the band King Missile (of "Detachable Penis" fame), **Bradford Reed** made his own instrument—a four-foot-high, double-necked string contraption. He often plucks and bows self-penned tunes on his "Pencilina" just outside the Astor Place subway stop.
- The **DDT Dancers** (stands for "doing damage together") are a flashback to the *Wild Style* era. The Bronx troupe has appeared in music videos (Usher) and NBA halftime shows. The group's mix of athleticism and choreography is a Times Square–station crowd pleaser.
- Even when music teacher **Gene Ghee** is playing the *I Love Lucy* theme, the tone from his soprano sax is oh-so-sweet. He's had more than 40 years of practice: Ghee backed the Isley Brothers while in high school, but now he solos at Jay Street–Borough Hall.
- Tall, dark and handsome twin brothers **Gabriel and Guillermo Ariza** hail from Colombia. The duo sing and strum rumba and flamenco at Grand Central, Penn Station and Union Square stations.
- After she was struck by a cab, budding modern dancer **Natalia Paruz** found a new calling as a saw musician. She played Lincoln Center's Avery Fisher Hall in December 2002; you can find her at Grand Central, Times Square and Union Square.

**Monkey business** No wonder so many men wander into FAO Schwarz's Barbie Store: She's cute—and for sale.

# Sightseeing



## Feature boxes



**This bud's for you** Something is always in bloom at the Brooklyn Botanic Garden.

# Museums

From Manets and Monets to mummies—New York City museums have it all

Many consider New York to be the museum capital of the world. After all, there are more than 60 institutions holding treasures such as Gutenberg Bibles, ancient Etruscan jewelry, Plains Indian buckskins and Fabergé eggs. Of course, art lovers who've toured Paris, Rome or London may argue about New York's position in the world's rankings, but one thing is beyond dispute: The city's museums offer something for everybody, whether one wishes to examine classic oil paintings and cutting-edge video installations, trace the history of various ethnicities, or catch a favorite *I Love Lucy* rerun.

Along upper Fifth Avenue is **Museum Mile**, a strand of major repositories of world culture. There's also a growing concentration of museums in Long Island City, Queens, among them the **Museum of Modern Art** (MoMA). Great collections can be viewed all over town, from the **Brooklyn Museum of Art** to Staten Island's **Jacques Marchais Museum of Tibetan Art**, with many offering activities beyond viewing paintings, installations and sculptures—there are exhibits to touch, gardens to stroll in and fine cafés where you can refuel.

The buildings themselves are equally impressive and eclectic. Uptown, the distinctive white spiral of the **Guggenheim** never fails to make passersby—tourists and jaded locals alike—stop and stare. The gray granite cube of the **Whitney Museum of American Art**, with its Cyclops's-eye window and concrete moat, is no less stunning. And when the sun goes down, the illuminated globe of the **Rose Center for Earth and Space** is simply breathtaking.

Attempting to cram several museum visits into a single day can be exhausting. Similarly, it's usually self-defeating to try to view every major exhibition in one visit to the larger museums, such as the **Metropolitan Museum of Art** and the **American Museum of Natural History**. Even comparably small venues like the Whitney can wear you out, so make sure to pace yourself: A host of excellent museum cafés and restaurants allow convenient breaks. Great places for a respite include Sarabeth's at the Whitney, Café Sabarsky at the **Neue Galerie**, the Museum Café in the **Morgan Library** and the **Jewish Museum**'s Café Weissman. While it might be tempting to save museums for a rainy day, remember that most sites offer glorious air-conditioned comfort on a hot summer day, and convivial warmth, come winter.

Although entry usually costs no more than the price of a movie ticket, admission prices may shock some visitors. This is because most New York museums are privately funded, with little or no government subsidies. Even so, a majority of the city's art institutions, including the Whitney, MoMA, the Guggenheim and the **International Center of Photography** *(see page 265)*, offer at least one evening a week when admission is either free or a voluntary donation. And while the city's crown jewel, the Metropolitan Museum, has a suggested $12 donation for adults, you can pay what you wish at all times. That's right—you can experience one of the world's finest museums for as little as 25 cents! (You're certain to get much more than two bits' worth of culture.)

## CRITICS' PICKS Museums

These museums are the best...

**...for spine-tingling dinosaurs**
American Museum of Natural History, *see page 41*

**...for immigrant history**
Lower East Side Tenement Museum, *see page 51*

**...for Mondays (when most institutions are closed)**
MoMA QNS, *see page 46*

**...for when you want your mummy**
The Metropolitan Museum of Art, *see page 44*

**...for peace and quiet**
The Frick Collection, *see page 43*

**...for a titillating time**
The Museum of Sex, *see page 53*

**...for a postmuseum picnic**
The Cloisters, *see page 41*

**...for viewing classic sitcoms**
The Museum of Television & Radio, *see page 57*

**...for Viennese decadence**
Neue Galerie, *see page 50*

Many of New York's best-loved venues—among them the **Frick Collection**, the Morgan Library, the **Schomburg Center for Research in Black Culture**, the Whitney and the Guggenheim—began as private collections. **The Cloisters**, at the northern reaches of Manhattan in Fort Tryon Park, was oil magnate John D. Rockefeller's gift to New York. Its reconstructed monastery holds the Met's beautiful collection of medieval art. In summer, bring a picnic lunch and bask in the garden, which affords spectacular views of the Hudson River and the rocky cliffs of the Palisades in New Jersey.

While you may relish the freedom of exploring museums on your own, consider that many institutions give tours that are fun and educational. For example, the audio tour at the provocative **Ellis Island Museum** and the guided tours at the **Lower East Side Tenement Museum** and the **Museum of Jewish Heritage**, all provide visitors with fascinating insights into NYC's immigrant roots.

Across the Hudson, New Jersey's **Liberty Science Center** is an unexpected pleasure, with its interactive exhibits and rooftop terrace overlooking Manhattan and the Statue of Liberty. You can take the **NY Waterway ferry** *(see page 132)* and admire Lady Liberty along the way.

As accomplished as they are, the city's museums rarely rest on their laurels—the scene is always shifting. One of the most dramatic recent examples of this is the American Museum of Natural History's construction of the Rose Center for Earth and Space. During 2002, the **Museum of Sex** opened its doors on Fifth Avenue, and the Brooklyn Museum began restoration of its Beaux Arts facade. Not to be outdone, the MoMA, the **Museum for African Art** and the **Isamu Noguchi Garden Museum**—all currently getting new or redesigned permanent homes—put down temporary stakes in Long Island City, joining the

> ▶ See chapter **Art Galleries** for more places to view art.
> ▶ For other sights and neighborhoods to explore, see chapters **Downtown**, **Midtown**, **Uptown**, **Brooklyn**, **Queens**, **The Bronx** and **Staten Island**.
> ▶ See ***Time Out New York*** for reviews and listings of current exhibitions.
> ▶ For dining options near museums, see chapter **Restaurants**.

**Animal house** Beastly mosaics mark the subway stop for the Natural History museum.

**P.S. 1 Contemporary Art Center** and the **American Museum of the Moving Image**.

But the game of musical museums doesn't stop there. The **Dahesh Museum** moved from Fifth Avenue to a larger venue on Madison Avenue, and the American Craft Museum renamed itself the **Museum of Arts and Design**. Eventually, it will relocate to Columbus Circle (near the AOL Time Warner building), in a vacant white-marble building designed by MoMA's original architect, Edward Durrell Stone. In spring 2003, Chelsea's **Dia Center for the Arts** will open a satellite facility in Beacon, New York, on the Hudson River, about 60 miles north of the city. There's even been talk of converting the six-story brownstone that once housed the Russian Tea Room (which closed in 2002) into a new museum of golf.

No matter which institutions you choose to visit, don't hesitate to bring your kids; the majority of venues have special events for children (*see chapter* **Kids' Stuff**).

Most New York museums are closed on New Year's Day, Presidents' Day, Memorial Day, Independence Day, Labor Day, Columbus Day, Thanksgiving and Christmas *(see* **Holidays**, *page 358)*. Some change their hours in summer; it's wise to check before setting out.

Security guards at all public institutions will ask you to open your purse or backpack for inspection; all bags must be checked, along with umbrellas, but there's no charge for the coatrooms. Most museums also provide free wheelchairs.

## Major institutions

### American Museum of Natural History

*Central Park West at 79th St (212-769-5000, recorded information 212-769-5100; www.amnh.org). Subway: B, C to 81st St–Museum of Natural History; 1, 9 to 79th St. Sun–Thu 10am–5:45pm; Fri, Sat 10am–8:45pm. Suggested donation $12, seniors and students $9, children $7. AmEx, MC, V.*

The thrills begin when you cross the threshold of the Theodore Roosevelt Rotunda and are confronted with a towering barosaur, rearing high on its hind legs to protect its young from an attacking allosaurus (similar to a tyrannosaur, but smaller). It's an impressive welcome to the largest museum of its kind in the world (and a reminder to visit the dinosaur halls on the fourth floor). During the museum's mid-1990s renovation (by the firm responsible for much of the Ellis Island Museum restoration), several specimens were remodeled in light of recent discoveries. The T-rex, for instance, was once believed to have walked upright, Godzilla-style; it's much more menacing now as it stalks, head down, with its tail parallel to the ground. The rest of the site is equally dramatic. The Hall of Biodiversity examines world ecosystems and environmental preservation. The spectacular $210 million **Rose Center for Earth and Space**—dazzling to come upon at night—is a giant silvery globe where you can learn about the universe through 3-D shows in the Hayden Planetarium and light shows in the Big Bang Theater. The museum's dazzling collection of gems includes the obscenely large Star of India sapphire, and enough diamonds and pearls to make Tiffany & Co. look like a Piercing Pagoda. An IMAX theater shows bigger-than-life nature programs, and there are always innovative temporary exhibitions, in addition to an easily accessible research library with vast photo and print archives, and a friendly, helpful staff.

### Brooklyn Museum of Art

See **Art and soul**, page 44.

### The Cloisters

*Fort Tryon Park, Fort Washington Ave at Margaret Corbin Plaza (212-923-3700; www.metmuseum.org). Travel: A to 190th St, then take the M4 bus or follow Margaret Corbin Dr north (about the length of five city blocks) to the museum. Mar–Oct Tue–Sun 9:30am–5:15pm; Nov–Feb Tue–Sun 9:30am–4:45pm. Suggested donation $12 (includes admission*

**Star search** The 3-D presentations at the Rose Center for Earth and Space at the American Museum of Natural History teaches science fans the secrets of the universe.

**You break it, you buy it** The Frick Collection's Fragonard Room is filled with elegant 18th-century furniture and restored rococo masterpieces.



*to the Metropolitan Museum of Art on the same day), seniors and students $7, under 12 free if accompanied by an adult. Cash only.*

The Cloisters houses the Met's medieval art and architecture collections in a bucolic park overlooking the Hudson River. A path winds through the tranquil grounds, bringing you to a castle that seems to have survived from the Middle Ages, even though it was built a mere 60 years ago. (It is constructed from pieces of five medieval cloisters from France.) Don't miss the famous "Unicorn Tapestries" or *The Annunciation Triptych* by Robert Campin.

## Cooper-Hewitt, National Design Museum

*2 E 91st St at Fifth Ave (212-849-8400; www.si.edu/ndm). Subway: 6 to 96th St. Tue 10am–9pm; Wed–Fri 10am–5pm; Sat 10am–6pm; Sun noon–5pm. $8, seniors and students $5, under 12 free. Tue 5–9pm free. Cash only.*

The Smithsonian's National Design Museum was once the home of industrialist Andrew Carnegie, whose architects responded to his request for "the most modest, plainest and most roomy house in New York" by designing a 64-room mansion in the style of a 19-century Georgian country estate. Recent exhibitions have included the first public viewing of early 20th-century Austrian, Czech and German glass, and a full-scale retrospective of furniture, dinnerware and appliances by the American designer Russel Wright. This is the only museum in the U.S. to collect examples of historical and contemporary design as well as domestic and industrial design. From April through September it will host the **National Design Triennial**, to explore breaking developments in architectural, interior and landscape design, as well as advances in graphics and fashion. Before you go, check out the website's terrific virtual tours. Sign language interpretation is available upon request *(212-849-8387).*

## Frick Collection

*1 E 70th St between Fifth and Madison Aves (212-288-0700; www.frick.org). Subway: N, R, W to Fifth Ave–59th St; 6 to 68th St–Hunter College. Tue–Sat 10am–6pm; Fri 10am–9pm; Sun 1–6pm. $12, seniors and students $5, children 10–16 must be accompanied by an adult, under 10 not admitted. Cash only.*

The opulent residence that houses this private collection of great masters from the 14th through the 19th centuries is more like a stately home than a museum (the dwelling was built for industrialist Henry Clay Frick). The firm of Carrére & Hastings designed the 1914 structure in an 18th-century European style.

Even if it didn't contain world-class paintings, sculpture and furniture by Rembrandt, Vermeer, Renoir, and the French cabinetmaker Jean-Henri Riesener, the museum would still be a must-see for its interior court and reflecting pool, which offer a welcome respite from New York's hectic streets.

### Guggenheim

See **Solomon R. Guggenheim Museum**, page 47.

### Metropolitan Museum of Art

*1000 Fifth Ave at 82nd St (212-535-7710; www.metmuseum.org). Subway: 4, 5, 6 to 86th St. Tue–Thu, Sun 9:30am–5:30pm; Fri, Sat 9:30am–9pm. Suggested donation $10, seniors and students $5, under 12 free. Cash only. No strollers on Sundays.*

It could take days, even weeks, to cover the Met's 1.5 million square feet of exhibition space, so it's best to be selective. Several enthralling temporary exhibitions are on view at any given time. Egyptology fans should head straight for the glass-walled atrium housing the Temple of Dendur. There are excellent collections of African, Oceanic and Islamic art, along with more than 3,000 European paintings from the medieval through the fin de siècle periods, including major works by Titian, Brueghel, Rembrandt, Vermeer, Goya, Manet and Degas. The Greek and Roman halls have received a graceful face-lift; the incomparable collection of medieval armor—a huge favorite with both adults and children—was recently enriched by new gifts



## Art and soul

**The Brooklyn Museum of Art's vast holdings rival anything found on Museum Mile. And there's dancing, too!**

The Brooklyn Museum of Art has a lot going for it: a magnificent late-19th-century Beaux Arts building; world-class collections of ancient and modern works; and an ongoing $55 million renovation of the entrance pavilion and plaza. There are even free dance parties every month.

About the only problem with the BMA is the "B." Since it's not located in Manhattan, the 178-year-old landmark is often overlooked by art connoisseurs who head straight for Museum Mile, unaware that the holdings here rival those of venerable venues such as the Metropolitan Museum of Art. (And the BMA is a mere 30-minute subway ride from midtown.)

Even its recent moment in the sun brought more infamy than fame. In 1999, a British exhibition called "Sensation" included Chris Ofili's painting *The Holy Virgin Mary*, decorated with elephant dung; it so angered former mayor Rudolph Giuliani (he called it "sick stuff") that he tried to cut off the BMA's financing. For a time, the firestorm drew crowds (and protesters), but today, the museum is rarely overrun, and the 560,000-square-foot space feels downright intimate.

That's all the better for adventurous art lovers, who have plenty to choose from in 2003. Among the museum's remarkable assets is a 4,000-piece Egyptian collection. Much of it has been in storage for years, but more than 1,500 treasured antiquities will go on long-term view *(starting April 12)*, including a gilded-ebony statue of Amenhotep III and, on the ceiling, a large-scale rendering of an ancient map of the cosmos.

A public study area will open in the Luce Center for American Art *(November)*. The space will add 3,000 objects—arranged in a spectacular glass-walled, open-shelf display—to the existing fifth-floor installation of important pieces from the museum's collections of painting, sculpture and decorative art. Located near the Rodin sculpture court, the center will include work by artists such as Thomas Eakins, Winslow Homer, Alex Katz, Barbara Kruger, Gaston Lachaise and Larry Rivers.

As the first New York institution to establish a collection of vintage photographs, the BMA's holdings in photography and printmaking run deep. There's an equally impressive display of European painting and sculpture; a new installation will show masterworks by Cezanne, Courbet, Degas and Monet *(beginning in August)*. But don't pass up the impressive African and Pacific Island galleries, or the outstanding sampling of Native American and Pre-Colombian textiles and art.

A wealth of temporary exhibitions is planned for 2003. The "Last Expression" *(Mar 7–Jun 15)* is a showing of artworks made by Holocaust victims while interned at Auschwitz and will feature many pieces never before seen by the public. "Pulp Art" *(Mar 21–Jul 20)* is a collection of paintings made for pulp magazine covers in the 1930s and '40s. In 2004 the museum will salute African-American fashion designer Patrick Kelly, who produced some of the most exuberant and influential

of European, North American, Japanese and Islamic arms. The Met has also made significant additions to its galleries of 20th-century art, including video artist Bill Viola's moving homage to Breughel. Contemporary sculptures are displayed each year in the Iris and B. Gerald Cantor Roof Garden *(May–Oct),* the perfect place to grab a sandwich and a beer or cocktail while surveying the skyscrapers soaring above Central Park. Foreign-language tours are available *(212-570-3711).*

**Planned 2003 exhibitions:** The Annenberg Collection of Impressionist and Postimpressionist Art, on loan from Philadelphia, returns this year *(May–mid-Nov).* A blockbuster show, "Manet/Velázquez," is also in the works *(Mar 4–Jun 8).* There will be special exhibitions of Chinese porcelain *(through Jul 13)* as well as works by Paul Klee *(Jun 3–Aug 17).* The Great Hall and the Howard Gilman Gallery will feature a major retrospective of the contemporary photographs of Thomas Struth *(Feb 4–May 18),* and later, the Howard Gilman Gallery will mount a full-scale retrospective of photographer Charles Sheeler *(Jun 3–Aug 17).* In the Costume Institute, "Goddess" examines how the dress of ancient Greece and Rome influenced art and design for centuries to come *(May 1–Aug 3).* A retrospective of the paintings of Dutch virtuoso Hendrik Goltzius will appear in the Robert Lehman Galleries *(Jun 26–Sept 8).*

**Party arty** A couple cozies up to a classic at First Saturday, the Brooklyn Museum of Art's monthly shindig. The museum is undergoing a $55 million renovation.

fashions of the 1980s before he died from AIDS in 1990 *(Mar 5–May 30).*

If you want to rub noses (and who knows what else) with cute city singles, check out the monthly **First Saturday** party *(6–11pm).* The free schmoozefest offers live dance music, screenings of film classics, art lectures and wine tastings.

The museum is also giving its facade a $55 million makeover that will add a glass pavilion to its entrance and a new public plaza to the drive leading up to it. Construction should be complete by early 2004, with two plaza fountains shooting ribbons of water, and a new exterior staircase providing views of the restored lobby on ground level. Until then, visitors must enter through the parking lot at the rear of the museum. But the approach isn't so grim as it may sound: The path running directly from the subway on Eastern Parkway borders the exquisite **Brooklyn Botanic Garden** *(see* **Seasons in the sun**, *page 113).*

### The Brooklyn Museum of Art

*200 Eastern Pkwy at Washington Ave, Prospect Heights, Brooklyn (718-638-5000; www.brooklynart.org). Subway: 2, 3 to Eastern Pkwy–Brooklyn Museum. Wed–Fri 10am–5pm; Sat, Sun 11am–6pm; first Saturday of each month 11am–11pm. $6, seniors and students $3, under 12 free. Cash only.*

Sightseeing

### The Morgan Library

*29 E 36th St between Madison and Park Aves (212-685-0008; www.morganlibrary.org). Subway: 6 to 33rd St. Tue–Thu 10:30am–5pm; Fri 10:30am–8pm; Sat 10:30am–6pm; Sun noon–6pm. $8, seniors and students $6, under 12 free. Cash only.*

This complex houses a fabulous archive of rare books, illuminated manuscripts and prints, making it both a museum *and* an extraordinary literary-research facility. Banker and financier J.P. Morgan Jr. had the Classical Revival structure built in 1928, next to the CharlesMcKim–designed Italianate building that had been his father's private library, to make the collection available to the public. A marble rotunda with a carved 16th-century Italian ceiling separates the three-tiered library from the deep-red study. The standouts include three Gutenberg Bibles, original Mahler manuscripts and the gorgeous silver, copper and cloisonné 12th-century Stavelot triptych. Guided tours are available Tuesdays through Fridays at noon. There's also a modern conservatory, with a tranquil courtyard café.

### Museum of Modern Art, Queens

*45-20 33rd St off Queens Blvd, Long Island City, Queens (212-708-9400; www.moma.org). Subway: 7 to 33rd St. Mon, Thu, Sat 10am–5pm; Fri 10am–7:45pm. $12, seniors and students $8.50, under 12 free. Fri 4–7:45pm voluntary donation. Cash only.*

The Museum of Modern Art contains the world's finest, most comprehensive holdings of 20th-century art, including an unsurpassed collection of photography. The museum has moved from its West 53rd Street home to the former Swingline staple factory in Long Island City, Queens, where it will stay until 2005, when expansion of to the midtown headquarters is complete. The low-slung electric-blue building now known as MoMA QNS is just a 15-minute subway ride from midtown, not far from MoMA's affiliate, **P.S. 1 Contemporary Art Center** *(see below)*. Due to space restrictions, only highlights of the permanent collection (in addition to temporary and traveling exhibitions) are on display. But what highlights! They include the best of Cezanne, Matisse, Picasso, Van Gogh (his *Starry Night* is here), Giacometti, Pollock, Rothko and Warhol, among many others. Back in Manhattan, the museum's outstanding Film and Media department (it has more than 14,000 films) has taken over the Gramercy Theater *(see* **Museum of Modern Art**, *page 283)*, where it will continue to host 20-plus screenings each week for the duration of MoMA's reconstruction.

**Planned 2003 exhibitions:** Despite a diminished space, nothing has stopped MoMA from mounting the buzz-worthy temporary exhibitions it's known for. A must-see for 2003 is "Matisse Picasso." The blockbuster show, which focuses on the complex, competitive relationship between the two masters, has wowed crowds in London and Paris; its nearly 140 pieces include paintings, sculptures and works on paper *(Feb 13–May 19)*. The great German Expressionist painter Max Beckmann will be the subject of an important, far-reaching exhibition *(Jun 26–Sept 29)*, while "Ansel Adams at 100" is the first major critical evaluation of the American photographer since his death in 1984 *(Jul 10–Nov 3)*. And contemporary art enthusiasts will enjoy a sweeping survey of print works by New York's own Kiki Smith *(Dec–Feb 2004)*.

## Cheap tix

If you're planning a multimuseum tour to cover several days—not to mention a visit to the Empire State Building or a Circle Line tour—consider buying a **CityPass** for $38 *(children 12–17 $31)*. Similarly, the **New York Pass** covers admission to more than 40 of the city's top cultural and popular attractions, with added discounts and unlimited public transportation. The card costs $39 for the day *(children 2–12 $21)* and $119 for the week *(children $84)*. Compare benefits and purchase cards at www.citypass.com and www.newyorkpass.com.

### New Museum of Contemporary Art

*583 Broadway between Houston and Prince Sts (212-219-1222; www.newmuseum.org). Subway: F, V, S to Broadway–Lafayette St; N, R, W to Prince St; 6 to Bleecker St. Tue–Sun noon–6pm; Thu noon–8pm. $6, under 18 free. Thu 6–8pm, $3. AmEx, DC, Disc, MC, V.*

Now under a new administration, this 25-year-old Soho institution has found its footing and matured into a showcase for contemporary art of significant international import. Its mid-career retrospectives of artists often underrecognized in the U.S.—from South Africa's William Kentridge to Los Angeles' Paul McCarthy and New York's Carroll Dunham—attract serious crowds who no longer dismiss the place as trendy or flaky. The 24-hour street-level window displays are also hard to beat; below-stairs, the Zenith Media Lounge holds regular Friday-night events and is perhaps the premier spot in the city for edgy, digitally based art. No admission fee is required for entrance to the museum's terrific art bookstore, open seven days.

### P.S. 1 Contemporary Art Center

*22-25 Jackson Ave at 46th Ave, Long Island City, Queens (718-784-2084; www.ps1.org). Subway: E, V to 23rd St–Ely Ave; G to Long Island City–Court Sq; 7 to 45th Rd–Court House Sq. Mon–Thu noon–6pm. Suggested donation $5, seniors and students $2. Cash only.*

Cutting-edge shows and an international studio program make any visit to this freewheeling contemporary-art space a treasure hunt, with artwork turning up in every corner, including the stairwells, roof and basement. In a distinctive Romanesque Revival building, whose maze of exhibition rooms

**The squeal world** Studio Museum in Harlem shows edgy works like Gary Simmons's *Here, Piggy Piggy,* inspired by characters from the film *Deliverance.*



still bear evidence of the high school it once was, P.S. 1 mounts shows that appeal to adults and children alike. P.S. 1 became an affiliate of MoMA in 1999, but has a wholly independent schedule of temporary exhibitions and a decidedly global worldview.

## Solomon R. Guggenheim Museum

*1071 Fifth Ave at 89th St (212-423-3500; www.guggenheim.org). Subway: 4, 5, 6 to 86th St. Wed–Sat 10am–5:45pm; Fri 10am–8pm. $15, seniors and students $8, under 12 free and must be accompanied by an adult. Fri 6–8pm voluntary donation. AmEx, MC, V.*

Even if your hectic museum-hopping schedule doesn't allow time to view the collections, you must visit this uptown museum's white spiral of a building, coiled among the 19th-century mansions on Fifth Avenue's Museum Mile. Designed by Frank Lloyd Wright, the Guggenheim itself is a stunning piece of art. In addition to works by Manet, Kandinsky, Picasso and Chagall, the museum owns Peggy Guggenheim's trove of Cubist, Surrealist and Abstract Expressionist works and the Panza di Biumo collection of American Minimalist and Conceptual art from the 1960s and '70s. In 1992, a ten-story-tower addition provided space for a sculpture gallery (with views of Central Park), an auditorium and a café. Since then, the Guggenheim has drawn increasing notoriety, thanks in large part to its ambitious global expansion, its penchant for sweeping historical presentations (5,000 years of Chinese art), calculated celebrations of pop culture (Norman Rockwell, motorcycles and Giorgio Armani), and in-depth retrospectives of major contemporary artists such as Robert Rauschenberg and Nam Jun Paik.

**Planned 2003 exhibitions:** The Guggenheim canceled or postponed several exhibitions due to funding problems in the wake of September 11, 2001, but the museum bounced back in 2002 and shows no signs of slowing down in 2003. Matthew Barney's epic retrospective features his five-part film series The Cremaster Cycle, as well as sculpture and still photographs *(Feb–Aug)*. There will be an exhibit from acclaimed video artist Pierre Huyghe *(Feb 14–May 18),* who received the museum's 2002 Hugo Boss Prize, as well as a close look at the Suprem-atist work of Kasimir Malevich, the grand old master of the Russian avant-garde *(May 22–Sept 4).*

## Studio Museum in Harlem

*144 W 125th St between Malcolm X (Lenox Ave) and Adam Clayton Powell Jr Blvds (Seventh Ave) (212-864-4500; www.studiomuseuminharlem.org). Subway: A, C, B, D, 2, 3 to 125th St. Wed, Thu noon–6pm; Fri noon–8pm; Sat, Sun 10am–6pm; guided tours by appointment. $5, seniors $3, under 12 $1. Cash only.*

It may be small, but size is no measure of this venue's importance to, or impact on, the cultural life of the city. When Studio Museum opened in 1968, it was the first black fine-arts museum in the country, and it remains the place to go for historical insight into

African-American art and the art of the African diaspora. Under the leadership of director Lowery Sims (late of the Met) and star chief curator Thelma Golden (formerly of the Whitney), the neighborhood favorite has evolved into the city's most exciting showcase for contemporary African-American artists. Several are graduates of the museum's prestigious and ultra-competitive artists-in-residence program.

**Planned 2003 exhibitions:** The year's first major show is "Challenge of the Modern: African-American Artists 1925–1945" *(Jan 23–Mar 30)*. Also in the works is a retrospective of painter Frederick J. Brown—"Portraits in Jazz, Blues and Other Icons" *(Apr 23–Jun 29)*. The architectural show "Harlem Envisioned" focuses on the future of the historic neighborhood *(Jul 26–Sept 28)*.

Sightseeing

### Whitney Museum of American Art

*945 Madison Ave at 75th St (212-570-3600, recorded information 212-570-3676; www.whitney.org). Subway: 6 to 77th St. Tue–Thu, Sat, Sun 11am–6pm; Fri 1–9pm. $12, seniors and students $9.50, under 12 free. Fri 6–9pm voluntary donation. $6 for day pass to Kaufman Astoria Film Studios. AmEx, MC, V.*

Like the Guggenheim, the Whitney is set apart by its unique architecture: a gray granite cube with an all-seeing, upper-story window "eye," designed by Marcel Breuer. When Gertrude Vanderbilt Whitney, a sculptor and art patron, opened the museum in 1931, she dedicated it to living American artists; its first exhibition showed the work of eight such talents. Today, the Whitney holds about 12,000 pieces by nearly 2,000 artists, including Alexander Calder, Willem de Kooning, Edward Hopper (the museum holds his entire estate), Jasper Johns, Alice Martin, Alice Neel, Louise Nevelson, Georgia O'Keeffe, Claes Oldenburg and John Sloan; many are now on continuous view in the refurbished fifth-floor galleries. A second-floor screening room provides an important showcase for American independent film and video artists. Still, the museum's reputation rests mainly on its temporary shows, particularly the exhibit everyone loves to hate: the **Whitney Biennial**. Held in even-numbered years, it remains the most prestigious (and controversial) assessment of contemporary American art in the U.S. Sarabeth's, the museum's café, is open daily till 4:30pm and offers homey—if pricey—food. The Whitney's midtown branch, in an office-lobby gallery, mounts four shows a year of solo projects by contemporary artists. At the main building, there are free guided tours daily and live art performances on Friday nights.

**Planned 2003 exhibitions:** Architecture fans will enjoy an exhibition displaying the works of the progressive design team Elizabeth Diller and Ricardo Scofidio *(Mar 1–Jun 1)*. The sculpture of Elie Nadelman will inhabit the third floor *(Mar 27–Oct 31)*. The image of American society as a whole, as expressed in its art of the last decade, is the subject of "The American Effect" *(summer)*. Also look for "Ellsworth Kelly: Red Blue Green" *(Aug 14–Nov 2)*.

**Other location** • *Whitney Museum of American Art at Philip Morris, 120 Park Ave at 42nd St (212-878-2550). Subway: S, 4, 5, 6, 7 to 42nd St–Grand Central. Mon–Wed, Fri 11am–6pm; Thu 11am–7:30pm. Sculpture court Mon–Sat 7:30am–9:30pm; Sun 11am–7pm. Free.*

## Art & design

### American Academy of Arts and Letters

*155th St between Broadway and Riverside Dr (212-368-5900). Subway: 1 to 157th St. Mid-Mar–mid-Jun Thu–Sun 1–4pm. Free.*

This organization honors 250 American writers, composers, painters, sculptors and architects. Henry James, Mark Twain and Edith Wharton were once members; today's list includes John Guare, Alison Lurie, Terrence McNally and Kurt Vonnegut. It's not technically a museum, but the academy mounts annual exhibitions that are open to the public. A magnificent research library of original manuscripts and first editions is open by appointment only.

### American Folk Art Museum

*45 W 53rd St between Fifth and Sixth Aves (212-977-7170; www.folkartmuseum.org). Subway: E, V to Fifth Ave–53rd St. Tue–Sun 10am–6pm; Fri 10am–8pm. $9, seniors and students $5, under 12 free. Fri 6–8pm free. AmEx, MC, V.*

Art is everywhere in the American Folk Art Museum (formerly the Museum of American Folk Art). Designed by architects Billie Tsien and Tod Williams, the museum's new eight-floor home *(see* **New Folk's home,** *page 26)* is four times larger than the original Lincoln Center location (now a branch of the museum) and includes a café. The exhibits are impressive; among the more recent breakthrough shows was a retrospective of self-taught Chicago-based outsider artist Henry Darger, whose delightfully disturbing work remains in the collection. The range of decorative, practical and ceremonial folk art encompasses pottery, trade signs, delicately stitched log-cabin quilts and even windup toys. Check the website or call for a schedule of public programs, including lectures, demonstrations and performances.

**Other location** • *2 Lincoln Sq, Columbus Ave between 65th and 66th Sts (212-595-9533). Subway: 1, 9 to 66th St–Lincoln Ctr. Mon 11am–6pm; Tue–Sun 11am–7:30pm. $3 suggested donation. Cash only.*

### Dahesh Museum

*580 Madison Ave between 56th and 57th Sts (212-759-0606; www.daheshmuseum.org). Subway: E, V to Lexington Ave–53rd St; 6 to 51st St. Tue–Sat 11am–6pm.*

Admission to this specialized venue, which houses an extensive private collection of 19th- and early 20th-century European academic art, has always been free, but that may change in spring 2003 when it reopens after completing renovation. No matter the price, this collection warrants a visit: Orientalism, landscapes, scenes of rural life and historical or mythical images painted by fascinating but neglected artists whose work you probably won't find in other museums. Check the website or call for up-to-date hours and exhibition information.

### Forbes Magazine Galleries

*62 Fifth Ave at 12th St (212-206-5548). Subway: L, N, Q, R, W, 4, 5, 6 to 14th St–Union Sq. Tue, Wed, Fri, Sat 10am–4pm. Free. Under 16 must be accompanied by an adult. No strollers, no photos.*

The late magazine publisher Malcolm Forbes assembled this wonderfully personal private collection. Besides toy boats and soldiers, the galleries showcase historic presidential letters and—best of all—a dozen Imperial Easter eggs and other intricate pieces by the famous Russian jeweler and goldsmith Peter Carl Fabergé. Gallery hours are subject to change, so call before visiting.

### Isamu Noguchi Garden Museum

*36-01 43rd Ave at 36th St, Long Island City, Queens (718-721-1932; www.noguchi.org). Travel: 7 to 33rd St. Mon, Thu, Fri 10am–5pm; Sat, Sun 11am–6pm. Suggested donation $5, seniors and students $2.50. Cash only.*

Aside from his famous lamps, sculptor Isamu Noguchi designed stage sets for Martha Graham and George Balanchine, as well as furniture, sculpture parks and immense objects of great simplicity and beauty. The artist's Astoria studios, where his work is shown in a serene garden setting, are closed for renovation until the spring of 2004, when it will reopen with a show of Noguchi's travel photographs and drawings. Meanwhile, this temporary loft space in Long Island City features selected sculptures from the museum's permanent collection. Guided tours begin at 2pm.

**What's old is Neue** The Neue Galerie spotlights Austrian artists such as Dagobert Peche. This show included his exuberantly decorative furniture, textiles, ceramics and wallpaper.

Sightseeing

## Municipal Art Society

*457 Madison Ave between 50th and 51st Sts (212-935-3960, tour information 212-439-1049; www.mas.org). Subway: E, V to Fifth Ave–53rd St; 6 to 51st St. Mon–Wed, Fri, Sat 11am–5pm. Free.*

This center for urban design, founded in 1980, functions as a gallery, bookshop and lecture forum. It specializes in exhibitions on architecture, public art and community-based projects. The society's greatest attraction may be its location: inside the historic Villard Houses, opposite St. Patrick's Cathedral *(see page 91)*.

## The Museum at FIT

*Seventh Ave at 27th St (212-217-7999; www.fitnyc.edu). Subway: 1, 9 to 28th St. Tue–Fri noon–8pm; Sat 10am–5pm. Free.*

The Fashion Institute of Technology houses one of the world's most important collections of costumes and textiles, curated by the influential fashion historian Valerie Steele. Recently, many exhibitions have been devoted to a single designer's work, though several have had a broader scope: the history of corsets; a look at the importance of the little black dress; and the influence of British fashion.

## The Museum of Arts and Design

*40 W 53rd St between Fifth and Sixth Aves (212-956-3535; www.americancraftmuseum.org). Subway: E, V to Fifth Ave–53rd St; N, R, W to 49th St. Sun–Wed 10am–6pm; Thu 10am–8pm. $8, seniors and students $5, under 12 free. Thu 6–8pm pay what you wish. Cash only.*

Formerly the American Crafts Museum, this is the country's leading museum for 20th-century crafts in clay, cloth, glass, metal and wood. It changed its name last year to emphasize correspondences between art, design and craft. The museum features temporary shows on four spacious floors, and one or two annual exhibitions from the permanent collection concentrate on a specific medium. Browse the gift shop for some unexpectedly stylish jewelry and ceramics.

## National Academy of Design

*1083 Fifth Ave at 89th St (212-369-4880; www.nationalacademy.org). Subway: 4, 5, 6 to 86th St. Wed, Thu, Sat, Sun noon–5pm; Fri 10am–6pm. $8, seniors and students $4.50, children 6–16 free. Fri 5–8pm free. Cash only.*

Housed in an elegant Fifth Avenue townhouse, the Academy comprises the School of Fine Arts and a museum containing one of the world's foremost collections of 19th- and 20th-century American art (painting, sculpture, architectural drawing and engraving). The permanent collection includes works by Mary Cassatt, John Singer Sargent and Frank Lloyd Wright. The temporary exhibitions are always strong.

## Neue Galerie

*1048 Fifth Avenue at 86th St (212-628-6200; www.neuegalerie.org). Subway: 4, 5, 6 to 86th St. Mon, Sat, Sun 11am–6pm; Fri 11am–9pm. $10, seniors and students $7, children 12–16 must be accompanied by an adult, children under 12 not admitted. AmEx, MC, V.*

This elegant recent addition to the city's museum scene is the only museum in New York devoted entirely to 20th-century German and Austrian fine and decorative arts. The brainchild of the late art dealer Serge Sabarsky and cosmetics mogul Ronald S. Lauder, the Neue Galerie—located in a renovated brick-and-limestone mansion built by the architects of the New York Public Library—has the largest concentration of works by Gustav Klimt and Egon Schiele outside Vienna. There's also a bookstore, design shop and the popular Café Sabarsky *(212-288-0665)*. Have hot chocolate and a piece of Sacher torte, or a full meal of tafelspitz (boiled beef with horseradish).

## Nicholas Roerich Museum

*319 W 107th St at Riverside Dr (212-864-7752; www.roerich.org). Subway: 1, 9 to 110th St–Cathedral Pkwy. Tue–Sun 2–5pm. Donation requested.*

Nicholas Roerich was a Russian-born philosopher, artist, architect, explorer, pacifist and scenery painter who collaborated with Diaghilev, Nijinsky and Stravinsky. The Roerich Peace Pact of 1935, an international agreement on the protection of cultural treasures, earned him a Nobel Peace Prize nomination. Roerich's wife bought this charming townhouse specifically to exhibit her late husband's possessions. Paintings are mostly from Roerich's Tibetan travels and reveal his interest in mysticism. It's a fascinating place, though the patron's intriguing life story tends to overshadow the collection.

## Queens Museum of Art

*New York City Building, park entrance on 49th Ave at 111th St, Flushing Meadows–Corona Park, Queens (718-592-9700; www.queensmuse.org). Subway: 7 to 111th St. Tue–Fri 10am–5pm; Sat, Sun noon–5pm. Suggested donation $5, seniors and students $2.50, under 5 free. Cash only.*

Located on the site of the 1939 and 1964 World's Fairs, the Queens Museum holds one of the area's most amazing sights: a miniature model of New York City that is accurate down to the square inch. It's surprisingly affecting when the ambient light turns day to night (dusk falls every 15 minutes). The model is also constantly updated, so the Towers of Light that were the city's first memorial to the lives lost at the World Trade Center will remain in place until Lower Manhattan is rebuilt.

**Planned 2003 exhibitions:** The museum is emerging as a place for hometown artists to display site-specific work. You can check out a show devoted to photographer Wendy Ewald's collaborations with children from local Arab-American communities *(Mar–Jun)*. Other highlights include the designs and paintings Salvador Dalí made for his Surrealist Dream of Venus pavilion for the 1939 World's Fair *(Jun 22–Sept 28)*, and important pieces from Joan Jonas, a founder and leading proponent of performance and video art *(Oct 12–Jan 11, 2004)*.

**Mural, mural on the wall** The Lower East Side Tenement Museum recreates the harsh life and strategies for survival of immigrant families in the late 19th century.

## Arts & culture

### Historical

#### American Museum of Natural History

See page 41.

#### Fraunces Tavern Museum

*54 Pearl St at Broad St (212-425-1778; www.frauncestavernmuseum.org). Subway: J, M, Z to Broad St; 4, 5 to Bowling Green. Tue, Wed, Fri 10am–5pm; Thu 10am–7pm; Sat 11am–5pm. $3, seniors and children $2. Cash only.*

This tavern used to be George Washington's watering hole and was a meeting place for anti-British groups before the Revolution. Most of the artifacts are displayed in period rooms in this 18th-century mansion, which has been partially reconstructed. A working restaurant is still part of the building and serves hearty American fare; call 212-968-1776 for information.

#### Lower East Side Tenement Museum

*90 Orchard St at Broome St (212-431-0233; www.tenement.org). Subway: F to Delancey St; J, M, Z to Delancey–Essex Sts. Visitor center Tue–Fri 1–4pm; Sat, Sun 11am–4:30pm. $9, seniors and students $7. AmEx, MC, V.*

This 1863 tenement building, in the heart of what was once Little Germany, is accessible by guided tour only. Hour-long tours recount the true stories of a Sicilian Catholic family, a German-Jewish dressmaker and an Orthodox Jewish brood. Other tours include "Getting By: Weathering the Great Depressions of 1873 and 1929," and "Piecing It Together: Immigrants in the Garment Industry." Book ahead— the tours regularly sell out. The museum also has a gallery, shop and video room, and leads walking tours of the Lower East Side.

#### Merchant's House Museum

*29 E 4th St between Bowery and Lafayette St (212-777-1089; www.merchantshouse.com). Subway: F, V, S to Broadway–Lafayette St; 6 to Bleecker St. Mon, Thu–Sun 1–5pm. $5, seniors and students $3, children under 12 free. Cash only.*

New York's only preserved 19th-century family home, Merchant's House Museum is stocked with the same furnishings and decorations that filled the house when it was inhabited from 1832 to 1933. Seabury Tredwell is the merchant in question. He made his fortune selling hardware and bought this elegant late Federal–Greek Revival house in 1835.

#### Mount Vernon Hotel Museum and Garden

*421 E 61st St between First and York Aves (212-838-6878; www.merchantshouse.com). Subway: N, R, W to Lexington Ave–59th St; 4, 5, 6 to 59th St. Tue–Sun 11am–4pm. $5, seniors and students $4, children under 12 free. AmEx, Disc, MC, V.*

Formerly known as the Abigail Adams Smith Museum, this structure was built in 1799 as a carriage house for Smith (daughter of John Adams, the second president of the U.S.) and her husband, Colonel William Stevens Smith. It served as a hotel from 1826 to 1833, and has been designated a historic landmark. The museum is filled with period articles and furniture, and is run by the Colonial Dames of America.

### Museum of American Financial History

*28 Broadway at Beaver St (212-908-4110; www.financialhistory.org). Subway: 2, 3 to Wall St; 4, 5 to Bowling Green. Tue–Sat 10am–4pm. Suggested donation $2.*

The permanent collection, which traces the development of Wall Street and American financial markets, includes ticker tape from the morning of October 29, 1929, an 1867 stock ticker and the earliest known photograph of Wall Street.

### Museum of the American Piano

*291 Broadway at Reade St, entrance on Reade St (212-406-6060; www.museumforpianos.org). Subway: N, R, W to City Hall; 4, 5, 6 to Brooklyn Bridge–City Hall. Mon–Sat 10am–5pm. $8, seniors and students $5; lecture and demonstration of instruments $16, seniors and students $9, advance reservation required. Cash only.*

Dedicated to exhibiting, restoring and teaching the preservation of historical pianos and musical instru-

## Bell bottoms

The real inventor of the telephone is no longer on hold

Ring, ring, ring. Hello? Alexander Graham Bell? We've got news for you, buddy: You've been disconnected. On June 11, 2002, Congress passed House Resolution 269 declaring that Italian-American inventor Antonio Meucci—who has a museum dedicated to him on Staten Island—was the true inventor of the telephone.

The resolution was introduced by Rep. Vito Fossella a few months prior to its passage, but the battle had been dragging on since 1885, when Meucci (1808–1889) first took Bell to court. Since 1919, the Order of the Sons of Italy in America has maintained the little Staten Island house where Meucci lived almost half his life (it was turned into a museum in 1956), and it has long sought recognition for the inventor.

As the story goes, the Italian immigrant developed the prototype for the telephone years before Bell's famous phone call, but he couldn't afford to obtain a patent. "The point of the matter is that Meucci had all the paperwork," says Joseph Sciame, president and CEO of the Garibaldi-Meucci Museum. "What he didn't have was the money." Pitted against Bell's fancy lawyers in an 1885 trial, Meucci lost his claim to the invention, despite nearly 50 declarations in favor of Meucci, his detailed notes (dated decades before Bell's telephone) and a written letter of support from Thomas Edison. In the end, Bell made the Italian immigrant look like a delusional fool with a string telephone, and Meucci's claim was never settled.

The debate was revived in 1976, with then-senator Alfonse D'Amato at the front lines, but D'Amato left office before his resolution passed. Rep. Fossella picked up the mantle and, in fall 2002, finally pushed HR269 through the House. The win brought relief and vindication to Sciame and his organization, but he realizes that, for some, this turn of events won't seem like an important call. "When people say, 'So what?' my point is 'So it corrects the annals of history, and more than that, it tells that justice can be achieved in this great country of ours,'" Sciame says. "Plus, it creates a lot of different opportunities for that little house where he lived." Still, even with this victory, the Order of the Sons of Italy and the Garibaldi-Meucci Museum have only gone one third of the way. The Senate and the President still have to sign off on the idea—and that could take another 117 years.

**Pat. pending** After 117 years, history answers Antonio Meucci's call.

### Garibaldi-Meucci Museum

*420 Tompkins Ave at Chestnut Ave, Staten Island (718-442-1608; www.garibaldimeuccimuseum.org). Travel: Staten Island Ferry, then S78 bus to Chestnut Ave. Tue–Sun 1–5pm. Suggested donation $3. Cash only.*

ments, this museum recently moved into new downtown digs. Along with an exhibition about the history of pianos, the museum holds a daily lecture and demonstration of instruments; it also offers self-guided tours.

### Museum of the City of New York

*1220 Fifth Ave between 103rd and 104th Sts (212-534-1672; www.mcny.org). Subway: 6 to 103rd St. Wed–Sat 10am–5pm; Sun noon–5pm. Suggested admission $7; seniors, students and children $4; families $12. Cash only.*

Several ongoing exhibitions showcase the epic history of New York City, including its various arts, subcultures and unique personalities. On permanent display is "New York Toy Stories," a look at the city's depiction in countless children's books.

### Museum of Sex

*233 Fifth Ave at 27th St (information 212-689-6337; tickets 866-667-3984; www.museumofsex.com). Subway: N, R, W, 6 to 28th St. Mon, Tue 10am–6:30pm, Thu–Sun 10am–9pm. $17; Mon, Tue, Thu, Fri before noon $12. All visitors must be 18 or over.*

This museum opened to mixed reviews in the fall of 2002 with the inaugural exhibition "NYC Sex: How New York City Transformed Sex in America" *(through July 2, 2003)*. Don't expect flashy design and pornographic content; the institution has opted for a respectable presentation of historical documents and items—many of which were too risqué to be made public in their own time—that explore prostitution, burlesque theater, birth control, obscenity and fetishism. A series of group walking tours (entitled "Street Walking") is available.

### National Museum of the American Indian

*George Gustav Heye Center, Alexander Hamilton Custom House, 1 Bowling Green between Broadway and Whitehall Sts (212-514-3700, 212-514-3888; www.nmai.si.edu). Subway: N, R, W to Whitehall St; 4, 5 to Bowling Green. Mon–Wed, Fri–Sun 10am–5pm; Thu 10am–8pm. Free.*

This branch of the Smithsonian Institution occupies two floors of the grand rotunda in the 1907 Custom House, located just off Battery Park and New York Harbor. Its permanent collection of rare documents and artifacts offers trenchant insight into Native American history and crafts. Of special interest is "All Roads Are Good," which reflects the personal choices of storytellers, weavers, anthropologists and tribal leaders. Only 500 of the collection's 1 million objects are displayed at any time, perhaps a reason why the museum seems intimate, despite the building's lofty proportions.

### New-York Historical Society

*2 W 77th St at Central Park West (212-873-3400; www.nyhistory.org). Subway: B, C to 81st St–Museum of Natural History; 1, 9 to 79th St. Tue–Sun 10am–5pm. $6, seniors and students $4, children under 12 free when accompanied by an adult. Cash only.*

New York's oldest museum, founded in 1804, was one of America's first cultural and educational institutions. With the opening of its new 17,000-square-foot gallery space, the Henry Luce III Center for the Study of American Culture, the NYHS can finally display a sizable share of its treasures. Highlights include George Washington's Valley Forge camp cot, the desk at which Clement Clarke Moore supposedly sat when he wrote "A Visit from St. Nicholas" (" 'Twas the night before Christmas…") and the world's largest collection of Tiffany lamps—132 of them. On permanent display: "Kid City," a reproduction of the corner of Broadway and West 82nd Street in 1901, in which kids can open doors, look into mailboxes and "shop" from stores to learn more about New York past and present.

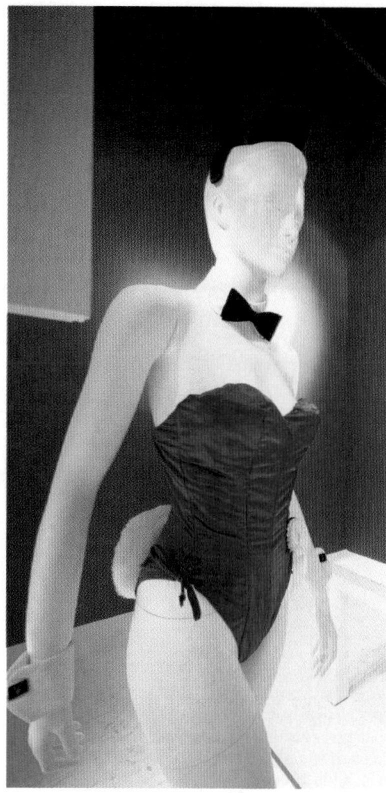

**Rabbit redux** Ogle an original Playboy bunny costume at the Museum of Sex.

### Skyscraper Museum

*2 West St at Battery Pl (212-968-1961; www.skyscraper.org). Museum to open in spring 2003.*

Until it moves into its new home in Battery Park City, the Skyscraper Museum maintains a strong Web presence and occasionally holds exhibitions at other

**The Norse pole** Film fests, photos, paintings—Scandinavia House has all things Nordic.

museum venues. The permanent facility will have two galleries: one for temporary exhibitions and one for the museum's main exhibition "Skyscraper/City," which illustrates the evolution of New York's skyline—past, present and future—through photos, architectural drawings, builders' records and other artifacts.

### South Street Seaport Museum

*Visitors' center, 12 Fulton St at South St (212-748-8600; www.southstseaport.org). Subway: A, C to Broadway–Nassau St; J, M, Z, 2, 3, 4, 5 to Fulton St. Apr 1–Sept 30 10am–6pm. Oct 1–Mar 31 Mon, Wed–Sun 10am–5pm. $5, students $4, children under 12 free. AmEx, MC, V.*

The museum sprawls across 11 blocks along the East River—an amalgam of galleries, historic ships, 19th-century buildings and a visitors' center. It's fun to wander around the rebuilt streets and pop in to see an exhibition on marine life and history before climbing aboard the four-masted 1911 *Peking.* The Seaport itself is pretty touristy, but it's still an intriguing place to spend an afternoon. There are plenty of cafés near the Fulton Fish Market building.

### The Statue of Liberty and Ellis Island Immigration Museum

See **Ain't no way to treat a Lady**, page 62.

### Waterfront Museum

*699 Columbia St, Gowanus Industrial Park, Red Hook, Brooklyn (718-624-4719; www.waterfrontmuseum.org). Travel: F, G to Smith–9th Sts; then B77 bus to Conover St; walk down Conover St to waterfront. Call or visit website for schedule. Barge admission varies with event.*

Located on the historic 1914 Lehigh Valley Railroad Barge, Waterfront Museum documents New York's history as a port of call. The wooden barge, the only one of its kind afloat today, is listed on the National Register of Historic Places. Summer weekend activities include a music series and circus performances. Views of Manhattan and New York Harbor are superb, but the museum is open only during events, or by appointment. In June 2002, the barge was hauled to Albany to have a wood-eating shipworm problem treated and to undergo preservation work. Events will resume in May 2003.

## International

### Asia Society and Museum

*725 Park Ave at 70th St (212-517-2742; www.asiasociety.org). Subway: 6 to 68th St–Hunter College. Tue–Thu, Sat, Sun 11am–6pm; Fri 11am–9pm. $7, seniors and students $5, children under 16 free. Fri 6–9pm free. Cash only.*

The Asia Society plays an important role in fostering Asian-American relations. It sponsors study missions and conferences, and promotes public programs on both continents. The newly renovated headquarters' expanded galleries show major art exhibitions from public and private collections, including the permanent Mr. and Mrs. John D. Rockefeller III collection of Asian art. Asian musicians and performers often entertain here.

### China Institute

*125 E 65th St between Park and Lexington Aves (212-744-8181; www.chinainstitute.org). Subway: F to Lexington Ave–63rd St; 6 to 68th St–Hunter College. Mon, Wed, Fri, Sat 10am–5pm; Tue, Thu 10am–8pm. Suggested donation $3, seniors and students $2, children under 12 free. AmEx, MC, V.*

Consisting of just two small gallery rooms, the China Institute is somewhat overshadowed by the Asia Society. But its rotating exhibitions, ranging from works by female Chinese artists to selections from the Beijing Palace Museum, are compelling. The institute also offers lectures and courses on subjects such as calligraphy, Confucianism and cooking.

### El Museo del Barrio

*1230 Fifth Ave between 104th and 105th Sts (212-831-7272; www.elmuseo.org). Subway: 6 to 103rd St. Wed–Sun 11am–5pm. $5, seniors and students $3, children under 12 free, when accompanied by an adult. AmEx, MC, V.*

At the top of Museum Mile, not far from Spanish Harlem (the neighborhood from which it takes its name), El Museo del Barrio is dedicated to the work of Latino artists in the United States, as well as that of Latin Americans. Frida Kahlo and Diego Rivera were the subject of a recent show, and a permanent exhibition explores the history of the Taino culture. Programming is typically contemporary and consciousness-raising; El Museo also sponsors annual community events such as the celebration of the Mexican Day of the Dead *(Nov 1)*.

### French Institute–Alliance Française

*22 E 60th St between Madison and Park Aves (212-355-6100; www.fiaf.org). Subway: N, R, W to Fifth Ave–59th St; 4, 5, 6 to 59th St. Mon–Thu 9am–8pm; Fri, Sat 9am–5pm. Free.*

Welcome to the New York home for all things Gallic: The institute (a.k.a. the Alliance Française) holds the city's most extensive all-French library and offers numerous language classes and cultural seminars. There are also French film screenings *(see page 283)* and live dance, music and theater performances. The institute also organizes the city's jubilant Bastille Day street festival in July.

### Goethe-Institut/ German Cultural Center

*1014 Fifth Ave at 82nd St (212-439-8700). Subway: 4, 5, 6 to 86th St. Gallery Mon, Wed, Fri 10am–5pm; Tue, Thu 10am–7pm. Library Tue, Thu noon–7pm; Wed, Fri noon–5pm. Free.*

Goethe-Institut New York is just one branch of a German multinational cultural organization founded in 1951. Located across the street from the Metropolitan Museum of Art in a landmark Fifth Avenue mansion, it mounts shows featuring German-born contemporary artists, as well as concerts, lectures and film screenings *(see page 283)*. A library offers books in German or English, in addition to German periodicals, videos and audiocassettes.

### Hispanic Society of America

*Audubon Terrace, Broadway between 155th and 156th Sts (212-926-2234; www.hispanicsociety.org). Subway: 1 to 157th St. Tue–Sat 10am–4:30pm; Sun 1–4pm. Free.*

The Society has the largest combined collection of Spanish art and manuscripts outside Spain. Keep an eye out for two portraits by Goya and the striking bas-relief of Don Quixote in the lobby. The collection is dominated by religious artifacts, including 16th-century tombs from the monastery of San Francisco in Cuéllar, Spain.

### Jacques Marchais Museum of Tibetan Art

*338 Lighthouse Ave between Richmond Rd and Terrace Cts, Staten Island (718-987-3500; www.tibetanmuseum.com). Travel: Staten Island Ferry, then S74 bus to Lighthouse Ave and a*

**Analyze these** Robert De Niro's coolest big-screen duds are on display at the American Museum of the Moving Image.

*15-minute walk up the hill. Wed–Sun 1–5pm. $5, seniors and students $3, children under 12 $2. MC, V.*

This mock Tibetan temple merits the hour-and-a-half trip from Manhattan. It was even worth a much longer trip for the Dalai Lama, who visited in 1991. The tiny museum contains a striking Buddhist altar and the largest collection of Tibetan art in the West, including religious objects, bronzes and paintings. In October, the museum hosts an annual Tibetan festival.



### Japan Society

*333 E 47th St between First and Second Aves (212-752-3015; www.japansociety.org). Subway: E, V to Lexington Ave–53rd St; 6 to 51st St. Tue–Fri 11am–6pm; Sat, Sun 11am–5pm. $5, seniors and students $3. Cash only.*

The Japan Society presents performing arts, lectures, exchange programs and special events, plus exhibitions two times a year. The gallery shows traditional and contemporary Japanese art and the film center is a major showcase for Japanese cinema in the U.S. *(see page 283)*. There's also a language center and a library (open to members and students) in the lower lobby.

### Jewish Museum

*1109 Fifth Ave at 92nd St (212-423-3200; www.jewishmuseum.org). Subway: 4, 5 to 86th St; 6 to 96th St. Mon–Wed 11am–5:45pm; Thu 11am–8pm; Fri 11am–3pm; Sun 10am–5:45pm. $8, seniors and students $5.50, children under 12 free when accompanied by an adult. Pay what you wish Thu 5–8pm. Cash only.*

The Jewish Museum, housed in the 1908 Warburg Mansion, presents a fascinating collection of art, artifacts and media installations. Recent exhibitions have included shows of Marc Chagall, Charlotte Salomon and Chaim Soutine. The museum commissions a contemporary artist or a group of artists to install a new show each year, and the results are always stellar. The permanent exhibition tracks the Jewish cultural experience through exhibits that range from a filigreed silver circumcision set and an interactive Talmud to a Statue of Liberty Hanukkah lamp. Most of this eclectic collection was rescued from European synagogues before World War II. You can refuel at the underground Café Weissman.

### Museum for African Art

*36-01 43rd Ave at 36th St, Long Island City, Queens (718-784-7700; www.africanart.org). Subway: 7 to 33rd St. Mon, Thu, Fri 10am–5pm; Sat, Sun 11am–6pm. $5; seniors, students and children $2.50. MC, V ($10 minimum).*

This attraction recently moved from Soho to new digs in Long Island City, which has become an art nexus since MoMA QNS opened last year. Exhibits change about twice a year, and the quality of the work—often from exhilarating private collections—is exceptional. There's an unusually good bookshop, with a children's section. The arts, history and cultural programs are also popular.

### Museum of Chinese in the Americas

*70 Mulberry St at Bayard St, second floor (212-619-4785). Subway: J, M, Z, N, Q, R, W, 6 to Canal St; S to Grand St. Tue–Sun noon–5pm. Suggested donation $3, seniors and students $1, children free.*

Located in a century-old former schoolhouse on the culturally rich Lower East Side, the two-room museum concentrates on the experience of Chinese immigrants and Chinese-American history.

### Museum of Jewish Heritage: A Living Memorial to the Holocaust

*18 First Pl at Battery Pl (212-509-6130; www.mjhnyc.org). Subway: 1, 9 to South Ferry; 4, 5 to Bowling Green. Sun–Wed 10am–5:45pm; Thu 10am–8pm; Fri, eve of Jewish holidays 10am–3pm (until 5pm in the summer). $7, seniors and students $5, children under 5 free. Sundays free. Last admission one hour before closing. AmEx, MC, V.*

You don't have to be Jewish to appreciate the contents of this institution, built in a six-sided shape that recalls the Star of David. Opened in 1997, it offers one of the most moving cultural experiences in the city. There are 2,000 photographs, hundreds of cultural artifacts and plenty of archival films that vividly detail the horrors of the Holocaust. The exhibition continues beyond those dark times to days of renewal, ending in an upper gallery that is flooded with daylight and gives views of Lady Liberty in the harbor. A rotating temporary display (on topics such as forced Jewish labor in Hungary) adds further depth to the experience. Closed-captioned video is available. Advance ticket purchase is recommended for large groups; call the museum box office *(212-945-0039)*.

### Scandinavia House: The Nordic Center in America

*58 Park Ave between 37th and 38th Sts (212-779-3587; www.scandinaviahouse.org). Subway: S, 4, 5, 6, 7 to 42nd St–Grand Central. Tue–Sat 11am–6pm. Suggested donation $3, seniors and students $2.*

You'll find all things Nordic—from Ikea designs to the latest in Finnish film—at this new $20 million center, the leading cultural link between the United States and the five Scandinavian countries (Denmark, Finland, Iceland, Norway and Sweden). Scandinavia House features exhibitions, films, concerts, lectures, symposia and readings for all ages. The AQ Café, operated by the renowned NYC restaurant **Aquavit** *(see page 197)*, is a cool lunch spot.

### Yeshiva University Museum

*Center for Jewish History, 15 W 16th St between Fifth and Sixth Aves (212-294-8330; www.yu.edu/museum). Subway: F, V to 14th St; L to Sixth Ave. Tue–Thu, Sun 11am–5pm. $6; seniors, students and children $4; children under 5 free. Cash only.*

The museum usually hosts one major exhibition a year and several smaller ones, mainly on Jewish themes. It's located inside the Center for Jewish History, a separate organization that holds educational and cultural programs as well as exhibitions of its own.

## Media

### American Museum of the Moving Image

*35th Ave at 36th St, Astoria, Queens (718-784-0077; www.ammi.org). Subway: G, R, V to Steinway St. Tue–Fri noon–5pm; Sat, Sun 11am–6pm. $8.50, seniors and students $5.50, children 5–18 $4.50, children under 5 free. Cash only. No strollers.*

About a 15-minute subway ride from midtown Manhattan, AMMI is one of the city's most dynamic institutions. Built within the restored complex that once housed the original Kaufman Astoria Studios *(see page 117),* it offers an extensive daily program of films and videos. The core interactive exhibition, "Behind the Screen," offers insight into every aspect of the mechanics and history of film production, including directing, sound mixing and marketing. You can also try your hand at several video games in the exhibit on the history of digital entertainment. The museum has a café, but you may want to try one of the great Greek restaurants nearby (*see chapter* **Restaurants, Queens**).

### The Museum of Television & Radio

*25 W 52nd St between Fifth and Sixth Aves (212-621-6800; www.mtr.org). Subway: B, D, F to 47–50th Sts-Rockefeller Ctr; E, V to Fifth Ave–53rd St. Tue, Wed, Sat, Sun noon–6pm; Thu noon–8pm; Fri noon–9pm. $6, seniors and students $4, children under 13 $3. Cash only.*

This nirvana for boob-tube addicts and pop-culture junkies contains an archive of more than 100,000 radio and TV programs. Head to the fourth-floor library to search the computerized system for your favorite *Star Trek* or *I Love Lucy* episode, then walk down one flight to take a seat at your assigned console. (The radio listening room operates the same way.) There are also theaters screening modern cartoons, public seminars and special presentations (for instance, a collection of Woody Allen's TV appearances).

## Military

### *Intrepid* Sea-Air-Space Museum

*USS Intrepid, Pier 86, 46th St at the Hudson River (212-245-0072; www.intrepidmuseum.org). Travel: A, C, E to 42nd St–Port Authority, then M42 bus to Twelfth Ave. Apr 1–Sept 30 Mon–Fri 10am–5pm; Sat, Sun 10am–7pm. Oct 1–Mar 31 Tue–Sun 10am–5pm. Last admission one hour before closing. $13; seniors, veterans and students $9; children ages 6–11 $6, ages 2–5 $2, children under 2 and servicepeople on active duty free. AmEx, MC, V.*

This museum is located on the World War II aircraft carrier *Intrepid,* whose decks are crammed with space capsules and various aircraft. There are plenty of audiovisual shows, as well as hands-on exhibits appealing to children and adults.

**All hands on deck** Test your sea legs with the interactive exhibits aboard the *Intrepid*.

**Book 'em** The NYPD Museum holds badges and law-enforcement volumes in custody.

## New York Public Library

The vast New York Public Library, founded in 1895, comprises four major research libraries and 85 local and specialty branches, making it the largest and most comprehensive library system in the world. The holdings grew from the combined collections of John Jacob Astor, James Lenox and Samuel Jones Tilden. Today, the system contains 52 million items, including more than 18 million books. About a million items are added to the collection each year. Unless you're interested in a specific subject, your best bet is to visit the system's flagship, officially called the Humanities and Social Sciences Library. Information on the entire system is at www.nypl.org.

### Donnell Library Center

*20 W 53rd St between Fifth and Sixth Aves (212-621-0618). Subway: E, V to Fifth Ave–53rd St. Mon, Wed, Fri 10am–6pm; Tue, Thu 10am–8pm; Sat 10am–5pm. Free.*

This branch of the NYPL has an extensive collection of records, films and videotapes, with appropriate screening facilities. The Donnell specializes in foreign-language books—in more than 80 languages—and there's a children's section of more than 100,000 books, films, records and cassettes, as well as the original Winnie the Pooh dolls.

### Humanities and Social Sciences Library

*455 Fifth Ave at 42nd St (recorded information 212-869-8089). Subway: B, D, F, V to 42nd St; 7 to Fifth Ave. Tue, Wed 11am–7:30pm; Thu–Sat 10am–6pm. Free.*

This landmark Beaux Arts building is what most people mean when they say "the New York Public Library." The famous stone lions out front are wreathed with holly at Christmas; during the summer, people relax on the steps or sip drinks at outdoor tables beneath the arches. Free guided tours (11am and 2pm) include the renovated Rose Main Reading Room and the Bill Blass Public Catalog Room, where you can surf the Internet. Special exhibitions are frequent and worthwhile, and lectures in the Celeste Bartos Forum are always well attended.

### Library for the Performing Arts

*40 Lincoln Center Plaza between 63rd and 64th Sts (212-870-1630). Subway: 1, 9 to 66th*

*St–Lincoln Ctr. Tue, Wed, Fri, Sat noon–6pm; Thu noon–8pm Free.*
After a three-year, $37 million renovation, this facility is one of the great research centers in the field of performing arts. The library contains audio- and videotapes, films, letters and manuscripts. The Rodgers and Hammerstein Archive Collection of Recorded Sound has 500,000 recordings. Visitors can check out books, scores and recordings, or attend concerts and lectures in the Bruno Walter Auditorium.

### Schomburg Center for Research in Black Culture

*515 Malcolm X Blvd (Lenox Ave) at 135th St (212-491-2200). Subway: 2, 3 to 135th St. Tue, Wed noon–8pm; Thu, Fri noon–6pm; Sat 10am–6pm. Free.*
This extraordinary trove of vintage literature and historical memorabilia relating to black culture and the African diaspora was founded in 1926 by its first curator, bibliophile Arthur Schomburg. The center hosts jazz concerts, films, lectures and tours.

### Science, Industry and Business Library

*188 Madison Ave between 34th and 35th Sts (212-592-7000). Subway: 6 to 33rd St. Tue–Thu 10am–8pm; Fri, Sat 10am–6pm. Free.*
The world's largest public information center devoted to science, technology, business and economics occupies the first floor and lower level of the old B. Altman & Co. department store. Opened in 1996, the Gwathmey Siegel–designed branch of the NYPL has a circulating collection of 50,000 books and an open-shelf reference collection of 60,000 volumes. To help small-business owners, the library also focuses on digital technologies and the Internet, and offers free access to more than 100 electronic databases. Free 30-minute tours are given on Tuesdays and Thursdays at 2pm.

## Science & technology

### Liberty Science Center

*251 Phillip St, Jersey City, NJ (201-200-1000; www.lsc.org). Travel: PATH to Pavonia/Newport, then NJ Transit (Hudson-Bergen Light Rail) to Liberty State Park. 9:30am–5:30pm. $10, seniors and children 2–18 $8; combined entry to center and IMAX movie $16.50, seniors and children 2–18 $14.50. AmEx, Disc, MC, V.*
This excellent museum has innovative exhibits and America's largest, most spectacular IMAX cinema. From the observation tower, you get great views of Manhattan and an unusual sideways look at the Statue of Liberty. The center emphasizes hands-on science, so get ready to elbow your way past the excited kids. On permanent view is "E-Quest: Exploring Earth's Energy." On weekends, take the NY Water-way ferry *(see page 132)*.

### New York Hall of Science

*47-01 111th St at 46th Ave, Flushing Meadows–Corona Park, Queens (718-699-0005; www.nyhallsci.org). Subway: 7 to 111th St. Sept–Jun Tue, Wed 9:30am–2pm; Thu–Sun 9:30am–5pm. Jul, Aug Mon 9:30am–2pm; Tue–Fri 9:30am–5pm; Sat, Sun 10:30am–6pm. $7.50, seniors and students $5, children 2–4 $2.50. Sept 1–Jun 30 Thu 2–5pm free. Science playground $3 (open Mar–Dec, weather permitting). AmEx, MC, V.*
Opened at the 1964–65 World's Fair, the New York Hall of Science keeps a large collection of interactive exhibits; it's considered one of the top science museums in the country. The emphasis is on education, and displays demystify science for the children who usually fill the place. The 30,000-square-foot outdoor science playground is the largest of its kind in the Western Hemisphere.

## Urban services

### New York City Fire Museum

*278 Spring St between Hudson and Varick Sts (212-691-1303; www.nycfiremuseum.org). Subway: C, E to Spring St; 1, 9 to Houston St. Tue–Sat 10am–5pm; Sun 10am–4pm. Suggested donation $4, seniors and students $2, children under 12 $1. AmEx, MC, V.*
An active firehouse from 1903 to 1954, the museum presents an equal measure of the gadgetry and pageantry associated with New York fire fighting since Colonial times. There are a few vintage fire engines and several displays of fire-fighting ephemera dating back 100 years. The museum is also compiling a permanent exhibit about NYC firefighters' heroic work following the World Trade Center attack.

### New York City Police Museum

*100 Old Slip between South and Water Sts (212-480-3100; www.nycpolicemuseum.org). Subway: 2, 3 to Wall St. Tue–Sun 10am–5pm. Suggested donation $5, seniors $3, children 6–18 $2.*
The NYPD's tribute to itself features exhibits on the history of the department and the tools (and transportation) of the trade. It's the only place in the city where the public can buy officially licensed NYPD paraphernalia, such as a police-logo golf shirt.

### New York Transit Museum

*Corner of Boerum Pl and Schermerhorn St, Brooklyn Heights, Brooklyn (718-243-8601; www.mta.info/museum). Subway: A, C, G to Hoyt-Schermerhorn. Museum will reopen in spring 2003. Call or visit website for details.*
The Transit Museum, located underground in an old 1930s subway station, is closed for renovation until spring of 2003. The museum's gallery at Grand Central Terminal remains open. A recent exhibition looked at the history of elevated trains in the city.
**Other location •** *Grand Central Terminal, 42nd St at Park Ave, adjacent to stationmaster's office off the Grand Concourse (212-878-0106). Subway: S, 4, 5, 6, 7 to 42nd St–Grand Central. Mon–Fri 8am–8pm; Sat 10am–6pm. Free.*

# Downtown

From the dignified architecture of the Financial District to the punk playground of the East Village—everything's waiting for you below 14th Street



New York City's most diverse concentration of neighborhoods and people is in lower Manhattan. You can get lychee ice cream in Chinatown and then walk two blocks to Mulberry Street to buy fresh *sfogliatella* in one of Little Italy's pastry shops. Or peruse boutiques stocked with expensive designer goods in Soho and Nolita, then head a few blocks east to the tattoo and piercing parlors on St. Marks Place in the East Village. In one afternoon, you may walk for hours ogling the architecture in the bustling Financial District, then wander north to enjoy a leisurely coffee in a Greenwich Village café.

Downtown is also where the Twin Towers once stood. In August 2002, New York Governor George Pataki, New Jersey Governor James E. McGreevey and New York City Mayor Michael Bloomberg proclaimed that, to commemorate the heroes of September 11, 2001, a viewing wall would be erected by the Port Authority. This site is now crowded with locals and visitors who come to reflect and pay their respects. In 2002, the World Monument Fund's list of 100 Most Endangered Sites included a special "101st Site"—Historic Lower Manhattan. The gesture was both an homage to the World Trade Center and a tribute to an area that contains six historic districts and 65 landmarks.

## Battery Park

It's most obvious that you're on an island when you explore the southern tip of Manhattan. The Atlantic breeze blows in over New York Harbor, covering the same route taken by the hope-filled millions who arrived here by sea. Trace their journey past the golden torch of the **Statue of Liberty**, through the immigration and quarantine center of **Ellis Island** and on to the statue-dotted promenade of Battery Park. Today, few steamships chug in; instead, the harbor is filled during summer with sailboats and Jet Ski riders who jump the wakes left by motorboats. Seagulls perch on the promenade railing, squawking at fishermen whose lines might snag a shad or a striped bass (while Hudson River is cleaner than it's been in years, State Health Department officials advise against eating its fish more than once a month).

The promenade is also a stage for applause-hungry performers, who entertain people waiting to be ferried to the Statue of Liberty and Ellis Island. The park itself often plays host to international touring events such as the **Cirque du Soleil** *(see page 296)*, as well as free outdoor music on summer evenings. **Castle Clinton**, situated inside the park, was built in 1811 to defend the city against possible attacks by the British. The castle has since been a theater and an aquarium, but now serves as a visitors' center, with historical displays, a bookstore and a ticket booth for the Statue of Liberty and Ellis Island tours *(see* **Ain't no way to treat a Lady**, *page 62)*. To the west is **Pier A** *(22 Battery Pl at West St)*, Manhattan's last Victorian-era pier shed; it's being restored and will someday house restaurants and historic vessels.

Whether or not you join the crowds making their way to Lady Liberty, you can head east around the shore where several ferry terminals jut out into the harbor. The 1954 Whitehall Ferry Terminal is where you board the famous—and free—**Staten Island Ferry** *(see page 132)*. The 20-minute ride to Staten Island offers an unparalleled view of the downtown Manhattan skyline, and of course, a look at the iconic statue. The terminal, which was damaged by fire in 1991, remains open as it undergoes reconstruction. When it is completed later this year, visitors will enter a 75-foot-high hall that will give glorious views of the Manhattan skyline and New York Harbor. In the years before the Brooklyn Bridge was built, the beautiful **Battery Maritime Building** *(11 South St between Broad and Whitehall Sts)* served as a terminal for many ferry services between Manhattan and Brooklyn.

At the southeastern end of the Battery Park promenade is **American Park at the Battery** *(see page 179)*; the restaurant's outdoor patio overlooks the harbor and is a primo spot to sip a cocktail.

Another patch of grass lies north of Battery Park: The triangle of Bowling Green, the city's oldest extant park. It's the front lawn of the beautiful 1907 Beaux Arts Alexander Hamilton Custom House, home to the **National Museum of the American Indian** *(see page 53)*. On the north side of the triangle, sculptor Arturo DiModica's muscular bronze bull represents the snorting power of Wall Street (understandably, the city has never commissioned a bear statue).

Other historical sights are close by: the rectory of the **Shrine of Elizabeth Ann Seton** (a 1793 Federal building dedicated to the first American-born saint) and **New York Unearthed**, a tiny gallery of urban archaeological finds from the area. The **Fraunces Tavern Museum** *(see page 51)* is a restoration of the alehouse where George Washington celebrated his victory over the British. After a bite, you can examine the Revolution-era relics displayed in the tavern's period rooms.

The **Stone Street Historic District** surrounds one of Manhattan's oldest roads. The once derelict bit of Stone Street between Coenties Alley and Hanover Square was recently resurfaced with granite paving blocks and outfitted with faux-gaslight lampposts. Upscale businesses such as the **Fragments** jewelry store *(see page 227)* and the **Stone Street Tavern** *(52 Stone St between Coenties Alley and Hanover Sq, 212-425-3663)* have moved in.

### Battery Park

*Between State St, Battery Pl and Whitehall St. Subway: N, R, W to Whitehall St; 4, 5 to Bowling Green.*

The seagulls and fishermen are sure signs of the Atlantic Ocean's proximity, just beyond the Verrazano-Narrows Bridge. The harbor itself is gorgeous, and one of the most peaceful experiences you can have in the city is to sit on a bench and look toward the Statue of Liberty, Ellis Island, Staten Island and all the boats bobbing on the water.

### New York Unearthed

*17 State St between Broadway and Whitehall St, behind Shrine of Elizabeth Ann Seton (212-748-8628). Subway: N, R, W to Whitehall St. Free.*

The **South Street Seaport Museum**'s *(see page 54)* tiny archaeology offshoot has 6,000 years' worth of finds that document New York history.

### Shrine of Saint Elizabeth Ann Seton

*7 State St between Broadway and Whitehall St (212-269-6865). Subway: N, R, W to Whitehall St. Mon–Fri 6:30am–5pm; Saturdays before and after 12:15pm Mass; Sundays before and after 9am and noon Masses. Free.*

A socialite who converted to Catholicism and the first native-born American to be canonized, Seton founded a religious community and a school for women.

### The Statue of Liberty & Ellis Island Immigration Museum

See **Ain't no way to treat a Lady**, page 62.

## Battery Park City & Ground Zero

The streets are once again bustling around Ground Zero, a year and a half after the attack on the World Trade Center. People in nearby offices are back at work and residents have

**America or bust** A Battery Park monument honors Italian explorer Giovanni da Verrazano, leader of the first European expedition to sail into New York Harbor in 1524.

returned home. Tourists now come down to the site's memorial to pay their respects to the more than 2,800 people who lost their lives. To accommodate visitors, a group of architects (Elizabeth Diller, Kevin Kennon, David Rockwell and Ricardo Scofidio), city agencies and private contractors built a 16-foot-high viewing platform in December 2001. Gradually, the city has embarked on the huge task of rebuilding the area. (For more on the plans for Ground Zero, *see* **The Sky's the Limit**, *page 28*).

The World Trade Center was Battery Park City's portal to the rest of Manhattan—residents would walk across two covered pedestrian bridges to take the subways that stopped beneath the WTC. After the events of September 11, construction crews worked around the clock to rebuild the damaged portions of the subway. The recovery and cleanup of the area progressed at break-neck speed, and was completed on May 30, 2002. All stations were reopened in September 2002, except for the Cortlandt Street station on the 1 and 9 line. Completed in 1988, the **World Financial Center** is an expression of the city-within-a-city concept. Architect Cesar Pelli's four glass-and-granite postmodern office towers—each crowned with a geometric form—surround an upscale retail area, a series of plazas with terraced restaurants and a marina, where water taxis to New Jersey are docked. The glass-

**Paying respects** Visitors gather at the Ground Zero Viewing Platform.

## Ain't no way to treat a Lady

### Sadly, the inside of the Statue of Liberty is closed, but it's still possible to keep company with New York's most famous dame

When you're in New York, a visit to Liberty and Ellis Islands is practically mandatory. Unfortunately, due to security concerns, the Statue of Liberty's museum, pedestal and crown are now closed to visitors. However, the grounds of Liberty Island remain open. When weather and staffing permit, national park rangers offer an outdoor tour that is a highly enjoyable stop on the way to Ellis Island *(see below)*. For the curious, here are a few facts and figures about Lady Liberty.

**Date construction began** 1875, in Paris, France

**Date completed** July 1884

**The design team** Frédéric-Auguste Bartholdi, sculptor; Richard Morris Hunt, architect of the base; and Alexandre-Gustave Eiffel, engineer

**Presented to America** July 4, 1884, by the people of France, in recognition of the friendship established between the two countries during the American Revolution

**Transport** In 1885, the French shipped Liberty to New York in 350 pieces.

**Materials** Copper, steel and concrete

**Color** The statue's shell is copper, which oxidizes and turns green when exposed to the elements.

**Crown** The seven points of her crown represent both the world's seven seas (Antarctic, Arctic, Indian, North and South Atlantic, North and South Pacific) and the seven continents (Africa, Antarctica, Asia, Australia, Europe, North and South America).

**Height** The statue is 151 feet from head to toe. The length of her hand is 16 feet, five inches, and her index finger is eight feet long.

**Weight** The copper weighs 62,000 pounds (31 tons), the steel is 250,000 pounds (125 tons) and the concrete foundation 54 million pounds (27,000 tons), for a total weight of 54,312,000 pounds (27,156 tons).

**Clothing** Liberty wears the outfit of a classical Roman deity: a *palla* (a cloak that is fastened on her left shoulder with a clasp) over a *stola* (which falls in many folds at her feet).

**Shoes** The length of her sandal is 25 feet, which would equal a U.S. women's shoe size of 879.

roofed **Winter Garden**, a popular venue for concerts and other forms of entertainment, was badly damaged in the WTC attack. But things move quickly in New York: The Winter Garden resumed its performance schedule in September 2002, and restaurants and shops such as **SouthWest NY** *(212-945-0528)* and **Century 21** (*22 Cortlandt St at Broadway, 212-227-9092*) started reopening as early as February 2002.

**Battery Park City** was devised by then Governor Nelson Rockefeller as the site of apartment housing and schools; its public plazas, restaurants and shopping areas were designed to link with the World Financial Center. The most impressive aspects of Battery Park City are its esplanade and park, which run north of the Financial Center along the Hudson River, and connect to Battery Park at the south. In addition to supplying inspiring views of the sunset behind **Colgate Center** (look for the huge Colgate sign and clock) and Jersey City, New Jersey, across the river, the esplanade is a paradise for bikers, in-line skaters and joggers—though plain old walking is fun too. There's a lot of exposed flesh on sultry weekends.

Wealthy Wall Streeters live in the residential area of Battery Park City; a portion of the high rents is intended to subsidize public housing elsewhere in the city, though the $276 million paid since 1992 has largely gone to other city services. To outsiders, the community seems isolated (it lies *west* of West Street), and its planned-community aspect feels more suburban than urban.

The northern end of the park (officially called **Nelson A. Rockefeller Park**) features the large **North Lawn**, which becomes a surrogate beach in summer. Sunbathers, kite fliers and soccer players vie for a patch of grass. Basketball and handball courts, concrete tables with chess and backgammon boards painted on them, and playgrounds with swings round out the recreational options. Tennis courts and baseball fields are nearby, just off West Street at Murray Street. The park ends at Chambers Street, but links with piers to the north, which are slowly being claimed for public use and will eventually become the **Hudson River Park** (for more on the park, *see* **A river runs near it**, *page 72)*. Situated between Battery Park City and Battery Park

**Chains** The broken links at her feet represent Liberty breaking the bonds of slavery.

**Torch** The statue's full name is *Liberty Enlightening the World.* She holds the lighted cresset to illuminate the struggle for freedom.

**Engraving** Emma Lazarus's 1883 poem, which includes the celebrated phrase "Give me your tired, your poor/Your huddled masses yearning to breathe free," is on a plaque on the pedestal.

**Statue of Liberty/Ellis Island**

*(212-363-3200; www.nps.gov/stli; www.ellisisland.com). 9:30am–5pm. Free. Travel: N, R, W to Whitehall St; 4, 5 to Bowling Green, then Statue of Liberty Ferry (212-269-5755), departing every 45 minutes from gangway 4 or 5 in Battery Park, at the southern tip of Manhattan. 9am–3:30pm; last trip out 3:30pm, last trip back 5:15pm. Ferry tickets $10, seniors $8, children 3–17 $4, under 2 free. Purchase tickets at Castle Clinton in Battery Park.*

On the way back to Manhattan, the tour boat takes you to the Immigration Museum on Ellis Island, through which more than 12 million people entered the country. The exhibitions are an evocative, moving tribute to those who headed for America with dreams of a better life. The $5 audio tour, narrated by Tom Brokaw, is excellent, and available in five languages.

**It ain't easy being green** The elements have given Lady Liberty's copper shell its characteristic bright patina.

**Stars and stocks forever** The NYSE is the nerve center of the U.S. economy.

are the inventively designed **South Cove** area, the **Robert F. Wagner Jr. Park** (an observation deck offers fabulous views of the harbor and the Verrazano-Narrows Bridge) and New York City's Holocaust museum, the **Museum of Jewish Heritage** *(see page 56)*. The entire park area is dotted with sculpture, such as Tom Otterness's whimsical installation *The Real World*. The park hosts outdoor cultural events during the warmer months.

### Battery Park City Authority

*212-417-2000; www.batteryparkcity.org.*
The neighborhood's official website lists events and has a great map of the area.

### Lower Manhattan Cultural Council

*212-219-9407; www.lmcc.net.*
An information service for artists and the public, the LMCC offers information on cultural events happening in and around lower Manhattan.

### World Financial Center & Winter Garden

*From Hudson River to West St between Albany and Vesey Sts (212-945-0505; www.worldfinancialcenter.com). Subway: N, R, W to Rector St; 4, 5 to Wall St. Free.*
Phone for information about free events, which range from concerts to flower shows.

### World Trade Center Viewing Platform

*Church St at Fulton St. Subway: Subway: N, R, W to Rector St; 4, 5 to Wall St. Free.*
At press time, visitors were required to obtain free tickets at the **South Street Seaport** ticket booth *(see page 66)*. Every day, tickets are distributed for each half-hour block, noon to 8pm the same day, or 9 to 11:30am the next day. Visitors should not arrive at the platform more than 15 minutes before their allotted time.

## Wall Street

Since the city's earliest days as a fur-trading post, wheeling and dealing has been New York's prime pastime, and commerce the backbone of its prosperity. **Wall Street** (or merely "the Street," if you wish to sound like a trader) is the thoroughfare synonymous with the world's greatest den of capitalism.

Wall Street itself is actually less than a mile long; it took its name from a wooden defensive wall that the Dutch built in 1653, to mark what was then the northern limit of New Amsterdam. The tip of Manhattan is generally known as the Financial District. In the days before telecommunications, financial institutions established their headquarters here to be near the seaport action. This was where corporate America made its first audacious architectural assertions; there are many impressive buildings built by grand old banks and businesses.

Notable structures include the former Merchants' Exchange at 55 Wall Street (now the **Regent Wall Street**; *see page 141*), with its stacked rows of Ionic and Corinthian columns, giant doors and an interior rotunda that holds 3,000 people; the **Equitable Building** *(120 Broadway between Cedar and Pine Sts)*, whose greedy use of vertical space helped instigate the zoning laws now governing skyscrapers (stand across the street from the building to get the optimum view); and **40 Wall Street** (today owned by real-estate tycoon Donald Trump), which in 1929 went head-to-head with the Chrysler Building in a battle for the title of "world's tallest building." (The Empire State Building trounced them both a year later.)

The Gothic Revival spire of the Episcopalian **Trinity Church** rises at the western end of Wall Street. It was the island's tallest structure when completed in 1846 (the original burned in 1776 and a second was demolished in 1839). Stop in and see brokers praying that the market gets bullish, or stroll through the adjacent cemetery, where cracked and faded tombstones mark the final resting places of dozens of past city dwellers, including signers of the Declaration of Independence and the U.S. Constitution. **St. Paul's Chapel**, a satellite of Trinity, is an oasis of peace modeled on London's St. Martin-in-the-Fields. The chapel is New York City's only extant pre-Revolutionary building (it dates to 1766), and one of the finest Georgian structures in the country. Miraculously, both landmark churches survived the nearby World Trade Center attack. Although mortar fell from their facades, the steeples remained intact—and St. Paul's Waterford crystal chandeliers hung in without a crack.

A block east of Trinity Church, the **Federal Hall National Memorial** is a Greek Revival shrine to American inaugural history—sort of. This is the spot where Washington was sworn in as the country's first president on April 30, 1789. The original building was demolished in 1812.

The nerve center of the U.S. economy is the **New York Stock Exchange**. Unfortunately, the Exchange is no longer open to the public for security reasons. Not to worry: People-watching on the street outside the NYSE is still a great spectator sport. It's an endless pageant of power, as besuited brokers march up and down Broad Street. For a lesson on Wall Street's influence through the years, check out the **Museum of American Financial History**.

The **Federal Reserve Bank**, a block north on Liberty Street, is an imposing structure built in the Florentine style. It holds the nation's largest store of gold—just over 9,000 tons—in a vault five stories below street level (you might have seen Jeremy Irons clean it out in *Die Hard 3*).

**Taking stock** Weary financial workers hit the Street at the market's close.

### Federal Hall National Memorial

*26 Wall St at Nassau St (212-825-6888). Subway: 2, 3, 4, 5 to Wall St. Mon–Fri 9am–5pm. Free.*

### Federal Reserve Bank

*33 Liberty St between Nassau and William Sts (212-720-6130). Subway: 2, 3, 4, 5 to Wall St. Tours Mon–Fri on the half hour, 9:30am–2:30pm. Free.*
The free one-hour tours through the bank—and its gold vaults—must be arranged at least two weeks in advance; tickets are sent by mail.

### Museum of American Financial History

*See page 52 for listing.*
This tiny museum and gift shop are located on the ground floor of the Standard Oil Building, the original site of John D. Rockefeller's office. Walking tours are conducted every Friday at 10am.

### St. Paul's Chapel

*211 Broadway between Fulton and Vesey Sts (212-602-0874; www.stpaulschapel.org). Subway: A, C to Broadway–Nassau St; J, M, Z, 2, 3, 4, 5 to Fulton St. Mon–Sat 9am–3pm; Sun 7am–3pm.*

### Trinity Church Museum

*Broadway at Wall St (212-602-0872; www.trinitywallstreet.org). Subway: N, R, W to Rector St; 2, 3, 4, 5 to Wall St. Mon–Fri 9–11:45am, 1–3:45pm; Sat 10am–3:45pm; Sun 1–3:45pm; closed during concerts. Free.*
The small museum inside Trinity Church chronicles the parish's past and the role it has played in New York's history.

## The Seaport

While New York's importance as a port has diminished, its initial fortune rolled in on the salt water that crashes around its natural harbor. The city was perfectly situated for trade with Europe; after 1825, goods from the Western Territories arrived via the Erie Canal and Hudson River. And because New York was the point of entry for millions of immigrants, its character was formed primarily by the waves of humanity that arrived at its docks.

The **South Street Seaport** is the best place to see this seafaring heritage. Redeveloped in the mid-1980s, the Seaport is an area of reclaimed and renovated buildings converted to shops, restaurants, bars and a museum. It's not an area that New Yorkers often visit, though it is rich in history. The Seaport's public spaces are a favorite with street performers, and the shopping area of Pier 17 is little more than a picturesque tourist trap of a mall by day and an after-work watering hole by night; outdoor concerts in the summer do attract locals from all over the city. Antique vessels are docked at other piers. The **Seaport Museum** *(see page 54)* details New York's maritime history and is located within the restored 19th-century buildings at **Schermerhorn Row** *(2–18 Fulton St, 91–92 South St and 189–195 Front St)*, which were constructed on landfill in 1812. At 11 Fulton Street, the **Fulton Market** (with gourmet food stalls and seafood restaurants that open onto the cobbled streets in summer) is a great place for slurping oysters and people-watching. Familiar national chain shops such as J. Crew and Abercrombie & Fitch line the surrounding streets. If you enter the Seaport area from Water Street, the first thing you'll notice is the whitewashed ***Titanic* Memorial Lighthouse**, erected the year after the great ship went down and moved to its current location in 1976. The area offers fine views of the **Brooklyn Bridge** *(see page 109)*. The smell on South Street is a clear sign that the **Fulton Fish Market**, America's largest, is nearby. Opened in 1836, the market sold fish fresh from the sea until 1930, when fishing boats stopped docking here. Today, fish are trucked in and out by land. Go now to see the frantic predawn dance of the wholesalers and the fantastic variety of fish—the market will move to Hunts Point in the Bronx when a new facility is completed in 2004.

### Fulton Fish Market

*Pier 16, South St at Fulton St (212-406-4985). Subway: A, C to Broadway–Nassau St; J, M, Z, 2, 3, 4, 5 to Fulton St. 3:30–11:30am.*

Get up early; most of the Fulton Fish Market's action occurs before sunrise. But don't ask about the market's long-alleged Mafia ties—you could wind up sleeping with the fishes.

### South Street Seaport

*From Water St to the East River, between John St and Peck Slip (212-SEAPORT; www.southstseaport.org). Subway: A, C to Broadway–Nassau St; J, M, Z, 2, 3, 4, 5 to Fulton St. 11am–6pm.*

## Civic Center & City Hall

The business of running New York takes place among the many grand buildings of the Civic Center. This area was the budding city's northern boundary in the 1700s. When **City Hall** was completed in 1812, its architects were so confident the city would grow no farther north, they didn't bother to put any marble on its northern side. The building, a beautiful blend of Federal form and French Renaissance details, is unfortunately closed to the public (except for scheduled group tours). **City Hall Park**, which was treated to a $30 million renovation in 1999, has a granite time wheel that displays the park's history. For years, the steps of City Hall and the park have been the site of press conferences and political protests. Under former mayor Rudolph Giuliani, the steps were closed to such activity, though civil

**A light to remember** The *Titanic* Memorial Lighthouse, at the South Street Seaport entrance, commemorates the 1912 tragedy.

libertarians successfully defied the ban in April 2000. The much larger **Municipal Building**, which faces City Hall and reflects it architecturally, houses other civic offices, including the marriage bureau, which can churn out newly-weds at a remarkable clip.

**Park Row**, east of the park and now lined with cafés and electronics shops, once held the offices of 19 daily papers and was known as Newspaper Row. It was also the site of Phineas T. Barnum's sensationalist American Museum, which burned down in 1865.

Facing the park from the west is Cass Gilbert's famous **Woolworth Building** *(233 Broadway between Barclay St and Park Pl)*, a vertically elongated Gothic cathedral–style office building that has been called the Mozart of skyscrapers. Its beautifully detailed lobby is open to the public during business hours.

The houses of crime and punishment are also located in the Civic Center around Foley Square—once a pond and later the site of the city's most notorious slum of the 19th century, Five Points. These days, you'll find the State Supreme Court housed in the **New York County Courthouse** *(60 Centre St at Pearl St)*, a hexagonal Roman revival building whose beautiful interior rotunda is decorated with a mural called *Law Through the Ages*. The **United States Courthouse** *(40 Centre St between Duane and Pearl Sts)* is crowned with a golden pyramid-topped tower above a Corinthian temple. Next to City Hall is the old New York County Courthouse, more popularly known as the 1872 **Tweed Courthouse**, a symbol of the runaway corruption of mid-19th-century municipal government. Boss Tweed, leader of the political machine Tammany Hall, pocketed $10 million of the building's huge $14 million cost. The remainder was still enough to buy a beautiful edifice; the Italianate detailing is exquisite. A recent $90 million renovation has restored much of the structure's luster. (The building now houses the Board of Education.) The **Criminal Courts Building and Bernard Kerik Detention Complex** *(100 Centre St between Hogan Pl and Worth St)* is the most intimidating in the district. Built of great slabs of granite with looming towers that guard the entrance, this is NYC justice at its most Kafkaesque. The Ziggurat-topped building is familiarly known as "the Tombs," a reference not only to the architecture of its predecessor (a long-gone building inspired by a photograph of an Egyptian tomb) but to its once deathly prison conditions; it holds 800 prisoners today. Formerly called the Manhattan House of Detention, it was renamed in honor of former Police Commissioner Bernard Kerik in 2002.

**Hall of fame** You can't fight City Hall, but you can admire its majestic design—part Federal, part French Renaissance.

All of these courts are open to the public, weekdays from 9am to 5pm, though only some of the courtrooms allow visitors. Your best bets for legal drama are the Criminal Courts, where, if you can't slip into a trial, you can at least observe hallways full of legal wheeler-dealers and the criminals they represent. Or for a grim twist on dinner theater, check out the weeklong, all-night parade of pleas at **Arraignment Court** in the same building.

A major archaeological site, the **African Burial Ground** *(Duane St between Broadway and Lafayette St)*, is the remnant of a five-and-a-half-acre cemetery where 20,000 African men, women and children were buried. The cemetery, which closed in 1794, was unearthed during construction of a federal office building in 1991 and designated a National Historic Landmark.

### City Hall

*City Hall Park between Broadway and Park Row (212-788-3000; www.nyc.gov). Subway: J, M, Z to Chambers St; 2, 3 to Park Pl; 4, 5, 6 to Brooklyn Bridge–City Hall.*
City Hall, at the northern end of the park, houses the mayor's office and the legislative chambers of the City Council, and is thus ringed with news vans waiting for Hizzoner to appear. The pretty landscaping and abundant benches make the park a popular lunchtime spot for area office workers. For group tours of City Hall, call two weeks in advance.

## Tribeca & Soho

Tribeca (Triangle Below Canal Street) today is a textbook example of the process of gentrification in lower Manhattan. It's very much as Soho (South of Houston Street) was 20

**The outsiders** Bargain hunters in Soho sample a sidewalk vendor's wares.

years ago: A few pockets are deserted and abandoned—the cobbles dusty and untrodden, and the cast-iron architecture chipped and unpainted—while the rest throbs with energy. Unlike Soho, however, the rich and famous have been the pioneers here: Harvey Keitel, Ed Burns (in JFK Jr.'s old apartment), Richard Serra and many other celebrities live in the area. There is a host of haute restaurants, including **Danube** and **Nobu** *(see pages 179 and 180),* and posh bars, especially near the corner of North Moore Street and West Broadway. Clubs such as **The Knitting Factory** *(see page 310)* contribute to the culture.

The buildings here are generally larger than those in Soho; particularly toward the river, many are warehouses rapidly being converted to condos. There is fine small-scale cast-iron architecture along White Street and the parallel thoroughfares, including 85 Leonard Street, the only remaining cast-iron building attributable to James Bogardus, the developer of this building method, which prefigured the technology of the skyscraper (for more about the city's architecture, *see page 20*). On nearby Harrison Street sits a row of well-preserved Federal townhouses (though a 1970s-era middle-income housing project looms overhead).

As in Soho, you'll find galleries, salons, furniture stores, spas and other businesses that cater to the neighborhood's stylish residents, but fewer of Tribeca's emporiums are outposts of mall-like chains.

Tribeca is also the unofficial headquarters of New York's film industry. Robert De Niro's **Tribeca Film Center** *(375 Greenwich St at Franklin St)* houses screening rooms and production offices in the old Martinson Coffee Building. His **Tribeca Grill** *(212-941-3900)* is on the ground floor. In addition, De Niro is one of the sponsors of the **Tribeca Film Festival** *(see page 282),* which draws an eager crowd to the neighborhood in May. Also in the Film Center are the Queens-bred industry heavies Bob and Harvey Weinstein and the main offices of their company, Miramax. A few blocks away, **The Screening Room** *(see page 281)* shows art-house films in an upstairs theater and serves solid American cuisine in its tasteful dining room.

Soho—New York's glamorous downtown shopping destination—was once an industrial zone known as Hell's Hundred Acres. In the 1960s, Soho was earmarked for destruction, but the neighborhood's signature cast-iron

► To further explore Soho's art scene, see chapters **Art Galleries** and **Museums**.
► Learn more about Soho buildings and other downtown structures in chapter **Architecture**.
► For Soho, Nolita and Tribeca shops so fabulous you'll not miss the dollars spent, see chapter **Shopping & Services**.

warehouses were saved by the many artists who inhabited them. (Urban-planning theorist Chester A. Rapkin coined the name Soho in a 1962 study on the neighborhood.) The **King and Queen of Greene Street** *(respectively, 72–76 Greene St between Broome and Spring Sts, and 28–30 Greene St between Canal and Grand Sts)* are two prime examples of cast-iron architecture. As loft living became fashionable and the buildings were renovated for residential use, landlords were quick to sniff the profits of gentrification. Today, Soho is a playground for the young, beautiful and rich. Walk around the cobbled streets, among the elegant buildings, boutiques and bistros, and you can try the lifestyle on for size. Most of the galleries that made Soho an art hot spot in the 1980s have decamped to cheaper (and now cutting-edge) neighborhoods like West Chelsea and Dumbo in Brooklyn (see chapter **Art Galleries**).

Surprisingly, plenty of sweatshops remain in Soho, especially near Canal Street—though the buildings may also house businesses such as graphic-design studios, magazine publishers and record labels.

Upscale hotels, such as **The Mercer**, **SoHo Grand** and **60 Thompson** *(see page 139)* have opened in the area, and the shop names run from Banana Republic and Old Navy to Marc Jacobs and Cartier. Soho is also the place to go for high-end home furnishings at design stores such as **Moss** *(see page 242)*. West Broadway, Soho's main shop-lined thoroughfare, is a magnet for out-of-towners—on the weekend, you're as likely to hear French, German and Italian as you are Brooklynese.

Two museums also make Soho their home—**New Museum of Contemporary Art** *(see page 46)* and the small, increasingly popular **New York City Fire Museum** *(see page 59)*, a former fire station that houses a collection of antique engines dating to the 1700s.

To the west of West Broadway, tenement- and townhouse-lined streets contain remnants of the Italian community that once dominated this area. Elderly men and women walk along Sullivan Street to the **St. Anthony of Padua Roman Catholic Church** *(155 Sullivan St at West Houston St)*, which was dedicated in 1888. You'll still find some old-school neighborhood flavor in businesses such as **Joe's Dairy** *(156 Sullivan St between Houston and Prince Sts, 212-677-8780)*, **Pino's Prime Meat Market** *(149 Sullivan St between Houston and Prince Sts, 212-475-8134)* and **Vesuvio Bakery** *(160 Prince St between Thompson St and West Broadway, 212-925-8248)*.

## Little Italy & Nolita

Little Italy, which once ran from Canal to Houston Streets between Lafayette Street and the Bowery, hardly resembles the insular community portrayed in Martin Scorsese's *Mean Streets*—Italian families have fled to the suburbs, Chinatown has crept north, and rising rents have forced mom-and-pop businesses to surrender to the stylish boutiques of Nolita (North of Little Italy, a misnomer since it actually lies within). "It's all restaurants and clothes—and who can fit into them?" moans one lifelong resident of Mott Street. Another telling change in the 'hood: **St. Patrick's Old Cathedral** *(260–264 Mulberry St between Houston and Prince Sts)* gives services in English and Spanish, not Italian. Completed in 1815 and restored after a fire in 1868, this was New York's premier Catholic church until it was demoted, upon consecration of the Fifth Avenue cathedral of the same name. But ethnic pride remains. Italian-Americans flood in from the outer boroughs to show their love for the old neighborhood during **The Feast of San Gennaro** *(see page 253)* every September. In summer, Luca Pizzaroni, a filmmaker from Rome, screens an open-air Italian-film series in the **De Salvio Playground** *(Mulberry St at Spring St)*. Aside from the tourist-oriented Italian cafés and restaurants on Mulberry Street *(between Canal and Houston Sts)*, there are pockets of the characteristic lifestyle. The elderly locals still buy olive oil and fresh pasta from venerable shops such as **DiPalo's Fine Foods** *(206 Grand St at Mott St)* and sandwiches packed with Italian meats and cheeses at **Italian Food Center** *(186 Grand St at Mulberry St)*.

Of course, Little Italy is the site of several notorious Mafia landmarks. The **Ravenite Social Club** *(247 Mulberry St between Prince and Spring Sts)* was celebrity don John Gotti's headquarters from the mid-1980s until his arrest in 1990; it's now occupied by the

### BEST VIEW Ritzy vista

**From the Rise Bar in the Ritz-Carlton New York, Battery Park**

Sip a potent martini at this sophisticated 14th-floor bar, which offers an elegant vantage point for gazing at the Statue of Liberty, Ellis Island, the Hudson River, Governor's Island and New Jersey. During the summer, cool off on the outdoor terrace. *See page 139 for listing.*

accessories boutique **Amy Chan** *(see page 226).* Mobster Joey Gallo was shot to death in 1972 while celebrating his birthday with his family at **Umberto's Clam House**, which has since moved around the corner *(178 Mulberry St at Broome St, 212-431-7545).* The Italian eateries in the area are mostly undistinguished, overpriced grill-and-pasta houses, but two reliable choices are **Il Cortile** *(125 Mulberry St between Canal and Hester Sts, 212-226-6060)* and **Benito One** *(174 Mulberry between Broome and Grand Sts, 212-226-9171).* Drop in at one of the many small cafés lining the streets, such as **Caffè Roma** *(385 Broome St at Mulberry St, 212-226-8413),* which opened in 1891, for an Italian soda or dessert and espresso. For a real drink, head to the bar **Mare Chiaro** *(see page 172),* once a favorite of Frank Sinatra. A new generation has discovered it, but plenty of old-timers (including a few portrayed in the Frank Mason painting on the wall) still visit.

Chichi restaurants and boutiques seem to open daily in Nolita (*see chapter* **Shopping & Services**). Elizabeth, Mott and Mulberry Streets—between Houston and Spring Streets in particular—are now the source of everything from perfectly cut jeans to handblown glass. The young, the insouciant and the vaguely European congregate outside eateries such as **Cafe Habana** and **Cafe Gitane** *(see page 181).* Long before the Nolita boom, the grand former **Police Headquarters Building** *(240 Centre St between Broome and Grand Sts)* had already been converted into luxe co-op apartments, in 1988.

## CRITICS' PICKS Bars

These are the best spots below 14th Street...

**...for nursing a hangover**

Prune (see page 189) serves nine different Bloody Mary potions for a bit of the hair of the dog.

**...for sampling suburbia**

Welcome to the Johnsons (see page 173) mixes *That '70s Show* with a punk-rock crowd.

**...for celebrating your birthday**

Chateau (see page 278) has hosted many celebrity soirees, including one of J. Lo's.

**...for hanging with the high-tech–meets–indie crowd**

Void (see page 277) lures avant-garde imbibers (Björk!) to its digital-video workshops.

**...for tripping back in time**

Chumley's (see page 169), a former speakeasy, takes you back to Prohibition days.

**...for Latin lovers**

Cafe Habana packs in sexy people, spicy food and stiff drinks (see page 181).

**...for midnight snacking**

Florent (see page 192) attracts late-night diners and bar hoppers seeking one last drink.

**...for dreaming about the apartment you'll never be able to afford**

Lounge in luxury at APT (see page 277).

**...for drinking with benefits**

During happy hour, Suba (see page 185) serves free tapas with every drink.

**...for jazz-loving insomniacs**

Smalls (see page 315) offers a rotation of live shows until 8am!

## Chinatown

Take a few steps south of Broome Street west of Broadway and you will feel as though you've entered a completely different country. You won't hear much English spoken along these crowded streets, which are lined with stands stocked with fish, fruit and vegetables. Manhattan's Chinatown is the largest Chinese-immigrant community outside Asia. Even though some residents decamp to four other Chinatowns in the city (two in Queens and two in Brooklyn), a steady flow of new arrivals keeps the original expanding. The tenements and high-rise buildings around East Canal Street house about 150,000 legal (and about 100,000 illegal) Chinese. Many work here and never leave the neighborhood. Chinatown's busy streets get even wilder during the Chinese New Year festivities in January or February, and around the Fourth of July, when the area is the city's best source of (illegal) fireworks.

Food is everywhere. The markets on **Canal Street** sell some of the best, most affordable seafood and fresh produce in the city—you'll see buckets of live eels and crabs, neatly stacked greens and piles of hairy rambutans. Street vendors sell satisfying snacks, such as bags of sweet egg pancakes. There are also countless restaurants. Mott Street—from Worth to Kenmare Streets—is lined with Cantonese and Szechuan places, as is East Broadway. Adding to the mix are increasing numbers of

Indonesian, Malaysian, Thai and Vietnamese eateries and stores.

Canal Street is a bargain-hunter's paradise: It's infamous as a source of knock-off designer items, such as handbags and perfumes. The area's gift shops are stocked with inexpensive Chinese products, from good-luck charms to kitschy pop-culture paraphernalia. One of Chinatown's best shops is the bi-level **Pearl River Mart** *(see page 243)*. It brims with food, dishware, dresses, traditional musical instruments and videos.

Historical sites of interest include **65 Mott Street** *(between Bayard and Pell Sts),* the city's first building erected in 1824 specifically as a tenement. Chinatown's oldest continuously run shop, **32 Mott Street General Store** *(between Chatham Sq and Pell St),* has been owned by the Lee family for three generations. The store, founded in 1891, has been at this location since 1899—note the peeling tin ceiling and carved arch made of wood brought over from China. Locals come to buy housewares and porcelain figurines. The antiques shop **Chu Shing** *(12 Mott St between Chatham Sq and Mosco St, 212-227-0279)* was once the New York office of the Chinese revolutionary Dr. Sun Yat-sen, known as the father of modern China.

**Wing Fat Shopping** is a strange little underground mall with a history. Enter through doors at Chatham Square (to the right of the OTB parlor at No. 8) and descend the stairs to your left—you'll find businesses such as the Foot Reflexology Center and Tin Sun Metaphysics, a well-known feng shui agency. The tunnel is rumored to have been a stop on the Underground Railroad, 25 years before the Chinese began populating this area in the 1880s. In 1906, the tunnel connected the Chinese Opera house at 5 Doyers Street with an actors' residence on the Bowery. Members of two rival tongs (Chinese organized-crime groups) staged a savage gun battle during an opera. At least four people were killed, and the gunmen escaped down the tunnels.

A statue of the Chinese philosopher marks **Confucius Plaza** at the corner of Bowery and Division Streets. **Columbus Park** at Bayard and Mulberry Streets is where elderly men and women gather around card tables to play mah-jongg and dominoes (you can hear the clacking tiles from across the street), while younger folks practice martial arts. On weekends, the place is jam-packed with families taking a break from shopping. The **Museum of Chinese in the Americas** *(see page 56)* hosts exhibitions and events that explore the Chinese immigrant experience in the Western Hemisphere. In the **Eastern States Buddhist Temple of America,** you'll be dazzled by the glitter of hundreds of Buddhas and the smell of incense. Near the Manhattan Bridge, **Mahayana Temple Buddhist Association** is a larger temple.

**Miracle on ice** Chinatown's markets have a seemingly endless supply of fresh fish.

For a different perspective on Chinatown culture, visit the noisy, dingy **Chinatown Fair**, an amusement arcade where some of the East Coast's best *Street Fighter* players congregate. Older kids hit Chinatown for liquid entertainment; the **Double Happiness** bar *(173 Mott St between Broome and Grand Sts, 212-941-1282)* is a popular nightspot for downtown denizens of all ethnic groups.

### Chinatown Fair

*8 Mott St at Chatham Sq. Subway: J, M, Z, N, Q, R, W, 6 to Canal St.*

### Eastern States Buddhist Temple of America

*64B Mott St between Bayard and Canal Sts (212-966-6229). Subway: J, M, Z, N, Q, R, W, 6 to Canal St. 9am–7pm.*

**Mahayana Temple Buddhist Association**

*133 Canal St at Bowery, No. 33 (212-925-8787). Subway: J, M, Z, N, Q, R, W, 6 to Canal St; S to Grand St. 8am–6pm.*

## Lower East Side

The Lower East Side tells the story of New York's immigrants, millions upon millions of whom poured into the city in the late 19th and 20th centuries. The area is densely populated with a patchwork of strong ethnic communities, and it's great for dining and exploration. Today, Lower East Side residents are largely Asian and Latino families, with an increasing number of fresh-from-college kids sharing small apartments. The early settlers were mostly Eastern European Jews. Mass tenement housing was built to accommodate the 19th-century influx of immigrants, which included many German, Hungarian, Irish and Polish families. The unsanitary, overcrowded conditions, documented near the end of that century by Jacob A. Riis in *How the Other Half Lives,* outraged reformers, who prompted the introduction of building codes. To better understand how these immigrants lived, visit the **Lower East Side Tenement Museum** *(see page 51).*

Between 1870 and 1920, hundreds of synagogues and religious schools were established. Yiddish newspapers were published, and associations for social reform and cultural studies flourished, along with vaudeville and Yiddish theaters. (The Marx Brothers, Jimmy Durante, Eddie Cantor, and George and Ira Gershwin were just a few of the entertainers who once lived in this district.) Today, only about 10 percent of the current population is Jewish; the **Eldridge Street Synagogue** finds it hard to round up the ten adult males required to conduct a service. Despite a shrinking congregation, the synagogue has not missed a Sabbath or holiday service in 115 years. Remarkably, in October 2001, a white-tiled *mikvah* (a small pool that collects rainwater used to cleanse Orthodox Jewish women after their menstrual cycles), was unearthed behind the synagogue; it is believed to be the oldest one of its kind in New York, dating back to 1887. **First Shearith Israel Graveyard** has gravestones that date back to 1683.

Puerto Ricans and Dominicans began to move to the Lower East Side after World War II. Colorful awnings characterize the area's bodegas (corner groceries). Many restaurants serve Caribbean standards, such as rice and beans with fried plantains. In the summer, the streets throb with the sounds of salsa and merengue as residents hang out, savor ices, drink beer and play dominoes.

Beginning in the 1980s, a new breed of immigrants began moving in: young artists,

# A river runs near it

### Urbanites welcome the parks, piers and beaches of the Hudson River Project

One of the most densely populated areas in the country is about to acquire a bit more breathing room. The Hudson River Park Trust is transforming a five-mile stretch along the waterfront from Battery Park to 59th Street into a park for all of New York City to enjoy. The project, which is scheduled to be completed in 2005, will add 550 acres of open space to Manhattan. "The park will ensure that the Hudson River is part of our everyday lives," Governor George Pataki has said. "The river won't be just a waterway that we see from the car, but a source of family fun, economic opportunity and inspiration."

For centuries, the Hudson was a major trade route, first for Algonquin tribes, and later, for Dutch and English settlers. But by the mid-20th century, as other waterways opened and railroads were laid down, the piers and shoreline were vacated and the docks used as parking lots.

Since the 1980s, civic groups have pushed for the area to be converted to a public park. Their efforts resulted in the passage of the Hudson River Park Act in 1998. The legislation reserves extensive portions of the waterfront exclusively for public recreation, significantly limits commercial activity on the land, and states that all money made within the park must be spent on the project's construction, maintenance and operation.

The park's first section was completed this spring. The area, which is adjacent to the West Village, contains a children's playground, a large lawn, concession stands and an artificial turf for sports. In addition, the stretch also offers access to three reconstructed piers; one of them, **Pier 54** *(W 13th St at West Side Hwy),* holds the

**Final home** First Shearith Israel Graveyard is the city's oldest Jewish cemetery.

musicians and other sensitive types attracted by low rents. Bars, boutiques and music venues that catered to this crowd sprang up on Ludlow Street and the surrounding area, creating an annex of the East Village; this scene is still thriving, though rents have risen sharply. For live music, check who's playing at **Arlene Grocery** *(see page 307),* the **Bowery Ballroom** *(see page 307)* and **Tonic** *(see page 313).*

The Lower East Side's reputation as a haven for political radicals lives on at the squat **ABC No Rio** *(156 Rivington St between Clinton and Suffolk Sts; www.abcnorio.org),* which also houses a gallery and performance space. The arts organization is in the process of legally taking ownership of the building from the city.

Despite the trendy shops that have cropped up along the block, Orchard Street below Stanton Street remains the heart of the **Orchard Street Bargain District**, a row of stores selling utilitarian goods. This is the place for cheap hats, luggage, sportswear and T-shirts. In the 1930s, Mayor Fiorello La Guardia forced pushcart vendors off the streets into large, indoor marketplaces. Although many of these structures are now a thing of the past, **Essex Street Markets** *(120 Essex St between Delancey and Rivington Sts)* is still going strong as a purveyor of all things Latino, from chorizo to religious icons.

Many remnants of the neighborhood's Jewish roots remain. One of the Lower East Side's most famous eateries is the proudly shabby **Sammy's Steak House** *(157 Chrystie St between Delancey and Rivington*

archway that welcomed home the survivors of the *Titanic*. Workers will overhaul ten more piers before the project is completed. "Standing at the end of a 1,000-foot pier and looking back at the skyline is a unique and amazing experience," says Alex Dudley, spokesperson for the Hudson River Park Trust. "We can't wait for all New Yorkers to discover it."

For sports enthusiasts, a number of Hudson River Park facilities are already open. At Pier 63, hoop lovers can perfect their dunk at **BasketBall City** *(23rd St at West Side Hwy, 212-924-4040),* which contains six air-conditioned, full-size basketball courts. Baseball players can "batter up" at **Pier 40**'s batting cages *(Houston St at West Side Hwy; www.pier40.org),* and Tiger Woods wanna-bes can aim for a hole-in-one at the miniature golf course at **Pier 25** *(North Moore St at West Side Hwy; www.manhattanyouth.org).* If you don't leave home without your skateboard, tear up the free skate park located in front of **Pier 26** (*North Moore St at West Side Hwy).* Other activities include gymnastics, ice-skating and rock climbing at **Chelsea Piers' Pier 61** (*see page 328 for listing);* volleyball at **Pier 25**; and kayaking at **Piers 26** and **40** *(see also page 330).* In the future, water babies will be able to splash about on public beaches near 34th Street and at Gansevoort Peninsula.

Nautical enthusiasts may appreciate a tour of the ***Intrepid*** **Sea-Air-Space Museum** *(see page 57)* as well as historic ships such as the ***Frying Pan*** and the ***John Jay Harvey*** historic fireboat *(both at Pier 63),* and the ***Yankee*** *(at Pier 25),* a 94-year-old ferry that served in both World Wars and was one of the earliest Statue of Liberty ferries.

The project is also constructing several playgrounds and community gardens where visitors will be able to relax, watch the sun set and take in great views of the Statue of Liberty. "For years, the people of New York City have been cut off from the Hudson," says Dudley. "The park restores their access to this beautiful waterway."

For a guide to the park, visit the website at www.hudsonriverpark.org.

*Sts, 212-673-0330),* where hearty servings of Eastern European fare are served with a jug of schmaltz (chicken fat) and a bottle of vodka. If you prefer "lighter" food, **Katz's Delicatessen** *(see page 185)* sells someof the best pastrami in New York (Meg Ryan's famous faux-orgasm scene in *When Harry Met Sally...* was filmed here). People come from all over for the fresh, crunchy dills at **Guss' Pickles** *(see page 239),* another Lower East Side landmark. For dinner, try the nostalgic American cuisine at **Lansky Lounge & Grill** *(104 Norfolk St between Delancey and Rivington Sts, 212-677-9489),* a swinging speakeasy-style club named for the late Jewish mobster Meyer Lansky (for more neighborhood treats, *see* **Lower East Side snacks**, *below*).

Sightseeing

### Eldridge Street Synagogue

*12 Eldridge St between Canal and Division Sts (212-219-0888; www.eldridgestreet.org). Subway: F to East Broadway. Tours Tue, Thu 11:30am, 2:30pm and by appointment; Sun 11am–3pm on the hour. $4, seniors and students $2.50.*

This beautifully decorated building was the pride of the Jewish congregation that once filled it. Services are conducted in the *beth hamedrash* (house of study) on the ground floor.

### First Shearith Israel Graveyard

*55–57 St. James Pl between James and Oliver Sts. Subway: J, M to Bowery; S to Grand St.*

This is the burial ground of the oldest Jewish community in the United States—Spanish and Portuguese Jews who escaped the Inquisition.

# The Village

## East Village

Scruffier than its western counterpart, the East Village has a long history as a countercultural hotbed. Originally considered part of the Lower East Side, the neighborhood boomed in the 1960s when writers, artists and musicians moved in and turned it into the hub for the countercultural revolution. (Allen Ginsberg lived at 437 East 12th Street, between First Avenue and Avenue A, until his death in 1997.) Many famous clubs and coffeehouses thrived,

## CRITICS' PICKS Lower East Side snacks

**Authentic Belgian fries at Pomme-Pomme**

*195 E Houston St between Ludlow and Orchard Sts (646-602-8140).*

Who needs ketchup? You have more than 30 sauces to choose from at this take-out joint.

**Grilled cheese sandwich at Grilled Cheese NYC**

*168 Ludlow St between Houston and Stanton Sts (212-982-6600).*

Cheese pressed between two warm slices of bread is treated like an arty new invention at this eatery. They don't butter the bread, so it's as healthy as a grilled *fromage* can be.

**Homemade brownies at Angelina's**

*188 Orchard St between Houston and Stanton Sts (212-979-5564).*

These delicious delights taste like they're right out of the oven.

**Homemade tortilla chips and guacamole at San Loco Mexico**

*111 Stanton St between Essex and Ludlow Sts (212-253-7580).*

The guacamole is made with fresh avocados, spices and the juice of just-squeezed limes. It comes with four different homemade sauces: mild, hot, serious and stupid.

**Old-fashioned taffy at Economy Candy**

*108 Rivington St between Essex and Ludlow Sts (212-254-1832).*

Feel like a kid again as you chew on taffy and ogle the large candy bins filled with chocolates, PEZ and jelly beans.

**Romanian *karnatzlack* at Sammy's Steak House**

*157 Chrystie St between Rivington and Delancey Sts (212-673-0330).*

This "garlic lovers" appetizer is shaped like a sausage and combines beef, veal, onions and lots of garlic.

**Tea sandwiches at Teany**

*90 Rivington St between Ludlow and Orchard Sts (212-475-9190).*

The mini-sandwiches at this tiny tea shop, owned by electronic musician Moby, go great with any of the restaurant's 94 teas.

**Toasted peanut-butter, honey & banana sandwich at Pink Pony**

*176 Ludlow St between Houston and Stanton Sts (212-253-1922).*

Get a warm, mushy feeling from this scrumptious sandwich, which is served at a bar that's always in full swing.

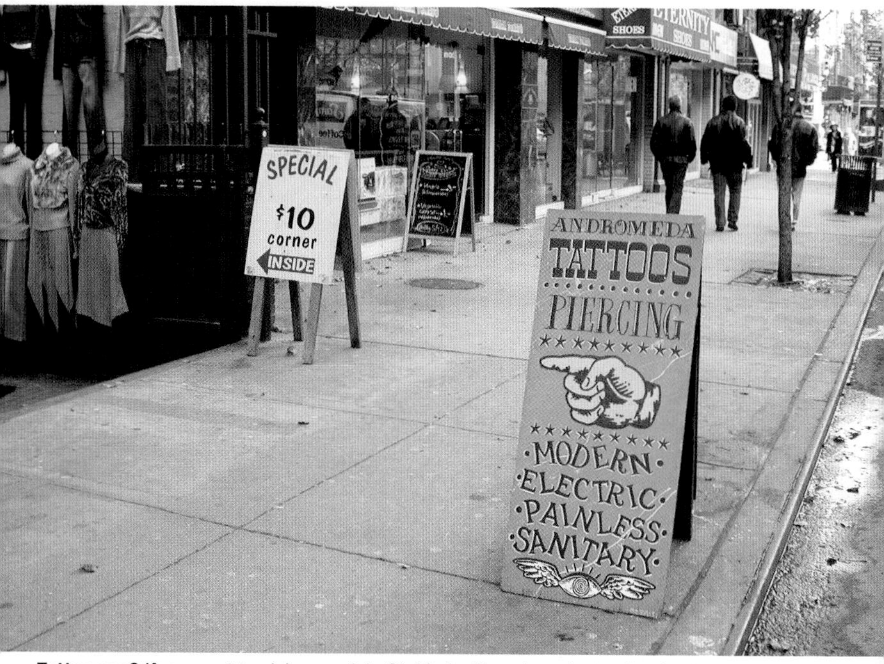


**Tattoo you?** If you want to sink some ink, St. Marks Place has plenty of parlors.

including the Fillmore East rock theater on Second Avenue between 6th and 7th Streets (now demolished), and the Dom *(23 St. Marks Pl)*, where the Velvet Underground was a regular headliner; it's now being turned into condos. In the '70s, the neighborhood took a dive as drugs and crime prevailed—but that didn't stop the influx of artists and punk rockers. In the early '80s, East Village galleries were among the first to display the work of groundbreaking artists Jean-Michel Basquiat and Keith Haring.

Today, the area east of Broadway between Houston and 14th Streets is no longer quite so edgy, though remnants of its spirited past endure. Now you'll find a generally amiable population of ravers, punks, yuppies, hippies, homeboys, vagrants and trustafarians—wanna-be bohos who live off trust funds. This motley crew has crowded into the neighborhood's tenements—next to a few elderly residents, who tend to be holdouts from previous waves of immigration. Check out the indie record shops, bargain restaurants, grungy bars, punky clubs and funky, cheap clothing stores.

**St. Marks Place** *(8th St between Lafayette St and Ave A)* is the main drag. In previous years, Trotsky ran a printing press (1917) and W.H. Auden lived (1953–72) at 77 St. Marks Place—now home to the regional Mexican restaurant **La Palapa** *(see page 188)*—but the street is generally less highbrow now. Lined with stores, bars and street vendors, St. Marks is packed until the wee hours with crowds browsing for bargain T-shirts, records and books. The more interesting places are to the east; you'll find cafés and shops on and around Avenue A between 6th and 10th Streets. Since tattooing became legal in New York City in 1997 (it had been banned since 1961), a number of parlors have opened up, including the famous **Fun City** *(see page 247)*, whose awning advertises CAPPUCCINO & TATTOO.

**Astor Place**, with its revolving cube sculpture, is always swarming with young skateboarders and other modern-day street urchins. It is also the site of Peter Cooper's recently refurbished **Cooper Union**, the city's first free private college. Opened in 1859, it's now a design and engineering college (and still free). In the 19th century, Astor Place marked the boundary between the ghetto to the east and some of the city's most fashionable homes, such as **Colonnade Row** *(428–434 Lafayette between Astor Pl and W 4th St)*. To the west facing these was the distinguished Astor Public Library, which theater legend Joseph Papp rescued from demolition in the 1960s. Today it's the **Public Theater**—a haven for first-run American plays, the producer of the **New York Shakespeare Festival** *(see page 335)* and the home of trendy **Joe's Pub** *(see page 309).*

East of Lafayette Street on the Bowery are several missionary organizations that cater to the down-and-out, the sole vestiges of the street's notorious past. In recent years, a few restaurants have also set up shop. Hallowed **CBGB** *(see page 307),* the birthplace of American punk, still packs in guitar bands, both new and used. Many other local bars and clubs successfully apply the formula of cheap beer and loud music, including the **Continental** and the **Mercury Lounge** *(see pages 309 and 312).*



East 7th Street is a Ukrainian stronghold; the focal point is the Byzantine-looking **St. George's Ukrainian Catholic Church** at No. 16–20, built in 1977 but appearing considerably more dated. Across the street, there is often a long line of beefy fraternity types waiting to enter **McSorley's Old Ale House** *(see page 172),* which touts itself as the city's oldest pub in a single location (1854); it still serves just one kind of beer—its own brew. For those who would rather shop than sip, eclectic boutiques of young designers and vintage clothing dealers dot 7th, 8th and 9th Streets.

Curry Row, on 6th Street between First and Second Avenues, is one of several Little Indias in New York. Roughly two dozen Indian restaurants sit side by side, though contrary to a popular joke, they do not share a single kitchen. (Not many are commendable except for diners on an extremely tight budget.) And if you're wondering about the row of shiny Harleys on 3rd Street between First and Second Avenues, the New York chapter of the **Hell's Angels** is headquartered here.

**Alphabet City**, on Avenues A through D, stretches toward the East River. The largely working-class Latino population is being overtaken by professionals willing to pay higher rents. Avenue C is known as "Loisaida Avenue," the phonetic spelling of "Lower East Side" when pronounced with a clipped Spanish accent. The neighborhood's long, rocky romance with heroin is pretty much a thing of the past.

Although it's rough around the edges, Alphabet City has its attractions. Two churches on 4th Street are built in the Spanish-colonial style: **San Isidro y San Leandro** *(345 E 4th St between Aves C and D)* and **Iglesia Pentecostal Camino Damasco** *(289 E 4th St between Aves B and C).* **The Nuyorican Poets Cafe** *(see page 268),* a 28-year-old clubhouse for espresso-drinking beatniks, is famous for its slams, in which performance poets do lyric battle before a score-keeping audience. **Tompkins Square Park** has historically been the site of demonstrations and rioting. The last uprising was nearly a decade ago, when the city decided to evict the park's

**Touched by an Angel** Don't get too close to that shiny Harley—it belongs to a member of Hell's Angels. The bikers' New York headquarters are on East 3rd Street.

**Land of the free** Cooper Union, an art-and-science college in the East Village, provides full scholarships for all students.

squatters and renovate it to suit the area's increasingly affluent residents.

North of Tompkins Square, around First Avenue and 11th Street, are remnants of earlier communities: discount fabric shops, Italian cheese shops, Polish restaurants and two great Italian patisseries. Visit **DeRobertis** *(176 First Ave at 11th St, 212-674-7137)* and **Veniero's Pasticceria and Caffe** *(342 E 11th St at First Ave, 212-674-7264)* for wonderful pastries and old-world ambience.

### St. Mark's Church in-the-Bowery

*See* **Danspace Project**, *page 345.*

St. Mark's was built in 1799 on the site of Peter Stuyvesant's farm. Stuyvesant, one of New York's first governors, is buried in the cemetery, along with many of his descendants. Today the church is the East Village's unofficial cultural center, its space rented by arts groups, such as the experimental theater troupe **Ontological at St. Mark's** *(212-420-1916).*

### Tompkins Square Park

*From 7th to 10th Sts, between Aves A and B. Subway: 6 to Astor Pl.*

The community park of the East Village, Tompkins Square is one of the liveliest layabout zones in the city. Latino bongo beaters, longhairs with acoustic guitars, punky squatters, mangy dogs, the neighborhood's yuppie stroller-pushers and its homeless mingle on the grass under huge old trees. In summer, the park's southern end is often the site of musical performances, while the northern part is the province of basketball, handball and hockey enthusiasts.

## Greenwich Village

The middle section of "the Village" has seen some serious partying over the years. Stretching from Houston Street to 14th Street, between Broadway and Sixth Avenue, Greenwich Village's leafy streets have inspired bohemian lifestyles for almost a century. It's a place for idle wandering, for people-watching from sidewalk cafés, for candlelit dining in clandestine restaurants, and for hopping between bars and cabaret venues. The Village gets mobbed in mild weather and has lost some of its quaintness, but much of what has always attracted painters and poets to New York still exists. Sip a fresh roast in honor of the Beats—Jack Kerouac, Allen Ginsberg and their buddies—as you sit in their former haunts. Kerouac's favorite was **Le Figaro Café**, at the corner of Bleecker and MacDougal Streets. The **Cedar Tavern** *(82 University Pl between 11th and 12th Sts, 212-929-9089),* which moved from its original location at the corner of 8th Street, is where the leading figures of Abstract Expressionism's boys' club discussed how best to throw paint: Franz Kline, Jackson Pollock and Larry Rivers drank under this banner in the 1950s.

The hippies who tuned out in **Washington Square** are still there in spirit, and often in person: The park hums with musicians and street artists (though the once-ubiquitous pot dealers have become victims of strict policing and hidden surveillance cameras). Chess hustlers and students from **New York University** join in, along with today's new generation of idlers: hip-hop kids who drive down to West 4th Street in their booming Jeeps, and Generation Y skateboarders who clatter around the fountain and near the base of the **Washington Arch** (a modest-size Arc de Triomphe completed in 1895 in honor of George Washington). Renovation of the arch started almost a dozen years ago, but the money ran out and the structure is *still* fenced off. The project will take another year.

The Village has been fashionable since the 1830s, when the wealthy built handsome townhouses around Washington Square. Some of these properties are still privately owned and occupied; many others have become part of the New York University campus. Several literary figures, including Henry James,

► More information on downtown dining and nightlife can be found in chapters **Restaurants**, **Bars** and **Music**.

► A complete review of the Stonewall and other gay establishments can be found in chapter **Gay & Lesbian**.

Herman Melville and Mark Twain, lived on or near the square. In 1871, the local creative community founded the **Salmagundi Club**, America's oldest artists' club, which is now situated north of Washington Square on Fifth Avenue (No. 47). The landmark building hosts exhibitions, lectures and demonstrations. Take advantage of the evening and weekend sketch classes.

Greenwich Village continues to change with the times. The latest adaptation: The house where Edgar Allan Poe lived for approximately six months in 1845 (on West 3rd Street between Sullivan and Thompson Streets) was razed so that a law-school building could be built on the site. Fortunately, after a battle with community preservation groups, NYU has agreed to retain and incorporate portions of the building's historic facade.

Eighth Street is presently a long procession of cheap-jewelry vendors, piercing parlors, punky boutiques and shoe stores; in the 1960s, it was the closest New York got to San Francisco's Haight Street. Jimi Hendrix's **Electric Lady Studios** is still at No. 52; Bob Dylan lived at and owned 94 MacDougal Street through much of the '60s, performing in Washington Square Park and at clubs such as **Cafe Wha?** on MacDougal Street, between Bleecker and West 3rd Streets. Once the stamping ground of Beat poets and jazz musicians, **Bleecker Street** *(between La Guardia Pl and Sixth Ave)* is now a dingy stretch of poster shops, cheap restaurants and music venues for the college crowd. The famed **Village Gate** jazz club was once at the corner of Bleecker and Thompson Streets; it's now a CVS pharmacy, but the old sign is still up.

In the triangle formed by Sixth Avenue, Greenwich Avenue and 10th Street, you'll see the Neuschwansteinesque **Jefferson Market Library** (a branch of the New York Public Library), which has served as a courthouse and a women's prison. Enjoy its lovely flower-filled garden facing Greenwich Avenue. On Sixth Avenue at 4th Street, stop by "the Cage," outdoor basketball courts where you can witness or join some hot hoop action (if you've got the moves).

### Jefferson Market Library

*425 Sixth Ave between 9th and 10th Sts (212-243-4334). Subway: A, C, E, F, V, S to W 4th St. Library open Mon, Wed noon–8pm; Tue, Thurs 10am–6pm; Fri noon–6pm; Sat 10am–5pm. Free.*

This library has served the Greenwich Village community for 30 years. The 1877 building is based on one of crazy King Ludwig's Bavarian castles.

### Salmagundi Club

*47 Fifth Ave at 12th St (212-255-7740; www.salmagundi.org). Subway: L, N, Q, R, W,*

**Bright lights, pig city** Getting lost in the West Village is easy, but this Washington Street mural lets you know you've reached the Meatpacking District.

**Pastis, not pasties** Sleek eateries replaced trannie hookers in the Meatpacking District.

*4, 5, 6 to 14th St–Union Sq. Open for exhibitions only; phone for details. Free.*
The club, which has an elegant 19th-century interior, is home to artistic and historical societies.

### Washington Square Park

*From Fifth Ave to MacDougal St, between Waverly Pl and W 4th St. Subway: A, C, E, F, V, S to W 4th St.*
Located in the middle of Greenwich Village, this is the city's second-most-famous park. Musicians ring the park's center and street performers work around (and in) the fountain; the southwest corner is home to die-hard chess players. Plunk down on a bench for some of the best people-watching on Earth.

## West Village & Meatpacking District

While the West Village now harbors plenty of celebrities (from Gwyneth Paltrow to Ed Koch), it has managed to retain a humble everyone-knows-each-other feel. The area west of Sixth Avenue to the Hudson River, below 14th Street to Houston Street, still retains the features that molded the Village's character and gave it shape. Only in this neighborhood could West 10th Street cross West 4th Street, and Waverly Place cross Waverly Place. Locals fill the bistros and bars that line Bleecker and Hudson Streets, the area's main thoroughfares.

The northwest corner of this area is known as the **Meatpacking District**—it's been a primarily wholesale meat market since the 1930s. Until the 1990s, it was also a prime haunt for prostitutes, many of them transsexual. In recent years, the atmospheric cobblestoned streets have seen the arrival of a new type of tenant: The once lonely **Florent** *(see page 192),* a 24-hour French diner that opened in 1985, is now part of a chic scene that includes swinging watering hole **APT** *(see page 277)* and the restaurant **Pastis** *(see* **Balthazar**, *page 185).* The district also lures the fashion faithful with hot destinations like **Alexander McQueen**, **Jeffrey New York**, **Stella McCartney** *(see pages 211, 210 and 213),* and the rockin' **Dernier Cri** *(869 Washington St between 13th and 14th Sts, 212-242-6061).* As building owners raise rents, the meat dealers and artists' studios are moving out. Ten years ago, there were approximately 100 wholesale companies in the area; today, the number is down to about 30. Residents have started the Save Gansevoort Market campaign to obtain landmark status for the neighborhood.

On the corner of Bethune and Washington Streets is **Westbeth**, a block-long building formerly owned by Bell Labs (it's where the vacuum tube and the transistor were invented); the late-19th-century structure was converted to affordable lofts for artists in 1969 (Diane Arbus, Gil Evans, and Merce Cunningham lived and worked in the Westbeth community; *see page 345*). The development of luxury condos along Washington Street have led to griping that the neighborhood's bohemian appeal is diminishing. Yet several historic nightlife spots are alive and well: The **White Horse Tavern** *(567 Hudson St at 11th St, 212-989-3956)* is where poet Dylan Thomas went on his last drinking binge before his untimely death in 1953. Earlier in the century, John Steinbeck and John Dos Passos passed time at **Chumley's** *(see page 169),* a Prohibition-era speakeasy, still unmarked at 86 Bedford Street. On and just off Seventh Avenue South are jazz and cabaret clubs, including **Smalls** and the **Village Vanguard** *(see pages 315 and 316).*

The West Village is also a renowned gay neighborhood, though much of the scene has moved to Chelsea (*see chapter* **Gay & Lesbian**). **The Stonewall** *(see page 290)* on Christopher Street is next to the original Stonewall Inn, the sight of the 1969 rebellion, which marked the birth of the gay-liberation movement. There are as many same-sex couples strolling along Christopher Street as straight ones, and plenty of shops, bars and restaurants that are out and proud.

# Midtown

At the city's center, corporate America and world-famous culture set the pace



During weekday hours, midtown (roughly 14th to 59th Streets) is all business. Thousands of commuters pour in each morning and scurry to the towering office buildings of international corporations, record companies, advertising agencies, and book and magazine publishers. Garment manufacturers have long clustered in the area on and around Seventh Avenue (a.k.a. Fashion Avenue). Midtown is where you'll find most of the city's department stores, the luxury retailers of Fifth Avenue and landmarks such as the Empire State Building, Carnegie Hall and Rockefeller Center. It's also where many of the city's large hotels are located. Every night, locals and visitors alike gravitate to the high voltage of Times Square. This sanitized tourist hub is no longer the seedy attraction it once was: Families have plenty of places where they can eat, shop for music and home electronics, or see movies and Broadway shows.

## Flatiron District & Union Square

This style enclave at midtown's southern end is giving downtown a run for its money when it comes to coolness.The Flatiron District, which runs from 14th to 29th Streets, between Fifth Avenue and Park Avenue South, is full of retail stores that are often less expensive but just as style-conscious as those below 14th Street. The area is compact enough for tourists to hit all the sights on foot, and after a long day, there are numerous watering holes where pedestrians can rest their tired feet.

As Broadway cuts diagonally through Manhattan, it creates a public square wherever it intersects an avenue. Two such places, Union Square at 14th Street and Madison Square at 23rd, once marked the limits of a ritzy 19th-century shopping district known as Ladies' Mile. Extending along Broadway and west to Sixth Avenue, this collection of huge retail palaces (the first Macy's store was on Sixth Avenue between 13th and 14th Streets) attracted the "carriage trade"—wealthy ladies who bought the latest fashions and household goods from all over the world. By 1914, most of the department stores had moved north, leaving behind the proud cast-iron buildings that once housed them. Today, the area is again a shopping destination. The eclectic home-design store **ABC Carpet & Home** *(see page 240)* is in a beautiful 1882 terra-cotta-and-brick building at the corner of Broadway and 19th Street. Clothing store **Paul Smith** *(see page 221),* shoe boutique **Otto Tootsi Plohound** *(see page 229)* and many other upscale shops showcase the season's latest designs on lower Fifth Avenue; Sixth Avenue (which borders the Chelsea neighborhood; *see page 91*) is dotted with such chain-store behemoths as Old Navy and Bed, Bath & Beyond.

Union Square is named after neither the Union of the Civil War nor the lively labor rallies that once took place there, but simply for the union of Broadway and Bowery Lane (now Fourth Avenue). From the 1920s until the early 1960s, it had a reputation as a political hot spot, a favorite location for rabble-rousing oratory. Drug dealers ruled the park until the 1980s, when a renovation paved the way for gentrification. These days, the square is surrounded by the **W Union Square** hotel *(see page 139),* the giant **Zeckendorf Towers** residential complex *(1 Union Sq East and 1 Irving Pl between 14th and 15th Sts),* a **Virgin Megastore** *(see page 243),* a **Barnes & Noble** bookstore *(see page 235)*—in a handsome 1881 redbrick building that once housed the popular magazine *Century*—and many restaurants, including the touted **Union Square Cafe** *(see* **Blue Smoke**, *page 195)* and **Olives NY** *(W Union Square Hotel, 201 Park Ave South at 17th St, 212-353-8345).* While the square itself is now best known as the site of the Union Square Greenmarket—an excellent farmers' market—citizens still congregate to protest or to make a statement. After the World Trade Center attack, thousands of mourners gathered for candlelight vigils, and more recently, for antiwar marches. In summer, the outdoor **Luna Park** bar *(50 E 17th St between Broadway and Park Ave South)* beckons the cocktail crowd, while skateboarders practice wild tricks

► To find a place to stay while visiting midtown, see chapter **Accommodations**.
► For information on multimuseum discount packages, see **Cheap tix**, page 46.
► The area's museums are all detailed in chapter **Museums**.

**Greens party** Union Square's Greenmarket bursts with local organic produce.

on the steps and railings on the square's southern edge.

At the northern end of the neighborhood, just south of **Madison Square** *(from Fifth to Madison Aves, between 23rd and 26th Sts)*, is the famously triangular Renaissance palazzo **Flatiron Building**. Once named the Fuller Building after its original owners, it was the world's first steel-frame skyscraper. The area was christened in honor of the structure, and is peppered with boutiques, bookshops, photo studios and labs, not to mention wandering models. In the mid-1990s, big Internet-related companies, such as Doubleclick, began colonizing the lofts on Fifth Avenue and Broadway, earning the district a new nickname: Silicon Alley. Even though many dot-coms went bust and others have decamped to surrounding neighborhoods, the moniker remains in use.

Madison Square is also rich in history. It was the site of P.T. Barnum's Hippodrome and the original Madison Square Garden—the scene of prize fights, lavish entertainment and a scandalous society murder. After years of neglect, statue-filled Madison Square finally got a face-lift in 2001, and the vicinity bordering the park's east side is a dining hot spot. For years, the area was notable only for the presence of imposing structures such as the **New York Life Insurance Company** building *(51 Madison Ave between 26th and 27th Sts)* and the **Appellate Court** *(35 E 25th St at Madison Ave)*, but upscale restaurants, such as **Tabla** *(see* **Blue Smoke**, *page 195)*, have injected some café-society chic into this once-staid district.

### Flatiron Building

*175 Fifth Ave between 22nd and 23rd Sts. Subway: N, R, W, 6 to 23rd St.*

Completed in 1903, the Flatiron was one of the earliest buildings to use an interior steel cage for support. Designed by Daniel H. Burnham & Co., its exterior echoes the traditional Beaux Arts facades of the time. Unfortunately, tours of the interior are not given, but for more information on the building's history, see chapter **Architecture**.

### Union Square Greenmarket

*North end of Union Square, 17th St between Union Sq West and Union Sq East (212-477-3220). Subway: L, N, Q, R, W, 4, 5, 6 to 14th St–Union Sq. Mon, Wed, Fri, Sat 8am–6pm.*

## Chelsea

Chelsea is the city's epicenter of gay life *(see chapter* **Gay and Lesbian***)*, but residents of all stripes inhabit the region between 14th and 29th Streets, west of Fifth Avenue. There's a generous assortment of lively bars and restaurants, mostly clustered on Eighth Avenue. Chelsea's western warehouse district, which is currently home to fashionable lounges and nightclubs, is being developed for residential use. Pioneering cultural spaces, such as the **Dia Center for the Arts** *(see page 262)*, have led the art crowd northward, and the whole area has become a hot gallery zone.

**Cushman Row** *(406–418 W 20th St between Ninth and Tenth Aves)*, in the Chelsea Historic District, is an example of how Chelsea looked when it was developed in the mid-1800s—a grandeur that was destroyed 30 years later when noisy elevated railways were built, overshadowing the area and stealing the sunlight. Just north, occupying an entire block, is the **General Theological Seminary**, its garden a sublime retreat. The seminary's land was part of the estate known as Chelsea, owned by Clement Clarke Moore, a wealthy biblical scholar to whom "Account of a Visit from Saint Nicholas" (better known as "The Night Before Christmas") is attributed. The 1929 Art Deco **Empire Diner** *(210 Tenth Ave at 22nd St, 212-243-2736)* was once a lonely eating outpost for pre- and postclubbers. Lately, it's been joined by a host of other restaurants, including the beautiful-people hot spot **The Park** *(see page 194)* and the American bistro **The Red Cat** *(see* **The Harrison**, *page 180)*.

At Sixth Avenue near 27th Street, the concrete disappears beneath the palm leaves, decorative grasses and colorful blooms of Chelsea's flower district. Sixth Avenue in the mid-20s is full of antiques showrooms, which sell everything from old posters to classic furniture. The **Annex Antiques Fair & Flea Market** *(see page 238)* operates year-round on weekends in an empty parking lot on 25th Street. Like other pockets of Chelsea, the area attracts media: Minimalists will appreciate the stark interior and soaring ceilings of the new **Art Directors Club**, a nonprofit organization and gallery serving the visual-communications industry. It's downstairs from the indie-music heavyweight **Caroline Distribution**, which supplies music outlets with records from such labels as Astralwerks (Beth Orton, Röyksopp) and Steve Shelley's Smells Like Records (Two Dollar Guitar).

At the **Chelsea Hotel** *(see page 141)*, many famous people have checked in—some of whom never checked out, such as Nancy Spungen, who was stabbed to death by boyfriend Sid Vicious. Stop by for a peek at the curious artwork and grunge-glamorous guests, and a drink at the luxe basement lounge **Serena** *(see page 175)*. On Eighth Avenue is the **Joyce Theater** *(see page 343)*, a stunning renovated Art Deco cinema now devoted to dance; on 19th Street, the **Bessie Schönberg Theater** *(219 W 19th St between Seventh and Eighth Aves, 212-691-6500)* is where **Dance Theater Workshop** performs *(see page 345)*, poets recite and mimes do...well, whatever mimes do. Farther toward the river on 19th Street is

**Eminent Victorians** Rows of graceful brick houses line Chelsea's 22nd Street.

**The Kitchen** *(see page 341)*, an experimental arts center with a penchant for video.

**Chelsea Market** is in the former Nabisco plant, where the first Oreo cookie was made in 1912. The block-long building on Ninth Avenue is a conglomeration of 17 structures built between the 1890s and 1930s. A gourmet food arcade on the ground floor offers artisanal bread, fresh lobster, wine, hand-decorated cookies and imported Italian foods, among other things. The building has also become a media center: Oxygen Media and NY1 News have offices inside.

The **Starrett-Lehigh** building *(601 W 26th St at Eleventh Ave)* is the perfect barometer of the high-pressure real-estate market. Until 1999, the 1930s structure—acclaimed as a masterpiece of the International Style—was a neglected $6-a-square-foot industrial loft and warehouse. Today, companies such as Martha Stewart Living Omnimedia and Hugo Boss pay more than $30 per square foot for raw space.

You can watch the sunset from one of the Hudson River piers; they were once terminals for the world's grand ocean liners (the *Titanic* was scheduled to dock here). Most are now in a state of disrepair, though development has

- ▶ Contemporary art lovers should explore the far-western area of Chelsea. See chapter **Art Galleries** for listings.
- ▶ For more information on Chelsea's gay nightlife, see chapter **Gay & Lesbian**.

transformed the four between 17th and 23rd Streets into a sports center and TV-studio complex called **Chelsea Piers** (*see chapter* **Sports & Fitness**).

### The Art Directors Club

*106 W 29th St between Sixth and Seventh Aves (212-643-1440; www.adcny.org). Subway: 1, 9 to 28th St. Mon–Fri 10am–6pm.*

This nonprofit organization has been providing encouragement, support and resources to visual-communications artists since 1920, but its new gallerylike space and calendar of events are anything but dated. This year, the club will exhibit the most provocative work of the Fashion Institute of Technology design class. In early summer, the 82nd Annual Awards Exhibition will honor the world's best advertising, graphic design, illustration, photography and new media.

### Chelsea Historic District

*From Ninth to Tenth Aves between 20th and 22nd Sts. Subway: C, E to 23rd St.*

You'll find a range of architecture: Greek and Gothic Revival, Italianate and apartment buildings from the 1800s.

### Chelsea Market

*75 Ninth Ave between 15th and 16th Sts (www.chelseamarket.com). Subway: A, C, E to 14th St; L to Eighth Ave. Mon–Sat 8am–7pm; Sun 10am–6pm.*

### General Theological Seminary

*Ninth Ave between 20th and 21st Sts (212-243-5150; www.gts.edu). Subway: C, E to 23rd St. Mon–Fri noon–3pm; Sat 11am–3pm. Free.*

## Gramercy Park

You need a key to get past the gates of Gramercy Park, a tranquil square at the bottom of Lexington Avenue, between 20th and 21st Streets. Who gets a key? Only people who live in the beautiful townhouses and apartment buildings that flank the park—or those who stay at the **Gramercy Park Hotel** *(see page 141)*. Anyone, however, can enjoy the charm of the surrounding district, between Park Avenue South and Third Avenue. Gramercy Park was developed in the 1830s as an imitation of a London square. **The Players**, at 16 Gramercy Park South, is housed in an 1845 brownstone that was owned by actor Edwin Booth; the 19th-century superstar was the brother of Abraham Lincoln's assassin, John Wilkes Booth. Edwin had it remodeled as a club for theater professionals (Winston Churchill and Mark Twain were members). No. 15 is the Gothic Revival **National Arts Club**, whose members often donate impressive works in lieu of annual dues. Its bar has what may be the only original Tiffany stained-glass ceiling left in the city.

**Irving Place**, leading south from the park to 14th Street, is named after Washington Irving. Although the author of *The Legend of Sleepy Hollow* didn't actually live on this street, it does have a literary past. O. Henry wrote "The Gift of the Magi" at **Pete's Tavern** *(129 E 18th St at Irving Pl, 212-473-7676)*, whose owners insist that their alehouse—and not **McSorley's** *(see page 172)* or the **Ear Inn** *(326 Spring St between Greenwich and Washington Sts, 212-431-9750)*—is the oldest bar in town. Near the corner of 15th Street, **Irving Plaza** *(see page 309)*, a medium-size live-music venue, hosts big-name acts (from Fischerspooner to Willie Nelson). At the corner of Park Avenue South and 17th Street, stands the final headquarters of the once-omnipotent Tammany Hall political machine. Built in 1929, the building now contains the **Union Square Theater** and **New York Film Academy**.

The **Theodore Roosevelt Birthplace** is now a small museum. The president's actual birthplace was demolished in 1916 but has since been fully reconstructed, complete with period furniture and a trophy room. The low, fortresslike **69th Regiment Armory** *(68 Lexington Ave between 25th and 26th Sts)*, currently used by the New York National Guard, was the site of the sensational 1913 Armory Show that introduced Americans to Cubism, Fauvism, work from the precocious Marcel Duchamp and other artistic innovations. This tradition continues at the annual **Armory Show** (*see page 255)*.

### National Arts Club

*15 Gramercy Park South between Park Ave South and Irving Pl (212-475-3424; www.nationalartsclub.org). Subway: 6 to 23rd St. Open for exhibitions only.*
See page 267.

### Theodore Roosevelt Birthplace

*28 E 20th St between Broadway and Park Ave South (212-260-1616; www.nationalartsclub.org). Subway: 6 to 23rd St. Mon–Fri 9am–5pm; tours of period rooms 10am–4pm on the hour. $3, under 17 free. Cash only.*

## Kips Bay & Murray Hill

Until recently, the area from 23rd to 40th Streets, between Park Avenue and the East River, was considered a nondescript neighborhood dominated by large apartment buildings and hospitals. But the slightly below-market rents and explosion of restaurants on nearby Park Avenue South have attracted stylish residents such as designer John Bartlett. This newly popular neighborhood now has an acronym: Nomad (North of Madison Square Park). The southern portion, known as Kips Bay (after Jacobus Henderson Kip, whose 17th-century farm once covered the area), is largely residential. Third Avenue is the main thoroughfare, and it's where you'll find ethnic eateries representing a variety of Eastern cuisines, including Afghan, Tibetan and Turkish, along with sleek nightspots such as **Spread**, a restaurant and lounge in the hotel **Marcel** *(see page 157)*, and the **Rodeo Bar** *(see page 317)*, a Texas-style roadhouse that offers food and live roots music. Lexington Avenue between 27th and 30th Streets is dubbed Curry Hill because of the many Indian restaurants and grocery stores offering inexpensive food, spices and imported goods. A shopping complex on Second Avenue includes the multiscreen **Loews Kips Bay** theater *(570 Second Ave at 31st St, 212-447-9425)* and a **Borders** bookstore *(see page 235)*. First Avenue in the 20s and 30s has unrivaled medical facilities: Mt. Sinai–New York University Medical Center, the city-run Bellevue Hospital Center and the chief medical examiner's office are here.

Murray Hill stretches from 30th to 40th Streets. Townhouses of the rich and powerful were once clustered around Park and Madison Avenues. While it's still a fashionable neighborhood, only a few streets retain the elegance that once made it a tony address. **Sniffen Court** *(150–158 E 36th St between Lexington and Third Aves)* is an unspoiled row of 1864 carriage houses, located within spitting distance of the Queens-Midtown Tunnel's ceaseless traffic (for places to stay in this area, *see* **Hill street news**, *page 154*).

The charming **Morgan Library** *(29 E 36th St between Madison and Park Aves; see page 46)* is the reason most visitors come to the area. Two elegant buildings (one of which was J. Pierpont Morgan's personal library), are linked by a modern glass cloister and house the silver and copper collections, manuscripts, books and prints owned by the notorious banker.

## Herald Square & the Garment District

Seventh Avenue in the 30s has a stylish (if rarely used) moniker: Fashion Avenue. The surrounding area is the Garment District, where midtown office buildings stand amid the buzzing activity of a manufacturing industry that's been around for a century. Its streets are permanently gridlocked by delivery trucks and crowded with workers pushing racks of clothes. Shabby wholesale clothing stores and fabric shops line the streets (especially 38th and 39th Streets), along with specialty shops selling lace, buttons or Lycra swimsuits. At Seventh Avenue and 27th Street is the **Fashion Institute of Technology** *(see page 50)*, a state college where aspiring Calvin Kleins and Anna Suis (both FIT graduates) dream up the modes of tomorrow. The school's gallery mounts stellar exhibitions.

Plunked at the corner of Broadway and 34th Street, and stretching all the way to Seventh Avenue, **Macy's** *(see page 210)* is still the biggest—and busiest—department store in the world. Across the street is the younger, trendier **H&M** *(see page 210)*, located in the Marbridge Building, which recently got a $24 million makeover. Herald Square, the site of this retail wonderland, is named for a long-gone newspaper. The southern section is known as

**Herald angels** Vendors make once-dodgy Herald Square a congenial place to rest and refuel.

**Electric avenue** The showiest hawkers in the Times Square area are now major corporations.

Greeley Square, after Horace Greeley, the owner of the *Herald*'s rival, the *Tribune,* which employed Karl Marx as a columnist. *Life* magazine was based around the corner on 31st Street, and its cherubic mascot can still be seen over the entrance of what is now the **Herald Square Hotel** *(see page 159)*. Once an area to be avoided, the squares now offer bistro chairs and rest areas for weary pedestrians. East of Greeley Square, the many restaurants and shops of Koreatown line 32nd Street.

The giant doughnut of a building on Seventh Avenue between 31st and 32nd Streets is the sports and entertainment arena, **Madison Square Garden** *(see page 325)*. It occupies the site of the old Pennsylvania Station—the McKim, Mead & White architectural masterpiece that was razed in the 1960s by the Pennsylvania Railroad, an act that brought about the creation of the Landmarks Preservation Commission (for more on the city's architecture, *see chapter* **Architecture**). The railroad terminal's name has been shortened (as if in shame) to Penn Station, and it now lies beneath the Garden, where it serves approximately 600,000 people daily—more than any other station in the country. Fortunately, the aesthetic tide turned in 2000, with the approval of a $788 million restoration-and-development project to move Penn Station back home, so to speak, to the **General Post Office** *(421 Eighth Ave between 31st and 33rd Sts, 212-967-8585)*, which was designed by the original Pennsylvania Station architects in 1913 to complement the majestic structure. The project will connect the post office's two buildings with a soaring glass-and-nickel–trussed ticketing hall and concourse. When finally realized in 2005, the new Penn Station will offer Amtrak service and rail links to Newark, La Guardia and JFK airports; the current Penn Station will continue as a hub for New Jersey Transit, the Long Island Rail Road and the subways.

### Herald Square

*Junction of Broadway and Sixth Ave at 34th St. Subway: B, D, F, V, N, Q, R, W to 34th St–Herald Sq.*

## Broadway & Times Square

Around 42nd Street and Broadway, which is often called "the crossroads of the world," the night is illuminated not by the moon and stars but by acres of blinking, glaring neon. Even native New Yorkers are electrified by the larger-than-life light show of this buzzing core of entertainment and tourism. Perhaps no area represents the city's glitter and grit like Times Square.

Originally called Long Acre Square, Times Square was renamed after *The New York Times* moved to the site in the early 1900s, announcing its arrival with a spectacular New

Year's Eve fireworks display. *The Times* erected the world's first zipper sign on its building at 1 Times Square, and the circling messages—from the Crash of 1929 and JFK's assassination to the World Trade Center attack—have been known to stop midtown masses in their tracks. The Gray Lady is now located on 43rd Street between Seventh and Eighth Avenues (and has an $84 million plan to build a new tower on Eighth Avenue between 40th and 41st Streets), but the sign and New Year's Eve celebrations remain at the original locale. Times Square is really just an elongated intersection where Broadway crosses Seventh Avenue, but it's the epicenter of the Theater District. More than 30 grand stages used for dramatic productions are situated on the streets that cross Broadway—which is also another name for the area (*see chapter* **Theater & Dance**). The peep shows—what's left of Times Square's once-famous sex trade—are now relegated to Eighth Avenue *(see* **Times a-changin'**, *below)*.

The area's transformation began in 1990, when the city condemned most of the properties along 42nd Street between Seventh and Eighth Avenues (a.k.a. the Deuce). A few years later, the city changed its zoning laws, making it harder for adult-entertainment establishments to operate. The grimy Times Square of the 1970s and '80s is now undeniably safer and cleaner. To see how much has changed, stop by Show World, a former porn emporium that currently sells tourist trinkets and hosts short (nonporn) film series and (fully clothed) Off-Off Broadway performances. But there are still a few places in and around The Deuce which aim to satisfy carnal cravings.

The streets west of Eighth Avenue are filled with eateries catering to theatergoers. Restaurant Row—West 46th Street between

## Times a-changin'

### Catch a peep at midtown's sex trade, such as it is, before it's gone forever

The 37 million tourists who flock to Times Square every year hoping to be mesmerized by the bright lights of this bustling epicenter won't be disappointed. That is, if G-rated entertainment is their idea of a good time. Once a den of prostitutes, peep shows and perversion, "the Deuce" *(42nd St between Seventh and Eighth Aves)* is now crowded with chain restaurants, video arcades, respectable clothing stores and commercial movie multiplexes. This must make former mayor Rudy Giuliani stand tall with pride.

Shortly after taking the oath of office, Hizzoner pushed a law stipulating that no sex-related business could be located within 500 feet of a school, a church, a park or another X-rated business. The law also mandated that no more than 40 percent of any store's inventory (books, videotapes, etc.) could be X-rated. After a series of court challenges, the antiporn law went into effect in August 1998.

Mainstream commerce has been booming in Times Square ever since. Many of the city's sex-related enterprises (including the arty, ironic downtown scene that featured tattooed dancers of all body types) have closed because of the new zoning laws, gone out of business due to rising rents or relocated to industrial areas in the outer boroughs. Since many New Yorkers profess nostalgia for the lost *Midnight Cowboy* grit of old, scuzzy Times Square, one can't help but be curious about what's left.

The last vestiges of midtown's X-rated diversions are grouped along Eighth Avenue between 39th and 44th Streets, like a carnal food court in the middle of a suburban mall. But visitors hungry for a truly down-and-dirty experience may not be sated. "Tourists come in and say, 'This is *it*?'" says the manager of **The Playground** *(634 Eighth Ave between 40th and 41st Sts, 212-391-9722)*, one of the few remaining peep clubs where a bow-tied emcee clutching a mike loudly beckons potential clients to go upstairs as they enter. Upstairs, you'll find not very enthusiastic strippers who writhe behind glass while the customer sits in broom-closet–size booths—$3 for topless, $5 for bottomless and $15 to go into a "fantasy booth" where, for five minutes, a woman will say whatever a paying customer wants to hear. Watching HBO's *G-String Divas* series is more titillating.

The Playground should not be confused with **The Playpen** *(693 Eighth Ave between 43rd and 44th Sts)*, where more energetic ladies perform live (no glass partition) for $5 a dance and a mandatory 20-buck tip. **Euroworld** *(632 Eighth Ave between 40th and 41st Sts, 212-221-8814)* has booths for watching X-rated videos at the rate of one dollar for every three minutes; an attendant regularly wipes down the seats.

Eighth and Ninth Avenues—has an unbroken string of them.

As you'd expect, office buildings in the area are filled with entertainment companies: recording studios, theatrical management companies, record labels and screening rooms. **The Brill Building** *(1619 Broadway at 49th St)* boasts a rich history, having long been the headquarters of music publishers and arrangers. Such luminaries as Lieber and Stoller, Phil Spector and Carole King wrote and produced their hits within. Visiting rock royalty and aspiring musicians drool over the selection of new and vintage guitars, and countless other instruments for sale along 48th Street, just between Sixth and Seventh Avenues.

Two recent additions to the area are the 110,000-square-foot **Toys R Us** flagship store *(see page 238),* which has a 60-foot-tall indoor Ferris wheel, and the colorful 863-room **Westin** hotel *(see page 153),* which opened in November 2002.

At the southwestern end of the square is the home base of **MTV** *(1515 Broadway at 44th St),* which often sends camera crews into the street to tape segments. During warmer months, crowds of screeching teens congregate under the windows of the network's second-floor studio, hoping for a wave from guest celebrities inside.

The glittering glass case of magazine-publishing giant **Condé Nast** *(Broadway at 43rd St)* looms across the street at 4 Times Square. This structure's outer layer includes tiny sunlight-capturing cells that generate some of the energy needed for the building's day-to-day operations. In the same building is the **Nasdaq MarketSite**. The multimedia "electronic stock market" dominates Times Square with its eight-story-tall, 9,800-square-foot cylindrical video screen.

**Swing low** Playboys may find Playground's strippers less frisky than the sign suggests.

Some shops, such as **Peepworld** *(691 Eighth Ave between 42nd and 43rd Sts, 212-262-0178)* and **Xcellent Video** *(630 Eighth Ave between 40th and 41st Sts, 212-354-1826)* obey the 40-percent rule by mixing kung fu videos or even tourist trinkets with their efficiently categorized skin flicks—making for some curious juxtapositions. They also sell a wide variety of sex toys. You may ask yourself, Why go to **Madame Tussaud's Wax Museum** *(see page 88)* to ogle the untouchable likeness of Elle Macpherson, when, only a block away, you can pick up a vibrating love doll molded to the exact dimensions of your favorite porn star?

Those in the market for live physical contact can head to **Stiletto Gentleman's Club** *(698 Eighth Ave between 43rd and 44th Sts, 212-581-0805),* which offers all-nude lap dancing. Over on Broadway are the slightly more "respectable" topless clubs **Flashdancers** *(1674 Broadway between 52nd and 53rd Sts, 212-977-8160)* and **Lace** *(725 Seventh Ave between 48th and 49th Sts, 212-764-6969),* which has a $300 "Champagne Room" where patrons may purchase a private dance.

While it is odd to exit these dark adult playpens and blink in the wholesome light of surrounding family eateries, mainstream cinemas and well-scrubbed tourists, what remains of seedy Times Square may not be all that different from the sex trade found at the desolate edges of any American town. Perhaps you might consider sublimating desire at the new **Museum of Sex** *(see page 53),* for a broader, historical look at the vagaries of sex in the city. Or, if you're wondering where the city's alternakids go to get their freak on, check out the burgeoning New Burlesque movement *(see **Fringe Scene**, page 32).*

**Madame Tussaud's New York**, a Gothamized version of the London-based wax museum chain, has an "Opening Night Party" room containing New York personalities such as Woody Allen and Barbra Streisand, along with the glamorous likes of Princess Diana and RuPaul. Check out the museum's latest inductees: wrestler–turned–movie-star The Rock, Robin Williams, and Matthew Broderick and Nathan Lane, formerly of the Broadway smash *The Producers*.

Nightlife in the square is dominated by theaters and theme restaurants. For a shot of vein-popping adrenaline—and entertainment at its most outrageous—stop by World Entertainment's **The World** *(1501 Broadway between 43rd and 44th Sts, 212-398-2563)* for some burgers and body slams.

Make a brief detour uptown on Seventh Avenue, just south of Central Park, for a glimpse of the great classical-music landmark **Carnegie Hall** *(see page 318)*. Across the street is the celebrated sandwich shop **Carnegie Deli** *(854 Seventh Ave at 55th St, 212-757-2254)*.

West of Times Square, past the curious steel spiral of the Port Authority Bus Terminal on Eighth Avenue and the Lincoln Tunnel's often traffic-knotted entrance, is an area historically known as Hell's Kitchen. During the 19th century, an impoverished Irish community lived here amid gangs and crime. Following the Irish were Italians, Greeks, Puerto Ricans, Dominicans and other ethnic groups. It remained rough-and-tumble (providing the backdrop for the hit musical *West Side Story*) through the 1970s, when, in an effort to invite gentrification, neighborhood activists renamed it Clinton, after DeWitt Clinton Park on Eleventh Avenue between 52nd and 54th Streets. Crime has abated and these days, Clinton's pretty tree-lined streets and neat redbrick apartment houses are filled with a diverse group of old-timers, actors and professionals. Ninth Avenue is the area's main drag, known for its inexpensive restaurants and bars catering to a young crowd. There's also a small Cuban enclave around Tenth Avenue in the mid-40s, an otherwise desolate stretch of the city.

**Rabbit season** Ride a menagerie of mounts on Bryant Park's antique carousel.

South of 42nd Street, the main attraction is the **Jacob K. Javits Convention Center** *(Eleventh Ave between 34th and 39th Sts)*. This glass palace, designed by James Ingo Freed of I.M. Pei & Partners, hosts conventions and trade shows. Among the Hudson River piers is the **Circle Line** terminal *(see page 131)* on 42nd Street at Pier 83. At the end of 46th Street, the aircraft carrier *Intrepid* houses the **Sea-Air-Space Museum** *(see page 57)*.

### Madame Tussaud's New York

*234 W 42nd St between Seventh and Eighth Aves (800-246-8872; www.madame-tussauds.com). Subway: N, Q, R, W, S, 1, 2, 3, 9, 7 to 42nd St–Times Sq. 10am–8pm. $17–$22, children under 3 free.*

### New York City's Official Visitor Information Center

See page 375.

### Show World

*669 Eighth Ave between 42nd and 43rd Sts (212-247-6643). Subway: A, C, E to 42nd St–Port Authority. 24hrs.*

### Times Square

*Times Square Visitors' Center, 1560 Broadway between 46th and 47th Sts, entrance on Seventh Ave (212-768-1560). Subway: N, R, W to 49th St; 1, 9 to 50th St. 8am–8pm.*

## Fifth Avenue

This majestic thoroughfare is the route of the city's many parades and marches. It runs past chic stores and some of the most recognizable buildings and public spaces in town.

The **Empire State Building** at 34th Street is visible from all over the city (and lit at night in various colors, according to the holiday or special event). However, it's only at the corner of Fifth Avenue and 34th Street that you can truly appreciate its height. Situated smack dab in the center of midtown, its observatory offers brilliant views in every direction.

Impassive stone lions guard the steps of the **New York Public Library** at 41st Street

**Clash of titans** St. Patrick's Cathedral faces Rockefeller Center vying for your attention.

*(see page 58).* This beautiful Beaux Arts building provides a quiet escape from the noise outside. The Rose Main Reading Room, on the library's top floor, is a hushed sanctuary of 23-foot-long tables and matching oak chairs where people read, write and research. Behind the library is **Bryant Park**, a well-cultivated lawn sprinkled with lunching office workers during the warm months; the park also houses the ivy-covered American restaurant **Bryant Park Cafe and Grill** *(25 W 40th St between Fifth and Sixth Aves, 212-840-6500)* and hosts a dizzying schedule of free entertainment (for specific events, see chapter **By Season, Summer**). Across 40th Street at No. 40, **The Bryant Park** *(see page 153)* is a new hotel built within the former American Radiator Building. Designed by architect Raymond Hood in the mid-1920s, the building's near-black brick, trimmed in gold leaf, seems to exemplify the term *Gotham.* Inside this luxurious hotel are the **Cellar Bar** lounge *(212-642-2260)* and **Ilo** *(212-642-2255),* a high-class, French-infused American restaurant. At **The Algonquin** *(see page 151),* scathing wit Dorothy Parker and friends held court at Alexander Woollcott's Round Table.

The city's jewelry trade is located along the 47th Street strip known as Diamond Row. In front of glittering window displays, you'll see Orthodox Jewish traders with precious gems in their pockets, doing business in the street.

Veer off Fifth Avenue into the 19 buildings of **Rockefeller Center** *(from 48th to 51st Sts)* and you'll understand why this masterful use of public space is so lavishly praised. As you stroll down the Channel Gardens, the stately Art Deco GE Building gradually appears above you. The sunken plaza in the center is the winter site of an oft-packed **ice-skating rink** *(see page 239)*. A giant **Christmas tree** looms above it all each December *(see page 254)*. Gathered around the plaza's perimeter are the International Building and its companions. The center is filled with murals, sculptures, mosaics, metal-work and enamels. Of special note are José María Sert's murals in the GE Building and Sol LeWitt's primary-colored mural *Wall Drawing #896 Colors/Curves* in the lobby of Christie's auction house at 20 Rockefeller Plaza.

On weekday mornings, a crowd gathers at the **NBC** television network's glass-walled ground-level studio (where the *Today* show is shot), at the southwest corner of Rockefeller Plaza and 49th Street. When taping ends, the same throng—along with thousands of other pedestrians—treks to the chain stores above and below Rockefeller Center. At Sixth Avenue and 50th Street is **Radio City Music Hall**, the world's largest cinema when it was built in 1932. This Art Deco jewel was treated to a $70 million restoration in 1999; the home of the legendary Rockettes is a stellar example of the benefits of historic preservation.

Across Fifth Avenue from Rockefeller Center is the beautiful Gothic Revival **St. Patrick's Cathedral**, the largest Catholic cathedral in the United States.

Several museums are just a few blocks north of Rockefeller Center: the newly built **American Folk Art Museum** *(see* **New Folk's home**, *page 26)*, the **Museum of Arts and Design** (formerly known as the American Craft Museum; *see page 50*) and the **Museum of Television & Radio** *(see page 57)*. **The Museum of Modern Art**'s location on West 53rd Street is closed for renovation until 2005. MoMA has temporarily moved to Long Island City, Queens *(see* **Modern convenience**, *page 118)*. One more bit of culture before you shop: In the 1920s, 52nd Street was Swing Street, a row of speakeasies and jazz clubs. All that's left is the **'21' Club** (at No. 21; *see page 198*), long a power-lunch spot; its $29 hamburger is almost worth the price.

► For more on modern and postmodern buildings in midtown, see chapter **Architecture**.

**Rockette-fueled** Radio City Music Hall is home to the famous dance troupe.

The blocks of Fifth Avenue between Rockefeller Center and Central Park boast expensive retail palaces offering everything from Rolexes to gourmet chocolate. Along the stretch between **Saks Fifth Avenue** *(at 50th St; see page 211)* and **Bergdorf Goodman** *(at 58th St; see page 209)*, the rents are among the highest in the world, and you'll find such names as **Cartier**, **Gucci**, **Tiffany & Co.** and

**Versace**, as well as the first U.S. outpost of Swedish clothing giant H&M and the **National Basketball Association**'s official store. The pinnacle of this clustering trend is the soaring brass spine of **Trump Tower** *(725 Fifth Ave at 56th St)*, an ostentatious pink-marble shopping mall built by "the Donald."

Fifth Avenue is crowned by Grand Army Plaza at 59th Street. A statue of General Sherman presides over this public space; to the west is the elegant **Plaza Hotel** *(see page 161)*; to the east is the can't-miss **FAO Schwarz** toy store *(see page 238)*.

### NBC

*30 Rockefeller Plaza, 49th St between Fifth and Sixth Aves (212-664-3700; www.shopnbc.com). Subway: B, D, F, V to 47–50th Sts–Rockefeller Ctr. Tours Mon–Sat 8:30am–5:30pm; Sun 9:30am–4:30pm. $17.50, seniors and children $15. Children under 6 not admitted.*

Peer through the *Today* show's studio window with a horde of fellow onlookers, or pay admission for a guided tour of the interior studios. (For information on more NBC show tapings, *see page 283*).

### New York Public Library

See **Humanities and Social Services Library**, page 58.

### Radio City Music Hall

*See page 313 for listing. Tour tickets $16, children under 12 $10.*

### Rockefeller Center

*From 48th to 51st Sts between Fifth and Sixth Aves (212-632-3975; www.rockefellercenter.com). Subway: B, D, F, V to 47–50th Sts–Rockefeller Ctr. Free.*

Guided tours are available for $10 per person at the **NBC Experience Store** *(30 Rockefeller Plaza)*. Call 212-664-3700 for more information.

### St. Patrick's Cathedral

*Fifth Ave between 50th and 51st Sts (212-753-2261). Subway: B, D, F to 47–50th Sts–Rockefeller Ctr; E, V to Fifth Ave–53rd St. Free. 6:30am–9:30pm. Call for tour dates and times. Services Mon–Fri 7, 7:30, 8, 8:30am, noon, 12:30, 1, 5:30pm; Sat 8, 8:30am, noon, 12:30, 5:30pm; Sun 7, 8, 9, 10:15am, noon, 1, 4, 5:30pm.*

## Midtown East

Grand Central Terminal, a 1913 Beaux Arts station, is the city's most spectacular point of arrival (though only commuter trains operate within). The station stands at the junction of 42nd Street and Park Avenue, the latter rising on a cast-iron bridge and literally running around the terminal. Thanks to a 1998 renovation, the terminal has itself become a destination, with upscale restaurants and bars such as the ornate cocktail lounge **Campbell Apartment** *(see page 174)*, star chef Charlie Palmer's **Métrazur** *(East Balcony, 42nd St between Fifth and Madison Aves, 212-687-4600)* and **Michael Jordan's—The Steak House NYC** *(West Balcony, 212-655-2300)*. There's even the food hall **Grand Central Market**, which sells gourmet goodies from New York and around the world, and the Lower Concourse food court offers sophisticated, fairly priced lunch options. A quirky historical note: The constellations of the winter zodiac on the ceiling of the main concourse are backward—a mistake made by the original artist.

East 42nd Street holds still more architectural distinction, in the Romanesque Revival hall of the former **Bowery Savings Bank** (at No. 110, now a special-events space owned by the Cipriani restaurant family) and the Art Deco detail of the **Chanin Building** (No. 122). Completed in 1930, the gleaming chrome **Chrysler Building** (at the corner of Lexington Avenue) pays homage to the automobile. Architect William van Alen outfitted the base of the main tower with brickwork cars, complete with chrome hubcaps and radiator-cap eagles enlarged to vast proportions and projected over the edge as "cargoyles." The building's needle-sharp stainless-steel spire was added to the original plan so that the finished building would be taller than 40 Wall Street, which was under construction at the same time. Philip Johnson's **Chrysler Trylons**—three blue-gray glass pyramids—rest between the Chrysler Building and 666 Third Avenue. This retail pavilion is Johnson's "monument to 42nd Street." **The *Daily News* Building** (No. 220), another Art Deco gem designed by Raymond Hood, was immortalized in the *Superman* films and still houses a giant globe in its lobby, though its tabloid namesake no longer has offices there.

The street ends at **Tudor City**, a pioneering 1925 residential development that's a high-rise version of Hampton Court in England. This neighborhood is dominated by the **United Nations** and its famous glass-walled Secretariat building *(UN Plaza between 42nd and 48th Sts)*. You won't need your passport, but you are leaving U.S. soil when you enter the UN complex—this is an international zone, and the vast buffet at the **Delegates Dining Room** *(fourth floor, 212-963-7626)* puts multiculturalism on the table. Optimistic sculptures dot the grounds, and the Peace Gardens along the East River bloom with delicate roses. The serenity is trumped, however, by the 72-story **Trump World Tower** *(First Ave between 47th and 48th Sts)*, the world's tallest residential building. Even a coalition of high-powered area residents, including newsman Walter Cronkite, couldn't prevent Trump from erecting it.

Rising behind Grand Central Terminal, the **MetLife Building** *(see page 26)* was once the world's largest office tower. Its most celebrated tenants are the peregrine falcons that nest on the roof, living off pigeons that they kill in midair. Glittering **230 Park Avenue** is directly north. Built by the architects of Grand Central, the building's details were later flashily gilded by the Helmsley corporation.

On Park Avenue, amid the blocks of international corporate headquarters, is the **Waldorf-Astoria** *(see page 147).* The famed hotel was originally located on Fifth Avenue, but was demolished in 1929 to make way for the Empire State Building; it was rebuilt on this spot in 1931. Many of the city's most famous International Style office buildings are also in the area. Built in 1952, **Lever House** *(390 Park Ave between 53rd and 54th Sts)* was the first, and most graceful, glass box on Park Avenue. The 1958 **Seagram Building** *(375 Park Ave between 52nd and 53rd Sts),* designed by Ludwig Mies van der Rohe and others, is a stunning bronze-and-glass tower that contains the landmark restaurant **The Four Seasons** *(see page 200).* A postmodern Chippendale crown tops Johnson's '80s-era **Sony Building** *(550 Madison Ave between 55th and 56th Sts).* Inside is Sony's **Wonder Technology Lab** *(see page 299),* a hands-on thrill zone of innovative technology.

The newest addition to this cluster of dazzling architecture is the **LVMH Tower** *(see page 22).* Designed by Christian de Portzamparc, the youngest architect to be awarded the Pritzker Prize, the U.S. headquarters for the French conglomerate Louis Vuitton Moët Hennessy is a reworked vision of Art Deco.

Taking advantage of what was already in place, the **Bridgemarket** complex *(First Ave at 59th St),* opened in 1999 in what was once a farmers' market under the Queensboro Bridge. The space now contains a **Terence Conran Shop** *(see page 242)* and **Guastavino Restaurant** *(212-980-2455),* named for the maker of the tiles that line its curved ceilings. The Spanish builder's legacy can also be seen in the **Grand Central Oyster Bar & Restaurant** *(see page 200)* and at **Ellis Island** *(see* **Ain't no way to treat a Lady,** *page 62).*

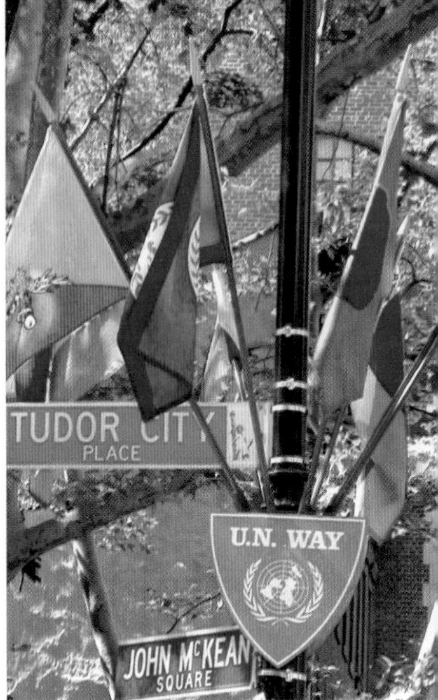

**Heraldry square** Colorful banners announce the block occupied by immense Tudor City.

## BEST VIEW High society

### From a balcony in Grand Central Terminal

Cipriani Dolci is situated in the west balcony of Grand Central's Main Hall, which affords patrons the chance to admire the terminal's splendor. The long, narrow space evokes a first-class railroad car, complete with a glass-enclosed train track embedded in the floor, and the design ensures no bad seats. For the cost of a club sandwich (which runs $17.50, more than a round-trip ticket to Larchmont), you'll get a vivid view of the world whizzing by, especially at rush hour.

*Grand Central Terminal, West Balcony, 23 Vanderbilt Ave at 43rd St (212-973-0999; www.grandcentralterminal.com). Subway: S, 4, 5, 6, 7 to 42nd St–Grand Central.*

### Grand Central Terminal

*From 42nd to 44th Sts between Vanderbilt and Lexington Aves. Subway: S, 4, 5, 6, 7 to 42nd St–Grand Central.*
For tour information, call 212-697-1245.

### United Nations Headquarters

*First Ave at 46th St (212-963-7713; www.un.org). Subway: S, 4, 5, 6, 7 to 42nd St–Grand Central. 9:30am–4:45pm. Free. Guided tours every half hour: $8.50, seniors $7, students $5; children under 5 not permitted.*

# Uptown

Central Park's beauty, Madison Avenue's glamour, Harlem's urban style—venture north of 59th Street to enjoy the broadest range of the city's attractions



To many, the term *uptown* conjures visions of a tony community populated by the richest of the rich—limousines, white-gloved doormen and little old ladies walking toy poodles. But if you visit the various neighborhoods north of 59th Street, you'll notice a diverse landscape. Sure, you can gaze at Renaissance masterpieces in the **Metropolitan Museum of Art**, but you could also examine spray-paint spectaculars at the **Graffiti Hall of Fame**. Above the frenetic business centers of the Financial District and midtown, uptown moves at a slower, saner pace. And **Central Park**, the gateway to the island's northern half, is where New Yorkers go to breathe easy.

## Central Park

"Once around the park, driver." The request has been made countless times by lovers canoodling in cabs or snuggling in horse-drawn buggies. The park is, of course, Central Park, the crown jewel of the city's parks system, and even locals have been known to pony up $40 for a 20 minute clip-clopping carriage ride with that someone special *(see page 133).*

As natural as it appears, this 843-acre patch of the great outdoors was made by man. Make that *two* men. It took 20 years for journalist and landscape architect Frederick Law Olmsted and architect Calvert Vaux to create this mowable masterpiece. Park construction began in 1840, and recent research reveals that a community known as Seneca Village—made up of 1,600 free blacks, along with Irish and German immigrants—was leveled 17 years later *(see* **The secrets of Central Park**, *page 96).*

The park is filled with landmarks. **Strawberry Fields**, near the West 72nd Street entrance, memorializes John Lennon, who lived in the nearby **Dakota** *(see page 100).* Also known as the "international garden of peace," the sanctuary's mosaic of the word *imagine* was donated by the city of Naples, Italy, and more than 160 species of flowers and plants from all over the world bloom here, including jetbead, roses, and of course, strawberries.

In summer, kites, Frisbees and soccer balls fly every which way in **Sheep Meadow**, which begins at 65th Street. The sheep are gone (they grazed until the 1930s), replaced with sunbathers improving their tans and scoping out the throngs of thongs. The hungry (and flush) can repair to glitzy **Tavern on the Green** *(Central Park West at 67th St, 212-873-3200).* A short stroll to the south, kids line up for a ride on **The Friedsam Memorial Carousel**. (For more park activities for children, *see page 300.*) Come winter, ice skaters lace up at nearby **Wollman Memorial Rink** *(see page 98).*

East of Sheep Meadow, between 66th and 72nd streets, is **The Mall**, where you'll find volleyball courts and a hot-hot-hot roller-disco area (with not-to-be-missed costumes and acrobatics). Behind the **Naumburg Bandshell** is **Rumsey Playfield**—site of the annual **Central Park SummerStage** *(see page 252),* an eclectic series of free and benefit concerts held throughout the warmer months. One of

**Greece is the word** Take the highway to Hellas in the Met's Jaharis Galleries.

Sightseeing

the most popular meeting places in the park is **Bethesda Fountain and Terrace**, near the center of the 72nd Street Transverse Road. North of the fountain is the **Loeb Boathouse** *(see page 327),* where you can rent a rowboat to take out on the **Lake**, which is crossed by the elegant **Bow Bridge**. The nearby **Boat House in Central Park** restaurant *(Central Park Ln, Park Drive North at 72nd St, 212-517-2233)* offers a mesmerizing park view to go with its first-rate surf-and-turf menu.

Farther uptown is the popular **Belvedere Castle**, which houses the **Henry Luce Nature Observatory**; the **Delacorte Theater** *(see* **The secrets of Central Park**, *page 98),* which mounts performances during the summer New York Shakespeare Festival; and the **Great Lawn**, a sprawling stretch of grass that hosts New York Philharmonic concerts and other events. Several years ago, the **Reservoir** was renamed in honor of the late Jacqueline Kennedy Onassis, who used to jog around it.

### Central Park Zoo/Wildlife Center

See page 303.

### Charles A. Dana Discovery Center

*Park entrance on Fifth Ave at 110th St (212-860-1370). Subway: 6 to 110th St. Apr–Oct 11am–5pm; Nov–Mar 11am–4pm. Free.*

Stop in for weekend family workshops, cultural exhibits and outdoor performances on the plaza.

### The Dairy

*Mid-park at 64th St (212-794-6564). Subway: A, C, B, D, 1, 9 to 59th St–Columbus Circle; N, R, W to Fifth Ave. Apr–Oct Tue–Sun 10am–5pm; Nov–Mar Tue–Sun 10am–4pm. Free.*

Built in 1872 to show city kids where milk comes from (cows, in this case), The Dairy is now the park's information center, complete with an interactive exhibit and a history video. Milk it for all it's worth.

### Henry Luce Nature Observatory

*Belvedere Castle, mid-park at 79th St (212-628-2345). Subway: B, C to 81st St–Museum of Natural History; 6 to 77th St. Apr–Oct Tue–Sun 10am–5pm; Nov–Mar Tue–Sun 10am–4pm. Free.*

Kids enjoy the hands-on "Woods and Water" exhibit that surveys the park's variety of plants and animals. Learn bird-watching techniques on ranger-led walks that start at the Castle every Wednesday at 8am. On Hawk Watch (September to November), park rangers give presentations and help visitors spot raptors from the roof. You can also pick up a bird-watching kit that includes binoculars, maps and bird-identification guides.


▶ For more information on the museums in this section, see chapter **Museums**.
▶ Chapter **Art Galleries** has additional listings for uptown dealers.
▶ Shopping for high fashion? See **Suit yourself**, page 218.


## Upper East Side

Once Central Park opened in 1859, New York society was ready to move north. By the mid-1800s, the city's most affluent residents had built mansions along Fifth Avenue, and by the beginning of the 20th century, the superrich had warmed to the (initially appalling) idea of living in apartment buildings—provided they were near the park. Many grand edifices were thus constructed along Fifth Avenue and the surrounding area.

Scores of New York socialites still call the Upper East Side home, many taking up residence on a strip known as the Gold Coast—Fifth, Madison and Park Avenues from 61st to 80th Streets. Billionaire mayor Michael Bloomberg lives in a Beaux Arts mansion at 17 East 79th Street, and financial advisor Jeffrey Epstein resides on East 71st Street in a 45,000-square-foot eight-story mansion, purported to be the largest private house in Manhattan. The area also cultivates a cultural elite (Woody Allen and writer Joan Didion call it home). It's no surprise that the neighborhood's zip code, 10021, is the city's wealthiest; the median household income is $155,693.

Residents of the area's stately mansions, townhouses and luxury apartments include stock society figures such as the ladies-who-lunch and young scions who spend their inheritance on **Madison Avenue**. The upscale shopping strip from East 57th to 79th Streets is anchored by such luxe merchants as Donna Karan and Barneys *(see page 209)*. Heads of corporations take advantage of tax write-offs to fund the area's many cultural institutions. Their philanthropic gestures, made during the past 130 years, helped create the many art collections, museums and cultural institutions that attract visitors to the area known as **Museum Mile**, a geographical designation and promotional slogan that includes the **Metropolitan Museum of Art**, the Frank Lloyd Wright–designed **Guggenheim Museum** and the **Frick Collection** (for complete listings, *see chapter* **Museums**).

In addition to bankrolling art museums, the neighborhood's monied class has used its loot to promote the cultures and languages of foreign lands. The **Asia Society** *(725 Park*

**Fun central** Uptown's Central Park holds plenty of pleasures. Clockwise from top left: loungers on the Great Lawn; a fire-eater at Bethesda Fountain; boaters from Loeb Boathouse; roller boogie near the Mall.

*Ave between 70th and 71st Sts)*, founded by David Rockefeller, features a garden court and café. Nearby are the **China Institute in America** *(125 E 65th St between Park and Lexington Aves)* and the **Americas Society** *(680 Park Ave between 68th and 69th Sts)*, the latter dedicated to the nations of Central and South America, as well as Canada and the Caribbean. On Fifth Avenue at 79th Street, you'll find the **Ukrainian Institute** *(www.ukrainianinstitue.org)*, and the **Goethe-Institut/German Cultural Center** *(see page 55)* is at 83rd Street.

Uptown seems less grand (and less stuffy) on Lexington Avenue, where **Bloomingdale's** teases your wallet at 59th Street *(see page 209)*. This area also hums with history. **The Mount Vernon Hotel Museum** *(421 E 61st St between First and York Aves)*, one of eight 18th-century houses left in the city, was built as a coach house in 1799 and became a country inn in the 1820s. Tallulah Bankhead, Montgomery Clift, Kim Novak and Eleanor Roosevelt lived along the tree-lined stretches of brownstones known as the **Treadwell Farm Historic District** *(61st and 62nd Sts between Second and Third Aves)*.

The riches of the Rockefellers underwrites **The Rockefeller University**, a medical research institution. Its **Founder's Hall**, built in 1906, is a national historic landmark; it can be reached by walking east through the 66th Street entrance at York Avenue. Medical facilities dominate several blocks, including the **New York Hospital/Cornell Medical Center**, into which the city's oldest hospital was incorporated.

## The secrets of Central Park

### New York's slice of Eden harbors more than bladers, bikers and joggers

Central Park, which officially celebrates it's 150th birthday this year, is a welcome respite from the overwhelming pace of New York City life—a leafy haven away from blaring taxis and the obscenities spewed by their drivers. But it's much more than a place to take a leisurely walk. Here are some of the park's mysteries, unearthed.

#### GET READY TO ROCK

At the north end of Central Park, just west of the Harlem Meer, is **Worthless Boulder**. The ten-foot-tall rock is scarred with chalk—marking the places where rock climbers have clung to its face. Until the late 1990s, junkies and hookers favored the spot, which was clogged with foliage and sprinkled with broken glass. By forming alliances with the Park Department, the city's tight-knit climbing community reclaimed the rock and cleared the area of brush and debris. Wood chips cushion the ground beneath the most technically challenging part of the face, known as Mean Green. Climbers can now hang here and elsewhere in the park in safety. The **North Meadow Recreation Center** *(mid-park at 97th St, 212-348-4867; www.climbnyc.com)* has an indoor climbing wall and instructor on hand from Tuesday to Saturday.

#### JUST LIKE STARTING OVER

Every day, pilgrims come to the John Lennon *Imagine* mosaic in **Strawberry Fields** and leave behind tributes to their fallen idol: paintings, bouquets of flowers, candles, poetry. Where does it all go? Every day, a Parks Department employee collects this devotional farrago—mostly wilted flowers and melted candles—and dumps it into a sanitation truck. The more elaborate treasures, like framed artworks, are taken to the park's Mineral Springs building, where they're held and displayed in the hopes that the artists will claim them. When they go unclaimed, these items join the other debris in the trucks, which haul everything to a collection center in Queens. Then it's all loaded onto barges—to be sent off to landfills as close as Staten Island or as far away as Mississippi.

#### SENECA VILLAGE PEOPLE

It's no secret that New York had a pre–Civil War African-American settlement, which once stretched from 81st to 89th Streets, between Seventh and Eighth Avenues, before it was razed in 1857 to make room for Central Park. But little is known about the people who lived there. Three scholars have spearheaded an archaeological effort to solve the mystery of Seneca Village—Diana Wall, an anthropology professor at City College; Nan Rothschild, an anthropology professor at Barnard; and Cynthia Copeland of the New-York Historical Society.

After poring over hundreds of 19th-century documents—mostly land surveys, and census and church records—the trio has

**The Rockefeller University**
*1230 York Ave between 63rd and 68th Sts (212-327-8000; www.rockefeller.edu). Subway: 6 to 68th St– Hunter College.*
Monthly exhibitions are open to the public.

## Yorkville

The eastern and northeastern parts of the Upper East Side are residential, home of many of the city's professionals. There are countless places to dine and drink, from society hangouts **Elaine's** *(see page 202)* and **Orsay** *(1057 Lexington Ave at 75th St, 212-517-6400)* to cheap ethnic places like **Saigon Grill** *(1700 Second Ave at 88th St, 212-996-4600)* and groovy spots like **The Auction House** bar *(300 E 89th St between First and Second Aves, 212-427-4458).*

The area extending from the 70s to 96th Street, east of Lexington Avenue, is known as Yorkville and was, at one time, a quaint, predominantly German riverside hamlet. In the late 1800s, 86th Street was the Hauptstrasse of Manhattan, filled with German restaurants, beer gardens, and food and clothing shops. Subsequent waves of Hungarians and Yugoslavs followed. Today, there are just a few reminders of that Old World legacy: **Schaller & Weber** *(Second Ave between 85th and 86th Sts, 212-879-3047),* a homey grocery, has been selling 75 different varieties of German sausage and cold cuts since 1937; and **Heidelberg** *(1648 Second Ave between 85th and 86th Sts, 212-628-2332),* where dirndled waitresses serve wurst and sauerbraten. Another treasure is the **Elk Candy Company** *(1628 Second*

pieced together clues about Seneca's inner workings. Not only were African-Americans the village's main occupants, they were also its primary landowners. In the 1800s, men of color needed to own at least $250 in property to be eligible to vote in New York State elections. To qualify, several black entrepreneurs bought cheap land in Seneca. Many of the black landowners were also landlords—to whites. (At that time, most New Yorkers would not rent or sell to Irish immigrants.) All Angels, the largest congregation of Seneca's three churches, mirrored the local ethnic diversity: African-Americans, German-Americans and Irish-Americans all worshiped together. And there was at least one interracial celebrated wedding in the village.

The scholars believe that many more valuable clues remain buried beneath Central Park's landscape. They plan to take soil core samples in summer 2003 to get a better idea of whether excavation is warranted, and if so, where to begin.

### SNACK ATTACK

You're in mid-stroll, feeling peckish, but you can't stomach another mystery-meat hot dog. Rejoice. Central Park holds one of the city's best crêpe makers: Madeleine Bernard. Her kiosk, **Chez Madeleine** *(59th St at Central Park West, Tue–Sun 9:30am–7pm)*, serves hearty, crisp crêpes, available with sweet or savory fillings.

Or you can have your meal come to you. **It's a Wrap** *(2012 Broadway between 68th and 69th Sts, 212-362-7922; Sun–Thu 8am–10pm; Fri, Sat 8am–11pm)* delivers its sandwich-in-a-tortilla to four spots in the park: Bethesda Fountain, Delacorte Theater, Sheep Meadow and Strawberry Fields. All you need is money and a cell phone.

### WATCH THE BIRDIE

Central Park is one of the country's best bird-watching spots, with more than 200 different species sighted in a given year. For a chronicle of daily aviary life, head to the **Loeb Boathouse** *(see page 327).* There, on an oval wooden table near the self-serve snack bar, you'll find a beat-up blue binder—*Central Park Bird Register & Nature Notes*—with detailed entries on the activities of warblers, owls and hawks. How detailed? On October 23, 2002, one watcher reported seeing an "immature redtailed hawk trying to hunt pigeons on Cedar Hill. Missed one, flew to killing tree, perched for five minutes." Among the journal's contributors is former president Jimmy Carter, who wrote about his own redtail sighting in 1998.

The best place for birding is in the **Ramble**, a strip of the park between 72nd and 81st Streets. Another prime viewing spot is the north end of the park, above 103rd Street. Peak migration seasons are the best time to glimpse exotic species—April and May in the spring, September and October in the fall. For bird-watching and tour information, call the **American Museum of Natural History** *(see page 41)* or the **New York City Audubon Society** *(212-691-7483).* See also **Henry Luce Nature Observatory**, page 94.

### PSSST. BET YOU DIDN'T KNOW...

• Hunting is illegal in all NYC parks, but visitors to the sprawling **Harlem Meer** can enjoy catch-and-release fishing, courtesy of the **Central Park Conservancy** *(212-310-6639;* ▶

*Ave between 84th and 85th Sts, 212-585-2303),* which is known for its marzipan. As recently as the mid-1990s, there were five Hungarian-food establishments; only the **Yorkville Meat Emporium** remains *(1560 Second Ave at 81st St, 212-628-5147).* Run by brothers Laszlo and Ferenc Gubicza, the shop's house-made cold cuts, fresh meat and large stock of famous Szeged paprika and prepared dishes (including a peppery goulash) attract a Hungarian-speaking clientele from across the city.

In the tiny **Henderson Place Historic District** *(East End Ave between 86th and 87th Sts),* stand two dozen handsome Queen Anne row houses. Commissioned by furrier John C. Henderson, their turrets, double stoops and slate roofs remain intact, and the cul-de-sac looks much as it did in 1882. Across the street is **Gracie Mansion**, New York's official mayoral residence since 1942 and the only Federal-style mansion in Manhattan still used as a home (Mayor Bloomberg, resides in his townhouse though, and uses the mansion only for special events). The yellow house with green shutters, built in 1799 by Scottish merchant Archibald Gracie, is the focal point of tranquil Carl Schurz Park, named in honor of a German immigrant, newspaper editor and U.S. senator.

### Gracie Mansion

*Carl Schurz Park, 88th St at East End Ave (212-570-4751). Subway: 4, 5, 6 to 86th St. Mar–Nov Tue for group tours (25–50 people, by reservation only); Wed for individuals 10, 11am, 1, 2pm. Park closes at 1am daily. $4, seniors $3, students and children under 12 free.*

## ▸ The secrets of Central Park (continued)

*www.centralparknyc.org).* Free rods and bait will help you land largemouth bass, catfish and bluegills. Just be sure to return them quickly to the deep!

- In 1880, Egypt gave the United States an **obelisk**, nicknamed "Cleopatra's Needle," that dates from 1500 BC. It took four months to transport the 71-foot granite structure from the Hudson to its present location in the park near the Metropolitan Museum of Art; workers rolled it over cannonballs.
- In preparation for British attack during the War of 1812, the city built **Blockhouse No. 1**, just south of Warriors' Gate at the park's northern end. The fortification never saw combat; now it's the only vacant structure in the park.
- ***Still Hunt***, a lifelike (and life-size) bronze statue of a panther poised to pounce, near East Drive and 76th Street, was created by the sculptor Edward Kemeys in 1881. Because of its stealthy positioning, high on a rock outcropping, it's been startling joggers ever since.
- Those tiny brass arrows inlaid in the sidewalks throughout the park aren't telling you where to go. They direct Parks Department workers to utility boxes.
- When Henry Bacon designed the park's original lampposts in 1907, he affixed to each one a waist-high number that tells the nearest cross street. Lamppost 6725, for example, is near 67th Street. You'll never get lost again.

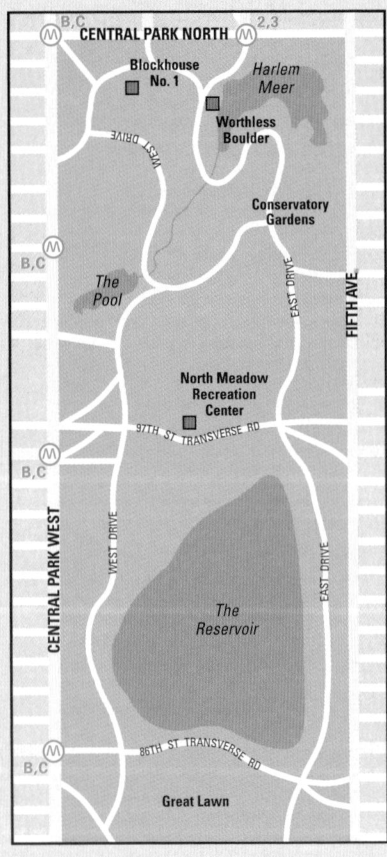

Gracie Mansion's upstairs living quarters are open to the public for the first time since Mayor La Guardia moved there in 1942. The tour also winds through the mayor's living room, a guest suite and smaller bedrooms. A $7 million restoration has spruced up the house. Look at the library's windows for the etched autographs of three naughty girls: Millie (the granddaughter of Noah Wheaton, who owned the house in the 1800s), Margie (the daughter of Mayor John Lindsay) and Caroline (Rudolph Giuliani's daughter). Reservations are a must.

**Empty seat** Savor the view Mayor Bloomberg is missing outside Gracie Mansion.

## Roosevelt Island

Roosevelt Island, a submarine-shaped East River isle, was called Minnehannonck ("island place") by the Indians, who sold it to the Dutch (in a vast creative leap, they renamed it Hog Island). The Dutch farmed the island, as did Englishman Robert Blackwell, who moved there in 1686. His family's rebuilt clapboard farmhouse is in Blackwell Park, adjacent to Main Street (the one and only commercial strip).

In the 1800s, a lunatic asylum, a smallpox hospital, prisons and workhouses were built on what was then known as Welfare Island. The weathered—and technically off-limits—remains of these structures are at the island's southern and northern ends. Charles Dickens visited the island in the 1840s and was disturbed by its "lounging, listless, madhouse air." In an early example of investigative journalism, reporter Nellie Bly feigned insanity and had herself committed to the asylum for ten days in 1887, then wrote an exposé of the conditions in what she described as a "human rat trap."

Roosevelt Island became a state-planned residential community in the 1970s (people started moving into apartments in 1975, and 9,500 people now live there). The best way to see the island is to take the tram that crosses the East River from Manhattan. Roosevelt Island and the cable cars have appeared in a host of films, including *Spider-Man* and *Before Night Falls.* You can also take the F train for a nonscenic (but faster) ride. The riverfront promenades afford panoramas of the skyline and East River. On the east side, wander down the **Meditation Steps** for river views (located just north of the tram stop), or take one of the river-hugging paths around the island.

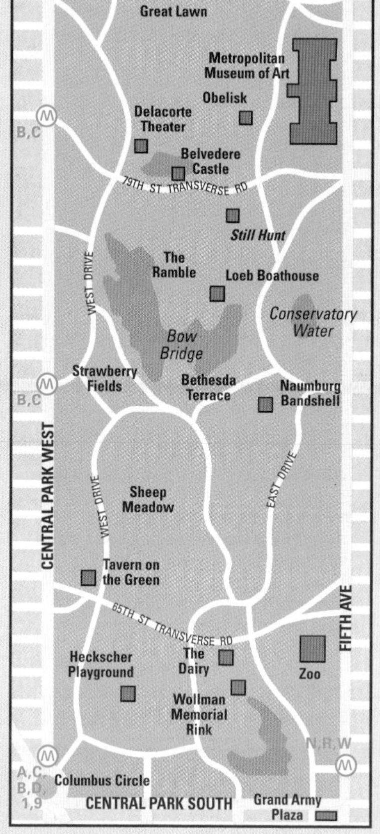


### Roosevelt Island Operating Corporation

*591 Main St (212-832-4540; www.rioc.com). Mon–Fri 9am–5pm.*
Call for details of events and free maps of the island.

### Roosevelt Island Tramway

*Embark at Second Ave and 60th St in Manhattan. $1.50. Subway tokens only.*

**A street named desire** At Madison Avenue's tony boutiques—from Armani to Yves Saint Laurent—well-heeled shoppers find plenty to pique their interest.

## Upper West Side

The Upper West Side is as much a state of mind as a geographic appellation. Its residents have long been thought of as intellectually and politically liberal, but that spirit has waned somewhat as rents have risen. European immigrants were drawn here during the late 19th century by the building boom, that was sparked by the completion of Central Park, the subway, as well as by Columbia University's relocation to the area. Today, the neighborhood, and it's main artery, Broadway, are crowded with restaurants, bars, bookstores—and celebrities, such as gadfly filmmaker Michael Moore *(Bowling for Columbine)*, comic Jerry Seinfeld and *Doonesbury* creator Garry Trudeau.

The Upper West Side story begins at **Columbus Circle**, where Broadway meets 59th Street, Eighth Avenue, Central Park South and Central Park West—a rare rotary in a city of right angles. This hub is undergoing major changes. At 1 Columbus Circle, on the former site of the New York Coliseum (torn down in 2000), is the partially built $1.7 billion **AOL Time Warner** headquarters. Scheduled to open in late 2003, the massive complex will house AOL Time Warner; an auditorium for **Jazz at Lincoln Center**; a **Mandarin Oriental Hotel**; highly anticipated restaurants from chefs Thomas Keller, Masa Takayama and Jean-Georges Vongerichten; and shops, shops and more shops.

Across from a 700-ton statue of Christopher Columbus is 2 Columbus Circle, an odd and nearly windowless structure built as a modern-art gallery by Huntington Hartford in 1964. The **Museum of Arts and Design** *(see page 50)* has bought the building, and after renovation, will move into its new home in 2005. The circle also bears Donald Trump's signature: He converted the former Gulf & Western Building into the pricey **Trump International Hotel & Tower** *(see page 161)*, which houses the acclaimed French-inflected restaurant **Jean Georges** *(see* **JoJo**, *page 202)*.

The Upper West Side's cultural nexus is **Lincoln Center** *(see page 320)*, a complex of concert halls and auditoriums that are the heart and soul of classical music and high-brow culture in the city. Its buildings are linked by sweeping, barren public plazas and filled with sensitive-looking music types; in summer, amateur dancers gather in the plaza to dance alfresco at **Midsummer Night Swing** *(see page 252)*. Completed in 1968, the center is ready for a face-lift: a $1 billion redevelopment is in the works, which would include a redesign of public spaces, basic refurbishment of the various aging halls and construction of new buildings (such as a permanent home for the City Opera).

While not as immediately fashionable as Fifth Avenue, the Upper West Side did catch on quickly once the park was completed. Magnificent apartment buildings rose high above **Central Park West**. **The Dakota**, on 72nd Street, is largely known as the setting for *Rosemary's Baby* and the site of John Lennon's murder in 1980 (Yoko Ono still lives in the building). As one of New York's first luxury apartment buildings, the structure accelerated the westward migration. (After it was completed in 1884, New Yorkers sniffed that it was so far north, it might as well be in the Dakotas.) The building at **55 Central Park West** *(at 66th St)* is best remembered for its role in *Ghostbusters*. Built in 1930, it was the first Art Deco building on the block; within two years, five others had joined it on CPW: **Century Apartments** *(at 62nd St)*, **Majestic Apartments** *(between 71st and 72nd Sts)*, **241 Central Park West** *(at 84th St)*, **The Eldorado** *(between 90th and 91st Sts)* and **The Ardsley** *(at 92nd St)*. The massive twin-towered **San Remo Apartments** (at 74th St) date from 1930 and are so exclusive that even Madonna had to settle for the waiting list.

The **New-York Historical Society** *(see page 53)* is the oldest museum in the city. Across the street, the **American Museum of Natural History** *(see page 41)* attracts visitors with its IMAX theater (which shows Oscar-winning nature documentaries) and permanent rain forest exhibit, as well as its formidable wildlife dioramas, dinosaur skeletons and ethnological collections. The 2000 opening of the museum's **Rose Center for Earth and Space**, which includes the retooled **Hayden Planetarium** *(see page 40)*, has meant an astronomical leap in visitors—but it's well worth suffering the crowds to marvel at this installation.

Amsterdam and Columbus, the avenues west of Central Park West, experienced a renaissance when Lincoln Center was erected in the 1960s. The neighborhood now teems with restaurants, gourmet food shops and boutiques, while many of the old, inhabitants and shops remain. A popular Sunday outing is still the Columbus Avenue stroll, which typically starts at the **Flea Market** at 84th Street *(see page 238)*. If you head south, stop for an iced cappuccino in the back garden of **Café La Fortuna** *(69 W 71st St between Central Park West and Columbus Ave, 212-724-5846)*, a neighborhood favorite for more than 70 years.

On Broadway, the notoriously crowded **72nd Street subway station**, which opened in 1904, is notable for its Beaux Arts entrance. The station is undergoing a $53 million renovation and expansion, to be completed in summer 2003. It's part of **Sherman Square**, named after the Civil War general. The opposite triangle, at the intersection of Broadway and 73rd Street, is called **Verdi Square**. The name fits, geometry notwithstanding: In the nearby **Ansonia Hotel** *(2109 Broadway between 73rd and 74th Sts)*, resident Enrico Caruso was known to keep other inhabitants entertained—and awake—with renditions of his favorite arias. Other luminary occupants have included Babe Ruth, Igor Stravinsky and Arturo Toscanini.

**The Beacon Theatre** *(see page 307)*, once a fabulous movie palace, is now a concert venue, hosting the likes of Beck and Sheryl Crow, with an annual two-week stand by the Allman Brothers every spring. Across the street, the gourmet markets **Fairway** *(2127 Broadway at 74th St, 212-595-1888)* and **Citarella** *(2135 Broadway at 75th St, 212-874-0383)* vie for hungry shoppers. Fairway is known citywide for its produce, Citarella for its seafood and meat departments. A few blocks

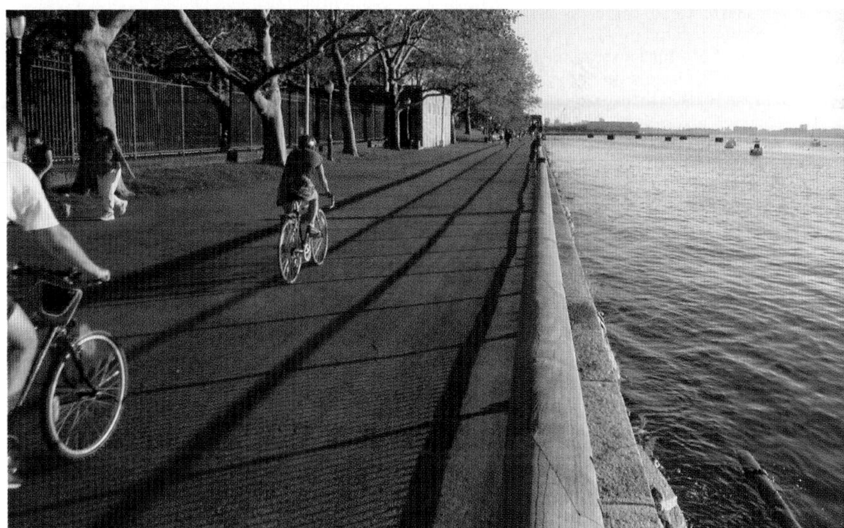

**Different spokes** Cyclists can catch fresh breezes (really!) on the Hudson River promenade.

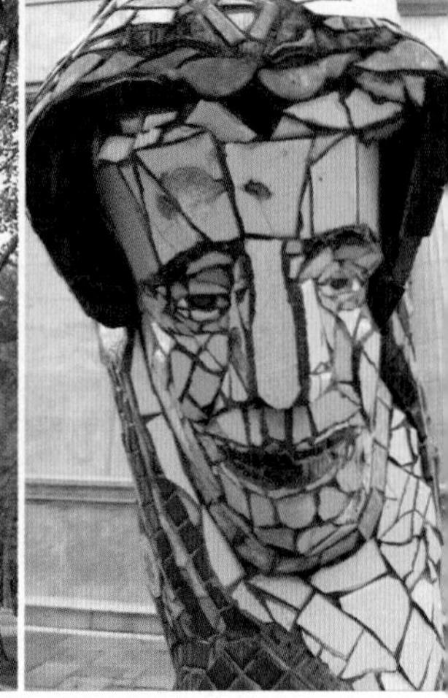

**Grant's wish** The resting place of Ulysses S. Grant, former president and Civil War general, is bordered by a whimsical mosaic sculpture that doubles as seating.

north are the **Children's Museum of Manhattan** *(see page 298)*; **H&H Bagels** *(2239 Broadway at 80th St, 212-595-8000)*, the city's largest purveyor of New York's favorite nosh; **Zabar's** *(see page 240)*, a supplier of more than 250 types of cheese, hand-sliced smoked fish, prepared foods and kitchen equipment; and the legendary **Barney Greengrass—The Sturgeon King** *(541 Amsterdam Ave between 86th and 87th Sts, 212-724-4707)*, an old-time cafeteria-style restaurant with a marvelous smoked-salmon–and–bagel platter.

**Riverside Park**, a sinuous Olmsted-designed stretch of riverbank between Riverside Drive and the Hudson River, runs from 72nd to 153rd Streets. You'll probably see yachts berthed at the 79th Street Boat Basin, along with several houseboats; there's also an open-air café in the adjacent park (open during summer). Several park sites provide havens for reflection. The **Soldiers' and Sailors' Monument** *(89th St at Riverside Dr)* honors Union soldiers who died in the Civil War, and a 1908 memorial pays tribute to fallen firemen *(100th St at Riverside Dr)*. The park is also home to **Grant's Tomb**, the mausoleum of former President Ulysses S. Grant. Behind the structure is a folk-art garden of multicolored mosaic benches, created by 3,000 volunteers (many of them neighborhood children) in a 1970s antivandalism project launched by Chilean-born artist Pedro Silva.

### General Grant National Memorial

*Riverside Dr at 122nd St (212-666-1640). Subway: 1, 9 to 125th St. 9am–5pm. Free.*

Who's buried in Grant's Tomb? Technically, nobody—the crypts of Civil War hero and 18th president Ulysses S. Grant and his wife, Julia, are in full aboveground view.

### Soldiers' and Sailors' Monument

*Riverside Dr at 89th St. Subway: 1, 9 to 86th St.*

The 1902 monument was designed by French sculptor Paul E.M. DuBoy (who also co-designed the Ansonia Hotel) and pays tribute to Civil War dead.

## Morningside Heights

Morningside Heights runs from 110th to 125th streets, between Morningside Park and the Hudson River, and is dominated by **Columbia University**. One of the oldest universities in the U.S., Columbia was chartered in 1754 as King's College (the name changed after the Revolutionary War). It moved to its present location in 1897. Thanks to Columbia's large student population and that of its sister school, **Barnard College**, the area has an academic feel, with bookshops and cafés lining Broadway and the quiet, leafy streets toward the west, overlooking Riverside Park.

**Miss Mamie's Spoonbread Too** *(366 W 110th St between Columbus and Manhattan Aves, 212-865-6744)* is *the* place for chicken and ribs. The blocks of Broadway between 110th and 116th Streets are packed with restaurants and cafés. **The West End** *(2911 Broadway between 113th and 114th Sts, 212-662-8830)* is notable for its $6 pitchers of Bud (Monday through Friday 5 to 7pm and 9 to 11pm), live jazz and its heritage—it was a hangout for the original Beats. **Mondel Chocolates** *(2913 Broadway at 114th St, 212-864-2111)* has been sating students' candy cravings since 1943.

The neighborhood has two immense houses of worship. **The Riverside Church** was built with Rockefeller money and contains the world's largest carillon and bell. Ride to the top of the 21-story steel-frame tower for commanding views of the city and the Hudson.

The hammering and chiseling at the enormous Episcopal **Cathedral of St. John the Divine** will continue well into this century. Construction began in 1892 in Romanesque style, was put on hold for a Gothic Revival redesign in 1911, then ground to a halt in 1942, when the United States entered World War II. Work resumed in earnest in 1979, but a fire in 2001 destroyed the church's gift shop (and badly damaged two 17th-century Italian tapestries), further delaying completion. When its towers and great crossing are finally finished, New York will have a church to rival the grandeur of Paris's Notre Dame. In addition to Sunday services, the cathedral hosts concerts, tours and on occasion, memorial services for the rich and/or famous.

### Cathedral of St. John the Divine

*1047 Amsterdam Ave at 112th St (212-316-7540; www.stjohndivine.org). Subway: B, C, 1, 9 to 110th St–Cathedral Pkwy. Mon–Sat 7am–6pm; Sun 7am–7pm. July–Aug closes daily at 6pm. Services Mon–Sat 8am, 12:15, 5:30pm; Sun 8, 9, 9:30 (Spanish). Tours Tue–Sat 11am; Sun 1pm. $3.*

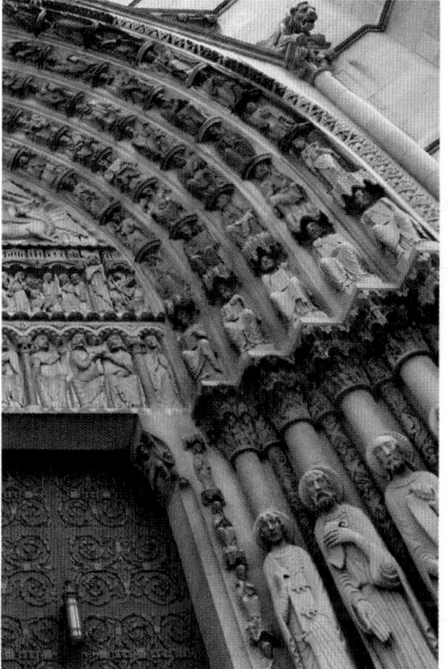

**Guardian angel** Progressive Riverside Church towers over Morningside Heights.

### Columbia University

*From Amsterdam Ave to Broadway, between 114th and 120th Sts (212-854-1754; www.columbia.edu). Barnard College entrance on Broadway, just north of 116th St (212-854-5262). Subway: 1, 9 to 116th St–Columbia University.*

### The Riverside Church

*Riverside Dr at 120th St (212-870-6700; www.theriversidechurchny.org). Subway: 1, 9 to 125th St. 9am–5pm.*



## Harlem

Ten years on, the second Harlem Renaissance is going strong. Former President Bill Clinton has an office in the neighborhood *(55 W 125th St between Fifth Ave and Malcolm X Blvd [Lenox Ave]),* the Harlem USA mall is packed with chain stores, and everywhere you turn, long-neglected brownstones are being renovated.

But despite the retail explosion and influx of development money, there remains a psychological divide between Harlem and the rest of Manhattan—a rift that local entrepreneurs are eager to overcome. Violent crime remains low (though it's not uncommon to find a shop locked—the salesperson buzzes you in). And while many locals complain of about ballooning rents, the infiltration of superstores, the Caucasian invasion and simultaneous watering-down of black culture, this neighborhood remains the heart and soul of Black America. Harlem's avenues are filled with Afrocentric culture, its institutions and streets are named for African-American luminaries, and of course, its soul-food restaurants serve the world's best pork chops and collard greens.

Harlem was originally composed of country estates, but when the subways arrived at the turn of the 20th century, the area was developed with white middle-class New Yorkers in mind. When the whites failed to fill the townhouses, speculators began renting them to African-Americans. The area's population doubled during the 1920s and '30s, a growth that coincided with a great exodus of blacks from the south and a cultural explosion known as the Harlem Renaissance. The poets, writers, artists and musicians living in this bohemian republic ushered in the Jazz Age.

Today, several musical genres inform Harlem's soundtrack—jazz, rap, reggae and merengue, the latter courtesy of the Cubans and Dominicans who have joined the Latin population of **Spanish Harlem**, the section east of Fifth Avenue and above 96th Street. **La Marqueta**, Park Avenue's multistore food emporium located between 110th and 116th Streets, pampers patrons with fresh fruits, vegetables, spices and meats. Those seeking more knowledge about the area can check out **El Museo del Barrio** *(see page 55)*, Spanish Harlem's community museum on Fifth Avenue at 104th Street, or the **Hispanic Society of America** *(see page 55)*.

The **Graffiti Hall of Fame**, on 106th Street between Madison and Park Avenues, is actually a schoolyard. The interior and exterior walls present the work of new and old-school "writers," such as the Tats Cru; it's also the site of impromptu artists' gatherings in the summer.

**Malcolm Shabazz Masjid**, the silver-domed mosque of the late Malcolm X's ministry, awaits you at 116th Street and Malcolm X Boulevard (Lenox Avenue). Just down the street is the **Malcolm Shabazz Harlem Market** *(52–60 W 116th St between Fifth Ave and Malcolm X Blvd [Lenox Ave], 212-987-8131)*, where street vendors who once lined Harlem's main drags now hawk T-shirts, tapes and (purportedly) African souvenirs. **Amy Ruth's** *(113 W 116th St between Malcolm X Blvd [Lenox Ave] and Adam Clayton Powell Jr. Blvd [Seventh Ave], 212-280-8779)* is Al Sharpton's favorite restaurant; join him for the signature dish—fried chicken with waffles. A few blocks north is the glorious, storied **Lenox Lounge** *(see page 177)*, where Billie Holiday and Miles Davis performed and Malcolm X worked as a hustler. You can still hear great live jazz here at Roy Campbell's Monday Night Jam. While the tourist-heavy clientele at nearby **Sylvia's** *(328 Malcolm X Blvd [Lenox Ave] between 126th and 127th Sts, 212-996-0660)*, is not New York–authentic, the soul food is, and the Sunday gospel brunch is a feast for the ears, eyes and palate.

Harlem's historic districts continue to grow increasingly gentrified. The **Mount Morris** area *(from Malcolm X Blvd [Lenox Ave] to Mount Morris Park West, between 119th to 125th Streets)* offers a host of groovy new boutiques and restaurants. **Harlemade** *(174 Malcolm X Blvd [Lenox Ave] between 118th and 119th Sts, 212-987-2500; www.harlemade.com)* sells T-shirts with afro-headed silhouettes, postcards, books and other neighborhood-related memorabilia. **Xukuma** *(183 Malcolm X Blvd [Lenox Ave] at 119th St, 212-222-0490)*, a delightful home-design shop that carries its own line of body products, would seem right at home in Soho. Just five years ago, finding bistro food or a cup of espresso was unheard of in Harlem; now you can get both at the new cafés **Native** *(161 Malcolm X Blvd [Lenox Ave] at 118th St, 212-665-2525)*, with its "all world" menu, and **Sette Pani** *(196 Malcolm X Blvd [Lenox Ave] at 119th St, 917-492-4806)*, which serves tempting pastries and sandwiches.

Another area with a historic past is Strivers' Row, also known as the **St. Nicholas Historic District** *(138th and 139th Sts between Adam Clayton Powell Jr. [Seventh Ave] and Frederick Douglass Blvds [Eighth Ave])*. It consists of two strips of magnificent neo-Georgian houses developed in 1891 by David H. King Jr. (who

**Shop to it** The Malcolm Shabazz Harlem Market is stocked with African arts and crafts.

also constructed Stanford White's Madison Square Garden). In the 1920s, prominent members of the black community such as Eubie Blake and W. C. Handy lived in this area, and you can still see signs on the gates that read WALK YOUR HORSES. As new residents with disposable cash move in, so do young establishments like the stylish boutique **Grandview** *(2531 Frederick Douglass Blvd [Eighth Ave] between 135th and 136th Sts),* which looks like it could have been imported from Nolita. Owner Veronica Jones sells eclectic contemporary clothing and accessories by largely African-American designers, including Byron Lars and Tracy Reese.

Harlem has also become a destination for art lovers. Most of the exhibitions at the critically praised **Studio Museum in Harlem** *(see page 47)* are generated by local talent. Meanwhile, Harlem's rich history lives on in the **Schomburg Center for Research in Black Culture**. Part of the New York Public Library system, it's the largest research collection devoted exclusively to African-American culture, with archives that include audio and visual recordings of black musicians, plus speeches by leaders ranging from Marcus Garvey to Jesse Jackson. The **Abyssinian Baptist Church**, at 138th Street, houses a small museum dedicated to Adam Clayton Powell Jr., the first black member of the New York City Council and the neighborhood's U.S. congressman from 1946–70.

Harlem's main commercial drag is 125th Street, and the **Apollo Theater** *(see page 307)* has historically been its focus. For some 40 years after it began presenting live shows in the 1930s, the Apollo was the world's most celebrated venue for black music. No longer the force it was, the theater nonetheless continues to feature live performances by superstars such as Mary J. Blige, George Clinton and the Temptations. Tours run daily; call 212-531-5337 for details.

The **Cotton Club** *(666 W 125th St at Riverside Dr, 212-663-7980)* is another music landmark. Originally located on 142nd Street, it was the neighborhood's premier nightclub from the 1920s to the '50s. Dubbed the Aristocrat of Harlem, the club launched the careers of entertainment royalty such as Cab Calloway, Dorothy Dandridge and Duke Ellington; today, it's a showcase for live blues and jazz. **Showman's** *(375 W 125th St at Frederick Douglass Blvd [Eighth Ave], 212-864-8941)* remains a smoke-filled house of swinging music and tap dancing.

There's plenty of modern-day consumerism amid 125th Street's revered music venues. The **Harlem USA** mall *(300 W 125th St between Adam Clayton Powell Jr. [Seventh Ave] and Frederick Douglass [Eighth Ave] Blvds; www.harlem-usa.com),* across the street from the Apollo, features a Magic Johnson movie theater *(Frederick Douglass Blvd [Eighth Ave] at 124th St, 212-665-8742)* and the Hue-Man bookstore, the country's third-largest store specializing in African-American titles. The mall also houses retail megastores like Old Navy, Modell's and a Disney outpost.

**Your name here** Everyday people become stars at the Apollo's famous amateur night.

True jazz fans may want to step onto the stoop at 17 East 126th Street, between Fifth and Madison Avenues. It was here, in 1958, that nearly 60 jazz greats gathered for a world-famous *Esquire* magazine photo. The event was the subject of a mid-1990s documentary titled *A Great Day in Harlem.*

The area west of St. Nicholas Avenue, between 125th and 155th Streets, is known as **Hamilton Heights**, after Alexander Hamilton, who owned a farm here. The same architect responsible for City Hall designed Hamilton's Federal-style home, called **Hamilton Grange**. Now incongruously wedged between a church and an apartment building, the woodframe house will be moved to a more suitable setting in nearby St. Nicholas Park by 2004. In this gentrified section of Harlem is the Gothic Revival–style **City College**, the City University of New York's northernmost outpost in Manhattan. On the campus, check out the **135th Street Gatehouse**, on Convent Avenue at 135th Street. In the 1880s, the Gatehouse was instrumental in bringing water from the Croton Reservoir to New York City.

Since this is Harlem, even Hamilton's old stamping grounds have excellent eats. **Londel's Supper Club** *(see page 203)*, owned by former police officer Londel Davis, serves some of the best blackened catfish in town. And the area comes alive at night, especially at the legendary **St. Nick's Pub** *(773 St. Nicholas Ave at 149th St, 212-283-9728)*, where you can hear live jazz every night except Tuesday.

A little farther north, **Audubon Terrace** *(Broadway at 155th St)* contains a double cluster of Beaux Arts buildings, which were part of artist John James Audubon's estate. Now they're an unusual group of museums that includes the Hispanic Society of America *(see page 55)*.

### The Abyssinian Baptist Church

*132 W 138th St between Malcolm X (Lenox Ave) and Adam Clayton Powell Jr. Blvds (Seventh Ave) (212-862-7474; www.abyssinian.org). Subway: B, C, 2, 3, to 135th St. Mon–Fri 9am–5pm. Services Sun 9, 11am.*
The Abyssinian is celebrated for its history and rousing gospel choir. Arrive a half hour early on Sunday to guarantee a seat.

### Hamilton Grange National Memorial

*287 Convent Ave between 141st and 142nd Sts (212-283-5154). Subway: A, C, B, D, 1, 9 to 145th St. Fri–Sun 9am–5pm.*
Some of the household objects inside were actually used by Alexander Hamilton.

## BEST VIEW Span-tastic

**From the George Washington Bridge**
The view of the mile-long George Washington Bridge is lovely, especially at night when the structure glitters like a diamond necklance. But equally impressive is the view *from* the 72-year-old suspension bridge. Walk halfway to New Jersey and look south to see the Manhattan skyline and the mighty Hudson River flowing toward New York Harbor. Turn around and glimpse the forefront of the scenic Hudson River Valley, with the rocky cliffs of the Palisades on the left.
*Subway: A to 181st St; walkway entrances on Cabrini Blvd at 178th or 179th Sts.*

### Schomburg Center for Research in Black Culture

*See page 59 for listing.*
Security is strict—be prepared to check large bags and coats; you're given a clear plastic bag in which to carry necessities.

## Washington Heights & Inwood

The area from 155th Street north to Dyckman Street is called **Washington Heights**; venture any higher than that and you're in **Inwood**, Manhattan's northernmost neighborhood. A growing number of artists and young families are moving to these parts, attracted by Art Deco buildings, big parks, spacious and hilly streets, and comparatively low rents.

The island narrows this far north, and the parks on either side culminate in the wilderness of **Inwood Hill Park**. Some believe the legendary 1626 transaction between Peter Minuit and the Munsee Indians for the purchase of a strip of land called "Manahatta" took place at this location—a plaque at the southwest corner of the ball field at 214th Street marks the purported spot of the trade. The 196-acre refuge contains the island's last swath of forest. In June 2002, the Urban Park Ranger's Wildlife Management Program introduced four fledgling eagles to the park. By September, three had left the nest for wild lives as far as 30 miles away (one was recuperating in captivity after breaking its leg). Largely due to the efforts of Frederick Law Olmsted, the area was not leveled in the 1800s—the house-size, glacier-deposited boulders (called erratics) were a factor too. Today, with a bit of imagination, you can hike in this mossy forest and see a bit of the beautiful land the Munsees called home.

**High Bridge** *(Amsterdam Ave at 177th St)* will give you an idea how New York used to get its water. This aqueduct carried water across the Harlem River from the Croton Reservoir in Westchester County to Manhattan. The central piers were replaced in the 1920s to accommodate passing ships. Another bridge dominates Washington Heights—the **George Washington Bridge**, which connects New York to New Jersey. A pedestrian walkway allows for dazzling views of Manhattan, and it's a popular route for bicyclists, too. Under the bridge on the east side is a diminutive lighthouse—those who know the children's story *The Little Red Lighthouse and the Great Gray Bridge* will recognize it immediately.

The main building of **Yeshiva University** *(2540 Amsterdam Ave at 187th St)* is one of

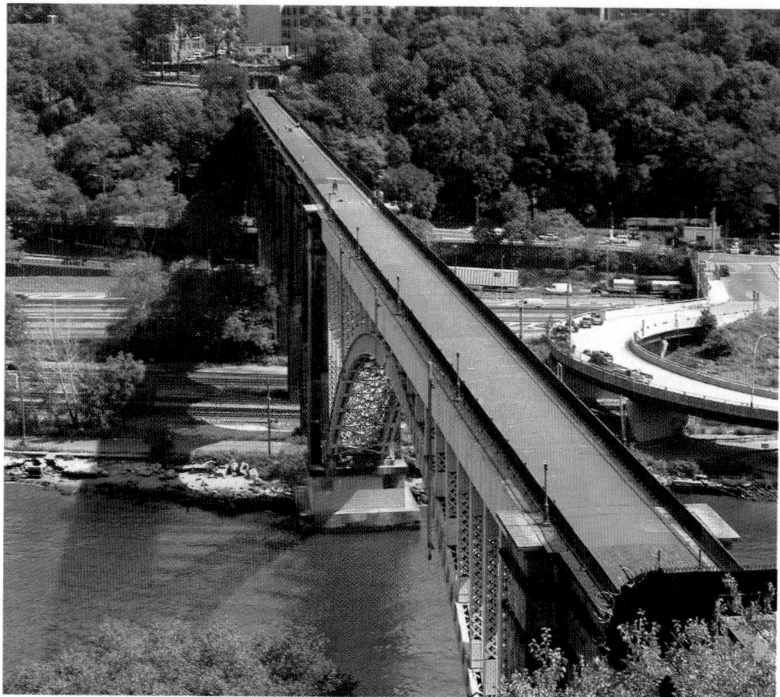

**The high road** The spectacular High Bridge Aqueduct, which once carried fresh water to Manhattan from the upstate Croton Reservoir, can be viewed from High Bridge Park.

the local oddities, a Romanesque Revival–style orange-brick structure decorated with turrets and minarets. **The Cloisters** *(see page 41)*, at the northern edge of flower-filled Fort Tryon Park, is a reconstructed monastery incorporating several original medieval cloisters that the Rockefeller clan shipped over from Europe. It seems custom-designed for romantic picnics.

The neighborhood has two significant American historic sites. **Dyckman House**, a circa-1785 Dutch farmhouse with a high-shouldered gambrel roof and flared eaves, is the oldest surviving home in Manhattan and something of a lonely sight on busy Broadway. In 1915, when the house was threatened with demolition, the Dyckman family's descendants purchased it and filled it with heirlooms. **Morris-Jumel Mansion** was where George Washington planned for the battle of Harlem Heights in 1776, after the British colonel Roger Morris moved out. The handsome 18th-century Palladian-style villa also has fantastic views. Cross the street to see **Sylvan Terrace**, which boasts the largest continuous strip of old wooden houses in Manhattan.

### Dyckman Farmhouse Museum

*4881 Broadway at 204th St (212-304-9422). Subway: A to 207th St–Inwood. Tue–Sat 10am–4pm. Free.*
The period furnishings are beautiful, but most intriguing are the Indian artifacts and Revolutionary War memorabilia in the Relic Room.

### George Washington Bridge

See **Span-tastic**, page 106.

### Inwood Hill Park

*Entrance on 207th St at Seaman Ave. Visitors' center on 218th St at Indian Rd (212-304-2365). Subway: A, 1, 9 to 207th St.*

### Morris-Jumel Mansion

*65 Jumel Terr between 160th and 162nd Sts (212-923-8008; www.morrisjumel.org). Subway: C to 163rd St–Amsterdam Ave. Wed–Sun 10am–4pm. $3, seniors and students $2. MC, V accepted in gift shop and for group admissions.*
Built in 1765, the mansion is Manhattan's only surviving pre-Revolutionary house. Now surrounded by brownstones, it originally sat on a 160-acre estate that stretched from river to river.

# Brooklyn

No longer in Manhattan's shadow, Kings County offers boutiques, cool clubs, historical sights and restaurants galore



After 14 years of construction, which claimed the lives of some 20 men, the Brooklyn Bridge was opened to the public in 1883. The 1,595-foot span of steel cable and stone ranked as the world's longest bridge, and experts proclaimed it a technological marvel. But a joke of the time told of a Manhattanite who visited the finished structure, learned of its long, accident-riddled history, and remarked, "All that trouble, just to get to Brooklyn?"

Brooklyn is a punch line no more. Once a self-styled "city of homes and churches," it's currently the most populous of New York's five boroughs, with 2.5 million residents. Just in the last decade, the area has grown at a pace unparalleled since 1898, when it was incorporated into New York City. (Brooklyn residents, most of whom were less than thrilled with the merger, called it "The Great Mistake of '98.")

The late 1990s were boom years for the borough, as start-up businesses and studio-starved artists flooded the westernmost regions. Lured by the quick commute and (slightly) lower rents, these settlers brought with them money and style, and Brooklyn became the "new Manhattan." But the area is more than a haven for hip émigrés. The range of cultures and lifestyles is vast (nearly 100 ethnic groups fly the colors of their homelands), creating distinct neighborhood identities.

The best way to get to know Kings County is to become familiar with its disparate geographies, cultures and communities. For further research, or to request a calendar of events, contact **Brooklyn Information and Culture** *(647 Fulton St between Ashland and Rockwell Pls, 718-855-7882; www.brooklynx.org).*

## Brooklyn Heights & Dumbo

Now the borough's toniest neighborhood, Brooklyn Heights was born in 1814, when entrepreneur Robert Fulton's first steam-powered ferry linked Manhattan to the sleepy fishing village on western Long Island. The streets of Brooklyn Heights—particularly Cranberry, Hicks, Pierrepont and Willow—are lined with beautifully maintained Greek revival and Italianate row houses dating to the 1820s. In 1965, 30 blocks were designated Brooklyn's first historic district. Today, Henry and Montague Streets are the main drags, packed with shops, restaurants and bars.

When it was completed in 1881, the building that houses **The Brooklyn Historical Society** was the first structure in New York to use locally produced terra-cotta on its facade. The George B. Post–designed creation is currently undergoing an extensive restoration and is scheduled to reopen in 2003 with the interactive multimedia exhibit "Brooklyn Works: 400 Years of Making a Living in Brooklyn." Also in the area is the dignified **Plymouth Church of the Pilgrims**, established in 1847 under the ministry of abolitionist Henry Ward Beecher, brother of American writer Harriet Beecher Stowe.

The remnants of Brooklyn's past as an independent city can be found downtown. The grand **Borough Hall** *(209 Joralemon St at Fulton St)* sits in the center. Completed in 1848, the Greek Revival edifice—later crowned with a Victorian cupola— was renovated in the late 1980s. The hall is linked to the **New York State Supreme Court** *(360 Adams St)* by **Cadman Plaza**, where farmers peddle fresh produce on Tuesdays, Thursdays and Saturdays. Nearby is the massive Romanesque Revival **U.S. Post Office** *(271-301 Cadman Plaza East between Johnson and Tillary Sts)*, which is getting a major makeover.

Brooklyn's main business district is on Jay Street in **MetroTech Center**. A common provides a shady place to rest between 2 MetroTech and **Polytechnic University**, the nation's second-oldest private science-and-engineering school. At the easternmost edge of the common is **Wunsch Hall** *(311 Bridge St at Johnson St)*. Long before it became part of the university campus, the 1846 Greek Revival building was the home of the Bridge Street African Wesleyan Methodist Episcopal Church, a stop on the Underground Railroad. (The congregation moved to Bedford-Stuyvesant in 1938.)

► For more on the Brooklyn Museum of Art, see **Art and soul**, page 44.
► The **Brooklyn map** is on pages 402–403.
► For kid-friendly activities, see chapter **Kids' Stuff**.

**Urban spanning** The Brooklyn Heights Promenade gives a splendid view of lower Manhattan.

Sightseeing

A town obsessed with getting from place to place in a hurry deserves a museum on the subject. **New York Transit Museum** *(see page 59),* located in a decommissioned subway station, is in the midst of a full-scale renovation, and is slated to reopen in the spring of 2003.

Brooklyn Heights has more than history on its side; it offers spectacular views of Manhattan. You can catch a great glimpse of the Financial District skyline from the **Brooklyn Heights Promenade** *(see* **Best view**, *below).* Another fine perch is **Fulton Ferry Landing**, located below the Brooklyn Bridge, which juts into the East River at Old Fulton and Water Streets—it's a prime spot for snapping photos or hitching a ride with the **New York Water Taxi** *(see page 132).* Also nearby: the upscale restau-rant **River Café** *(1 Water St at Old Fulton St, 718-522-5200).* The beautiful view and equally lovely menu cushion the blow of the bill.

If Brooklyn Heights is too ritzy for your blood, you might feel more at home in the gruff but lovable neighborhood of **Dumbo** (Down Under the Manhattan Bridge Overpass). Artists flocked here in the 1970s and '80s, drawn by the cobblestoned streets and warehouse loft spaces, and they kept on coming through the go-go '90s. The **Dumbo Arts Center** promotes the work of community artists through its gallery and sponsorship of the annual **Dumbo Art Under the Bridge** festival *(see page 253),* during which artists open their studios to the public.

Speaking of works of art, pizza lovers in Dumbo should sample a coal-fired pie at venerable **Grimaldi's** *(see* **The upper crust**, *page 190).* After the meal, slam dancers and technophiles can hit the **Lunatarium** *(see page 275),* a multimedia museum–dance club located in a 20,000-square-foot penthouse.

Of course, no trip to Brooklyn would be complete without a walk on the **Brooklyn Bridge**. The vision of German-born civil engineer John Augustus Roebling (who did not live to see its com-pletion), the structure was the first to use steel cables. It connects downtown Brooklyn with Manhattan, providing glorious views of the Statue of Liberty and the New York Harbor; as you walk along its promenade, you'll see plaques detailing the story of the bridge's construction.

## BEST VIEW Hit the Heights

**Brooklyn Heights Promenade**

This most romantic of New York City photo ops features a panorama that sweeps from the Verrazano-Narrows Bridge and New York Harbor, to the Statue of Liberty, skyline of lower Manhattan and the Brooklyn Bridge. Plentiful benches make the promenade a comfortable spot for lunching locals, strolling families and cuddling couples.

*Furman St between Cranberry and Remsen Sts, Brooklyn Heights, Brooklyn. Subway: 2, 3 to Clark St. Walk toward the East River; main entrance is on Montague St.*

### Brooklyn Bridge

*Subway: A, C to High St; J, M, Z to Chambers St; 4, 5, 6 to Brooklyn Bridge–City Hall.*

**The Brooklyn Historical Society**
*128 Pierrepont St at Clinton St, Brooklyn Heights (718-222-4111; www.brooklynhistory.org). Subway: M, N, R, W to Court St; 2, 3, 4, 5 to Borough Hall. Mon, Thu–Sat noon–5pm. $2.50; Mondays free. Cash only.*

**Dumbo Arts Center**
*30 Washington St between Plymouth and Water Sts, Dumbo (718-694-0831; www.dumboartscenter.org). Subway: F to York St. Mon, Thu–Sun noon–6pm.*

**Plymouth Church of the Pilgrims**
*75 Hicks St between Cranberry and Orange Sts, Brooklyn Heights (718-624-4743; www.plymouthchurch.org). Subway: A, C to High St; 2, 3 to Clark St. Free tours by appointment only.*

## Carroll Gardens & Cobble Hill

Nowhere is Brooklyn's rapid gentrification more apparent than on **Smith Street**, also known »as Brooklyn's Restaurant Row. The eateries, shops and nightspots have transformed a formerly decaying strip into one of the city's hottest commercial corridors. As recently as a decade ago, denizens of the surrounding African-American, Irish, Italian and Latino neighborhoods were well advised to avoid this street at night. But soaring Manhattan rents, along with the late 1990s urban-renewal project that decked Smith Street with handsome new sidewalks and wrought-iron street lamps, lured the young and trend-conscious. Pioneering restaurants like the neighborhood bistro **Patois** *(No. 255, 718-855-1535)* and the Franco-Vietnamese **Uncle Pho** *(No. 263, 718-855-8787)* paved the way for an explosion of dining and shopping options that now draw Manhattanites in a reverse bridge-and-tunnel trek.

Many purveyors are artists and designers selling their own wares; they stand, sometimes uneasily, shoulder to shoulder with Latino restaurants, bodegas, junk stores and social clubs that have survived the transition. Playful, pretty women's clothing is for sale at **Frida's Closet** *(No. 296, 718-855-0311)* and **Stacia** *(No. 267, 718-237-0078)*, and no fashion-conscious visitor should miss **Refinery** *(No. 254, 718-643-7861)*, the source of the vintage-fabric handbags that swing from the shoulders of neighborhood art-chicks and stroller-pushing mamas alike. **Halcyon** *(see page 278)*, a space-age furniture store–coffeehouse–nightspot–vinyl emporium, features some of New York's best DJs spinning after dark; by day, it's a cool place to sip java and maybe find that *Jetsons* sofa you've been looking for. **Robin des Bois** *(see page 205)* serves French bistro fare amid supercool 20th-century vintage furniture (also for sale) and offers some of the city's best al fresco dining in its verdant, sunny backyard, called Sherwood Forest.

Other Smith Street eats can be had at **Café LuluC** *(No. 214, 718-625-3815)*, a casual French-Cuban spot with a garden and friendly waiters in guayaberas; and **Panino'teca 275** *(No. 275, 718-237-2728)*, whose Italian-style pressed sandwiches go well with a glass of Chianti. For more refined choices, try **The**

**The breakfast club** Part café, record shop, nightspot *and* used-furniture store, Halcyon serves a low-key Sunday brunch called Hangover Café.

**Always fresh, never crude** The Refinery's inspired selections are fashionista faves.

**Grocery** *(see page 204)*, **Restaurant Saul** *(No. 140, 718-935-9844)* and **Smith Street Kitchen** *(No. 174, 718-858-5359)*, where fresh fish is the order of the day.

Smith Street isn't the only road to culinary riches. If you're seeking some world-class tabouli, the mile-long stretch of Atlantic Avenue between Henry and Nevins is the place. To the west, between Henry and Court Streets, is a cluster of excellent, mostly Middle Eastern food markets and restaurants. The granddaddy of them all is **Sahadi Importing Company** *(No. 187, 718-624-4550)*, a 50-year-old neighborhood institution that sells olives, spices, cheeses, nuts and other gourmet treats; **Malko Karkenny Bros**. *(No. 174, 718-834-0845)* and **Hanshali International Foods** *(No. 197, 718-625-2400)* offer many savory selections as well.

Italian-food lovers may want to head to **Court Street** in Carroll Gardens, where Italian-American roots run deep. Buy a prosciutto loaf from the **Caputo Bakery** *(No. 329, 718-875-6871)*, pick up freshly made buffalo mozzarella at **Caputo's Fine Foods** *(No. 460, 718-855-8852)*, grab an aged *soppressata* salami from **Esposito and Sons** *(No. 357, 718-875-6863)*, and relax in **Carroll Park** *(between Carroll and President Sts)* to watch the old-timers play bocce.

## Park Slope

Welcome to Brooklyn's burbs. **Park Slope** has a upscale feel and is loaded with charming brownstones, coffeeshops and restaurants, such as **al di là** *(248 Fifth Ave at Carroll St, 718-783-4565)* and **Max & Moritz** *(426A Seventh Ave between 14th and 15th Sts, 718-499-5557)*.

The Slope's biggest draw may be **Prospect Park**. Central Park is bigger and more famous, but Prospect Park has a rustic quality that its rectangular sibling to the west lacks. It's a great place to bird-watch, boat or hike amid the waterfalls, reflecting pools and wildlife habitats of the recently restored **Ravine**. Central Park architects Frederick Law Olmsted and Calvert Vaux designed this 526-acre encore to be enjoyed from a saddle; you can rent horses at nearby **Kensington Stables** *(see page 329)*, or hop on a bike and pedal alongside bladers and runners. On Sundays, from mid-May through October, the Congo Square Drummers and Dancers gather in a section called **Drummers Grove**, north of the Parkside–Ocean Avenue entrance; onlookers are encouraged to join in and dance. Children enjoy riding the hand-carved horses of the park's antique **Carousel**, located at the intersection of Empire Boulevard and Flatbush Avenue. Kids can play with animals in the **Prospect Park Wildlife Center** *(718-399-7339)*, and every July, young anglers compete in **R.H. Macy's Fishing Contest** near the Lake at the park's southern end.

Another verdant expanse, **Green-Wood Cemetery**, is a ten-minute walk from Prospect Park. A century ago, this 478-acre site vied with Niagara Falls as New York state's greatest tourist attraction. Filled with Victorian mausoleums, cherubs and gargoyles, Green-Wood is the resting place of more than a half million New Yorkers, including Jean-Michel Basquiat, Leonard Bernstein and Mae West.

The central branch of the **Brooklyn Public Library** *(see page 268)* sits near Prospect Park's main entrance and the massive Civil War memorial arch at **Grand Army Plaza** *(at the intersection of Flatbush Ave, Eastern Pkwy and Prospect Park West)*. The library's Brooklyn Collection includes thousands of artifacts, manuscripts and photos that trace the borough's history. Just around the corner is the tranquil **Brooklyn Botanic Garden** *(see* **Seasons in the sun**, *page 112)* and the **Brooklyn Museum of Art** *(see* **Art and soul**, *page 44)*.

Architecture buffs should consider a tour of Victorian Flatbush, just south of Prospect Park. The homes are extravagant, and no two are alike (the developer wouldn't allow it). On the last Sunday in April, the Flatbush Development Corporation *(718-859-3800)* sponsors a tour of mansions that once housed the city's elite, including reporter Nellie Bly, silent-film star Mary Pickford and the Guggenheims.

### Brooklyn Botanic Garden

See **Seasons in the sun**, page 112.

### Green-Wood Cemetery

*25th St at Fifth Ave, Green-Wood Heights (718-768-7300; www.green-wood.com). Subway: M, R, W to 25th St. 8am–4pm. Free.*

**Prospect Park**
*Main entrance: Flatbush Ave at Grand Army Plaza, Prospect Heights (general information 718-965-8999, Prospect Park Wildlife Center 718-399-7339; www.prospectpark.org). Subway: F to 15th St–Prospect Park; Q, S to Prospect Park; 2, 3 to Grand Army Plaza.*

## Fort Greene & Williamsburg

**Fort Greene** boasts distinguished Victorian brownstones and a rich history of African-American arts and entrepreneurship: Spike Lee, Branford Marsalis, Chris Rock and Richard Wright have all called this neighborhood home. **Fort Greene Park** *(from DeKalb to Myrtle Aves, between St. Edwards St and Washington Park)* was conceived in 1847 at the behest of poet Walt Whitman (then the editor of the *Brooklyn Daily Eagle*); its master plan was fully realized by Olmsted and Vaux in 1867. At the center of the park stands the **Prison Ship Martyrs Monument**, erected in 1909 in memory of more than 11,000 American prisoners who died on British ships that were anchored nearby during the Revolutionary War.

More history awaits just a block away. The **Lafayette Avenue Presbyterian Church** was founded by a group of abolitionists; Abraham Lincoln's oldest son, Robert Todd Lincoln, broke ground in 1860. Its subterranean

# Seasons in the sun

The Brooklyn Botanic Garden is bloomin' beautiful all year long

It was designed to be a sanctuary, but Prospect Park can get a little raucous, with its fair-weather riot of concerts, bike riders and in-line skaters. Respite seekers need only slip inside the Brooklyn Botanic Garden, an intimate emerald triangle abutting the park's east side. The exhaustive rules—no picnicking, no pets, no Frisbees—make the 93-year-old garden a placid retreat. But you need not limit your visits to warmer months; the grounds are gorgeous in January as well. Here are some blossom highlights by season.

**SPRING**
In the boulder-scattered Rock Garden, melting snow gives way to spring's floral flourish of narcissi, snowdrops, aconites and hellebores.

**Flower children** You can take a self-guided tour of the Japanese Hill-and-Pond Garden.

**Garden variety** No matter when you visit, BBG's gates open to an array of flora.

In April, Magnolia Plaza's namesake trees turn a brilliant pink, and cherry blossoms erupt in the newly restored Japanese Hill-and-Pond Garden, one of the most celebrated Japanese gardens outside Asia. Come May, purple lilacs, magenta and red azaleas, and tulips in a broad palette of colors bloom throughout the garden. Be sure to stroll among the more than 45,000 bluebells in Bluebell Wood.

**SUMMER**
The Cranford Rose Garden rings in summer with countless roses blooming on 5,000 bushes. A sea of English marigolds unfolds in the Shakespeare Garden, which features more than 80 varieties of flora cited in the Bard's poems and plays. Midsummer is perfect for a trip to the Fragrance Garden, a tactile and aromatic display that includes

Sightseeing

tunnel once served as a stop on the Underground Railroad. The church is restoring its celebrated stained-glass windows, created by Louis Comfort Tiffany.

A year after the church was established, the **Brooklyn Academy of Music** *(see page 318)* was founded in Brooklyn Heights, later moving to its current site on Fort Greene's southern border. America's oldest operating performing-arts center, BAM offers cutting-edge performance art, theater and music, including the renowned Brooklyn Philharmonic. Every fall, from October through December, the **Next Wave Festival** showcases contemporary experimental works of dance, music and theater. **BAM Rose Cinemas** *(see page 281)* is both a first-run theater and Brooklyn's art-house film center. The BAMcafé serves dinner and drinks on performance nights and presents live music on weekends. Should you desire something sinful after all that culture, the world-famous cheesecake at **Junior's Restaurant** *(386 Flatbush Ave at DeKalb Ave, 718-852-5257)* is just three blocks away.

More aggressively cool than Fort Greene is **Williamsburg**, Brooklyn's bohemian nexus. It wasn't always this way. The waterfront location made Billyburg ideal for industry, and after the Erie Canal linked the Atlantic Ocean with the Great Lakes in 1825, it became a bustling port. Companies such as Domino Sugar and

petunias, heliotropes and Mexican evening primroses. The garden was designed for visitors with disabilities: Labels are in braille, and flowers are grown in elevated beds to be more easily viewed from wheelchairs. In August, lotuses and water lilies take center stage in the Botanic Garden's two huge lily ponds.

**AUTUMN**

In September, miniatures and floribundas appear in the Cranford Rose Garden. Asters and goldenrods emerge in the Native Flora Garden, which shows off the vast biodiversity of the New York metropolitan area. A collage of fall colors explodes in October and November: Stand on the Overlook walkway to glimpse golden ginkgo trees and sorrel trees burning a fiery crimson.

**WINTER**

In December, the show moves indoors to the Steinhardt Conservatory, the garden's $25 million greenhouse complex, where holiday

**Greenhouse effect** Yucca blooms all year long in the Steinhardt Conservatory.

**Nice pad** Goldfish glide in the two pools found in Lily Pool Terrace.

greens and flowers are showcased. (The Conservatory's lower-level gallery exhibits nature-inspired artwork year-round.) In January and February, the Robert W. Wilson Aquatic House in the Conservatory boasts blooming orchids, and the Helen Mattin Warm Temperate Pavilion features South African bulbs such as Cape cowslips and butterfly irises. For the hale and hearty, the chilly grounds offer a spare, silent beauty: striking evergreens, skeletal cherry trees and snow-dusted yew hedges.

**Brooklyn Botanic Garden**

*900 Washington Ave between Carroll and Crown Sts, with additional entrances on Eastern Pkwy and Flatbush Ave, Prospect Heights (718-623-7200; www.bbg.org). Subway: C to Franklin Ave, then S to Botanic Garden; 2, 3 to Eastern Pkwy–Brooklyn Museum. Apr–Sept Tue–Fri 8am–6pm; Sat, Sun, holidays 10am–6pm. Oct–Mar Tue–Fri 8am–4:30pm; Sat, Sun, holidays 10am–4:30pm. Adults $3, seniors and students $1.50, under 16 free. Tuesdays, Sat 10am–noon, free.*

**Academy rewards** BAM booms all kinds of sounds, from experimental to classical.

pharmaceuticals giant Pfizer started here. Then, in the 20th century, companies began abandoning enormous industrial spaces in the neighborhood. The beloved **Brooklyn Brewery** *(79 North 11th St, 718-486-7422; www.brooklynbrewery.com)* is located in a former ironworks factory. Visit during happy hour on Friday evenings, or take a factory-and-tasting tour on Saturday; art shows and block parties are held year-round.

Williamsburg is among New York's curious multiethnic amalgams. To the south, Broadway divides a vibrant Latino neighborhood from a lively community of Hasidic Jews, while the northern half extending into **Greenpoint** is largely Polish. The north side also has deep Italian roots, which are celebrated during the first two weeks of July at **Our Lady of Mt. Carmel Feast and Bazaar**, centered on the eight blocks surrounding **Our Lady of Mt. Carmel Church** (*1 Havemeyer St at North 8th St, 718-384-0223).* The festival features dining, music and dancing.

Some of the city's trendiest clubs and restaurants can be found along North Sixth Street, or off the main drag of Bedford Avenue, including **Galapagos** *(see page 309),* **Luxx** *(see page 275)* and **SEA** *(114 North 6th St at Berry St, 718-384-8850).* And Williamsburg is home to the distinctly untrendy gustatory treasure **Peter Luger** *(see page 205),* which grills the best steak (porterhouse only) in New York City.

The area also has dozens of art galleries, such as **Momenta Art** and **Pierogi 2000** *(see page 263),* as well as several performance spaces like **Northsix** *(see page 313)* and **Warsaw at the Polish National Home** *(see page 314).* The **Williamsburg Art & Historical Center**, in a landmarked bank building, is the core of the area's art scene and displays works by local and international artists; it also hosts a dizzying program of dance, digital art, film, music, performance art, theater and video.

### Lafayette Avenue Presbyterian Church

*85 South Oxford St at Lafayette Ave, Fort Greene (718-625-7515; www.lapcbrooklyn.org). Subway: C to Lafayette Ave; G to Fulton St. Tours by appointment only.*

### Williamsburg Art & Historical Center

*135 Broadway at Bedford Ave, Williamsburg (718-486-7372; www.wahcenter.org). Subway: J, M, Z to Marcy Ave. Sat, Sun noon–6pm and by appointment.*

## Bedford-Stuyvesant, Crown Heights & Flatbush

Although it was made famous for racial tension in *Do the Right Thing,* Bed-Stuy is in fact a tight-knit and often very welcoming African-American community whose size rivals that of Harlem. Join the annual **Brownstoners of Bedford-Stuyvesant Inc. House Tour** *(718-574-1979),* held the third Saturday in October, rain or shine; it's a great way to see the area's historic homes. Another attraction, the **Concord Baptist Church of Christ**, offers uplifting gospel music from one of the biggest (and loudest) African-American congregations in the U.S.

There's plenty to do south of Bed-Stuy in the largely West Indian neighborhoods of **Crown Heights** and **Flatbush** (both also have sizable Jewish populations). Calypso and soca music blare from open windows, and it seems like every block features a storefront selling spicy jerk chicken or meat patties. In Flatbush, try the sublime oxtail soup at Caribbean eatery **Sybil's** *(2210 Church Ave at Flatbush Ave, 718-469-9049).*

### Concord Baptist Church of Christ

*833 Marcy Ave (Gardner C. Taylor Blvd) between Madison and Putnam Aves, Bedford-Stuyvesant (718-622-1818). Subway: A, C to Nostrand Ave. Call for service times.*

## Bay Ridge, Bensonhurst & Gravesend

These three neighborhoods are always hopping. **Bay Ridge** and **Bensonhurst** were the settings for *Saturday Night Fever,* and the disco in which John Travolta boogied down remains—it's now a gay club called **Spectrum** *(802 64th St at Eighth Ave, 718-238-8213).* Before the neighborhood served as a hangout for would-be Tony Maneros, it was a Dutch settlement; in the 19th century, it became a summer retreat for moneyed Manhattanites. You can still find grand old homes along the quiet suburban streets, including the **Howard E. and Jessie Jones**

**House** *(8220 Narrows Ave at 83rd St)*, an arts-and-crafts mansion known locally as the Gingerbread House.

There are a host of eating options on the main drags of Third, Fourth and Fifth Avenues, between Bay Ridge Parkway and 88th Street. For authentic Lebanese, try **Karam** *(8519 Fourth Ave between 85th and 86th Sts, 718-745-5227)*, and 89-year-old favorite **Hinsch's Confectionery** *(8518 Fifth Ave between 85th and 86th Sts, 718-748-2854)* froths a mean egg cream.

You can see the **Verrazano-Narrows Bridge** from just about anywhere in Bay Ridge. Completed in 1964, it connects Brooklyn and Staten Island. **Fort Hamilton**, named after founding father Alexander Hamilton, sits at the foot of the bridge. The fort is the second oldest continuously garrisoned federal post in the country.

If you find Manhattan's Little Italy too touristy, check out Bensonhurst's rendition on a stretch of 18th Avenue known as **Cristoforo Colombo Boulevard** *(between 68th and 77th Sts)*. There are social clubs, delis stocked with pasta, shops selling Italian music, and **Villabate Pasticceria & Bakery** *(7117 18th Ave between 71st and 72nd Sts, 718-331-8430)*, where Italian-speaking crowds shout out their orders of pastries and marzipan. On Wednesdays, Thursdays and Saturdays, carnivores brave the long lines at **John's Deli** *(2033 Stillwell Ave at 86th St, 718-372-7481)* for the daily special: thinly sliced roast beef, melted mozzarella and sautéed onions on a crusty roll.

**Gravesend** was founded in 1643 by Lady Deborah Moody, a rich widow and radical Protestant who was the first woman to charter land in the New World. The **Hicks-Platt House** *(17 Gravesend Neck Rd between McDonald Ave and Van Sicklen St)*, a 17th-century house (marred by a fake-stone veneer) is on what was reputedly the Moody farm. Lady Moody is buried in the cemetery across the street. Today, locals stop at **Joe's of Avenue U** *(287 Ave U between Lake St and McDonald Ave, 718-449-9285)* for pasta *con le sarde* (fresh sardines) and *arancini* (rice balls).

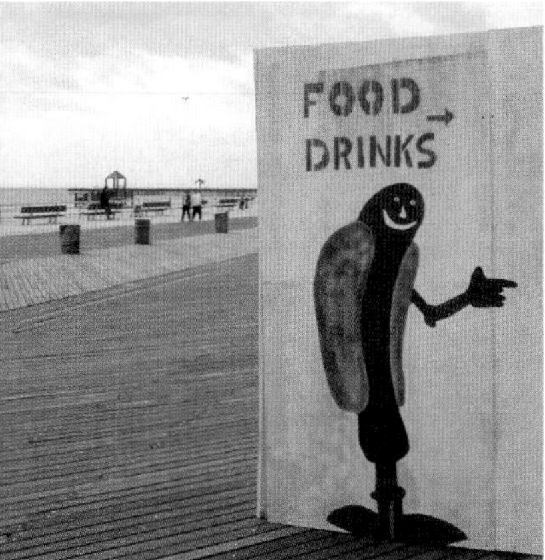


**Hot diggity dog!** Frankly speaking, Coney Island has plenty of mouthwatering snacks.

## Brighton Beach & Coney Island

**Brighton Beach**, south of Gravesend, is known as Little Odessa because of its large population of Russian immigrants. You can wander the aisles of **M&I International Foods** *(249 Brighton Beach Ave between Brighton 1st and Brighton 2nd Sts, 718-615-1011)*, a huge Russian deli and grocery, or make a reservation at one of the local nightclubs. Dress is formal, food and vodka are plentiful, and dancing goes until the wee hours.

**Coney Island**, on the peninsula just west of Brighton Beach, is a summertime destination. After decades of decay, the weirdly wonderful community known for its amusement park, beach and boardwalk has made a comeback. The biggest improvement is **KeySpan Park** *(see page 324)*, home to the **Brooklyn Cyclones**, a minor-league baseball affiliate of the New York Mets. If you're a thrill seeker, take a spin in the Cyclone at **Astroland Amusement Park** *(see page 296)*; a ride on the 75-year-old wooden roller coaster lasts only two minutes, but the first drop is nearly vertical, and the cars clatter along the 2,640 feet of track at speeds up to 60 miles per hour.

After your ride, grab a hot dog at **Nathan's Famous** *(1310 Surf Ave at Stillwell Ave, 718-946-2202; www.nathansfamous.com)*, and take a stroll along the boardwalk. You'll soon hit the **New York Aquarium** *(see page 303)*, where you can marvel at the famous beluga whales. From July through early September, you can boogie to house music on the boardwalk at the **Black Underground** dance party *(Sat 3–9pm)* at 10th Street. And there is always the (fairly tame) **Sideshows by the Seashore** put on by **Coney Island USA**, an organization that keeps the torch for early 20th century Coney Island burning.The **Mermaid Parade** *(see page 352)* and **Nathan's Famous Fourth of July Hot Dog Eating Contest** *(see page 352)* are two popular annual Coney Island events.

### Coney Island USA

*1208 Surf Ave at W 12th St, Coney Island (718-372-5159; www.coneyislandusa.com). Subway: W to Stillwell Ave–Coney Island. Call for show times and schedules. $5, under 12 $3.*

# Queens

A tour of NYC's fastest-growing borough is like a trip around the world

In his 1949 essay *Here Is New York,* E.B. White wrote of not one but three cities—that of the commuter, the native and the settler. The last was the greatest, he concluded, because theirs was "the city of final destination, the city that is a goal…Commuters give the city its tidal restlessness; natives give it solidity and continuity; but the settlers give it passion."

A half century later, settlers are still bringing passion to New York, but instead of making their homes in Manhattan, more and more are moving to the outer boroughs—and to blue-collar Queens, where housing is more affordable and neighborhoods are being revitalized. The borough's population jumped 14 percent from 1990 to 2000, to 2.2 million, which would make it America's fourth largest city if it stood alone.

Yet if it weren't for Kennedy and La Guardia airports, few visitors would set foot in Queens. To them—and to many Manhattan-centric New Yorkers—it's undiscovered territory.

The most sprawling borough (120 square miles), Queens is also the most ethnically diverse—a third of its inhabitants are foreign-born, and many neighborhoods have formed along ethnic lines, including Astoria (Greek), Corona (Italian), Jackson Heights (Colombian and Indian), Maspeth (Polish-Lithuanian), Richmond Hill (Indo-Caribbean) and Woodside (Irish).

***Sum* kind of wonderful** Main Street is packed with winning Asian restaurants.

Amid such diversity, it's no wonder the public library system circulates materials in 70 languages and boasts the most extensive Chinese-language collection in the United States. Likewise, the Queens dining scene rivals Manhattan's in variety: Albanian, Chinese, Greek, Indian, Korean, Latin American and Pakistani restaurants, take-out joints and markets line the main thoroughfares.

This dramatic cultural confluence plays out against a relatively mundane landscape. Because Queens developed dramatically after World War II, much of its architectural landscape lacks the 19th-century grandeur that defines Manhattan. Although there are scattered oases of 1920s-era garden apartments worthy of the National Historic Register—such as those in Bay Ridge, Forest Hills Gardens, Jackson Heights and Sunnyside Gardens—you'll encounter endless blocks of unremarkable redbrick houses and apartment buildings and large swaths of current and past industrial areas. Still, Queens is not short on charm. Take a walk through Astoria, the largest Greek community outside of Greece, and you'll find grape arbors and fig trees planted in backyards, and fruit-and-spice–scented tobacco wafting from a number of Greek and Middle Eastern cafés.

Besides immigration, the biggest boom to hit Queens is the art scene, especially with the arrival of **MoMA Queens** *(see* **Modern convenience**, *page 118),* the temporary site of the **Museum of Modern Art** *(see also page 46).* Many other museums, galleries, performance spaces and parks now inhabit once-abandoned factories, warehouses and outdoor areas along unused waterfront lots.

The logical first stop is Long Island City, the neighborhood closest to Manhattan, and the hub of the borough's growing art community. **P.S. 1 Contemporary Art Center** *(see page 46),* a former public school converted into a gallery and studio space, is an affiliate of MoMA. The center's open workshops, multimedia galleries and avant-garde exhibitions attract artists and visitors from around the world.

**It's a small world after all** Take a relaxing stroll through Flushing Meadows–Corona Park.

On weekends, the free Queens Artlink bus runs from Manhattan to P.S. 1 and other select cultural destinations in the area *(see* **Borough haul**, *page 301),* including MoMA QNS. Those who like their high art high-tech can visit the nearby **Center for the Holographic Arts** *(45-10 Court Sq off Jackson Ave, 718-784-5065; www.holocenter.com),* the only venue of its kind in the city. If you think bigger is better, there's the 4.5-acre **Socrates Sculpture Park** on the banks of the East River. The large-scale works of established and lesser-known artists dot the large field, which is also the site of a summertime film-and-concert series.

Long before Hollywood became the movie capital of the world, there was Astoria, adjacent to Long Island City. W.C. Fields, Gloria Swanson, Rudolph Valentino and the Marx Brothers made films at **Kaufman Astoria Studios** *(34-12 36th St between 34th and 35th Aves, 718-706-5300; www.kaufmanastoria.com),* which opened in 1920 and is the largest filmmaking facility on the East Coast. The Children's Television Workshop (producers of *Sesame Street*), the Lifetime Network, a recording studio and a 14-screen movie theater are based here. The studio is closed to the public, but the complex also includes the **American Museum of the Moving Image** *(see page 57),* where you can learn about the history and process of film and TV production or inspect famous props such as the swivel-headed Linda Blair dummy from *The Exorcist*.

Long Island City's **Silvercup Studios** *(42-22 22nd St between Queens Plaza South and 43rd Ave),* which opened in 1983, is now the largest independent full-service film and television studio in the northeastern United States. *Sex and the City* and *The Sopranos* are produced inside, and past movies include *Men in Black* and *Do the Right Thing*. Unfortunately, tours are not available.

The formerly rural area of Astoria was developed by its first commercial resident: the **Steinway Piano Factory**, one of the world's premier piano makers. Tours of the working factory let you get up close (with goggles) to the craftsmen assembling pianos piece by piece.

You *must* eat Greek when in Astoria, which has attracted immigrants from Hellas since the 1920s. The best bets include **S'Agapo** *(34-21*


► The **Queens street map** is on page 404.
► For a guide to MoMA QNS, see **Modern convenience**, page 118.
► For dining options in Queens, see chapter **Restaurants**. Also see ***Time Out New York Eating & Drinking Guide*** or **eatdrink.timeoutny.com**.

*34th Ave at 35th St, 718-626-0303),* which serves a mean homemade spanakopita; beloved **Elias Corner** *(see page 206);* casual **Taverna Kyklades** *(33-07 Ditmars Blvd between 32nd and 33rd Sts, 718-545-8666);* and 1950s-hep **Café Bar** *(32-90 34th Ave between 35th and 36th Sts, 718-204-5273),* a good place for coffee, cocktails and conversation. **Titan** *(25-56 31st St at Astoria Blvd, 718-626-7771)*is the place to stock up on all your favorite Greek staples, from olives to lavender soap.

The 7 train, which runs above ground in Queens and offers lovely views of the Manhattan skyline, is known as the International Express—almost every stop takes you to a different ethnic community. Among the first few stops after Long Island City (40th Street to 61st Street–Woodside stations) are **Sunnyside** and **Woodside**, which are loaded with Irish pubs. If you fancy a bite of black pudding, stop by one of the many Irish bakeries, delis and restaurants. But the Emerald Isle isn't the only country represented: **Cornel's Garden Romanian** Restaurant *(46-04 Skillman Ave at 46th St, 718-786-7894),* **Dazies Italian Restaurant** *(39-41 Queens Blvd between 39th and 40th Sts, 718-786-7013)* and **Nazar Turkish Cuisine** *(42-03 Queens Blvd at 42nd St, 718-392-3838)* are just a few of the places serving excellent food at reasonable prices.

So many dining options make it easy to go from gourmet to gourmand. A good way to burn calories is to stroll around **Sunnyside Gardens** (begins on 43rd Street at Skillman Avenue), a 77-acre historic district of tree-shaded streets, garden apartments and homes. Or take a walk to the renowned **Thalia Spanish Theater**, which presents flamenco and tango performances, musical concerts, zarzuela (Spanish operetta) and bilingual plays such as *Picasso's Guernica.*

For a touch of India, explore **Jackson Heights**. When you exit the 74th Street–Broadway subway station, you'll encounter residents wearing shimmering saris and elaborate gold jewelry. You can fill up on curry at **Delhi Palace** *(37-33 74th St between Roosevelt and 37th Aves, 718-507-0666)* or

## Modern convenience

### MoMA is very much at home in its temporary Queens digs

It's strange to think that many of the Museum of Modern Art's most prized possessions—among them Henri Matisse's *Dance* and Picasso's *Les Demoiselles d'Avignon*—are, at this very moment, hanging in a converted stapler factory in Long Island City. Their new home, MoMA QNS, is a temporary exhibition space built to keep collections accessible to the public while the 53rd Street building is closed for renovation and expansion.

Thanks to architect Michael Maltzan, who designed the lobby and exterior, art lovers are learning to enjoy the ride on the 7 train. (There's also a free shuttle that runs between West 53rd Street and MoMA QNS; *see* **Borough haul**, *page 301.*) Working in a style that might be called "cinematic picturesque," he's made the process of getting to the art an experience that owes as much to the long tracking shot that opens Orson Welles's *A Touch of Evil* as to any architectural precedent.

The sequence begins when the blue-and-white MoMA QNS logo, painted on the building's roof, first comes into view from the 7 train's elevated track, and it doesn't end until you've walked a couple hundred feet, through a carefully delineated series of spaces, into the heart of the building. Along the way, you're guided past a Dominican diner, the employee entrance, the mezzanine MoMA shop, the coat check, a wall of projected videos, the ticket counter and a kind of gallery-within-the-gallery that's earmarked for special installations. What this extension of the entrance experience accomplishes (apart from making you aware that it's taking place) isn't obvious. But it is a distinctive, formal experiment in a linear, scaled horizontal movement that is rare in a city obsessed with verticality.

The actual exhibition spaces, in contrast, are purposely unobtrusive and nondescript: simple concrete floors, painted plasterboard walls, unfinished ceilings. The galleries are designed to be easily reconfigured as shows change and pieces from the permanent collection are rotated. This straightforward spatial dynamic seems somewhat anti-climactic after all the architecture (with a capital "A") out front, and it reminds you that you're still in a faux-stucco, single-story box in an industrial part of town—a space not unlike the spare, loftlike interiors of Chelsea's commercial galleries.

the **Jackson Diner** *(37-47 74th St between Roosevelt and 37th Aves, 718-672-1232).* At **Patel Brothers** *(37-27 74th St between Roosevelt and 37th Aves, 718-898-3445),* you'll discover an amazing range of hard-to-find Indian spices, groceries and beauty items.

Jackson Heights' historic district extends for 30 blocks and encompasses 500 apartment buildings and houses. These English garden-style homes and large apartment complexes were built during the first half of the 20th century as models of urban planning. Most are not open to the public, but the **Jackson Heights Beautification Group** *(212-439-8784; www.preserve.org/jhbg)* sponsors tours of select garden courtyards each June. Another option is **Cooper Union** *(212-353-4000; www.cooper.edu),* which also offers tours throughout the year.

An Asian community thrives in the heart of **Flushing**, whose Main Street is packed with Chinese, Korean and Vietnamese restaurants and food stores. For dim sum, bring a big appetite to **C&J Restaurant** *(136-14 38th Ave at Main St, 718-353-3366),* where narrow aisles are choked with carts laden with dumplings, savory rice noodles and heaps of clams steamed in an aromatic sauce. For Korean food in large family-size portions, there's **Kum Gang San** *(138-28 Northern Blvd at Union St, 718-461-0909).*

Most of Queens' historic buildings are also in Flushing. The **Friends Meeting House** was built in 1694 by religious activist John Bowne. It's still used as a Quaker gathering place, making it one of the oldest active houses of worship in the U.S. Next door is **Kingsland Homestead**, a 1785 farmhouse that serves as headquarters for the Queens Historical Society. **Flushing Town Hall**, an 1862 Romanesque Revival building, contains the Flushing Council on Culture and the Arts and presents art exhibits and concerts.

The **Queens Botanical Garden** offers a 39-acre reprieve from the bustle of Main Street. It was originally created as a horticultural display for the 1939 World's Fair (the pair of blue Mount Atlas cedars punctuating the

**MoMA said knock you out** The Museum of Modern Art's temporary home in Queens thrills visitors, whether they're approaching on the 7 train or exploring the sights within.

At first blush, the selections from the permanent collection seem radically, delightfully out of place. In an ironic inversion of Warhol's induction of the Brillo box into the temple of modernism, some of the holiest 20th-century icons are submerged in the benign neutrality of this big unfinished shed. The result is that familiar paintings and sculptures look remarkably fresh. Shorn of institutional context, it's easier to recall, for example, that Pollock's canvases looked radical back in the 1950s.

When the new building in Manhattan is finished in 2005, be ready for full institutional grandeur. Until then, this curious outpost should be able to take up the slack.

For contact information, directions and a preview of exhibits planned for 2003, *see page 46.*

entrance were planted then; the garden site was later reoriented for the 1964 World's Fair). Although it can't compete with the size and scope of its rivals in Brooklyn and the Bronx, the Queens Botanical Garden sets itself apart by reflecting the borough's ethnic mix.

**Flushing Meadows–Corona Park**, a 1,255-acre expanse of fields and lakes, contains **Shea Stadium**, home of the New York Mets *(see page 324)* and the **United States National Tennis Center** *(see* **U.S. Open**, *page 326)*, where the U.S. Open is played every summer. The 1939 and 1964 World's Fairs were held in Corona Park (then known as Flushing Meadows Park), and a few massive structures remain, most famously the mammoth stainless-steel Unisphere globe. A 1939 pavilion now contains the **Queens Museum of Art** *(see page 50)*, where the main attraction is the *Panorama of the City of New York*—an intricately detailed, 9,335-square-foot architectural scale model of the five boroughs, originally built for the 1964 World's Fair and updated several times since. The **Queens Theatre in the Park**, designed by Philip Johnson, is an indoor amphitheater that hosts dance, theater and comedy performances (often for half what you'd pay for Manhattan shows).

On weekends, picnicking families and soccer-playing teams of transplanted South Americans flock to Corona Park. At the eastern edge is the **New York Hall of Science** *(see page 59)*, an acclaimed interactive museum for kids of all ages. If you hear the sound of barking California sea lions, you're near the **Queens Zoo** (also known as the Queens Wildlife Center). Opened for the 1964 World's Fair, the zoo is home to North American animals such as woolly-headed bison, bald eagles and bears—and Otis the coyote, who was found wandering in Central Park in 1999.

The only working farm in the city is southeast of Corona, near the Long Island border. The 47-acre **Queens County Farm Museum**, in Floral Park, has tours, seasonal events and workshops for adults and kids. Near Kennedy Airport, the tidal wetlands of the **Jamaica Bay Wildlife Refuge** provide prime perches for bird-watching, especially in May and September.

If you're a gambler, you can press your luck at the **Aqueduct** racetrack *(see page 326)*, site of Thoroughbred racing from October through May.

### Flushing Meadows–Corona Park

*Between Jewel Ave and Northern Blvd, Corona. Subway: 7 to Willets Point–Shea Stadium.*

### Flushing Town Hall

*137-35 Northern Blvd, Flushing (718-463-7700; flushingtownhall.org). Subway: 7 to Flushing–Main St. Mon–Fri 10am–5pm; Sat, Sun noon–5pm. $3, seniors and students $2, children $1. AmEx, MC, V.*

### Friends Meeting House

*137-16 Northern Blvd between Main and Union Sts, Flushing (718-358-9636). Subway: 7 to Flushing–Main St.*
Tours by appointment only.

### Jamaica Bay Wildlife Refuge

*Cross Bay Blvd at Broad Channel, Jamaica (718-318-4340). Travel: A, S to Broad Channel, then walk on Noel Rd to Cross Bay Blvd; cross it and turn right, then walk a half mile until you see the trailhead on your left. 8:30am–5pm. Free.*
You can spot pairs of osprey, a fish-eating hawk that has bounced back from near-extinction. Migratory species, including the long-legged curlew sandpiper, appear in spring and early fall. Guided walks, lectures and other nature activities are available.

### Kingsland Homestead/ Queens Historical Society/ Weeping Beech Park

*143-35 37th Ave at Parsons Blvd, Flushing (718-939-0647). Subway: 7 to Flushing–Main St. Mon–Fri 9:30am–5pm. Tours Tue, Sat, Sun 2:30–4:30pm. $3. Cash only.*

**P.S., I love you** Visitors adore the edgy exhibits at P.S. 1 Contemporary Art Center.

**Bird's-eye view** The Queens Zoo aviary allows visitors a close look at fine feathered friends.

Built in 1785 by a wealthy Quaker, Kingsland House was moved to its present site in 1968. The Queens Historical Society now uses it for exhibitions detailing local history.

### Queens Botanical Garden

*43-50 Main St between Dahlia and Elder Aves, Flushing (718-886-3800; www.queensbotanical.org). Subway: 7 to Flushing–Main St. Apr–Oct Tue–Fri 8am–6pm; Sat, Sun 8am–7pm. Nov–Mar Tue–Fri 8am–4:30pm. Open on Monday holidays. Free.*

### Queens Council on the Arts

*79-01 Park Ln South at 80th St, Woodhaven (718-647-3377; www.queenscouncilarts.org). Subway: J to 85th St–Forest Pkwy. Mon–Fri 9am–4:30pm.*
This organization provides exhaustive details, updated daily, on all cultural events in the borough.

## BEST VIEW Three for all

### From Gantry Plaza State Park

This 2.5-acre park offers three views in one: the Manhattan skyline, Roosevelt Island and the Brooklyn waterfront. The space is the first phase in a plan to create a 25-acre park system on the Long Island City shore. The park has four piers, one of which is reserved for fishing, and two railroad gantries hark back to the area's industrial past.
*48th Ave at the East River, Long Island City, Queens. Travel: 7 to Vernon Blvd–Jackson Ave, then walk toward the river.*

### Queens County Farm Museum

*73-50 Little Neck Pkwy, Floral Park (718-347-3276; queensfarm.org). Travel: E, F to Kew Gardens–Union Tpke, then Q46 bus to Little Neck Pkwy. Mon–Fri 9am–5pm outdoor grounds only; Sat, Sun 10am–5pm tours of farmhouse and museum galleries. Voluntary donation.*

### Queens Theatre in the Park

*Corona Park, trolley picks up at subway station one hour before each show (718-760-0064; www.queenstheatre.org). Subway: 7 to Willets Point–Shea Stadium; take Shea Stadium exit to meet shuttle. Show times and prices vary.*

### Queens Zoo

*53-51 111th St in Corona Park (718-271-1500; www.wcs.org). Subway: 7 to 111th St. Mon–Fri 10am–4:30pm; Sat, Sun, holidays 10am– 4:30pm. $2.50, seniors $1.25, children 50¢. Cash only.*

### Socrates Sculpture Park

*Broadway at Vernon Blvd, Long Island City (718-956-1819; www.socratessculpturepark.org). Travel: N, W to Broadway, then Q104 bus to Vernon Blvd; Queens Artlink shuttle, see* **Borough haul**, *page 301.* *9am–sunset. Free.*

### Steinway Piano Factory

*1 Steinway Pl between 19th Ave and 38th St, Astoria (718-721-2600; www.steinway.com). Subway: N, W to Ditmars Blvd. Free tours by appointment only.*
Call ahead: The four-hour tours fill up quickly.

### Thalia Spanish Theatre

*41–17 Greenpoint Ave between 41st and 42nd Sts, Sunnyside (718-729-3880; www.thaliatheatre.org). Subway: 7 to 40th St; take southeast exit. Show times vary. Tickets $20–$25. AmEx, MC, V.*

# The Bronx

Get back to nature in the borough that's one-quarter parkland

The Bronx is so named because the area once belonged to the family of Jonas Bronck, a Swede from the Netherlands who built his farm in 1639. As Manhattan's rich moved into baronial mansions on Fifth Avenue, a similar metamorphosis took place here. Consequently, the Bronx contains some of the city's most important popular-culture landmarks, including the Bronx Zoo, New York Botanical Garden and Yankee Stadium.

**Yankee Stadium** *(see page 324)* sits at 161st Street. When there are no day games, the Yankee Organization gives tours of the clubhouse, dugout and the famous right-field fence with its "short porch"—a within-regulation 295 feet from home plate—that proved helpful to Babe Ruth when he was setting his home-run records. The coolest way to get to a game is by boat: NY Waterway *(see page 132)* will ferry you from Manhattan or New Jersey to the stadium and back aboard the *Yankee Clipper.*

Walk a couple of blocks past Yankee Stadium to 1005 Jerome Avenue at 162nd Street to see the **Park Plaza Apartments**, with its intricate brick patterns, terra-cotta friezes, gargoyles, and squirrel and owl statuettes. Designed by Marvin Fine and Horace Ginsberg, the eight-story landmark building stretches almost two-thirds of a block. If you can sneak a peek into the lobby, you'll notice a mosaic floor and elegant archways with recessed lighting leading to each wing of the complex.

For an eyeful of Art Deco buildings, take a stroll along the **Grand Concourse**, the west Bronx's four-mile main drag, which stretches from 138th Street to Mosholu Parkway. During the 1930s, when Deco was the rage, the borough experienced a building boom. At the time, the 182-foot-wide boulevard was known as the Champs-Elysées of the Bronx, because of its urban vibe and jazzy designs.

At the Concourse's intersection with 161st Street, you'll find the most eye-catching edifices: **888 Grand Concourse** has a concave entrance of gilded mosaic, topped by a curvy metallic marquee (though it could use a good shine). Inside, the mirrored lobby's central fountain and sunburst-patterned floor give any hotel on Miami's Ocean Drive a run for its money. The nearby **Executive Towers** *(1020 Grand*

**Fishing for a compliment** The mosaic murals at 1150 Grand Concourse exemplify the Art Deco architectural style of the area's building boom during the 1930s.

*Concourse at 165th St)* is a gleaming 1960s high-rise featuring a landscaped forecourt, wave-shaped balconies, a marble entryway and larger-than-life gilded statues. And **1150 Grand Concourse** at 167th Street is bedecked with sawtooth-patterned windows, a marine-themed mosaic entrance, and a circular lobby with mahogany-paneled elevators and painted murals.

The grandest building on the Grand Concourse is the landmark **Andrew Freedman Home**, a 1924 limestone palazzo between McClennan and 166th Streets. In his will, mysterious millionaire Freedman stipulated that the bulk of his $7 million be used to build a retirement home for wealthy people who had fallen on hard times. Today, it still houses the elderly—but a dramatic reversal of fortune is no longer a residency requirement.

The **Bronx Museum of the Arts**, which turned 30 in 2001, is housed in a former synagogue. Peer behind the security counter at the entrance to see a piece of the original wall, with an inscription in Hebrew. The museum focuses on contemporary work, with exhibitions such as "The Commodification of Buddhism," which features works by Asian artists.

The **Hall of Fame for Great Americans**, modeled after Rome's Pantheon, is on the Bronx Community College campus. Designed by Stanford White, it was the country's first-ever hall of fame when it opened in 1901, with the bronze busts of 29 inductees, including George Washington and Ralph Waldo Emerson. The busts are by sculptors such as Daniel Chester French and Augustus Saint-Gaudens. The group that elected additions to the hall disbanded in 1976 (due to lack of funds). The hall is a pleasant enough rotunda, but it isn't a destination in itself.

A ride north on the Bx1 bus will drop you near the Gothic-style campus of **Fordham University** *(441 E Fordham Rd between Washington and Third Aves)*, a Jesuit institution founded in 1841. Some buildings date to 1836, when this was a private estate, including the Greek Revival Rose Hill Administration Building. Call security ahead of time *(718-817-2222)* if you wish to visit; they'll put your name on a list at the gate.

The small wooden farmhouse at East Kingsbridge Road and Grand Concourse is the **Edgar Allan Poe Cottage**, where the writer spent the last years of his life, from 1846 to 1849. It was moved in 1913 from its original location in Fordham village to its present spot and converted to a museum.

The Bronx's population is largely Latino, and nightlife centers around **Jimmy's Bronx Cafe** *(281 W Fordham Rd between Broadway and Cedar Ave, 718-329-2000)*. Jimmy Rodriguez opened the club in an old car dealership off the Major Deegan Expressway. The menu is Caribbean seafood, and weekend salsa nights are a big draw.

Farther north lies Riverdale, one of the city's most beautiful neighborhoods. It sits atop a hill overlooking the Hudson River, and its huge homes on narrow, winding streets have offered privacy to the famous and the obscure. **Wave Hill**, a former private estate that is now a cultural center, is the best-known house in the area. Its illustrious past tenants include Theodore Roosevelt, Arturo Toscanini and Mark Twain. Wave Hill's 28 acres of cultivated gardens and urban woodland provide lovely views of the river. The art gallery shows nature-themed exhibits, and the organization presents concerts and performances year-round, including a dance program in the summer *(see page 127)*.

Some of Riverdale's other high points include the mansion on **Independence Avenue** where the young John F. Kennedy lived *(5040 Independence Ave at 252nd St)* from 1926 to 1928 while attending the nearby Riverdale Country School. Just above 252nd Street is a peak that offers one of the best views of the Hudson River Valley and Riverdale's manors.

If you crave a day outdoors on foot or bike, the Hudson River–hugging **Riverdale Park** *(between 232nd and 254th Sts)* has quiet pathways. Enter this swath of forest preserve at either end of Palisade Avenue. Both meandering roads are dotted with country estates and old barns that have been converted into homes. **Spaulding Lane**, off 248th Street, is blessed with a gurgling stream and waterfall; and on **Ladd Road** (north of 255th Street), three modernist houses sit like serene Buddhas in the woods.

In the 1,100-acre **Van Cortlandt Park** *(Broadway at 249th St)*, cricket teams are a common sight. (To learn about golf in the park, *see* **Still Vanny after all these years**, *page 330*). The **Van Cortlandt House**, a fine example of pre-Revolutionary Georgian architecture, was built by Frederick Van Cortlandt in 1748 as the homestead of his wheat plantation; tours of the luxuriously furnished interior are offered.

For a different perspective on Bronx life, visit **Van Cortlandt Village** and the **Amalgamated and Park Reservoir Houses** *(between Sedgwick Ave and Van Cortlandt Park South, 718-796-9300)*. Nestled between Van Cortlandt Park and Jerome Park Reservoir, this community was founded on socialist principles in 1927. To this day, the 6,000 residents—a mix of old-timers, young families and singletons—buy apartments for an astonishingly low price (a one-bedroom goes for $8,000, with a monthly maintenance fee of $400 to $500) and sell them back to the development, for no profit, when they leave. The picturesque brick apartment blocks and lively playgrounds have made the village a model for cooperative development, a movement that lost steam in the late '60s with the less-idealistic creation of the epic **Co-op City** in the northeast Bronx, which was built to keep the fleeing middle-class tax base in the city.

The **New York Botanical Garden** is the place to enjoy nature at its flowering best. The 250-acre area includes 48 gardens and plant collections, and the last 50 uncut acres of a forest that once covered all of New York City. You can follow winding trails through the unbelievably quiet woods. The Bronx River flows through the property and creates a small waterfall. From March through June, the "Spring at the Garden" exhibit showcases acres of colorful flowers, including snowdrops, daffodils, tulips, irises, anemones and scilla. At the **Enid A. Haupt Conservatory**, which opened in 1902, the "World of Plants" exhibit takes you on an ecotour through tropical, subtropical and desert environments.

The borough's most famous attraction, the **Bronx Zoo**, opened in 1899 and is still the largest urban zoo in the U.S. The highlight is the **Congo Gorilla Forest**—and ultimately, you won't mind the wait and additional fee. In the Gorilla Encounter Tunnel, a glass-encased walkway, you're bound to get close to one of the endangered lowland gorillas. The Skyfari tram is the best way to traverse the 265-acre zoo. If you take the Bengali Express Monorail, try to get a seat in a front car; passengers in the back often can't see what the guide is pointing out, and by the time the train advances, the animals might have moved away.

Head to nearby **Belmont**, a mostly Italian-American neighborhood, after visiting the garden or zoo. It's predominantly residential, but the main street, lively **Arthur Avenue**, is New York's most authentic "little Italy" and the place to go for every edible delicacy. Browse and graze at the **Arthur Avenue Retail Market** *(Crescent Ave at 186th St)*, a bazaar built in the 1940s by former mayor Fiorello La Guardia to get pushcarts off the street. (Take note: The street shuts down on Sunday.) Inside is **Mike's Deli** *(2344 Arthur Ave between 183rd and 186th Sts, 718-295-5033)*, where Italian men ply you with compliments and prosciutto (get the trademark *schiacciata* sandwich of grilled vegetables). At the **Arthur Avenue Café** *(2329 Arthur Ave between 185th and 186th Sts, 718-562-0129)*, sip an espresso that blows Starbucks' away. The observant eye can still pick out Belmont's old-world traces. A sunken garden peeks from behind the houses on tiny Adams Place between Crescent Avenue and Grote Street, and the shrubs and trees surrounding **Pizza Margherita** *(673 E 187th St at Cambreleng Ave, 718-295-2902)* make the spot seem more like a Capri cliffside eatery than a pizzeria on a busy Bronx street.

Not far away is New York's own little Lourdes. At **St. Lucy's Roman Catholic Church** *(833 Mace Ave at Bronxwood Ave, 718-882-0710)*, people line up to take water from Our Lady of Lourdes Grotto, opened in 1939. The faithful believe that the water has healing powers, even though it comes from the city's public water supply. (By the way, the church makes no claims about the water.)

**Hunts Point**, to the south, may look like an industrial wasteland, but it's where grocers, butchers and top restaurateurs arrive at the crack of dawn to buy wholesale produce and meat. **New York City Terminal Market** *(234–237 Hunts Point Ave at Halleck St, 718-542-4115)* is the city's largest produce emporium and **Hunts Point Cooperative Market** *(355 Food Center Dr at Halleck St, 718-842-7466)* sells meat. In 2004, the famous **Fulton Fish Market** *(see page 66)* will also move to Hunt's Point. These markets are open to the public (but you can only buy in bulk). The rest of Hunts Point is accessible by subway, but the markets are best visited by car—one with a big trunk.

A new arts movement is germinating in Hunts Point. In 1994, artists converted a 12,000-square-foot industrial building to create **The Point** *(940 Garrison Ave at Manida St, 718-542-4139; www.thepoint.org)*, a performance space, gallery and business incubator. The arts-and-advocacy center holds a monthly break-dancing performance called "Breakbeats," and leads a weekly walking tour, "Mambo to Hip-Hop," that covers the history of locally born music genres.

## BEST VIEW Nature in the Bronx

**From New York Botanical Garden Café**

Bronx Borough Historian Lloyd Ultan knows the area's highs and lows. His favorite view in the borough is in the middle of the Botanical Garden *(see above)*. From the patio behind the restaurant, look across the Bronx River Gorge. Within the pristine forest, you'll spot a sheer rock face and rushing rapids.

**Slippery when wet** Aristide Maillol's *The River* is part of an exhibition of MoMA sculptures on display at the New York Botanical Garden through August 2003.

At **BAAD!**, the Bronx Academy of Arts and Dance, creative types stage performances and more than a dozen painters and sculptors work in its studios. BAAD! annually presents "BAAD! Ass Women," a celebration of works by women; the "Boogie Down Dance Series," a spring festival of dance; and "Out Like That," a gay and lesbian arts festival.

For music of a more traditional—and spiritual—kind, visit the **Corpus Christi Monastery** on Sunday morning for Mass or in the afternoon, when the cloistered Dominican nuns sing the office. During the music-filled services, the 1889 church is lit mostly by candles which cast lovely shadows on the mosaic floor.

The Bronx is also home to the city's biggest bucolic playground: **Pelham Bay Park**, a sprawling wilderness in the northeast corner of the borough. You're best off with a car or bike if you want to explore the 2,765 acres, once home to the Siwonay Indians. Pick up a map at the **Ranger Nature Center** (near the entrance on Bruckner Blvd at Wilkinson Ave) in the park's southern zone. You can also visit the **Bartow-Pell Mansion** on the southeastern part of the park. Inside this 1830s Greek Revival manor, rooms are furnished as they were in the 19th century. Maintained by the International Garden Club since 1914, the mansion's grounds include gardens, a fountain and a carriage house.

For shore lovers, the park offers 13 miles of coastline, which wends along the Hutchinson River to the west and Long Island Sound and Eastchester Bay to the east. In summer, locals crowd man-made **Orchard Beach**. Created by city planner **Robert Moses** in the 1930s (the sand came from New Jersey and Queens), this salty crescent has been called the Riviera of the Bronx. Grills and picnic tables line the woods next to the parking lot (which costs $6 per day).

Perhaps the most unexpected section of the Bronx is **City Island**, a small isle on Long Island Sound that's about 45 minutes by train and bus from midtown Manhattan. Settled in 1685, it was once a prosperous shipbuilding center with a busy fishing industry. Now it offers New Yorkers a slice of New England–style recreation—it's packed with marinas, seafood restaurants, nautical-themed bars, six yacht clubs and a couple of sail makers. Join the crowds at **Johnny's Famous Reef Restaurant** *(2 City Island Ave at Belden's Pt, 718-885-2086)* for steamed clams, a cold beer and nice views.

Although few commercial fishermen remain, you'd hardly know that when walking into the

**Georgian on my mind** Contemplate pre-Revolutionary architecture at 1748 Van Cortlandt House.

Boat Livery *(663 City Island Ave at Bridge St, 718-885-1843),* a bait-and-tackle shop and bar. The place has changed so little over the past decades that the boat-rental price painted next to the door still reads $2 PER DAY. The bar, locally known as the Worm Hole, serves $1 beers (in plastic cups) that you can drink on the dock while you watch boats return at sunset.

You'll also find one of the city's best record stores—the two-story **Moon Curser Records** *(229 City Island Ave between Centre and Schofield Sts, 718-885-0302).* Octogenarian owner Roger Roberge does a remarkable job of schooling his customers in jazz, Latin jazz, salsa, merengue, soul and funk. He doesn't carry CDs or cassettes, only vinyl and sheet music. You'll likely walk away from the store with hot music you would have never thought to buy.

## Bartow-Pell Mansion

*895 Shore Rd North at Pelham Bay Park (718-885-1461). Travel: 6 to Pelham Bay Park, then W45 bus (ask driver to stop at the Bartow-Pell Mansion; bus does not run on Sunday), or take a cab from the subway station. Wed, Sat, Sun noon–4pm. $2.50, $1.25 seniors and students, under 12 free. Cash only.*

## Bronx Academy of Arts and Dance (BAAD!)

*841 Barretto St between Garrison and Lafayette Aves (718-842-5223; www.bronxacademyofartsanddance.org). Subway: 6 to Hunts Point Ave. Hours and prices vary by event.*

## Bronx County Historical Society Museum

*Valentine-Varian House, 3266 Bainbridge Ave between Van Cortlandt Ave and 208th St (718-881-8900; www.bronxhistoricalsociety.org).*

*Subway: D to Norwood–205th St. Mon–Fri for group tours by appointment only; Sat 10am–4pm; Sun 1–5pm. $3, seniors and students $2.*
This 1758 fieldstone house is a fine example of the pre-Revolutionary Federal style.

### Bronx Museum of the Arts

*1040 Grand Concourse at 165th St (718-681-6000). Subway: B, D, 4 to 161st St–Yankee Stadium. Wed noon–9pm; Thu–Sun noon–6pm. $5, seniors and students $3, under 12 free.*

### Bronx Zoo/Wildlife Conservation Society

*Bronx River Pkwy at Fordham Rd (718-367-1010; www.bronxzoo.org). Subway: 2 to Pelham Parkway, 5 to E 180th St. Apr–Oct Mon–Fri 10am–5pm; Sat, Sun, holidays 10am–5:30pm. Nov–Mar 10am–4:30pm. $11, seniors $7, under 12 $6. Wednesdays free. Some rides and exhibitions are $2–$3 extra. Cash only.*

### City Island

*Travel: 6 to Pelham Bay Park, then Bx29 bus to City Island. Call the City Island Chamber of Commerce (718-885-9100; www.cityisland.com) for information about events and activities.*

### Corpus Christi Monastery

*1230 Lafayette Ave at Barretto St (718-328-6996). Subway: 6 to Hunts Point Ave. Morning prayer 6am, Mass 7:15am, night prayer 5, 7pm; Sun Mass 8:15am.*

### Edgar Allan Poe Cottage

*Grand Concourse at Kingsbridge Rd (718-881-8900). Subway: B, D, 4 to Kingsbridge Rd. Sat 10am–4pm; Sun 1–5pm. $3, seniors and students $2.*

### Grand Concourse

*Between 138th St and Mosholu Pkwy. Subway: 4 to 149 St–Grand Concourse or 161st St–Yankee Stadium.*

### Hall of Fame for Great Americans

*Bronx Community College, University Ave at 181st St, Hall of Fame Terrace. Travel: B, D to 182nd–183rd Sts; 4 to 183rd St. 10am–5pm. Free.*

### New York Botanical Garden

*Bronx River Parkway at Fordham Rd (718-817-8700; www.nybg.org). Travel: B, D, 4 to Bedford Park Blvd, then Bx26 bus; Metro-North Harlem Line local from Grand Central Terminal to New York Botanical Garden. Apr–Oct Tue–Sun, Monday holidays 10am–6pm. Nov–Mar Tue–Sun 10am–4pm. $3, seniors and students $2, children $1, under 2 free. Wed all day, Sat 10am–noon free. Cash only.*
The basic $3 fee only allows access to the grounds. The $10 Garden Passport also includes admission to the adventure garden and conservatory. A one-way Metro-North ticket is $3.50 to $4.75 (depending on time of day), or purchase a $14 Getaway ticket, which includes round-trip travel plus a Garden Passport.

### Pelham Bay Park

*718-430-1890. Subway: 6 to Pelham Bay Park.*

### Van Cortlandt House Museum

*Van Cortlandt Park, Broadway at 246nd St, Riverdale (718-543-3344). Subway: 1, 9 to 242nd St–Van Cortlandt Park. Tue–Fri 10am–3pm; Sat, Sun 11am–4pm. $2, seniors and students $1.50, under 12 free. Cash only.*

### Wave Hill

*249th St at Independence Ave (718-549-3200; www.wavehill.org). Travel: Metro-North Hudson Line local from Grand Central Terminal to Riverdale. Apr 15–Oct 14 Tue, Thu–Sun 9am–5:30pm; Jun, Jul Wed 9am–9pm. Oct 15–Apr 14 Tue–Sun 9am–4:30pm. Open Memorial Day, Labor Day and Columbus Day 9am–5:30pm. $4, seniors and students $2, under 6 free. Tue, Sat 9am–noon free. Nov 15–Mar 14 free. Cash only.*

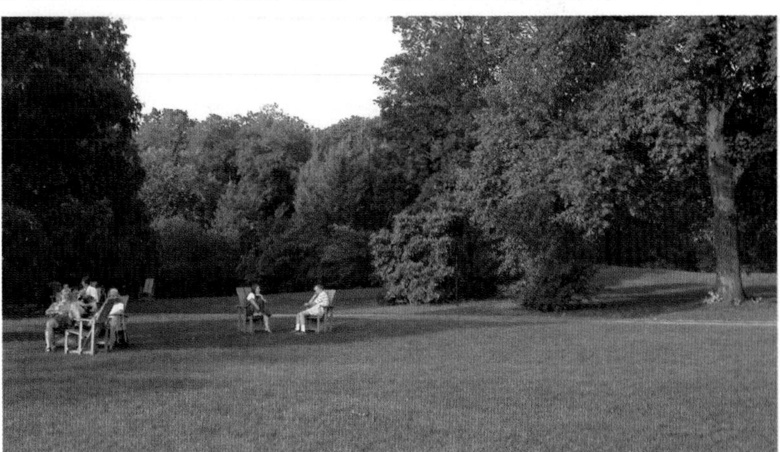

**Catch the wave** If the weather is nice, you can relax on the lawn at Wave Hill in Riverdale.

Sightseeing

# Staten Island

Looking for tranquil beaches, lush parks and historic houses? Hop a ferry to New York's most overlooked borough.



Staten Island has a love-hate relationship with the rest of the city—with the emphasis on hate. Residents continue to accuse City Hall of taking their taxes to pay for the rest of New York's problems, and giving them nothing in return but garbage. (The infamous Fresh Kills landfill is one of the world's largest man-made structures—it closed in early 2001, only to be reopened to receive rubble from the World Trade Center.) Driving through Staten Island's tree-lined suburbs, with their open spaces and vast parks, one can understand why many of its inhabitants are so eager to bail out on the other boroughs.

Staten Island was one of the first places in North America to be settled by Europeans. Giovanni da Verrazano sailed into the Narrows—the body of water separating the island from Brooklyn—in 1524, and his name graces the suspension bridge that connects the two boroughs today. Henry Hudson christened the island "Staaten Eylandt" (Dutch for "State's Island") in 1609. The Duke of York sponsored a sailing competition in 1687, with Staten Island as the prize. The Manhattan representatives won the race, and since then, it has been governed from Gotham.

You reach the island from Manhattan via the **Staten Island Ferry** *(see page 132)*. The free ride from lower Manhattan passes by the Statue of Liberty before sailing into the St. George ferry terminal, next to which sits the **Richmond County Bank Ballpark**, home to the **Staten Island Yankees** *(see* **Treasure island**, *page 130)*. Like the Bronx, the borough has a zoo; it's much smaller and less expensive but perfect for families with young children. **The Staten Island Zoo**'s Children's Center is modeled after a New England farm and features domestic farm animals from around the globe.

The **Snug Harbor Cultural Center**, opened in 1833, was originally a maritime hospital and a home for retired sailors. It comprises 26 buildings—grand examples of various periods of American architecture—in an 83-acre park. In 1976, the city took over the site and converted it into a cultural center, which now sponsors exhibitions and hosts arts events. Near the lighthouse at the island's highest point is the **Jacques Marchais Museum of Tibetan Art** *(see page 56)*, a collection of art and cultural treasures from the Far East. Its Buddhist temple is one of New York's most tranquil sanctuaries.

**Historic Richmond Town** is a large museum of 28 restored buildings, some dating back to the 17th century. Many of the buildings have been moved here from elsewhere on the island. Visit the courthouse, general store, bakery and tinsmith, as well as private homes.

During the Revolutionary War, Billop House (now **Conference House**) was the site of a failed peace conference between the Americans, led by Benjamin Franklin and John Adams, and England's Lord Howe. The 1680 building, which is the oldest manor house in New York City, has been turned into a museum featuring Colonial furniture and (it is said) a few ghosts. If you need a history break, head to adjacent **Tottenville Beach**; the sandy shore is perfect for sunbathing or a late-afternoon stroll.

If all the fresh air makes you hungry, Staten Island has a number of notable dining options. **Denino's** *(524 Port Richmond Ave between Hooker Pl and Walker St, 718-442-9401)* in Port Richmond bakes one of the best pizzas in New York City. To sample eclectic, seasonal cuisine, make a reservation at the popular **Aesop's Tables** *(1233 Bay St at Maryland Ave, 718-720-2005)*. **The Parsonage** *(74 Arthur Kill Rd at Clarke Ave, 718-351-7879)* offers sedate country dining in an 1855 house.

## BEST VIEW Cool cottage

**From Alice Austen House**

Take in the panoramic vista of Upper New York Bay from the front lawn of this Victorian cottage. Once the home of photographer Alice Austen, the place now displays her trove of 3,000 glass-plate negatives depicting life during the late 19th and early 20th centuries.

*2 Hylan Blvd between Bay and Edgewater Sts (718-816-4506). Staten Island Ferry, then S51 bus to Hylan Blvd. Mar–Dec Thu–Sun noon–5pm (closed major holidays). $2 suggested donation.*

**Cozy cove** Snug Harbor Cultural Center showcases both contemporary art and historic American architecture.

### Conference House (Billop House)

*7455 Hylan Blvd at Craig Ave (718-984-2086). Travel: Staten Island Ferry, then S78 bus to Craig Ave. Apr 1–Dec 15 Fri–Sun 1–4pm. $3, seniors and children $2.*

### Historic Richmond Town

*441 Clarke Ave between Arthur Kill and Richmond Rds (718-351-1611). Travel: Staten Island Ferry, then S74 bus to St. Patrick's Pl. Sept–Jun Wed–Sun 1–5pm. Jul–Aug Mon, Wed–Sat 10am–5pm; Sun 1–5pm. $5, seniors $4, under 18 $3.50, under 5 free. Cash only.*

Seven houses are open to the public, including Guyon-Lake-Tysen House, a wooden farmhouse with Dutch and Flemish influences, built in 1740 for a French Huguenot. During summer, actors dressed in 19th-century garb linger in the doorways, ready to answer questions about the site.

### Staten Island Zoo

*614 Broadway between Forest Ave and Victory Blvd (718-442-3100; www.statenislandzoo.org). Travel: Staten Island Ferry, then S48 bus to Broadway. 10am–4:45pm. $5, seniors $4, children 3–15 $3, Wednesdays after 2pm free. Cash only.*

## Snug Harbor Cultural Center

The complex includes **The Newhouse Center for Contemporary Art**, which exhibits post-1945 art with a special emphasis on Staten Island and underrecognized artists. You can attend films and spoken-word performances in the 200-seat Veterans Memorial Hall, or hear chamber music, jazz and opera in the Music Hall, the city's second-oldest music venue (built in 1892). There are also a number of affiliated organizations on the grounds of the Cultural Center complex, including the **Art Lab**, the **John A. Noble Maritime Collection**, the **Staten Island Botanical Garden** and the **Staten Island Children's Museum**.

### Snug Harbor Cultural Center

*1000 Richmond Terr (718-448-2500, 718-815-SNUG for tickets; www.snug-harbor.org) Travel: Staten Island Ferry, then Snug Harbor trolley or S40 bus to Snug Harbor Rd. Grounds dawn–dusk free. Galleries Jun 1–Sept 1 Mon–Fri 11am–5pm; Sat 11am–7pm; Sun 11am–5pm. Sept 2–May 31 Wed–Sun 11am–5pm. $2, senior $1, under 10 free. AmEx, MC, V. Music Hall call or check website for concert show times and prices.*

### The Art Lab

*Building H (718-447-8667). Mon 4–8pm; Tue–Thu 10am–8pm; Fri–Sun 10am–5pm. Gallery admission free; life-drawing class (Thu 7–10pm) $9. MC, V.*

This nonprofit gallery and art school features local artists and offers classes in fine arts, crafts, graphics and photography for all ages. Courses run for ten weeks, but Thursday's life-drawing workshop accepts walk-in students who wish to attend a single class.

### The John A. Noble Maritime Collection

*Building D (718-447-6490; www.noblemaritime.org). Thu–Sun 1–5pm. $3, seniors and students $2, under 10 free. AmEx, MC, V.*

Housed in one of the former dormitories for retired sailors, this collection showcases maritime art.

### The Staten Island Botanical Garden

*Building H, visitors' center (718-273-8200; www.sibg.org). Dawn–dusk. Grounds admission free, certain gardens $1–$5. AmEx, MC, V.*

The Staten Island Botanical Garden includes the Chinese Scholar's Garden; the White Garden, inspired by Vita Sackville-West's garden at Sissinghurst Castle, in England; and the Secret Garden, complete with a child-size castle, maze and walled garden.

### The Staten Island Children's Museum

*(718-273-2060). Sept 2–Jul 4 Tue–Sun noon–5pm; Jul 5–Sept 1 Tue–Sun 11am–5pm. $5, under 1 free. Wednesdays seniors free. AmEx, Disc, MC, V.*

## CRITICS' PICKS Treasure island

Two more reasons to head across the water to Staten Island.

### Staten Island Yankees Baseball at Richmond County Bank Ballpark

*75 Richmond Terr at Bay St Staten Island (718-720-YANKS). Travel: Staten Island Ferry to St. George Terminal. Jun–Sept. $8, $10.*

The Single A affiliate of the Major League Yankees has achieved nearly the same level of success as its parent team, winning league championships in 2000 and 2002. Catch a pop foul at the beautiful new stadium of the "Baby Bombers."

### Wildlife trails at High Rock Park

*200 Nevada Ave between High Rock Park and Rockland Ave (718-667-2165). Travel: Staten Island Ferry, then S74 bus to Rockland Ave and walk or take S57 to Nevada Ave. Park 9am–dusk; Visitors' center Mon–Fri 9am–5pm.*

This 90-acre park is part of the Greenbelt, Staten Island's 2,800 acres of parkland. Hike the mile-long Swamp Trail; climb Todt Hill, the highest natural point on the Eastern seaboard between Maine and Miami; or explore three gardens, each planted with unique species.

# Tour New York

By bike, boat, bus or on foot, New York City will thrill you at every turn

There are 8 million stories in the naked city, and almost as many ways to explore it. New York is a mosaic of cultures and people, and offers a kaleidoscope of tours to show them off. Gaze at the towering silver spires by boat, glide through the Central Park greenery by bike, or lace up your tennies and explore the city's historic neighborhoods on foot. New York has to be seen to be believed—here's how to view it up close.

## By bicycle

For more city biking, see page 327.

### Bike the Big Apple

*877-865-0078; toursbybike.com. Fri–Sun 10am–2pm. Mon–Thu by appointment only. $49–$79, includes bicycle and helmet rental fee. Custom tours by appointment. Call or visit website for meeting locations. AmEx, DC, Disc, MC, V.*

Licensed guides Bruce, Joel and Keith treat cyclists to gently paced, half- and full-day rides through New York's neighborhoods. See the leaves change color on the "Foliage Tour," or stop off for the city's best Italian ice on a tour of Queens. Check the website's calendar for seasonal events.

### Central Park Bicycle Tours

*Meet outside 2 Columbus Circle, Broadway at 59th St (212-541-8759; www.centralparkbiketour.com). Subway: A, C, B, D, 1, 9 to 59th St–Columbus Circle. Apr–Dec 10am, 1, 4pm. Jan–Mar by appointment only. $35, under 15 $20, includes bicycle rental fee. AmEx, Disc, MC, V.*

This leisurely two-hour tour visits the John Lennon memorial at Strawberry Fields, Belvedere Castle and other Central Park attractions. There's plenty of rest time when the guide stops to talk, and Spanish-language tours are available. Film buffs will enjoy the two-hour "Central Park Movie Scenes Bike Tour," and hard-core bikers should consider the three-hour Manhattan Island Bicycle Tour ($45, weekends by appointment only, ten-person minimum).

**Yankee clipper** Circle Line cruises offers remarkable views of the New York skyline.

## By boat

### Bateaux New York

*Chelsea Piers, Pier 62, 23rd St at West Side Hwy (212-352-2022, 866-211-3806; www.bateauxnewyork.com). Subway: C, E to 23rd St. Memorial Day–Labor Day noon–2pm, 8–11pm. Sept–May noon–2pm, 7–10pm Lunch cruises $46; dinner cruises $103–$117. AmEx, DC, Disc, MC, V.*

Savor your meal against a skyline backdrop while traveling in a glass-covered vessel. The à la carte American menu has French and Mediterranean influences. After dinner, you can shake it to Broadway, jazz and blues tunes on the dance floor. Tax and service charges are included in the prices. Call or check website for a complete schedule and updated cruise information.

### Circle Line Cruises

*Pier 83, 42nd St at Twelfth Ave (212-563-3200; www.circleline.com). Subway: A, C, E to 42nd St–Port Authority. Three-hour tour $25, seniors $20, under 12 $12; evening cruise $20, seniors $17, under 12 $10; speedboat $16, children $10. Call or visit website for schedule. AmEx, DC, Disc, MC, V.*

Circle Line's three-hour circumnavigation of Manhattan is one of the best and cheapest ways to take in the city's sights. You can behold midtown's urban jungle, or watch Columbia University's rowing teams practicing in their sculls. A two-hour cruise sticks to lower and mid-Manhattan (the "harbor lights" version sails at sunset from May to October). For a quick adventure (April to October), there's a roaringly fun 30-minute ride on a speedboat called the *Beast*. Call or check website for departures.

► If you plan on visiting several museums *and* taking one of the boat tours, see **Cheap tix**, page 46, for reduced-fare passes.

► To explore Manhattan's shoreline by kayak, see page 330.

Sightseeing

**Other location** • *South Street Seaport, Pier 16, South St between Burling Slip and Fulton St (212-563-3200). Subway: A, C to Broadway–Nassau St; J, M, Z, 2, 3, 4, 5 to Fulton St. Mid-Mar–Dec one-hour cruise $13, seniors $11, children $7; speedboat $16, children $10. May–Sept two-hour live-music and DJ party cruises $20–$40. Call or visit website for schedule. AmEx, DC, Disc, MC, V.*

Sightseeing

### New York Water Taxi

*Fulton Ferry Landing, Brooklyn (212-742-1969; www.nywatertaxi.com). Subway: A, C to High St; 2, 3 to Clark St. Mon–Fri 6:30am–7pm; Sat, Sun 11am–8pm. $3–$8. All-day pass: $15, seniors and children under 12 $12. AmEx, MC, V.*

If you can't find a cab, fear not—hope floats. The city's newest taxi is still yellow and checkered, but it glides on the water, offers great views, and even has a small café and bar. Launched in September 2002, New York Water Taxis run weeklong, with services in lower Manhattan and Brooklyn during rush hours and expanded service on the west side at midday and on weekends. Tickets for casual travel are sold on the landings and on the boats. Call or visit website for schedules and fares.

**Other locations** • *Pier A, Battery Park. Subway: 1, 9 to South Ferry; N, R, W to Whitehall St; 4, 5 to Bowling Green.* • *North Cove Marina, Battery Park. Subway: A, C, 1, 2, 3, 9 to Chambers St; E to World Trade Ctr; N, R, W to Cortlandt St.* • *Pier 11, Wall St at the East River. Subway: 2, 3 to Wall St; J, M, Z to Broad St.* • *Chelsea Piers, Pier 62, W 22nd St at the Hudson River. Subway: C, E to 23rd St.* • *Pier 84, W 44th St at the Hudson River. Subway: A, C, E to 42nd St–Port Authority.*

### NY Waterway

*Pier 78, 38th St at West Side Hwy (800-53-FERRY; www.nywaterway.com). Subway: A, C, E to 42nd St–Port Authority. Call for seasonal schedule. Ninety-minute New York Harbor cruise: $19, seniors $16, children $9. AmEx, Disc, MC, V.*

For a concise, scenic overview of downtown, take this guided 90-minute cruise; the close-up of Lady Liberty is worth the price alone. Or choose the two-hour ride for a complete circuit of Manhattan. From May to September, twilight cruises are available, as are all-day sightseeing tours up the Hudson.

**Other location** • *South Street Seaport, Pier 17, South St at Beekman St. Subway: A,C to Broadway–Nassau St; J, M, Z, 2, 3, 4, 5 to Fulton St.*

### Staten Island Ferry

*South St at Whitehall St (718-727-2508; www.siferry.com). Subway: 1, 9 to South Ferry; 4, 5 to Bowling Green. 24 hours. Free.*

The poor man's Circle Line is plenty of fun, provided you bring the one you love. No-cost (and unguided) panoramas of lower Manhattan and the Statue of Liberty turn a trip on this commuter barge into a romantic sojourn—especially at sunset. True, Staten Island isn't as sexy as Manhattan, but it has a great personality. Boats depart South Ferry at Battery Park throughout the day. Call or visit the website for a schedule and updated information.


► Follow the path of your favorite writer by joining one of the literary walking tours on page 268.

► For more information on New York walking tours, see the Around Town section of ***Time Out New York***.


### World Yacht

*Pier 81, 41st St at West Side Hwy (212-630-8100; www.worldyacht.com). Subway: A, C, E to 42nd St–Port Authority. Call for seasonal schedule. $41.90–$79. AmEx, Disc, MC, V.*

If you're not interested in a guided boat tour, then a three-hour dinner or two-hour brunch cruise around lower Manhattan will let you enjoy the sights while you linger over a meal. Even though "The Best of New York" menu was designed by such renowned chefs as David Burke, Christian Delouvrier, Andrew DiCataldo and Todd English, you can tell that they aren't supervising the preparations (which are made off-boat and warmed after the boat sets sail).

## By bus or limo

### D3 Busline

*212-533-1664; www.d3busline.com. Call for meeting locations and times. Fri, Sat. $60. AmEx, MC, V.*

This isn't your grandma's double-decker. A night out on D3's "trans-lounge limo bus" includes an open bar, a DJ and VIP entrance into select Manhattan hot spots. The service is also available for private functions and corporate rentals.

### Gray Line

*777 Eighth Ave between 47th and 48th Sts (800-669-0051; www.graylinenewyork.com). Subway: A, C, E to 42nd St–Port Authority. 7:30am–7:30pm. $35–$79. AmEx, Disc, MC, V.*

Gray Line offers more than 20 bus tours, from a basic two-hour ride to the monster "Manhattan Comprehensive," which lasts eight-and-a-half hours and includes a three-course lunch in Times Square. Call or visit the website for a schedule and prices.

**Other location** • *Times Square Visitors' Center, Broadway between 46th and 47th Sts (800-669-0051). Subway: N, R, W to 49th St; 1, 9 to 50th St. 7:30am–5:30pm. $35–$79. AmEx, Disc, MC, V.*

### Limo Tours

*212-779-1122; www.limotours.com. Call for meeting location. Tours 8:30am, 1pm. Reservations required. $60. AmEx, MC, V.*

Notwithstanding their association with proms, limos mean luxury—at least they do at Limo Tours. Among many options is the four-hour "VIP Grand Limo Tour," which covers Manhattan from Battery Park to Harlem, and makes several stops, including Central Park's Strawberry Fields and Grant's Tomb. There's also a stop near the Brooklyn Bridge that offers a great photo op of lower Manhattan.

**Don't pay the ferryman** Passengers on the Staten Island Ferry ride for free.

## By copter, carriage or rickshaw

### Liberty Helicopter Tours

*VIP Heliport, West Side Hwy at 30th St (212-967-4550; www.libertyhelicopters.com). Subway: A, C, E to 34th St–Penn Station. 9am–9pm. Reservations required. $49–$275. AmEx, MC, V.*

If you blanch at the thought of a bumpy ride in a small, wind-whipped chopper, have no fear. The Liberty helicopters are larger than most, and provide a fairly smooth flight. Durations vary, but even the shortest ride (five minutes) is long enough to get a thrilling close-up view of the Statue of Liberty.

### Manhattan Carriage Company

*200 Central Park South at Seventh Ave (212-664-1149). Subway: B, D, E to Seventh Ave; N, Q, R, W to 57th St. 10am–2am. $40 per 20-minute ride. Extended rides must be prebooked. Hours and prices vary during holidays. AmEx, MC, V.*

The beauty of Central Park is even more romantic from the seat of a horse-drawn carriage. (First, visit www.aspca.org/media/carriagehorse.pdf to learn how to make the ride as humane as it is quaint.)

### Manhattan Rickshaw Company

*212-604-4729; www.manhattanrickshaw.com. $20 minimum fare for prearranged pickups. Cash only.*

Manhattan Rickshaw's pedicabs operate primarily around the Empire State Building and Times Square, but they're also in Soho and Greenwich Village. If you see one that's available, hail the driver. (Fares start at $8 and are determined before the ride.) For a prearranged pickup, make reservations at least 24 hours in advance.

## By foot—walking tours

### Big Apple Greeter

*1 Centre St at Chambers St, suite 2035 (212-669-8159; www.bigapplegreeter.org). Subway: J, M, Z to Chambers St; 4, 5, 6 to Brooklyn Bridge–City Hall. Mon–Fri 9:30am–5pm; recorded information at other times. Free.*

The guides at Big Apple Greeter don't want you to merely enjoy New York—they want you to fall in love with it. Instead of herding groups from corner to corner, the program introduces visitors to one of 500 friendly volunteers, giving adventurers a chance to see the city that lies beyond the tourist traps. Visit Vinny's mom in Bensonhurst, or have Renata show you around Polish Greenpoint. The service is free, conducted in any of several languages, and can be tailored to visitors with disabilities. Call or write *(1 Center St, suite 2035, New York, NY 10007)* three to four weeks in advance to book yourself a New York pal.

### ChinatownNYC.com Walking Tours

*Tour meets at Kim Lau Memorial Arch, Chatham Sq (212-571-2016; www.chinatownnyc.com). Subway: J, M, Z to Chambers St; 4, 5, 6 to Brooklyn Bridge–City Hall. Wed 9am. $15. Cash only.*

Irrepressible Jami Gong, an aspiring actor-comic and licensed guide, gives an insider's tour of Chinatown, where he was born and raised. He's happy to customize group tours that include a feast at one of Chinatown's many restaurants. Call or register online.

### Foods of New York Walking and Tasting Tours

*Tour meets on Bleecker St between Sixth and Seventh Aves (212-239-8561; www.foodsofny.com). Subway: 1, 9 to Christopher St–Sheridan Sq. Tue–Sun 11am–2pm. Reservations required. Call for schedule. $35, all tastings included. AmEx, Disc, MC, V.*

On these delicious outings, your food-savvy guide walks you through some of the best restaurants and food shops in Greenwich Village. Rocco's Bakery, Joe's Pizza and the eateries of Cornelia Street are typical destinations. Arrive hungry—you'll sample at least nine different foods.

### Greenwich Village Pub Crawl

*New Ensemble Theatre Company (212-613-5796). Tour meets at the White Horse Tavern, 567 Hudson St at 11th St. Subway: 1, 9 to Christopher St–Sheridan Sq. Sat 2pm. $15, seniors and students $9. Reservations requested.*

Local actors from the New Ensemble Theatre Company lead you through the haunts of famous writers. Stops include Chumley's (a former speakeasy) and the Cornelia Street Cafe. Imbiber beware: The ticket price does not include drinks.

### Harlem Heritage Tours

*230 W 116th St between Malcolm X Blvd (Lenox Ave) and Adam Clayton Powell Jr. Blvd (Seventh Ave), suite 5C (212-280-7888; www.harlemheritage.com). $10–$95. Call for times and locations. AmEx, MC, V.*

Now operating 30 different tours, Harlem Heritage

Sightseeing

…e soul of Harlem. On Friday and …gs, "Jazz Nights in Harlem" features …as the Apollo Theater and the Hotel …ed by dinner at Sylvia's and live music at a ja… The Sunday "Harlem Gospel Walking Tour" takes in a Baptist church service with gospel music, a tour of churches and lunch.

### Municipal Art Society Tours

*457 Madison Ave between 50th and 51st Sts (212-935-3960, recorded information 212-439-1049; www.mas.org). Subway: E, V to Fifth Ave–53rd St; 6 to 51st St. Call or visit website for meeting locations, prices and schedule. AmEx, MC, V.*

The society organizes informative tours, including hikes in Greenwich Village, Murray Hill and Park Slope. It also offers a free tour of Grand Central Terminal on Wednesdays at 12:30pm and private tours by appointment.

### New York City Cultural Walking Tours

*212-979-2388; www.nycwalk.com. Public tour Sun 2pm. $10, $30 per hour for a private individual or group tour. Cash only.*

Alfred Pommer's tours explore the architecture and history of many New York neighborhoods—Soho, Little Italy, Murray Hill, Upper East Side. Call or visit website for meeting locations of public tours.

### New York Curmudgeon Tours

*400 W 43rd St at Ninth Ave, suite 27M (212-629-8813; users.erols.com/wawalters/curmudgeon). Mar–Nov Sat, Sun 10am.Call or visit website for meeting locations. $20. Cash only.*

Bill Walters, a seasoned theater professional, guides you past many of New York's famous Broadway theaters, from those on 42nd Street to the Ed Sullivan, home to Late Show with David Letterman. He brings the city's entertainment scene to life by combining an insider's personal experience with historical tidbits.

### NYC Discovery Walking Tours

*212-465-3331. Sat, Sun. Call for meeting locations and schedule. $12, food tour $17. Cash only.*

These two-hour weekend walking tours come in six varieties: American history (American Revolution to Civil War), biography (George Washington to John Lennon), culture (art to baseball), indoor winter tours (for example, "The Secrets of Grand Central"), neighborhood (Soho to the Upper West Side), and tasting-and-tavern (food-and-drink landmarks). The company has 75 year-round selections; private tours are available by appointment.

### Rock & Roll Walking Tour

*Rock Junket NYC (212-696-6578; www.rockjunket.com). Check website for meeting locations. Sat 1pm. $20. Cash only.*

Rocker tour guides Bobby Pinn and Ginger Ail lead this East Village walking tour of legendary rock, punk and glam sites from the 1960s to the present.

### Wall Street Walking Tour

*Tour meets at U.S. Custom House, 1 Bowling Green between State and Whitehall Sts (212-606-4064). Subway: N, R, W to Whitehall St; 4, 5 to Bowling Green. Thu, Sat noon. Free.*

Explore Wall Street's wealth of history with this free 90-minute tour. The guides and routes change weekly. Destinations typically include the New York Stock Exchange, Trinity Church and Ground Zero.

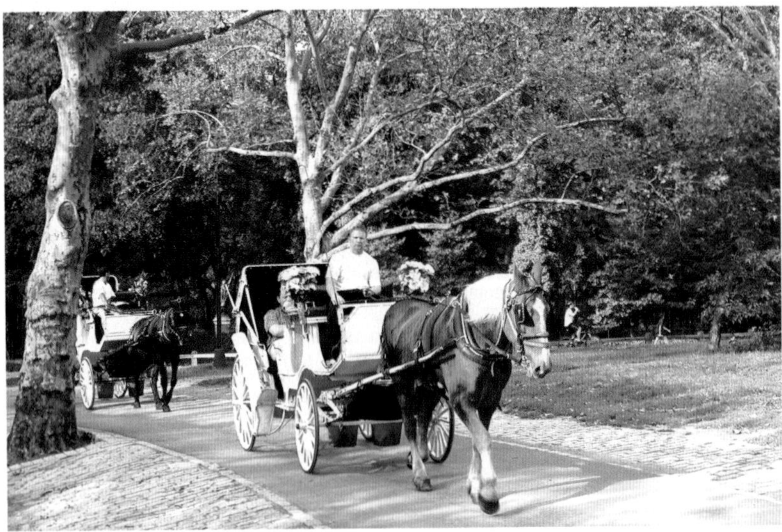

**Once around the park** A carriage tour is a lovely way to see Manhattan's greener pastures.

# Necessities



## Feature boxes



**Take your licks** Dylan's Candy Bar is a sugar rush for kids of every age.

# Accommodations

Room rates are rising, but trenchant travelers can still score savings

"If you build it, they will come" could have been the mantra of hoteliers in 2000, when it was difficult to find a place to stay in New York, and rates averaged $250 a night. Prices and occupancy fell, along with the economy, in early 2001. September 11 further lowered (by a tenth) that year's average occupancy rate to 73 percent (still high compared to many other cities), and the median room rate dropped to $192.

Bookings started picking up again by the end of 2001. The prices quoted here, while not guaranteed, give a good estimate of what you can expect if you call a particular hotel. And if you know how and where to look, there are slashed room rates, package deals and special promotions available.

Most high-end hotels publicize only their "rack rates," hoping that if occupancy is bad (and thus availability is good) their potential customers will be pleasantly surprised when they receive a better price than they anticipated. So when you're contacting a hotel to inquire about costs, make sure to ask about special promotions and package deals. In the worst-case scenario, you'll be met with a scoff; in the best case, you'll score a bargain. It's still a renter's market, so you may be able to make the economy's pain your gain.

Start your hotel search by choosing an area that interests you. Each neighborhood offers a variety of distinctive places to stay *(see* **Hill street news**, *page 154)*. New York has the greatest proportion of small-chain and independent hotels of any big city in the country, with nearly half of its properties unaffiliated with a national or international chain. Spearheaded by stylish boutique hotels such as Ian Schrager's Morgans (which opened in 1985), the indie-hotel movement has a strong presence in Manhattan.

While the current air of competition within the industry works in your favor, finding holiday lodging in Manhattan is never easy. There will be times when getting a room in the city is more difficult than hailing a cab at rush hour. In that case, go online, where hotel-reservation agencies offer deals—even when everyone else swears the city is booked solid.

One more caveat: New York's 13.25 percent room tax may cause sticker shock for the uninitiated. There's also a $2-per-night occupancy tax. And ask in advance about unadvertised costs—phone charges, minibars, faxes—or you might not find out about them until checkout. Telephone tip: The toll-free 800, 877 and 888 numbers listed work only within the United States.

### HOTEL-RESERVATION AGENCIES

These companies book blocks of rooms in advance and thus can offer reduced rates. Discounts cover most price ranges, including economy; some agencies claim savings of up to 65 percent, though 20 percent is more likely. If you know where you'd like to stay, call a few

## CRITICS' PICKS Inn crowd

These are the best hotels...

**...for feeling eco-friendly**
The Benjamin Hotel (see page 153) is Ecotel-certified.

**...for a fast-drawing bath**
The Four Seasons Hotel (see page 145) has tubs that fill in just 60 seconds.

**...for a lovers' tryst**
The Library Hotel (see page 154) writes the book on romance with its Erotica package.

**...for jet-set pets**
The SoHo Grand (see page 139) and Sofitel (see page 153) welcome furry companions.

**...for fine in-room dining**
The New York Palace (see page 147) offers room service from Le Cirque 2000.

**...for seeing red**
The Time (see page 149) provides guest rooms furnished entirely in blue, yellow or red.

**...for help with downloading your new MP3s**
The Ritz-Carlton New York (see pages 139 and 161) has a "technology butler."

**...for movie mavens**
Woody Allen used Hotel 17 (see page 143) to film *Manhattan Murder Mystery.*

**...for courting the luck of the Irish**
The Fitzpatrick Grand Central Hotel (see page 151) offers the Liam Neeson suite.

**In the money** The Wall Street Inn's lobby befits its setting in a former bank building.

agencies before booking, in case the hotel is on their list. If you simply want the best deal, mention the part of town you prefer and the rate you're willing to pay, and see what's available. The following agencies work with select New York hotels and are free of charge, although a few require you pay for your rooms in advance.

### Accommodations Express

*801 Asbury Ave, sixth floor, Ocean City, NJ 08226 (800-277-1064, 800-971-7666; www.accommodationsexpress.com).*

### Central Reservation Service

*159 Lookout Pl, suite 201, Maitland, FL 32751 (407-740-6442, 800-555-7555; fax 407-740-8222; www.reservation-services.com).*

### Express Hotel Reservations

*3825 Iris Ave, Boulder, CO 80301 (303-440-8481, 800-407-3351; www.express-res.com).*

### Hotel Reservations Network

*8140 Walnut Hill Ln, suite 800, Dallas, TX 75231 (214-369-1264, 800-715-7666; www.hoteldiscount.com).*

### HotRes.com

*1011 High Ridge Rd, Stamford, CT 06905 (203-329-1130; hotres@hotres.com, www.hotres.com).*

► For hotel listings with direct links to booking, visit www.timeout.com/newyork.

### Quikbook

*381 Park Ave South, third floor, New York, NY 10016 (212-779-ROOM, 800-789-9887; www.quikbook.com).*

### timeoutny.com

The *Time Out New York* website offers online reservations to more than 200 hotels. You can search by date of arrival or by name of hotel. Disclosure: *TONY* receives a commission from sales made through our partner hotel reservation sites.

## STANDARD HOTEL SERVICES

All hotels have air-conditioning—a relief in summer—unless otherwise noted. In the categories **Deluxe**, **Stylish**, **First-class**, **Business** and **Boutique**, all hotels have the following services and amenities (unless otherwise noted): alarm clock, cable TV, concierge, conference facility, fax (in business center or in room), hair dryer, in-room safe, laundry, minibar, modem line, radio, one or more restaurants, one or more bars and room service. Additional services are noted at the end of each listing.

Most hotels in all categories have access for the disabled, nonsmoking rooms, and an iron and ironing board in the room or on request. Call to confirm.

"Breakfast included" may mean coffee and toast, or croissants, fresh orange juice and cappuccino. While many hotels boast a "multilingual" staff, the term is used loosely.

## Downtown & below 23rd Street

### Deluxe

#### The Ritz-Carlton New York, Battery Park

*2 West St at Battery Pl (212-344-0800; fax 212-344-3801; www.ritz-carlton.com). Subway: 4, 5 to Bowling Green. Single/double $229–$535, suite $600–$4,500. 298 rooms. AmEx, DC, Disc, MC, V.*

See **The Ritz-Carlton New York, Central Park**, page 161.

### Stylish

#### The Inn at Irving Place

*56 Irving Pl between 17th and 18th Sts (212-533-4600, 800-685-1447; fax 212-533-4611; www.innatirving.com). Subway: L, N, Q, R, W, 4, 5, 6 to 14th St–Union Sq. Single/double $325–$415, suite from $475–$495. 12 rooms. AmEx, DC, MC, V.*

For Victorian charm, book a room at this 19th-century townhouse near Gramercy Park. It's one of Manhattan's smallest inns and also one of its most romantic. Instead of a front desk, there's a parlor with a blazing fireplace. Some rooms are small, but many are furnished with four-poster beds. The Madame Wollenska suite has a pretty window seat. The inn is a hideaway for models and chic Hollywood types. Rates include Continental breakfast. Tea at **Lady Mendl's** *(212-533-4466)* is an event.

**Hotel services** *Conference facility. Tearoom. 24-hour dry cleaning. Valet.* **Room services** *CD player. VCR.*

#### The Mercer

*147 Mercer St at Prince St (212-966-6060, 888-918-6060; fax 212-965-3838). Subway: N, R, W to Prince St. Single/double $395–$565, suite $1,100–$1,600. 75 rooms. AmEx, DC, Disc, MC, V.*

The Mercer's location in the center of Soho gives this 75-room gem a leg up on its closest competitors, 60 Thompson and the SoHo Grand. Rooms feature high-speed Internet access, high-tech amenities, furniture made from African wood and oversized bathrooms. The restaurant, **Mercer Kitchen** *(212-966-5454)*, serves Jean-Georges Vongerichten's notion of casual American cuisine.

**Hotel services** *Book-and-magazine library in lobby. CD-and-video library. Free access to nearby gym. Multilingual baby-sitters.* **Room services** *Cassette and CD players. Fireplace in some rooms. Laptop computer on request. VCR.*

#### 60 Thompson

*60 Thompson St between Broome and Spring Sts (212-431-0400, 877-431-0400; fax 212-431-0200; www.60Thompson.com). Subway: C, E to Spring St. Single/double $370–$450, suite $520–$630, penthouse suite $3,500. 100 rooms. AmEx, DC, Disc, MC, V.*

This recent Soho entrant has added 100 rooms to the neighborhood. Since it's the tallest building in the vicinity, the views extend north to the Empire State Building and can be enjoyed from the rooftop bar, A60. Guests enter through an outdoor garden café. Thomas O'Brien of Aero Studios designed the Thompson Chair (available for purchase) nestled in each guest room. You'll feel pampered by nice touches such as down duvets, Philosophy toiletries and a pantry stocked with goodies from gourmet-grocer Dean & DeLuca.

**Hotel services** *Cell-phone rental. DVD library. Laptop computer on request. Parking. Valet.* **Room services** *CD and DVD players. Microwave oven on request. VCR. Voice mail.*

#### SoHo Grand Hotel

*310 West Broadway between Canal and Grand Sts (212-965-3000, 800-965-3000; fax 212-965-3244; www.sohogrand.com). Subway: A, C, E, 1, 9 to Canal St. Single/double $259–$429, suite $1,599–$1,899. 369 rooms. AmEx, DC, Disc, MC, V.*

The SoHo Grand's striking design pays homage to the neighborhood's contemporary-art community and to the area's past as a manufacturing district. A dramatic stairway of bottle glass and cast iron leads from the street level up to the elegant lobby and reception desk, where a monumental clock looms. Rooms are decorated in soothing grays and beiges, with photos from local galleries on the walls. In 2000, its sister location, the Tribeca Grand Hotel, was the first major hotel to open in the fashionable triangle below Canal Street.

**Hotel services** *Fitness center. Pets allowed. 24-hour dry cleaning.* **Room services** *VCR. Voice mail.*

**Other location** • *Tribeca Grand Hotel, 2 Sixth Ave between Church and White Sts (212-519-6600, 877-519-6600; fax 212-519-6700; www.tribecagrand.com). Subway: C, E to Canal St. Single/double $259–$599, suite $499–$1,049. 203 rooms. AmEx, DC, Disc, MC, V.*

#### W Union Square

*201 Park Ave South at 17th St (212-253-9119; fax 212-253-9229). Subway: L, N, Q, R, W, 4, 5, 6 to 14th St–Union Sq. Single/double $299–$499, suite $599–$1,800. 270 rooms. AmEx, DC, Disc, MC, V.*

See **W New York–Times Square**, page 151.

### Business

#### The Holiday Inn Wall Street

*15 Gold St at Platt St (212-232-7700, 800-HOLIDAY; fax 212-425-0330; www.holidayinnwsd.com). Subway: A, C to Broadway–Nassau St; J, M, Z, 2, 3, 4, 5 to Fulton St. Single/double $169–$349, suite $500–$700. 138 rooms. AmEx, DC, Disc, MC, V.*

Slightly cheaper than most of its neighbors, this Holiday Inn is good for the business traveler with a family in tow: It offers special weekend rates, and children under 18 stay for free (a roll-away bed is $25 a night). If you book a single, however, expect one of the smallest rooms in the city—some are only 275 square feet. Keeping up with the e-times, this site has

Necessities

**Cheap chic** The affordable Larchmont is in a 1910 Beaux Arts building in the Village.

automated check-in and check-out kiosks and "virtual office" rooms that include high-speed Internet access, an eight-foot L-shaped desk, ergonomic chair and unlimited office supplies.
**Hotel services** *CD library. Fitness center. Gift shop. Parking.* **Room services** *CD player. Cordless phone. Nintendo. Voice mail. Web TV.*

### The Regent Wall Street

*55 Wall St between Hanover and William Sts (212-845-8600, 800-545-4000; fax 212-845-8601; www.regenthotels.com). Subway: 2, 3 to Wall St. Single/double $495–$995 (weekend rates $245–$495), suite $525–$995. 144 rooms. AmEx, DC, Disc, MC, V.*
The first five-star hotel in the Financial District, and the first hotel ever on Wall Street, the Regent opened in December 1999 after an $80 million remodeling of the historic building it occupies. Built in 1842, the Regent Wall Street was originally the Merchants' Exchange. From 1863 to 1899, it was the U.S. Custom House. The 12,000-square-foot ballroom, with 60-foot-high Corinthian columns, marble walls and an elliptical dome, was designated one of the city's most important historic public spaces by the Landmarks Preservation Commission. Rooms are exquisitely decorated and comfortable, offering great views, tubs for two and all the business accoutrements your broker heart desires. The hotel's **55 Wall Street** restaurant *(212-699-5555)* boasts a dramatic stone balcony, where you may dine on American cuisine among the soaring pillars.
**Hotel services** *Baby-sitting. Beauty salon. Fitness center. Gift shop. Parking. Spa. Valet.* **Room services** *CD and DVD players. Voice mail.*

### The Wall Street Inn

*9 South William St at 85 Broad St (212-747-1500; fax 212-747-1900). Subway: 2, 3 to Wall St; 4, 5 to Bowling Green. Single/double $249–$450. Call for corporate and weekend rates. 46 rooms. AmEx, DC, Disc, MC, V.*
This boutique hotel, in the landmark Stone Street district, is the reincarnation of an 1830 Lehman Brothers Bank building. To reach beyond the financiers who make up 98 percent of the clientele, the hotel offers hefty discounts on weekends. There's no restaurant or room service, but breakfast is included.
**Hotel services** *Conference facility. Fitness center. Video library.* **Room services** *VCR. Voice mail.*

## Less than $200

### Chelsea Hotel

*222 W 23rd St between Seventh and Eighth Aves (212-243-3700; fax 212-675-5531; www.chelseahotel.com). Subway: C, E, 1, 9 to 23rd St. Single/double from $135, suite $325. 400 rooms. AmEx, DC, Disc, MC, V.*
Built in 1884, the famous redbrick building oozes history. In 1912, *Titanic* survivors stayed here for a few days; other former residents include Mark Twain, Dylan Thomas, O. Henry and Brendan Behan. No evidence remains of the hotel's most infamous association: the murder of Nancy Spungen by Sex Pistol Sid Vicious. The lobby doubles as an art gallery, showing work by past and present guests, and rooms are large, with high ceilings. Most rooms, but not all, have a private bathroom and air conditioner. The cocktail lounge **Serena** *(see page 175)* lures a sleek crowd to the basement.
**Hotel services** *Beauty salon. Concierge. Restaurant.* **Room services** *Kitchenettes or refrigerators in some rooms. Modem line.*

### Cosmopolitan

*95 West Broadway at Chambers St (212-566-1900, 888-895-9400; fax 212-566-6909; www.cosmohotel.com). Subway: A, C, 1, 2, 3, 9 to Chambers St. Single/double $109–$159. 115 rooms. AmEx, DC, MC, V.*
It's not luxurious, but this little hotel is immaculate and well-maintained, with rock-bottom rates. Open continuously since the 1850s, it's located within easy walking distance of Chinatown, Little Italy, Soho and the South Street Seaport.
**Hotel services** *Concierge. Discount parking. Safe.* **Room services** *Modem line. Voice mail.*

### Gramercy Park Hotel

*2 Lexington Ave at 21st St (212-475-4320, 800-221-4083; fax 212-505-0535; www.gramercyparkhotel.com). Subway: 6 to 23rd St. Single/double $160–$185, suite $210–$240. 455 rooms. AmEx, DC, Disc, MC, V.*
This hotel is in a surprisingly quiet location adjoining the small green oasis of Gramercy Park (to

► For more accommodations, see chapter **Gay & Lesbian**.

Necessities

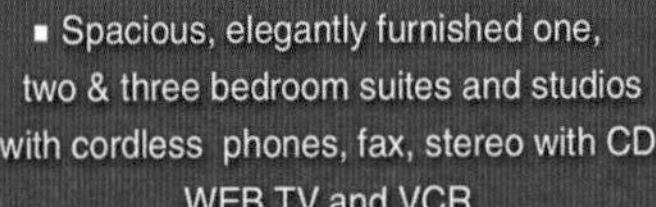

which only hotel guests and neighboring residents receive a key). Last year, the entire hotel was renovated. Guests vary from business travelers to rock stars, and the piano bar is a favorite local hangout for young media types and tipsy senior citizens.
**Hotel services** *Bar. Beauty salon. Dry cleaning. Gift shop. Laundry drop-off. Newsstand/ticket desk. Restaurant. Valet.* **Room services** *Room service. Voice mail.*

### Howard Johnson's Express Inn

*135 E Houston St between First and Second Aves (212-358-8844; www.hojo.com). Subway: F, V to Lower East Side–Second Ave. Single/double $109–$169. 45 rooms. AmEx, Disc, MC, V*

Forget the funky orange roof and bright turquoise walls that made you love (or loathe) HoJo in the 1970s; this Houston Street version is earth-toned and frill-free. The fixtures in the basic rooms are blessedly new: The bed is firm, linens are fresh and the cheaply framed landscape prints are not half-bad. Plus, the shower is sparkly clean with strong water pressure. The highest-end rooms have two double beds and a Jacuzzi.
**Hotel services** *Complimentary breakfast. Fax.* **Room services** *Alarm clock. Hair dryer. Voice mail.*

### Union Square Inn

*209 E 14th St between Second and Third Aves (212-614-0500; www.unionsquareinn.com). Subway: L to Third Ave; N, Q, R, W, 4, 5, 6 to 14th St–Union Sq. Single/double $99–$139. 41 rooms. AmEx, MC, V.*

See **Murray Hill Inn**, page 155.

### Washington Square Hotel

*103 Waverly Pl between Fifth and Sixth Aves (212-777-9515, 800-222-0418; fax 212-979-8373; www.washingtonsquarehotel.com). Subway: A,C, E, F, V, S to W 4th St. Single/double $131–$165, quad $188. 170 rooms. AmEx, MC, V.*

Bob Dylan and Joan Baez lived in this Greenwich Village hotel when they sang for change in nearby Washington Square Park. Rooms are no-frills (though clean and recently renovated), and hallways are so narrow that you practically open your door into the opposite room. Rates include breakfast—or splurge on the Sunday jazz brunch at **North Square** *(212-254-1200),* the restaurant and lounge next door.
**Hotel services** *Complimentary breakfast. Fitness center.* **Room services** *Modem line. Voice mail.*

## Budget

### Chelsea Lodge

*318 W 20th St between Eighth and Ninth Aves (212-243-4499; www.chelsealodge.com). Subway: C, E to 23rd St. Single/double with shared bath $90–$105, deluxe with private bath $135–$150, suite with private bath $195–$225 (each additional person $15; maximum four guests). 26 rooms. AmEx, DC, Disc, MC, V.*

In the spring of 1998, husband-and-wife team Paul and G.G. Weisenfeld turned a landmark brownstone into a European-style inn for budget travelers. Guests can choose among 22 rooms and four suites kitted out in classic Americana. Although most are fairly small, the rooms are so aggressively charming, you need to book well in advance.
**Room services** *Cable TV. Hair dryer. VCR and kitchenette in suites.*

### Hotel 17

*225 E 17th St between Second and Third Aves (212-475-2845; fax 212-677-8178; www.hotel17.citysearch.com). Subway: L to Third Ave, N, Q, R, W, 4, 5, 6 to 14th St–Union Sq; Single/double $60–$90, triple $80–$120. 140 rooms. MC, V.*

Behold the ultimate dive hotel, and one of the coolest places to stay if you're an artist, musician or model; everyone on the underground circuit knows the place. Madonna posed here for a magazine shoot, and Woody Allen used the location for *Manhattan Murder Mystery.* The decor is classic shabby-chic, with labyrinthine hallways leading to high-ceilinged rooms filled with discarded dressers, gorgeous old fireplaces, velvet curtains and 1950s wallpaper. Ignore the permanent NO VACANCY sign, and expect to share the hallway bathroom with other guests. The affiliated **Hotel 31** *(see page 159)* has less style cachet, but suffices as a budget hotel in midtown.
**Hotel services** *Air-conditioning. Self-serve laundry.* **Room services** *Alarm clock. Cable TV. Hair dryer.*



### Larchmont Hotel

*27 W 11th St between Fifth and Sixth Aves (212-989-9333; fax 212-989-9496; www.larchmonthotel.com). Subway: F, V to 14th St; L to Sixth Ave. Single $70–$95, double $90–$115, queen $109–$125. 60 rooms. AmEx, DC, Disc, MC, V.*

This attractive, affordable hotel is housed in a renovated 1910 Beaux Arts building on a quiet side street. Guests enter through a hallway adjacent to

**Holiday** Stay at hip dive Hotel 17, where Madonna once pouted for a photo shoot.

the lobby, making the place feel like a private apartment building. Some rooms are small, but all are clean. Each is equipped with a washbasin, robe and pair of slippers, though not one has a private bath.
**Hotel services** *Kitchenette on some floors. Safe.* **Room services** *Radio. Voice mail.*

### Off-Soho Suites Hotel

*11 Rivington St between Bowery and Chrystie St (212-979-9808, 800-633-7646; fax 212-979-9801; www.offsoho.com). Subway: J, M to Bowery; S to Grand St. Suite with shared bath $119, with private bath $209. 38 rooms. AmEx, MC, V.*
A good value for suite accommodations, Off-Soho is perfectly situated if you're into bars, clubbing and the Soho scene. All suites are roomy, clean and bright, with fully equipped kitchens and polished wooden floors.
**Hotel services** *Café. Fitness room. Safe. Self-serve laundry.* **Room services** *Alarm clock. Microwave. Modem line. Refrigerator. Room service.*

## Hostels

### Bowery's Whitehouse Hotel of New York

*340 Bowery between 2nd and 3rd Sts (212-477-5623; fax 212-473-3150; www.whitehousehotelofny.com). Subway: F, V, S to Broadway–Lafayette St; 6 to Bleecker St. Single/double: $27–$53, triple $70. 250 rooms. AmEx, DC, Disc, MC, V.*
Built in 1917 as housing for railroad workers, the Bowery's Whitehouse Hotel offers cheap, safe and private rooms at rates that are almost unheard of downtown. Although small, the units (and bed linens) are clean, the mattresses are comfortable, and your property will be safe. A microwave and large-screen TV are available in the lounge at all hours. If you sit down with one of the resident old-timers (about 45 people live here permanently), you'll hear one-of-a-kind stories of the city.
**Hotel services** *Internet access in lobby. Luggage storage. Safety boxes. Self-serve laundry. TV in lobby.*

# Midtown

## Deluxe

### Four Seasons Hotel

*57 E 57th St between Madison and Park Aves (212-758-5700, 800-332-3442; fax 212-758-5711; www.fourseasons.com). Subway: N, R, W to Lexington Ave–59th St; 4, 5, 6 to 59th St. Single/double $495–$795, suite $1,350–$9,500. 368 rooms. AmEx, DC, Disc, MC, V.*
Renowned architect I.M. Pei's sharp geometric design (in neutral cream and honey tones) is sleek and modern, befitting this favorite haven of media moguls. The rooms are among the largest in the city, with bathrooms of Florentine marble and tubs that fill in just 60 seconds. Views of Manhattan from the higher floors are superb, especially if you're looking out from the balcony of the hotel's new royal suite, which measures 2,000 square feet.
**Hotel services** *Baby-sitting. Complimentary video library. Currency exchange. Fitness center. Gift shop. Parking. Spa. 24-hour dry cleaning.* **Room services** *High-speed Internet access. Nintendo. VCR in suites; otherwise on request. Voice mail.*

**Edible poetry** Guests at the Kitano devour the creations of chef Nadaman Hakubai.

### The Kitano

*66 Park Ave at 38th St (212-885-7000, 800-548-2666; fax 212-885-7100; www.kitano.com). Subway: S, 4, 5, 6, 7 to 42nd St–Grand Central. Single/double $480–$605, suite $715–$2,100. 149 rooms. AmEx, DC, Disc, MC, V.*
The Kitano has a Japanese aesthetic—warm mood lighting, rich mahogany paneling, smooth stone floors, complimentary green tea and an authentic tatami suite. It is also home to the Japanese restaurant **Nadaman Hakubai** *(212-885-7111).*
**Hotel services** *Baby-sitting. Dry cleaning. Gift shop. Laundry drop-off.* **Room services** *Safe. Voice mail.*

### Le Parker Meridien

*118 W 57th St between Sixth and Seventh Aves (212-245-5000, 800-543-4300; fax 212-708-7471; www.parkermeridien.com). Subway: F, N, Q, R, W to 57th St. Single/double $325–$365, suite $450–$2,500. 731 rooms. AmEx, DC, MC, V.*
The No. 1 draw at this midtown classic is the rooftop pool. The award-winning breakfast at **Norma's** *(212-708-7460),* complete with smoothie shots, "red berry risotto oatmeal" and Hudson Valley duck confit hash, comes in a close second, and the nameless burger joint in the lobby rounds out the trifecta.

► For more hotels in midtown, see **Hill street news**, page 154.

**Hotel services** *Cell-phone rental. Currency exchange. Fitness center. Parking. Spa.* **Room services** *DVD player. High-speed Internet access. Room service. Voice mail.*

### New York Palace

*455 Madison Ave between 50th and 51st Sts (212-888-7000, 800-697-2522; fax 212-644-5750; www.newyorkpalace.com). Subway: E, V to Fifth Ave–53rd St. Single/double $450–$710, suite $900–$7,000. 896 rooms. AmEx, DC, Disc, MC, V.*

The Palace—once the Villard Houses, a cluster of mansions designed by McKim, Mead & White—is home to the acclaimed **Le Cirque 2000** *(see page 200)*. It's nearly impossible to make a last-minute reservation at the restaurant, but guests in the tower suites don't have to worry—Le Cirque will deliver to your room.

**Hotel services** *Currency exchange. Fitness center. 24-hour dry cleaning.* **Room services** *Dual-line phones. Fax/copier. Voice mail.*

### The Waldorf-Astoria

*301 Park Ave at 50th St (212-355-3000, 800-924-3673; www.waldorf.com). Subway: E, V to Lexington Ave–53rd St; 6 to 51st St. Single $275–$450, double $300–$450, suite $400–$900. 1,425 rooms. AmEx, DC, Disc, MC, V.*

The famous Waldorf salad made its debut in 1896 at what was then the city's largest hotel. Demolished to make way for the Empire State Building, a new Art Deco Waldorf reopened in 1931, and continued to cater to New York's high society (former guests include Princess Grace, Cary Grant, Sophia Loren and a long list of U.S. presidents). It's where visiting dignitaries stay when in town for United Nations meetings.

**Hotel services** *Beauty salon. Cell-phone rental. Fitness center with steam rooms. Valet parking.* **Room services** *Kitchenette in some suites. VCR on request. Voice mail. Web TV.*

## Stylish

### Chambers

*15 W 56th St between Fifth and Sixth Aves (212-974-5656; fax 212-974-5657; www.chambershotel.com). Subway: F to 57th St; N, R, W to Fifth Ave–59th St. Single $275–$350, double $350–$400, studio $350–$450, suite $650–$1,600. 77 rooms. AmEx, DC, Disc, MC, V.*

The mood at the Chambers is artist's loft–meets–Fifth Avenue wallet. Rooms are warmer than you'd expect from such a design-oriented hotel: Stainless-steel fixtures and track lighting are cozied up by taupe-and-purple bedding, rugs and plenty of textured wood. If all that doesn't engage your attention, the creative American dishes at the hotel's restaurant, **Town**, will *(see page 198)*.

**Hotel services** *Baby-sitter. Complimentary passes to New York Sports Club. Computer rental. Valet parking.* **Room services**. *CD-and-DVD library. Cordless telephone. Internet access.*

**Urban bloom** Tulips and other fresh blossoms adorn the rooms of City Club.

### City Club Hotel

*55 W 44th St between Fifth and Sixth Aves (212-921-5500, 888-256-4100; fax 212-575-2758; www.cityclubhotel.com). Subway: B, D, F, V to 42nd St; 7 to Fifth Ave. Single/double $275–$375, duplex suite $600. 65 rooms. AmEx, DC, MC, V.*

Neither a boutique hotel nor a full-blown luxury palace, City Club aims to be something in between. Guests enjoy a blend of high fashion and contemporary comfort in the well-appointed rooms as well as the personalized service. Chef Daniel Boulud's **DB Bistro Moderne** *(see page 197)*, the hotel's restaurant, serves American classics with a French twist.

**Hotel services** *Complimentary access to nearby gym. Discount parking.* **Room services** *CD and DVD players. Cordless phone. High-speed Internet access.*

### Dylan

*52 E 41st St between Madison and Park Aves (212-338-0500, 800-555-DYLAN; fax 212-338-0569; www.dylanhotel.com). Subway: S, 4, 5, 6, 7 to 42nd St–Grand Central. Single/double $295–$395, suite $650–$1,200. 107 rooms. AmEx, DC, Disc, MC, V.*

The once-crumbling 1903 Beaux Arts brick-and-limestone building—with a grand marble staircase that spirals up three floors from the lobby—has undergone a $30 million restoration. Fabrics in rooms and public spaces are soft and rich: velvet, suede, silk, mohair and chiffon.

**Hotel services** *Fitness center. Parking. Safe.* **Room services** *Safe. Voice mail.*

### Flatotel

*135 W 52nd St between Sixth and Seventh Aves (212-887-9400; www.flatotel.com). Subway: N, R, W to 49th St; 1, 9 to 50th St. Single/double $199–$349, suite $299–$499. 288 rooms. AmEx, DC, MC, V.*

The flat in Flatotel refers to the word's British usage—the building was a condominium complex before becoming a hotel in 1994. After a recent two-year renovation, it's a cosmopolitan lodge with glossy granite floors and a backlit walnut bar. Pumping with techno beats, the loungey lobby provides cowhide-and-leather couches with cozy nooks for cocktailing and

canoodling. **Moda** *(212-887-9880)*, the on-site eatery, serves Italian-inspired fare like foie gras *panna cotta* in a tea-light–decked space. For postwork drinks, head to Loggia, Moda's new alfresco atrium.
**Hotel services** *Business center. Fitness center.* **Room services** *High-speed Internet access. Room service. Safe. Voice mail.*

## The Hudson

*356 W 58th St between Eighth and Ninth Aves (212-554-6000; fax 212-554-6001; www.ianschragerhotels.com). Subway: A, C, B, D, 1, 9 to 59th St–Columbus Circle. Single/double $175–$260, suite $295–$3,500. 803 rooms. AmEx, DC, Disc, MC, V.*
Ian Schrager opened his fourth New York property in 2000. (The other three are **Morgans**, **The Paramount** and **The Royalton**.) The stylish hotel has a lush interior courtyard with enormous potted trees, a rooftop terrace that overlooks the Hudson River and a glass-roofed lobby crawling with imported English ivy and beautiful people. The in-house **Hudson Cafeteria** and **Hudson Bars** attract the famous and their fans.
**Hotel services** *Cell phone rental. Currency exchange. Fitness center.* **Room services** *CD player. High-speed Internet access. Voice mail.*
**Other locations** • *Morgans, 237 Madison Ave between 37th and 38th Sts (212-686-0300, 800-334-3408; fax 212-779-8352). Subway: S, 4, 5, 6, 7 to 42nd St–Grand Central. Single $225–$325, double $250–$350, suite $325–$425. 113 rooms. AmEx, DC, Disc, MC, V.* • *The Paramount, 235 W 46th St between Broadway and Eighth Ave (212-764-5500, 800-225-7474; fax 212-354-5237). Subway: N, R, W to 49th St. Single $165–$245, double $195–$280, suite $400–$550. 600 rooms. AmEx, DC, Disc, MC, V.* • *The Royalton, 44 W 44th St between Fifth and Sixth Aves (212-869-4400, 800-635-9013; fax 212-575-0012). Subway: B, D, F, V to 42nd St; 7 to Fifth Ave. Single $295–$395, double $345–$415, suite $425–$625. 169 rooms. AmEx, DC, MC, V.*

**All decked out** Lounge chairs await you on the Hudson's rooftop terrace.

## The Mansfield

*12 W 44th St between Fifth and Sixth Aves (212-944-6050, 877-847-4444; fax 212-764-4477; www.boutiquehg.com). Subway: B, D, F, V to 42nd St; 7 to Fifth Ave. Single/double $250–$355, suite $410–$1,000. 124 rooms. AmEx, DC, Disc, MC, V.*
See **The Roger Williams**, page 156.

## The Time

*224 W 49th St between Broadway and Eighth Ave (212-320-2900, 877-846-3692; fax 212-245-2305; www.thetimeny.com). Subway: C, E, 1, 9 to 50th St; N, R, W to 49th St. Single/double $189–$239, suite $289–$379, penthouse suite $2,500–$6,000. 193 rooms. AmEx, DC, Disc, MC, V.*
Designer Adam Tihany says of this stylish Times Square hotel, "The idea is to truly experience a

**Three-color theory** Each suite at the Time hotel is decorated in blue, red or yellow.

color—to see it, feel it, taste it, smell it and live it." This experience includes guest rooms furnished entirely in the primary color of your choice, accented with artfully placed jelly beans of that hue and a chromatically inspired scent and reading material. Sound like a bit much? You can always chill out in the hotel's neutral public spaces.
**Hotel services** *Cell-phone rental. Fitness center. Shopping services.* **Room services** *CD player. VCR. Voice mail.*

### W New York—Times Square

*1567 Broadway at 47th St (212-930-7400; 877-W-HOTELS; fax 212-930-7500; www.whotels.com). Subway: N, R, W to 49th St; 1, 9 to 50th St. Single/double $259–$339, suite $499–$2,500. 509 rooms. AmEx, DC, Disc, MC, V.*
The W brand is like a gigolo, spawning progeny around the world and coining its own smooth-guy lingo (the lobby is the "living room," and housekeepers are "stylists"). NYC's fifth and flashiest location has a street-level vestibule with a waterfall but no front desk. Hop in an elevator, which delivers you to seventh-floor reception. To your right, W paradise: a massive sprawl of white leather seating and resin alcoves swarming with *Sex and the City* types. Each room features a floating-glass desk and sleek bathroom, but it's the boat-size bed and bed-to-ceiling headboard mirror that get the mind racing. Steve Hanson's vertiginous bi-level temple of seafood, **Blue Fin** *(212-918-1400)*, serves grade-A sushi, triple-tiered shellfish castles and stellar booze.
**Hotel services** *Fitness center. Gift shop. Spa. Valet parking.* **Room services** *DVD. VCR. Video library.*
**Other locations** • *W New York–The Court, 130 E 39th St between Park and Lexington Aves (212-685-1100; fax 212-889-0287). Subway: S, 4, 5, 6, 7 to 42nd St–Grand Central. Single/double $239–$359, suite $379–$799. 198 rooms. AmEx, DC, Disc, MC, V.* • *W New York–The Tuscany, 120 E 39th St between Park and Lexington Aves (212-686-1600; fax 212-779-7822). Subway: S, 4, 5, 6, 7 to 42nd St–Grand Central. Single/double $279–$379, suite $399–$899. 122 rooms. AmEx, DC, Disc, MC, V.* • *W New York, 541 Lexington Ave at 49th St (212-755-1200, fax 212-319-8344). Subway: E, V to Lexington Ave–53rd St; 6 to 51st St. Single/double $229–$339, suite $359–$1,800. 758 rooms. AmEx, DC, Disc, MC, V.*

## First-class

### The Algonquin

*59 W 44th St between Fifth and Sixth Aves (212-840-6800, 800-555-8000; fax 212-944-1618; www.algonquinhotel.com). Subway: B, D, F, V to 42nd St; 7 to Fifth Ave. Single/double $229–$329, suite $329–$429. 174 rooms. AmEx, DC, Disc, MC, V.*
Arguably New York's most famous literary landmark, this was where Dorothy Parker, Robert Benchley and other wits of the 1920s and '30s gathered to gossip and parry at the legendary Round Table in the **Oak Room** *(212-419-9331)*. The rooms are on the small side but cheerful and charming, and the hallways are covered with *New Yorker*–cartoon wallpaper. On some Monday evenings, there are readings by local authors, and cabaret singers perform Tuesday through Saturday *(see page 269)*.
**Hotel services** *Cell-phone rental. 24-hour dry cleaning. 24-hour fitness center.* **Room services** *CD player and VCR in suites. Refrigerator in suites, otherwise on request. Voice mail.*

### Fitzpatrick Grand Central Hotel

*141 E 44th St between Lexington and Third Aves (212-351-6800, 800-367-7701; fax 212-818-1747; www.fitzpatrickhotels.com). Subway: S, 4, 5, 6, 7 to 42nd St–Grand Central. Single/ double $335, suite $435. 155 rooms. AmEx, DC, Disc, MC, V.*
You can't miss the fact that this family-run East Sider is Irish-owned: There are kelly-green carpets with a Book of Kells pattern in the lobbies…and a Liam Neeson penthouse suite. **The Wheel Tapper Pub** *(212-351-6800)* serves bangers, rashers, soda bread and high tea.
**Hotel services** *Cell-phone rental. Free access to nearby gym. In-room massage. 24-hour dry cleaning. Valet.* **Room services** *Computer. Data port in room. DVD rental. WebTV.*
**Other location** • *Fitzpatrick Manhattan, 687 Lexington Ave between 56th and 57th Sts (212-355-0100, 800-367-7701; fax 212-308-5166). Subway: E, V to Lexington Ave–53rd St; 4, 5, 6 to 59th St. Single/double $335, suite $365. 92 rooms. AmEx, DC, Disc, MC, V.*

**Dubya** Like a certain commander-in-chief, the W hotel chain aims for worldwide domination (W Times Square, above).

### Hotel Elysée

*60 E 54th St between Madison and Park Aves (212-753-1066; fax 212-980-9278). Subway: E, V to Lexington Ave–53rd St; 6 to 51st St. Single/double $295–$345, suite $425–$525. 101 rooms. AmEx, DC, Disc, MC, V.*

This is a charming hotel with an attentive staff. The quarters are furnished with antiques and Italian-marble bathrooms; some rooms have colored-glass conservatories and terraces. It's popular with publishers, so don't be surprised if you see a famous author enjoying the complimentary afternoon tea. Downstairs is the **Monkey Bar** *(212-838-2600)*, where a well-coiffed clientele dines on American cuisine. For Elysée's sister hotels, see **Casablanca**, page 153, **The Library Hotel** and **The Giraffe**, page 154.

**Hotel services** *Baby-sitting. Free access to nearby gym. Valet parking.* **Room services** *Kitchenette in suites. VCR. Voice mail.*

### The Iroquois

*49 W 44th St between Fifth and Sixth Aves (212-840-3080, 800-332-7220; fax 212-398-1754; www.iroquoisny.com). Subway: B, D, F, V to 42nd St; 7 to Fifth Ave. Single/double $199–$395, suite $349–$695. 114 rooms. AmEx, DC, Disc, MC, V.*

The Iroquois, once a budget hostelry, has morphed into a full-service luxury hotel. A mahogany paneled library, marble-lined bathrooms and a polished-stone lobby are just part of a $13 million renovation that did away with an archaic barbershop and a photographer's studio. **Triomphe** *(212-453-4233)* is the hotel's French-accented American restaurant.

**Hotel services** *Cell-phone rental. Fitness center. Parking. 24-hour dry cleaning. Video library.* **Room services** *CD player. 24-hour room service. Voice mail.*

### The Michelangelo

*152 W 51st St between Sixth and Seventh Aves (212-765-1900, 800-237-0990; fax 212-581-7618; www.michelangelohotel.com). Subway: N, R, W to 49th St; 1, 9 to 50th St. Single/double $195–$495, suite $395–$1,200. 178 rooms. AmEx, DC, Disc, MC, V.*

This appealing little haven in the Theater District welcomes guests with a lobby filled with peach marble, oil paintings, giant potted palms and overstuffed, rose- and salmon-toned couches. The sizable rooms are decorated in styles ranging from French country to Art Deco; each includes two TVs (one in the bathroom), a fax machine, a terry-cloth robe and a giant tub. Complimentary breakfast comes with espresso, cappuccino and Italian pastries. The hotel also has fully equipped apartments for extended stays, with full or limited hotel service *($3,500–$9,000 per month).*

**Hotel services** *Baby-sitting. Complimentary limousine service to Wall St (Mon–Fri). 24-hour dry cleaning. 24-hour fitness center.* **Room services** *CD player. Complimentary newspaper and shoe shine. Laptop computer and printer on request.*

### The Roger Smith

*501 Lexington Ave between 47th and 48th Sts (212-755-1400, 800-445-0277; fax 212-758-4061; www.rogersmith.com). Subway: E, V to Lexington Ave–53rd St; 6 to 51st St. Single/double $195–$295, suite $249–$435. 135 rooms. AmEx, DC, Disc, MC, V.*

The Roger Smith, which is popular with touring bands, is owned by the family of sculptor-painter James Knowles, and a few of his pieces decorate the lobby. Many of the large rooms have been recently renovated, and each is uniquely furnished. The staff is helpful, breakfast is included, and there's a library of free videos and books for those who want to stay in for the night.

**Hotel services** *Baby-sitting. Valet parking. Video library.* **Room services** *Coffeemaker. Free local phone calls. Kitchenette with microwave oven in suites. VCR. Voice mail.*

### The Shoreham

*33 W 55th St between Fifth and Sixth Aves (212-247-6700). Subway: E, V to Fifth Ave–53rd St; F to 57th St. Single $229–$299, double $300–$450, suite $450–$1,500. 174 rooms. AmEx, DC, Disc, MC, V.*

See **The Roger Williams**, page 156.

### The Warwick New York

*65 W 54th St at Sixth Ave (212-247-2700, 800-223-4099; fax 212-713-1751; www.warwickhotels.com). Subway: E, V to Fifth Ave–53rd St; F to 57th St. Single/double $295–$395, suite $500–$1,275. 426 rooms. AmEx, DC, MC, V.*

Built by William Randolph Hearst in 1927 and later frequented by Elvis and the Beatles, the Warwick is still polished and gleaming. The rooms are exceptionally large by midtown standards. Ask for a view of Sixth Avenue (double-glazed windows keep out the noise). The top-floor Suite of the Stars has a wraparound balcony, which was once the home of Cary Grant.

**Hotel services** *Baby-sitting. Fitness center. Parking.* **Room services** *Voice mail. Room service.*

## Business

### Beekman Tower Hotel

*3 Mitchell Pl, 49th St at First Ave (212-355-7300; 800-ME-SUITE; fax 212-753-9366; www.mesuite.com). Subway: E, V to Lexington Ave–53rd St; 6 to 51st St. Studio suite $209–$360, one-bedroom $219–$400, two-bedroom $478–$680. 174 rooms. AmEx, DC, Disc, MC, V.*

Built in 1928, the Beekman's distinctive tower is an Art Deco landmark. This pleasant hotel is a member of the family-owned Manhattan East Suites, the city's largest all-suite hotel group (it has nine other properties in the city, including **The Benjamin** *(see page 153)* Rooms include kitchenettes. **The Top of the Tower** restaurant *(212-980-4796)* on the 26th floor has a terrace with panoramic views.

**Hotel services** *Ballroom. Fitness center. Parking. Valet.* **Room services** *Kitchenette. Voice mail.*

**High times** The new 45-story Westin hotel is a standout, even in Times Square.

### The Benjamin

*125 E 50th St at Lexington Ave (212-715-2500, 888-4-BENJAMIN; fax 212-465-3697; www.thebenjamin.com). Subway: E, V to Lexington Ave–53rd St; 6 to 51st St. Single/double $260–$530, suite $530–$1,100. 209 rooms. AmEx, DC, Disc, MC, V.*

Now occupying the famous landmark building that once housed the Hotel Beverly (which Georgia O'Keeffe used to paint from her apartment across the street), the Benjamin has reclaimed its heritage while evolving into a fully equipped executive-suite hotel, featuring a state-of-the-art communications system. And for the green at heart: The Benjamin is Ecotel-certified.

**Hotel services** *Fitness center. Spa.* **Room services** *Cordless phone. High-speed Internet access. Kitchenette. Safe. Voice mail. Web TV.*

### Sofitel

*45 W 44th St between Fifth and Sixth Aves (212-354-8844; fax 212-782-3002; www.sofitel.com). Subway: B, D, F, V to 42nd St; 7 to Fifth Ave. Single/double/suite $209–$699. 398 rooms. AmEx, DC, Disc, MC, V.*

Part of a French chain, Sofitel New York is a 30-story luxury business hotel with a wonderful brasserie, **Gaby** *(212-782-7149)*, a piano bar and 52 suites with stunning views of midtown Manhattan. Rooms are contemporary and tasteful, decorated in warm, earthy colors with mahogany furniture and understated floral bedding—a perfect retreat from the hustle and bustle of Times Square.

**Hotel services** *Parking. Pets allowed.* **Room services** *Dataport. Internet access.*

### The Westin at Times Square

*270 W 43rd St at Eighth Ave (888-627-7149; fax 212-201-4669; www.westinny.com). Subway: A, C, E to 42nd St–Port Authority. Single/double $289–$439; suite $519–$1,657. 863 rooms. AmEx, DC, Disc, MC, V.*

Open since October 2002, the Westin's 45 stories assert its presence even in the heart of Times Square. The spacious rooms have black slate entryways, flat-screen TVs and desks set up for laptops. Try to score a room with a view; all above the 15th floor have unobstructed vistas of Times Square or the Hudson River.

**Hotel services** *Fitness center. Gift shop.* **Room services** *Cordless phone with voice mail. High-speed Internet access. Safe.*

## Boutique

### The Bryant Park

*40 W 40th St between Fifth and Sixth Aves (212-642-2200). Subway: B, D, F, V to 42nd St; 7 to Fifth Ave. Single/double $295–$395, suite $495–695. 129 rooms. AmEx, DC, MC, V.*

Former Ian Schrager partner Philip Pilevsky has converted the 1924 American Radiator Building, designed by Raymond Hood, into his first New York property. Just across the street from lovely Bryant Park, this luxe spot has a prime location and excellent amenities (and guests such as John Travolta). Chef Rick Laakkonen designed the menus at **Ilo** *(212-642-2255)*, an upscale American Creative restaurant, and **Cellar Bar** *(212-642-2260)*, the hotel's vaulted lounge.

**Hotel services** *Boardroom with video conferencing. Fitness center. Screening room. Spa.* **Room services** *Intrigue System (includes digitally downloaded movies).*

### Casablanca Hotel

*147 W 43rd St between Sixth Ave and Broadway (212-869-1212, 800-922-7225; fax 212-391-7585; www.casablancahotel.com). Subway: B, D, F, V to 42nd St. N, Q, R, W, S, 1, 2, 3, 9, 7 to 42nd St–Times Sq; Single/double $159–$265, suite $265–$375. 48 rooms. AmEx, DC, MC, V.*

Run by the same people who own **Hotel Elysée** *(see page 152)*, **The Library Hotel** and **The Giraffe** *(see page 154)*, this 48-room hotel in the Theater District has a cheerful Moroccan theme. **Rick's Café** (get it?) serves free wine and cheese Monday through Saturday. Breakfast is included.

**Hotel services** *Business center. Cybercafé. Free access to nearby gym. 24-hour dry cleaning. Valet. Video library.* **Room services** *VCR. Voice mail.*

### The Gorham New York

*136 W 55th St between Sixth and Seventh Aves (212-245-1800, 800-735-0710; fax 212-582-8332; www.gorhamhotel.com). Subway: F, N, Q, R, W to 57th St. Single/double $200–$420, suite $235–$460. 115 rooms. AmEx, DC, MC, V.*

At the Gorham, opposite the City Center theater, the small lobby's marble floors, maple walls and slightly worn oriental carpets lend it a European ambience. The rooms, though not luxurious, are large by New York standards, and there's a kitchenette (refrigerator, sink and microwave) in each.

**Hotel services** *Baby-sitting. Dry cleaning. Fitness center.* **Room services** *Nintendo. Safe. VCR on request. Voice mail.*

### The Library Hotel

*299 Madison Ave at 41st St (212-983-4500; fax 212-449-9099; www.libraryhotel.com). Subway: S, 4, 5, 6 to 42nd St–Grand Central; 7 to Fifth Ave. Single/double $265–$295, suite $345–$395. 60 rooms. AmEx, DC, MC, V.*

If you want to bone up on your French lit, check into the mahogany-rich Library, which is organized according to the Dewey decimal system. You'll find the Anthropology room on the Science floor—and it's stocked with the appropriate books. The 1912 tapestry-brick building was treated to a $10 million renovation before it opened in mid-2000. Rates include breakfast and evening wine and cheese in the second-floor Reading Room. **The Giraffe**, one of the Library's sister hotels, offers similar services in a European Moderne setting in the up-and-coming Rose Hill area.

**Hotel services** *Baby-sitting. Business center. Free access to nearby gym. Parking. Ticket desk.* **Room services** *CD player. VCR. Voice mail.*

**Other location** • *The Giraffe, 365 Park Ave South at 26th St (212-685-7700, 877-296-0009; www.hotelgiraffe.com). Subway: 6 to 28th St. Single/double $325–$425, suite $475–$575. 73 rooms. AmEx, DC, MC, V.*

### The Muse

*130 W 46th St between Sixth and Seventh Aves (212-485-2400). Subway: B, D, F, V to 47–50th Sts–Rockefeller Ctr. Single/double $285–$355, suite $450–$600. 200 rooms. AmEx, DC, Disc, MC, V.*

This 200-room concierge-style hotel aims to anticipate guests' every whim (rooms are equipped with feather beds and Philosophy toiletries), but the real news is the restaurant **District** *(212-485-2999),*

## Hill street news

A fashionable home for new hotels is the once-staid Murray Hill

Given the rising rents and the demand for space in Manhattan, it's a stretch to say that any centrally located area was only recently "discovered" or developed. Let's just call Murray Hill a late bloomer. The community is named for Robert Murray, who lived in what is now the Financial District and, in the 1750s, built his country estate in the area that spans the lower East 30s. The neighborhood became largely residential when other prominent, wealthy families moved in, including the Astors and John Pierpont Morgan.

Murray Hill's boundaries run from 30th to 40th Streets between Fifth Avenue and the East River. The community remains primarily residential, and is therefore sometimes overlooked by both tourists and natives. But in the last few years, hoteliers have wised up, buying and renovating in this inviting area. The neighborhood is home to Koreatown (which has great cheap eats), and the Empire State Building (which has great views). The wide price range and dense cluster of hotels speak to the diversity of the people it attracts: business people, fashionistas and, we're guessing, you.

### The Avalon

*16 E 32nd St between Fifth and Madison Aves (212-299-7000; fax 212-299-7001; www.theavalonny.com). Subway: 6 to 33rd St. Single/double $195–$215, suites $225–$425. 100 rooms. AmEx, DC, Disc, MC, V.*

Open since April 1998, the Avalon caters mostly to business customers during the week. The 20 rooms and 80 suites are large by Manhattan standards, and there are direct-dial phone lines in each. Executive suites have separate office areas with computers and fax/printer/scanner machines. **The Avalon Bar and Grill** (located on the lobby level and available for room service) has a "fresh American" menu of healthy dishes made with organic ingredients from local farmers' markets.

**Hotel services** *Complimentary breakfast. Conference facility. Restaurant.* **Room services** *High-speed internet. Minibar. Voice mail.*

### Clarion Park Avenue

*429 Park Ave South between 29th and 30th Sts (212-532-4860, 800-446-4656; fax 212-545-9727; www.bestnyhotels.com). Subway: 6 to 28th St. Single $105–$259, double $115–$299. 60 rooms. AmEx, DC, Disc, MC, V.*

run by chef Sam DeMarco, known for inventive American cooking. Guests can get in-room spa treatments like hour-long massages for $140. **Hotel services** *Cell-phone rental. Fitness center. Valet parking.* **Room services** *CD player. Safe. VCR. Voice mail.*

By the book Every room in the Library Hotel is stocked for your reading pleasure.

## Comfortable

### Clarion Hotel Fifth Avenue

*3 E 40th St between Fifth and Madison Aves (212-447-1500, 800-228-5151; fax 212-213-0972). Subway: B, D, F, V to 42nd St; 7 to Fifth Ave. Single/double $149–$239. 189 rooms. AmEx, DC, Disc, MC, V.*

The Clarion is a stone's throw from the New York Public Library and Bryant Park. Request room numbers that end in three to six (the higher the floor, the better) for a street view and plenty of light; back rooms are darker and look into offices. Ask about corporate and weekend rates, and catch a meal at **Salmon River** *(212-481-7887)*, the hotel's seafood restaurant. **Hotel services** *Dry cleaning. Parking. Restaurant.* **Room services** *Fax. Radio. Room service. Voice mail.*

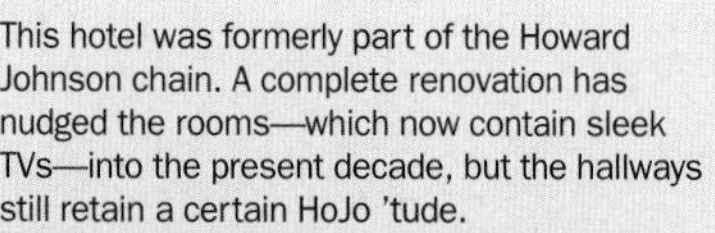

This hotel was formerly part of the Howard Johnson chain. A complete renovation has nudged the rooms—which now contain sleek TVs—into the present decade, but the hallways still retain a certain HoJo 'tude.
**Hotel services** *Complimentary breakfast. Valet parking.* **Room services** *Modem line. Radio. Safe. Voice mail.*

### Hotel Grand Union

*34 E 32nd St between Madison and Park Aves (212-683-5890; fax 212-689-7397; www.hotelgrandunion.com). Subway: 6 to 33rd St. Single/double $90, twin/triple $110, quad $125. 96 rooms. AmEx, DC, Disc, MC, V.*

You won't find many bells and whistles at the Hotel Grand Union, but you will find spacious rooms with clean, private bathrooms for the same price that similar hotels might charge for shared bathrooms. The rooms quickly fill with tourists, so reserve at least a month in advance. The helpful staff will book tours for you and provide useful New York advice.
**Hotel services** *Concierge. Safe.* **Room services** *Modem line. Refrigerator. Voice mail.*

### Le Marquis

*12 E 31st St between Fifth and Madison Aves (212-889-6363; fax 212-889-6699; www.lemarquisny.com). Subway: 6 to 33rd St. Single/double $179–$300. Suite $279–$450. 131 rooms. AmEx, DC, Disc, MC, V.*

You're issued a personal direct-dial telephone line upon check-in at Le Marquis, the first of many comforts proffered by this deluxe hotel. The rooms, though small, are appointed with luxury linens, Frette bathrobes, DVD players and Aveda bath products. The building was built in 1906, but the hotel has been recently renovated; modern rooms are designed in white, khaki and light blue with black-and-white photographs of New York streetscapes on the walls. The 12:31 bar offers cocktails and a light food menu. Turndown service leaves chocolate on your pillow and a next-day weather forecast—hope for rain so you can stay in bed all day.
**Hotel services** *Bar. Conference facility. Fitness center. Restaurant.* **Room services** *Alarm clock. Complimentary DVD library. High-speed internet. Minibar. Safe.*

### Murray Hill Inn

*143 E 30th St between Lexington and Third Aves (212-683-6900, 888-996-6376; fax 212-545-0103; www.murrayhillinn.com). Subway: 6 to 28th St. Double with shared bath $75–$95, single/double with private bath $95–$125. 45 rooms. AmEx, MC, V.*

Located on a quiet, tree-lined street in midtown within walking distance of the Empire State Building and Grand Central Terminal, this inn is a good value. Rooms are basic, but neat and clean; most come with private bathrooms, and all have sinks. Discounted weekly and monthly rates are available. Book ▶

## Comfort Inn Manhattan

*42 W 35th St between Fifth and Sixth Aves (212-947-0200, 800-228-5150; fax 212-594-3047; www.comfortinnmanhattan.com). Subway: B, D, F, V, N, Q, R, W to 34th St–Herald Sq. Single/double $129–$349. 130 rooms. AmEx, DC, Disc, MC, V.*

This small, family-oriented hotel is around the corner from Macy's and the Empire State Building. The front-desk clerk Alex, a hotel fixture for more than a decade, is a hoot. Rates include breakfast.

**Hotel services** *Concierge. Continental breakfast.* **Room services** *Alarm clock. Hair dryer. Safe. Voice mail.*

## Hotel Edison

*228 W 47th St at Broadway (212-840-5000, 800-637-7070; fax 212-596-6850; www.edisonhotelnyc.com). Subway: N, R, W to 49th St; 1, 9 to 50th St. Single $150, double $170 ($15 for each extra person, four-person maximum), suite $175–$220. 1,000 rooms. AmEx, DC, Disc, MC, V.*

After a two-year renovation, the Edison and its Art Deco lobby are decidedly spruced up. Rooms are standard, but theater lovers won't find a more convenient location. The coffeeshop **Cafe Edison** *(212-840-5000)*, just off the lobby, is a longtime favorite of Broadway actors and their fans—Neil Simon was so smitten with the place that he put it in a play.

**Hotel services** *Bar. Currency exchange. Restaurant. Safe. Travel/tour desk.* **Room services** *Cable TV. Hair dryer. Voice mail.*

## Hotel 41

*206 W 41st St between Seventh and Eighth Aves (877-847-4444; fax 212-302-0895; www.hotel41.com). Subway: N, Q, R, W, S, 1, 2, 3, 9, 7 to 42nd St–Times Sq. Single/double $119–$299, suite $269–$489. 47 rooms. AmEx, DC, MC, V.*

Open only since August 2002, Hotel 41 looks as if it might accept payment in francs. The lobby is small and sleek, and the white-walled chambers channel that Swiss combination of efficiency and charm. Reading lamps protrude from pale-wood headboards. Triple-paned windows effectively block out the cacophony from Times Square below. The front desk has a CD/DVD library, and rooms come complete with DirectTV and Internet access.

**Hotel services** *Baby-sitting. Bar. Complimentary breakfast. Dry cleaning. Laundry drop-off.* **Room services** *Cable TV. CD player. Safe. VCR. Video library.*

## ▸ Hill street news (continued)

well in advance or try the sister locations, **Union Square Inn**, **Amsterdam Inn** and **Central Park Hostel** *(See pages 143 and 164)*.

**Hotel services** *Air-conditioning. Complimentary breakfast. Currency exchange.* **Room services** *Cable TV. Hair dryer.*

### Park South Hotel

*122 E 28th St between Park Ave South and Lexington Ave (212-448-0888, 800-315-4642; www.parksouthhotel.com). Subway: 6 to 28th St. Single/double $199–$260, suite $325–$345. 143 rooms. AmEx, DC, Disc, MC, V.*

One of the city's newest boutique hotels, Park South gives a nod to old New York. The restored 1906 building has a mezzanine library crammed with books on historic Gotham, and the walls are covered with nearly 100 images from the New-York Historical Society. The rooms—decorated in warm amber and brown—and the dazzling views of the Chrysler Building conjure sentimental feelings about the city. The hotel's restaurant, **Black Duck** *(212-204-5240)*, serves traditional American fare.

**Hotel services** *Complimentary breakfast. Conference facility. Dry cleaning. Fitness center.* **Room services** *DVD player. Fax/copier. Internet access.*

### The Roger Williams

*131 Madison Ave at 31st St (888-448-7788; fax 212-448-7007; www.rogerwilliamshotel.com). Subway: 6 to 33rd St. Single/double $225–$245. Suite $405–$475. 187 rooms. AmEx, DC, Disc, MC, V.*

Popular with the fashion industry, the small and stylish Roger Williams offers complimentary espresso and cappuccino, and a glass of champagne upon check-in to warm you amid the cool decor and even cooler clientele. The facade resembles that of a sleek Madison Avenue office building, and the lobby displays paintings and sculpture from a local gallery. The amenities (such as free bottled water and 300-thread–count linens) make you feel as though you're in your own home—if you're lucky enough to live like this. Each room on the penthouse level has access to comfy deck chairs (and free sunscreen) on a shared wraparound terrace. **The Franklin**, **Hotel Wales**, **Mansfield** and **Shoreham** *(see pages 162, 149 and 152)* are also part of the Boutique Hotel Group, and are located near Museum Mile; some rooms in the Hotel Wales have views of Central Park.

**Hotel services** *Business center. Concierge. Fitness center. Meditation room.* **Room services** *Alarm clock. Room service. Voice mail.*

### ThirtyThirty

*30 E 30th St between Madison Ave and Park Ave South (212-689-1900; fax 212-689-0023; www.stayinny.com). Subway: 6 to 28th St. Single/double $110–$215. Suites $160–$305. 262 rooms. AmEx, DC, Disc, MC, V.*

## Hotel Metro

*45 W 35th St between Fifth and Sixth Aves (212-947-2500, 800-356-3870; fax 212-279-1310; www.hotelmetronyc.com). Subway: B, D, F, V, N, Q, R, W to 34th St–Herald Sq. Single/double $145–$325, suite $200–$400. 184 rooms. AmEx, DC, MC, V.*

It's not posh, but the Metro has good service and a convenient location near the Empire State Building. The lobby exudes a charming retro feel, rooms are small but neat and clean, and the roof terrace offers splendid views (not to mention a rooftop bar). **Metro Grill** *(212-947-2500)* is in the lobby.

**Hotel services** *Complimentary breakfast. Fitness center. Library. Restaurant and bar. Ticket desk.* **Room services** *Modem line. Refrigerator. Room service. Voice mail.*

## La Quinta Manhattan

*17 W 32nd St between Fifth Ave and Broadway (212-736-1600, 800-567-7720; fax 212-790-2758). Subway: B, D, F, V, N, Q, R, W to 34th St–Herald Sq. Single/double $99–$329, triple/quad $109–$399. 182 rooms. AmEx, DC, Disc, MC, V.*

This is a good-value hotel with a stylish Beaux Arts facade and a black-and-gray marble lobby. The new restaurant in the lobby, **Dae Dong** *(212-967-1900)*, serves Japanese and Korean cuisine.

**Hotel services** *Fitness center. Gift shop. Ticket desk.* **Room services** *High-speed Internet access. Voice mail.*

## The Marcel

*201 E 24th St at Third Ave (212-696-3800; fax 212-696-0077; www.nycityhotels.com). Subway: 6 to 23rd St. Single/double $90–$220. 97 rooms. AmEx, DC, Disc, MC, V.*

One of the few hotels in this bustling part of the city, the sleek Marcel is frequented by fashion-industry types for its easy access to the downtown, Flatiron, Gramercy and midtown districts. The compact rooms have nice design touches; those facing Third Avenue are noisy but have the best views. **Spread** *(212-683-8880)*, the hotel's sexy lounge, serves pricey designer nibbles, but guests looking for dining alternatives will find many options on Park Avenue South, just a short walk away.

**Hotel services** *Dry cleaning. 24-hour cappuccino bar. Video library.* **Room services** *Alarm clock. CD player. Dataport. Modem line. Nintendo. Radio. VCR on request.*

**Modern lug** The spare lobby of ThirtyThirty provides ample room for hauling suitcases.

ThirtyThirty boasts a stylish modern feel and little extras designed to lure budget business customers, as do the other uptown locations, **Habitat Hotel** *(see page 164)* and **On the Ave** *(see page 162)*. Upbeat ambient music sets the tone in the spare, fashionable lobby, which stretches from 29th to 30th Streets. "Executive Floor" rooms are slightly larger than the rest and have a workspace with a desk and extensions for a phone and laptop.

**Hotel services** *Concierge. Fax. Florist. Free passes to nearby gym.* **Room services** *Alarm clock. Cable TV. Room service. Voice mail.*

### Metropolitan Hotel

*569 Lexington Ave at 51st St (212-752-7000, 800-836-6471; fax 212-753-7253). Subway: E, V to Lexington Ave–53rd St; 6 to 51st St. Single/double $159–$259, suite $229–$699. 722 rooms. AmEx, DC, Disc, MC, V.*

In 2000, the hotel underwent a $17 million renovation that returned the building to its original Coffeeshop Moderne look (architect Morris Lapidus designed many of the '50s-era hotels). Toiletries in the business-class rooms are just like those at home: Besides soap and shampoo, guests will find cotton balls, Q-tips and a nail file.

**Hotel services** *Baby-sitting. Fitness center. Manicurist. Valet.* **Room services** *Room service. Voice mail.*

### The Roosevelt Hotel

*45 E 45th St at Madison Ave (212-661-9600, 888-TEDDY-NY; fax 212-885-6162; www.theroosevelthotel.com). Subway: S, 4, 5, 6, 7 to 42nd St–Grand Central. Single/double $179–$289, suite $205–$2,000. 1,040 rooms. AmEx, DC, Disc, MC, V.*

Built in 1924, this enormous hotel was once a haven for celebs and socialites (Guy Lombardo did his first New Year's Eve "Auld Lang Syne" broadcast from here). Nostalgic grandeur lives on in the lobby, with its 27-foot fluted columns, acres of marble and huge sprays of flowers. The Palm Room serves snacks under a blue-sky mural, and the **Madison Club Lounge** *(212-885-6192)* serves cocktails in a clubby setting adorned with stained-glass windows.

**Hotel services** *Baby-sitting. Ballroom. Bar. Concierge. Conference facility. Fitness center. Restaurant. Valet. Valet parking.* **Room services** *Kitchenette and VCR in suites. Modem line. Room service. Voice mail.*

### Wellington Hotel

*871 Seventh Ave at 55th St (212-247-3900, 800-652-1212; fax 212-581-1719; www.wellingtonhotel.com). Subway: B, D, E to Seventh Ave; N, Q, R, W to 57th St. Single/double $159–$250, suite $189–$250. 600 rooms. AmEx, DC, Disc, MC, V.*

Wellington has some fetching old-fashioned touches (like a gold-domed lobby ceiling with a chandelier), though everything's a tad frayed around the edges. Still, it's close to Broadway and Central Park, and you can dine on-site at **Molyvos** *(see page 198)*, one of the city's best Greek restaurants.

**Hotel services** *Bar. Beauty salon. Coffeeshop. Restaurant. Transportation desk.* **Room services** *Refrigerator in some rooms. Room service.*

### Wyndham Hotel

*42 W 58th St between Fifth and Sixth Aves (212-753-3500, 800-257-1111; fax 212-754-5638; www.wyndham.com). Subway: F to 57th St; N, R, W to Fifth Ave–59th St. Single/double $140–$170, suite $195–$250. 204 rooms. AmEx, DC, Disc, MC, V.*

Popular with actors and directors, the Wyndham has generous-sized rooms and suites with walk-in closets. The decor is worn but homey. This is a good midtown location—you can walk to the new **American Folk Art Museum** *(see page 48)*, Fifth Avenue shopping and many Broadway theaters—and it's reasonably priced, so book well ahead.

**Hotel services** *Bar. Beauty salon. Restaurant.* **Room services** *Refrigerator in suites. Voice mail.*

## Budget

### Broadway Inn

*264 W 46th St at Eighth Ave (212-997-9200, 800-826-6300; fax 212-768-2807; www.broadwayinn.com). Subway: A, C, E to 42nd St–Port Authority. Single/double $99–$185, suite $199–$275. 41 rooms. AmEx, DC, Disc, MC, V.*

In contrast to Times Square's megahotels, this inn feels small and personal—think Off Broadway rather than the Great White Way. The warm lobby has exposed-brick walls, ceiling fans, shelves loaded with books you can borrow, and a hospitable front-desk staff. The basic guest rooms and suites get a lot of natural light and are fairly priced. But beware: The stairs are steep, and the inn has no elevator.

**Hotel services** *Complimentary breakfast. Concierge. Safe.* **Room services** *Kitchenette in suites. Radio.*

### Carlton Arms Hotel

*160 E 25th St at Third Ave (212-679-0680; www.carltonarms.com). Subway: 6 to 23rd St. Single with shared bath $70, with private bath $85; double with shared bath $90, with private bath $100; triples $110–$120. 54 rooms. MC, V.*

The Carlton Arms is a cheerful, basic budget hotel popular with Europeans (you should reserve at least two months in advance). The themed rooms and corridors are brightly decorated, each by a different artist. Units are redesigned every few years—check out the English cottage room, gussied up in a convincing Tudor style. Discounts are offered for students, overseas guests and patrons on weekly stays. Only some rooms have air-conditioning, but all have character.

**Hotel services** *Café. Telephone in lobby.* **Room service** *Sink.*

### The Chelsea Star Hotel

*300 W 30th St at Eighth Ave (212-244-7827; fax 212-279-9018; www.starhotelny.com). Subway: A, C, E to 34th St–Penn Station. Dorm room $35, single/double with shared bathroom $59–$79, suite with private bath $129–$175. 18 rooms. AmEx, Disc, MC, V.*

This hotel has earned its name—it was one of Madonna's first New York residences. The small room she called home has a gritty view of Madison Square Garden, and the slight seediness of the location is part of the experience. (You'll also find theme rooms dedicated to *Star Trek, Madame Butterfly* and Cleopatra.) A roof deck and dorm room make the Chelsea Star one of the city's best deals for hostelers. The hotel also offers discounted weekly and monthly rates for one-bedroom apartments.

**Charge it** You may use your credit card to stay in the Rhino Room at the Carlton Arms Hotel.

**Hotel services** *Internet access in hallways. Safe.* **Room services** *Air-conditioning. Cable TV. Modem line in apartments.*

## The Gershwin Hotel

*7 E 27th St between Fifth and Madison Aves (212-545-8000; fax 212-684-5546; www.gershwinhotel.com). Subway: N, R, 6 to 28th St. $40 per person in 4- to 8-bed dorm, $109–$209 for one to three people in private room, suite $189–$289. 150 rooms. AmEx, MC, V.*

The bohemian Gershwin offers extremely reasonable accommodations just off Fifth Avenue. The lobby is hung with Lichtenstein and Warhol works, and the hallways display a large photography collection. The hotel is popular with young student types who have little need for luxuries. If you can afford a suite, book the Lindfors (named after the building's designer), which has screen-printed walls and a nifty sitting room. Poetry readings and stand-up comedy take place in the evenings.

**Hotel services** *Concierge. Conference facility. Dry cleaning. Roof garden. Transportation desk.* **Room services** *Alarm clock. Modem line. TV in private rooms. Voice mail.*

## The Herald Square Hotel

*19 W 31st St between Fifth Ave and Broadway (212-279-4017, 800-727-1888; fax 212-643-9208; www.heraldsquarehotel.com). Subway: B, D, F, V, N, Q, R, W to 34th St–Herald Sq. Single/double $60–$120, triple $130, quad $140. 130 rooms. AmEx, Disc, MC, V.*

The Herald Square Hotel was the original *Life* magazine building, and it retains its cherub-adorned entrance. All rooms were renovated in 1999, and most have private bathrooms; corridors are lined with framed *Life* illustrations. It's a good deal, so book well in advance. There are discounts for students.

**Hotel services** *Safe. Ticket desk.* **Room services** *Modem line. Radio. Voice mail.*

## Hotel 31

*120 E 31st St between Park Ave South and Lexington Ave (212-685-3060). Subway: 6 to 33rd St. Single/double $85–$120, triple $130. 70 rooms. MC, V.*

See **Hotel 17**, page 143.

## Pickwick Arms

*230 E 51st St between Second and Third Aves (212-355-0300, 800-742-5945; fax 212-755-5029;*

*www.pickwickarms.com). Subway: E, V to Lexington Ave–53rd St; 6 to 51st St. Single $79–$109, double $129–$150. 370 rooms. AmEx, DC, MC, V.*

The rooms may be small, but they are clean. And although the hotel is in a rather quiet district, restaurants, movie theaters, Radio City Music Hall and the United Nations are all within walking distance. Most of the rooms have private bathrooms, but some share an adjoining facility, while others share a bathroom down the hall. There are two restaurants within the hotel, as well as a rooftop garden.

**Hotel services** *Bar. E-mail access in lobby. Restaurant. Safe.* **Room services** *Cable TV. Voice mail.*

### Red Roof Inn

*6 W 32nd St between Fifth Ave and Broadway (212-643-7100, 800-RED-ROOF; fax 212-643-7101; www.redroof.com). Subway: B, D, F, V, N, Q, R, W to 34th St–Herald Sq; 6 to 33rd St. Single/double $110–$290. 171 rooms. AmEx, DC, Disc, MC, V.*

This branch of the U.S. motel chain surpasses its brethren with a black-and-beige lobby that's smart and sleek. It's also one of the best deals in town. In the middle of Koreatown, the converted office building is centrally located and close to good Korean restaurants, many of which are open all night. Each room that ends in six has a minifridge and microwave oven. For quiet, book a room at the back.

**Hotel services** *Bar. Concierge. Conference room. Safe. 24-hour fitness center.* **Room services** *Refrigerator and microwave oven in some rooms. Web TV.*

### The Wolcott Hotel

*4 W 31st St between Fifth Ave and Broadway (212-268-2900; fax 212-563-0096; www.wolcott.com). Subway: B, D, F, V, N, Q, R, W to 34th St–Herald Sq. Single/double $100–$120, suite $110–$150. 159 rooms. AmEx, MC, V.*

The ornate gilded lobby comes as a surprise in this Garment District hotel, where celebs of another age, such as Edith Wharton and *Titanic* survivor Washington Dodge, once stayed. The rooms are on the small side, but inexpensive.

**Hotel services** *Concierge. Fitness center. Self-serve laundry. Ticket desk.* **Room services** *Modem line. Safe. Voice mail. Web TV.*

## Hostels

### Chelsea Center

*313 W 29th St between Eighth and Ninth Aves (212-643-0214; fax 212-473-3945; www.chelseacenterhostel.com). Subway: A, C, E to 34th St–Penn Station. $25–$30 per person in dorm. 20 beds. Cash only.*

The Chelsea Center is a small, welcoming hostel with clean bathrooms and a patio garden in the back. It has the feel of shared student housing. Since there are a limited number of beds in each dorm, book at least a week in advance. There's no curfew or air-conditioning, and the price includes Continental breakfast. All rooms are nonsmoking. There is also an East Village location, for which bookings should be made through the Chelsea Center.

**Hotel services** *Fax. Garden patio. Kitchen facilities. TV room.*

### YMCA (Vanderbilt)

*224 E 47th St between Second and Third Aves (212-756-9600; fax 212-752-0210; www.ymcanyc.org). Subway: S, 4, 5, 6, 7 to 42nd St–Grand Central. Single/double $64–$80, suite $134. 370 rooms. AmEx, MC, V.*

This cheerful YMCA's more expensive quarters have sinks, but the rooms aren't very large—the beds barely fit into some of them. Book well in advance by writing to the reservations department, including a deposit for one night's rent. All rooms allow smoking and only the suites have private baths.

**Hotel services** *Air-conditioning. Fitness facilities. Luggage room. Self-serve laundry.* **Room services** *Alarm clock. TV.*

# Above 59th Street

## Deluxe

### The Carlyle

*35 E 76th St between Madison and Park Aves (212-744-1600, 800-227-5737; fax 212-717-4682; www.thecarlyle.com). Subway: 6 to 77th St. Single/double $495–$795, suite $850–$3,200. 180 rooms. AmEx, DC, Disc, MC, V.*

One of New York's most sumptuous and glamorous hotels, the Carlyle has attracted famous guests for more than 70 years—especially those who value privacy. The ground floor has been recently renovated, including the lobby (with its Matisse and Picasso artworks) and **Bemelmans Bar**, which was named for Ludwig Bemelmans, the creator of the children's book *Madeline,* and is lined with murals he painted in 1947, when he lived at the hotel *(see page 269)*. Some bathrooms feature whirlpools and all are stocked with Kiehl's products.

**Hotel services** *Fitness center. Parking. Restaurant. 24-hour dry cleaning.* **Room services** *CD player. VCR. Voice mail.*

### The Mark

*25 E 77th St between Fifth and Madison Aves (212-744-4300, 800-843-6275; fax 212-472-5714; www.themarkhotel.com). Subway: 6 to 77th St. Single $525–$600, double $545–$575, suite $665–$2,500. 177 rooms. AmEx, DC, Disc, MC, V.*

Towering potted palms and arched mirrors line the entryway to this cheerful European-style Upper East Side hotel. The marble lobby, decorated with 18th-century Piranesi prints and Veuve Clicquot magnums, is usually swarming with dressy international guests and white-gloved bellmen. Especially popular are the clubby Mark's Bar and the more elegant restaurant, **Mark's** *(212-879-1864)*.

**Hotel services** *Cell-phone rental. Currency exchange. Fitness center. Free shuttle to Wall Street.*

**Girl power** The Madeline series illustrator lends charm to the Carlyle's Bemelmans Bar.

*24-hour dry cleaning.* **Room services** *Kitchenette. Printer. VCR. Web TV.*

### The Pierre Hotel

*2 E 61st St at Fifth Ave (212-838-8000, 800-PIERRE-4; fax 212-826-0319; www.fourseasons.com/pierre). Subway: N, R, W to Fifth Ave–59th St. Single $425–$950, double $475–$995, suite $625–$3,800. 201 rooms. AmEx, DC, Disc, MC, V.*

The Pierre has been seducing guests since 1930 with its service and discreet, elegant atmosphere. Front rooms overlook Central Park, and some of Madison Avenue's most famous stores are only a block away. Besides dry cleaning, the hotel offers hand laundering for precious garments.

**Hotel services** *Baby-sitting. Beauty salon. Business service. Cell-phone rental. Currency exchange. Fitness center. Parking. Theater desk. 24-hour dry cleaning.* **Room services** *High-speed Internet access. In-room exercise equipment. VCR on request. Voice mail.*

### The Plaza Hotel

*768 Fifth Ave at 59th St (212-759-3000, 800-759-3000; fax 212-759-3167; www.fairmont.com). Subway: N, R, W to Fifth Ave–59th St. Single/double $429–$869, suite $909–$1,600. 807 rooms. AmEx, DC, Disc, MC, V.*

Ideally located for a shopping spree, the Plaza Hotel is across the street from Central Park and minutes from Fifth Avenue's most exclusive stores. The hotel, built in 1907, is renowned for its baroque splendor; 200 rooms and suites have their original marble fireplaces. After a day of rigorous consumption, unwind at the 8,000-square-foot spa, or with wine and brasserie food at **ONE c.p.s** *(212-583-1111)*, the restaurant in what was once the Edwardian Room.

**Hotel services** *Baby-sitting. Fitness center. Salon. Spa. Ticket desk. 24-hour dry cleaning.* **Room services** *VCR on request. Voice mail.*

### The Ritz-Carlton New York, Central Park

*50 Central Park South between Fifth and Sixth Aves (212-308-9100; fax 212-877-6465; www.ritz-carlton.com). Subway: F to 57th St; N, R, W to Fifth Ave–59th St. Single/double $650–$975, suite $1,395–$12,500. 277 rooms. AmEx, DC, Disc, MC, V.*

Gilded doors swing open, a beaming doorman greets you, and bejeweled patrons drift through the high-ceilinged lobby of this renovated 1930s hotel. Frill seekers will adore the sleeping quarters, which are outfitted with pristine bed dressing and vases of fresh flowers. The swank, on-site La Prairie at the Ritz-Carlton Spa offers treatments like a champagne-and-caviar firming facial and jet-lag therapy. The hotel's dining hall, **Atelier** *(212-521-6125)*, has suede walls, a chef formerly of Jean Georges and entrées like squab and foie gras *croustillant.* In what seems to be a bid to update its old-school image, all Ritz-Carltons (for the Battery Park location, *see page 161*) now employ a "technology butler."

**Hotel services** *Cell-phone rental. Currency exchange. Dry cleaning. Fitness center with on-call personal trainers. Free overnight shoe shine. Free shuttle within midtown. Laundry drop off.* **Room services** *DVD player. High-speed Internet access. Safe.*

### Trump International Hotel & Tower

*1 Central Park West at Columbus Circle (212-299-1000, 888-448-7867; fax 212-299-1150; www.trumpintl.com). Subway: A, C, B, D, 1, 9 to 59th St–Columbus Circle. Single/double $525–$575,*

*suite $795–$1,650. 167 rooms. AmEx, DC, Disc, MC, V.*
Donald Trump's glass-and-steel skyscraper towers over Columbus Circle, just steps from Central Park. Inside, all is subdued elegance, from the small marble lobby to the suites equipped with fax machines, Jacuzzis and floor-to-ceiling windows. Each guest is assigned a personal assistant to cater to his or her whims, and a chef will come to the room to cook on request. Better yet, head downstairs to **Jean Georges** *(see* **JoJo**, *page 202),* named for its four-star chef, Jean-Georges Vongerichten.
**Hotel services**. *Cell-phone rental. Currency exchange. Fitness center. Personal attaché service.* **Room services** *CD player. Computer. Kitchenette. Telescope. VCR. Voice mail.*

## Stylish

### On the Ave Hotel

*2178 Broadway at 77th St (212-362-1100, 800-509-7598; fax 917-441-0295; www.ontheave-nyc.com). Subway: 1, 9 to 79th St. Single/double $159–$280, suite $215–$320, penthouse suite $300–$450. 250 rooms. AmEx, DC, Disc, MC, V.*
On the Ave brings some sorely needed style to the Upper West Side's stodgy hotel scene. Its most winning attractions are "floating beds," industrial-style bathroom sinks and three floors that offer 23 penthouse rooms and suites, each with fantastic balcony views of Central Park, the Hudson River and beyond. (All guests have access to a balcony on the 16th floor.) Original artwork and innovative touches, such as individual breakfast trays that can double as laptop desks, embellish the minimalist decor. The hotel is part of Citylife Hotel Group, which also owns **ThirtyThirty** *(see page 156)* and **Habitat Hotel** *(see page 164).*
**Hotel services** *24-hour dry cleaning and laundry. Valet.* **Room services** *High-speed Internet access. Room service. VCR. Voice mail.*

### The Franklin

*164 E 87th St at Lexington Ave (212-369-1000, fax 212-369-8000). Subway: 4, 5, 6 to 86th St. Single/double $210–$295. 48 rooms. AmEx, DC, Disc, MC, V.*
See **The Roger Williams**, page 156.

### The Hotel Wales

*1295 Madison Ave between 92nd and 93rd Sts. (212-876-6000). Subway: 6 to 96th St. Single/double $235–$320, double $20 per extra person in room, suite $335–$450. 87 rooms. AmEx, MC, V.*
See **The Roger Williams**, page 156.

## Business

### The Bentley

*500 E 62nd St at York Ave (212-644-6000, 888-66HOTEL; fax 212-751-7868; www.nychotels.com). Subway: N, R, W to Lexington Ave–59th St; 4, 5, 6 to 59th St. Single/double $135–$245, suite $225–$575. 197 rooms. AmEx, DC, Disc, MC, V.*
This slender 21-story, glass-and-steel hotel, located as far east as you can go on the Upper East Side, offers

**Glass eye** Oversized windows provide impressive views from On the Ave's 16th-floor suite.

sweeping views of the East River and the Queensboro Bridge. Converted from an office building in 1998, the Bentley is an ideal getaway for tired execs: It has soundproof windows and blackout shades. The mahogany-paneled library houses a complimentary cappuccino bar, and there's a nearby spot for sophisticated souvenir shopping—around the corner at designer **Terence Conran**'s shop *(see page 242).*
**Hotel services** *Complimentary breakfast.* **Room services** *CD and DVD players. Nintendo.*

### The Phillips Club

*155 W 66th St between Broadway and Amsterdam Ave (212-835-8800, 877-854-8800; fax 212-835-8850; www.phillipsclub.com). Subway: 1, 9 to 66th St–Lincoln Ctr. Suite $420–$1,300. 120 rooms. AmEx, DC, Disc., MC, V.*
Perhaps the classiest of New York's growing number of extended-stay hotels, the Phillips Club is on the Upper West Side, across from Lincoln Center and two blocks from Central Park. Suites are available for transient visits, leasing and club ownership, which functions like a time-share. Each suite has a full kitchen and includes access to the Reebok Club. The high-end Balducci's market on the ground floor ensures that all the ingredients for a fancy home-cooked meal are close at hand. The gourmet grocer also provides room service.
**Hotel services** *Baby-sitting. Dry cleaning. Fitness center. Spa.* **Room services** *CD player. Room service.*

## Boutique

### Hotel Plaza Athénée

*37 E 64th St between Madison and Park Aves (212-734-9100, 800-447-8800; www.plaza-athenee.com). Subway: F to Lexington Ave–63rd St. Single/double $480–$515, suite $1,100–$3,600. 152 rooms. AmEx, DC, Disc, MC, V.*
Hotel Plaza Athénée is one of the few boutique hotels to stray from the modernist course. Situated steps off posh Park Avenue on a quiet residential block, this European-style hotel impresses discerning guests upon arrival; the lobby features Italian-marble floors, French antique furnishings and hand-painted tapestries. The 113 recently renovated guest rooms are just as luxurious: Fresh-cut flowers scent the bathrooms and plush robes are a courtesy. Visitors lucky enough to afford one of the 39 suites (Charlize Theron posed in one during a *Vanity Fair* fashion shoot) may be treated to a terrace and a solarium. Only the suites have pantries equipped with a stove and refrigerator, but all guests can enjoy the hotel's creative American restaurant, **Arabelle** *(212-606-4647).*
**Hotel services** *Fitness center. Overnight shoe shine.* **Room services** *CD player. Complimentary newspaper. Speakerphone. Voice mail.*

### The Lowell Hotel

*28 E 63rd St between Madison and Park Aves (212-838-1400, 800-221-4444; fax 212-605-6808). Subway: N, R, W to Lexington Ave–59th St; 4, 5, 6 to 59th St. Single/double $445–$575, suite $775–$4,575. 70 rooms. AmEx, DC, Disc, MC, V.*
Renovated in 2000, this petite charmer is in a landmark Art Deco building. Rooms feature marble baths and Scandinavian down comforters; there are even wood-burning fireplaces in the suites. The gym suite (which has two private baths and a personal gym) has lodged Michelle Pfeiffer and Arnold Schwarzenegger, among other fitness enthusiasts.
**Hotel services** *Baby-sitting. Cell-phone rental. Currency exchange. Fitness center.* **Room services** *CD player. DVD player on request. VCR. Voice mail.*

### The Melrose Hotel

*140 E 63rd St between Lexington and Third Aves (212-838-5700; www.melrosehotel.com). Subway: N, R, W to Lexington Ave–59th St; 4, 5, 6 to 59th St. Single/double $199–$340, suite $450–$1,800. 306 rooms. AmEx, DC, Disc, MC, V.*
The Melrose opened June 2002 in the Barbizon Hotel building, which from 1927 to 1981 was an exclusive women-only hotel that played host to Grace Kelly and Liza Minnelli. The place has been spiffed up with cherry-wood furniture and gilded mirrors, and the marble floor in the lobby was restored to its original splendor. Tower suites boast landscaped balconies with Corinthian pillars and dizzying views of city lights. Every detail is deluxe: Bathrooms are stocked with spa products from Gilchrist & Soames of London.
**Hotel services** *Bar. Fitness center. Ticket desk. Valet service.* **Room services** *CD player. High-speed Internet access. VCR. Voice mail.*

## Comfortable

### The Empire Hotel

*44 W 63rd St between Broadway and Columbus Ave (212-265-7400, 888-822-3555; fax 212-315-0349; www.empirehotel.com). Subway: 1, 9 to 66th St–Lincoln Ctr. Single/double $100–$249, suite $400–$1,000. 381 rooms. AmEx, DC, Disc, MC, V.*
The Empire sits opposite Lincoln Center and near a number of decent pretheater restaurants (*see chapter* **Restaurants, Upper West Side**). Wood paneling and velvet drapes make for a surprisingly baronial lobby. The rooms are clean and tasteful, with plenty of chintz and floral prints.
**Hotel services** *Bar. Currency exchange. Dry cleaning. Fitness center. Gift shop. Theater/tour ticket desk. Video rental.* **Room services** *Cassette and CD players. Modem line. Two-line phones. VCR. Voice mail.*

### The Lucerne

*201 W 79th St at Amsterdam Ave (212-875-1000, 800-492-8122; fax 212-721-1179; www.newyorkhotel.com). Subway: 1, 9 to 79th St. Single/double $180–$345, suite $170–$635. 187 rooms. AmEx, DC, Disc, MC, V.*
From the outside, the landmark Lucerne, with its ornate columns and elaborate prewar facade, recalls the heyday of high-society New York. The rooftop patio offers views of Central Park and the Hudson River, and Lincoln Center is nearby. The Lucerne is

Necessities

part of the Empire Hotel Group and has six sister locations (for more info, visit the website).
**Hotel services** *Cell-phone rental. Concierge. Fitness center. Parking.* **Room services** *Nintendo. Radio. Room service. Safe. Voice mail. Web TV.*

### The Mayflower Hotel

*15 Central Park West at 61st St (212-265-0060, 800-223-4164; fax 212-265-0227; www.mayflowerhotel.com). Subway: A, C, B, D, 1, 9 to 59th St–Columbus Circle. Single/double $200–$265, suite $320–$1,200. 365 rooms. AmEx, DC, Disc, MC, V.*
This musicians' haven faces Central Park and is just a few blocks from Lincoln Center. The views of the park are spectacular from the front rooms, which cost a small amount more. The **Conservatory Café** *(212-581-0896)* on the first floor is a nice spot for a light breakfast.
**Hotel services** *Bar. Currency exchange. Fitness center. Restaurant.* **Room services** *Room service. VCR on request. Voice mail.*

## Less than $200

### Amsterdam Inn

*340 Amsterdam Ave at 76th St (212-579-7500; fax 212-579-6127; www.amsterdaminn.com). Subway: 1, 9 to 79th St. Single/double with shared bath $85, with private bath $99–$129. AmEx, MC, V.*
See **Murray Hill Inn**, page 155.

### Excelsior Hotel

*45 W 81st St between Central Park West and Columbus Ave (212-362-9200, 800-368-4575; fax 212-721-9224; www.excelsiorhotelny.com). Subway: B, C to 81st St–Museum of Natural History; 1, 9 to 79th St. Single/double $159–$199, suite $239–$439. 195 rooms. AmEx, DC, Disc, MC, V.*
On the Upper West Side, where hotels are scarce, the Excelsior offers a prime location just steps from Central Park and across the street from the American Museum of Natural History. The rooms are reliable and renovated but still affordable.
**Hotel services** *Concierge. Fitness center. Gift shop. Library. Valet.* **Room services** *Computers in many rooms. Modem line. Nintendo. Voice mail. Web TV.*

### Habitat Hotel

*130 E 57th St at Lexington Ave (212-753-8841; www.habitatny.com). Subway: N, R, W to Lexington Ave–59th St; 4, 5, 6 to 59th St. Single/double $89–$129, deluxe/suites $169–$199. 350 rooms. AmEx, DC, Disc, MC, V.*
Similar to **Thirty Thirty** *(see page 157)*, Habitat's $20 million overhaul turned what was once a dilapidated women's residence into a stylish, reasonable hotel. Keep in mind that space is tight.

### Hotel Beacon

*2130 Broadway between 74th and 75th Sts (212-787-1100, 800-572-4969; fax 212-787-8119; www.beaconhotel.com). Subway: 1, 2, 3, 9 to 72nd St. Single/double $145–$185, suite $185–$325. 242 rooms. AmEx, DC, Disc, MC, V.*
If you're looking for a break from the throngs of tourists clogging Times Square—or if you want to see how many Gothamites live—consider the Beacon. It's in a desirable residential neighborhood and only a short walk from Central Park, Lincoln Center and the famous Zabar's food market. The hallways have been refurbished, and the rooms, which vary in decor, are clean and spacious. There is an Internet center on the second floor, and guests will be able to purchase passes to the new Synergy gym opening on the hotel's ground level. The Beacon is the tallest building in the area, so rooms are sunny and the windows offer views of the neighborhood.
**Hotel services** *Laundry. Safe.* **Room services** *Kitchenette. Microwave oven. Radio. Voice mail.*

### Hotel Belleclaire

*250 W 77th St at Broadway (212-362-7700; fax 212-362-1004; www.hotelbelleclaire.com). Subway: 1, 9 to 79th St. Single/double $99–$159, suite $169–$229. 240 rooms. AmEx, DC, Disc, MC, V.*
Located near the Museum of Natural History, Lincoln Center and Central Park, Belleclaire is a steal in a neighborhood that generally prices out budget travelers. Housed in a landmark building, the hotel has character despite its lack of luxury. Rooms that end with a six have cozy king-sized beds with down comforters, and beige and bright-green Art Deco–style interiors. Decorations are spare but rooms are clean, well-kept and have refrigerators.
***Hotel services:*** *Air conditioning. Business center. Fitness center. Gift shop.* ***Room services:*** *Alarm clock. Cable TV. Hair dryer. Refrigerator. Voice mail.*

### Riverside Towers Hotel

*80 Riverside Dr at 80th St (212-877-5200, 800-724-3136; fax 212-873-1400). Subway: 1, 9 to 79th St. Single $84, double $89, suite $99–$119. 120 rooms. AmEx, DC, Disc, MC, V.*
The Riverside offers a good rate for the Upper West Side, and it's one of the few hotels in Manhattan located on the Hudson River. The views are fine, and there's a quiet park across the street, but accommodations are basic. This is strictly a place to sleep.
**Hotel services** *Fax. Safe. Self-serve laundry.* **Room services** *Microwave and refrigerator in suites.*

## Hostels

### Central Park Hostel

*19 W 103rd St at Central Park West (212-678-0491; www.centralparkhostel.com). Subway: B, C to 103rd St. $25 for a bed. Cash or traveler's checks only.*
See **Murray Hill Inn**, page 155.

### Hostelling International New York

*891 Amsterdam Ave at 103rd St (212-932-2300; fax 212-932-2574; www.hinewyork.org). Subway: 1, 9 to 103rd St. Dorm rooms $29–$38; family room $120, private room with bath $135. 624 rooms. AmEx, DC, MC, V.*
This gargantuan 624-bed hostel takes up an entire city block. Once a residence for elderly women, the gabled redbrick building retains an institutional

**Limb shady** Trees and umbrellas cool off Hostelling International New York's patio.



feel. Rooms are spare, but immaculate and air-conditioned, affording a pleasant stay. There is a community kitchen, a large enclosed garden, a selection of volunteer programs, and organized low-budget sightseeing trips for guests. All rooms are nonsmoking.

**Hotel services** *Café. Cafeteria. Conference facility. Fax. Game room. Library. Lockers. Self-serve laundry. Shuttles. Travel bureau. TV lounge.*

### International House

*500 Riverside Dr at 125th St (212-316-8473, in summer 212-316-8436; fax 212-316-1827). Subway: 1, 9 to 125th St. Single $115–$125, double/suite $125–$140. 11 rooms. MC, V.*

No, you won't run into W.C. Fields here, but this hostel is located on a peaceful block overlooking Grant's Tomb and the small but well-tended Sakura Park. A subsidized cafeteria serves main dishes for around $5. Only suites have private bathrooms. The best time to book is summer, when foreign graduate students and visiting scholars check out. Summer single rates drop super low.

**Hotel services** *Bar. Cafeteria. Conference facility. Fax. Game room. Self-serve laundry.* **Room services** *TV.*

### Jazz on the Park Hostel

*36 W 106th St between Central Park West and Manhattan Ave (212-932-1600; fax 212-932-1700; www.jazzhostel.com). Subway: B, C to 103rd St. 4- to 12-bed dorm room $27–$37, 2-bed dorm room $80 (double occupancy). 310 beds. MC, V.*

A cozy old-school hostel just off Central Park West, Jazz on the Park employs a friendly neighborhood staff. The basic rooms can be cramped (use the private lockers) but the price is a bargain. You can occasionally hear live jazz on the weekends and attend summer-evening barbecues on a second-floor terrace. The basement lounge hosts local jazz acts and karaoke, and serves bottled beer out of a cooler. Book in advance.

**Hotel services** *Bike and in-line–skate rental (summer only). Café. Complimentary breakfast. Internet access. Private lockers. Self-serve laundry. TV room.*

### YMCA (West Side)

*5 W 63rd St between Central Park West and Broadway (212-875-4100; fax 212-875-1334; www.ymcanyc.org). Subway: A, C, B, D, 1, 9 to 59th St–Columbus Circle. Rooms with shared bath $72–$89; rooms with private bath $105–$140. 540 rooms. AmEx, MC, V.*

A cavernous building near Central Park and Lincoln Center, this Y's rooms are simple and clean. Book well in advance. A deposit is required to hold a reservation. Most of the rooms have shared bathrooms and all are air-conditioned.

**Hotel services** *Cafeteria. Concierge. Fitness facilities. Self-serve laundry.* **Room services** *Air-conditioning. Cable TV.*

## Brooklyn

### Akwaaba Mansion

*347 MacDonough St between Lewis and Stuyvesant Aves, Bedford-Stuyvesant (718-455-5958; fax 718-774-1744; www.akwaaba.com). Subway: A, C to Utica Ave. Weekdays $120–$135, weekends $135–$150. Four rooms. MC, V.*

This restored 1860s mansion, whose name means "welcome" in Ghanaian, showcases the handiwork of Monique Greenwood, former editor-in-chief of *Essence* magazine, and her husband, Glenn Pogue. Greenwood's decorating sense is meticulous: Akwaaba's guest suites are furnished with antiques and individually themed. The spacious Ashante Suite, for example, is accented with African artifacts and textiles. Stays include a hearty Southern-style breakfast served in the impressive dining room or on the porch. There's also the **Akwaaba** restaurant *(393 Lewis Ave between Decatur and MacDonough Sts, 718-774-1444)* down the street for anyone who can't get enough Southern cooking. Around the corner is Greenwood's latest venture, **Mirrors Coffeehouse** *(401 Lewis Ave between Decatur and MacDonough Sts, 718-771-0633)*, where an incredible red-velvet cake is served.

**Hip flop fabulous** The Harlem Flophouse raises the bar for cool uptown digs.

### Angelique Bed & Breakfast

*405 Union St between Hoyt and Smith Sts, Carroll Gardens (718-852-8406). F, G to Carroll St. Single $100, double $150. Six rooms. AmEx, DC, Disc, MC, V.*
Housed in an 1889 brownstone in charming Carroll Gardens, Angelique is a comfy quasi-Victorian–style establishment. Children and pets are welcome, and several rooms accommodate two adults and two children for an extra charge of $25 per child. On a warm summer day, you may relax in the back garden or take the F train four stops to Prospect Park. And you'll eat like a king (or queen)—the B-and-B is just around the corner from Smith Street, one of Brooklyn's most happening restaurant rows.

### Awesome Bed & Breakfast

*136 Lawrence St between Fulton and Willoughby Sts, Downtown Brooklyn (718-858-4859; www.awesome-bed-and-breakfast.com). Subway: A, C, F to Jay St–Borough Hall; M, N, R, W to Lawrence St; 2, 3, 4, 5 to Borough Hall. Single/double $79–$99, triple/quads $120–$145. Six rooms. MC, V.*
While it doesn't quite live up to its name, this second-floor guest house brims with character. Theme rooms include Ancient Madagascar and Aurora Borealis (also known as the "groovy room"), which has purple walls and lots of daisies. The snazzy bathrooms are communal. Breakfast is included and served at 8am. Nearby is Montague Street—Brooklyn Heights' main drag—and the Promenade.

### Bed & Breakfast on the Park

*113 Prospect Park West between 6th and 7th Sts, Park Slope, Brooklyn (718-499-6115; www.bbnyc.com). Subway: F to Seventh Ave. $125–$300. Eight rooms. AmEx, MC, V accepted, but checks preferred.*
Staying at this 1895 brownstone is like taking up residence on the set of *Moulin Rouge*. The parlor floor is crammed with elaborately carved antique furniture and accessorized with Oriental carpets, candelabra and porcelain figurine tchotchkes: Guest rooms are outfitted with cozy love seats, swooping damask drapery, canopy beds overflowing with lacy French linens, and a plethora of paintings. As the name suggests, this impressive inn is situated right on Prospect Park. The **Brooklyn Museum of Art** *(see page 45)* and Park Slope's boutique-laden Seventh Avenue are within walking distance.

### New York Marriott Brooklyn

*333 Adams St between Tillary and Willoughby Sts, Brooklyn Heights (718-246-7000; fax 718-246-0563; www.marriott.com). Subway: A, C, F to Jay St–Borough Hall; 2, 3, 4, 5 to Borough Hall. Single/double $239–$289, suite $399–$449. 376 rooms. AmEx, DC, Disc, MC, V.*
You'll get just what you'd expect from a Marriott: all the usual amenities, including a restaurant, fitness center, business and conference facilities, and a recently upgraded pool. Nearby is the landmark haute-Southern **Gage & Tollner** restaurant *(372 Fulton St between Jay and Smith Sts, 718-875-5181)*. A five-minute walk will take you to busy Montague Street and the sweeping view of Manhattan from the Brooklyn Heights Promenade.

## Bed & breakfast services

New York's bed-and-breakfast scene is deceptively large. There are thousands of rooms available, but since there isn't a central B-and-B organization, some may be hard to find. Many B-and-Bs are unhosted, and breakfast is usually Continental (if it's served at all). They often offer a more personal ambience than a hotel. Prices are not necessarily low, but B-and-Bs are a good way to feel less like a tourist and more like a New Yorker. Sales tax of 8.25 percent is added on hosted bed-and-breakfast rooms, but not on unhosted apartments if you stay for more than seven days. Ask about decor, location and amenities when booking, and if safety is a concern, find out whether the building has a 24-hour doorman. One caveat: Last-minute changes can be costly; some agencies charge a fee for cancellations less than ten days in advance. More B-and-Bs are in the chapter **Gay & Lesbian**—and they welcome straight guests too.

### A Hospitality Company

*247 W 35th St, fourth floor, New York, NY 10001 (800-987-1235; fax 212-965-1149; www.hospitalityco.com). Studio $99–$165, one-bedroom apartment $125–$195, two-bedroom apartment $275–$375. AmEx, Disc, MC, V.*

A Hospitality Company has more than 500 furnished apartments available for nightly, weekly or monthly stays, from Soho lofts to Upper East Side walk-ups, and is popular among visiting artists (one opera diva requested a grand piano during her stay). Every place has cable TV, and many have VCRs and stereos. The nightly rate often includes Continental breakfast.

### All Around the Town

*270 Lafayette St, suite 804, New York, NY 10012 (800-443-3800; fax 212-675-6366; david.aroundtown@att.net). Studio $120–$175, one-bedroom apartment $150–$280. AmEx, DC, MC, V.*

This agency can arrange accommodations in most Manhattan neighborhoods in unhosted furnished apartments. There is a three-night minimum; ask about reduced rates for monthly stays.

### At Home in New York

*P.O. Box 407, New York, NY 10185 (212-956-3125, 800-692-4262; fax 212-265-8539; athomeny@erols.com). Hosted single/double $90–$150, unhosted studio $120–$165, unhosted 1-bedroom apartment $135–$225, unhosted 2-bedroom apartment $200–$400. Cash only (AmEx, MC, V can be used to guarantee rooms).*

At Home has reasonably priced rooms in about 300 properties; most are in Manhattan, with a few in Brooklyn, Queens and Staten and Roosevelt Islands. The two-night minimum can be waived for last-minute bookings.

### Bed and Breakfast in Manhattan

*P.O. Box 533, New York, NY 10150 (212-472-2528; fax 212-988-9818). Hosted $100–$120, unhosted $125–$400. Cash only.*

Each of this organization's 100 or so properties has been personally inspected by the owner, who also helps travelers select a site in the neighborhood best suited to their interests.

### Bed & Breakfast (& Books)

*35 W 92nd St, apartment 2C, New York, NY 10025 (212-865-8740 phone and fax, call Mon–Fri 10am–5pm; bedbreakfastbook@aol.com). Hosted single $85–$120, hosted double $120–$135, unhosted studio $120–$160, unhosted 1-bedroom apartment from $160, unhosted 2-bedroom apartment from $250. Cash or traveler's checks only (AmEx, DC, Disc, MC, V can be used to guarantee rooms).*

Several hosts in this organization are literary types—hence the bookish title. There are 40 hosted and unhosted rooms, and the minimum stay is two nights.

### CitySonnet

*Village Station, P.O. Box 347, New York, NY 10014 (212-614-3034; fax 425-920-2384; mail@citysonnet.com; www.citysonnet.com). Bed-and-breakfast room $80–$165, artist's loft $135–$175, private apartments $135–$375. AmEx, Disc, MC, V.*

This friendly artist-run agency specializes in downtown locations, but has properties all over Manhattan. The B-and-B rooms and short-term apartment rentals are priced according to room size, number of guests and whether the bathroom is private or shared with other guests. Hosts provide neighborhood information and Continental breakfast. All rooms are private and completely furnished.

### The Harlem Flophouse

*242 W 123rd St between Adam Clayton Powell (Seventh Ave) and Frederick Douglass Blvds (Eighth Ave) (212-662-0678; www.harlemflophouse.com). Subway: A, B, C, D to 125th St. One room, separate bath. Single $65, double $90. Four rooms. MC, V.*

The beautiful brownstone that houses the Harlem Flophouse had been chopped into more than a dozen bed-size rooms when its current owner, René Calvo, bought it in 2000. Calvo restored the place to its original condition and converted it into a B-and-B. Guest rooms are handsome but spare, and feature hammered tin ceilings and antique cabinetry. They're accessorized with curios like radios and dime novels from the Harlem Renaissance era. The inn, whose name testifies to the building's former function, is a fun if slightly rough-hewn base from which to explore ever-changing Harlem.

### The Urban Jem Guest House

*2005 Fifth Ave between 124th and 125th Sts (212-831-6029; www.urbanjem.com). Subway: 2, 3 to 125th St. Single/double with shared bath $95–$120, suite for up to four people $200–$220, studio apartment with private kitchen and bath $105–$130; minimum two-night stay on weekends and holidays. Four rooms. AmEx, Disc, MC, V.*

Proprietors Jane Mendelson and Oklahoma Simms's renovated 19th-century brownstone is just a block from Bill Clinton's 125th Street office. The nearby Synergy Gym offers daily guest passes; Simms runs a car service, and there is also a small library of Harlem-oriented travel, photo, documentary and fiction books. Each of the four rooms is clean and well-appointed, with Afrocentric art on the walls and original marble mantelpieces. The parlor floor, which overlooks Fifth Avenue, is also the site of regular jazz performances.

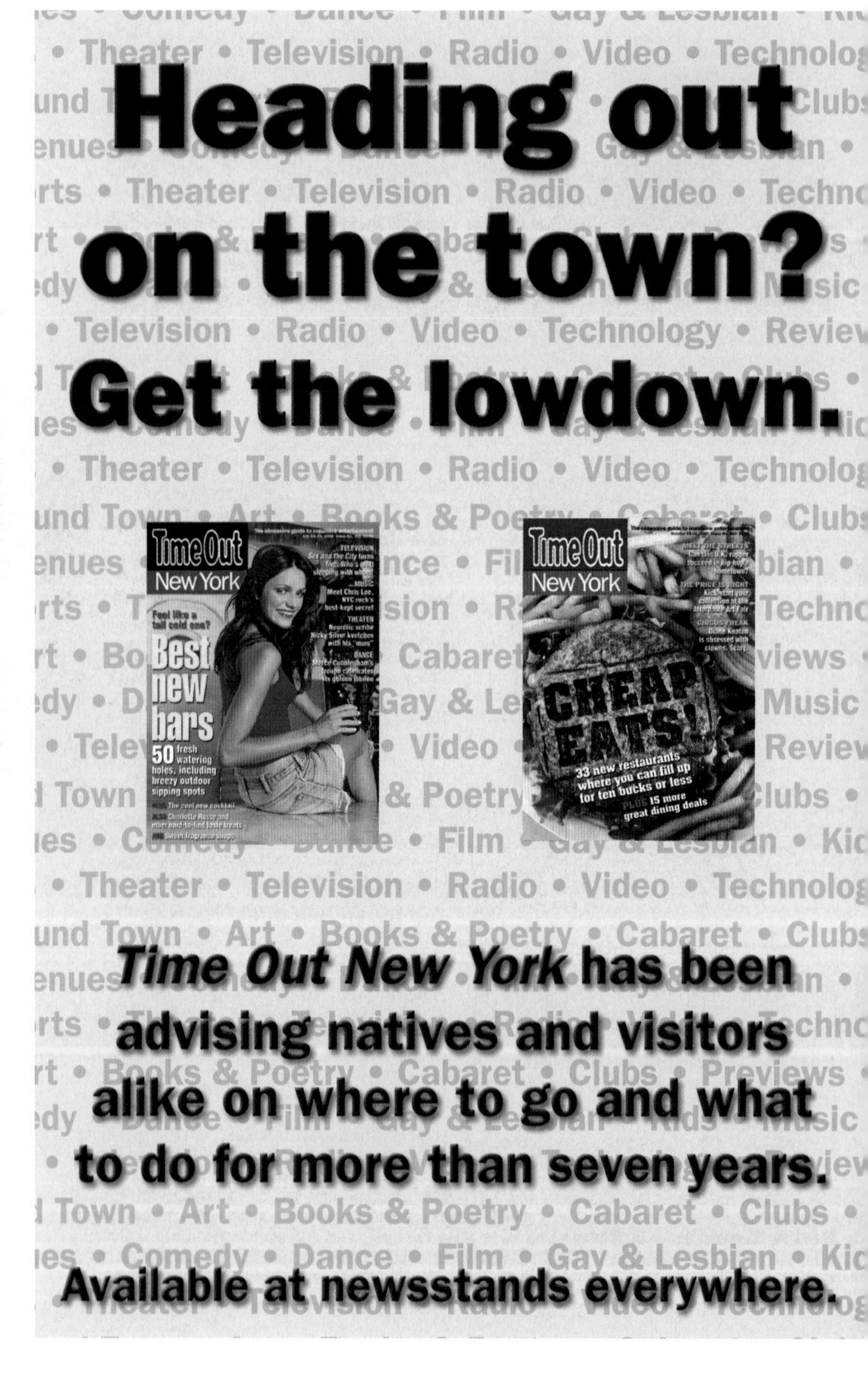
Heading out on the town?
Get the lowdown.
Time Out New York
Best new bars
CHEAP EATS!
Time Out New York has been advising natives and visitors alike on where to go and what to do for more than seven years.
Available at newsstands everywhere.

# Bars

Pick your poison: New York City drinking establishments are as diverse as the millions of people who imbibe here

Whether you're partial to cocktails at a posh hotel lounge, the latest vintage at a comfortable wine bar or a pint of beer at a dark, seedy dive, you've come to the right town to quench your thirst.

## Downtown

### APT

See page 277.

### Bauhaus

*196 Orchard St between Houston and Stanton Sts (212-477-1550). Subway: F, V to Lower East Side–Second Ave. Wed, Thu 5:30pm–2am; Fri, Sat 5:30pm–4am; Sun 3pm–midnight. Average drink: $7. AmEx, Disc, MC, V.*

Created by two FIT interior-design grads, Bauhus is a stylized, ambitious bar. DJs (including Astralwerks' Brian Beck) spin high-quality electronica and house on the ground floor, while the downstairs lounge, Narnia, is a more exclusive affair.

### Baraza

*133 Ave C between 8th and 9th Sts (212-539-0811). Subway: L to First Ave; 6 to Astor Pl. 7:30pm–4am. Average drink: $5. Cash only.*

Back when Avenue C was sleazy, those in the know flocked to this relaxed Latin American party place. Four years later, the vibe is still dead-on, with DJs spinning Afrocuban, Brazilian, merengue and salsa.

### Bar 89

*89 Mercer St between Broome and Spring Sts (212-274-0989). Subway: N, R, W to Prince St; 6 to Spring St. Mon–Thu noon–1:30am; Fri, Sat noon–2:30am. Average drink: $9. AmEx, MC, V.*

Bar 89's gimmick is its unisex bathroom with transparent stall doors that turn opaque when you lock them. Other noteworthy features: model types three-deep at the bar, delicious sandwiches and appetizers, and a terrific selection of single-malt Scotch.

### Blind Tiger Alehouse

*518 Hudson St at 10th St (212-675-3848). Subway: 1, 9 to Christopher St–Sheridan Sq. Mon–Fri noon–4am; Sat, Sun 1pm–4am. Average drink: $4.50. AmEx, Disc, MC, V.*

Blind Tiger serves Belgian bottled beers and microbrews that flow from 24 taps and two hand-drawn pumps. The epic happy-hour specials have cultivated a devoted following.

### Chateau

See page 278.

**A loo with a view** Never fear—the clear-glass bathroom doors at Bar 89 frost over when you lock them.

### Chibi's Bar

*238 Mott St between Prince and Spring Sts (212-274-0025). Subway: N, R, W to Prince St. Tue–Thu, Sun 6pm–midnight; Fri 3pm–1am; Sat 3pm–midnight. Average drink: $10. AmEx, MC, V ($20 minimum).*

Jazz plays softly in this dim Japanese hideaway. Select from 18 sakes and enjoy a free plate of mushroom dumplings on Tuesday and Wednesday nights. There's also a small selection of wine and beer.

### Chumley's

*86 Bedford St between Barrow and Commerce Sts (212-675-4449). Subway: 1, 9 to Christopher St–Sheridan Sq. Mon–Thu 4pm–midnight; Fri 4pm–2am;*

► For more bar listings, see chapters **Cabaret & Comedy**, **Clubs**, **Gay & Lesbian** and **Music**.

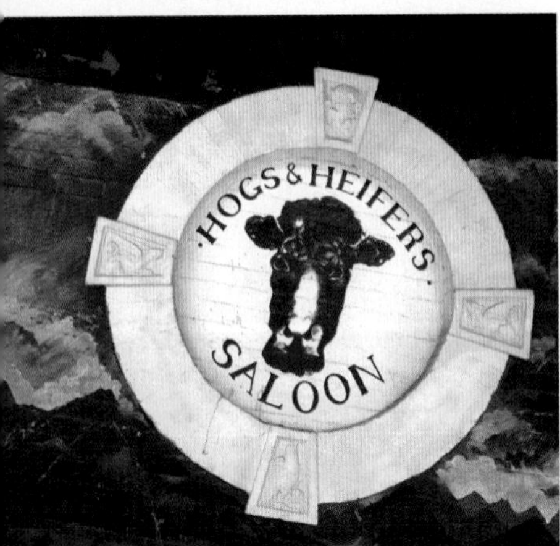


**Cowboy way** Sample some good ol' country attitude at Hogs & Heifers.

*Sat 11am–2am; Sun 11am–midnight. Average drink: $6. Cash only.*
Opened in 1922, Chumley's is home to as many tales as taps (eight beers are home-brewed). It's known as a writers' pub; F. Scott Fitzgerald and David Mamet have indulged here. The lack of a sign and two separate doors (in and out) betray the bar's speakeasy roots.

**Decibel**
*240 E 9th St between Second and Third Aves (212-979-2733). Subway: 6 to Astor Pl. Mon–Sat 8pm–3am; Sun 8pm–1am. Average drink: $9. AmEx, DC, Disc, MC, V.*
It's a thrill to descend the narrow staircase into the shrouded subterranean grotto of Decibel, which leads to a cavern furnished with high-backed booths. Bring a willing accomplice, and tackle the intimidatingly large sake menu.

**Fanelli Cafe**
*94 Prince St at Mercer St (212-226-9412). Subway: N, R, W to Prince St. Mon–Thu 10am–2:30am; Fri, Sat 10am–3am; Sun 11am–12:30am. Average drink: $6. AmEx, MC, V.*
Expect international chitchat at charming, grungy old Fanelli, a boxing-themed corner pub. In the two rooms (the back one is all tables), you may dine on

# Rosé-colored glasses

## New York wine bars cultivate a new generation of relaxed oenophiles

New Yorkers have developed an acute taste for the grape, as evidenced by the rabbitlike proliferation of wine bars. Three years ago, there might have been a half dozen in the whole city. That figure is now closer to 30, and climbing by the week.

The French and Italians honed the wine-bar concept, but it seems made for New York. These dark, cozy boîtes require very little space, attract a sophisticated, often chiefly female crowd, and stay open till the wee hours. And in NYC, no one has to drive home.

**The Bar@Etats-Unis**
*242 E 81st St between Second and Third Aves (212-396-9928). Subway: 6 to 77th St. Mon–Sat noon–midnight; Sun 5pm–midnight. Average drink: $10. AmEx, DC, MC, V.*
This tiny, civilized venue has a strong wine list that includes many French vintages.

**Bar Veloce**
*175 Second Ave between 11th and 12th Sts (212-260-3200). Subway: L to Third Ave; 6 to Astor Pl. 5pm–3am. Average drink: $8. AmEx, MC, V.*
The East Village original, with its mod look and fine selection of medium-priced Italian glasses, has spawned a twin in Nolita *(17 Cleveland Pl between Kenmare and Spring Sts, 212-966-7334)*. Both feature translucent backlit wine racks.

**D.O.C.**
*83 North 7th St at Wythe Ave, Williamsburg, Brooklyn (718-963-1925). Subway: L to Bedford Ave. 6pm–1am. Average drink: $6. Cash only.*
Manhattan can't have all the fun. Williamsburg now has its own wine bar. D.O.C. sticks with Italian wines, which is appropriate given the intimate Tuscan-farmhouse decor.

**Enoteca I Trulli**
*124 E 27th St between Park Ave South and Lexington Ave (212-481-7372). Subway: 6 to 28th St. Mon–Thu noon–10:30pm; Fri noon–11pm; Sat 5–11pm. Average drink: $9. AmEx, DC, MC, V.*
If you like what you drink here—and you may choose from 500 bottles and 50 glasses—the nearby wine store, Vino, sells the same selections at retail.

**Flute**
For this sparkling-wine bar, see page 174.

tolerably good grub. Music-lovers take note: There is none.

### Fez

*Inside Time Cafe, 380 Lafayette St at Great Jones St (212-533-2680). Subway: F, V, S to Broadway–Lafayette St; 6 to Bleecker St. Sun–Thu 6pm–2am; Fri 5:30pm–4am; Sat 6pm–4am. Average drink: $6. AmEx, MC, V.*
See page 309.

### Hogs & Heifers

*859 Washington St at 13th St (212-929-0655). Subway: A, C, E to 14th St; L to Eighth Ave. Mon–Fri 11am–4am; Sat 1pm–4am; Sun 2pm–4am. Average drink: $5. Cash only.*
We're happy to report that western-themed biker bar Hogs & Heifers is aging disgracefully. Yes, the barmaids still dance on the countertops and discarded bras dangle from lamps. Uptowners have their own location too *(see page 177)*.

### Idlewild

*145 E Houston St between Eldridge and Forsyth Sts (212-477-5005). Subway: F, V to Lower East Side–Second Ave. Tue–Sat 8pm–3am. Average drink: $6.AmEx, DC, MC, V.*
This is a jet-set theme bar, so fasten your seat belts and enjoy the ride. Drinks are incomparably better (albeit pricier) than those on your average flight to Miami.

### Joe's Pub

See page 271.

### Lakeside Lounge

*162 Ave B between 10th and 11th Sts (212-529-8463). Subway: L to First Ave; 6 to Astor Pl. 4pm–4am. Average drink: $4. AmEx, MC, V.*
Avenue B may have become polluted with snooty bars, but Lakeside Lounge remains proudly unpolished. Its juke is the best in town.

### Liquor Store Bar

*235 West Broadway at White St (212-226-7121). Subway: A, C, E to Canal St; 1, 9 to Franklin St. Noon–4am. Average drink: $5. Cash only.*
After selling packaged booze for many years, this site evolved into a mellow drinking spot. The building dates back to 1804 and the sidewalk seating is great for enjoying a Speckled Hen Ale.

**Wine seller** Peruse the walls of the Nolita branch of Bar Veloce for a delicious Italian vintage.

### Morrell Wine Bar and Café

*1 Rockefeller Plaza, W 49th St between Fifth and Sixth Aves (212-262-7700). Subway: B, D, F, V to 47–50th Sts–Rockefeller Ctr. Mon–Sat 11:30am–11pm; Sun noon–6pm. Average drink: $17. AmEx, DC, Disc, MC, V.*
The adjacent Morrell & Company is one of the city's most celebrated wine stores, and its formidable offerings are often uncorked in the cafe. Provided you have the cash (some exclusive pours push past $100), you'll taste wines that may never again be available by the glass. In early 2003, a larger branch is slated to open at 900 Broadway at 20th St.

### Rhône

*63 Gansevoort St between Greenwich and Washington Sts (212-367-8440). Subway: A, C, E to 14th St; L to Eighth Ave. Mon–Sat 5:30pm–4am. Average drink: $8. AmEx, MC, V.*
New York has fallen in love with Rhône wines, and some of America's best imports can be found in this airy, zinc-filled warehouse. Come with a group, enjoy the shareable plates of meats and cheeses, and talk very loudly.

### 'ino

*21 Bedford St between Sixth Ave and Downing St (212-989-5769). Subway: 1, 9 to Houston St. Mon–Fri 9am–2am; Sat, Sun 11am–2am. Average drink: $8. Cash only.*
'ino is so tiny, its logo doesn't even rate a capital letter. A dozen different bottles of Italian wine are open at all times, served with just enough *panini* or bruschetta to keep you in your seat.

Necessities

**Ten heads are better than one** Chat up the beer-loving locals at McSorley's Old Ale House.

### Lit

*93 Second Ave between 5th and 6th Sts (212-777-7987). Subway: F, V to Lower East Side–Second Ave; 6 to Astor Pl. Mon–Sat 5pm–4am; Sun 9pm–4am. Average drink: $5. AmEx, MC, V ($20 minimum).*

Fledgling Lit manages to break the mold with its hush-hush weekly basement parties, thronged with close pals, graffiti artists and musicians. In the rear is the Fuse Gallery, supported by part of the bar's proceeds. So take a seat and down a pint—for art's sake.

### The Lotus Club

*35 Clinton St at Stanton St (212-253-1144). Subway: F to Delancey St; J, M, Z to Delancey–Essex Sts. Mon–Sat 7:30am–4am; Sun 9am–2am. Average drink: $5. AmEx, Disc, MC, V.*

The Lotus Club has long been a no-frills café and bar where laid-back erstwhile alternakids linger endlessly over coffee or beer.

### Mare Chiaro

*176½ Mulberry St between Broome and Grand Sts (212-226-9345). Subway: J, M, Z, N, Q, R, W, 6 to Canal St; S to Grand St. Mon–Thu 10am–1am; Fri, Sat 10am–2am; Sun noon–1am. Average drink: $4. Cash only.*

Scenes from *Donnie Brasco* and the *Godfather* trilogy were shot here. Given the grizzled old-timer blindly pouring cocktails with a fat cigar between his lips, you can count on getting whacked pretty quick—and for cheap.

> ► For a comprehensive guide to notable New York bars, pick up a copy of the ***Time Out New York Eating & Drinking 2003 Guide***, or subscribe to the online version at **eatdrink.timeoutny.com**.

### Max Fish

*178 Ludlow St between Houston and Stanton Sts (212-529-3959). Subway: F, V to Lower East Side–Second Ave. 5:30pm–4am. Average drink: $4. Cash only.*

If only *all* Lower East Side hangouts were still packed to the gills with boys flaunting messy hair and girls wearing spinster glasses. The sticker-collaged pool table complements the jukebox that plays tunes from esoteric bands.

### McSorley's Old Ale House

*15 E 7th St between Second and Third Aves (212-473-9148). Subway: F, V to Lower East Side–Second Ave; N, R, W to 8th St–NYU. Mon–Sat 11am–1am; Sun 1pm–1am. Average drink: $1.75. Cash only.*

Established in 1854, McSorley's is the city's longest-running pub in a single location. Irish waiters in gray coats part the sea of drinkers to pack table-tops with pints of McSorley's Dark (smooth and sweet) and Light (smooth with a bite) Ales.

### Ñ

*33 Crosby St between Broome and Grand Sts (212-219-8856). Subway: 6 to Spring St. Sun–Thu 5pm–2am; Fri, Sat 5pm–4am. Average drink: $7. Cash only.*

Ñ is one of Soho's treasured hideaways. The crowd is mostly art-centered early-thirties folks who travel in small packs. A menu of intriguing alcoholic potations and Spanish tapas has two highlights: fruity sangria and *gambas al ajillo* (garlicky shrimp).

### Opium Den

*29 E 3rd St between Bowery and Second Ave (212-505-7344). Subway: F, V to Lower East Side–*

*Second Ave; 6 to Bleecker St. Mon–Sat 8pm–4am. Average drink: $6. AmEx, MC, V.*
Illuminated by candlelight and decorated with hardwood and polished steel, this seductive lounge can become an expensive habit.

### Plant Bar

*217 E 3rd St between Aves B and C (212-375-9066). Subway: F, V to Lower East Side–Second Ave. 7pm–4am. Average drink: $5. Cash only.*
The brainchild of trendsetting DJs Marcus and Dominique of Plant Music, Plant Bar is a major house-music haunt for East Village hipsters. A backlit terrarium lends the place an underwater feel.

### Pravda

*281 Lafayette St between Houston and Prince Sts (212-226-4944). Subway: F, V, S to Broadway–Lafayette St; N, R, W to Prince St; 6 to Bleecker St. Mon–Wed 5pm–1am; Thu 5pm–2:30am; Fri, Sat 5pm–3:30am; Sun 6pm–1am.*
While the 1990s retro-Russian trend has fizzled, this sleek underground caviar bar endures. There are plenty of flavorful concoctions, but with 70 varieties of vodka, you're better off ordering the classic vodka martini (served in a miniature shaker).

### Sway

*305 Spring St between Greenwich and Hudson Sts (212-620-5220). Subway: C, E to Spring St; 1, 9 to Canal St. 11pm–4am. Average drink: $8. AmEx, DC, MC, V.*
If you can get into Sway (which is like saying "If you can get into Harvard"), you'll have no complaints. The DJs spin a heavy beat and the bartenders are gracious in this mood-of-Morocco room.

### Théo

See page 187.

### Uncle Ming's

*225 Ave B between 13th and 14th Sts (212-979-8506). Subway: L to First Ave. 6pm–4am. Average drink: $6. AmEx, MC, V.*
Formerly home to an illegal after-hours club, Uncle Ming's has no sign out front. To reach the lounge (which is hidden above a liquor store), you have to climb a dark staircase. The room is stocked with antique couches, cheap drinks and an East Village–cool crowd.

### Von Bar

*3 Bleecker St between Bowery and Elizabeth St (212-473-3039). Subway: F, V, S to Broadway–Lafayette St; 6 to Bleecker St. Sun–Thu 5pm–2am; Fri, Sat 5pm–4am. Average drink: $7. AmEx, DC, Disc, MC, V.*
Soft sofas and a mild-mannered clientele make this dark den ideal for a get-to-know-you drink. Grab a glass of wine from the bar and cozy up on a couch.

### Welcome to the Johnsons

*123 Rivington St between Essex and Norfolk Sts (212-420-9911). Subway: F to Delancey St; J, M, Z to Delancey–Essex Sts. Mon–Fri 3pm–4am; Sat, Sun 1pm–4am. Average drink: $4. Cash only.*
If you're feeling completely out of touch with suburbia, treat yourself to a can of Pabst Blue Ribbon ($1.50 during happy hour) at Welcome to the Johnsons, which also offers a Pac-Man and a rockin' crowd.

**Fruity call** Sangria-loving locals flock to Ñ in Soho, to snack, sip and be merry.

### Zum Schneider

*107–109 Ave C at 7th St (212-598-1098). Subway: F, V to Lower East Side–Second Ave; L to First Ave. Mon–Thu 5pm–2am; Fri 4pm–2am; Sat, Sun 1pm–4am. Average drink: $6. Cash only.*

This Bavarian beer hall is as squeaky-clean as its patrons. The suds (12 German brands on tap) are cold, the service is decent, and the various meaty platters (wursts, Bavarian meat loaf, etc.) enhance the brew.

## Midtown

### Aubette

*119 E 27th St between Park Ave South and Lexington Ave (212-686-5500). Subway: 6 to 28th St. Mon–Fri 5pm–4am; Sat, Sun 7pm–4am. Average drink: $10. AmEx, MC, V.*

Young professionals nip into candlelit Aubette for flavored martinis, 22 wines by the glass, soulful music and plenty of eye contact. Come winter, grab a prime seat by the fireplace.

## CRITICS' PICKS Bar drinks

These are the best watering holes...

**...for the original bloody mary**
King Cole Bar *(see page 175)* invented the drink, but christened it the Red Snapper.

**...for a twist on the tired Cosmo**
Cellar Bar *(see right)* makes a mean Razmopolitan.

**...for a memorable mojito**
Isla *(see page 192)* purees the mint for extra punch.

**...for a local microbrew**
Blind Tiger Alehouse *(see page 169)* has Brooklyn and Southampton brews on tap.

**...for a glass of sangria**
Pipa *(see page 196)* makes it with ultrafresh fruit and a touch of cinnamon.

**...for a flight of sake**
Decibel *(see page 170)* offers 80 traditional kinds, served with contemporary attitude.

**...for a flaming mai tai**
Tiki Room *(see page 176)* serves it frozen *and* on fire in a 32-ounce tiki bowl.

**...for the city's priciest cocktail**
The World Bar's *(see page 176)* blend of premium Champagnes and juices rings in at $50!

### Campbell Apartment

*Grand Central Terminal, off the West Balcony, 15 Vanderbilt Ave at 43rd St (212-953-0409). Subway: S, 4, 5, 6, 7 to 42nd St–Grand Central. Mon–Sat 3pm–1am; Sun 3–10pm. Average drink: $12. AmEx, MC, V.*

From 1923 to 1941, this was the private office and salon of New York Central Railroad trustee John Campbell. The space oozes robber-baron chic, with wrought iron, wood detailing on the balcony and an incredible wall of backlit windows behind the bar. Catch live music on Saturdays—as a performance venue, it's fantastic.

### Cellar Bar

*Bryant Park Hotel, 40 W 40th St between Fifth and Sixth Aves (212-642-2260). Subway: B, D, F, V to 42nd St; 7 to Fifth Ave. Mon 5pm–midnight; Tue–Sat 5pm–2am. Average drink: $11. AmEx, DC, MC, V.*

At this stunning Mediterranean-style bar, you can recline beneath vaulted ceilings and snack on creations from the adjoining restaurant Ilo *(212-642-2255)*.

### Divine Bar

*244 E 51st St between Second and Third Aves (212-319-9463). Subway: E, V to Lexington Ave–53rd St; 6 to 51st St. Mon–Wed 5pm–1am; Thu, Fri 5pm–2am; Sat 7pm–3am; Sun 7pm–1am. Average drink: $7. AmEx, DC, MC, V.*

Gilt mirrors, fireplaces and dark beams form a backdrop for midtown workers in this buzzing bar. Choose from 60 wines and 40 beers.

**Other location** • *236 W 54th St at Eighth Ave (212-265-WINE). Subway: C, E, 1, 9 to 50th St. Mon–Wed noon–1am; Thu, Fri noon–3am; Sat 5pm–3am; Sun 5pm–1am. Average drink: $7. AmEx, DC, MC, V.*

### Flute

*40 E 20th St between Broadway and Park Ave South (212-529-7870). Subway: N, R, W, 6 to 23rd St. Mon–Sat 5pm–4am; Sun 7pm–4am. Average drink: $12. AmEx, DC, MC, V.*

A suited waiter whisks you to an intimate corner nook where you open the four-page menu devoted to sparkling wine. What will it be? An $8 glass of the Barnaut Blanc de Noirs or a $220 bottle of Dom?

**Other location** • *205 W 54th St between Seventh Ave and Broadway (212-265-5169). Subway: B, D, E to Seventh Ave. 5pm–4am. Average drink: $12. AmEx, DC, MC, V.*

### Fusion

*818 Tenth Ave between 54th and 55th Sts (212-397-1133). Subway: C, E to 50th St. Sun–Thu 4pm–2am; Fri, Sat 4pm–4am. Average drink: $6. MC, V.*

Fusion is sexy: Bright red-and-turquoise walls in the front bar, a 1950s-style lounge and a garden with potted palms and whirling metal fans. Enjoy fancy cocktails, Cuban eats and a cool crowd.

### Glass

*287 Tenth Ave between 26th and 27th Sts (212-904-1580). Subway: 1, 9 to 28th St. Mon–Wed 5pm–2am; Thu–Sat 5pm–4am. Average drink: $8. AmEx, MC, V.*

**Green light** The traffic at Plant slows down to look at the glass-encased faux foliage.

Architect Thomas Seeser designed Glass's mod grey-and-white interior with custom-made cocktail tables and curvy padded-bench seating. Young gallery hoppers stargaze in the bamboo garden.

### Hudson Bars

*The Hudson, 356 W 58th St between Eighth and Ninth Aves (212-554-6343). Subway: A, C, B, D, 1, 9 to 59th St–Columbus Circle. Mon–Sat 4pm–2am; Sun 4pm–1am. Library noon–2am. Average drink: $12. AmEx, DC, Disc, MC, V.*

Like a lime-green stairway to heaven, an escalator leads to the lobby of Ian Schrager's Hudson Hotel, where you'll find three separate bars. Most dazzling is the postmodern Hudson Bar, with its ceiling fresco by Francesco Clemente and glowing glass floor. The Library Bar marries class (leather sofas) with kitsch (photos of cows wearing pillbox hats). April through October, take in some fresh air at Private Park, the leafy outdoor garden-bar lit by candle chandeliers.

### King Cole Bar

*St. Regis Hotel, 2 E 55th St between Fifth and Madison Aves (212-339-6721). Subway: E, V to Fifth Ave–53rd St. Mon–Thu 11:30am–1am; Fri, Sat 11:30am–2am; Sun noon–midnight. Average drink: $14. AmEx, DC, Disc, MC, V.*

As you'd expect at a grand hotel bar, there are mahogany walls and leather club chairs, a famous mural (Maxfield Parrish), a jacket requirement and a male-to-female ratio of four to one.

### Metro Grill

*Hotel Metro, 45 W 35th St between Fifth and Sixth Aves (212-947-2500). Subway: B, D, F, V, N, Q, R, W to 34th St–Herald Sq. Noon–midnight. Average drink: $7. AmEx, DC, MC, V.*

These days, it seems like every midtown watering hole is attached to a hotel, but this rooftop annex of the Hotel Metro *is* one of the best outdoor bars in the city.

### Oak Bar

See page 269.

### Open

*559 W 22nd St between Tenth and Eleventh Aves (212-243-1851). Subway: C, E to 23rd St. Tue–Thu, Sun 11am–2am; Fri, Sat noon–4am. Average drink: $7. AmEx, MC, V.*

Open's glass doors slide back for full street exposure and river breezes. The alluring space is inspired by Montreal airport lounges from the 1970s.

### The Park

See page 194.

### Passerby

*436 W 15th St between Ninth and Tenth Aves (212-206-7321). Subway: A, C, E to 14th St; L to Eighth Ave. Mon–Sat 6pm–2am. Average drink: $8. AmEx, MC, V.*

The unmarked Passerby was originally created as a clubhouse for artists represented by the adjacent gallery, Gavin Brown's Enterprise. The flashing colored floor panels create a warm glow.

### Serena

*Chelsea Hotel, 222 W 23rd St between Seventh and Eighth Aves (212-255-4646). Subway: C, E, 1, 9 to 23rd St. Mon–Fri 6pm–4am; Sat 7pm–4am. Average drink: $8. AmEx, MC, V.*

Even though Serena is housed in the infamous Chelsea Hotel, you'll find few punk-rock alums in this polished postyuppie hideaway. The neighborhood's moderately stylish set indulges in drinks with names like Pink Bitch, while eating cornmeal-crusted chicken fingers with spicy sweet-potato dip.

### Single Room Occupancy

*360 W 53rd St between Eighth and Ninth Aves (212-765-6299). Subway: B, D to Seventh Ave; C, E to 50th St. Mon–Thu 7:30pm–3am; Fri, Sat 7:30pm–4am. Average drink: $7. AmEx.*

This narrow bar changes its colored lighting seasonally. Behind a series of square windows is a gallery, which sometimes features go-go dancers or a DJ.

### Suede

*161 W 23rd St between Sixth and Seventh Aves (212-633-6113). Subway: F, V, 1, 9 to 23rd St. Mon–*

*Fri 5pm–4am; Sat, Sun 10pm–4am. Average drink: $10. AmEx, MC, V.*
Designer vodkas, velvet ropes and a minimalist design supply Suede with all the requisites of a pretentious "look at me" bar—except that it isn't. Modeling contract or not, you'll get an actual smile from the bartender as he collects your nine bucks for a glass of the house chardonnay.

### Tao
*42 E 58th St between Madison and Park Aves (212-888-2288). Mon, Tue 11:30am–1am; Wed–Fri 11:30am–2:30am; Sat 5pm–2:30am; Sun 5pm–1am. Average drink: $10. AmEx, DC, MC, V.*
Curly bamboo, glowing lanterns and a 16-foot, 4,000-pound stone Buddha statue make this an unforgettable dining spot. The two bars overlook the high-ceilinged dinning room, where you can feast on Kobe beef and other Pan-Asian fare for the elite.

### Tiki Room
*4 W 22nd St between Fifth and Sixth Aves (646-230-1444). Subway: F, V, N, R, W to 23rd St. Tue–Fri 5pm–4am; Sat 8pm–4am. Average drink: $8. AmEx, MC, V.*
The Tiki Room is a lush lounge where you can sip Honolulu Hangovers and mai tais while munching on tropical treats. The walls are lined with flat-screen TVs playing surf videos, and the center of the bar showcases an 18-foot tiki idol.

### The World Bar
*Trump World Tower, 845 United Nations Plaza, First Ave at 48th St (212-935-9361). Subway: E, V to Lexington Ave–53rd St; 6 to 51st St. 1pm–1am. Average drink: $12. AmEx, DC, MC, V.*
This elegant cocktail lounge is unfortunately located on the ground floor of the Trump World Tower. If it were on the 90th floor, it could have $17 million views (the price of apartment 90B). Instead, you'll have to make do with drinks from around the world—French 75s, negronis, sangrias.

## Uptown

### The Boat Basin Café
*79th St at the Hudson River (212-496-5542). Subway: 1, 9 to 79th St. May–Oct noon–midnight. Average drink: $5.50. AmEx, MC, V.*
Watch the sun set over boats in their slips at this often-crowded outdoor café at the edge of Riverside Park. Order a beer and burger—it's what they do best.

### Eden Bar & Café
*2728 Broadway at 105th St (212-865-5565). Subway: 1, 9 to 103rd St. Mon–Thu 5pm–4am; Sat, Sun 5:30pm–4am. Average drink: $6. AmEx, Disc, MC, V.*

**United libations** The World Bar serves drinks and drunks from all over the globe.

Remove its crowd and Eden looks like an attempt to Soho-fy the Upper West Side. Enter through a velvet curtain and sit at the stone-slab bar or in the dark lounge in the rear. Eden is upscale, but it's also a neighborhood hang, featuring live Latin, blues and reggae.

### Fez Over Time Cafe

*2330 Broadway at 85th St (212-579-5100). Subway: 1, 9 to 86th St. Sun–Wed 6pm–midnight; Thu 6pm–2am; Fri, Sat 6pm–4am. Average drink: $6. AmEx, MC, V.*

On weeknights, Moroccan-themed Fez Over Time Cafe is a great place to settle in for a tête-à-tête, but on weekends, it's standing-room only. This is the uptown sister to the downtown original *(see page 171).*

### Hogs & Heifers North

*Hogs & Heifers North, 1843 First Ave at 95th St (212-722-8635). Subway: 6 to 96th St. Tue–Sat 4pm–4am. Average drink: $5. Cash only.*

See page 171.

### Lenox Lounge

*288 Malcolm X Blvd (Lenox Ave) between 124th and 125th Sts (212-427-0253). Subway: 2, 3 to 125th St. Noon–3:30am. Cover varies. Average drink: $5. AmEx, DC, MC, V.*

This famous Harlem bar–lounge–jazz club welcomes a mix of old-school cats, locals and quiet booze hounds. Billie Holiday and Miles Davis are just two big names who have graced the Lenox Lounge stage.

### Roof Garden at the Metropolitan Museum of Art

*1000 Fifth Ave at 82nd St (212-535-7710). Subway: 4, 5, 6 to 86th St. Roof Garden May–Oct Tue–Thu 4–8:45pm; Fri, Sat 3–8:45pm; Sun 11am–5:15pm. Average drink: $7. AmEx, DC, Disc, MC, V.*

Sip while surveying the magnificent skyscrapers rising above Central Park. Beer, cocktails and virgin piña coladas are available, but it's more swish to swan around with a flute of Champagne.

### Soha

*988 Amsterdam Ave between 108th and 109th Sts (212-678-0098). Subway: 1, 9 to 110th St–Cathedral Pkwy. 4pm–4am. Average drink: $4. AmEx, DC, MC, V.*

Soha's funky magnetism draws crowds from the Upper West Side and Harlem. The style is as diverse as the clientele—walls are exposed brick, faux-wood siding and chalkboards. There's live music on Sunday and Monday evenings.

## Brooklyn

### Bar Below

*209 Smith St at Baltic St, Carroll Gardens, Brooklyn (718-694-2277). Subway: F, G to Bergen St. Sun–Thu 7pm–2am; Fri, Sat 7pm–4am. Average drink: $6. Cash only.*

Plenty of white tile and aqua lights lend this small bar an indoor-pool effect. Generously portioned cocktails also make a splash.

**Tempted** Seductive pleasures lie behind the apple-red curtain at Eden Bar & Café.

### Brooklyn Brewery Tasting Room

*79 North 11th St between Berry St and Wythe Ave, Williamsburg, Brooklyn (718-486-7422). Subway: L to Bedford Ave. Fri 6–10pm; Sat noon–5pm. Average drink: $3. AmEx, MC, V.*

Scope out the crowd during games of pool. As the evening wears on, the DJ's soft-rock selections segue into old-school funk. The makeshift bar serves house brews for a steal—two drafts for $5.

### Galapagos

*See page 309 for listing.*

Nothing gets a Manhattanite over the river like Galapagos. One night you'll hear a staged reading of a new play. The next, a punk band, a string quartet and a folk–and–hip-hop showcase. The gorgeous interior has a reflecting pool and walls of candles.

### The Stinger Club

*241 Grand St between Driggs Ave and Roebling St, Williamsburg, Brooklyn. (718-218-6662). Subway: L to Bedford Ave. 6pm–4am. Average drink: $5. Cash only.*

This is the only place in Williamsburg (or even Manhattan) where you can hear live bluegrass or reggae while eating hot dogs or jerk chicken. Rotating DJs and bands are the crème de l'hood.

# Restaurants

## Whatever your hunger, New York's myriad eateries can satisfy it

This town is a food-lover's paradise, with cuisines—and price points—so numerous and varied, it's no wonder that New Yorkers eat out as much as they do; there are just too many delicacies to pass up. City dwellers are also more than willing to travel to satisfy their cravings, so don't hesitate to let your appetite guide you to culinary adventures in all five boroughs.

If you wish to dine at one of the city's premier restaurants—especially the establishments listed in **Star chefs** *(see page 196)*—you'll need to book a table a month in advance (and often settle for eating at 6 or 10pm). Many smaller restaurants and bistros seat on a first-come, first-served basis, so be prepared to wait at a crowded bar (or outside on the sidewalk). Be mindful that the restaurant world is volatile: Call ahead to see if the place that was sizzling last week still serves the type of food we describe…or if it's even in business.

Establishments are grouped by geography for your convenience. To find restaurants by category, see the index on page 206. And remember, tipping is a must at New York restaurants *(see* **Tax & tipping**, *page 189)*.

A note on smoking: To the relief of some and the sharp dismay of others, Mayor Bloomberg recently urged the city council to pass legislation that effectively bans smoking in most of the city's restaurants and bars, possibly as early as March 2003. So ask before you light up: You may have to take your pleasure on the street.

**Whisper, don't shout** Subtlety triumphs at Tribeca's urbane retreat the Harrison.

## Tribeca & South

### American Park at the Battery

*Battery Park, across from 17 State St at Pearl St (212-809-5508). Subway: N, R, W to Whitehall St; 4, 5 to Bowling Green, 1, 9 to South Ferry. Mon–Sat 11:30am–10pm; Sun 11:30am–3pm. Average main course: $25. AmEx, Disc, MC, V.*

The massive American Park, with the air of a docked luxury liner, provides waterfront tables where you may sip wine, nibble on *frutti di mare* at the raw bar and gaze out over New York Harbor. Chef Rad Matmati includes earthy basics, such as braised short ribs and roasted rack of lamb, but his focus is fish. Tuesday through Saturday, enjoy live jazz and cabaret in the Park Grill, the more casual lower tier of the terrace. Reserve the novel "water table" in advance; it seats parties of up to 14 around a shallow pool that dishes float in—an aquatic lazy Susan.

### Danube

*30 Hudson St at Duane St (212-791-3771). Subway: A, C, 1, 2, 3, 9 to Chambers St. Mon–Sat 5:30–11:30pm. Average main course: $30. Five-course prix fixe: $80. AmEx, DC, Disc, MC, V.*

You will swoon for owner David Bouley's stunning vision of Austrian cuisine, capably executed by executive chef Mario Lohninger. Lacquered Klimt-like murals and divinely smooth lavender suede couches mix past and present in a fashion that reflects the cuisine. The "Monarchie" side of the menu includes

► For reviews of the newest restaurants, see the latest issue of ***Time Out New York.***
► The thousands of reviews in ***Time Out Eating & Drinking Guide*** are available on newsstands and at **eatdrink.timeoutny.com**.
► For more neighborhood favorites, see individual borough chapters in **Sightseeing**, page 37.

**Pig heaven** Pico's John Villa knows his way around a suckling porker.

traditional Viennese offerings, such as the tender Wiener schnitzel. The "Impressions" section is more fusion-friendly, with playful dishes like the Waltz of Salads: beef strudel and oxtail jam on a bed of marinated celery salad, foie gras terrine with rhubarb, and gently heated shrimp with snow peas. The result is revelatory fin de siecle decadence. To taste French food for the new millennium, try **Bouley** *(120 West Broadway at Duane St, 212-964-2525).*

## Fresh

*105 Reade St between Church and West Broadway (212-406-1900). Subway: N, R, W to City Hall; 1, 2, 3, 9 to Chambers St. 5–11pm. Average main course: $30. AmEx, MC, V.*

For fresher fish, you'd have to eat on the boat. Chef Martin Burge has connections with the city's most scrupulous seafood supplier and cooks only the best of the daily catch. On one evening, he served a refreshing, tangy ceviche of Boston mackerel, Japanese snapper and royal red shrimp, as well as a smooth gazpacho stocked with tender white slivers of Maryland blue crab. A filling *financier* packed with figs and petite late-harvest grapes make for a fine finish.

## The Harrison

*355 Greenwich St at Harrison St (212-274-9310). Subway: 1, 9 to Franklin St. Mon 5:30pm–midnight; Tue–Thu noon–2:30pm, 5:30–11:30pm; Fri, Sat noon–2:30pm, 5:30pm–midnight. Average main course: $22. AmEx, DC, Disc, MC, V.*

Chef-owner Jimmy Bradley's talent is to give a neighborhood the restaurant it wants but didn't know it deserved. For Tribeca, the Harrison arrived just in time. As at its beloved Chelsea sister, **The Red Cat** *(227 Tenth Ave between 23rd and 24th Sts, 212-242-1122),* the food seduces quietly. Entrées—ricotta *cavatelli* pasta, meaty skate paired with grapefruit, crisp baby red mullet—are sensible but never dull.

## Les Halles Downtown

*15 John St between Broadway and Nassau St (212-285-8585). Subway: A, C to Broadway–Nassau St; J, M Z, 2, 3, 4, 5 to Fulton St. Noon–midnight. Average main course: $14. AmEx, DC, Disc, MC, V.*

See page 195.

## Le Zinc

*139 Duane St between Church St and West Broadway (212-513-0001). Subway: A, C, 1, 2, 3, 9 to Chambers St. Sun–Thu 8am–2am; Fri, Sat 8am–3am. Average main course: $17. AmEx, DC, Disc, MC, V.*

Three-year-old Le Zinc, the disarmingly down-market sibling of David and Karen Waltuck's sumptuous **Chanterelle** *(2 Harrison St at Hudson St, 212-966-6960),* brings class to the masses. The spare space features a new zinc-topped bar and walls papered with old gallery posters, but that's as fancy as it gets. The food is a mix of peasant stock (pot roast, goulash), classic bistro (terrines, sautéed skate) and down-home American (bacon cheeseburger, fried catfish)—dishes that make well-mannered adults hum with pleasure as they tuck into their meals.

## Nobu

*105 Hudson St at Franklin St (212-219-0500). Subway: 1, 9 to Franklin St. Mon–Fri 11:45am–2:15pm, 5:45–10:15pm; Sat, Sun 5:45–10:15pm. Average hot dish: $16. Average sushi meal: $27. AmEx, DC, MC, V.*

Nobu is the stuff of legend—the most famous Japanese restaurant in America, a magnet for celebrities and the place that has no qualms about making you wait a month for a table (unless, of course, you're Gwyneth Paltrow). But here's a trick: Simply show up, say, on a Monday night around 9pm. Diners without reservations are seated at the sushi bar on a first-come, first-served basis, and you might even nab a table, should there be a cancellation. The talents in the kitchen continue to produce masterpieces from Japan-by-way-of-Peru. Nobu's signature black cod with miso, a hunky fish shellacked in sticky-sweet glaze, is elevated to an untouchable delicacy. If you seek a more down-to-earth experience, **Next Door Nobu** *(105 Hudson St at Franklin St, 212-334-4445)* shares Nobu's prep kitchen and offers an everyman version of its parent's cuisine.

## Odeon

*145 West Broadway between Duane and Thomas Sts (212-233-0507). Subway: A, C, 1, 2, 3, 9 to Chambers St. Mon–Fri noon–2am; Sat, Sun 11am–2am. Average main course: $18. AmEx, DC, Disc, MC, V.*

Brunch is a great time to bask in this legendary bistro—sunlight streams in through the Art Deco room, the noise level is low, and the feel is one of ease and comfort (potent, spicy Bloody Marys contribute to the warm glow). Dinner is prime time for indulging your meat lust with the famous steak frites au poivre or a roasted free-range chicken. Even the sweet-pea risotto is flavorful with *jambon de* Bayonne. Although Odeon's glorious art-snob days are gone, the food retains its star power.

### Pico

*349 Greenwich St between Harrison and Jay Sts (212-343-0700). Subway: 1, 9 to Franklin St. Mon–Thu noon–2:30pm, 6–10:30pm; Fri noon–2:30pm, 6–11:30pm; Sat 11:30am–3pm, 6–11:30pm; Sun 11:30am–3pm, 5–10pm. Average main course: $27. AmEx, DC, MC, V.*

Chef John Villa takes cues from all over Portugal to put his own refined spin on what is essentially country cooking. A chickpea soup sounds typically homey, but when Villa gets his hands on it, the production stars cinnamon, short ribs and fresh morels. Lift the half-cylinder dome of crackling skin covering the suckling pig to find delicate pork pieces and spinach leaves graced by a wildflower-honey sauce. Pico is one of the very few places in town where you'll find top-quality Portuguese wines.

## Chinatown & Little Italy

### Bread

*20 Spring St between Elizabeth and Mott Sts (212-334-1015). Subway: N, R, W to Prince St; 6 to Spring St. Mon–Sat noon–11pm; Sun noon–10pm. Average sandwich: $8. AmEx, Disc, MC, V.*

This tiny, chic white-and-silver *paninoteca*–café–wine bar succeeds in part because of a reliance on fine ingredients: fresh-baked *ciabatta* and raisin-walnut bread, authentic prosciutto *di Parma,* mozzarella and taleggio. Bread fills densely flavored sandwiches with everything from pesto chicken and avocado to goat cheese and shiitakes—then presses them in a *panini* grill. The ravioli bolognese starter is robustly flavored, and a spread of savory *speck,* salami, prosciutto, grilled zucchini and Brie is so fresh, you'll think you died and went to Parma.

### Cafe Gitane

*242 Mott St at Prince St (212-334-9552). Subway: N, R, W to Prince St; 6 to Spring St. 9am–midnight. Average main course: $8. Cash only.*

Across the street from St. Patrick's Old Cathedral and tree-filled cemetery, Cafe Gitane teems with hip-hugger-clad beauties. In summer, they lounge on benches outside, sipping strong coffee. Inside, the pace is leisurely—this café caters to those who like to linger. (If you're on the go, there's a walk-up coffee window.) The menu is a variety show of fresh French- and Mediterranean-inspired snacks and more substantial bites.

### Cafe Habana

*17 Prince St at Elizabeth St (212-625-2001). Subway: N, R, W to Prince St; 6 to Spring St. 9am–midnight. Average main course: $10. AmEx, DC, MC, V.*

There's nowhere to hide in this sexy, casual Cuban café. You'll be squeezed into a room packed with *very* beautiful people, but you'll soon be eyeing the hot little *nuevo cubano* menu. An appetizer of chicken tacos with cilantro, lime and tomatillo salsa is spicier than the usual Caribbean version. All of the elements in the blue-cornmeal cake—sun-dried tomatoes, goat cheese and black beans—meld together for surprisingly subtle flavor. There's also take-out next door *(229 Elizabeth St between Houston and Prince Sts, 212-625-2002)*—a counter locals swear by for a quick bite.

### Dim Sum Go Go

*5 East Broadway between Catherine and Oliver Sts (212-732-0797). Subway: F to East Broadway; J, M, Z, N, Q, R, W, 6 to Canal St. 10am–11pm. Average main course: $10. Average dim sum: $3.50. AmEx, MC, V.*

Glance at Dim Sum Go Go's dumplings and expect to be smitten by their cunning shapes and flavors. Chef Charn-Hing Man offers diners a higher order of playful dim sum—chive-shrimp *shumai,* duck skin and crabmeat with spinach dough—but if



## CRITICS' PICKS Chain reaction

Every day, tourists line up at recognizable chain restaurants because they are… recognizable. Here are a few alternatives that serve true New York flavor.

**Instead of Chevy's Fresh Mex**, try **Mi Cocina** *(57 Jane St at Hudson St, 212-627-8273),* a bright, regional-Mexican eatery with killer food and a renowned *mole* sauce. No chimichangas, but there is a delicious chicken enchilada doused in thick peanut sauce, and *carnes à la parrilla,* seasoned skirt steak served with tortillas.

**Instead of Olive Garden**, try **Becco** *(355 W 46th St between Eighth and Ninth Aves, 212-397-7597),* a popular Italian eatery minus the corporate feel. Follow salt-cod *brandade* and silky buffalo mozzarella with familiar dishes like veal parmigiana, served on the bone and covered with creamy fontina.

**Instead of TGI Friday's**, try **Frankie & Johnnie's Steakhouse** *(269 W 45th St at Eighth Ave, 212-997-9494),* a crusty 76-year-old red-meat joint in a former speakeasy. Sirloins are thick, aged and perfectly charred from a run under the broiler. Accompany your steak with heaping à la carte hash browns and Caesar salad.

Brasserie
Les Halles™
Voted
"Best French Bistro/Brasserie"
by Time Out readers, 2001 and 2002
©
Non-stop
noon to midnight
open 7 days
AMERICAN BEEF
FRENCH STYLE
New York
411 Park Ave. S. @ 29th St.
212-679-4111
New York Downtown
15 John Street
212-285-8585
www.LesHalles.net
Miami, FL
2415 Ponce de Leon
305-461-1099
Washington, DC
1201 Penn. Ave.
202-347-6848

"Best Turk Around"
ZAGAT 1999
Turkish
Kitchen
386 E 3rd Av (btw.27&28)
Tel: (212) 679 6633

you're venturing into the regular menu, steer toward the bamboo-heart soup with shredded pork or even the unusual Go Go hamburger—a house specialty served in a steamed Chinese bun. The setting is as sleek and mod as the cuisine is inventive.

### Le Jardin Bistro

*25 Cleveland Pl between Kenmare and Spring Sts (212-343-9599). Subway: 6 to Spring St. Sun–Thu noon–3pm, 6–10pm; Fri, Sat noon–3pm, 6–11pm. Average main course: $20. AmEx, DC, Disc, MC, V.*

The *jardin* in question happens to be one of the loveliest outdoor eating spaces in Manhattan: In nice weather, the back garden, with its ivy-covered trellises and French street signs, feels like Paris in spring. The menu of bistro classics, like the lean hanger steak and fat mussels, remains solid. Best of all, both dishes come with Le Jardin's killer frites, which are pencil-thin, crisp and salty. The only thing better might be the oversized crème brûlée, a great excuse to dawdle on a warm, breezy evening.

### New York Noodle Town

*28½ Bowery at Bayard St (212-349-0923). Subway: J, M, Z, N, Q, R, W, 6 to Canal St. Sun–Thu 9am–3:30am; Fri, Sat 9am–4:30am. Average main course: $9. Cash only.*

Although the name would suggest otherwise, New York Noodle Town's specialty is barbecued meat. As at many Chinatown restaurants, you'll find reddish-brown ducks, chickens, loins of pork and sides of crisp baby pig hanging in the window—but what's different here is the rare subtle flavor and succulence of the offerings. Noodles are served in fragrant broths with dumplings; panfried until crunchy; or stir-fried with vegetables and meat or seafood. The focus is on the food, not the ambience, and the kitchen keeps cooking well past midnight, when other nearby restaurants are fast asleep.

### Ping's

*22 Mott St between Mosco and Pell Sts (212-602-9988). Subway: J, M, Z, N, Q, R, W, 6 to Canal St. Mon–Thu 10am–midnight; Fri, Sat 10am–2am; Sun 9am–midnight. Average main course: $11. AmEx, MC, V.*

At Ping's, the draw is well-prepared exotic seafood, like spiced baby silver fish—bitesized pieces of boneless smelt, deep-fried to a golden yellow. Or try the duck's-tongue appetizer in a peppery batter or big steamed oysters with Ping's famous XO sauce (a spicy concoction that includes dried shrimp, scallops and garlic). An entrée of sliced, sautéed conch is set off by snappy snow peas and a tangy fermented shrimp sauce.

### Vietnam Restaurant

*11 Doyers St between Bowery and Pell St (212-693-0725). Subway: J, M, Z, N, Q, R, W, 6 to Canal St. Sun–Thu 11am–9:30pm; Fri, Sat 11am–10:30pm. Average main course: $7. AmEx.*

Come with a gang to casual, subterranean Vietnam, because you're going to want to sample as much as possible. Can't-miss entrées include salmon fried with vegetables and drenched in a thick, robust black-bean sauce, and a steaming bowl of curried-duck and noodle soup, accompanied by a dipping sauce of lime juice and black pepper. Here's a side serving of history: In the early 1900s, Doyers Street was nicknamed the "Bloody Angle." Apparently, a gang member named Mock Duck would squat in the middle of the dogleg alley, close his eyes and fire his guns in both directions. Today, you'll be hit with only good food.

**Not by Bread alone** Luigi Comandatore takes refreshment at his *paninoteca* Bread.

## Lower East Side

### AKA Café

*49 Clinton St between Rivington and Stanton Sts (212-979-6096). Subway: F, V to Lower East Side–Second Ave. Mon–Fri noon–4:30pm, 6pm–midnight; Sat 6pm–midnight; Brunch Sun 11:30am–4pm. Average sandwich: $8. AmEx, MC, V.*

Brought to you by the owners of **71 Clinton Fresh Food** *(71 Clinton St between Rivington and Stanton Sts, 212-614-6960)* and **Alias** *(76 Clinton St at Rivington St, 212-505-5011),* AKA Café is part of the street's restaurant boomlet. Chef Scott Ehrlich's menu is a shortlist of sophisticated but bargain-priced soups, salads, empanadas and sandwiches. His ceviche of fluke and Scotch bonnet peppers is sublime at a mere $7. Roasted squid stuffed with chickpeas and basil will set you back $12. The portions aren't huge, but the creations are wonderfully complex: AKA's postmodern PB&J features focaccia smeared with chunky almond butter, then draped with thin slices of lamb's tongue and topped with red-currant glaze.

### Congee Village

*100 Allen St between Broome and Delancey Sts (212-941-1818). Subway: F to Delancey St; J, M, Z to Delancey–Essex Sts. 10:30am–2am. Average main course: $10. AmEx, Disc, MC, V.*

There's no bad food at Congee Village; in fact, just

about every dish is sublime. Start with congee, of course, a thick porridge of rice gruel that can play host to a variety of ingredients, as in the "three-meat version" with pork, chicken and duck. If the waitress is in a good mood, she might recommend salty chicken prepared with ginger, scallions and soy—so simple, yet so good. You may squirm at some of the selections—pig intestines and steamed fish heads—but most of the food is accessible. This place will make a congee fan of you yet.

### Katz's Delicatessen

*205 E Houston St at Ludlow St (212-254-2246). Subway: F, V to Lower East Side–Second Ave. Sun–Tue 8am–10pm; Wed, Thu 8am–11pm; Fri, Sat 8am–3am. Average sandwich: $10.50 AmEx, MC, V ($20 minimum).*

This cavernous old dining hall is a repository of living history. Arrive at 11am on a Sunday morning, and the line may be out the door. Grab a ticket and approach the long counter. First, a hot dog. The weenies here are without peer; crisp-skinned, all-beef dogs that are worth the $2.50 each. Then shuffle down and order your legendarily shareable sandwich. Roast beef goes quickly and the brisket rates, but don't forsake horseradish. And the pastrami? It's simply da best.

### Oliva

*161 E Houston St at Allen St (212-228-4143). Subway: F, V to Lower East Side–Second Ave. Sun–Thu 11:30am–3:30pm, 5:30pm–midnight; Fri, Sat 11:30am–3:30pm, 5:30pm–1am. Average main course: $17. AmEx.*

At this casual but food-serious restaurant, you'll find sumptuous Basque fare, like garlic shrimp *a la plancha,* laden with paprika and olive oil, and served atop dark-green Swiss chard with a hint of garlic. The paella *de mariscos'* fragrant saffron rice is adorned with shrimp, mussels, calamari, clams and chorizo. Succulent pieces of filet mignon with brandy sauce and green peppercorns are served alongside *papas bravas*—fried potato with aioli and a touch of chili sauce. Stylish downtowners (with that sangria glow) eat it all up.

### Paladar

*161 Ludlow St between Houston and Stanton Sts (212-473-3535). Subway: F, V to Lower East Side–Second Ave. Sun–Wed 5:30–11:30pm; Thu–Sat 5:30pm–2am. Average main course: $13. Cash only.*

The menu at funky pastel Paladar offers fresh twists on spicy standards, including a ceviche of tangy shrimp and scallops, a sweet plantain "canoe" stuffed with savory stewed codfish, and braised short ribs simmered in a taste-bud–popping *ancho*-chili broth. Mix and match appetizers and fruity drinks to fuel your fiesta.

### Suba

*109 Ludlow St between Delancey and Rivington Sts (212-982-5714). Subway: F to Delancey St; J, M, Z to Delancey–Essex Sts. Sun–Wed 6–11pm; Thu–Sat 6pm–midnight. Bar Sun–Thu 6pm–2am; Fri, Sat 6pm–4am. Average main course: $21. AmEx, MC, V.*

The Lower East Side's nightlife supports all manner of shtick, but how many places can claim a moat? At Suba, a narrow pool surrounds the subterranean dining room, and submerged lights project dancing white ripples on the brick walls. This dazzling effect, along with the adventurous French-influenced Spanish menu, lends glamour to dining in a basement. Chef de cuisine Alain Allaire throws in a few touches from the Americas (grilled sardines in chipotle sauce, with red cabbage, red beans and guacamole; herbed chicken breast with Idiazábal cheese, broccoli rabe and almond mashed potatoes). Those who don't want to dive into a whole meal can nibble on tapas in one of the two (waterless) lounges.

## Soho



### Balthazar

*80 Spring St between Broadway and Crosby St (212-965-1414). Subway: N, R, W to Prince St; 6 to Spring St. Mon–Thu 7:30–11:30am, noon–5pm, 5:45pm– 1:30am; Fri 7:30–11:30am, noon–5pm, 5:45pm–2:30am; Sat 7:30am–3:30pm, 5:45pm–2:30am; Sun 7:30am–3:30pm, 5:30pm–12:30am. Average main course: $21. AmEx, MC, V.*

After more than five years, people still jostle for cocktails at the 25-foot zinc-topped bar of this classic

**Cinderella complex** Soho's Cendrillon enchants with nuanced Filipino cooking.

brasserie. The Parisian touches always impress: battered mirrors, Art Deco lighting, waiters in white bistro-length aprons. See-and-be-seen types don't usually have sound food judgment, but this crowd knows the score. The three-tiered raw-seafood tower, Le Balthazar, is an awesome sight (about nine oyster varieties are available on any given day). Chèvre-and-caramelized-onion tart, duck shepherd's pie and weekly specials like Saturday's braised short ribs are compelling. For more casual food and just as much of a scene, try sister restaurant **Pastis** *(9 Ninth Ave at Little West 12th St, 212-929-4844)* in the Meatpacking District.

### Cendrillon

*45 Mercer St between Broome and Grand Sts (212-343-9012). Subway: J, M, Z, N, Q, R, W, 6 to Canal St. Tue–Fri noon–4pm, 6–11pm; Sat, Sun 11am–5pm, 6–11pm. Average main course: $18. AmEx, DC, Disc, MC, V.*

A few blocks from West Broadway's strip mall, there's a lofty hideaway filled with some of the city's best Pan-Asian cuisine. The emphasis is on Filipino cooking, which draws largely from Latin influences. Tender barbecued spareribs cooked in a "Chinese smokehouse" are paired with mashed taro and sweet potatoes. Paella with black rice—a squid-ink–tinged bed for spiced crab, shrimp and Manila clams—calls for sake (there are good ones) instead of sangria. Specials like *lechón de leche* (roasted suckling pig) and an addictive green-papaya relish are fairy-tale good.

**Mind the store** Pick up Asian groceries and a quick bite at Soho's Kelley and Ping.

### Herban Kitchen

*290 Hudson St at Spring St (212-627-2257). Subway: C, E to Spring St; 1, 9 to Canal St. Mon–Fri 11am–11pm, Sat 5pm–midnight. Average main course: $17. AmEx, DC, Disc, MC, V.*

Herban Kitchen—a country-kitchen display with exposed brick, high ceilings, flickering votives and brown-paper tablecloths—serves vegetarian-friendly, healthy food that is as pleasing as the relaxed ambience. Pot-au-feu is a rich sage-broth stew studded with white beans, fennel, root vegetables and homemade mushroom-ravioli triangles; juicy herb-crusted catfish is served with butternut-squash puree and roasted plum tomatoes. The extensive wine and beer list has many organic selections.

### Ideya

*349 West Broadway between Broome and Grand Sts (212-625-1441). Subway: A, C, E, 1, 9 to Canal St. Mon–Wed 1–11pm; Thu, Fri 1pm–midnight; Sat 11:30am–midnight; Sun 11:30am–11pm. Average main course: $18. AmEx, DC, MC, V.*

The mobs and snobs of Soho seem miles away when you kick back with a tart caipirinha at this island-themed bistro. The walls are lined with tropical graffiti murals by New York artist Daze, and Brazilian jazz keeps everyone—including the first-rate guayabera-clad servers—in the groove. The menu encompasses various Caribbean influences, from Bahamian salt-cod fritters and Jamaican duck patties to Trinidad-style potato-and-vegetable stew and Mexican seafood *taquitos*. All are a pleasant change from the usual *cosa*.

### Kelley and Ping

*127 Greene St between Houston and Prince Sts (212-228-1212). Subway: F, V, S to Broadway–Lafayette St; N, R, W to Prince St; 6 to Bleecker St. 11:30am–11pm. Average main course: $6. AmEx, MC, V.*

Savvy locals and trendy tourists swarm this noodle shop, which is nearing institution status after ten years. They walk past the shelves of Asian groceries and peruse the menu of Thai, Vietnamese and Chinese dishes, waiting in front of the glassed-in counter of noodles and vegetables ready for stir-fry. There's something for everyone, including many vegetarian dishes and a variety of noodles (wheat, egg or rice).

### Palacinka

*28 Grand St between Thompson St and Sixth Ave (212-625-0362). Subway: A, C, E, 1, 9 to Canal St. Sun–Wed 10:30am–11pm; Thu–Sat 10:30am–midnight. Average crêpe: $7.50. Cash only.*

All glinting tin tables and gorgeous Europeans, this spot is enchanting. Crêpes are Palacinka's pride and joy (and the meaning of the eatery's Czech name)—they're good and cheap, and they come two to a plate, with a side of mesclun salad. The savory crêpes mix tarragon-herbed chicken with goat cheese and peppers, and portobello mushrooms with potatoes, mozzarella and pesto. Sweet crêpes range from the classic lemon, butter and sugar to a luscious filling of chestnut paste with crème fraîche.

### Pintxos

*510 Greenwich St between Canal and Spring Sts (212-343-9923). Subway: C, E to Spring St; 1, 9 to Houston St. Mon–Thu 11:30am–10pm; Fri, Sat 3–11pm. Average main course: $17. AmEx, MC, V.*

Pintxos is perhaps the best of several new Basque eateries. Owner Javier Ortega was trained in San Sebastian, Spain, where he honed his talent for infusing simple ingredients with magic. An appetizer of grilled chorizo has you begging for seconds, as do *piquillo* peppers stuffed with salt cod. *Pintxos* means "tapas" in Basque, and you could easily make a meal of the ones here, though the main courses deserve top billing. Try squid in its own ink over a bed of rice, or sea bass in parsley-and-garlic green sauce. The superb (and cheap) red wine has Pintxos buzzing with handsome regulars well into the night.

### Théo

*325 Spring St between Greenwich and Washington Sts (212-414-1344). Subway: C, E to Spring St. Sun–Thu 6pm–midnight; Fri, Sat 6pm–1am. Bar 6pm–2am. Average main course: $21. AmEx, MC, V.*

From the same people who gave sushi a sleek nightclub vibe at **Bond St.** *(6 Bond St between Broadway and Lafayette St, 212-777-2500),* Théo seems like the center of a hipster galaxy. The kitchen doles out cute bar food to go with whimsical cocktails in the blood-red lounge upstairs, while it riffs on traditional favorites in the dining room downstairs. The mac-and-cheese ravioli is addictive, and tender duck breast over potato, mango and apple mash is a standout.

## East Village

### Angelica Kitchen

*300 E 12th St between First and Second Aves (212-228-2909). Subway: L to First Ave; N, Q, R, W, 4, 5, 6 to 14th St–Union Sq. 11:30am–10:30pm. Average main course: $10. Cash only.*

Votive candles and yogic atmosphere make Angelica Kitchen more hippie than hip. The initiated have been coming since the 1970s for clever dishes that could convert even a die-hard carnivore. A 34-term cheat sheet on the back of the menu explains what *umeboshi* and *konbu* are, and why they're good for you. Still, you might think you're downing a Reuben when you bite into the fresh sourdough baguette layered with baked, marinated tempeh slices under homemade mushroom gravy; it's served with raw spinach, ruby kraut and mashed potatoes. With options like these, who needs meat?

### A Salt & Battery

*80 Second Ave between 4th and 5th Sts (212-254-6610). Subway: F, V to Lower East Side–Second Ave. Noon–10pm. Average main course: $10. AmEx, MC, V.*

See page 190.

### Casimir

*103–105 Ave B between 6th and 7th Sts (212-358-9683). Subway: F, V to Lower East Side–Second Ave; 6 to Astor Pl. Mon–Fri 5:30pm–1am; Sat, Sun 11am–4pm, 5:30pm–1am. Average main course: $15. AmEx.*

Call it laissez-faire, or call it insouciance—whatever the word, popular Casimir is relaxed. Young, lanky French servers do their best to show the East Village crowd that this gig isn't their *real* job. Thankfully, the kitchen staff is professional, producing generous, delicious dishes. The filet mignon with pepper-and-cognac sauce and the sesame-crusted tuna are seared on the outside and rare within. Slightly thick frites, served in pails, are salty and crunchy. And the steak tartare, capably seasoned, is cool and lean. Half of the restaurant is a Moroccan-themed cocktail lounge that spills onto the sidewalk, but in summer, try to snag an umbrellaed table on the small rear patio.

### Dok Suni's

*119 First Ave between St. Marks Pl and E 7th St (212-477-9506). Subway: F, V to Lower East Side–Second Ave; 6 to Astor Pl. Sun, Mon 4:30–11pm; Tue–Sat 4:30pm–midnight. Average main course: $13. Cash only.*

Dok Suni's might look like a dimly lit haunt for smoking indie-rockers. It might sound like a dive bar with a well-considered, fully loaded jukebox. But it smells like the dynamite-in-the-mouth Korean-food joint that it is. If you're just becoming familiar with this cuisine, Dok Suni's dazzling selections will ensure further exploration. If you're an old pro at rolling sticky rice, beef and spicy *banchan* into a lettuce leaf, then have your favorites served by an attractive, superhip waitstaff. Former design student Jenny Kwak founded the place in 1993 and in 1999 opened the even slicker **Do Hwa** in the West Village *(55 Carmine St between Bedford St and Seventh Ave South, 212 414-1224).*

### Five Points

*31 Great Jones St between Bowery and Lafayette St (212-253-5700). Subway: F, V, S to Broadway–Lafayette St; 6 to Bleecker St. 5pm–midnight. Average main course: $21. AmEx, DC, MC, V.*

Four years on, Five Points has become a fantastic neighborhood restaurant. Handsome, vaguely nautical and completely unpretentious, it's the kind of seductive place where you can take a seat at the bar, order an oversized martini and slurp oysters (a buck apiece from 5 to 7pm). Marc Meyer's well-conceived American food is spiked with Mediterranean accents. The menu changes daily, but staples include a nicely chewy grilled hanger steak, seasoned with garlic and rosemary, and buttermilk-marinated chicken, which has a Mediterranean tinge of honey, cinnamon and cardamom.

### Gotham Bar and Grill

*12 E 12th St between Fifth Ave and University Pl (212-620-4020). Subway: L, N, Q, R, W, 4, 5, 6 to 14th St–Union Sq. Mon–Thu noon–2:30pm,*

*5:30–10pm; Fri noon–2:30pm, 5:30–11pm; Sat 5:30–11pm; Sun 5:30– 10:00pm. Average main course: $34. AmEx, DC, MC, V.*

Chef Alfred Portale, the father of vertical food, is still in Gotham's kitchen most weeknights, and the food is as mesmerizing as ever. Every ingredient is a superlative: the softest rack of lamb, the most succulent shrimp, the sweetest scallop. Plates are constructed with precision—lobster tails are placed in a circular design that's sculptural as much as architectural. Atop their pedestal of roasted fingerling potatoes, cabbage, whole garlic cloves and flageolets, the crustaceans seem to be in a natural environment all their own. On weekends, a steady stream of limousines pulls up to the entrance, disgorging unfamous people young and old, ready to partake of a legend.

### Jewel Bako

*239 E 5th St between Second and Third Aves (212-979-1012). Subway: 6 to Astor Pl. Mon–Sat 6:30–10:30pm. Average sushi meal (8 pieces, 1 roll): $24. AmEx, DC, MC, V.*

The space is a stunning Kubrick-meets-Kurosawa bamboo tunnel, and chef Kazuo Yoshida's sushi and sashimi is just as awe-inspiring. *Omakase* starts at $50, and for that, Yoshida makes dishes with the day's best seafood (up to 50 varieties)—say, jack mackerel, fluke and fatty tuna laced with barley miso, trefoil or *shiso*. Seasonal appetizers include tilefish cooked on its plate in hot sesame oil, and an almost whipped *toro* tartare topped with fresh ginger and creamy avocado sauce.

**Dark and handsome** Dok Suni's lends a little atmosphere to terrific Korean home cooking.

### Jules Bistro

*65 St. Marks Pl between First and Second Aves (212-477-5560). Subway: L to First Ave; 6 to Astor Pl. Mon–Fri 11:30am–4:30pm, 5:30pm–1:30am; Sat, Sun 11:30am–4:30pm, 5pm–1am. Average main course: $14. AmEx.*

Despite being located on St. Marks Place, this is one of the city's most effortlessly charming restaurants, frequented by a crowd of locals and French expats. Even the by-the-numbers live jazz will seem inspired as you sip a glass of wine on the small terrace, or chug a Leffe behind a beaded curtain indoors. The menu combines the familiar (house-made pâté, *moules frites,* hanger steak) with enough idiosyncrasy to tease bistro habitués: The nicely fatty duck is sweetened with dried apricots and figs in Armagnac sauce; grilled tuna steak is accompanied by buttery quinoa.

### La Palapa

*77 St. Marks Pl between First and Second Aves (212-777-2537). Subway: 6 to Astor Pl. Mon–Fri noon–midnight; Sat, Sun 11am–midnight. Average main course: $15. AmEx, DC, MC, V.*

La Palapa's earth tones, well-spaced tables and subdued lighting make you feel like you're in a thatched-roof hut (a.k.a. *palapa*) on a balmy beach. Grilled Muscovy duck with sesame seeds is rich and juicy when ordered medium-rare and drizzled with the robust bitter-chocolatelike *mole* that La Palapa is known for. Swiss chard and toasted–pumpkin-seed sauce add a nice bite to the mild cod fillet. If poet W.H. Auden were alive and still living upstairs, he'd ruminate about the sublime food at La Palapa for inspiration.

### Mama's Food Shop

*200 E 3rd St between Aves A and B (212-777-4425). Subway: F, V to Lower East Side–Second Ave. Mon–Sat 11am–10:30pm. Average main course: $8. Cash only.*

When you get a hankering for some down-home cooking, you're going to want this Mama to adopt you. The no-fuss, no-frills cafeteria-style canteen serves only the basics—fried or grilled chicken, hearty meat loaf, lumpy mashed potatoes—but they're more than basically good. Not too many people's mamas can improve on the amazing macaroni and cheese. Vegetarians pile plates with garlic-studded broccoli, fresh corn salad, couscous and many other meat-free sides. But don't get picky or make special requests; as the menu states, just "shut up and eat it!" **Stepmama** *(199 E 3rd St between Aves A and B, 212-228-2663),* across the street, serves sandwiches.

### Moustache

*265 E 10th St between First Ave and Ave A (212-228-2022). Subway: L to First Ave; 6 to Astor Pl. Noon–midnight. Average main course: $10. Cash only.*

You'll have to leave Manhattan to find Middle Eastern food this good at such reasonable prices. The nutty hummus is excellent, and the spinach-and-chickpea salad is tangy; all of the appetizers should be scooped up with excellent piping-hot pita. One of Moustache's specialties is "pitza," which comes with a wide variety of toppings. Perhaps best of all is the *ouzi,* a bowl-shaped pastry containing a delicious mix of rice, chunks of chicken, raisins and vegetables. Finish your meal with a sugary dessert and a powerful cup of equally sweet Turkish coffee.

### Patio Dining

*31 Second Ave between 1st and 2nd Sts (212-460-9171). Subway: F, V to Lower East Side–Second Ave. Tue–Sat 6–11pm. Average main course: $17.*

Here's a reincarnation that's infinitely easier to stomach than Shirley MacLaine's. Mugsy's Chow-Chow, the beloved East Village temple of cheap Italian eats, has been reborn as Patio Dining. Hardly anything has changed in the decor of this wood-paneled nook, but the food has more dimension: Chef Sara Jenkins is turning out robust, market-fresh Mediterranean fare. Expect wholesome, elegant dishes like seared venison with chanterelles and Tuscan sulfur beans, and *pennette* with pea shoots and Parmesan. The adjoining bar is a supremely pleasant spot to kick back pre- or postmeal.

### Prune

*54 E 1st St between First and Second Aves (212-677-6221). Subway: F, V to Lower East Side–Second Ave. Mon–Thu 6–11pm; Fri, 6pm–midnight; Sat 10am–3:30pm, 6pm–midnight; Sun 10am–3:30pm, 5–10pm. Average main course: $21. AmEx, MC, V.*

At tiny Prune, there's nothing cute or safe about chef-owner Gabrielle Hamilton's daring food. Juicy roasted suckling pig is complemented by a spicy salad of pickled tomatoes, black-eyed peas and aioli; rich, plump sweetbreads are topped with bacon; and the "bacon chop" is a pork chop wrapped in bacon. Vegetarians will do well with side options like roasted beets aioli or shoots of white and green asparagus in fennel butter. Show up on weekend mornings for such delights as whitefish and lox, the popular sausages and oysters and at least one of the nine Bloody Mary variations. Prune thoughtfully supplies a chaser with each: Red Stripe in a shot glass.

### Strip House

*13 E 12th St between Fifth Ave and University Pl (212-328-0000). Subway: L, N, Q, R, W, 4, 5, 6 to 14th St–Union Sq. Tue–Thu noon–3pm, 5:30–11pm; Fri noon–3pm, 5:30–11:30pm; Sat 5:30–11:30pm; Sun 5:30–11pm. Average main course: $26. AmEx, Disc, MC, V.*

This place may have the best steak in Manhattan. The New York strip for two, a magnificent hunk of beef, is carved tableside into perfect, four-inch-deep squares that are charred crisp and salty on the outside, garnet-red within. Start with chef David Walzog's creative take on a classic tomato-and-onion salad, then pair your meat with luscious truffled, creamed spinach and goose-fat–fried potatoes. What distinguishes Strip House from its competitors is the restaurant itself. Think Hugh Hefner, circa 1962—a spacious cocktail lounge, red-velvet walls, burgundy quilted-leather banquettes, terrazzo floors and a put-you-in-the-mood glow that permeates the whole house.

### Supper

*156 E 2nd St between Aves A and B (212-477-7600). Subway: F, V to Lower East Side–Second Ave. Sun–Thu 11am–1am; Fri, Sat 11am–2am. Average main course: $10. Cash only.*

*Strozzapreti,* a pasta called "the timely priest stranglers" is the most politically charged dish on the menu—in terms of titles. As for taste, it's just one among many provocations at Supper. Take the spaghetti *al limone,* a sprightly union of citrus and Parmesan, or salmon *tagliata,* two pink hunks of fish with arugula and a pestolike fava-bean puree. Supper may be dressed up with chandeliers, tapestried booths and a regal back room with a glassed-in wine cellar, but thanks to its raucous open kitchen and neighborly prices, casual wins out.

### Trattoria Paolina

*175 Ave B at 11th St (212-253-2221). Subway: L to First Ave. Open daily 11am–4pm, 6pm–midnight. Average main course: $11. Cash only.*

This fire-engine-red spot is appointed with sporty touches like piles of little cars, a huge mobile of artwork and a rack of Italian comic books. Try the asparagus, made wonderfully goopy by a sunny-side-up egg (plus butter and Parmesan); the spaghetti carbonara; or pork loin with milk-and-spinach sauce. Trattoria Paolina delivers down-home Italian cooking in a laid-back setting with playful decor.

## West Village

### Annisa

*13 Barrow St between Bleecker and W 4th Sts (212-741-6699). Subway: A, C, E, F, V, S to W 4th*

## Tax & tipping

Few New York restaurants add a service charge to the bill (unless your party is of eight or more), but it is customary to pay 15 to 20 percent of the bill total as a tip. The easiest way to figure out the amount is to double the 8.25-percent sales tax. Complain all you want if you feel service is under par, but only in the most extreme cases should you withhold a tip. Remember that servers are paid *far* below minimum wage, and rely on tips to pay the rent. Don't forget to tip bartenders ($1 a drink). The person who delivers your Chinese food probably receives no salary at all and relies entirely on tips ($2 is considered a good amount). Don't give out-of-towners a bad name.

*St. Mon–Sat 5:30–10pm; Sun 6:30–9:30pm. Average main course: $26. AmEx, DC, MC, V.*
Chef Anita Lo's menu draws inspiration from France, Japan and 21st-century New York, so expect some wild-card action. To wit: seared foie gras with soup dumplings and jicama; cod with artichoke gratin and Meyer lemon; miso-marinated sablefish with crisp deep-fried tofu in a bonito-kelp broth; and roasted veal with sweetbreads, lobster and mushrooms. All the dishes are carefully and exquisitely prepared. Even after one of the five- or seven-course tasting menus—which Lo often improvises according to available ingredients—you won't feel weighted down.

### A Salt & Battery

*112 Greenwich Ave between 12th and 13th Sts (212-691-2713). Subway: A, C, E to 14th St; L to Eighth Ave. Noon–10pm. Average main course: $10. AmEx, MC, V.*
A Salt & Battery, a candidate for silliest restaurant pun ever, is about as authentic as any non–U.K. fish-and-chips joint could be. The batter is light and crisp, the cod tender and the chips Brit-style soggy, even before you douse them with malt vinegar. Stick with the basic cod, or try the more intensely flavored chunks of batter-dipped cod roe—wrapped in a London newspaper, of course.

### Babbo

*110 Waverly Pl between MacDougal St and Sixth Ave (212-777-0303). Subway: A, C, E, F, V, S to W 4th St. Mon–Sat 5:30–11:30pm; Sun 5–11pm. Average main course: $27. Average pasta: $19. AmEx, Disc, MC, V.*
As Babbo regulars know, ordering grows more frustrating upon each visit. Once you taste a Babbo dish, such as lamb's-tongue salad painted with the thick yolk of a poached egg, or saucy parcels of beef-cheek ravioli, you must order it again. Mario Batali's gnocchi are as fluffy as down pillows and blanketed with tender shreds of oxtail. Two-Minute Calamari—a spicy red soup exploding with caper berries and rings of squid—is a bowlful of fireworks. Order it all— if the Lord smites you for gluttony, at least you'll leave this world with a smile. If you can't get a reservation, try one of Batali's other superb restaurants: the casual Roman trattoria **Lupa** *(170 Thompson St between Bleecker and Houston Sts, 212-982-5089)* or the midtown seafood haven **Esca** *(402 W 43rd St at Ninth Ave, 212-564-7272).*

Necessities

# The upper crust

## Where to get authentic New York pizza—and not just by the slice

Pizza has come a long way. According to legend, it was around 500 B.C. when Darius the Great's peckish Persian soldiers first slathered dough on their shields, topped them with cheese and dates, and baked them over campfires. So after 2,500 years of culinary evolution, you'd think that finding a good piece of pie in one of the world's most advanced cities would be easy.

While there are hundreds of choices, eating pizza in New York is not the same as eating New York pizza. The quintessential pie is characterized by a thin crust layered with fresh homemade ingredients, adorned with classic toppings like pepperoni and Italian sausage, and cooked at an intense heat, usually in a coal-fired brick oven. From this inferno emerges a crisp, almost burned creation—a smoky revelation for those whose taste buds have been numbed by a lifetime of gimmicky chain pies and stale, reheated slices (not to mention pizza pitas, pizza pockets, pizza turnovers, pizza wraps and pizza-on-a-stick).

Makers of real New York pizza don't just toss a pie in the oven and then sneak out for a smoke. They're craftsmen. During the three minutes a pizza spends baking at John's Pizzeria, the kitchen's "stick men" never rest—they manipulate the pie, moving it to and from the oven's hot spots, opening and shutting the door to regulate the 900-degree heat, all in an effort to produce an evenly charred crust.

Then why are there so many parlors making (and reheating) ho-hum pie? "Most places haven't been around that long," explains Robert Vittoria, co-owner of John's, which has been in his family since 1946. "They don't have the know-how. You don't just say, 'Hey, let's open a pizza place and make money.' You have to know what you're doing."

Fortunately, there *are* pizzerias that know exactly what they're doing. Here are some of New York's finest.

### Grimaldi's

*19 Old Fulton St between Front and Water Sts, Brooklyn Heights, Brooklyn (718-858-4300). Subway: A, C to High St; F to York St. Mon–Thu 11:30am–11pm; Fri 11:30am–midnight; Sat noon–midnight; Sun noon–11pm. Large plain pizza: $14. Cash only.*
A front-runner for the title of New York Pizza

**Crisp in the first degree** Fish-and-chips pack a whopping crunch at A Salt & Battery.

## Bar Pitti

*268 Sixth Ave between Bleecker and Houston Sts (212-982-3300). Subway: A, C, E, F, V, S to W 4th St; 1, 9 to Houston St. Noon–midnight. Average main course: $15. Cash only.*

The harried servers at Bar Pitti zip by, even though there's barely enough space between tables to maybe, *maybe,* let Lara Flynn Boyle slip through unscathed. Regardless of seating, you'll fall for this rustic next-door sister to the refined **Da Silvano** *(260 Sixth Ave between Bleecker and Houston Sts, 212-982-2343)* and casual **Da Silvano Cantinetta** *(260 Sixth Ave between Bleecker and Houston Sts, 212-844-0282).* Northern Italian specials include a variety of tempting fish, meat and pasta dishes. Fish courses are dreamy—oven-roasted fillet of sea bass with olive oil and rosemary, for example—if on the small side. That's not necessarily a bad thing, as it allows room for the superb *panna cotta,* which is baked to a creamy consistency, chilled and drenched in chocolate sauce.

## Blue Hill

*75 Washington Pl between Washington Sq West and Sixth Ave (212-539-1776). Subway: A, C, E, F, V, S to W 4th St. Mon–Sun 5:30–11pm. Average main course: $24. AmEx, DC, MC, V.*

This critically praised modern bistro relies upon a smartly appointed dining room, a knowledgeable waitstaff and food that is creative but not forced.



Mecca, Grimaldi's tops its creations with a thin sheet of mozzarella that accentuates the savory homemade sauce.

### John's Pizzeria

*278 Bleecker St at Jones St (212-243-1680). Subway: A, C, E, F, V, S to W 4th St; 1, 9 to Christopher St–Sheridan Sq. Mon–Sat 11:30am–11:30pm; Sun noon–11:30pm. Large plain pizza: $11. Cash only.*

The gas-powered Rays and Pizza Huts of the world can't compete with the coal-fueled flavor of John's glistening pies. You can count on sweet sauce, fresh mozzarella and a thin crust that's both charred and chewy.

### Lombardi's

*32 Spring St between Mott and Mulberry Sts (212-941-7994). Subway: 6 to Spring St. Mon–Thu 11:30am–11pm; Fri, Sat 11:30am–midnight; Sun 11:30am–10pm. Large plain pizza: $14. Cash only.*

Lombardi's has history. It was America's first pizzeria—opened in 1905 by Gennaro Lombardi—and remains one of the best. Taste the famous littleneck-clam pie and you'll know why.

### Patsy's Pizzeria

*2287 First Ave between 117th and 118th Sts (212-534-9783). Subway: 6 to 116th St. Mon–Thu 11am–midnight; Fri 11am–1am; Sat 11am–2am; Sun 1–11pm. Large plain pizza: $10. Cash only.*

This New York institution turns 70 in 2003. The herb-infused sauce is lovingly ladled onto a thin crust that tastes like cake, bread and cracker all rolled into one.

### Two Boots Pizzeria

*42 Ave A at 3rd St (212-254-1919) Subway: F, V to Lower East Side–Second Ave. Mon–Fri 5pm–midnight; Sun noon–11pm. Large plain pizza: $14. AmEx, Disc, MC, V.*

Two Boots may not be New York pizza by strict definition because of its gas ovens and exotic toppings. But this fun-loving minichain has become a cultural force in the city. If you only want a slice, try the Newman—it's topped with ricotta, *soppressata* and sweet Italian sausage named in honor of the *Seinfeld* postal worker character.

**Other locations** • *Two Boots to Go-Go, 74 Bleecker St between Broadway and Lafayette Sts (212-777-1033). Subway: F, V, S to Broadway–Lafayette St; 6 to Bleecker St.* • *Two Boots to Go West, 201 W 11th St at Seventh Ave (212-633-9096). Subway: L to Sixth Ave; 1, 2, 3, 9 to 14th St.* • *Two Boots, Grand Central Terminal, Lower Concourse, 42nd St at Park Ave (212-557-7992). Subway: S, 4, 5, 6, 7 to 42nd St–Grand Central.* • *Two Boots Rock Center, 30 Rockefeller Center, Lower Concourse (212-332-8800). Subway: B, D, F, V to 47–50th Sts–Rockefeller Ctr.* • *Two Boots Park Slope, 514 2nd St between Seventh and Eighth Aves, Park Slope, Brooklyn (718-499-3253). Subway: F to Seventh Ave.*

**Leaven on earth** Blue Ribbon Bakery's breads are always on the rise, and served with a generous mix of small dishes and upscale main courses from around the world.

Chefs Dan Barber and Mike Anthony find inspiration in the latest market ingredients: That salad of poached shrimp and buttery avocado, balanced with crisp, bracing ribbons of fennel, can only be had when it's absolutely fresh. Roasted chicken is so tender, you wonder if you've been cooking it wrong all these years. Visit any night of the week and you'll find a packed house.

## Blue Ribbon Bakery

*33 Downing St at Bedford St (212-337-0404). Subway: A, C, E, F, V, S to W 4th St; 1, 9 to Houston St. Tue–Thu noon–midnight; Fri noon–2am; Sat 11:30am–2am; Sun 11:30am–midnight. Average main course: $22. AmEx, DC, MC, V.*

In this brick-walled turn-of-the-century space, you can order roasted garlic, spread it on a slice of toasted challah bread, top it with another dish—say, succulent bone marrow—and then dip the whole thing into smooth red-wine sauce. The inspired kitchen staff doles out small plates of soul-pleasing food. Matzo-ball soup, chicken-salad sandwiches and garlic shrimp and chorizo are prepared with as much loving skill as the more upscale offerings, such as roasted duck in orange-cassis sauce. Vegetarians get their own menu section; the wine list is extensive; and locals love the weekend brunch. The Blue Ribbon family includes the chef hang-out **Blue Ribbon** *(97 Sullivan St between Prince and Spring Sts, 212-274-0404)*, **Blue Ribbon Sushi** *(119 Sullivan St between Prince and Spring Sts, 212-343-0404)* and **Blue Ribbon Brooklyn** *(280 Fifth Ave between Garfield Pl and 1st St, Park Slope, Brooklyn. 718-840-4040).*

## Florent

*69 Gansevoort St between Greenwich and Washington Sts (212-989-5779). Subway: A, C, E to 14th St; L to Eighth Ave. Mon 12:01–5am, 9am–midnight; Tue, Wed 9am–midnight; Thu–Sun 24hrs. Average main course: $15. Cash only.*

The trannies come and go, club kids disappear into K-holes, and chic boutiques open nearby—but through good times and bad in the Meatpacking District, Florent endures. Since 1985, it's been a reliable bistro, a community center of sorts and a renowned late-night hang. Regulars come for the dry-aged sirloin au poivre, served with frites and a vegetable; always-fresh *moules;* the jumbo burger on a Thomas' English muffin; and the artery-choking *boudin noir.* Florent also offers a children's menu in the form of an illustrated French lesson, so take the little ones during the day, when light streams lovingly into the restaurant.

## Isla

*39 Downing St between Bedford St and Seventh Ave South (212-352-2822). Subway: 1, 9 to Houston St. Tue–Thu 6pm–midnight; Fri, Sat 6pm–1am. Average main course: $23. AmEx, MC, V.*

Blue-and-white tile, aqua Formica and hanging orange lamps supply a 1950s Havana resort feel to this Cuban spot; chef Juventino Avila contributes his share of elegance and simplicity. A three-tiered appetizer special showcases crisp *croquetas de pollo* (chicken); skewers of grilled okra, each topped with a cherry tomato; and *masitas de puerco* (pork chunks) and shrimp, pungent with black-truffle sauce. Filet mignon, marinated in a classic garlic-vinegar-lemon-parsley *mojo,* is sensuously tart. The waitstaff takes such good care of you, you'll hardly miss the swimming pool.

## Mama's Food Shop

*222 Sullivan between Bleecker and W 3rd Sts (212-505-8123). Subway: A,C, E, F, V, S to W 4th St. Average main course: $9. Cash only.*
See page 188.

## Mary's Fish Camp

*64 Charles St at W 4th St (646-486-2185). Subway: 1, 9 to Christopher St–Sheridan Sq. Mon–Sat noon–3pm, 6–11pm. Average main course: $20. AmEx, MC, V.*
You know you're in the right seafood spot when irrepressible chef Mario Batali *(see* **Babbo**, *page 190)* is downing oysters at the next table. The kitchen does wonders with lobster, whether it's in a creamy potpie, placed over angel-hair pasta in a spicy tomato broth, lightly mixed with mayo and stuffed into a buttered roll, or served au naturel with drawn butter and lemon. Also noteworthy are the plump, crisp salt-crusted shrimp, the silky chowder loaded with clams, and the herb-stuffed, grilled whole fish. The best thing about Mary's (other than the food) is the casual milieu. It's the perfect place to repair to after a punishing day.

**Fantasy island** Isla's decor evokes a mid-century–modern resort in Cuba.

## Moustache

*90 Bedford St between Barrow and Grove Sts (212-229-2220). Subway: 1, 9 to Christopher St–Sheridan Sq. Noon–11pm. Average main course: $10. Cash only.*
See page 188.

## Negril Village

*70 W 3rd St between La Guardia Pl and Thompson St (212-477-2804). Subway: A, C, E, F, V, S to W 4th St. Mon–Fri noon–midnight; Sat, Sun noon–2am. Average main course: $20. AmEx, DC, Disc, MC, V.*
While many of New York's palm-covered Jamaican restaurants attempt to give you an authentic island experience, not all of them look so good doing it. Not only is Negril Village candlelit and sexy, it serves seriously delicious Jamaican food. Coconut shrimp are huge, crunchy delights, heightened by spicy pineapple salsa. Famished? Try the Jerk Treasure Chest, a toppling platter of shrimp, mussels, skewered chicken and strips of grilled sea bass and salmon, all smothered in a not-too-spicy jerk sauce.

## Piadina

*57 W 10th St between Fifth and Sixth Aves (212-460-8017). Subway: F, V to 14th St; L to Sixth Ave. 6–11:30pm. Average main course: $13. Cash only.*
This may seem like an ordinary Village Italian joint, but Piadina's food has acquired a certain cachet—Roberto Benigni stops by when he's in town (like the owners, he's from Rimini) and Elle Macpherson has been known to duck in for a bite. The restaurant is named after an Emilia-Romagna specialty: slices of stone-baked unleavened bread, filled with prosciutto, spinach, salami or cheese, and paired with tomato or arugula. Also recommended: house-made spinach gnocchi in pesto-tomato sauce and the daily risotto special. The wine list offers a fairly priced selection of Italian bottles.

## Tangerine

*228 W 10th St between Bleecker and Hudson Sts (212-463-8585). Subway: 1, 9 to Christopher St–Sheridan Sq. 5:30pm–midnight. Average main course: $16. AmEx, DC, M, V.*
Tangerine is one of those rare pleasures for the eyes *and* the palate. The owners are straight out of Thailand, which explains why this place has some of the better eats this side of Bangkok. The Purple Blossom appetizer—delicate chicken-filled dumplings in the shape of flowers—may well be the prettiest starter you'll ever devour. Entrées run from mainstay (seafood pad thai) to massive (an array of Tangerine Dream platters packed with soup, seafood, rice and meat). Dine downstairs in the sleek open room or take it upstairs to the sexy maroon-colored lounge, dotted with leafy bamboo plants and dimly illuminated by lanterns.

## Wallsé

*344 W 11th St at Washington St (212-352-2300). Subway: 1, 9 to Christopher St–Sheridan Sq. 5:30pm–midnight. Average main course: $23. AmEx, MC, V.*

Wallsé's chicly simple aesthetic (white walls, dark wood) and bold French-accented Austrian menu make for a fanciful dining experience. Chef-owner Kurt Gutenbrunner gives heavy, drab Austrian staples like boiled beef a swift kick in the lederhosen—his *tafelspitz* is served with apple-horseradish puree, a crunchy potato pancake and luxuriously soft creamed spinach. Fresh-herb spaetzle is topped with tender morsels of sautéed rabbit; an exquisite chestnut soup is topped with a cloud of white mushroom foam. The fluffy dessert dumplings, which combine quark (a soft, mild, unripened cheese) with bracing apricot puree, are deservedly famous.

### Washington Park

*24 Fifth Ave at 9th St (212-529-4400). Subway: A, C, E, F, V, S to W 4th St. Mon–Fri noon–2:30pm; Mon–Sat 5:30–11pm; Sun 5:30–10pm Average main course: $27. Five-course prix fixe: $59. AmEx, MC, V.*

After dropping off the food world's radar for a number of years, Jonathan Waxman resurfaced in April 2002 with Washington Park. Ever since, New Yorkers have been clamoring for a taste of the California cuisine that made him famous in the 1980s. Now, in his sunny corner restaurant, waiters clad in Thomas Pink shirts shuttle between the tiled open kitchen and linen-draped tables, set with Christofle silver. The ever-changing menu reads like a shopping list you'd take to a luscious farmer's market: foie gras with lamb's quarters and sweet-pea flowers; stuffed Catskill duck breast with wild asparagus and spring onions. Signature dishes include charcoal-grilled chicken with fries, and red-pepper pancakes with smoked salmon, crème fraîche and salmon roe.

## Chelsea

### AZ

*21 W 17th St between Fifth and Sixth Aves (212-691-8888). Subway: F, V to 14th St; L to Sixth Ave; 1, 9 to 18th St. Mon–Wed noon–2:30pm, 5:30–11pm; Thu, Fri noon–2:30pm, 5:30–11pm; Sat 5:30–11pm; Sun 5:30–10pm. Lounge Mon–Sat 5pm–2am; Sun 5pm–midnight. Average main course: $33. Three-course prix fixe: $57. AmEx, DC, Disc, MC, V.*

AZ's designers must have spent their formative years club-hopping in Hong Kong. A glass elevator whooshes you from an Asian-inspired ground-floor bar to a rooftop dining room enclosed by greenhouse-style glass. Waiters in bold red-and-blue vests look like they stepped out of a comic book. Chef Patricia Yeo cooks cleanly and cleverly. Plump gulf prawns are gently charred, laid in a pool of sweet tomato water and paired with tender wontons stuffed with fresh mashed soy beans. Among entrées, tea-smoked salmon is matched with green-tea–and–caramelized-onion risotto; the hefty, pillowy-soft pork chop arrives with a bundle of five-spice baby spareribs. At her new midtown venture, **Pazo** *(105 E 57th St between Park and Lexington Aves, 212-754-7470),* Yeo works similar magic on Mediterranean flavors.

**Waxing delicious** Jonathan Waxman is back and better than ever at Washington Park.

### Bottino

*246 Tenth Ave between 24th and 25th Sts (212-206-6766). Subway: C, E to 23rd St. Mon 6–11:30pm; Tue–Sat noon–11:30pm; Sun 6–10:30pm. Average main course: $24. AmEx, DC, Disc, MC, V.*

New York art dealers have made this Italian restaurant their dining cornerstone: Its effortlessly chic ambience is perfect for entertaining a world-famous curator, wealthy collector or vogue artist. Bottino's allure is largely based on a no-frills approach to sophistication (think Donna Karan in the kitchen). Basic dishes are best: light but luscious tuna tartare; a more filling-than-usual antipasto *misto;* grilled Norwegian salmon; roasted rack of lamb with rosemary and garlic. In Nolita, Bottino's strenuously cool little brother, **Bot** *(231 Mott St between Prince and Spring Sts, 646-613-1312),* serves similar Italian fare at slightly lower prices.

### The Park

*118 Tenth Ave at 17th St (212-352-3313). Subway: A, C, E to 14th St; L to Eighth Ave. 11:30am–1am. Average main course: $24. AmEx, DC, Disc, MC, V.*

Dig this soaring ex–taxi garage's glamorous pastiche style—equal parts 007, Southeast Asian kitsch, and '50s Palm Springs. Inside, you'll find Indonesian shell lamps, redwood-root benches, a taxidermist's songbirds, two sizable bars and a fashion-fabulous crowd. The menu is Cal-Med: minty scallop ceviche; steak tartare topped with a quail egg; braised lamb shank; and seared tuna with a tomato-olive mix. It's all likable, but no dish is as riveting or memorable as the stuff that surrounds you.

### Wild Lily Tea Room

*511 W 22nd St between Tenth and Eleventh Aves (212-691-2258). Subway: C, E to 23rd St. Tue–Sun 11am–10pm. Average main course: $11. MC, V.*

Located in art gallery central, Wild Lily pays due attention to design: The dark-wood furniture is clean and spare; a split-level dining area makes the narrow room seem spacious; and a gurgling goldfish pool adds to the tranquility. Careful thought is given to the composition of plates like pear salad with sugar-glazed walnuts and goat cheese, or a dumpling sampler of shrimp, crab, vegetable and shiitake fillings. All dishes are created to be accompanied by sake, and dessert specials are paired with specific tea recommendations.

## Gramercy & Flatiron

### Blue Smoke

*116 E 27th between Park Ave South and Lexington Ave (212-448-7711). Subway: 6 to 28th St. Mon–Thu noon–1am; Sun 5:30pm–1am. Average main course: $24. AmEx, Disc, MC, V.*

This new barbecue joint from high-end restaurateur Danny Meyer is set in a rustic, wooden dining room with modern touches. You'll find warm, puffy fry bread, succulent ribs smoked on the premises and—holy luncheon meat!—a fabulous hunk of smoked bologna, served on a crusty bun with coleslaw. The kitchen uses wood-burning smokers to slowly cook ribs, chicken and pork shoulder. Open late, the place is eminently hangoutable. You can pop in after visiting the **Jazz Standard** downstairs *(see page 314)*—*if* you've made a reservation: Blue Smoke is red-hot. Meyer's other renowned venues include the American creative restaurants **Eleven Madison Park** *(11 Madison Ave at 24th St, 212-889-0905)*, **Gramercy Tavern** *(see* **Craft**, *below)*, and **Union Square Cafe** *(21 E 16th St between Fifth Ave and Union Sq, 212-529-4400)*, and the Indian-fusion spot **Tabla** *(11 Madison Ave at 25th St, 212-889-0667)*.

### City Bakery

*3 W 18th St between Fifth and Sixth Aves (212-366-1414). Subway: L, N, Q, R, W, 4, 5, 6 to 14th St–Union Sq. Mon–Fri 7:30am–7pm; Sat 7:30am–6pm; Sun 9am–6pm. Salad bar: $11 per pound. AmEx, MC, V.*

Maury Rubin's City Bakery has homemade marshmallows, fudgy hot chocolate, way-better-than-mom's macaroni and cheese, sinful cookies and exceptionally fresh salads. While many eateries trumpet seasonal ingredients, City Bakery's allegiance to fresh-from-the-Greenmarket produce shows in nearly every dish. You pay by the pound for salad-bar items like roasted beets, fruit salad and roasted green tomatoes. There's much more than salad, though—catfish, jasmine rice with red beans and tofu—and whatever you choose, it's worth every penny.

### Craft

*43 E 19th St between Broadway and Park Ave South (212-780-0880). Subway: N, R, W, 6 to 23rd St. Mon–Thu noon–2pm, 5:30–10pm; Fri noon–2pm, 5:30–11pm; Sat 5:30–11pm; Sun 5:30–10pm. Average main course with one side: $36. AmEx, DC, Disc, MC, V.*

This restaurant's buzz (and the monthlong wait for a reservation) hasn't abated since it opened in 2001. In fact, chef-owner Tom Colicchio's experiment is so successful that imitators of his compose-it-yourself concept have sprung up all over the city. Colicchio serves organic, seasonal American cuisine in a modern setting with leather walls and rosy lighting. As the name implies, you craft your own meal, choosing ingredients and preparation method—to often thrilling ends. It's not as complicated as it sounds; the waitstaff is smart, informed and helpful, and a chef's tasting menu saves anyone who's at a loss. **Craftbar** next door *(47 E 19th St between Broadway and Park Ave South, 212-780-0880)* offers a conventional menu with an Italian bent—and it's kinder to your MasterCard. Colicchio is also responsible for the food at another of New York's finest restaurants: the refined, seductive **Gramercy Tavern** *(42 E 20th St between Broadway and Park Ave South, 212-477-0777)* and its more casual **Tavern Room**—a fantastic value.

### Havana Central

*22 E 17th St between Fifth Ave and Broadway (212-414-2298). L, N, Q, R, W, 4, 5, 6 to 14th St–Union Sq. Mon–Sat 7am–11:30pm. Average main course: $8. AmEx, DC, Disc, MC, V.*

Before opening this new tropical cafeteria, owner Jeremy Merrin spent nine months researching Cuban cuisine so he could get the arroz con pollo (chicken with rice) and *ropa vieja* (traditional stewed beef) just right. His Roots Trio is a great introduction to the Cuban "underground": deep-fried baby *criolla* potatoes, sweet potatoes and yuca, served in a cup with a wooden spoon.

### Les Halles

*411 Park Ave South between 28th and 29th Sts (212-679-4111). Subway: 6 to 28th St. Noon–midnight. Average main course: $19. AmEx, Disc, DC, MC, V.*

He has been busy eating monkey brains and still-beating cobra hearts for his latest book and Food Network TV series, *A Cook's Tour,* but Anthony Bourdain is still executive chef at one of the city's top brasseries. His kitchen sends out plate after plate of unadulterated classics: jumbo mussels that are as tender as tofu, and draped in silky, butter-enriched sauce; frisée salad with chewy *lardons;* and a sublime coq au vin, stocked with seared mushrooms, soft baby onions and more of those lardons. *Côte de boeuf* is epic, and the premium beef is sold for home cooking from an in-house icebox. The long saloon-style bar and quiet back dining room are pub-comfortable, as are the well-portioned dishes.

## Pipa

*ABC Carpet & Home, 38 E 19th St between Broadway and Park Ave South (212-677-2233). Subway: L, N, Q, R, W, 4, 5, 6 to 14th St–Union Sq. Mon–Thu noon–3:30pm, 6–11pm; Fri noon–3pm, 5:30pm–midnight; Sat 11am–3:30pm, 5:30pm–midnight; Sun 11am–3:30pm, 5:30–10pm. Average tapa: $11. AmEx, MC, V.*

### CRITICS' PICKS Star chefs

These are some of New York City's more famous chefs and the restaurants where they showcase their skills. Reservations can be tough to secure; call at least a month in advance.

**Dan Barber and Mike Anthony:** Blue Hill, page 191

**Mario Batali:** Babbo, page 190, Esca and Lupa

**David Bouley:** Danube, page 179, and Bouley

**Daniel Boulud:** DB Bistro Moderne, page 197, Café Boulud and Daniel

**Terrance Brennan:** Picholine, page 201, and Artisanal

**Tom Colicchio:** Craft, page 195, and Gramercy Tavern

**Alain Ducasse:** Alain Ducasse at the Essex House, page 197

**Anita Lo:** Annisa, page 189

**Nobu Matsuhisa:** Nobu, page 180

**Alfred Portale:** Gotham Bar and Grill, page 187

**Douglas Rodriguez:** Pipa and Chicama, see above

**Marcus Samuelsson:** Aquavit, page 197

**Jean-Georges Vongerichten:** JoJo, page 202, Jean-Georges and Vong

**Jonathan Waxman:** Washington Park, page 194

**Patricia Yeo:** AZ, page 194, and Pazo

**Geoffrey Zakarian:** Town, page 198

Chef-owner Douglas Rodriguez, whose Latino flagship **Chicama** is just around the corner *(35 E 18th St between Broadway and Park Ave South, 212-505-2233)*, has a seductive way of harmonizing seemingly divergent flavors at tapas-centric Pipa. Almond-stuffed dates are gift-wrapped with bacon and served in an endive cup. The creamy paella is packed with fresh seafood and chorizo; Rodriguez adds smoked paprika, which makes a delicious difference. The sangria comes in red or white and is presented in a glass pitcher with a giant cinnamon stick as a stirrer. This Pan-Latino master with a penchant for detail has four cookbooks under his belt, so the question remains, Where's the television show?

## Republic

*37 Union Sq West between 16th and 17th Sts (212-627-7168). Subway: L, N, Q, R, W, 4, 5, 6 to 14th St–Union Sq. Sun–Wed 11:30am–11pm; Thu–Sat 11:30am–midnight. Average main course: $8. AmEx, DC, MC, V.*

For little more than you'd spend at a no-ambience Chinatown joint, you can sit with a boisterous low-budget in-crowd at Republic's stylish communal tables and dig into big noodle bowls, such as coconut-milk broth with tender chicken pieces. Nonsoup items include pork—marinated in soy and garlic and grilled—served atop rice noodles. The recipes have been subtly altered to suit mainstream palates—dishes are slightly sweeter or less fishy than in a more authentic place, but who's complaining?

## Tamarind

*41–43 E 22nd St between Broadway and Park Ave South (212-674-7400). Subway: N, R, W, 6 to 23rd St. 11:30am–3pm, 5:30–11:30pm. Average main course: $22. AmEx, DC, Disc, MC, V.*

Tamarind isn't just one of the best Indian restaurants in the city; it's one of the best restaurants, period. The modern, bright dining room feels like a gallery for select craft pieces. Two chefs in white toques work the tandoor ovens, which issue forth hot, yeasty flatbreads, like addictive tamarind nan. Despite their complexity, dishes like dumplings made with lotus root and fresh cheese are somehow made to seem familiar. *Nawabi murgh ke* tikka is boneless chicken marinated in fenugreek. The adjacent tearoom serves six kinds of sandwiches; whole-wheat flatbread is wrapped around delectable fillings such as tandoori salmon or marinated lamb.

## TanDa

*331 Park Ave South between 24th and 25th Sts (212-253-8400). Subway: N, R, W, 6 to 23rd St. Mon– Fri noon–3am; Sat 6pm–3am. Average main course: $21. AmEx, Disc, MC, V.*

Brothers Andy and Chris Russell, former owners of the exclusive club Moomba, have done away with the velvet rope, but their new venue is hardly a dive. Posh TanDa, a restaurant-lounge, is named after a Vietnamese poet who wrote about food and wine as the essence of life. Chef Stanley Wong offers artfully executed dishes like Balinese roasted duck and tuna



Necessities

**No pipe dream** Impresario-chef Douglas Rodriguez, who makes ceviche sublime at the Nuevo Latino restaurant Chicama, takes on traditional Spanish cuisine here at Pipa.



tartare with wasabi and daikon—perfect fodder for escapist fantasies.

## Midtown West

### Alain Ducasse at the Essex House

*155 W 58th St between Sixth and Seventh Aves (212-265-7300). Subway: F, N, Q, R, W to 57th St. Mon–Sat 6:30–9:30pm. Prix fixe: $145–$280. AmEx, DC, Disc, MC, V.*

France's Alain Ducasse, the most celebrated chef on the Continent, swooped into the Essex House in 2000 and offered what was then the city's most expensive meal. The prices are still breathtaking, but so are the opulent spectacle and successive waves of astonishing food: One after another, dazzling dishes arrive, every morsel tasting as if it came from another world where foodstuffs are smaller and more flavorful than in our own. The incredibly gracious waitstaff never seems to hover (even when a table for two is attended by more than that number).

### Aquavit

*13 W 54th St between Fifth and Sixth Aves (212-307-7311). Subway: E, V to Fifth Ave–53rd St. Noon–2:30pm, 5:30–10:30pm. Three-course prix fixe: $69. Tasting menu: $85. AmEx, DC, Disc, MC, V.*

Swedish-Ethiopian chef Marcus Samuelsson has been seducing diners for nearly a decade with his artistic food fights (which end in dreamy détentes), and he shows no sign of resting on his laurels. At Aquavit, you enter an 1896 townhouse that once sheltered Rockefellers, then descend into a spacious, ultramodern atrium that complements Samuelsson's starkly bold, geometric creations. An adjacent café serves more straight-ahead Swedish food (gravlax, meatballs). Samuelsson is also credited with the menu at the **AQ Café** in Scandinavia House *(58 Park Ave between 37th and 38th Sts, 212-847-9745)*, where you may sample inventions such as salmon lasagna at deli prices.

### DB Bistro Moderne

*55 W 44th St between Fifth and Sixth Aves (212-391-2400). Subway: S, 4, 5, 6, 7 to 42nd St–Grand Central. Mon noon–2:15pm, 5:30–10pm; Tue–Sat noon–2:15pm, 5:30–11:15pm; Sun 4:30–10pm. Average main course: $29. AmEx, DC, Disc, MC, V.*

DB Bistro Moderne—chef Daniel Boulud's bridge to the haute couture Daniel and ready-to-wear Café Boulud—is so stylized that you might want to consult a copy of *Wallpaper* before you go. Fashionistas rave about the DB burger—braised short ribs, foie gras and black truffles wrapped in raw sirloin, then oven-roasted medium-rare. Forget frites; this burger comes with *pommes soufflées*. DB's changing cuisine is well-prepared and artfully presented, but you'll pay for all that glamour. For successively more sublime (and costly) dining experiences, reserve a spot at **Café Boulud** *(20 E 76th St between Fifth and Madison Aves, 212-772-2600)* or **Daniel** *(60 E 65th St between Madison and Park Aves, 212-288-0033)*.

### 44 & X Hell's Kitchen

*622 Tenth Ave at 44th St (212-977-1170). Subway: A, C, E to 42nd St–Port Authority. Mon–Wed 5:30pm–midnight; Thu, Fri 5:30pm–12:30am; Sat 11:30am–3pm, 5:30pm–12:30am; Sun 11:30am–3pm, 5:30–11pm. Average main course: $17. AmEx, MC, V.*

Forgive 44 & X the unevocative name—because it has style and the food is good. The white dining room is nearly bare but for an occasional wall sconce or stocky column, and clublike beats thump in the background. Chef Adam Fishbein cooks an appetizing menu of staples with Asian and Southwestern accents: *ancho*-chili–rubbed pork loin over cheddar grits; a beef fillet slathered with sweet tomato jam and served with mashed potatoes mixed with butter beans; and grilled short ribs over polenta. For Hell's Kitchen, it's all pretty heavenly.

### Island Burgers and Shakes

*766 Ninth Ave between 51st and 52nd Sts (212-307-7934). Subway: C, E to 50th St. Sun–Thu, Sat noon–10:30pm; Fri noon–11pm. Average burger: $7. Cash only.*

Surfboards on the wall in Manhattan? Righteous! Island Burgers and Shakes attracts everyone from creative cuties to smiling suits, and they love what they're eating: Ingredients are snappily fresh, and the dozens of burger permutations have names like Route 66 (avocado, Swiss cheese and bacon on rye) and Pop and Top's (Thai sauce, jalapeño and roasted peppers on the bread of your choice). Herbivores can make a meal out of Island's bushy salads, and all should savor the thick, creamy milk shakes.

### Molyvos

*871 Seventh Ave between 55th and 56th Sts (212-582-7500). Subway: B, D, E to Seventh Ave; N, Q, R, W to 57th St. Mon–Thu noon–3pm, 5:30–11:30pm; Fri, Sat noon–3pm; 5–midnight; Sun noon–11pm. Average main course: $24. AmEx, DC, Disc, MC, V.*

Molyvos presents refined versions of the Greek staples. The souvlaki is made with juicy beef tenderloin grilled over fruitwood; moussaka, layered with eggplant, potato, tomato and spiced lamb, is dressed with a tangy yogurt béchamel. In fact, all the lamb dishes—marinated shanks, leg of lamb or grilled baby chops—do justice to Greece's favorite meat. The fresh seafood scores too, especially grilled whole fish marinated in lemon, oregano and olive oil. In the dining room, romantic lighting softly illuminates tastefully placed tapestries, tiles and ceramics.

### Noche

*1604 Broadway at 49th St (212-541-7070). Subway: N, R, W to 49th St. Mon, Tue noon–2:30pm, 5–10pm; Wed–Fri noon–2:30pm, 5–11pm; Sat 5–11pm. Average main course: $21. AmEx, Disc, MC, V.*

At Noche, your eyes shoot straight to the top of the soaring four-story dining room, where a spaceship-size light fixture changes colors during the meal. Noche has reason to celebrate: Owner David Emil ran Windows on the World and Wild Blue atop the World Trade Center, and this is his first new eatery since their demise. Some former Windows staff are on board, including consulting chef Michael Lomonaco. Latin-inspired dishes, such as Chilean salmon with yuca or a tower of tender braised short ribs atop a sweet-corn cake, are accompanied by live music on Wednesday and Saturday nights.

### Pam Real Thai Food

*404 W 49th St between Ninth and Tenth Aves (212-333-7500). Subway: C, E, 1, 9, to 50th St. 11:30am–11pm. Average main course: $8. Cash only.*

It's nothing fancy to look at, but Pam Real Thai's authentic cooking has cultivated a loyal following of spicy-food fans. *Som tam* is a healthy heap of green papaya, tomato, skinny string beans, chili and peanuts. The crisp duck salad with red onion and pineapple slices is big enough for two. And seafood panang curry is spicy with calamari and shrimp in a paste of lime leaves, basil and cumin.

### Ruby Foo's

*1626 Broadway at 49th St (212-489-5600). Subway: N, R, W to 49th St; 1,2 to 50th St. Sun–Thu 11:30am–midnight; Fri, Sat 11:30am–1am. Average main course: $19. AmEx, MC, V.*
See page 202.

### Scotch Bonnet

*32 W 31st St between Fifth Ave and Broadway (212-594-7575). Subway: B, D, F, V, N, Q, R, W to 34th St–Herald Sq. Mon–Thu 11am–11pm; Fri 11am–2am; Sun 5–11pm. Average main course: $18. AmEx, Disc, MC, V.*

Befitting the vicious pepper it's named for, Scotch Bonnet has become one of the hottest Jamaican restaurants in town. Along with high-end Caribbean selections—subtly flavored codfish fritters and tangy, boneless jerk chicken—the menu is laced with other influences, like the fruity Cha Cha chicken, inspired by Chinese sweet-and-sour sauce. Vegetarians succumb to choices like brown-stew curried tofu and barbecued tofu with vegetables.

### Town

*Chambers Hotel, 15 W 56th St between Fifth and Sixth Aves (212-582-4445). Subway: E, V to Fifth Ave–53rd St. Mon–Sat 7:30–10am, noon–2pm, 5:30–10:30pm; Sun 11am–2pm, 5:30–9:30pm. Three-course prix fixe $68. AmEx, MC, V.*

This sexy hotel has a suitably modern restaurant, designed with neutral-fabric panels and straight lines. Upstairs, "bar chefs" mix Cosmopolitans with freshly squeezed blood-orange juice; downstairs, chef-owner Geoffrey Zakarian injects creative color into traditional plates. Arctic char is flavored with green tea and served with poached radishes and mussels in a sweet-onion broth; Shinshu apples, pea shoots and pistachios brighten the *merlu* (hake); a rich, earthy black-trumpet jus heightens the flavor of the organic rack of lamb. Among the stellar desserts are warm, deliquescent chocolate beignets.

### '21' Club

*21 W 52nd St between Fifth and Sixth Aves (212-582-7200). Subway: B, D, F to 47–50th Sts–Rockefeller Ctr; E, V to Fifth Ave–53rd St. Mon–Thu noon–2:30pm, 5:30–10pm; Fri noon–2:30pm, 5:30–11pm; Sat 5:30–11pm. Closed Saturdays Jun–Aug. Average main course: $39. AmEx, DC, Disc, MC, V.*

Want to feel like Charles Foster Kane (or at least Michael Bloomberg)? Go to '21'. After 74 years, it's still a clubby enclave for the powerful. Chef Erik Blauberg creates seasonal contemporary dishes, such as a crisped black sea bass in champagne sauce, and a neat arrangement of grilled game (house-made duck sausage, bacon-wrapped antelope medallions and a roll of pheasant, squab and foie gras). For the famous burger, a mix of ground lean meats (including dry-aged sirloin) gets a flavor boost from duck fat to create one of the city's best beef-and-bun sandwiches. Act like a regular and have an after-dinner drink in the front lounge, where original Remingtons line the walls. The luxurious new **Upstairs '21'**, serving more refined, inventive cuisine, opened in November 2002.

### Uncle Vanya Cafe

*315 W 54th St between Eighth and Ninth Aves (212-262-0542). Subway: C, E to 50th St. Mon–Sat noon–11pm; Sun 2–10pm. Average main course: $10. MC, V.*

If you've ever eaten good home cooking in Moscow or St. Petersburg, you'll recognize the dill-laden and sour-cream–daubed standards at Uncle Vanya Cafe. Your feast begins with dark Russian bread, along with a teapot of hot spiced chai. Next, try appetizers such as a sweet, garlicky beet salad embellished with tiny peas. Dishes are simple: The savory *golubtsy* is ground beef and rice wrapped in a cabbage leaf, soused with brothy tomato sauce and topped with sour cream. Anyone who loves babushka decor will thrill to the kitsch-filled, lino-floored dining room, trimmed with a fake-wood picket fence.

### Virgil's Real BBQ

*152 W 44th St between Sixth Ave and Broadway (212-921-9494). Subway: B, D, F, V to 42nd St; N, Q, R, W, S, 1, 2, 3, 9, 7 to 42nd St–Times Sq. Sun, Mon 11:30am–11pm; Tue–Sat 11:30am–midnight. Average main course: $16. AmEx, DC, Disc, MC, V.*

One wouldn't expect to find honest-to-God wood-fired barbecue in the heart of Times Square, but the piles of hickory logs and the smell of burning wood attest to Virgil's *bona fides*. Virgil's defies its tourist-central location by turning out some of the best brisket in the boroughs. The menu features Southern favorites from hoof to snout (well, almost)—biscuits and gravy, baby back ribs, Texas links and an ample selection of sides. Dedicated gluttons should consider the Pig Out, a sampler of ribs, chicken, brisket, pork and links.

## Midtown East

### Amma

*246 E 51st St between Second and Third Aves (212-644-8330). Subway: E, V to Lexington Ave–53rd St; 6 to 51st St. Noon–3pm; 5–11pm. Average main course: $12. AmEx, DC, Disc, MC, V.*

Named for the Hindi word for "mother," Amma offers carefully prepared home cooking, served in a softly lit room with mustard walls and orange Ultrasuede banquettes. On the menu are standards like moist, subtly flavored jumbo shrimp from the tandoor and spicy chicken vindaloo; more complex dishes include lamb cooked in a spot-on cardamom sauce, spiced to order. Portions are generous, so it's easy to overdo it with the appetizers, especially the addictive Bombay Behru—small lentil, corn and rice fritters mixed with chopped tomatoes, onions and a sweet sauce.

**Right on track** A New York classic, the Grand Central Oyster Bar & Restaurant serves New England chowder and dozens of varieties of fish and firm, briny mollusks.

**Brasserie**

*100 E 53rd St between Park and Lexington Aves (212-751-4840). Subway: E, V to Lexington Ave–53rd St; 6 to 51st St. Mon–Fri 7am–1am; Sat 11am–1am; Sun 11am–10pm. Average main course: $22. AmEx, DC, Disc, MC, V.*

Brasserie's location in the basement of Mies van der Rohe's Seagram Building, and a multimillion-dollar facelift—streamlined surfaces of steel, pear wood, chrome, glass and molded plastic—ensure its high style. Waiters constantly ferry the popular and dramatic seafood plateau: mounds of ice topped with oysters, shrimp, lobster, mussels and clams. Other brasserie classics (steak frites, filet mignon, chicken paillard and coq au vin) are guaranteed to satisfy. Narcissists will be pleased to see a blurred image of their entrance into the restaurant promenade across video screens over the bar.



**The Four Seasons Restaurant**

*99 E 52nd St between Park and Lexington Aves (212-754-9494). Subway: E, V to Lexington Ave–53rd St; 6 to 51st St. Mon–Fri noon–2:30pm, 5–9pm; Sat 5–11pm. Average main course: $42. Tasting menu: $125. AmEx, DC, Disc, MC, V.*

Famous almost from the minute it opened in 1959, the Four Seasons set the pace for turning the reassuring tradition once called "Continental" into truly great American cuisine. Luxurious ingredients are treated respectfully and spared the silly experiments: crisp Long Island duck (for two) is served with plum compote; the fillet of bison is complemented by Périgord-truffle sauce and foie gras. Philip Johnson created the elegant interiors of the Grill Room, where JFK celebrated his 45th birthday, and the serene Pool Room, where enormous trees, changed seasonally, dapple the room in leafy shadows.

**Grand Central Oyster Bar & Restaurant**

*Grand Central Terminal, Lower Concourse, 42nd St at Park Ave (212-490-6650). Subway: S, 4, 5, 6, 7 to 42nd St–Grand Central. Mon–Fri 11:30am–9:30pm; Sat noon–9:30pm. Average main course: $22. AmEx, DC, Disc, MC, V.*

This 90-year-old Grand Central Terminal institution is a portal to old New York. The boisterous lunch hour belongs to power brokers who feast on soothing Manhattan clam chowder and select from 20-odd varieties of oysters at the raw bar. During the less hectic evenings, out-of-towners gather under the vaulted Guastavino-tile ceilings. The list of market-fresh fish is dizzying (20 to 30 offerings is typical), and house specialties, such as *coquilles St. Jacques* and Maryland crab cakes, are staunchly old-fashioned.

**Le Cirque 2000**

*New York Palace Hotel, 455 Madison Ave between 50th and 51st Sts (212-303-7788). Subway: E, V to Lexington Ave–53rd St; 6 to 51st St. Mon–Sat 11:45am–2:30pm, 5:30–10pm; Sun 5:30–10pm. Average main course: $37. Tasting menu: $90. AmEx, DC, MC, V.*

**Maine event** Playful Le Cirque 2000 makes a seriously delicious lobster salad.

On the rota of haute-French heavies, no restaurant is so celebrated for festivity as Le Cirque 2000. The menu is upscale with mass appeal. Basics like tuna tartare and sautéed scallops are on the safe end, but there are also terrine of rabbit rillettes and venison, the famous Le Cirque sea bass (wearing a jacket of golden potato slices) and a duck triptych—a rosy breast seared just so, a leg confit and almost-liquid sautéed foie gras. The Chocolate Extravaganza is a mind-blowing composition of ice cream, molten cake and sculpted chocolate. Like all 20 or so desserts, it's a magnificent finish to a fairy-tale feast.

## Upper West Side

**A**

*947 Columbus Ave between 106th and 107th Sts (212-531-1643). Subway: B, C to 103rd St. Tue–Sat 6–10pm. Average main course: $9. Cash only.*

Wee little A, named for the train, offers French-Caribbean eats. The dining room is small, but the food has big flavor, as the patrons who cram into the four tables can attest. Chef-owner Marc Solomon established a fan base downtown at the late, lamented Les Deux Lapins, and now his groupies head north for his popular escargots stuffed in a conch shell, and Carib-style crêpes—the jerk chicken variety will blow your mind *and* your tongue. Do BYOB, but don't bring your credit cards; the place is cash-only.

**Aix**

*2398 Broadway at 88th St (212-874-7400). Subway: 1, 9 to 86th St. Mon–Fri 5pm–midnight; Sat 11am–4pm, 5–11pm. Average main course: $22. AmEx, MC, V.*

This two-story space was recently transformed into a warm, colorful new home for chef Didier Virot's

Provençal cooking, and the place has been mobbed ever since. On the inaugural menu: *pistou* with sardine tartare; *daurade* with fennel broth; and venison loin with quince-beet strudel. Relax in the sultry lounge or survey Broadway from the upstairs balcony.

### Cafe Luxembourg

*200 W 70th St between Amsterdam and West End Aves (212-873-7411). Subway: 1, 2, 3, 9 to 72nd St. 9am–midnight. Average main course: $22. Three-course prix fixe: $38.50. AmEx, DC, MC, V.*

At this neighborhood institution, the lighting is forgiving and the atmosphere is one of classy chaos. The nicely worn zinc-topped bar remains a popular gathering spot (though those ample naked women in the restaurant's longtime print ad have yet to show up). Steak frites are the benchmark of brasserie reliability, and Luxembourg's New York strip is topnotch. Seafood is also done well: A firm, moist red snapper fillet with fennel is splashed with tangy orange jus. The café is now open for breakfast every day, serving fluffy herbed omelettes and other first-rate selections.

### Compass

*208 W 70th St between Amsterdam and West End Aves (212-875-8600). Subway: 1, 2, 3, 9 to 72nd St. Mon–Sat 5–11pm; Sun 11:30am–2:30pm, 5–11pm. Average main course: $25. AmEx, DC, Disc, MC, V.*

The former Marika has found its way as Compass, offering slightly less expensive new American dishes: onion-crusted king salmon, grilled rabbit over polenta and skate with artichokes. The room is still sleek (with a few design tweaks and a more relaxed feel) but best of all, chef Neil Annis is clearly having fun now—and you can taste it.

### Ouest

*2315 Broadway between 83rd and 84th Sts (212-580-8700). Subway: 1, 9 to 86th St. Mon–Thu 5pm–11pm; Fri, Sat 5pm–midnight; Sun 10:30am–2pm, 5–10pm. Average main course: $24. AmEx, DC, Disc, MC, V.*

Ouest (pronounced "west") took the city by storm when it opened in 2001 on a stretch of Broadway that's been Blockbustered and Baby Gapped into suburban submission. No wonder patrons wait weeks for a table—it's fine dining in a playful setting. Chef and co-owner Tom Valenti concentrates on bold flavors that take you back in time. His trademark lamb shank appears on Mondays and Tuesdays, but it's surpassed by supple braised short ribs on a sheet of polenta. A rhubarb crumble and scoop of buttermilk-vanilla ice cream, wading in a ruby pool of strawberry sauce, is equal parts sweet, sour and crunch. "It's like something your mom used to make," says Valenti. We wish.

### Picholine

*35 W 64th St between Central Park West and Broadway (212-724-8585). Subway: A, C, B, D to 59th St–Columbus Circle; 1, 9 to 66th St–Lincoln Ctr. Tue–Sat 11:45am–2pm; Mon–Wed 5–11pm; Thu–Sat 5–11:45pm; Sun 5–9pm. Average main course: $35. Seven-course tasting menu: $125. AmEx, DC, MC, V.*

Chef-owner Terrance Brennan and chef de cuisine David Cox elevate Mediterranean cuisine to something sublime. The sea urchin *panna cotta* with lobster consommé and a whopping dollop of osetra caviar is one of the richest seafood starters on earth. Squab, shiny with a licorice lacquer, is sweet and tart with glazed turnips and spiced rhubarb. And don't forget the cheese. Obsessive maître *du fromage*

**Cooking with latitude** At the Upper West Side restaurant Compass, chef Neil Annis has found his direction with lively, inspired American cuisine.

**Mean green** Etats-Unis on the Upper East Side stirs a dead-on delicious mojito.

Max McCalman oversees a selection that puts lavish cheese carts back on the map. True cheese heads should book a table at Brennan's **Artisanal** *(2 Park Ave at 32nd St, 212-725-8585),* where 250 varieties of *fromage* and 150 wines (all available by the glass) are offered alongside robust Parisian bistro food.

### Ruby Foo's

*2182 Broadway at 77th St (212-724-6700). Subway: 1, 9 to 79th St. Sun–Thu 11:30am– 12:30am; Fri, Sat 11:30am–1am. Average main course: $17. AmEx, Disc, MC, V.*

Most New Yorkers pretend they'd never frequent a tourist haunt, but the Ruby Foo's chain is an exception. It's just glam enough to be self-mocking, and the menu reassures those who really care about what they eat. The East-by-Southeast fusion menu is designed for sharing—a whole table of cocktail tipplers can pick from utterly addictive tamarind-glazed baby back ribs; robust yet delicate shrimp-and-crabmeat dumplings; and crisp duck and seven-flavor beef with chili-lime sauce. Since the dining room is often mobbed, the counter seating is good for a spontaneous bite.

## Upper East Side

### Elaine's

*1703 Second Ave between 88th and 89th Sts (212-534-8103). Subway: 4, 5, 6 to 86th St. 6pm–2am. Bar 6pm–4am. Average main course: $23. AmEx, DC, Disc, MC, V.*

There are two Elaine's, really. There's the classic Elaine's of literary renown: the one where Ms. Kaufman herself sits at your table, conferring legitimacy; where everyone knows your name, rank and Q rating; where intellectuals banter about the legacy of Willie Morris. Then there's Elaine's-for-the-rest-of-us: a shambling restaurant where decent food—robust, lemony mussels, or a celebrated veal chop that's pink within, charred without—is served to out-of-towners, dating couples, everyday people. But you came to see the other Elaine's, right?

### Etats-Unis

*242 E 81st St between Second and Third Aves (212-517-8826). Subway: 6 to 77th St. 6–11pm. Average main course: $26. AmEx, DC, MC, V.*

As the name implies, the food at popular Etats-Unis is a mix of French and American with a daily-changing menu that relied on fresh, organic ingredients. Slow-cooked meat is a specialty—as in the superb beef ragout with handmade fettuccine, or the short ribs braised in beer for seven hours. Market-fresh seafood, like the steamed lobster, is cooked to perfection. The food is rich in flavor and satisfying, and the desserts—chocolate soufflé and date pudding—have their own neighborhood following. Slightly lighter, simpler food is available across the street at **Bar@Etats-Unis** *(see* **Rosé-colored glasses**, *page 170).*

### JoJo

*160 E 64th St between Lexington and Third Aves (212-223-5656). Subway: F to Lexington Ave–63rd St. Mon–Fri noon–2:30pm, 6–11pm; Sat noon–2:30pm, 5:30–11:30pm; Sun noon–2:30pm, 5:30–11pm. Average main course: $25. Tasting menu: $65. AmEx, DC, MC, V.*

Just about everything has been refurbished at Jean-Georges Vongerichten's reliable bistro, and the makeover has restored romance to this intimate townhouse setting. In the dark, luxurious downstairs area, you feel as if you're eating in an ambassador's private dining room, and the meal lives up to expectations. Dishes such as sautéed duck breast paired with a pastry parcel of pâtélike duck-leg will leave you wondering about the chef's tasty secret spices. For more of the Vongerichten empire, call well in advance for his masterful showpiece, **Jean Georges** *(Trump International Hotel and Tower, 1 Central Park West at Columbus Circle, 212-299-3900)* or visit his French-Thai restaurant, **Vong** *(200 E 54th St at Third Ave, 212-486-9592)* or his relatively casual Soho outpost, the **Mercer Kitchen** *(99 Prince St at Mercer St, 212-966-5454).*

### Sel et Poivre

*853 Lexington Ave between 64th and 65th Sts (212-517-5780). Subway: F to Lexington Ave–63rd St. Sun–Thu noon–10:30pm; Fri, Sat noon–11pm. Average main course: $21. AmEx, DC, MC, V.*

From the spreadable butter to the lovely pale-yellow walls hung with black-and-white French streetscapes, Sel et Poivre is practically perfect. Pureed red snapper and sea bass are blended with a tangy tomato broth to make a full-bodied soup. The accompanying plate of homemade croutons, mild mustard sauce and shredded Swiss cheese came with polite instructions from the waiter: "Spread ze sauce on ze crouton, top with *fromage,* and float in ze soup like little boats." The mushroom-leek risotto is rich, dense and tastes of dry white wine. Even the golden salted frites rank among the city's finest.

### Taco Taco

*1726 Second Ave between 89th and 90th Sts (212-289-8226). Subway: 4, 5, 6 to 86th St. Sun–Thu noon–11pm; Fri, Sat noon–midnight. Average main course: $8. Cash only.*

Piñata trimmings and crossover Latin music aside, Taco Taco is only slightly gringofied, and its menu includes some exceptional offerings. The potato-and-chorizo *taquito* appetizer comes smothered in guacamole, and the barbecued chipotle chicken has so much tangy sauce, sopping up the remains is almost required. (True to its name, Taco Taco also serves standard tacos and burritos.) It's not fancy, but you're guaranteed a bright atmosphere and energetic dishes at decent prices.

## Above 116th St

### Londel's

*2620 Frederick Douglass Blvd (Eighth Ave) between 139th and 140th Sts (212-234-6114). Subway: A, C, B, D to 145th St. Tue–Sat 11:30am–midnight; Sun 9am–5pm. Average main course: $20. AmEx, DC, Disc, MC, V.*

When Bill Clinton, lover of all foods Southern, visited this restaurant in 2001, he only had time to scarf salad and corn bread. Too bad, because Bubba missed out on some of the city's choicest soul-food eats. The fried chicken—best when accompanied by slightly sweet Belgian waffles—is molar-rattlingly crunchy, well-seasoned and way less oily than your average politician. Other staples prove just as tasty, including the cornmeal-crusted whiting fingers, blackened catfish fillet, and thick mac and cheese bound by crisped cheddar. Live music on Friday and Saturday nights—including jazz, R&B and gospel—adds to the downhome feel.

### M&G Soul Food Diner

*383 W 125th St at Morningside Ave (212-864-7326). Subway: A, C, B, D to 125th St. Mon–Thu 24hrs; Fri 12:01am–11:30pm; Sat, Sun 8:30am–11:30pm. Average main course: $9. Cash only.*

Served with a stack of fluffy pancakes, M&G's fried chicken is almost more crust than meat—and that's a good thing. The deeply seasoned, hot and crispy coating is a perfect foil for the sweet syrup drizzled over the pancakes—or try a mountain of mac and cheese or candied yams. The feel of M&G is as appealing as the food: faux-wood paneling; a Formica-topped lunch counter; a few tiny tables…and a hair-net–wearing staff, whose Richard Roundtree cool is matched only by that of the jukebox, stocked with the likes of Curtis Mayfield and Barry White.

### Republi'K

*114 Dyckman St at Nagle Ave (212-304-1717). Subway: A to Dyckman St. Mon–Thu 11am–11pm; Fri–Sun 1pm–6am. Average main course: $20. AmEx, Disc, MC, V.*

Call it an identity crisis or smart marketing: Republi'K

Necessities

## Cheap eats

The following restaurants offer main courses (or their equivalent) for $10 or less

is a pan-Latino restaurant, cafe and champagne bar rolled into one. The bar crowd can scarf down arroz con pollo in the cafe; the bling-bling set can order Crystal by the glass in the bubbly lounge; and food lovers can slip into ultrasuede banquettes for chef Ricardo Cardona's creations, such as yuca croquettes with lump crabmeat and avocado-lime aioli. Seek comfort in the *asopados*—soups served on weekends from 1am to 6am for hangover relief.

### Sugar Hill Bistro

*458 W 145th St between Amsterdam and Convent Aves (212-491-5505). Subway: A, C, B, D, 1, 9 to 145th St. Mon–Wed 5–10pm; Thu 5–11pm; Fri 5pm–midnight; Sat 11am–4pm, 5pm–midnight; Sun 11am–4pm, 5–10pm. Average main course: $23. AmEx, MC, V.*

The Sugar Hill Bistro evokes the days of the Harlem Renaissance, serving food for the stomach and culture for the soul. Works by notable African-American artists hang on the walls of this landmark townhouse, and they're all for sale. There are regular jazz nights, an R&B brunch on Saturday and a gospel brunch on Sunday (those who are overcome by the Spirit can perform during the open-mike segment). The elegant second-floor dining room serves sideways Southern dishes: blackened catfish topped with creamy champagne-shallot sauce, and shell steak with fried leeks.

**No greasy spoon** Williamsburg's Diner puts a sophisticated spin on the classics.

## Brooklyn

### Convivium Osteria

*68 Fifth Ave between Bergen St and St. Marks Pl, Park Slope, Brooklyn (718-857-1833). Subway: Q to Seventh Ave; 2, 3 to Bergen St. Tue–Thu 6–10pm; Fri, Sat 5:30–11pm; Sun 5:30–10pm. Average main course: $19. AmEx.*

Rustic Convivium is a sensualist's dream. The heavy oak tables, soft candlelight and assorted kitchen and farm tools on the walls make you feel like you've stopped at an old friend's European country home. The menu is a mix of Portuguese, Spanish and Italian influences: sumptuous grilled baby octopus, dressed with a mild vinaigrette and served on a bed of warm olives, celery and onions; magnificent prawns coated with coarse sea salt; a richly flavored pine-nut–crusted rack of lamb. Add a pleasant garden and thoughtful servers, and what could be more convivial?

### Diner

*85 Broadway at Berry St, Williamsburg, Brooklyn (718-486-3077). Subway: J, M, Z to Marcy Ave. Mon–Thu 11am–4pm, 6pm–midnight; Fri, Sat 11am–4pm, 6pm–1am; Sun 11am–4pm, 6pm–midnight. Average main course: $14. MC, V.*

When it opened in 1999, Diner showed everyone that it could be hip *and* grown-up. Models, photographers and fashion hounds (who came by car from Manhattan) were seated in vinyl-and-chrome booths near scruffy locals, where they sucked down mussels and top-shelf cocktails. Four years later, Diner has kept its cool under chef Caroline Fidanza, who turns out addictive burgers, fries and salads. Specials scrawled on your tabletop might include a deliriously light *branzino* (sea bass), served whole over spicy Spanish rice, or succulent pork chops soaked in a red-wine sauce.

### The Grocery

*288 Smith St between Sackett and Union Sts, Carroll Gardens, Brooklyn (718-596-3335). Subway: F, G to Carroll St. Mon–Thu 6–10pm; Fri 6–11pm; Sat 5:30–11pm. Average main course: $20. MC, V.*

From the serene green-gray walls and the kraft-paper menu covers to the chef who wanders out of the kitchen to personally deliver tastes of tomato–and–white-bean soup, this is an understated, fuss-free ideal of a restaurant. Basically, the Grocery serves food that you'd like to think you could make at home, but you really can't: Delicate pan-seared arctic char is smartly paired with a hearty potato *tortilla* and sautéed spinach in bacon vinaigrette; pasta is dappled with house-made sausage, white beans and kale. The Grocery can't help but corner its market.

### Madiba

*195 DeKalb Ave between Adelphi St and Carlton Ave, Fort Greene, Brooklyn (718-855-9190). Subway: C to Lafayette Ave; G to Clinton–Washington Aves. Mon 5:30pm–midnight; Tue–Thu noon–4pm, 5:30pm–midnight; Fri, Sat noon–4pm, 5:30pm–1am; Sun noon–4pm, 5:30–11pm. Average main course: $13. AmEx, DC, Disc, MC, V.*

Madiba not only serves good, rough-hewn South African cooking, it also has a relaxed vibe and entertainment by the likes of Ladysmith Black Mambazo and *Lion King* cast members. Dishes are marked by the cuisines of indigenous South Africans, colonists (Dutch, Huguenot, Brit) and indentured laborers (Malaysian and Indian). That means you can have ostrich carpaccio and vegetable samosas, Durban bunny chow (thick curry in a hollowed-out hunk of bread) and *bobotie* (a vaguely Malaysian-spiced meat loaf topped with sweet mango chutney). Enjoy them with one of the well-chosen South African wines.

### The Minnow

*442 9th St between Sixth and Seventh Aves, Park Slope, Brooklyn (718-832-5500). Subway: F to Seventh Ave. Mon 5:30–9:30pm; Wed, Thu 5:30–10:30pm; Fri 5:30–11pm; Sat 5–11pm; Sun 11:30am–2:30pm, 5–9:30pm. Average main course: $17. AmEx, DC, Disc, MC, V.*

This family-friendly eatery was among the first high-profile destinations in the Slope. The seafood-laden menu assembles a variety of ingredients: scallops in sweet brandy sauce with pumpkin puree; whole roasted sea bass topped with saffron-tomato rice and steamed vegetables. You can also create a D.I.Y. meal by choosing any seafood item, prepared in any style, with a choice of sides. How Craft-y.

### Moustache

*405 Atlantic Ave between Bond and Nevins Sts, Boerum Hill, Brooklyn (718-852-5555). Subway: M, N, R, W to Pacific St; Q, 2, 3, 4, 5 to Atlantic Ave. 11am–11pm. Average main course: $10. Cash only.*

See page 188.

### Peter Luger

*178 Broadway at Driggs Ave, Williamsburg, Brooklyn (718-387-7400). Subway: J, M, Z to Marcy Ave. Sun–Thu 11:30am–10pm; Fri, Sat 11:30am–11pm. Steak for two: $64.50. Cash only.*

Does Luger deserve its rep as one of the best steakhouses in America—nay, the world? You'll find few dissenters among those crowd the rustic, no-frills dining rooms to tear into dry-aged prime beef. Luger was established as a German beer hall in 1887, and eating here is a similarly communal and boisterous experience. The steakhouse serves but one cut: a porterhouse that's charbroiled black on the outside, tender and pink on the inside. Because most folks order the steak, menus are rarely used, though lamb chops and hamburgers are also well prepared. Service is notoriously slow and crotchety, but that's just part of the Luger legend.

### Robin des Bois

*195 Smith St between Baltic and Warren Sts, Carroll Gardens, Brooklyn (718-596-1609). Subway: F, G to Bergen St. Mon–Fri noon–midnight; Sat, Sun 11am–midnight. Average main course: $10. Cash only.*

Run by French expat Bernard Decanali, Robin des Bois quadruples as a beer-and-wine bar, café, gallery and antiques shop. On sunny weekend mornings, the sun-dappled garden is the most pleasant brunch spot around. After night falls, you get rustic French fare such as *croque-monsieur* and smoked duck (with potatoes, string beans and cranberry sauce) served on wooden slabs. Come winter, seat yourself at the communal table near the fireplace and warm up with hot, spiced red wine. This spot is unquestionably an original.

**Redistribution of wealth** Located on Brooklyn's Smith Street, Robin des Bois sells simple French cooking and quirky vintage furnishings—both are a steal.

**One-man show** The interior of the Egyptian café Mombar shows the careful attention of artist, owner, chef—and informal neighborhood counselor—Moustafa El Sayed.



### Tom's Restaurant

*782 Washington Ave between St. Johns and Sterling Pls, Prospect Heights, Brooklyn (718-636-9738). Subway: S to Park Pl; 2, 3 to Eastern Pkwy–Brooklyn Museum. Mon–Sat 6am–4pm. Average main course: $6. Cash only.*

This popular soda shop has survived the Depression, civil unrest and changing tastes. Since 1936, Tom's has flourished in part because owner Gus Vlahavas and his family treat every customer like a long-lost cousin. Cozy up to the well-worn black-marble counter and enjoy first-rate fountain service, all-day breakfast and fairly ambitious luncheonette fare, such as baked short ribs, crab cakes and roasted turkey. Gus's real specialties are sandwiches (particularly the beef brisket) and griddle items like lemon-ricotta pancakes and outrageously good waffles.

## Queens

### Elias Corner

*24-02 31st St at 24th Ave, Astoria, Queens (718-932-1510). Subway: N, W to Astoria Blvd. 4pm–midnight. Average main course: $14. Cash only.*

Elias Corner is Astoria's most beloved taverna devoted to grilled seafood. Arrive early or plan a weeknight dinner to avoid the long wait. There's little thought given to ambience and no menu, which means you select superbly fresh fish (or a cut of beef or lamb) from the display in front. Those platter-size salmon steaks are, in fact, single servings—and phenomenally flavorful ones at that. Perfectly crunchy fried potato rounds, called chips, along with a glass of Hellenic wine or beer, complete the meal. The line of people eager to eat will speed you along.

# Restaurants by cuisine

### Mombar

*25-22 Steinway St between 25th and 28th Aves, Astoria, Queens (718-726-2356). Subway: G, R, V to Steinway St. Tue–Sun 5–11pm. Average main course: $18. Cash only.*

There's no sign to mark the restaurant, but the gorgeous mosaic eye over the door hints at the spectacular food inside. Chef Moustafa El Sayed designed the tilework that graces the restaurant's walls and tables. In an open kitchen, he prepares Egyptian specialties like duck with molasses, or *mombar*—sausage stuffed with rice, dried meat and herbs, and served with chickpeas and fresh tomatoes. If you're lucky, El Sayed will offer to prepare a surprise for dessert, perhaps a piece of homemade pound cake topped with yogurt, tender pears and mango syrup.

### Ping's Seafood

*83-02 Queens Blvd at Goldsmith St, Elmhurst, Queens (718-396-1238). Subway: G, R, V to Grand Ave–Newtown. 8am–2am. Average main course: $11. AmEx.*

See page 183.

### Tournesol

*50-12 Vernon Blvd between 50th and 51st Aves, Long Island City, Queens (718-472-4355). Subway: 7 to Vernon Blvd–Jackson Ave. Tue–Thu noon–3pm, 5:30–11:30pm; Fri, Sat 11am–3:30pm, 5:30pm–midnight; Sun 11am–3:30pm, 5–10pm. Average main course: $13. Cash only.*

It takes guts to open a French bistro in Queens—even more to accept only cash. But this place can get away with it because soon the Gascon specials arrive: cassoulet and coq au vin just like you'd find in southwest France; buttery skate wing with apple-and-mango sauce; and duck confit, its glossy dark meat encased in crisp skin, served with cauliflower mousse.

## Bronx

### Dominick's

*2335 Arthur Ave between Crescent Ave and E 187th St, Bronx (718-733-2807). Travel: B, D, 4 to Fordham Rd, then Bx12 bus to Arthur Ave. Mon, Wed, Thu, Sat noon–10pm; Fri noon–11pm; Sun 1–9pm. Average main course: $15. Cash only.*

Dominick's has bragging rights: It's the most popular restaurant in what locals proudly call New York's *real* Little Italy. Neighborhood folk, out-of-towners and tracksuited wise guys gather at long, crowded tables to consume massive platters of veal parmigiana, steaming bowls of mussels marinara and linguine with white clam sauce. There are no menus, so mind your waiter.

### Frankie and Johnnie's Pine Restaurant

*1913 Bronxdale Ave between Matthews and Muliner Aves, Bronx (718-792-5956). Subway: 2, 5 to Bronx Park East. 10am–midnight. Average main course: $15. Cash only.*

This place could double as a baseball hall of fame—jerseys, bats and balls are lovingly preserved under glass. Guys from the House that Ruth Built even show up on occasion to chow down on the stadium-size plates of pasta, such as a trough of seafood Alfredo swimming with tiny scallops, shrimp and king-crab legs. If you're still hungry at dessert time, eat that extra helping on your dinner plate instead. The Entenmann's-like confections strike out.

# Shopping & Services

Hot deals, designer heels, facial peels—in New York, you better shop around

Many claim they come to New York for the museums and culture, to which we say "Ha!" They're really here for the shopping (especially now that the sales tax on shoes and clothing applies only to items costing more than $110). It helps to think like a New Yorker, whether you want to rifle through flea markets or try on $3,000 gowns on Madison Avenue. Here are a few tips.

### SHOP TILL YOU DROP

The best bargains don't just fall into your lap; you have to hunt them down. Shopping events like **Barneys'** semi-annual warehouse sale and designers' sample sales are some of the best sources of low-priced clothing by fashion's biggest names. To find out who's selling where, see the Check Out section in ***Time Out New York***. The **S&B Report** *($10; 877-579-0222; www.lazarshopping.com)* and the **SSS Sample Sales** hot line *(212-947-8748)* are also great discount resources. Sales are usually held in the designers' shops or rented loft spaces. Typically, the loft sales are not equipped with changing rooms, so bring a courageous spirit and wear appropriate undergarments.

As Soho and Nolita's storefronts fill up, trendy designers are going farther afield—in only a year's time, 14th Street west of Ninth Avenue has gone from Meatpacker Row to Boutique Central. To find out who's making waves in New York's fashion scene, visit the *TONY* website at www.timeoutny.com, click on Check Out and scan the archives.

Most downtown shops stay open an hour or two later than those uptown. Thursday is the universal—though unofficial—shop-after-work night; most stores remain open until at least 7pm.

Certain stores listed below have multiple locations. If a shop has more than a few branches, we'll tell you to check the business pages in the phone book for other addresses.

## Department stores

### Barneys New York

*660 Madison Ave at 61st St (212-826-8900). Subway: N, R, W to Fifth Ave–59th St; 4, 5, 6 to 59th St. Mon–Fri 10am–8pm; Sat 10am–7pm; Sun 11am–6pm. AmEx, MC, V.*

All the top designers are represented at this haven of New York style; at Christmastime, Barneys has the most provocative windows in town. The store also sells seductive home furnishings and fancy children's clothes. Its Co-op branches carry young designers, as well as secondary lines from heavies like Katayone Adeli and Marc Jacobs. Every February and August, the Chelsea Co-op hosts the Barneys Warehouse Sale, where prices are reduced 50 to 80 percent.

**Other locations** • *Barneys Co-op, 116 Wooster St between Prince and Spring Sts (212-965-9964). Subway: C, E, 6 to Spring St. Mon–Sat 11am–7pm; Sun noon–6pm.* • *Barneys Co-op, 236 W 18th St between Seventh and Eighth Aves (212-826-8900). Subway: 1, 9 to 18th St. Mon–Fri 10am–8pm; Sat 11am–7pm; Sun noon–6pm. AmEx, MC, V.*

### Bergdorf Goodman

*754 Fifth Ave at 57th St (212-753-7300). Subway: E, V to Fifth Ave–53rd St; N, R, W to Fifth Ave–59th St. Mon–Wed, Fri, Sat 10am–7pm; Thu 10am–8pm; Sun noon–6pm. AmEx, MC, V.*

While Barneys aims for a young, trendy crowd, Bergdorf's is dedicated to an elegant, understated one with money to spare. As department stores go, it's one of the best for clothing and accessories. The famed men's store is across the street.

### Bloomingdale's

*1000 Third Ave at 59th St (212-355-5900). Subway: N, R, W to Lexington Ave–59th St; 4, 5, 6 to 59th St. Mon–Fri 10am–8:30pm; Sat 10am–7pm; Sun 11am–7pm. AmEx, MC, V.*

Bloomie's is a gigantic, glitzy department store, offering everything from handbags and cosmetics to furniture and designer duds. Brace yourself for crowds—it ranks among the city's most popular tourist attractions, right up there with the Empire State Building. A downtown branch is expected to open in fall 2003.


▶ **Fashion**, starting on page 211, includes everything from trendsetting designers to vintage shops.

▶ **Accessories**, page 226, includes stores devoted to hats, jewelry and the like.

▶ **Health & Beauty**, page 231, lists recommended sites for haircuts, massages and other services.

▶ Looking for a camera, book, unique gift or something for your home? See **Objects of desire**, page 235.

▶ For wardrobe services such as clothing repair, shoe repair and dry cleaning, see **Directory**, page 376.


Necessities

**Orient express** An ample stock of loose teas is just one attraction at Japanese department store Takashimaya, which also sells fine jewelry, cosmetics, and men's and women's clothes.

### Felissimo

*10 W 56th St between Fifth and Sixth Aves (212-247-5656). Subway: F to 57th St; N, R, W to Fifth Ave–59th St. Mon–Thu, Sat noon–6pm; Fri noon–8pm. AmEx, MC, V.*

This five-story townhouse is a Japanese-owned, eco-savvy specialty store that stocks covetable items. Choose from jewelry, travel accessories, clothing, candles and collectibles. Assistance is available in nine languages.

### Henri Bendel

*712 Fifth Ave at 56th St (212-247-1100). Subway: E, V to Fifth Ave–53rd St; N, R, W to Fifth Ave–59th St. Mon–Wed, Fri, Sat 10am–7pm; Thu 10am–8pm; Sun noon–6pm. AmEx, DC, Disc, MC, V.*

Bendel's lavish quarters resemble a plush townhouse. There are elevators, but it's nicer to saunter up the elegant, winding staircase. Prices are comparable with those of other upscale stores, but merchandise seems more desirable here—must be those darling brown-striped shopping bags.

### H&M

*640 Fifth Ave at 51st St (212-489-0390). Subway: E, V to Fifth Ave–53rd St. Mon–Sat 10am–8pm; Sun 11am–7pm. AmEx, MC, V.*

This shockingly inexpensive Swedish megamart opened in 2000, and the three-story, 35,000-square-foot venue is always mobbed. Clothing is grouped by various house "brands," such as the trendy Impulse line and the sporty L.O.G.G. collection. There's also a large selection of undies and accessories. Check the phone book for other locations.

### Jeffrey New York

*449 W 14th St between Ninth and Tenth Aves (212-206-1272). Subway: A, C, E to 14th St; L to Eighth Ave. Mon–Wed, Fri 10am–8pm; Thu 10am–9pm; Sat 10am–7pm; Sun 12:30–6pm. AmEx, MC, V.*

Jeffrey Kalinsky, a former Barneys shoe buyer, was a pioneer in the Meatpacking District with his namesake shop, a branch of the Atlanta original. Designer clothing abounds—Alexander McQueen, Helmut Lang, Versace and Yves Saint Laurent. But the centerpiece is the shoe salon, which proffers Manolo Blahnik, Prada and Robert Clergerie.

### Macy's

*151 W 34th St between Broadway and Seventh Ave (212-695-4400). Subway: B, D, F, V, N, Q, R, W to 34th St–Herald Sq; 1, 2, 3, 9 to 34th St–Penn Station. Mon–Sat 10am–8:30pm; Sun 11am–7pm. AmEx, MC, V.*

Behold the real miracle on 34th Street. You'll find everything: designer labels and cheap imitations, a pet-supply shop, a restaurant in the cellar, a Metropolitan Museum of Art gift shop, a juice bar and—gulp—a McDonald's on the kids' floor. The store also offers Macy's by Appointment, a free service that allows shoppers to order goods or clothing over the phone and have it shipped anywhere in the world *(800-343-0121).*

### Saks Fifth Avenue

*611 Fifth Ave between 49th and 50th Sts (212-753-4000). Subway: E, V to Fifth Ave–53rd St. Mon–Wed, Fri, Sat 10am–7pm; Thu 10am–8pm; Sun noon–6pm. AmEx, DC, Disc, MC, V.*

Saks is the classic upscale American department store. It features all the big names in women's fashion (and some of the better lesser-known ones), one of the city's best shoe departments, an excellent menswear department, fine household linens and attentive customer service.

### Takashimaya

*693 Fifth Ave between 54th and 55th Sts (212-350-0100). Subway: E, V to Fifth Ave–53rd St. Mon–Sat 10am–7pm; Sun noon–5pm. AmEx, DC, Disc, MC, V.*

The first two floors of this Japanese department store provide 4,500 square feet of art gallery space, a men's and women's signature clothing collection, Japanese makeup and exotic plants; the top floor is devoted to beauty essentials. The basement's Tea Box café is a sanctuary for shoppers craving tea and a light meal.

## National chains

Many New Yorkers regard chain stores as unimaginative places to shop, but that doesn't mean you won't have to stand behind a long line of them while you make your way to the register. Stores such as **Banana Republic**, **Express**, **Old Navy** and **Victoria's Secret** are all over the city, including the shopping nexuses of Soho, Rockefeller and the areas surrounding Bloomingdale's and Macy's. To find the nearest location of your favorites, refer to the phone book.

# Fashion

## Trendsetters

### Alexander McQueen

*417 W 14th St between Ninth and Tenth Aves (212-645-1797). Subway: A, C, E to 14th St; L to Eighth Ave. Mon–Wed, Fri, Sat 11am–7pm; Thu 11am–8pm; Sun 12:30–6pm. AmEx, DC, Disc, MC, V.*

The rebellious Brit's new Meatpacking District boutique resembles a place of worship, with barrel-vaulted ceilings and quiet white lighting. But the clothing—topstitched denim skirts, brown-leather jeans—is far from monastic.

### Catherine

*468 Broome St at Greene St (212-925-6765). Subway: C, E to Spring St; N, R, W to Prince St. Mon–Sat 11am–7pm; Sun noon–7pm. AmEx, MC, V.*

Take refuge from Soho's chain-store madness at this colorful boutique, which showcases everything from tile-topped cocktail tables to beaded silk pillows—not to mention the breathtaking fashions of owner-designer Catherine Malandrino.

### Comme des Garçons

*520 W 22nd St between Tenth and Eleventh Aves (212-604-9200). Subway: C, E to 23rd St. Sun, Mon noon–6pm; Tue–Sat 11am–7pm. AmEx, DC, MC, V.*

This austere store is devoted to Rei Kawakubo's architecturally constructed designs for men and women. The boutique fits in well in west Chelsea: Kawakubo's clothing is hung like art, and the innovative space is very gallerylike.

### Diane von Furstenberg, the Shop

*385 W 12th St between Washington St and West Side Hwy (646-486-4800). Subway: A, C, E to 14th*

**It's a mod, mod world** Catherine Malandrino selects the best in fashion and design.

*St; L to Eighth Ave. Mon–Wed, Fri 11am–7pm; Thu 11am–8pm; Sat 11am–6pm; Sun noon–5pm. AmEx, MC, V.*
Although she's known for her classic wrap dress, Diane von Furstenberg has installed much more at this soigné space. Whether you go for ultrafeminine dresses or sporty knits, you'll emerge from the changing room feeling like a princess.

### Diesel

*1 Union Sq West at 14th St (646-336-8552). Subway: L, N, Q, R, W, 4, 5, 6 to 14th St–Union Sq. Mon–Fri 11am–9pm; Sat 10am–9pm; Sun 11am–8pm. AmEx, DC, Disc, MC, V.*
This 14,000-square-foot emporium will satisfy any denim craving you have. In addition to jeans and stylish accessories, there are shoes, underwear and outerwear. The 55 DSL line is carried exclusively at the Union Square store. Check the phone book for other locations.

### Earl Jeans

*160 Mercer St between Houston and Prince Sts (212-226-8709). Subway: F, V, S to Broadway–Lafayette St; N, R, W to Prince St; 6 to Bleecker St. Mon–Sat 11am–7pm; Sun noon–6pm. AmEx, DC, Disc, MC, V.*
Industrial design meets country comfort at this Soho shop, as with Earl's form-fitting jeans: Dark, light, stretchy or tight, you've got a good shot at scoring a new favorite pair.

### Katayone Adeli

*35 Bond St between Bowery and Lafayette St (212-260-3500). Subway: F, V, S to Broadway–Lafayette St; 6 to Bleecker St. Tue–Sat 11am–7pm. AmEx, MC, V.*
Katayone Adeli's collection pieces are available here, but for those perfect side-slit pants, you'll have to scour the racks at Barneys, Bergdorf's or Saks. Ditto for the bridge line, 2 by Katayone Adeli.

### Lucy Barnes

*117 Perry St between Greenwich and Hudson Sts (212-647-0149). Subway: A, C, E to 14th St; L to Eighth Ave; 1, 9 to Christopher St. Mon–Sat 11:30am–7:30pm; Sun noon–6pm. AmEx, MC, V.*
This homey shop, lit by crystal-trimmed hanging lightbulbs, looks primed for a tea party. Scottish designer Barnes's prim-with-a-twist threads include tulle blouses and patchwork skirts, with a sprinkling of vintage pieces.

### Philosophy di Alberta Ferretti

*452 West Broadway between Houston and Prince Sts (212-460-5500). Subway: C, E to Spring St; N, R, W to Prince St. Mon–Sat 11am–7pm; Sun noon–6pm. AmEx, MC, V.*
This two-story shop features mother-of-pearl–tinted walls and cascading water—elements that echo the layering, translucence and craft in Ferretti's collection of delicate womenswear.

### Stella McCartney

*429 W 14th St between Ninth and Tenth Aves (212-255-1556). Subway: A, C, E to 14th St; L to Eighth Ave. Mon–Wed, Fri, Sat 11am–7pm; Thu 11am–8pm; Sun 12:30–6pm. AmEx, DC, Disc, MC, V.*
Celeb designer McCartney, who won acclaim for her rock-star collections for Chloé, now showcases her line of glam-sprite womenswear, shoes and accessories at her first-ever store.

**Groove in the promised land** DJ Manchild spins while you spend at Diesel.

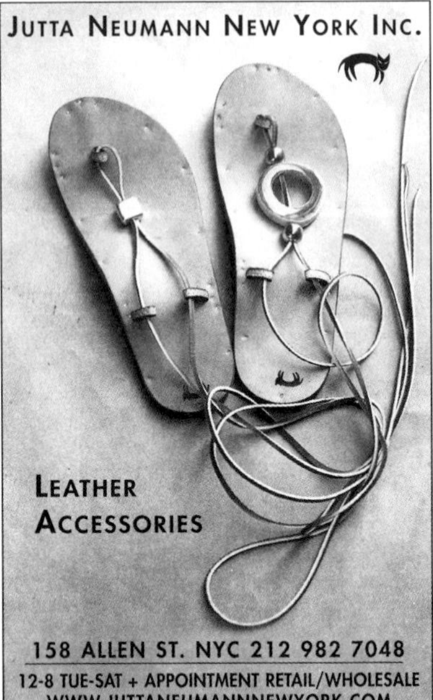
JUTTA NEUMANN NEW YORK INC.
LEATHER ACCESSORIES
158 ALLEN ST. NYC 212 982 7048
12-8 TUE-SAT + APPOINTMENT RETAIL/WHOLESALE
WWW.JUTTANEUMANNNEWYORK.COM

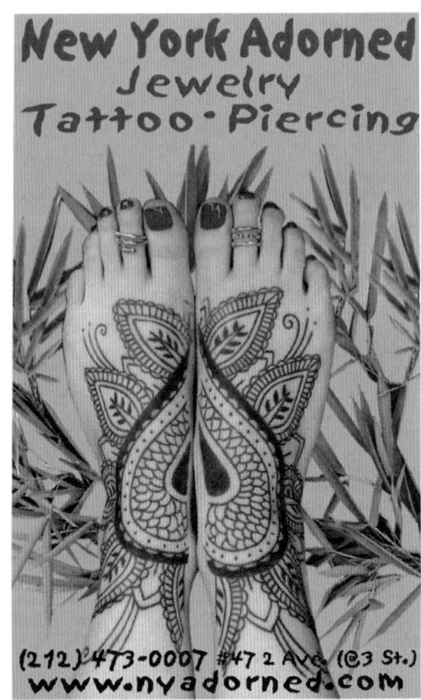
New York Adorned
Jewelry
Tattoo · Piercing
(212) 473-0007 #47 2 Ave. (@3 St.)
www.nyadorned.com

## Boutiques

### A.

*125 Crosby St between Houston and Prince Sts (212-941-8435). Subway: F, V, S to Broadway–Lafayette St; N, R, W to Prince St; 6 to Bleecker St. Mon–Sat 11am–7pm; Sun noon–6pm. AmEx, DC, Disc, MC, V.*

This sophisticated clothier showcases entire collections of emerging designers, including Sophia Kokosalaki, Carol Christian Poell and Raf Simons.

### Bird

*430 Seventh Ave between 14th and 15th Sts, Park Slope, Brooklyn (718-768-4940). Subway: F to 15th St–Prospect Park. Mon–Fri noon–8pm; Sat, Sun noon–6pm. AmEx, MC, V.*

It's an impeccable boutique for "real girls with real bodies" offering clothing from Built by Wendy, Milk Fed and Bird's own label.

### Bond 07

*7 Bond St between Broadway and Lafayette Sts (212-677-8487). Subway: F, V, S to Broadway–Lafayette St; 6 to Bleecker St. Mon–Wed, Fri, Sat 11am–7pm; Thu 11am–8pm; Sun noon–7pm. AmEx, Disc, MC, V.*

Selima Salaun, of famed **Le Corset** *(see page 219)* and **Selima Optique** *(see page 226)*, has branched out from undies and eyewear, this time offering a nice selection of clothing (Alice Roi, Colette Dinnigan), accessories and French furniture.

### Calypso on Broome

*424 Broome St between Crosby and Lafayette Sts (212-274-0449). Subway: 6 to Spring St. Mon–Sat 11am–7pm; Sun noon–6pm. AmEx, DC, MC, V.*

While customers can still shop at the original Calypso on Mott Street, this location (which is four times larger) features more upscale merchandise and different vendors. Stop by either shop for gorgeous slip dresses, suits, sweaters and scarves, many from little-known French designers. Check the phone book for other locations. (For children's clothing, *see* **Calypso Enfants**, *page 222*.)

### Castor & Pollux

*67½ Sixth Ave between Bergen St and Flatbush Ave, Park Slope, Brooklyn (718-398-4141). Subway: 2, 3 to Bergen St. Tue–Sat noon–8pm; Sun 1–6pm.*

Owners Kerrilyn Hunt and Anne-Catherine Luke named this tin-ceilinged boutique after the twin heroes of Greek mythology. The stock is eclectic, from old-school floral bedding to leather-trimmed fedoras, La Cosa tees and Rozae Nicols dresses.

### Erica Tanov

*204 Elizabeth St between Prince and Spring Sts (212-334-8020). Subway: N, R, W to Prince St; 6 to Spring St. Mon–Sat 11am–7pm; Sun noon–6pm. AmEx, Disc, MC, V.*

California-based designer Tanov's first New York store is so soothing, you'll be tempted to slip into one of her silk camisoles and stretch out on the antique bed. But then you'd miss out on the blood-red organza tops and paper-thin silk tunics.

### Hedra Prue

*281 Mott St between Houston and Prince Sts (212-343-9205). Subway: F, V, S to Broadway–Lafayette St; N, R, W to Prince St; 6 to Bleecker St. Mon–Sat 11am–7:30pm; Sun noon–6:30pm. AmEx, MC, V.*

A trip to Nolita isn't complete without a visit to Hedra Prue, which stocks the latest and greatest from young downtown designers, such as Ulla Johnson and Rebecca Taylor.

### Hotel Venus by Patricia Field

*382 West Broadway between Broome and Spring Sts (212-966-4066). Subway: C, E to Spring St. Mon–Fri, Sun 11am–8pm; Sat 11am–9pm. AmEx, Disc, MC, V.*

Patricia Field is brilliant at blending club and street fashions (check out the costumes that she assembles for *Sex and the City*). Her original mix of jewelry, makeup and club wear proves it.

### Intermix

*125 Fifth Ave between 19th and 20th Sts (212-533-9720). Subway: N, R, W, 6 to 23rd St. Mon–Sat 11am–8pm; Sun noon–6pm. AmEx, Disc, MC, V.*

The buyers know what they're doing at Intermix, selecting pieces from Catherine Malandrino, Paul & Joe, Trosman Churba, Urchin and Vanessa Bruno. See phone book for other locations.

### ISA

*88 North 6th St between Berry St and Wythe Ave, Williamsburg, Brooklyn (718-387-3363). Subway: L to Bedford Ave. Mon–Sat 1–10pm; Sun 1–7pm. AmEx, Disc, MC, V.*

Isa Saalabi and partner Holly Harnsongkram stock their warehouse-style shop with hip duds from Marc Jacobs, Sally Penn and ORFI.

### Kirna Zabête

*96 Greene St between Prince and Spring Sts (212-941-9656). Subway: C, E to Spring St; N, R, W to Prince St. Mon–Sat 11am–7pm; Sun noon–6pm. AmEx, MC, V.*

Founded by 28-year-old fashion veterans (not an oxymoron in NYC) Sarah Hailes and Beth Shepherd, Kirna Zabête includes more than 50 designers from around the globe, such as Balenciaga, Hussein Chalayan and Jean Paul Gaultier.

### Language

*238 Mulberry St between Prince and Spring Sts (212-431-5566). Subway: N, R, W to Prince St; 6 to Spring St. Mon–Wed, Fri, Sat 11am–7pm; Thu 11am–8pm; Sun noon–6pm. AmEx, DC, Disc, MC, V.*

Language is a clothing boutique, furniture store, art gallery and bookstore—a can't-miss for folks who buy into the lifestyle-shopping aesthetic.

**Unique boutique** Language is a one-stop shop for clothes, art, books and furniture.

### Min-K

*334 E 11th St between First and Second Aves (212-253-8337). Subway: L to First Ave; 6 to Astor Pl. 1–9pm. AmEx, DC, Disc, MC, V.*

Unless you shop in Tokyo or Seoul, you probably won't recognize any of the streetwear labels sold at this East Village boutique. Min-K owner Minge Kim designs much of the clothing; the rest is gathered on her frequent trips to Japan and Korea.

### Miss Sixty

*246 Mulberry St between Prince and Spring Sts (212-431-6040). Subway: N, R, W to Prince St; 6 to Spring St. Mon–Fri 12:30–8pm; Sat noon–8pm; Sun noon–7pm. AmEx, MC, V.*

Trendy Italian label Miss Sixty's first American outpost looks like a '50s-era vision of the future: A white, cube-shaped portal leading up to the second level could be the stairway to a spaceship. Denim, cut far south of the belly button, stars in curve-clinging jeans and microscopic minis. The new flagship store on West Broadway carries a line of luxury denim.

**Other location ●** *386 West Broadway between Broome and Spring Sts (212-334-9772). Mon–Sat 11am–8pm; Sun 11am–7pm. AmEx, MC, V.*

### M.Z.

*57 Clinton St between Rivington and Stanton Sts (212-228-3634). Subway: F to Delancey St; J, M, Z to Delancey–Essex Sts. Noon–7pm. AmEx, Disc, MC, V.*

M.Z. houses the handiwork of designer Michelle Zacks, who gives wardrobe basics a welcome kick in the pants. Coy flourishes abound—keyhole cutouts, a pearl chain here, a vintage button there. Contributions from pals include the skin-care line Beauty in Utility.

### Scoop

*1275 Third Ave between 73rd and 74th Sts (212-535-5577). Subway: 6 to 77th St. Mon–Fri 11am–8pm; Sat 11am–7pm; Sun noon–6pm. AmEx, DC, Disc, MC, V.*

Scoop is the ultimate fashion editor's closet. Clothing from Juicy Couture, Diane von Furstenberg, Philosophy and others are arranged by hue, not label. Next door is the men's shop.

**Other location ●** *532 Broadway between Prince and Spring Sts (212-925-2886). Subway: N, R, W to Prince St; 6 to Spring St. Mon–Sat 11am–8pm; Sun noon–7pm. AmEx, DC, Disc, MC, V.*

### Steven Alan

*103 Franklin St between Church St and West Broadway (212-343-0692). Subway: 1, 9 to Franklin St. Mon–Wed, Fri, Sat 11am–7pm; Thu noon–10pm; Sun 1–6pm. AmEx, MC, V.*

Style-mogul Alan has expanded to 2,200 square feet of Tribeca space (his diminutive Wooster Street shop now only carries the French designer Vanessa Bruno). Hip boys and girls from all over town still covet his stock, including APC, Development, Wink and Alan's own creations.

**Other location ●** *Vanessa Bruno, 60 Wooster St between Broome and Spring Sts (212-925-2886) Subway: C, E to Spring St; N, R, W to Prince St. Mon–Wed, Fri, Sat 11am–7pm; Thu noon–8pm; Sun noon–7pm. AmEx, MC, V.*

### Sude

*829 Ninth Ave between 54th and 55th Sts (212-397-2347). Subway: A, C, B, D, 1, 9 to Columbus Circle–59th St. Mon, Wed–Sun noon–8pm. AmEx, MC, V.*

Proprietor Sude Dellinger is boldly going where no boutique has gone before, presenting a small but brilliantly edited collection in fashion-starved Hell's Kitchen. Shop for jeans by Seven, tops by Juicy Couture and pieces from new designers such as Escape Velocity, MarieMarie and Leona Edmiston.

### TG-170

*170 Ludlow St between Houston and Stanton Sts (212-995-8660). Subway: F, V to Lower East Side–Second Ave. Noon–8pm. AmEx, MC, V.*

Terri Gillis has an eye for emerging designers: She was the first to carry Built by Wendy and Pixie Yates. Nowadays, you'll find Jared Gold, Liz Collins and United Bamboo hanging gracefully on the racks.

### Trash & Vaudeville

*4 St. Marks Pl between Second and Third Aves (212-982-3590). Subway: 6 to Astor Pl. Mon–Thu noon–8pm; Fri 11:30am–8:30pm; Sat 11:30am–9pm; Sun 1–7:30pm. AmEx, Disc, MC, V.*

This punk clubhouse has two floors of collar tips, jewelry, leathers, snakeskin boots, stretchy tube dresses and other Goth-rock necessities.

## Leather goods

### Carla Dawn Behrle

*134 W 26th St between Sixth and Seventh Aves, suite 1202 (212-243-8877). Subway: 1, 9 to 28th St. By appointment only. AmEx, MC, V.*

Carla Dawn Behrle's Chelsea shop features leather

pants and skirts, plus brightly colored stretch-leather tees and tanks that can be best described as chic duds for the next Bond girl (or boy). Just ask devotees Bono and Alicia Keys.

### Coach

*595 Madison Ave at 57th St (212-754-0041). Subway: N, R, W to Lexington Ave–59th St; 4, 5, 6 to 59th St. Mon–Sat 10am–8pm; Sun 11am–6pm. AmEx, Disc, MC, V.*

Coach's butter-soft leather briefcases, wallets and handbags have always been exceptional, but the Manhattan Coach stores now also stock the label's luxurious outerwear collection. Check the phone book for other locations.

### Jutta Neumann

*158 Allen St between Rivington and Stanton Sts (212-982-7048). Subway: F, V to Lower East Side–Second Ave. Tue–Sat noon–8pm. AmEx, MC, V.*

Jutta Neumann designs leather sandals and bags, as well as belts and jewelry. Haven't you always wanted the perfect leather choker?

### New York City Custom Clothing

*168 Ludlow St between Houston and Stanton Sts (212-375-9593). Subway: F, V to Lower East Side–Second Ave. By appointment only. Cash only.*

Fashion bugs buzz around Agatha Blois's shop to custom-order camouflage-print jackets with rabbit hoods and lace-up corsets with rose inlays.

## Lingerie

### La Perla

*777 Madison Ave between 66th and 67th Sts (212-570-0050). Subway: 6 to 68th St–Hunter College. Mon–Sat 10am–6pm; Sun noon–5pm. AmEx, MC, V.*

Every woman deserves the luxury of La Perla, a high-end line of Italian lingerie, but few can afford it. Bras start at about $150, and lace corsets can run more than $500.

### La Petite Coquette

*51 University Pl between 9th and 10th Sts (212-473-2478). Subway: N, R, W to 8th St–NYU.*

Necessities

## Suit yourself

New York City's top designers will leave you dressed to thrill

Calvin, Donna, Giorgio, Ralph—they're the designers we know and love (until our Visa bill arrives). But where to find them? Many top shops are clustered uptown on and around Fifth and Madison Avenues, as well as in Soho, though some are now making forays into Tribeca *(see* **Southern comforts**, *page 225)*. And **Stella McCartney** and **Alexander McQueen** have settled in the Meatpacking District *(see pages 213 and 211)*. No matter where you roam, you're bound to find something ready-to-wear. For bargains, try **Century 21** *(22 Cortlandt St at Broadway, 212-227-9092).*

### Uptown brands

Take an N, R or W train to Fifth Avenue and 59th Street.

**Burberry**
*9 E 57th St between Fifth and Madison Aves (212-371-5010).*

**Calvin Klein**
*654 Madison Ave at 60th St (212-292-9000).*

**Celine**
*667 Madison Ave between 60th and 61st Sts (212-486-9700).*

**Chanel**
*15 E 57th St between Fifth and Madison Aves (212-355-5050).*

**Chloé**
*850 Madison Ave at 70th St (212-717-8220).*

**Christian Dior**
*21 E 57th St between Fifth and Madison Aves (212-931-2950).*

**Dolce & Gabbana**
*816 Madison Ave between 68th and 69th Sts (212-249-4100).*

**Donna Karan**
*819 Madison Ave between 68th and 69th Sts (212-861-1001).*

**Fendi**
*720 Fifth Ave at 56th St (212-767-0100).*

**Giorgio Armani**
*760 Madison Ave at 65th St (212-988-9191).*

**Givenchy**
*710 Madison Ave at 63rd St (212-772-1040).*

**Gucci**
*685 Fifth Ave at 54th St (212-826-2600).*

**Louis Vuitton**
*703 Fifth Ave at 55th St (212-758-8877).*

*Mon–Wed, Fri, Sat 11am–7pm; Thu 11am–8pm; Sun noon–6pm. AmEx, MC, V.*
Cindy, Liv, Uma and Sarah Jessica join the throngs who flip through the panels of pinned-up bras and panties at La Petite Coquette. If your selection isn't in stock, owner Rebecca Apsan will order it for you.

### Le Corset by Selima
*80 Thompson St between Broome and Spring Sts (212-334-4936). Subway: C, E to Spring St. Mon–Sat 11am–7pm; Sun noon–7pm. AmEx, Disc, MC, V.*
In addition to Selima Salaun's slinky designs, this spacious boutique stocks antique camisoles, Renaissance-inspired girdles and comely lingerie.

### Mixona
*262 Mott St between Houston and Prince Sts (646-613-0100). Subway: F, V, S to Broadway–Lafayette St; N, R, W to Prince St; 6 to Bleecker St. Mon–Sat 11am–8:30pm; Sun 11am–7:30pm.*
This boutique boasts luxurious underthings by 30 designers, including Christina Stott's leather-trimmed mesh bras and Passion Bait's lace knickers.

### Only Hearts
*386 Columbus Ave between 78th and 79th Sts (212-724-5608). Subway: B, C to 81st St–Museum of Natural History; 1, 9 to 79th St. Mon–Sat 11am–8pm; Sun 11am–6pm. AmEx, Disc, MC, V.*
The dainty delicates at Only Hearts are the work of a hopeless romantic, designer Helena Stuart. The downtown store also carries her new ready-to-wear line, plus jewelry and shoes.
**Other location** • *230 Mott St between Prince and Spring Sts (212-431-3694). Subway: 6 to Spring St. Mon–Sat 11am–7pm; Sun noon–6pm. AmEx, MC, V.*

### Religious Sex
*7 St. Marks Pl between Second and Third Aves (212-477-9037). Subway: 6 to Astor Pl. Mon–Wed noon–8pm; Thu–Sat noon–9pm; Sun 1–8pm. AmEx, Disc, MC, V.*
Religious Sex is a playpen for your inner fetishist. The store carries mesh tops with *FUCK* printed all over them, panties the size of eye patches and rubber corsets that all but guarantee a dangerous liaison—or a rash.

**Oh, Donna** You'll leave Karan's flagship store looking like an uptown girl.

**Michael Kors**
*974 Madison Ave at 76th St (212-452-4685).*

**Moschino**
*803 Madison Ave between 67th and 68th Sts (212-639-9600).*

**Ralph Lauren**
*867 Madison Ave at 72nd St (212-606-2100).*

**Valentino**
*747 Madison Ave at 65th St (212-772-6969).*

**Versace**
*647 Fifth Ave between 51st and 52nd Sts (212-317-0224).*

**Yves Saint Laurent**
*855 Madison Ave between 70th and 71st Sts (212-988-3821).*

## Downtown brands

Take an N or R train to Prince Street, the 6 line to Spring Street, or the F, V or S lines to Broadway–Lafayette Street.

**agnès b.**
*103 Greene St between Prince and Spring Sts (212-925-4649).*

**Helmut Lang**
*80 Greene St between Broome and Spring Sts (212-925-7214).*

**Jill Stuart**
*100 Greene St between Prince and Spring Sts (212-343-2300).*

**Marc Jacobs**
*163 Mercer St between Houston and Prince Sts (212-343-1490).*

**Prada**
*575 Broadway at Prince St (212-334-8888).*

**Vivienne Westwood**
*71 Greene St between Broome and Spring Sts (212-334-5200).*

**Bare necessities** The slinky modern styles at Mixona put the *linger* in lingerie.

### 37=1

*37 Crosby St between Broome and Grand Sts (212-226-0067). Subway: F, V, S to Broadway–Lafayette St; 6 to Spring St. Wed–Fri 1–7pm; Sat, Sun 11am–7pm.*
In her Soho atelier, designer Jean Yu creates ethereal made-to-measure bras and panties from silk and chiffon—with no elastic in sight.

## Swimwear

### Malia Mills

*199 Mulberry St between Kenmare and Spring Sts (212-625-2311). Subway: 6 to Spring St. Tue–Sun noon–7pm. AmEx, MC, V.*
Ever since one of her designs made the cover of a *Sports Illustrated*'s swimsuit issue a few years ago, Malia Mills's swimwear has become a staple for folks who spend New Year's Eve on St. Bart's.

### OMO Norma Kamali

*11 W 56th St between Fifth and Sixth Aves (212-957-9797). Subway: F to 57th St; N, R, W to Fifth Ave–59th St. Mon–Sat 10am–6pm. AmEx, MC, V.*
This 18-year-old store carries new and vintage womenswear, menswear and accessories, plus Kamali's bathing-suit separates.

## Streetwear

### Adidas

*136 Wooster St between Houston and Prince Sts (212-777-2001). Subway: F, V, S to Broadway–Lafayette St; N, R, W to Prince St; 6 to Bleecker St. Mon–Sat 11am–7pm; Sun noon–5pm. AmEx, DC, MC, V.*
Soho players with an appetite for '70s street style have welcomed the first U.S. Adidas store with open arms. The boutique specializes in sneakers and sportswear emblazoned with the classic trefoil, rather than the soccer-jock line.

### Alife

*178 Orchard St between Houston and Stanton Sts (646-654-0628). Subway: F, V to Lower East Side–Second Ave. Tue–Sun noon–7pm. AmEx, MC, V.*
This shop sells footwear from Adidas, Converse and the house line Ritefoot; one-of-a-kind accessories by Nuflow and Suckadelic; Nixon watches; and rare Japanese action figures. For sneakers-only shopping, check out offspring **Alife Rivington Club** *(158 Rivington St between Clinton and Suffolk Sts, 212-375-8128).*

### Memes

*3 Great Jones St between Broadway and Lafayette St (212-420-9955). Subway: F, V, S to Broadway–Lafayette St; 6 to Bleecker St. Mon–Sat noon–8pm; Sun noon–7pm. AmEx, MC, V.*
Tetsuo Hashimoto's shop offers refined men's streetwear, but it's not uptight. You'll find Adidas and Kangol goods, as well as Addict, Dope, Soul Rebel, Thunder Thorn and WK Interact.

### Mr. Joe

*500 Eighth Ave between 35th and 36th Sts (212-279-1090). Subway: A, C, E to 34th St–Penn Station. 9:30am–8pm. AmEx, DC, Disc, MC, V.*
What started in 1975 as a spot to buy Converse sneakers and Jordache jeans has evolved into a destination for hip-hop shoes and clothing. DJ Clue and Mark Wahlberg are patrons.

### Phat Farm

*129 Prince St between West Broadway and Wooster St (212-533-7428). Subway: C, E to Spring St; N, R, W to Prince St. Mon–Sat 11am–7pm; Sun noon–6pm. AmEx, MC, V.*
This store showcases Def Jam Records impresario Russell Simmons's classy, conservative take on hip-hop couture: phunky-phresh oversized, baggy clothing, and for gals, the curvy Baby Phat line.

### Recon

*237 Eldridge St between Houston and Stanton Sts (212-614-8502). Subway: F, V to Lower East Side–Second Ave. Noon–7pm. AmEx, MC, V.*
The joint venture of famed graffiti artists Stash and Futura, Recon offers graf junkies a chance to admire the work of their favorite taggers on clothing and accessories.

### Stüssy

*140 Wooster St between Houston and Prince Sts (212-274-8855). Subway: N, R, W to Prince St. Mon–Thu noon–7pm; Fri, Sat 11am–7pm; Sun noon–6pm. AmEx, MC, V.*
Check out the fine hats, tees and other skate and surf wear that Sean Stüssy is famous for.

### Supreme

*274 Lafayette St between Houston and Prince Sts (212-966-7799). Subway: F, V, S to Broadway–Lafayette St; N, R, W to Prince St; 6 to Spring St. Mon–Sat 11:30am–7pm; Sun noon–6pm. AmEx, MC, V.*
This skate wear store is filled mostly with East Coast brands such as Chocolate, Independent, Zoo York and the shop's eponymous line.

### Triple Five Soul

*290 Lafayette St between Houston and Prince Sts (212-431-2404). Subway: F, V, S to Broadway–Lafayette St; N, R to Prince St; 6 to Bleecker St. Mon–Sat 11am–7:30pm; Sun noon–7pm. AmEx, MC, V.*
Clothing and accessories from New York designers fill the racks and shelves at this Soho streetwear store.

### Union

*172 Spring St between Thompson St and West Broadway (212-226-8493). Subway: C, E to Spring St. Mon–Sat 11am–7pm; Sun noon–7pm. AmEx, MC, V.*
This store is the exclusive New York dealer of The Duffer of St. George, the famed streetwear sold at British shops of the same name. Union also carries the Maharishi and Union labels.

**Clothes encounters** Soho's new Adidas store is the only one of its kind in the U.S.

## Menswear

Although chic department stores such as **Barneys New York** and **Bergdorf Goodman** *(see page 209)* have enormous men's sections, it's not always easy or comfortable for guys to seek out new duds. But at the following stores, it's the women who will find themselves killing time on the couch outside the dressing room. *(See also* **Streetwear**, *page 220.)*

### agnès b. homme

*79 Greene St between Broome and Spring Sts (212-431-4339). Subway: C, E to Spring St; N, R, W to Prince St. 11am–7pm. AmEx, MC, V.*
The films of Jean-Luc Godard and his contemporaries are clearly a primary inspiration for agnès b.'s designs. Men's basics include her classic snap-button cardigan sweater and striped, long-sleeve T-shirts.

### Brooks Brothers

*346 Madison Ave at 44th St (212-682-8800). Subway: S, 4, 5, 6, 7 to 42nd St–Grand Central. Mon–Wed, Fri, Sat 9am–7pm; Thu 9am–8pm; Sun noon–6pm. AmEx, Disc, MC, V.*
Prepsters head here for high-quality button-down shirts, chinos, affordable suits and classic tuxes. There's understated clothing for ladies too.
**Other location** • *666 Fifth Ave between 52nd and 53rd Sts (212-261-9440). Subway: E, V to Fifth Ave–53rd St. Mon–Fri 10am–8pm; Sat 10am–7pm; Sun 11am–7pm. AmEx, Disc, MC, V.*

### D/L Cerney

*13 E 7th St between Second and Third Aves (212-673-7033). Subway: 6 to Astor Pl. Noon–8pm. AmEx, MC, V.*
This shop specializes in timeless original designs for the stylish fellow, plus vintage menswear from the 1940s to the '60s. An adjacent shop carries D/L Cerney's new women's line.

### INA Men

See **INA**, page 224.

### Jack Spade

See **Kate Spade**, page 226.

### Paul Smith

*108 Fifth Ave between 15th and 16th Sts (212-627-9770). Subway: L, N, Q, R, W, 4, 5, 6 to 14th St–Union Sq. Mon–Wed, Fri, Sat 11am–7pm; Thu 11am–8pm; Sun noon–6pm. AmEx, Disc, MC, V.*
Stop by Paul Smith for the relaxed English-gentleman look, with designs and accessories combining elegance, quality and wit.

### Scoop Men

See **Scoop**, page 217.

Necessities

### Sean

*132 Thompson St between Houston and Prince Sts (212-598-5980). Subway: C, E to Spring St. Mon–Sat 11am–8pm; Sun noon–7pm. AmEx, MC, V.*

This is a place for gents who yearn to make a thrilling style statement on a Gap-size budget. Owner Sean Cassidy stocks his store with French designer Pierre Emile Lafaurie's suits, poplin shirts (in 23 colors!) and corduroy jackets.

**Other location** ● *224 Columbus Ave between 70th and 71st Sts (212-769-1489). Subway: B, C, 1, 2, 3, 9 to 72nd St. Mon–Sat 11am–8pm; Sun noon–7pm. AmEx, MC, V.*

### Seize sur Vingt

*243 Elizabeth St between Houston and Prince Sts (212-343-0476). Subway: F, V, S to Broadway–Lafayette St; N, R, W to Prince St; 6 to Bleecker St. Mon–Sat noon–7pm; Sun noon–6pm. AmEx, DC, Disc, MC, V.*

Men's shirts come in vibrant colors with impeccable touches: mother-of-pearl buttons and short square collars that look good with the top button undone. The women's line is also popular.

## CRITICS' PICKS Shopping

We suggest you spend your money here...

**...for high-design home accessories**
Lafco, page 224.

**...for unique sneaks**
Alife Rivington Club, page 220.

**...for soothing the savage sweet tooth**
Jacques Torres Chocolate, page 237.

**...for the fabulous fop**
Ted Baker London, above.

**...for Fluffy and Fido**
Fetch, page 245.

**...for cut-rate designer duds**
INA, page 224.

**...for happy wanderers**
Rand McNally Map & Travel Store, page 246.

**...for coatracks that symbolize man's inhumanity to man**
MoMA Design Store, page 241.

**...for couture lingerie**
37=1, page 220.

**...for stylish spectacles**
Selima Optique, page 226.

### Ted Baker London

*107 Grand St at Mercer St (212-343-8989). Subway: J, M, Z, N, Q, R, W, 6 to Canal St. Mon–Sat 11:30am–7pm; Sun noon–6pm. AmEx, DC, MC, V.*

This recently expanded shop has been popular in England for more than a decade. It now features the entire Ted Baker line, whose focus is short- and long-sleeved shirts in bright colors, plus crease-resistant Endurance suits.

### Thomas Pink

*520 Madison Ave at 53rd St (212-838-1928). Subway: E, V to Fifth Ave–53rd St. Mon–Wed, Fri 10am–7pm; Thu 10am–8pm; Sat 10am–6pm; Sun noon–6pm. AmEx, DC, MC, V.*

Pink's shirts are made in bold, dynamic colors that animate conservative suits. But the shop is no longer strictly for men: The women's department includes accessories, jewelry and—of course—shirts.

**Other location** ● *1155 Sixth Ave at 44th St (212-840-9663). Subway: B, D, F, V to 42nd St. Mon–Wed, Fri 10am–7pm; Thu 10am–8pm; Sat 10am–6pm; Sun noon–5pm. AmEx, DC, MC, V.*

## Children's clothes

For **Children's toys**, see page 238.

### Bonpoint

*1269 Madison Ave at 91st St (212-722-7720). Subway: 6 to 96th St. Mon–Sat 10am–6pm.AmEx, MC, V.*

Perfect for toddlers with expense accounts, this Upper East Side institution carries frilly white party dresses and starched sailor suits.

**Other location** ● *811 Madison Ave at 68th St (212-879-0900). Subway: 6 to 68th St–Hunter College. Mon–Sat 10am–6pm. AmEx, MC, V.*

### Calypso Enfants

*426 Broome St between Crosby and Lafayette Sts (212-966-3234). Subway: 6 to Spring St. Mon–Sat 11am–7pm; Sun noon–7pm. AmEx, MC, V.*

Fans of Calypso—and its ultrafeminine clothing, bags and accessories *(see* **Calypso on Broome**, *page 215)*—adore this Francophile children's boutique: The tiny wool coats look as if they leaped from the pages of *Madeline*.

### Lilliput

*240 Lafayette St (212-965-9201) and 265 Lafayette St (212-965-9567) between Prince and Spring Sts. Subway: N, R, W to Prince St; 6 to Spring St. Sun, Mon noon–6pm; Tue–Sat 11am–7pm. AmEx, Disc, MC, V.*

This style source sells "clothes for cool kids," plus accessories, bedding and toys.

### Space Kiddets

*46 E 21st St between Broadway and Park Ave South (212-420-9878). Subway: N, R, W, 6 to 23rd St. Mon, Tue, Fri, Sat 10:30am–6pm; Wed, Thu 10:30am–7pm. AmEx, MC, V.*

Space Kiddets clothing is cool, practical, comfortable and fun. In addition to unique toys, it features a preteen collection for girls.

### Z'Baby Company

*100 W 72nd St at Columbus Ave (212-579-2229). Subway: B, C, 1, 2, 3, 9 to 72nd St. Mon–Sat 10:30am–7:30pm; Sun 11am–6pm. AmEx, MC, V.*

Uptown yuppies clothe their newborns and kids (up to size seven) in Z'Baby's fashions. Sonia Rykiel is among the designers who trim their cuts down to size; others include Cakewalk, Geisswein and Lili Gaufrette. The new Z'Girl store extends the look to junior sizes.

**Other locations** • *996 Lexington Ave at 72nd St (212-472-2229). Subway: 6 to 68th St–Hunter College. Mon–Sat 10am–7pm; Sun noon–5pm. AmEx, MC, V.* • *Z'Girl, 976 Lexington Ave between 71st and 72nd Sts. Subway: 6 to 68th St–Hunter College. Mon–Sat 10am–7pm; Sun noon–5pm. AmEx, MC, V.*

## Maternity wear

### Liz Lange Maternity

*958 Madison Ave between 75th and 76th Sts (212-879-2191). Subway: 6 to 77th St. Mon–Fri 10am–7pm; Sat 10am–6pm; Sun noon–5pm. AmEx, MC, V.*

Liz Lange is the mother of hip maternity wear. Catering to high-profile moms such as Catherine Zeta-Jones and Iman, Lange creatively modifies nonpregnant styles.

### Pumpkin Maternity

*407 Broome St at Lafayette St (212-334-1809). Subway: 6 to Spring St. Mon–Sat noon–7pm; Sun noon–5pm. AmEx, Disc, MC, V.*

At former rocker Pumpkin Wentzel's store, you'll find casual, tailored, machine-washable essentials for the expectant mother, especially one who craves the feel of real denim against her skin.

## Vintage & discounted clothes

When trolling for secondhand clothes, remember the cardinal rule: The less you browse, the more you pay. Although we've included a few in our listings, the shops along lower Broadway tend to ask inflated prices for anything except the most mundane '70s disco shirts. The alternatives are the many small shops in the East Village and on the Lower East Side, where real bargains can be found. Goodwill and Salvation Army stores also warrant a rummage, as does any place with the word *thrift* in its name. Flea markets also have a lot of vintage and antique clothing.

### Alice Underground

*481 Broadway at Broome St (212-431-9067). Subway: N, R, W to Prince St; 6 to Spring St. 11am–7:30pm. AmEx, MC, V.*

**Kid frock** The chic boutique Calypso ensures that your *enfants* never look *terribles*.

This vintage mainstay houses gear from the 1940s through the oughts, in varied condition. Prices are high, but it's always worth rooting through the bins at the front and back for a bargain.

### Allan & Suzi

*416 Amsterdam Ave at 80th St (212-724-7445). Subway: 1, 9 to 79th St. Noon–6pm. AmEx, Disc, MC, V.*

Models drop off their worn-once Comme des Garçons, Gaultiers, Muglers and Pradas here. The platform-shoe collection is incomparable, as is a fab selection of vintage jewelry. There's also a branch in Asbury Park, New Jersey *(732-988-7372).*

### Domsey's Warehouse

*431 Broadway between Hewes and Hooper Sts, Williamsburg, Brooklyn (718-384-6000). Subway: G to Broadway; J, M to Hewes St. Mon–Fri 9am–6pm; Sat 10am–7pm; Sun 11am–5:30pm. Disc, MC, V.*

It's usually easy to turn up a funky find at Domsey's. Choose from a huge selection of used jeans, jackets, military and industrial wear, shoes, hats and a vast sea of Hawaiian shirts.

**Other location** • *1609 Palmetto St at Myrtle Ave, Ridgewood, Queens (718-386-7661). Subway: L to Myrtle Ave; M to Wyckoff Ave. Mon–Sat 10am–7pm; Sun 11am–5:30pm. Disc, MC, V.*

### Filthmart

*531 E 13th St between Aves A and B (212-387-0650). Subway: L to First Ave; N, Q, R, W, 4, 5, 6 to 14th St–Union Sq. Sun–Tue 1–7pm; Wed–Sat noon–8pm. AmEx, Disc, MC, V.*

This East Village store (co-owned by *Sopranos* star Drea de Matteo) specializes in white trash and rock memorabilia from the 1960s through the early '80s: lots of leather, denim and T-shirts.

### Foley & Corinna

*108 Stanton St between Essex and Ludlow Sts (212-529-2338). Subway: F to Delancey St; J, M, Z to Delancey–Essex Sts. Mon–Fri 1–8pm; Sat, Sun noon–8pm. AmEx, MC, V.*

Vintage-clothing fiends like Liv Tyler and Donna Karan know they can have it both ways here: Shoppers freely mix old (Anna Corinna's vintage finds) with new (Dana Foley's original creations, including lace tops, leather-belted pants and sheer wool knits) to compose a truly one-of-a-kind look.

### INA

*101 Thompson St between Prince and Spring Sts (212-941-4757). Subway: C, E to Spring St. Noon–7pm. AmEx, MC, V.*

For the past nine years, INA on Thompson Street has reigned supreme over the downtown consignment scene. The cheery Soho location features drastically reduced couture pieces, while the Nolita site carries trendier clothing. Be sure to visit the men's store on Mott Street.

**Other location** • *21 Prince St between Elizabeth and Mott Sts (212-334-9048). Subway: J, M to Bowery;*

## Southern comforts

**These five fabulous stores will put Tribeca on your shopping map**

When a hankering to shop strikes, you might be tempted to visit default destinations such as Madison Avenue's couture row and trend-central Soho. But if you haven't ventured below Canal Street, try Tribeca. Several fresh-faced boutiques have recently cropped up, joining established outposts that have only improved with age. Here are some of the neighborhood's most distinctive shops.

### Hattitude

*93 Reade St between Church St and West Broadway (212-571-4558). Subway: A, C, 1, 2, 3, 9 to Chambers St. Mon–Fri noon–7pm. AmEx, Disc, MC, V*

British milliner Wendy Carrington has been outfitting ladies with the perfect toque for seven years. Her boutique's shelves are packed with her own playful, brightly colored chapeaus as well as two other labels, Cigmond and Anne Depasquale. Any one of them can be customized. Current styles, such as jaunty silk-shantung newsboy caps, are mixed in with vintage gems, like a rhinestone-sprinkled 1920s paisley turban. Cases display seasoned costume jewelry, makeup mirrors and Jackie O.–style sunglasses.

### Lafco

*200 Hudson St between Canal and Vestry Sts (800-362-3677). Subway: A, C, E, 1, 9 to Canal St. Tue–Sat 11am–7pm; Sun noon–6pm. AmEx, MC, V.*

This sprawling store is the brainchild of housewares tastemaker Jon Bresler, who traverses the globe in search of design-forward wares that have yet to be showcased stateside. Modern home furnishings, like a steel-and-ultrasuede bed from Australia, take up the bulk of the space, with the rest dedicated to personal-care miniboutiques. Purchases can be shipped in less than a week, so your new flokati rug from Athens will be waiting for you when you get home. Don't miss the Santa Maria Novella fragrances—it's not just anywhere that you can find beauty products produced in an Italian monastery since 1210.

**That '70s shoe** Marmalade has some of the coolest retro heels and threads downtown.

*N, R, W to Prince St; 6 to Spring St. Sun–Thu noon–7pm; Fri, Sat noon–8pm. AmEx, MC, V. • INA Men, 262 Mott St between Houston and Prince Sts (212-334-2210). Subway: F, V, S to Broadway–Lafayette St; 6 to Bleecker St. Sun–Thu noon–7pm; Fri, Sat noon–8pm. AmEx, MC, V. • 208 E 73rd St between Second and Third Aves (212-249-0014). Subway: 6 to 77th St. Mon–Sat noon–7pm; Sun noon–6pm.*

### Keni Valenti Retro-Couture

*247 W 30th St between Seventh and Eighth Aves (212-967-7147). Subway: A, C, E, 1, 2, 3, 9 to 34th St–Penn Station. AmEx, DC, Disc, MC, V.*
This appointment-only showroom caters to models and actresses, but is great for anyone passionate about original Balenciaga, Courrèges and Halston. Prices start in the thousands.

### Nikki B.

*20 Harrison St between Greenwich and Hudson Sts (212-343-9731). Subway: A, C, E to Canal St; 1, 9 to Franklin St. Mon–Sat 11am–7pm. AmEx, DC, Disc, MC, V.*
It's easy to overlook this simple storefront on a dead-end block, and that would be a shame: Nikki Butler's accessories should be in everyone's closet. Her own designs—including aviator sunglasses with pastel leather stems and a bracelet strung with mother-of-pearl bird and fish charms—occupy prime real estate. Jill Stuart jeans and slouchy fringed shoulder bags by Katie Bloom blend in seamlessly.

### Tribeca Gardens

*100 Hudson St at Leonard St (212-966-4226). Subway: A, C, E to Canal St; 1, 9 to Franklin St. Mon–Fri 9am–6pm; Sat 10am–5pm. AmEx, MC, V.*
Every inch of Tribeca Gardens' interior drips with flora, including weeping willow boughs and potted topiaries. Gregarious owner Chris Giglio will happily explain each plant's origins and idiosyncrasies. Even the containers are stunning, from giant 600-year-old Malaysian kettles to simpler ceramic vases from the 1930s and '40s. At the back of the shop, cut flowers sit like ladies in waiting—peonies, roses of every hue, yellow hyacinths, white lilacs and more. Bouquets start at $50, but if you drop in, you can have a stem for as little as $1.

### Tribeca Issey Miyake

*119 Hudson St at North Moore St (212-226-0100). Subway: A, C, E to Canal St; 1, 9 to Franklin St. Mon–Sat 11am–7pm; Sun noon–6pm. AmEx, DC, MC, V.*
A collaboration between mega-architect Frank Gehry and forward-thinking fashion designer Issey Miyake is sure to be an eyeful. Once you've gawked at the striking titanium Gehry sculpture that snakes through the shop, you can admire the rest of the high-tech boutique. This flagship is jam-packed with Miyake's head-turning pieces, like a poppy-colored kimono-esque dress and men's sweaters that look like the stripes were spray-painted on. Miyake's APOC (A Piece of Cloth) project lets you customize garments of fray-proof fabric by cutting along perforated lines, turning, say, a long-sleeved top into a cap-sleeved one. Or skip the scissors—the designs are stunning as they are.

**Marmalade**

*172 Ludlow St between Houston and Stanton Sts (212-473-8070). Subway: F, V to Lower East Side–Second Ave. Sun–Thu 12:30–9pm. Fri, Sat noon–10pm. AmEx, MC, V.*

One of the cutest vintage-clothing stores on the Lower East Side, Marmalade also has some of the hottest 1970s and '80s threads below Houston Street. Whether you're in need of a slinky cocktail dress or a ruffled blouse, you'll find it amid the selection of well-cared-for, well-priced items. Accessories, an array of vintage shoes and a small selection of men's clothing are also available.

**Resurrection**

*217 Mott St between Prince and Spring Sts (212-625-1374). Subway: N, R, W to Prince St; 6 to Spring St. Mon–Sat 11am–7pm; Sun noon–7pm. AmEx, MC, V.*

This vintage boutique is a Pucci wonderland, where Anna Sui and Kate Moss come for 1960s and '70s clothing. The shop occupies a space that was reputedly a former funeral home. But have no fear: Katy Rodriguez's shop looks more like a jewel box than a haunted house.

# Accessories

## Eyewear emporiums

**Alain Mikli Optique**

*880 Madison Ave between 71st and 72nd Sts (212-472-6085). Subway: 6 to 68th St–Hunter College. Mon–Sat 10am–6pm; Sun noon–5pm. AmEx, MC, V.*

French frames for the bold and beautiful are available at this Madison Avenue outlet, including specs designed by architect Philippe Starck.

**Myoptics**

*123 Prince St between Greene and Wooster Sts (212-598-9306). Subway: N, R, W to Prince St. Mon–Sat 11am–7pm; Sun noon–6pm. AmEx, Disc, MC, V.*

Plastics are hot at Soho's Myoptics; look for styles by Blind, Oliver Peoples and Paul Smith. Check the phone book for other locations.

**Selima Optique**

*59 Wooster St at Broome St (212-343-9490). Subway: C, E to Spring St. Mon–Wed, Fri, Sat 11am–7pm; Thu 11am–8pm; Sun noon–7pm. AmEx, DC, Disc, MC, V.*

Selima Salaun's wear-if-you-dare frames are popular with famous four-eyes such as Lenny Kravitz and Sean Lennon (both of whom have frames named for them). Salaun also stocks Face à Face, Gucci, Matsuda and more. Check the phone book for other locations.

**Sol Moscot Opticians**

*118 Orchard St at Delancey St (212-477-3796). Subway: F to Delancey St; J, M, Z to Delancey–Essex Sts. Mon–Fri 9am–6pm; Sat 10am–6pm; Sun 9am–5pm. AmEx, DC, Disc, MC, V.*

This 77-year-old family-run emporium offers the same big-name frames you'll find uptown, for about 20 percent less. Sol Moscot also carries vintage glasses (starting at $49), wrap-shield sunglasses by Chanel and Gucci, and bifocal contacts.

**Other location** ● *69 W 14th St at Sixth Ave (212-647-1550). Subway: F, V to 14th St; L to Sixth Ave. Mon–Fri 10am–7pm; Sat 10:30am–6pm; Sun noon–5pm. AmEx, DC, Disc, MC, V.* ● *107-20 Continental Ave between Austin St and Queens Blvd, Forest Hills, Queens (718-544-2200). Subway: E, F, V, G, R to Forest Hills–71st Ave. Mon–Fri 10am–7pm; Sat 10am–5pm; Sun noon–5pm. AmEx, Disc, MC, V.*

## Handbags

See also **Leather goods**, page 217.

**Amy Chan**

*247 Mulberry St between Prince and Spring Sts (212-966-3417). Subway: F, V, S to Broadway–Lafayette St; N, R, W to Prince St; 6 to Spring St. Mon–Wed, Fri–Sun noon–7pm; Thu noon–8pm. AmEx, MC, V.*

Designer Amy Chan made her mark a few years back when she launched a collection of handbags made from Chinese silk, sari fabric and feathers; they're now the centerpiece of her Nolita store. She also sells clothing and jewelry for rocker chicks.

**Blue Bag**

*266 Elizabeth St between Houston and Prince Sts (212-966-8566). Subway: F, V, S to Broadway–Lafayette St; 6 to Bleecker St. Mon–Sat 11am–8pm; Sun noon–7pm. AmEx, Disc, MC, V.*

Blue Bag is the walk-in handbag closet of your dreams. Its delicious and ever-changing bags (not all blue) are popular with the likes of Cameron Diaz and Courtney Love.

**Destination**

*32–36 Little West 12th St between Ninth Ave and Washington St (212-727-2031). Subway: A, C, E to 14th St; L to Eighth Ave. Mon–Sat 11am–8pm; Sun noon–7pm. AmEx, MC, V.*

Those who drool over luscious ornaments will make a pilgrimage to the island's largest accessories boutique. The bags, shoes, hats and jewelry created by more than 30 designers include Vegas-worthy baubles and handbags crafted of film from Vietnamese movies.

**Kate Spade**

*454 Broome St at Mercer St (212-274-1991). Subway: N, R, W to Prince St; 6 to Spring St. Mon–Sat 11am–7pm; Sun noon–6pm. AmEx, MC, V.*

Popular handbag designer Kate Spade sells her classic boxy tote as well as other smart numbers in this sleek store. Spade also stocks shoes, pajamas and rain slickers. For her luggage line, see page 228. Accessories for men are sold at Jack Spade.

**Other location** ● *Jack Spade, 56 Greene St between Broome and Spring Sts (212-625-1820). Subway: C, E, 6 to Spring St; N, R, W to Prince St. Mon–Sat 11am–7pm; Sun noon–6pm. AmEx, MC, V.*

### Kazuyo Nakano

*223 Mott St between Prince and Spring Sts (212-941-7093). Subway: 6 to Spring St. Noon–7pm. AmEx, MC, V.*

Straight out of high school, Kazuyo Nakano worked on the assembly line at her father's kimono-bag factory in Kyoto. Now Nakano has her own handbag shop, selling her fun, functional designs. She has also launched a leather clothing collection.

## Hats

### Amy Downs Hats

*227 E 14th St between Second and Third Aves (212-358-8756). Subway: L to Third Ave; N, Q, R, W, 4, 5, 6 to 14th St–Union Sq. Tue–Sat 1–7pm. Cash only.*

Downs' soft wool and felt hats are neither fragile nor prissy.

**Hats *amore*** Choose from more than 20 designers at the Hat Shop in Soho.

### Arnold Hatters

*620 Eighth Ave between 40th and 41st Sts (212-768-3781). Subway: A, C, E to 42nd St–Port Authority. Mon–Sat 9am–7:15pm; Sun 10am–5pm. AmEx, DC, Disc, MC, V.*

At 76-year-old family-owned Arnold Hatters (the old sign outside says KNOX HATS), the selection includes Kangols (widest array in the USA), Stetsons, fedoras and spitfires. Call before you visit: The shop may move nearby in 2003.

### Eugenia Kim

*203 E 4th St between Aves A and B (212-673-9787). Subway: F, V to Lower East Side–Second Ave. Mon–Fri 11am–8pm; Sat, Sun noon–8pm. AmEx, MC, V.*

This is the source for Eugenia Kim's funky cowboy hats, newsboy caps, cloches and more.

### The Hat Shop

*120 Thompson St between Prince and Spring Sts (212-219-1445). Subway: C, E to Spring St. Mon–Sat noon–7pm; Sun 1–6pm. AmEx, MC, V.*

The Hat Shop offers customers creations from 20 different designers—plus the house line, Chapeau Chateau—and scads of personal attention, too.

## Jewelry

### Bulgari

*730 Fifth Ave at 57th St (212-315-9000). Subway: N, R, W to Fifth Ave–59th St. Mon–Sat 10am–5:30pm. AmEx, DC, Disc, MC, V.*

Bulgari offers some of the world's most beautiful adornments—everything from watches and chunky gold necklaces to leather goods and silk scarves and ties.

**Other location** ● *783 Madison Ave between 66th and 67th Sts (212-717-2300). Subway: 6 to 68th St–Hunter College. Mon–Sat 10am–5:30pm. AmEx, DC, Disc, MC, V.*

### Cartier

*653 Fifth Ave at 52nd St (212-446-3459). Subway: E, V to Fifth Ave–53rd St. Mon–Sat 10am–5:30pm. AmEx, DC, MC, V.*

Cartier bought its Italianate mansion, one of the few remnants of this neighborhood's previous life as a residential area, for $100 and two strands of oriental pearls in 1917. All the usual Cartier items—jewelry, silver, porcelain—are sold within. Check the phone book for other locations.

### Fragments

*116 Prince St between Greene and Wooster Sts (212-334-9588). Subway: C, E, 6 to Spring St; N, R, W to Prince St. Mon–Sat 11am–7pm; Sun noon–6pm. AmEx, MC, V.*

Over the years, Fragments buyer Janet Goldman has assembled an exclusive stable of more than 100 artists. The jewelers first offer their designs at the Soho store before Goldman sells them to department stores such as Barneys.

**Other location** ● *53 Stone St between Coenties Slip and Hanover Sq (212-269-3955). Subway: N, R, W to*

*Whitehall St; 4, 5 to Bowling Green. Mon–Wed, Fri 10am–5:30pm; Thu 11am–7pm. AmEx, MC, V.*

### Ilias Lalaounis

*739 Madison Ave between 64th and 65th Sts (212-439-9400). Subway: F to Lexington Ave–63rd St; N, R, W to Fifth Ave–59th St. Mon–Sat 10am–5:45pm. AmEx, MC, V.*

This Greek jewelry designer's work is inspired by his native country's ancient symbols, as well as by Native American and Arabic designs.

### L'Atelier

*89 E 2nd St between First Ave and Ave A (212- 677-4983). Subway: F, V to Lower East Side–Second Ave. Mon–Fri noon–7pm; Sat 2–7pm. AmEx, MC, V.*

All of the precious-metal pieces at this small East Village jewel box are made on-site.

### Me & Ro

*239 Elizabeth St between Houston and Prince Sts (917-237-9215). Subway: F, V, S to Broadway–Lafayette St; 6 to Bleecker St. Mon–Sat 11am–7pm; Sun noon–6pm. AmEx, MC, V.*

Michele Quan and Robin Renzi, the dynamic duo behind Me & Ro jewelry, are inspired by ancient Chinese, Tibetan and Indian traditions (like tying bells around the wrist as a form of protection).

### Piaget

*730 Fifth Ave at 57th St (212-246-5555). Subway: N, R, W to Fifth Ave–59th St. Mon–Fri 10am–6pm; Sat 10am–5:30pm. AmEx, DC, MC, V.*

This giant boutique full of glittering jewels would make anyone swoon—especially the person paying for that perfect diamond.

### Push

*240 Mulberry St between Prince and Spring Sts (212-965-9699). Subway: 6 to Spring St. Wed–Sat noon–7pm; Sun 1–6pm. AmEx, MC, V.*

Karen Karch's charming rings, most of which are simple, narrow diamond settings, make spending two months' salary on an engagement band an obsolete gesture.

### Reinstein/Ross

*122 Prince St between Greene and Wooster Sts (212-226-4513). Subway: N, R, W to Prince St. Mon–Sat 11:30am–7pm; Sun noon–6pm. AmEx, MC, V.*

Most of the sleek, handmade engagement rings and wedding bands here are made with the store's custom alloys, such as 22-karat "apricot" gold.

**Other location** ● *29 E 73rd St between Fifth and Madison Aves (212-772-1901). Subway: 6 to 77th St. Mon–Sat 11am–6:30pm. AmEx, MC, V.*

### Robert Lee Morris

*400 West Broadway between Broome and Spring Sts (212-431-9405). Subway: C, E to Spring St; N, R, W to Prince St. Mon–Fri 11am–6pm; Sat 11am–7pm; Sun noon–6pm. AmEx, Disc, MC, V.*

Robert Lee Morris remains one of the foremost contemporary jewelry designers; his bright Soho gallery is the only place where you can view his entire strong, striking line.

### Tiffany & Co.

*727 Fifth Ave at 57th St (212-755-8000). Subway: N, R, W to Fifth Ave–59th St. Mon–Fri 10am–7pm; Sat 10am–6pm; Sun noon–5pm. AmEx, DC, Disc, MC, V.*

Tiffany's heyday was around the turn of the last century, when Louis Comfort Tiffany, son of store founder Charles Lewis Tiffany, took the reigns and began designing his famous lamps and sensational Art Nouveau jewelry. Today, the big stars are Paloma Picasso and Elsa Peretti. Three stories are stacked with precious jewels, silver accessories, chic watches, stationery and porcelain.

## Luggage

### Bag House

*797 Broadway between 10th and 11th Sts (212-260-0940). Subway: L, N, Q, R, W, 4, 5, 6 to 14th St–Union Sq. Mon–Sat 11am–6:45pm; Sun 1–5:45pm. AmEx, MC, V.*

Find all sorts of bags, from the tiniest tote to something that could hold every towel in the Plaza.

### Flight 001

See page 246.

### Innovation Luggage

*300 E 42nd St at Second Ave (212-599-2998). Subway: S, 4, 5, 6, 7 to 42nd St–Grand Central. Mon–Fri 10am–8pm; Sat 11am–7pm; Sun 11am–5pm. AmEx, DC, Disc, MC, V.*

This chain carries the newest models of top-brand luggage, including Dakota, Swiss Army and Tumi. Check the phone book for other locations.

## Shoes

In addition to these shops, swing by **Barneys New York** *(see page 209)* or **Jeffrey New York** *(see page 210)*. For variety, **Saks Fifth Avenue** *(see page 211)* wins, toes down.

### Camper

*125 Prince St at Wooster St (212-358-1842). Subway: N, R, W to Prince St; 6 to Spring St. Mon–Sat 11am–8pm; Sun noon–6pm. AmEx, DC, MC, V.*

This large corner store stocks dozens of styles from its legendary line of Spanish casual shoes.

### Christian Louboutin

*941 Madison Ave between 74th and 75th Sts (212-396-1884). Subway: 6 to 77th St. Mon–Sat 10am –6pm. AmEx, MC, V.*

Serious shoe hounds should plan to drop several C-notes on Louboutin's irresistibly sexy red-soled shoes.

### Chuckies

*399 West Broadway between Broome and Spring Sts (212-343-1717). Subway: C, E to Spring St. Mon–Sat 11am–7:30pm; Sun noon–7:30pm. AmEx, MC, V.*

An alternative to department stores, Chuckies

carries high-profile labels for men and women. Stock ranges from old-school Calvin and Jimmy Choo to up-and-coming Ernesto Esposito.

**Other location** • *1073 Third Ave between 63rd and 64th Sts (212-593-9898). Subway: F to Lexington Ave–63rd St. Mon–Fri 10:30am–7:45pm; Sat, Sun 10:30am–7:30pm. AmEx, DC, Disc, MC, V.*

### Geraldine

*246 Mott St between Houston and Prince Sts (212-219-1620). Subway: F, V, S to Broadway–Lafayette St; N, R, W to Prince St. Mon–Sat 11:30am–7:30pm; Sun noon–6pm. AmEx, MC, V.*

Owner Bethany Mayer stocks cool creations from noted designers such as Olivia Morris, Chloé, Narcisco Rodriguez and Michel Perry.

### Jimmy Choo

*645 Fifth Ave, entrance on 51st St (212-593-0800). Subway: E, V to Fifth Ave–53rd St. Mon–Sat 10am–6pm. AmEx, MC, V.*

Jimmy Choo, famed for conceiving Princess Diana's custom shoe collection, is conquering America with his six-year-old emporium, which features chic boots, sexy pumps and kittenish flats—none selling for less than $350.

### Manolo Blahnik

*31 W 54th St between Fifth and Sixth Aves (212-582-3007). Subway: E, V to Fifth Ave–53rd St. Mon–Sat 10:30am–6pm. AmEx, MC, V.*

The high priest of glamour's timeless shoes will put style in your step and a dent in your wallet.

### Otto Tootsi Plohound

*137 Fifth Ave between 20th and 21st Sts (212-460-8650). Subway: N, R, W to 23rd St. Mon–Fri 11:30am–7:30pm; Sat 11am–8pm; Sun noon–7pm. AmEx, DC, Disc, MC, V.*

One of the best places for the latest shoe styles, Tootsi has a big selection of trendy (and slightly overpriced) imports for women and men. Check the phone book for other locations.

### Sigerson Morrison

*28 Prince St between Elizabeth and Mott Sts (212-219-3893). Subway: F, V, S to Broadway–Lafayette St; N, R, W to Prince St; 6 to Bleecker St. Mon–Sat 11am–7pm; Sun noon–6pm. AmEx, MC, V.*

Stop by this cultish women's shoe store for cleanly designed styles in the prettiest colors: baby blue, ruby red and shiny pearl.

**On your feet** Sigerson Morrison's unique styles and colors will make you take notice.

# Health & Beauty

## Bath, body & beauty booty

### Alcone

*235 W 19th St between Seventh and Eighth Aves (212-633-0551). Subway: 1, 9 to 18th St. Mon–Sat 11am–6pm. AmEx, MC, V.*

Frequented by makeup artists prowling for the German brand Kryolan and kits of fake blood and bruises, mere mortals shop at Chelsea's Alcone for its premade palettes (trays of a dozen or more eye, lip and cheek colors) and its own line of sponges.

### Aveda

*233 Spring St between Sixth Ave and Varick St (212-807-1492). Subway: C, E to Spring St; 1, 9 to Houston St. Mon–Fri 9am–9pm; Sat 9am–7pm; Sun 9am–6pm. AmEx, DC, Disc, MC, V.*

This is a spacious, tranquil boutique filled with an exclusive line of makeup, hair- and skin-care products, and massage oils made from flower and plant extracts. Check the phone book for other locations.

### Face Stockholm

*110 Prince St at Greene St (212-966-9110). Subway: N, R, W to Prince St. Mon–Wed, Fri, Sat 11am–7pm; Thu 11am–8pm; Sun 11am–6pm. AmEx, MC, V.*

Along with a full line of eye shadows, lipsticks, blushes and tools, Face offers two services: makeup applications and lessons.

**Other locations** • *687 Madison Ave at 62nd St (212-207-8833). Subway: F to Lexington Ave–63rd St; N, R, W to Fifth Ave–59th St. Mon–Wed, Fri 10am–6pm; Thu, Sat 10am–7pm; Sun noon–5pm. AmEx, MC, V.* • *226 Columbus Ave between 70th and 71st Sts (212-769-1420). Subway: B, C, 1, 2, 3, 9 to 72nd St. Mon–Sat 11am–7pm; Sun noon–6pm. AmEx, MC, V.*

**Scents and sensibility** Cinnamon, ginger and jasmine are behind Fresh's natural fragrances.

### Fresh

*1061 Madison Ave between 80th and 81st Sts (212-396-0344). Subway: 6 to 77th St. Mon–Sat 10am–7pm; Sun noon–6pm. AmEx, MC, V.*

Fresh is a Boston company that bases its soaps, lotions and other products on natural ingredients such as honey, milk, soy and sugar.

**Other locations** • *57 Spring St between Lafayette and Mulberry Sts (212-925-0099). Subway: 6 to Spring St. Mon–Sat 10am–8pm; Sun noon–6pm. AmEx, MC, V.* • *388 Bleecker St between Perry and W 11th Sts (917-408-1850). Subway: A, C, E to 14th St; L to Eighth Ave; 1, 9 to Christopher St–Sheridan Sq. Mon–Sat 11am–8pm; Sun noon–7pm. AmEx, MC, V.*

### Kiehl's

*109 Third Ave between 13th and 14th Sts (212-677-3171). Subway: L to Third Ave; N, Q, R, W, 4, 5, 6 to 14th St–Union Sq. Mon–Sat 10am–7pm; Sun noon–6pm. AmEx, MC, V.*

Now 152 years old, this institution remains a mob scene. Grab free samples of moisturizer, lip balm or Creme with Silk Groom, and you'll be hooked.

### M.A.C

*14 Christopher St at Gay St (212-243-4150). Subway: A, C, E, F, V, S to W 4th St. Mon–Sat 11am–7pm; Sun noon–6pm. AmEx, Disc, MC, V.*

Makeup Art Cosmetics, committed to the development of cruelty-free products, is famous for lipsticks and eye shadows that come in exotic colors. The Soho branch features nine makeover counters.

**Other locations** • *113 Spring St between Greene and Mercer Sts (212-334-4641). Subway: N, R, W to Prince St; 6 to Spring St. Mon–Sat 11am–8pm; Sun noon–6pm. AmEx, Disc, MC, V.* • *1 E 22nd St between Fifth Ave and Broadway (212-677-6611). Subway: N, R, W, 6 to 23rd St. Mon–Sat 10am–8pm; Sun noon–6pm. AmEx, Disc, MC, V.*

### Make Up Forever

*409 West Broadway between Prince and Spring Sts (212-941-9337). Subway: C, E to Spring St; N, R, W to Prince St. Mon–Sat 11am–7pm; Sun noon–6pm. AmEx, MC, V.*

Make Up Forever, a French line, is popular with glam women and drag queens alike. Colors range from bold purples and fuchsias to muted browns and soft pinks. The mascara is a must-have.

### Ricky's

*718 Broadway at Washington Pl (212-979-5232). Subway: N, R, W to 8th St–NYU. Mon–Fri 9am–10pm; Sat 10am–10pm; Sun 11am–9pm. AmEx, Disc, MC, V.*

Stock up on tweezers, cheap travel containers and makeup cases that look like souped-up tackle boxes. Ricky's in-house makeup line, Mattése, includes fake lashes and glitter nail polish. Check the phone book for other locations.

Necessities

### Sephora

*555 Broadway between Prince and Spring Sts (212-625-1309). Subway: N, R, W to Prince St. Mon–Thu 10am–8pm; Fri, Sat 10am–8:30pm; Sun 11am–7pm. AmEx, Disc, MC, V.*

Sephora, the French beauty chain that is slowly devouring America, has everything. The 8,000-square-foot makeup emporium looks like the first floor of a department store, but staffers hang back until you seek them out. The flagship store is at Rockefeller Center *(636 Fifth Ave between 50th and 51st Sts, 212-245-1633)*. Check the phone book for other locations.

### Shiseido Studio

*155 Spring St between West Broadway and Wooster St (212-625-8820). Subway: C, E to Spring St. Sun, Mon noon–6pm; Tue 11am–6pm; Wed–Sat 11am–7pm. Free.*

A beauty store that doesn't sell anything? It may sound crazy, but Shiseido has opened a 3,800-square-foot consumer learning center to educate shoppers. Visitors can take free skin-care classes and test more than 330 items—cosmetics, fragrances and tools.

### Shu Uemura

*121 Greene St between Houston and Prince Sts (212-979-5500). Subway: F, V, S to Broadway–Lafayette St. N, R, W to Prince St; 6 to Bleecker St. Mon–Sat 11am–7pm; Sun noon–6pm. AmEx, MC, V.*

The entire line of Shu Uemura Japanese cosmetics is for sale at this stark, well-lit Soho boutique. Most hit Shu Uemura for its blushes, brushes, eye shadows and lipsticks, but for a real eye-opening experience, check out the best-selling eyelash curler.

## Perfumeries

### Creed

*9 Bond St between Broadway and Lafayette St (212-228-1940). Subway: F, V, S to Broadway–Lafayette St; 6 to Bleecker St. Mon–Sat 11am–8pm; Sun noon–6pm. AmEx, MC, V.*

In this city, you'd be hard-pressed to find many affordable items that are two-and-a-half centuries old. But the arrival of 243-year-old English perfume house Creed in New York brought many pedigreed products. Customers are encouraged to create fragrance blends of their own.

**Other locations** • *680 Madison Ave between 61st and 62nd Sts (212-838-2780). Subway: N, R, W to Lexington Ave–59th St; 4, 5, 6 to 59th St. Mon–Sat 10am–7pm; Sun noon–6pm. AmEx, MC, V.* • *897 Madison Ave between 72nd and 73rd Sts (212-794-4480). Subway: 6 to 77th St. Mon–Sat 10am–7pm; Sun noon–6pm. AmEx, MC, V.*

### Demeter Fragrances

*83 Second Ave between 4th and 5th Sts (212-505-1535). Subway: F, V to Lower East Side–Second Ave. Mon–Fri 10am–6pm; Sat noon–7pm. MC, V.*

Follow your nose to Demeter Fragrances' anything-but-chichi boutique. In addition to famous single-note scents such as Crème Brûlée, Holy Water, Mushroom, Prune and Riding Crop, the shop carries Demeter's full range of bath and body products.

## Pharmacists

For 24-hour pharmacies, see page 365.

### C.O. Bigelow Apothecaries

*414 Sixth Ave between 8th and 9th Sts (212-533-2700). Subway: A, C, E, F, V, S to W 4th St. Mon–Fri 7:30am–9pm; Sat 8:30am–7pm; Sun 8:30am–5:30pm. AmEx, DC, Disc, MC, V.*

One of the grand old New York pharmacies, Bigelow is the place to find the latest creams, hair accessories, hygiene products, makeup, over-the-counter remedies, perfumes, soaps—you name it.

### Zitomer

*969 Madison Ave between 75th and 76th Sts (212-737-4480). Subway: 6 to 77th St. Mon–Fri 9am–8pm; Sat 9am–7pm; Sun 10am–6pm. AmEx, DC, Disc, MC, V.*

Zitomer stocks what seems like every beauty and health product under the sun. The second floor has kids' clothing, and there are toys on the third. The store also sells panty hose, socks and underwear.

## Salons & spas

### Salons

For a fraction of the usual price, some swanky salons free up their $200 chairs one night a week for those willing to become beauty guinea pigs for trainees. Not to worry—there's ample supervision, and the results are usually wonderful. All of the following salons have model nights, with prices starting at $30 (usually cash only). Phone for details, but know that you may face a three-month waiting list at famous places such as **Frédéric Fekkai Beauté de Provence** *(212-753-9500)* and **Louis Licari** *(212-758-2090)*.

### John Masters Salon and Spa

*77 Sullivan St between Broome and Spring Sts (212-343-9590). Subway: N, R, W to Prince St; 6 to Spring St. Mon–Fri 11am–6:30pm; Sat 10am–6:30pm; Sun noon–5:30pm. AmEx, MC, V.*

This salon has been inspired by nature, from its interior woodwork and waterfall, down to Masters' Organics line of skin- and hair-care products. Cuts start at $80, and the salon doubles as a spa, offering reflexology and massage.

### Miano Viel Salon and Spa

*16 E 52nd St between Fifth and Madison Aves, second floor (212-980-3222). Subway: E, V to Fifth Ave–53rd St. Tue 9am–6pm; Wed 9am–5pm; Thu, Fri 9am–7pm; Sat 9am–5pm. MC, V.*

You could pay more than $300 in one sitting, but Damien Miano and Louis Viel know how to treat tresses.

**Dye another day** Start with a cut at Ultra, a tiny salon popular with rockers.

### Privé

*310 West Broadway between Canal and Grand Sts (212-274-8888). Subway: A, C, E to Canal St. Mon 11am–5pm; Tue, Wed, Fri 10am–7pm; Thu 10am–10pm; Sat 10am–6pm. AmEx, MC, V.*

No need to go uptown for luxe locks. Laurent D., famous for tending to Gwyneth's mane, scored prime retail space in the SoHo Grand Hotel for his first New York salon. Haircuts with Laurent cost $225; cuts with other stylists range from $90 to $150. Highlights start at $125.

### Suite 303

*Chelsea Hotel, 222 W 23rd St between Seventh and Eighth Aves (212-633-1011). Subway: C, E, 1, 9 to 23rd St. Tue–Fri noon–6:45pm; Sat noon–5pm. MC, V.*

Owned by three ex-Recine's stylists, Suite 303 is located in the wonderfully spooky Chelsea Hotel. Haircuts start at $80; highlights start at $165.

### Ultra

*233 E 4th St between Aves A and B (212-677-4380). Subway: F, V to Lower East Side–Second Ave. Tue, Wed, Fri 11am–8pm; Thu noon–9pm; Sat 10am–5pm. AmEx, DC, Disc, MC, V.*

It's no wonder the music industry flocks to Ultra. This tiny salon's anonymous mint-green storefront has the feel of a low-profile club. Cuts start at $85 and color at $70, while highlights are $125 and up.

## Cheap cuts & blow-drys

### Astor Place Hair Stylists

*2 Astor Pl at Broadway (212-475-9854). Subway: N, R, W to 8th St–NYU; 6 to Astor Pl. Mon–Sat 8am–8pm; Sun 9am–6pm. Cash only.*

This is the classic New York hair experience. An army of barbers does everything from neat trims to shaved designs, all to pounding music—usually hip-hop. You can't make an appointment; just take a number and wait outside with the crowd. Sunday mornings are quiet. Cuts start at $12, blow-drys at $15, dreads at $75.

### Jean Louis David

*1180 Sixth Ave at 46th St (212-944-7389). Subway: B, D, F, V to 47–50th Sts–Rockefeller Ctr. Mon–Sat 10am–7pm. Disc, MC, V.*

Everything happens fast at this chain. Models flicker in and out of view on a television screen. Stylists scurry about in white lab coats. Best of all, a shampoo, mildly trendy cut (with clippers) and blow-dry can be yours, without an appointment, for $22.49. Check the phone book for other locations.

## Nails

### Rescue

*21 Cleveland Pl between Kenmare and Spring Sts (212-431-3805). Subway: 6 to Spring St. Mon–Fri 11am–8pm; Sat 10am–6pm. AmEx, MC, V.*

If your hands are in a state of emergency, run to Rescue. This charming garden-level space has been open for five years—and neighbors are still discovering its intensive treatments.

**Other location •** *Rescue Beauty Lounge, 8 Centre Market Pl between Broome and Grand Sts (212-431-0449). Subway: 6 to Spring St. Tue–Fri 11am–8pm; Sat, Sun 10am–6pm. AmEx, MC, V.*

## Spas

Feeling frazzled? After a day of battling city crowds, pamper your weary body with a spa visit. Most treatments start at $60, and no matter how relaxed you feel when you're done, don't forget to leave a tip (15 to 20 percent).

### Avon Salon & Spa

*Trump Tower, 725 Fifth Ave between 56th and 57th Sts, sixth floor (212-755-2866, 888-577-AVON). Subway: E, V to Fifth Ave–53rd St; N, R, W to Fifth Ave–59th St. Mon, Tue, Sat 8am–6pm; Wed, Thu, Fri 8am–8pm. AmEx, Disc, MC, V.*

Forget Skin-So-Soft Avon: This is the type of place you'd expect to find in glitzy Trump Tower. The salon offers face and body treatments, highlights from top colorist Brad Johns and the famous eyebrow waxings of Eliza Petrescu.

### Bliss 57

*19 E 57th St between Fifth and Madison Aves, third floor (212-219-8970). Subway: F to 57th St; E, V to Fifth Ave–53rd St. Mon–Fri 9am–8:30pm; Sat 9:30am–6:30pm. AmEx, Disc MC, V.*

This uptown sister of Soho's hippest spa is the ultimate in pricey retreats, providing your necessary coddling in record time. Want a manicure in tandem with your facial? Done. The "simultanebliss" combines an oxygen facial with a hot-cream manicure and pedicure. Just prepare to max out the plastic. **Other location** ● *568 Broadway between Houston and Prince Sts, second floor (212-219-8970). Subway: F, V, S to Broadway–Lafayette St; N, R, W to Prince St; 6 to Bleecker St. Mon–Fri 9:30am–8:30pm; Sat 9:30am–6:30pm. AmEx, MC, V.*

### Carapan

*5 W 16th St between Fifth and Sixth Aves, garden level (212-633-6220). Subway: L, N, Q, R, W, 4, 5, 6 to 14th St–Union Sq. 10am–9:45pm; retail store 10am–8pm. AmEx, MC, V.*

In the language of the Pueblo Indians, *carapan* means "a beautiful place of tranquillity where one comes to restore one's spirit." The cedar-scented salon offers reiki, craniosacral therapy and massage.

### Helena Rubinstein

*135 Spring St between Greene and Wooster Sts (212-343-9963). Subway: C, E, 6 to Spring St. Mon 11am–7pm; Tue–Fri 11am–8pm; Sat 10am–6pm; Sun 11am–6pm. AmEx, MC, V.*

In HR's bright and spacious street-level Beauty Gallery, you can dabble in its superb makeup line, then retreat downstairs to a plush oasis. Sink into the elegant lounge, flip through a magazine and snack on nuts, berries and fresh juice. Choose any one of the perfected "Art of Spa Rituals," such as the body soufflé wrap. To prepare for reentry into the real world, take a steam shower and indulge in the skin-care and perfume samples in the bathroom.

### The Mezzanine Spa at Soho Integrative Health Center

*62 Crosby St between Broome and Spring Sts (212-431-1600). Subway: 6 to Spring St. Tue, Wed noon–8pm; Thu, Fri 9am–8pm; Sat, Sun 10am–6pm. AmEx, MC, V.*

The brainchild of dermatologist Dr. Laurie Polis, the spa includes five facial rooms and a wet room for

## Butt, bath and beyond

New York spas offer much more than massages and mud packs

### High Thighs treatment at Bliss 57, $100

*See above.*

You may not be able to change your backside's size or shape, but you can do something about its smoothness. Bliss 57 offers a treatment called High Thighs—also known as a "buttcial"—in which microdermabrasion, massage and a stimulating mask are applied to the buttocks and thighs while you lie on a heated table. A final massage is the clincher in reducing the appearance of cellulite. The resulting rear is as smooth as a tot's tush.

### Gemstone Facial at Stone Spa, $125

*125 Fourth Ave between 12th and 13th Sts. Subway: L, N, Q, R, W, 4, 5, 6 to 14th St–Union Sq. Mon–Fri 9am–9pm; Sat, Sun 10am–8pm. MC, V.*

The spa that sparked the local hot-stone massage craze has found a new fetish in gemstones—water-crushed amethyst, aquamarine and citrine—dissolved in water. A facialist applies a series of towels soaked in the mineral solution, to soften skin and draw out impurities. Even the facial steam that follows is fortified—forced through pulverized tourmaline, espresso-style, with a specially modified steamer. Head and foot massages round out the treatment.

### Public Eye treatment at Inspiration, $65

*525 Broadway at Spring St, sixth floor (212-966-2611). Subway: N, R, W to Prince St; 6 to Spring St. Mon–Sat 11am–8:30pm. MC, V.*

This Soho spa revitalizes tired eyes and minimizes lines. After exfoliation and a smear of castor-bean cream, a pair of cold 24-karat gold spoons (alternated with heated spoons) are swirled over the eyes, brows and cheekbones. The corners of the eyes are then stimulated with a mild electric current.

### Truffle and Olive Oil Body Wrap at Brigitte Mansfield European Spa, $160

*37 Union Sq West between 16th and 17th Sts (212-366-0706). Subway: L, N, Q, R, W, 4, 5, 6 to 14th St–Union Sq. Tue–Fri 11am–10pm; Sat noon–8pm; Sun noon–6pm. AmEx, Disc, MC, V.*

Edibles have always had a place at spas (cucumber facials, ginger scrubs), but how about applying—not eating—black truffles, which are packed with skin-friendly minerals (who knew?). The aesthetician slathers a mix of warm paraffin, olive oil, truffle shavings and crushed almonds over your body, then cocoons you in thermal blankets for 20 minutes. When the paraffin forms a hard shell, it's cut away, and your treatment concludes with a light massage.

rinse-requiring services, such as the volcanic mud treatment. The signature therapy is the Diamond Peel: a device that exfoliates the face using suction and microcrystals.

### Prema Nolita

*252 Elizabeth St between Houston and Prince Sts (212-226-3972). Subway: F, V, S to Broadway–Lafayette St; 6 to Bleecker St. Call for hours. AmEx, MC, V.*

Owned by beauty-biz veterans Celeste Induddi and Betsy Olum, Prema Nolita may be the tiniest spa in the city. In the front of the shop, shelves display cult skin-care lines Astara and Jurlique. In the back, there's a single treatment room offering a lavish list of services, some of which use the house line's Prema Salt Glow Scrubs.

# Objects of Desire

## Books

This city truly is book country. Many shops are happy to mail your selections overseas (books shipped out of state don't get charged sales tax).

### Barnes & Noble

*33 E 17th St between Broadway and Park Ave South (212-253-0810). Subway: L, N, Q, R, W, 4, 5, 6 to 14th St–Union Sq. 10am–10pm. AmEx, Disc, MC, V.*

The nation's largest bookstore and the flagship of this chain (there are 20 in the five boroughs) is a good source for recent hardcovers—some discounted—and the record, tape and CD department has one of the largest classical music selections in the city. Check the phone book for other locations.

### Borders Books & Music

*576 Second Ave at 32nd St (212-685-3938). Subway: 6 to 33rd St. Mon–Sat 9am–11pm; Sun 10am–10pm. AmEx, Disc, MC, V.*

Borders is folksier than Barnes & Noble; even if you're searching for an obscure book, staffers usually come through, or try hard to. There's also an extensive selection of music and videos.

### Complete Traveller Bookstore

*199 Madison Ave at 35th St (212-685-9007). Subway: 6 to 33rd St. Mon–Fri 10am–6:30pm; Sat 10am–6pm; Sun 11am–5pm. AmEx, Disc, MC, V.*

All manner of travel-related texts are available.

### Shakespeare & Co.

*716 Broadway at Washington Pl (212-529-1330). Subway: N, R, W to 8th St–NYU; 6 to Astor Pl. Sun–Thu 10am–11pm; Fri, Sat 10am–midnight. AmEx, Disc, MC, V.*

Some rise by sin, and some by virtue fall, but Shakespeare & Co. has survived the chain-store onslaught. Check the phone book for other locations.

**The great wall** New releases at St. Mark's Bookshop are always thought-provoking.

### St. Mark's Bookshop

*31 Third Ave at Stuyvesant St (212-260-7853). Subway: 6 to Astor Pl. Mon–Sat 10am–midnight; Sun 11am–midnight. AmEx, Disc, MC, V.*

This is the place to spend your pennies if you're a young intellectual (or if you want to look like one). It's loaded with cultural and lit crit publications, and small- and university-press titles.

### Strand Book Store

*828 Broadway at 12th St (212-473-1452). Subway: L, N, Q, R, W, 4, 5, 6 to 14th St–Union Sq. Mon–Sat 9:30am–10:30pm; Sun 11am–10:30pm. AmEx, Disc, MC, V.*

Founded in 1927, the Strand is reputedly the second-largest used bookshop in the country, with more than 2.5 million titles, most sold at a discount.

**Other location** • *Strand Book Store Annex, 95 Fulton St between Gold and William Sts (212-732-6070). Subway: A, C to Broadway–Nassau St; J, M, Z, 2, 3, 4, 5 to Fulton St. Mon–Fri 9:30am–9pm; Sat, Sun 11am–8pm.*

### Unoppressive Non-Imperialist Bargain Books

*34 Carmine St between Bedford and Bleecker Sts (212-229-0079). Subway: A, C, E, F, V, S to W 4th St. Mon–Thu 11am–10pm; Fri 11am–midnight; Sat noon–midnight; Sun noon–10pm. AmEx, Disc, MC, V.*

This 11-year-old shop sells publishers' over-stock at bargain prices. The store has recently expanded and opened a children's bargain-books section next door.


▸ For tips on buying from street artists, see **Curb your enthusiasm**, page 260.

▸ For more bookstores, see chapters **Gay & Lesbian** and **Books & Poetry**.

## Cameras & electronics

When buying a major electronics item, check newspaper ads for price guidelines (start with the inserts in Sunday's *New York Times*). It pays to go to a well-known shop to get reliable advice about the device's compatibility with systems in the country where you plan to use it.

### Bang & Olufsen

*927 Broadway between 21st and 22nd Sts (212-388-9792). Subway: N, R, W to 23rd St. Mon–Wed, Fri 10am–7pm; Thu 10am–8pm; Sat 10am–6pm; Sun noon–5pm. AmEx, MC, V.*
Sleek and Danish-efficient, Bang & Olufsen's upscale home electronics are must-haves for any design-mad techie.
**Other location** • *952 Madison Ave at 75th St (212-879-6161). Subway: 6 to 77th St. Mon–Sat 10am–6:30pm; Sun noon–5pm. AmEx, MC, V.*

### B&H

*420 Ninth Ave between 33rd and 34th Sts (212-444-5040). Subway: A, C, E to 34th St–Penn Station. Mon–Thu 9am–7pm; Fri 9am–2pm; Sun 10am–5pm. AmEx, Disc, MC, V.*
If you can deal with the odd hours (B&H is also closed on all Jewish holidays), long lines and a bit of a schlep, this is the ultimate one-stop shop for all your photographic, video and audio needs.

### Harvey

*2 W 45th St between Fifth and Sixth Aves (212-575-5000). Subway: B, D, F, V to 42nd St; 7 to Fifth Ave. Mon–Wed, Fri 10am–7pm; Thu 10am–8pm; Sat 10am–6pm; Sun noon–5pm. AmEx, MC, V.*
Harvey offers chain-store variety without the lousy warranties and mass-market stereo components. There are lots of high-end products, but plenty of realistically priced items, too.
**Other location** • *ABC Carpet & Home, 888 Broadway at 19th St (212-228-5354). Subway: L, N, Q, R, W, 4, 5, 6 to 14th St–Union Sq. Mon–Fri 10am–8pm; Sat 10am–7pm; Sun 11am–6:30pm. AmEx, MC, V.*

### J&R

*23 Park Row between Ann and Beekman Sts (212-238-9000, 800-221-8180). Subway: A, C to Broadway–Nassau St; J, M, Z, 4, 5 to Fulton St; 2, 3 to Park Pl. Mon–Wed, Fri, Sat 9am–7pm; Thu 9am–7:30pm; Sun 10:30am–6:30pm. AmEx, Disc, MC, V.*



# Sugar shacks

In New York's finest chocolate shops, rich rewards await those who are cuckoo for cocoa

New York makes you feel like a kid in a giant candy store. While there's no shortage of delis and bodegas pushing ho-hum chocolates, you need not settle for the ordinary.

Enter tiny **Li-Lac Chocolates** and sniff the sweet smell of excess. Display cases in the 80-year-old Christopher Street shop are packed with homemade bars and truffles (even a chocolate Statue of Liberty), while shelves lining the perimeter offer goodies galore: caramel apples, jelly beans and all things Gummi.

By contrast, the East Village's **El Eden** specializes in highbrow truffles, including white chocolate with rosewater and zinfandel, and dark chocolate with marzipan and pistachio. Befitting its name, **Chocolate Bar** in the West Village makes a gargantuan block: layers of organic peanut butter and jelly are coated in Belgian chocolate, sprinkled with white-chocolate–cookie crumbles *and* drizzled with dark chocolate.

While Chocolate Bar updates classics, midtown's **Chocolat Bla Bla Bla** offers strange new delights, like cocoa-coated fusilli. Try the M&M's–inspired Sunny Seed Drops—addictive sunflower kernels dipped in chocolate and covered in a candy shell.

Chocolate Bla Bla Bla's cluttered, kid-friendly feel is in stark contrast to prim-and-proper **La Maison du Chocolat**, in Rockefeller Plaza. Your voice drops to a whisper as you enter this chocolate-colored temple and confront the square ganache-filled morsels—flown in weekly from Paris—lined up patiently, importantly, under glass. La Maison takes sweets seriously; at these prices, sowill you.

Don't let your confectionery quest end at the East River. **Jacques Torres Chocolate** in Brooklyn's Dumbo neighborhood blows through more than a ton of Belgian chocolate every month. Each load arrives on a flat from Europe and soon becomes the stuff of dreams: chocolate-covered apricots, milk chocolates, caramel- and fruit-filled chocolate bars and chocolate wafers. The chocolate cookie is a dense mound of fudgy goodness, and the "wicked" *ancho*-and-chipotle–spiked hot cocoa will make your heart race.

This block-long row of shops carries every electronic device you could possibly need (from PCs and TVs to CDs and nose-hair trimmers).

### The Wiz

*17 Union Sq West between 15th and 16th Sts (212-741-9500). Subway: L, N, Q, R, W, 4, 5, 6 to 14th St–Union Sq. Mon–Sat 9am–8:30pm; Sun 11am–7pm. AmEx, DC, Disc, MC, V.*
Thanks to the Wiz's claim that it will match or beat any advertised price on electronic equipment, even its toughest competitors have a hard time keeping up. Check the phone book for other locations.

## Gadget repairs

### Computer Solutions Provider

*45 W 21st St between Fifth and Sixth Aves, second floor (212-463-9744). Subway: F, V, N, R, W to 23rd St. Mon–Fri 9am–6pm. AmEx, MC, V.*
Specialists in Macs, IBMs and related peripherals, CSP's staffers can recover your lost data and soothe you through all manner of computer disasters.

### Photo-Tech Repair Service

*110 E 13th St between Third and Fourth Aves (212-673-8400). Subway: L, N, Q, R, W, 4, 5, 6 to 14th St–Union Sq. Mon, Tue, Thu, Fri 8am–4:45pm; Wed 8am–6pm; Sat 10am–3pm. AmEx, Disc, MC, V.*
Photo-Tech has been servicing the dropped, cracked and drowned since 1959. The shop has 19 on-site technicians and guarantees that your camera wrongs can be righted, regardless of the brand. Rush service is available.

## Photo processing

Photo-developing services are offered by most drugstores (CVS and Rite Aid, for example) and megastores, such as Kmart, but the best results should be expected from labs that develop on the premises.

### Duggal

*3 W 20th St between Fifth and Sixth Aves (212-242-7000). Subway: F, V, N, R, W to 23rd St. Mon–Fri 7am–midnight; Sat, Sun 9am–6pm. AmEx, MC, V.*
Duggal has amassed a large and dedicated following that includes artist David LaChapelle and companies like American Express and Armani. Started by Baldev Duggal more than 40 years ago, this around-the-clock shop focuses on the ability to develop any

**Haute chocolate** Sample a cup of cocoa at elegant La Maison du Chocolat.

### Chocolat Bla Bla Bla

*359 E 50th St between First and Second Aves (212-759-5976). Subway: E, V to Lexington Ave–53rd St; 6 to 51st St. Mon–Sat 11:30am–7pm. AmEx, MC, V.*

### Chocolate Bar

*48 Eighth Ave between Horatio and Jane Sts (212-366-1541). Subway: A, C, E to 14th St; L to Eighth Ave. Mon–Fri 7am–9pm; Sat 8am–9pm; Sun 8am–8pm. AmEx, MC, V.*

### El Eden

*443 E 6th St between First Ave and Ave A (212-979-9291). Subway: F, V to Lower East Side–Second Ave. Mon–Wed noon–7pm; Thu, Fri noon–9pm; Sat noon–8pm; Sun 1–8pm. AmEx, DC, Disc, MC, V.*

### Jacques Torres Chocolate

*66 Water St between Dock and Main Sts, Dumbo, Brooklyn (718-875-9772). Subway: A, C to High St; F to York St. Mon–Sat 9am–7pm. AmEx, MC, V.*

### La Maison du Chocolat

*30 Rockefeller Plaza at 49th St (212-265-0342). Subway: B, D, F, V to 47–50th Sts–Rockefeller Ctr. Mon–Sat 10am–7pm; Sun noon–6pm. Closed Sundays in summer. AmEx, MC, V.*
**Other location** • *1018 Madison Ave between 78th and 79th Sts (212-744-7117). Subway: 6 to 77th St. Mon–Sat 10am–7pm; Sun noon–6pm. AmEx, MC, V.*

### Li-Lac Chocolates

*120 Christopher St between Bleecker and Hudson Sts (212-242-7374). Subway: 1, 9 to Christopher St–Sheridan Sq. Mon–Fri 10am–8pm; Sat noon–8pm; Sun noon–5pm. AmEx, Disc, MC, V.*
**Other location** • *Grand Central Market, Lexington Ave at 43rd St (212-370-4866). Subway: S, 4, 5, 6, 7 to 42nd St–Grand Central. Mon–Fri 7am–9pm; Sat 10am–7pm; Sun 11am–6pm. AmEx, Disc, MC, V.*

type of film—and to do so flawlessly. The prices reflect such expertise.

## Children's toys

### Enchanted Forest

*85 Mercer St between Broome and Spring Sts (212-925-6677). Subway: N, R, W to Prince St; 6 to Spring St. Mon–Sat 11am–7pm; Sun noon–6pm. AmEx, DC, Disc, MC, V.*

Browse through a gallery of beasts, books and handmade toys in a magical forest setting.

### FAO Schwarz

*767 Fifth Ave between 58th and 59th Sts (212-644-9400). Subway: N, R, W to Fifth Ave–59th St. Mon–Wed 10am–7pm; Thu–Sat 10am–8pm; Sun 11am–6pm. AmEx, DC, Disc, MC, V.*

The famous toy emporium has been supplying kids with magnificent playthings since 1862. There are kites, dolls, games, miniature cars, toy soldiers, bath toys and so on. The store hosts a number of special events too. Check www.fao.com for the schedule.

### Kidding Around

*60 W 15th St between Fifth and Sixth Aves (212-645-6337). Subway: F, V to 14th St; L to Sixth Ave. Mon–Sat 10am–7pm; Sun 11am–6pm. AmEx, Disc, MC, V.*

Loyal customers frequent this quaint shop for toys and kids' clothing. A recent expansion added a play area in the back.

### Toys R Us Times Square

*1514 Broadway between 44th and 45th Sts (800-TOYS-R-US). Subway: N, Q, R, W, S, 1, 2, 3, 9, 7 to 42nd St–Times Sq. Mon–Sat 10am–10pm; Sun 11am–8pm. AmEx, Disc, MC, V.*

This flagship location is the world's largest toy store. Kids and families are greeted by an animatronic T-Rex dinosaur and can ride a 60-foot indoor Ferris wheel. Eat and drink at the café or snack at Candy Land (designed just like the board game), the store's very own sweetshop. Check the phone book for other locations.

## Flea markets

For bargain-hungry New Yorkers, rummaging through flea markets qualifies as religious devotion. What better way to walk off that Bloody Mary brunch than to wander among aisles of vintage vinyl records, eight-track tapes, clothes, books and furniture? Try looking below 14th Street along Sixth Avenue or Avenue A at night, or lower Broadway on weekend afternoons. Although not as common in Manhattan, stoop sales are held on Saturdays in parts of Brooklyn (Park Slope, especially) and Queens. Local free papers (usually found in grocery stores), provide the dates, hours and addresses. Sidewalk shopping is popular with locals—they're serious, so head out early.

### Annex Antiques Fair & Flea Market

*Sixth Ave between 24th and 26th Sts (212-243-5343). Subway: F, V to 23rd St. Sat, Sun sunrise–sunset. Cash only.*

Although the market has shrunk a bit due to neighborhood construction, designers and the occasional dolled-down celebrity hunt regularly (and early) at the Annex. Divided into scattered sections, one of which charges a $1 admission fee, the market has heaps of secondhand and antique clothing, old bicycles, platform shoes, birdcages and fab accessories. The nearby Garage indoor market—heavenly on a cold day—is a trove of unusual items.

**Other location ●** *The Garage, 112 W 25th St between Sixth and Seventh Aves (212-243-5343). Subway: F, V to 23rd St. Sat, Sun sunrise–sunset. Cash only.*

### Antique Flea & Farmers' Market

*P.S. 9, W 84th St at Columbus Ave (212-721-0900). Subway: B, C, 1, 9 to 86th St. Sat 10am–6pm. AmEx, MC, V accepted by some vendors.*

This is a small market, but one that's good for antique lace, silverware and tapestries. Fresh eggs, fish and vegetables are also available.

## Florists

Although every corner deli sells flowers—especially carnations—they usually last just a few days. For arrangements that stick around a while and aren't filled with baby's breath, buy from some of Manhattan's finer florists.

### Blue Ivy

*762 Tenth Ave between 51st and 52nd Sts (212-977-8858; 800-448-6355). Subway: C, E to 50th St. Mon–Sat 9:30am–6pm. AmEx, DC, Disc, MC, V.*

Simon Naut, a former chief floral designer for the Ritz-Carlton Hotel, joined forces with graphic artist Michael Jackson to open this upscale floral shop.

### Elizabeth Ryan Floral Designs

*411 E 9th St between First Ave and Ave A (212-995-1111). Subway: L to First Ave; 6 to Astor Pl. Mon–Fri 9am–6pm; Sat 10am–6pm. AmEx, Disc, MC, V.*

Elizabeth Ryan has arranged her shop like one of her gorgeous bouquets, and the result is intoxicating.

### Gotham Gardens

*325 Amsterdam Ave between 75th and 76th Sts (212-877-8908). Subway: 1, 2, 3, 9 to 72nd St. Tue–Sat 10am–8pm; Sun noon–6pm. AmEx, DC, MC, V.*

Assorted greenery lines the sidewalk out front, which makes Dan Dahl and Kevin Esteban's Upper West Side shop stick out like a green thumb. Their creations use complementary leaves such as galax and lemon, koala and lily grasses, and herbs like Spanish lavender and flowering oregano.

### Perriwater Ltd.

*960 First Ave at 53rd St (212-759-9313). Subway: E, V to Lexington Ave–53rd St; 6 to 51st St. Mon–Fri 9am–6pm; Sat 9am–6pm. AmEx, MC, V.*

**Bloom service** VSF specializes in flowers you might find in an English country garden.

Proprietor Patricia Grimley doesn't believe that white flowers should be reserved for weddings; she loves the pure effect of an all-white arrangement for any occasion.

### Renny

*505 Park Ave at 59th St (212-288-7000). Subway: N, R, W to Lexington Ave–59th St; 4, 5, 6 to 59th St. Mon–Sat 9am–6pm. AmEx, MC, V.*
"Exquisite flowers for the discriminating" is the slogan for this florist to the rich and famous.

### VSF

*204 W 10th St between Bleecker and W 4th Sts (212-206-7236). Subway: A, C, E, F, V, S to W 4th St. Mon–Fri 10am–5pm; Sat 11am–4pm. AmEx, Disc, MC, V.*
VSF ("very special flowers") favors Shakespearean-sounding flourishes such as lady's mantle, lamb's ears and waxy, green camellia foliage.

## Food & drink

Although New York is urban to the core, there is no shortage of farm-fresh, high-quality produce, meats and grains. Listed below are a few better-known city markets. Pick up a copy of the *Time Out New York Eating & Drinking Guide* for an exhaustive list of everything edible.

### Dean & DeLuca

*560 Broadway at Prince St (212-431-1691). Subway: N, R, W to Prince St. Mon–Sat 9am–8pm; Sun 9am–7pm. AmEx, MC, V.*
Dean & DeLuca's flagship store (the only one that isn't just a fancy coffee bar) continues to provide the most sophisticated collection of specialty food items in New York City. The grandiose appearance of the place and its epic range of products are reflected in the sky-high prices. But downtown residents and international visitors don't seem to mind. After all, where else can you be assured that you're choosing from the highest-quality goods on the market?

### Dylan's Candy Bar

*1011 Third Ave at 60th St (646-735-0078). Mon–Thu 10am–9pm; Fri, Sat 11am–11pm; Sun 11am–8pm. Subway: N, R, W to Lexington Ave–59th St. AmEx, MC, V.*
Dylan Lauren, the daughter of Ralph Lauren, opened this sweet dream of a candy shop in 2001. You'll find clever Candy Land decor, thousands of sugary snacks and a well-stocked soda fountain.

### Greenmarkets

*212-477-3220; www.cenyc.org.*
There are more than 20 open-air markets sponsored by city authorities in various locations and on different days. The largest and most famous is the one at Union Square *(17th St between Broadway and Park Ave South; Mon, Wed, Fri, Sat 8am–6pm),* where small producers of cheeses, flowers, herbs, honey and vegetables sell their wares from the backs of their flatbed trucks. Arrive early, before the good stuff sells out.

### Guss' Pickles

*85–87 Orchard St between Broome and Grand Sts (516-642-0233). Subway: F to to Delancey St; J, M, Z to Delancey–Essex Sts; S to Grand St. Mon–Thu, Sun 9:30am–6pm; Fri 9am–4pm. Cash only.*
After a sojourn at the Lower East Side Tenement Museum, this LES legend moved into a larger, renovated space. Fans can once again get the pickle king's complete line of sours and half-sours, pickled peppers, watermelon rinds and sauerkraut.

### Kam Man Food Products

*200 Canal St at Mott St (212-571-0330). Subway: J, M, Z, N, Q, R, W, 6 to Canal St. 8:30am–9pm. MC, V.*
This shop has a huge selection of fresh and preserved Chinese, Thai and other Asian foods, as well as utensils and kitchenware.

### McNulty's Tea and Coffee

*109 Christopher St between Bleecker and Hudson Sts (212-242-5351). Subway: 1, 9 to Christopher St–Sheridan Sq. Mon–Sat 10am–9pm; Sun 1–7pm. AmEx, DC, Disc, MC, V.*
The original McNulty began selling tea in 1895; in 1980, the shop was taken over by the Wong family. Coffee is sold here, of course, but the real draw is the tea, from the rarest White Flower Pekoe (harvested once a year in China and priced at $25 per quarter pound) or peach-flavored green tea (at $6 per quarter pound) to a basic Darjeeling or Fortnum & Mason box set.

### Myers of Keswick

*634 Hudson St between Horatio and Jane Sts (212-691-4194). Subway: A, C, E to 14th St; L to*

**Design for living** The downtown MoMA Design Store holds a trove of modern housewares and furniture, as well as a large selection of art, film and music books.

*Eighth Ave. Mon–Fri 10am–7pm; Sat 10am–6pm; Sun noon–5pm. AmEx, MC, V.*
This charming English market is a frequent stop for Brits and local Anglophiles. While some come looking for a hint of home or a jolly good meet-and-greet, others flock to the store for Cornish pasties and steak-and-kidney pies.

### Russ & Daughters
*179 E Houston St between Allen and Orchard Sts (212-475-4880). Subway: F, V to Lower East Side–Second Ave. Mon–Sat 9am–7pm; Sun 8am–6pm. AmEx, Disc, MC, V.*
You'll feel like a circus seal when the jovial men behind the counter of this legendary Lower East Side shop start tossing you bits of lox and gravlax, but who's complaining? Russ & Daughters, open since 1914, sells eight kinds of smoked salmon and many other Jewish foodstuffs, along with Russian and Iranian caviar.

### Zabar's
*2245 Broadway at 80th St (212-787-2000). Subway: 1, 9 to 79th St. Mon–Fri 8am–7:30pm; Sat 8am–8pm; Sun 9am–6pm. AmEx, MC, V.*
Zabar's is more than just a market—it's a New York landmark worthy of campaign stops by would-be elected officials. You might leave rather light in the wallet, but you can't argue with the topflight food. Besides the famous smoked fish and rafts of Jewish delicacies, Zabar's has fabulous bread, cheese and coffee selections. Plus, it's the only market of its kind that offers an entire floor of gadgets and housewares.

## Liquor stores

Most supermarkets and corner delis sell beer. To buy wine or spirits, you need to go to a liquor store (most don't sell suds), which are closed on Sundays.

### Astor Wines & Spirits
*12 Astor Pl at Lafayette St (212-674-7500). Subway: N, R, W to 8th St–NYU; 6 to Astor Pl. Mon–Sat 9am–9pm. AmEx, Disc, MC, V.*
This is a modern wine supermarket that would serve as the perfect blueprint for a chain, were it not for a law preventing liquor stores from branching out. There's a wide range of wines and spirits.

### Sherry-Lehmann
*679 Madison Ave at 61st St (212-838-7500). Subway: F to Lexington Ave–63rd St; N, R, W to Fifth Ave–59th St; 4, 5, 6 to 59th St. Mon–Sat 9am–7pm. AmEx, MC, V.*
Perhaps the most famous of New York's numerous upscale liquor stores, Sherry-Lehmann has a vast selection of bourbons, brandies, Champagnes, ports and Scotches, as well as a superb range of American, French and Italian wines.

### Vintage New York
*482 Broome St at Wooster St (212-226-9463). Subway C, E to Spring St; 1, 9 to Canal St. Mon–Sat 11am–9pm; Sun noon–9pm. AmEx, Disc, MC, V.*
Technically, Vintage is an outpost of an upstate winery, which means it's open for business on Sundays. One catch: It sells wines only from New York vineyards, but you can sample any wine before buying.
**Other location** • *2492 Broadway at 93rd St (212-721-9999). Subway 1, 2, 3, 9 to 96th St. Mon–Sat 11am–9pm; Sun noon–9pm. AmEx, Disc, MC, V.*

## Home & design

### ABC Carpet & Home
*888 Broadway at 19th St (212-473-3000). Subway: N, R, W to 23rd St. Mon–Fri 10am–8pm; Sat 10am–7pm; Sun 11am–6:30pm. AmEx, MC, V.*
The selection is unbelievable and so are the often steep prices. But this shopping landmark really does

have it all: accessories, linens, rugs, antique (Western and Asian) and reproduction furniture, and more. Bargains may be found at ABC's Bronx warehouse outlet and at its new Brooklyn location.
**Other location** • *20 Jay St at Plymouth St, Dumbo, Brooklyn (718-643-7400). Subway: A, C to High St; F to York St. Mon–Sat 10am–7pm; Sun 11–6pm.* • *1055 Bronx River Ave between Westchester Ave and Bruckner Blvd, Bronx (718-842-8772). Subway: 6 to Whitlock Ave. Mon–Fri 10am–7pm; Sat 9am–7pm; Sun 11am–6pm. AmEx, MC, V.*

### The Apartment
*101 Crosby St between Prince and Spring Sts (212-219-3066). Subway: F, V, S to Broadway–Lafayette St; 6 to Bleecker St. Mon, Tue by appointment only; Wed–Sat noon–7pm; Sun noon–6pm. AmEx, MC, V.*
If that East Village couch you're crashing on is cramping your style, drop by The Apartment. Owners Gina Alvarez and Stefan Boublil have designed this lifestyle shop to look like the Tribeca loft that the PYT in your office lives in with her perfect boyfriend. You, the shopper, are meant to lounge on the minimalist Dutch furniture as if chez *vous*. All that you see is for sale: the Moderno Lifestyle Emmanuele bed, the Duravit bathroom fixtures by Philippe Starck, everything.

### Area I.D. Moderne
*262 Elizabeth St between Houston and Prince Sts (212-219-9903). Subway: F, V, S to Broadway–Lafayette St; 6 to Bleecker St. Mon–Fri noon–7pm; Sat, Sun noon–6pm. AmEx, MC, V.*
Area I.D. sells home accessories and furniture from the 1950s, '60s and '70s, both vintage and reproduction. What sets this store apart is that all of its furniture has been re-upholstered in luxurious fabrics (Ultrasuede and mohair, for example). The store also carries a wide selection of fur throws and rugs.

### Bennison Fabrics
*Fine Arts Building, 232 E 59th St between Second and Third Aves, third floor (212-223-0373). Subway: N, R, W to Lexington Ave–59th St; 4, 5, 6 to 59th St. Mon–Fri 9:30am–5:30pm. AmEx, MC, V.*
Bennison is an unusual shop that sells a classic yet innovative range of decorative fabrics silk-screened in England. Prices are steep, and the textiles—often 70 percent linen, 30 percent cotton—end up in some of the best-dressed homes in town.

### Chelsea Garden Center Home Store
*435 Hudson St at Morton St (212-727-7100). Subway: 1, 9 to Houston St. Mon–Fri 11am–8pm; Sat, Sun 10am–7pm. AmEx, MC, V.*
The Chelsea Garden Center's 6,000-square-foot, sun-filled garden, home and lifestyle store has plenty of books, furniture, plants, pottery and tools that will brighten your host's pad. The uptown location focuses on outdoor plants.
**Other location** • *455 W 16th St between Ninth and Tenth Aves (212-929-2477). Subway: A, C, E to 14th St; L to Eighth Ave. 10am–6pm. AmEx, MC, V.*

### Felissimo
See page 210.

### Ingo Maurer, Making Light
*89 Grand St at Greene St (212-965-8817). Subway: A, C, E, J, M, Z, N, Q, R, W, 6 to Canal St. Tue–Sat 11am–7pm; Sun noon–6pm. AmEx, MC, V.*
Munich native Ingo Maurer's clever lamps and fixtures incorporate LED words, holograms and feathers. One of his creations hangs in the Library Bar at **The Hudson** hotel *(see page 149)*.

### King's Road Home
*42 Wooster St between Broome and Grand Sts. (212-941-5011). Subway: A, C, E, J, M, Z, N, Q, R, W, 6, 1, 9 to Canal St. Mon–Sat 11am–7pm; Sun noon–6pm. AmEx, DC, Disc, MC, V.*
British designer Christian Carlson brings the creative inspiration of London's King's Road to Soho at this stylish showroom. You'll find oversized furniture, innovative lighting fixtures and custom-designed upholstery. The store also follows a strict green policy (all wooden pieces are constructed from recycled or farm-raised woods).

### MoMA Design Store
*44 W 53rd St between Fifth and Sixth Aves (212-767-1050). Subway: E, V to Fifth Ave–53rd St. Sun–Thu, Sat 10am–6:30pm; Fri 10am–8pm. AmEx, MC, V.*
At the Museum of Modern Art's Design Store, you'll find calendars, coatracks, glasses, jewelry—you name it—in whimsical shapes and colors.

**British invasion** Designer Christian Carlson imports London chic at King's Road Home.

**Other location** • *81 Spring St at Crosby St (646-613-1367). Subway: 6 to Spring St. Mon–Fri 11am–7pm; Sat 11am–7pm; Sun noon–6pm. AmEx, MC, V.*

### Moss

*146–150 Greene St at Houston St (212-226-2190). Subway: F, V, S to Broadway–Lafayette St. Tue–Fri 11am–7pm; Sat noon–7pm; Sun noon–6pm. AmEx, Disc, MC, V.*
Do you insist on impeccable design for even the most prosaic objects? Murray Moss's museumlike emporium features the best of what the contemporary design world has to offer, including streamlined clocks, curvy sofas and funky saltshakers.

### Pondicherri

*454 Columbus Ave at 82nd St (212-875-1609). Subway: B, C to 81st St–Museum of Natural History. 10am–8pm. AmEx, Disc, MC, V.*
Pondicherri sells handcrafted Indian textiles sure to add flavor to any room, including patchwork duvet covers, multipatterned throw pillows and table linens.

### Portico Home

*72 Spring St between Broadway and Lafayette St (212-941-7800). Subway: 6 to Spring St. Mon–Sat 10am–7pm; Sun noon–6pm. AmEx, Disc, MC, V.*
Portico features modern-chic furniture, and bed and bath accessories. Check the phone book for other locations.

### The Terence Conran Shop

*407 E 59th St between First and York Aves (212-755-9079). Subway: N, R, W to Lexington Ave–59th St; 4, 5, 6 to 59th St. Mon–Fri 11am–8pm; Sat 10am–7pm; Sun noon–6pm. AmEx, MC, V.*
Sir Terence Conran returned to New York in fall 1999 with this witty design store under the Queensboro Bridge (in the '80s, Conran had shops around the city). As in Europe, he offers a vast selection of trendy products—new and vintage—for every room of the house: cabinets, dishes, lighting, rugs, sofas…the list goes on.

### Urban Archaeology

*143 Franklin St between Hudson and Varick Sts (212-431-4646). Subway: A, C, E to Canal St; 1, 9 to Franklin St. Mon–Fri 8am–6pm; Sat noon–6pm. AmEx, Disc, MC, V.*
Old buildings saved! Or rather, picked to pieces and sold for parts. This store carries refurbished architectural artifacts, from Corinthian columns and lobby-size chandeliers to bathtubs and doorknobs, as well as reproductions of favorites. There's a tile showroom on the second floor.
**Other location** • *239 E 58th St between Second and Third Aves (212-371-4646). Subway: N, R, W to Lexington Ave–59th St; 4, 5, 6 to 59th St. Mon–Fri 9:30am–5pm. AmEx, MC, V.*

### Waterworks Collection

*475 Broome St between Greene and Wooster Sts (212-274-8800). Subway: C, E to Spring St. Mon–Fri 9am–6pm; Sat 11am–6pm; Sun noon–5pm. AmEx, MC, V.*
Bathrooms can be the hardest rooms to furnish. With that in mind, the folks at Waterworks stock an array of items—from secretaries and plumbing accessories to silver-plated shaving brushes and soap dishes—make bathrooms pleasant. The showroom *(212-966-0605)*, which offers services for larger bathroom renovations, is located at 469 Broome Street at the corner of Greene Street.
**Other location** • *225 E 57th St between Second and Third Aves (212-371-9266). Subway: N, R, W to Lexington Ave–59th St; 4, 5, 6 to 59th St. Mon–Fri 9am–6pm; Sat 11am–6pm. AmEx, MC, V.*

### Wyeth

*315 Spring St at Greenwich St (212-243-3661). Subway: C, E to Spring St; 1, 9 to Canal St. Mon–Fri 11am–6pm; Sat noon–5pm and by appointment. AmEx, MC, V.*
This Soho shop is known for its collection of vintage 20th-century pieces, as well as its metal lamps, chairs and tables that have been stripped of old paint, sanded and burnished to a soft finish.

### Zipper

*333 Smith St between Carroll and President Sts, Carroll Gardens, Brooklyn (718-596-0333). Subway: F, G to Carroll St. Wed–Sat 11am–7pm; Sun noon–5pm. AmEx, MC, V.*
Zipper is bicoastal. The greenery-strewn Brooklyn outpost of the L.A. shop offers a perky hodgepodge of modernist furniture, accessories and gifts, from oversized rubber duckies ($15) to an alder-wood credenza with white quilted-leather doors ($3,500).

## Gift shops

### Breukelen

*369 Atlantic Ave between Bond and Hoyt Sts, Boerum Hill, Brooklyn (718-246-0024). Subway: A, C, G to Hoyt–Schermerhorn. Tue–Sat noon–7pm; Sun noon–6pm. AmEx, DC, MC, V.*
This contemporary-design store pops up unexpectedly in the middle of Atlantic Avenue's three-block stretch of antiques stores. While the collection isn't limited to any single style, all the objects—pet dishes, table lamps, tumblers—fit a simple, clean, pared-down aesthetic. The Manhattan branch specializes in furniture and is slightly more expensive.
**Other location** • *68 Gansevoort St between Greenwich and Washington Sts (212-645-2216). Subway: A, C, E to 14th St; L to Eighth Ave. Tue–Sat 11am–7pm; Sun noon–6pm. AmEx, MC, V.*

### Kar'ikter

*19 Prince St between Elizabeth and Mott Sts (212-274-1966). Subway: N, R, W to Prince St; 6 to Spring St. 11am–7:30pm. AmEx, MC, V.*
Babar and Astérix paraphernalia are the main draw at this Nolita housewares shop. But grown-up goodies are also available, such as Philippe Starck–designed flyswatters, colorful Mendolino toilet brushes and interior accessories by Alessi.

**Domestic bliss** Breukelen stocks beautiful gifts and objects for the home.

### Love Saves the Day

*119 Second Ave at 7th St (212-228-3802). Subway: 6 to Astor Pl. 1–9pm. AmEx, MC, V.*

This shop has more novelties than you can shake a Yoda doll at: Elvis lamps, ant farms, lurid machine-made tapestries of Madonna, glow-in-the-dark crucifixes, collectible toys and Mexican Day of the Dead statues. Vintage clothing is peppered throughout the store.

### Metropolitan Opera Shop

*136 W 65th St at Broadway (212-580-4090). Subway: 1, 9 to 66th St–Lincoln Ctr. Mon–Sat 10am–10pm; Sun noon–6pm. AmEx, Disc, MC, V.*

Located in the Metropolitan Opera at Lincoln Center, this shop sells CDs and cassettes of—you guessed it—operas. You can also find a wealth of opera books, memorabilia and DVDs. Kids aren't forgotten either: The store's children's department stocks plenty of educational CDs.

### Mxyplyzyk

*125 Greenwich Ave at 13th St (212-989-4300). Subway: A, C, E to 14th St; L to Eighth Ave. Mon–Sat 11am–7pm; Sun noon–5pm. AmEx, MC, V.*

The moniker doesn't mean anything, though it's similar to the name of a character from the Superman comics. Mxyplyzyk offers a slew of cool lighting, furniture, housewares, stationery, toys and plenty of novelty books—on topics such as paranoid taxi-driver wisdom.

### Pearl River Mart

*277 Canal St between Broadway and Lafayette St. (212-431-4770). Subway: J, M, Z, N, Q, R, W, 6 to Canal St 10am–7:30pm. AmEx, Disc, MC, V.*

This downtown emporium is crammed with all things Chinese—bedroom slippers, clothing, gongs, groceries, medicinal herbs, pots, stationery, teapots, woks and a lot more.

**Other location** • *200 Grand St between Mott and Mulberry Sts (212-966-1010). Subway: S to Grand St. 10am–7:30pm. AmEx, MC, V.*

### Pop Shop

*292 Lafayette St between Houston and Prince Sts (212-219-2784). Subway: F, V, S to Broadway–Lafayette St; 6 to Bleecker St. Mon–Sat noon–7pm; Sun noon–6pm. AmEx, MC, V.*

The art of famed pop iconographer Keith Haring lives on in this shop, which sells bags, jigsaw puzzles, pillows and T-shirts—all emblazoned with the sympathetic figures that helped define the '80s.

### White Trash

*304 E 5th St between First and Second Aves (212-598-5956). Subway: F, V to Lower East Side–Second Ave; 6 to Astor Pl. Mon–Sat 2–8:30pm; Sun 1–8pm. MC, V.*

White trash connoisseurs Kim Wurster and Stuart Zamsky opened this popular store, to the delight of everyone who pines for a high-low mix of Jesus night-lights, Noguchi lamps, 1950s kitchen tables and furniture from the likes of Eames and Saarinen.

# Music

## Superstores

### HMV

*300 W 125th St between Frederick Douglas and St. Nicholas Aves. (212 932-9619). Subway: A, C, E to 125th St. Mon–Thu 9am–10pm; Fri–Sat 9am–11pm; Sun 9am–9pm. AmEx, Disc, MC, V.*

HMV has a jaw-dropping selection of cassettes, CDs, videos and vinyl.

**Other location** • *565 Fifth Ave at 46th St. (212-681-6700). Subway B, D, F, V to 47–50th Sts–Rockefeller Ctr. Mon–Fri 8:30am–9pm; Sat 9am–10pm; Sun 11am–8pm. AmEx, Disc, MC, V.*

### J&R

See page 236.

### Tower Records

*692 Broadway at 4th St (212-505-1500, 800-648-4844). Subway: N, R, W to 8th St–NYU. 9am–midnight. AmEx, Disc, MC, V.*

Tower has all the current sounds on CD and tape. Visit the clearance store down the block *(22 E 4th St at Lafayette St, 212-228-5100)* for markdowns in all formats, including vinyl (especially classical). Check the phone book for other locations.

### Virgin Megastore

*52 E 14th St at Broadway (212-598-4666). Subway: L, N, Q, R, W, 4, 5, 6 to 14th St–Union Sq. Mon–Sat 9am–1am; Sun 10am–midnight. AmEx, Disc, MC, V.*

Besides a huge selection of music of all genres, Virgin Megastore has in-store performances and a great selection of U.K–imported CDs. Check out the Virgin

**Unchained melodies** Other Music, NYC's most famous indie record store, sells all genres, including ambient, noise and pop.

soda machine and the Virgin Megastore Cafe. Books and videos are also available.
**Other location** ● *1540 Broadway between 45th and 46th Sts (212-921-1020). Subway: N, Q, R, W, S, 1, 2, 3, 9, 7 to 42nd St–Times Sq. Sun–Thu 9am–1am; Fri, Sat 9am–2am. AmEx, Disc, MC, V.*

## Multigenre

### Bleecker Bob's

*118 W 3rd St between MacDougal St and Sixth Ave (212-475-9677). Subway: A, C, E, F, V, S to W 4th St. Sun–Thu noon–1am; Fri, Sat noon–3am. AmEx, Disc, MC, V.*
This is *the* place for hard-to-find music, especially if it's on vinyl.

### Etherea

*66 Ave A between 4th and 5th Sts (212-358-1126). Subway: F, V to Lower East Side–Second Ave. Sun–Thu noon–10pm; Fri, Sat noon–11pm. AmEx, DC, Disc, MC, V.*
Etherea stocks mostly electronic, experimental, indie, house and rock CDs.

### Mondo Kim's

*6 St. Marks Pl between Second and Third Aves (212-598-9985). Subway: 6 to Astor Pl. 9am–midnight. AmEx, MC, V.*
This minichain of movie-and-music stores offers a great selection for collector geeks: electronic, indie, kraut, prog, reggae, soul, soundtracks and used CDs. Check the phone book for other locations.

### Other Music

*15 E 4th St between Broadway and Lafayette St (212-477-8150). Subway: N, R, W to 8th St–NYU; 6 to Astor Pl. Mon–Fri noon–9pm; Sat noon–8pm; Sun noon–7pm. AmEx, DC, MC, V.*
This may be the the most famous nonchain record store in NYC. No other venue has risen to the challenge of the current genre mania quite like this joint. Owned by three former Kim's slaves, it stocks a full selection of ambient, French pop, indie, noise and psychedelia.

### St. Marks Sounds

*16 St. Marks Pl (212-677-2727) and 20 St. Marks Pl (212-677-3444) between Second and Third Aves. Subway: 6 to Astor Pl. Sun–Thu noon–8pm; Fri, Sat noon–9pm; Sun noon–9pm. Cash only.*
Sounds, consisting of two neighboring stores, is the best bargain on the block. The eastern branch trades and stocks jazz and international recordings; the western branch carries new releases.

### Subterranean Records

*5 Cornelia St between Bleecker and W 4th Sts (212-463-8900). Subway: A, C, E, F, V, S to W 4th St. Mon–Wed noon–9pm; Thu–Sat noon–10pm; Sun noon–7pm. MC, V.*
At this just-off-Bleecker shop, you'll find new, used and live recordings, as well as a large selection of imports. Vinyls (LPs and 45s) fill the basement.

## Classical

### Gryphon Record Shop

*233 W 72nd St between Broadway and West End Ave (212-874-1588). Subway: 1, 2, 3, 9 to 72nd St. Mon–Fri 9:30am–10pm; Sat 11am–7pm; Sun noon–6pm. MC, V.*
This solidly classical store has traditionally been vinyl only, but the nascent 21st century has swept in a wave of CDs. Gryphon also carries a sprinkling of jazz, as well as drama and film books.

## Electronica

### Dance Tracks

*91 E 3rd St at First Ave (212-260-8729). Subway: F, V to Lower East Side–Second Ave. Mon–Thu noon–9pm; Fri noon–10pm; Sat noon–8pm; Sun 1pm–6:30pm. AmEx, Disc, MC, V.*
Stocked with European imports hot off the plane (which are nearly as cheap to buy here), and with racks of domestic house, dangerously enticing bins of Loft/Paradise Garage classics and private decks to listen on, Dance Tracks is a must.

### Satellite Records

*259 Bowery between Houston and Stanton Sts (212-995-1744). Subway: F, V, S to Broadway–Lafayette St; 6 to Bleecker St. Mon–Sat 1–9pm; Sun 1–8pm. AmEx, Disc, MC, V.*
The racks are a mess, but sort through them and you'll likely find every 12-inch you've ever wanted.

## Hip-hop & R&B

### Beat Street Records

*494 Fulton St between Bond St and Elm Pl, Downtown Brooklyn (718-624-6400). Subway: A, C, G to Hoyt–Schermerhorn; 2, 3, 4, 5 to Nevins St. Mon–Sat 10am–7pm; Sun 10am–6pm. AmEx, DC, Disc, MC, V.*

Beat Street, a block-long basement with two DJ booths, has the latest vinyl to go with that phat new sound system. CDs run the gamut from dancehall to gospel, but the reggae boom shots, 12-inch singles and new hip-hop albums make this the first stop for local DJs seeking killer breakbeats and samples.

### Fat Beats

*406 Sixth Ave between 8th and 9th Sts, second floor (212-673-3883). Subway: A, C, E, F, V, S to W 4th St. Mon–Sat noon–9pm; Sun noon–6pm. MC, V.*

Fat Beats is the foundation of local hip-hop. Twin Technics 1200 turntables command the center of this tiny West Village shrine to vinyl. Everyone—Beck, DJ Evil Dee, DJ Premier, Mike D, Q-Tip—shops here regularly for treasured hip-hop, jazz, funk and reggae releases, as well as underground magazines like *Wax Poetics* and cult flicks such as *Wild Style.*

## Jazz

### Jazz Record Center

*236 W 26th St between Seventh and Eighth Aves, room 804 (212-675-4480). Subway: C, E to 23rd St; 1, 9 to 28th St. Mon–Sat 10am–6pm. Disc, MC, V.*

Quite simply, Jazz Record Center is the best jazz store in the city, selling current and out-of-print records, along with books, videos and other jazz-related merchandise. Worldwide shipping is available.

## World music

### World Music Institute

*49 W 27th St between Broadway and Sixth Ave, suite 930 (212-545-7536). Subway: N, R, W to 28th St. Mon–Fri 10am–6pm. AmEx, MC, V.*

The store is small, but if you can't find what you want, WMI's expert employees can order sounds from any remote corner of the planet and ship them to you, usually within two to four weeks.

## Specialty stores

### Arthur Brown & Brothers

*2 W 46th St between Fifth and Sixth Aves (212-575-5555). Subway: B, D, F, V to 47–50th Sts–Rockefeller Ctr; 7 to Fifth Ave. Mon–Fri 9am–6:30pm; Sat 10am–6pm. AmEx, DC, Disc, MC, V.*

Arthur Brown has one of the largest selections of pens anywhere, including Cartier, Dupont, Mont Blanc, Porsche and Schaeffer.

### Big City Kites

*1210 Lexington Ave at 82nd St (212-472-2623). Subway: 4, 5, 6 to 86th St. Mon–Wed, Fri 11am–6:30pm; Thu 11am–7:30pm; Sat 10am–6pm. Call for summer hours. AmEx, Disc, MC, V.*

Act like a kid again and go fly a kite. At Big City, there are more than 150 to choose from.

### Carrandi Gallery

*138 W 18th St between Sixth and Seventh Aves (212-206-0499, 212-242-0710). Subway: 1, 9 to 18th St. Tue, Wed, Fri, Sat noon–6pm; Thu noon–7pm. AmEx, MC, V.*

Carrandi stocks original advertising posters from both sides of the Atlantic, dating as far back as 1880.

### Evolution

*120 Spring St between Greene and Mercer Sts (212-343-1114). Subway: C, E to Spring St. 11am–7pm. AmEx, DC, Disc, MC, V.*

If natural history is your obsession, look no further. Fossils, giraffe skulls, wild boar tusks and insects mounted behind glass are among the items for sale in this relatively politically correct store—the animals died of natural causes or were "culled."

### Fetch

*43 Greenwich Ave between Charles and Perry Sts (212-352-8591). Subway: A, C, E, F, V, S to W 4th St; 1, 9 to Christopher St–Sheridan Sq. Mon–Fri noon–8pm; Sat 11am–7pm; Sun noon–6pm. AmEx, Disc, MC, V.*

This luxury shop for cats and dogs carries everything from silken coats and aromatherapy perfume for Fido to bone-shaped peanut-butter treats and Kitty Calamari—which can be eaten by people, too. *Bon appétit!*

**Bone-us** Fetch sells luxe leashes and snuggly sleep pads for pets of all sizes.

### Flight 001

*96 Greenwich Ave between Seventh and Eighth Aves (212-691-1001). Subway: A, C, E to 14th St; L to Eighth Ave. Mon–Fri 11am–8:30pm; Sat 11am–8:30pm; Sun noon–6pm. AmEx, DC, MC, V.*
This one-stop West Village travel shop carries the requisite travel guidebooks and chic luggage along with clever products such as vacuum-packed shower gel pouches and pocket-size aromatherapy kits. Did you forget something? Flight 001's "travel essentials" wall features packets of Woolite, minidominoes and everything in between.

### Game Show

*1240 Lexington Ave between 83rd and 84th Sts (212-472-8011). Subway: 4, 5, 6 to 86th St. Mon–Wed, Fri, Sat 11am–6pm; Thu 11am–7pm; Sun noon–5pm. AmEx, MC, V.*
Scads of board games are sold here, many of them guaranteed to leave you intrigued or even embarrassed (a few games are quite naughty).
**Other location** • *474 Sixth Ave between 11th and 12th Sts (212-633-6328). Subway: F, V to 14th St; L to Sixth Ave. Mon–Wed, Fri, Sat noon–7pm; Thu noon–8pm; Sun noon–5pm. AmEx, MC, V.*

### Jerry Ohlinger's Movie Material Store

*242 W 14th St between Seventh and Eighth Aves (212-989-0869). Subway: A, C, E, 1, 2, 3, 9 to 14th St; L to Eighth Ave. 1–7:45pm. AmEx, Disc, MC, V.*
Ohlinger has an extensive stock of "paper material" from movies past and present, including photos, posters, programs and fascinating celebrity curios.

### Kate's Paperie

*561 Broadway between Prince and Spring Sts (212-941-9816). Subway: N, R, W to Prince St; 6 to Spring St. Mon–Sat 10am–7pm; Sun 11am–7pm. AmEx, MC, V.*
Kate's is the ultimate paper mill—there are more than 5,000 papers to choose from. It's also the best outpost for stationery, custom printing, journals, photo albums and creative gift wrapping.
**Other locations** • *8 W 13th St between Fifth and Sixth Aves (212-633-0570). Subway: F, V to 14th St; L to Sixth Ave. Mon–Fri 10am–7pm; Sat 10am–6pm; Sun noon–6pm. AmEx, Disc, MC, V.* • *1282 Third Ave between 73rd and 74th Sts (212-396-3670). Subway: 6 to 77th St. Mon–Fri 10am–7pm; Sat, Sun 11am–6pm. AmEx, MC, V.*

### Nat Sherman

*500 Fifth Ave at 42nd St (212-764-5000). Subway: S, 4, 5, 6, 7 to 42nd St–Grand Central; 7 to Fifth Ave. Mon–Wed 9am–7pm; Thu, Fri 9am–7:30pm; Sat 10am–6:30pm; Sun 11am–5pm. AmEx, DC, MC, V.*
Nat Sherman, located across the street from the New York Public Library, specializes in slow-burning cigarettes, cigars and related accoutrements, such as cigar humidors and smoking chairs. Flick your Bic upstairs in the famous smoking room.

### Pearl Paint

*308 Canal St between Broadway and Church St (212-431-7932). Subway: J, M, Z, N, Q, R, W, 6 to Canal St. Mon–Fri 9am–7pm; Sat 10am–6:30pm; Sun 10am–6pm. AmEx, Disc, MC, V.*
This art-and-drafting supply commissary is bigger than a supermarket and sells everything you could possibly need to create your masterpiece.
**Other location** • *207 E 23rd St between Second and Third Aves (212-592-2179). Subway: 6 to 23rd St. Mon, Tue 8:45am–7pm; Wed–Fri 8:45am–6:30pm; Sat 9:45am–6pm; Sun 10am–5pm. AmEx, Disc, MC, V.*

**Ready, jet set, go!** Flight 001 stocks hip accessories for fashion-conscious travelers.

### Quark International

*537 Third Ave between 35th and 36th Sts (212-889-1808). Subway: 6 to 33rd St. Mon–Fri 10am–6:30pm; Sat noon–5pm. AmEx, DC, Disc, MC, V.*
If you're considering a foray into the spying game, check out Quark, where you can buy body armor or a high-powered bug. The store will even custom-bulletproof your favorite jacket.

### Rand McNally Map & Travel Store

*150 E 52nd St between Lexington and Third Aves (212-758-7488). Subway: E, V to Lexington Ave–53rd St; 6 to 51st St. Mon–Fri 9am–7pm; Sat 10am–6pm; Sun noon–5pm. AmEx, Disc, MC, V.*
Rand McNally stocks atlases, globes and maps—even those from rival publishers.

### Sam Ash Music

*155, 159, 160 and 163 W 48th St between Sixth and Seventh Aves (212-719-2299). Subway: B, D, F, V to 47–50th Sts–Rockefeller Ctr; N, R, W to 49th St. Mon–Fri 10am–8pm; Sat 10am–7pm; Sun noon–6pm AmEx, Disc, MC, V.*
This 78-year-old musical-instrument emporium dominates its midtown block with four neighboring shops. New, vintage and custom guitars are available, along with amps, DJ equipment, drums,

keyboards, recording equipment, turntables and all manner of sheet music.

**Other locations** • *2600 Flatbush Ave at Hendrickson Pl, Marine Park, Brooklyn (718-951-3888). Travel: 2, 5 to Flatbush Ave–Brooklyn College, then B41 bus to Kings Plaza. Mon–Fri 10am–9pm; Sat 10am–7pm; Sun noon–5pm. AmEx, Disc, MC, V.* • *113-25 Queens Blvd at 76th Rd, Forest Hills, Queens (718-793-7983). Subway: E, F to 75th Ave. Mon–Fri 10am–9pm; Sat 10am–7pm; Sun noon–6pm. AmEx, Disc, MC, V.*

### Sony Style

*550 Madison Ave between 55th and 56th Sts (212-833-8800). Subway: E, V to Fifth Ave–53rd St; N, R, W to Fifth Ave–59th St. Mon–Sat 10am–7pm; Sun noon–6pm. AmEx, DC, Disc, MC, V.*

For the latest in boom boxes, paper-thin TV screens and innovative headphones, stop by this interactive midtown flagship. Downstairs, you can watch one of the big-screen, surround-sound TVs while lounging on a Polo Ralph Lauren leather couch.

### Stack's Coin Company

*123 W 57th St between Sixth and Seventh Aves (212-582-2580). Subway: F, N, Q, R, W to 57th St. Mon–Fri 10am–5pm. Cash only.*

The oldest, largest coin dealer in the U.S., Stack's trades in rare coins from all over the world.

### Tiny Doll House

*1179 Lexington Ave between 80th and 81st Sts (212-744-3719). Subway: 6 to 77th St. Mon–Fri 11am–5:30pm; Sat 11am–5pm. AmEx, MC, V.*

Everything here is itty-bitty: miniature furniture and wares for dollhouses, including beds, chests, cutlery and kitchen fittings. Even adults will love it.

### Toys in Babeland

*94 Rivington St at Ludlow St (212-375-1701). Subway: F to Delancey St; J, M, Z Delancey–Essex Sts. Mon–Sat noon–10pm; Sun noon–7pm. AmEx, MC, V.*

This friendly Lower East Side shop caters to lesbians but accommodates all lifestyles. You can seek out sex toys, ask for advice, or browse the shelves of erotic fiction and instruction manuals.

### West Marine

*12 W 37th St between Fifth and Sixth Aves (212-594-6065). Subway: B, D, F, V, N, Q, R, W to 34th St–Herald Sq. Mon–Fri 10am–6pm; Sat, Sun 10am–3pm. AmEx, Disc, MC, V.*

Get basic seafaring supplies, deck shoes and fishing gear, or shell out $120 to $2,000 for a Global Positioning System.

## Sports

### Blades, Board and Skate

*659 Broadway between Bleecker and Bond Sts (212-477-7350). Subway: F, V, S to Broadway–Lafayette St; 6 to Bleecker St. Mon–Sat 10am–9pm; Sun 11am–7pm. AmEx, Disc, MC, V.*

This is where to go for in-line skates, skateboards, snowboards and the requisite clothing and gear. Check the phone book for other locations.

### Gerry Cosby & Company

*3 Pennsylvania Plaza, Madison Square Garden, Seventh Ave at 32nd St. (212-563-6464, 877-563-6464). Subway: A, C, E, 1, 2, 3, 9 to 34th St–Penn Station. Mon–Fri 9:30am–7:30pm; Sat 9:30am–6pm; Sun noon–5pm. AmEx, Disc, MC, V.*

Cosby has a huge selection of official team wear and other sporting necessities. The store remains open during—and until 30 minutes after—evening Knicks and Rangers games, just in case you're feeling celebratory.

### Niketown

*6 E 57th St between Fifth and Madison Aves (212-891-6453, 800-671-6453). Subway: N, R, W to Fifth Ave–59th St. Mon–Sat 10am–8pm; Sun 11am–7pm. AmEx, Disc, MC, V.*

Don't despair if you have difficulty choosing among the 1,200 models of footwear. A huge screen drops down every 23 minutes and plays a Nike ad to focus your desire.

### Paragon Sporting Goods

*867 Broadway at 18th St (212-255-8036). Subway: L, N, Q, R, W, 4, 5, 6 to 14th St–Union Sq. Mon–Sat 10am–8pm; Sun 11:30am–7pm. AmEx, DC, Disc, MC, V.*

Equipment and clothing for most any sport is available at this three-floor store. There's a good range of backpacks, bikes, climbing gear, shoes, skis, surf wear, swimwear and tennis rackets.

## Tattoos & piercing

Tattooing was made legal in New York in April 1998; piercing is completely unregulated, so mind your nipples.

### Fun City

*94 St. Marks Pl between First Ave and Ave A (212-353-8282). Subway: L to First Ave; 6 to Astor Pl. Sun–Thu noon–2am; Fri, Sat noon–4am. Cash only.*

It's no doctor's office, but the Fun City folks can be trusted for tattoos and custom piercings.

### New York Adorned

*47 Second Ave between 2nd and 3rd Sts (212-473-0007). Subway: F, V to Lower East Side–Second Ave. Sun–Thu 1–9pm; Fri, Sat 1–10pm. AmEx, MC, V.*

Along with piercing and the city's most exotic selection of jewelry, modern-primitive Adorned offers tattooing and mehndi designs.

### Venus Modern Body Arts

*199 E 4th St between Aves A and B (212-473-1954). Subway: F, V to Lower East Side–Second Ave. Sun–Thu 1–9pm; Fri, Sat 1–10pm. AmEx, Disc, MC, V.*

Venus has been tattooing and piercing New Yorkers since 1992, before body art became de rigueur. It offers an enormous selection of jewelry—diamonds in your navel and platinum in your tongue, anyone?

# Arts & Entertainment



## Feature boxes



**Stretching the pointe** NYC Ballet dancers Maria Kowroski and Albert Evans extend their skills in *Agon*.

# By Season

Spring, summer, fall or winter, something is always going on in New York City. Pick an event you like and book your trip.

Following are some of the city's popular annual happenings. Each chapter in the **Arts & Entertainment** section lists other seasonal events. Before you set out, you should confirm whether an event is still taking place.

## Spring

### St. Patrick's Day Parade

*Fifth Ave between 44th and 86th Sts (212-484-1222; www.nycvisit.com). Mar 17.*

New York becomes a sea of green for the annual Irish-American day, starting at 11am with the parade up Fifth Avenue and extending late into the night in bars all over the city.

### Ringling Bros. and Barnum & Bailey Circus Animal Parade

*34th St from the Queens-Midtown tunnel to Madison Square Garden, Seventh Ave at 32nd St. Late Mar–mid-April.*

Don't miss the free midnight parade of animals that opens and closes the show's run. For information on the circus, see page 296.

### Whitney Biennial

*See page 48 for listing.*

Every two years, the Whitney showcases what it deems to be the most important contemporary American art—regularly stirring up controversy. The next show will be held March through May 2004.

### New York International Auto Show

*Jacob K. Javits Convention Center, Eleventh Ave between 34th and 39th Sts; entrance on 35th St (800-282-3336; www.autoshowny.com). Subway: A, C, E to 34th St–Penn Station. Mid-April.*

More than 1,000 cars, trucks, SUVs and vans from the past, present and future are on display during this annual rite of spring.

### New York Antiquarian Book Fair

*Park Ave between 66th and 67th Sts (212-777-5218; www.sanfordsmith.com). Subway: 6 to 68th St–Hunter College. Mid-April.*

More than 200 international booksellers exhibit rare books, maps, manuscripts and more.



► For film festivals, see chapter **Film & TV**.

► For sports seasons, see chapter **Sports & Fitness**.

**Slow down, you move too fast** Bike New York riders are feelin' groovy as they pedal over the 59th Street Bridge into Queens.

### Easter Parade

*Fifth Ave between 49th and 57th Sts (212-484-1222; www.nycvisit.com). Subway: E, V to Fifth Ave–53rd St. Easter Sunday.*

The annual Easter Parade kicks off at 11am. Arrive early to secure a prime viewing spot around St. Patrick's Cathedral *(see page 91).*

### You Gotta Have Park

*Parks throughout the city (212-360-3456). May.*

This celebration of New York's public spaces takes place in the major parks of all five boroughs.

### Marijuana March

*Begins on Broadway at Houston St (212-677-7180; www.cures-not-wars.org). Subway: F, V, S to Broadway–Lafayette St; 6 to Bleecker St. First Saturday in May.*

This annual parade for pot legalization is sponsored by Cures Not Wars, an advocacy group devoted to alternative drug policies.

### Bike New York: The Great Five Boro Bike Tour

*Begins at Battery Park, finishes on Staten Island (212-932-2453; www.bikenewyork.org). Subway: 4, 5 to Bowling Green. Early May.*
Every year, thousands of cyclists take over the city for a 42-mile (68-kilometer) bike ride through the five boroughs. You must register in advance.

### Ninth Avenue International Food Festival

*Ninth Ave between 37th and 57th Sts (212-581-7029). Subway: A, C, E to 42nd St–Port Authority. Mid-May.*
Hundreds of stalls serve every type of food.

### Red Hook Waterfront Arts Festival

*Various locations, Red Hook, Brooklyn (718-287-2224). Subway: F, G to Carroll St or Smith–9th Sts. Mid-May.*
This annual open-air festival celebrates Red Hook's rebirth as an arts community with dance performances, poetry, music, public dancing, boat rides, workshops and food prepared by local vendors.

### Fleet Week

*See **Intrepid** Sea-Air-Space Museum, page 57, for listing. Last week in May.*
Hello sailor! Actually all branches of the military visit New York for this weeklong event honoring the armed forces. U.S. Navy vessels and ships from other countries cruise past the Statue of Liberty. Also, expect maneuvers, parachute drops and air displays.

### Lower East Side Festival of the Arts

*Theater for the New City, 155 First Ave at 10th St (212-254-1109; www.theaterforthenewcity.org). Subway: L to First Ave; 6 to Astor Pl. Last weekend in May.*
This celebration of the artistic diversity of the Lower East Side features performances by more than 20 theatrical troupes and appearances by local celebrities.

### Washington Square Outdoor Art Exhibit

*Various streets surrounding Washington Square Park (212-982-6255). Subway: A, C, E, F, V, S to W 4th St; N, R, W to 8th St–NYU. Late May or early June and late August.*
Since its inception in 1931, this outdoor exhibit has represented the vitality of New York City's emerging-art scene: one-of-a-kind crafts, graphics, paintings, photography, sculpture and watercolors.

## Summer

### Met in the Parks

*Staged at various locations (212-362-6000; www.metopera.org). June.*
The Metropolitan Opera presents two different operas at open-air evening concerts in Central Park and other parks throughout the five boroughs. The performances are free. To get a good seat, arrive several hours before the performance begins.

### Toyota Comedy Festival

*Various locations (888-33-TOYOTA; www.toyotacomedy.com). Early to mid-June.*
Hundreds of America's funniest men and women perform at venues around the city. The information line operates from May to mid-June only.

### JVC Jazz Festival

*Various locations (212-501-1390; www.festivalproductions.net). Mid-June.*
The JVC bash, a direct descendant of the original Newport Jazz Festival, is an NYC institution. Not only does the festival fill Carnegie and Avery Fisher Halls with big draws (Anita Baker, Ray Charles, Harry Connick Jr., Lena Horne), it also pays tribute to jazz's roots, hosting gigs in Harlem and at downtown clubs.

### Summer Restaurant Week

*Various locations (212-484-1222). Mid-June.*
You can get a three-course prix-fixe lunch at more than 100 of the city's best restaurants for the bargain price of $20.03 (the price reflects the year). For a list of participating restaurants, go to www.nycvisit.com and search for "restaurant week." You'll need to make reservations well in advance.

### Gay and Lesbian Pride March

*Begins on Fifth Ave at 52nd St, and heads south to Christopher St (212-807-7433; www.nycpride.org). Last Sunday in June.*

**Reeling** Awestruck audiences watch movies unspool at Bryant Park in summertime.

The Heritage of Pride organization rallies gays and lesbians to parade from midtown to Greenwich Village in commemoration of the 1969 Stonewall riots. Thousands of visitors come for the previous week's events, which include a packed club schedule and a dance party on the West Side piers.

### Midsummer Night Swing

*Lincoln Center Plaza, Broadway between 64th and 65th Sts (212-875-5766; www.lincolncenter.org). Subway: 1, 9 to 66th St–Lincoln Ctr. Late Jun–mid-Jul.*

Each night is devoted to a different style of dance, from swing to salsa. Performances are preceded by free dance lessons.

### Celebrate Brooklyn! Performing Arts Festival

*Prospect Park Bandshell, 9th St at Prospect Park West, Park Slope, Brooklyn (718-855-7882; www.celebratebrooklyn.org). Subway: F to Seventh Ave. Late Jun–late Aug Thu–Sat.*

Free outdoor events—music, dance, film and spoken word—are presented in Brooklyn's answer to Central Park. Admission is charged for a few benefit shows.

### Bryant Park Free Summer Season

*Bryant Park, Sixth Ave at 42nd St (212-768-4242; www.bryantpark.org). Subway: B, D, F, V to 42nd St; 7 to Fifth Ave. Jun–Aug.*

This park has a packed season of free classical music, jazz, dance and film. Best of all are the Monday-night al fresco movies.

### Central Park SummerStage

*Rumsey Playfield, Central Park, entrance on Fifth Ave at 72nd St (212-360-2777; www.summerstage.org). Subway: 6 to 77th St. Jun–Aug.*

Enjoy free afternoon concerts featuring a wide variety of music; admission is charged for a few benefit shows.

### River to River Festival

*Various venues on the west side of Manhattan, along the Hudson River (www.rivertorivernyc.org). Jun–Sept.*

Lower Manhattan organizations band together to present more than 500 free concerts and performances throughout the summer. The **Hudson River Festival** *(212-528-2733; www.hudsonriverfestival.com)* is part of this larger production and offers visual-arts shows, theater, dance and family events.

> ▶ See Around Town in ***Time Out New York*** for more seasonal events.
> ▶ Go to **www.timeoutny.com** and click on This Week's Pick's for *TONY* critics' picks for each day of the week.
> ▶ **NYC & Company** *(www.nycvisit.com)*, the convention and visitors' bureau, has additional info.

### Mermaid Parade

*Coney Island, Brooklyn (718-372-5159; www.coneyisland.com). Subway: W to Coney Island–Stillwell Ave. First Saturday after summer solstice.*

Coney Island's annual showcase of bizarreness consists of elaborate floats, paraders dressed as sea creatures and other kitschy celebrations. Call for details as the parade location varies from year to year.

### New York Shakespeare Festival

*See page 335 for listing.*

This free festival is one of the highlights of a Manhattan summer, with big-name stars pulling on their tights for a whack at the Bard. There are two plays each year, with at least one written by Shakespeare.

### Nathan's Famous Fourth of July Hot Dog Eating Contest

*Nathan's Famous, 1310 Surf Ave at Stillwell Ave, Coney Island, Brooklyn (718-946-2202). Subway: W to Coney Island–Stillwell Ave. Jul 4.*

The winner of this Coney Island showdown is the man or woman who can stuff the most wieners down his or her gullet in 12 minutes.

### Macy's Fireworks Display

*Location to be announced (212-494-4495). Jul 4 at 9:15pm.*

The highlight of Independence Day is this spectacular fireworks display. Look up in wonder as $1 million worth of pyrotechnics light up the night.

### Lincoln Center Festival

*See page 320 for listing.* *July.*

Dance, music, theater, opera and more are all part of this ambitious festival.

### New York Philharmonic Concerts

*Various locations (212-875-5709; www.newyorkphilharmonic.org). Jul, Aug.*

The New York Philharmonic presents a varied program of classical music in many of New York's larger parks. The bugs are just part of the deal.

### Seaside Summer and Martin Luther King Concert Series

*Brighton Beach, Brooklyn (718-469-1912). Travel: F to Ave X, then free shuttle bus to W 8th St–NY Aquarium. Jul, Aug.*

Free funk, soul and gospel acts perform near the water's edge in Brighton Beach.

### Mostly Mozart

*Avery Fisher Hall, Lincoln Center, 65th St at Columbus Ave (212-875-5399; www.lincolncenter.org). Subway: 1, 9 to 66th St–Lincoln Ctr. Late Jul–Aug.*

The Mostly Mozart festival mounts an intensive four-week schedule of works by the genius and his fellow wig-wearers.

### New York International Fringe Festival

*Various downtown locations (212-420-8877; www.fringenyc.org). August.*

**Teeny wienie winner** The diminutive Takeru Kobayashi triumphed in Nathan's 2002 hot dog eating contest by consuming 50 ½ franks.

The Fringe Festival is a major venue for up-and-coming talent in the performing-arts world; the Broadway hit *Urinetown* had its humble beginning here.

### Central Park Zoo Chill Out Weekend

*Central Park Wildlife Center, entrance on Fifth Ave at 64th St (212-861-6030). Subway: N, R, W to Fifth Ave–59th St. Early August.*

Stay cool on a hot day and check on the polar bears and penguins during Central Park Zoo's annual two-day party.

### Harlem Week

*Throughout Harlem (212-862-8477; www.harlemdiscover.com). Subway: B, C, 2, 3 to 135th St. Early to mid-August.*

The largest black and Latino festival in the world features music, film, dance, fashion and sports.

### U.S. Open

*For listing, see page 326.*

This Grand Slam event is one of the most entertaining tournaments on the international tennis circuit. Tickets are hard to come by for the later rounds.

### West Indian–American Day Carnival

*Eastern Pkwy from Utica Ave to Grand Army Plaza, Prospect Park, Brooklyn (718-625-1515). Subway: 3, 4 to Crown Hts–Utica Ave. Labor Day weekend.*

This energetic celebration of Caribbean culture includes steel drum performances all weekend, a children's parade on Saturday and a massive march of flamboyantly costumed revelers on Labor Day.

## Fall

### Downtown Arts Festival

*Various lower Manhattan locations (212-243-5050; www.downtownarts.org). September.*

This mammoth event offers art exhibitions, gallery tours, performance-art happenings, experimental video shows and readings.

### Broadway on Broadway

*43rd St at Broadway (212-768-1560). Subway: N, Q, R, W, S, 1, 2, 3, 9, 7 to 42nd St–Times Sq. Early or mid-September.*

The season's new theatrical productions offer a sneak preview right in the middle of Times Square.

### New York Is Book Country

*Various locations (www.nyisbookcountry.com). Mid- to late September.*

This literary festival ends with a massive street fair on Fifth Avenue from 48th to 57th Streets.

### Feast of San Gennaro

*Mulberry St from Canal to Houston Sts (212-768-9320; www.sangennaro.org). Subway: J, M, Z, N, Q, R, W, 6 to Canal St. Mid-September.*

This celebration honors the patron saint of Naples and offers game booths, rides and tons of Italian food.

### BARC's Annual Dog Parade, Show and Fair

*Begins on Wythe Ave at North 1st St, Williamsburg, Brooklyn (718-486-7489; www.barcshelter.org). Subway: L to Bedford Ave. Mid-October.*

The Brooklyn Animal Resource Coalition hosts this lovable mutt of a parade. At the dog show, pups vie for awards such as "best butt" and "best kisser."

### Dumbo Art Under the Bridge

*Various locations in Dumbo, Brooklyn (718-624-0831; www.dumboartscenter.org). Subway: A, C to High St; F to York St. Mid-October.*

Dumbo (Down Under the Manhattan Bridge Overpass) becomes one big art happening for a weekend, with open studios, DJs, fashion shows and dance, film, music and theater events.

### CMJ Music Marathon, MusicFest and FilmFest

*Various venues (917-606-1908; www.cmj.com). Late October.*

Bands play rock, indie rock, hip-hop, electronica and more during this industry schmoozefest hosted by trade publisher *College Music Journal*.

**White-elephant sale** Babar charms children with stories of his travels while browsers track down publishing novelties, rarities and bargains at the New York Is Book Country fair.



### Big Apple Circus

See page 296. Late Oct–early Jan.

### Village Halloween Parade

*Sixth Ave from Spring to 22nd Sts (www.halloween-nyc.com). Oct 31 at 7pm.*
Anyone can participate in this parade—just wear a costume and line up at the beginning of the route at 6pm with the rest of the fascinating characters.

### New York City Marathon

*Begins on the Staten Island side of the Verrazano-Narrows Bridge (212-860-4455; www.nycmarathon.org). First Sunday in November at 10:50am.*
A crowd of 30,000 marathoners runs through all five boroughs over a 26.2-mile (42-kilometer) course. The race ends at Central Park's Tavern on the Green.

### Macy's Thanksgiving Day Parade

*Central Park West at 77th St to Macy's, Broadway at 34th St (212-695-4400). Thanksgiving Day at 9am.*
The parade features enormous, inflated cartoon-character balloons, elaborate floats and Santa Claus. Stop by the inflation area the afternoon before to watch the balloons take shape on 77th and 81st Streets, between Central Park West and Columbus Avenue.

## Winter

### *The Nutcracker*

*New York State Theater, Lincoln Center, 63rd St at Columbus Ave (212-870-5570; www.lincolncenter.org). Subway: 1, 9 to 66th St–Lincoln Ctr. Thanksgiving–first week of January.*
The New York City Ballet's performance of this famous work, assisted by children from the School of American Ballet, is a much-loved Christmas tradition *(see also* **New York State Theater**, *page 344).*

### Radio City Christmas Spectacular

*Radio City Music Hall, 1260 Sixth Ave at 50th St (212-247-4777). Subway: B, D, F, V to 47–50th Sts–Rockefeller Ctr. Nov–early Jan.*
This famous long-running show features the fabulous high-kicking Rockettes.

### Christmas Tree-Lighting Ceremony

*Rockefeller Plaza, near Fifth Ave between 49th and 50th Sts (212-332-7654). Subway: B, D, F, V to 47–50th Sts–Rockefeller Ctr. First week of December.*
Five miles of lights festoon a giant evergreen in front of the GE Building. The tree, ice skaters and shimmering statue of Prometheus make this the city's most enchanting Christmas spot.

### *Messiah* Sing-In

*Avery Fisher Hall, Lincoln Center, 65th St at Columbus Ave (212-333-5333). Subway: 1, 9 to 66th St–Lincoln Ctr. Mid-December.*
About a week before Christmas, the National Choral Council rounds up 17 conductors to lead huge audiences in a rehearsal and performance of Handel's *Messiah*. No experience is necessary, and you can buy the score on-site. Call for date and time.

### New Year's Eve Ball Drop

*Times Square (212-768-1560; www.timessquarebid.org). Subway: N, Q, R, W, S, 1, 2, 3, 9, 7 to 42nd St–Times Sq. Dec 31.*
A traditional New York year ends and begins in Times

Square, culminating with the dropping of the ball. If teeming hordes of drunken revelers turn you on, by all means go. Expect very tight security.

### New Year's Eve Fireworks

*Central Park (212-423-2284; www.nyrrc.org). Dec 31.*
The best viewing points for this display are Central Park West at 72nd Street, Tavern on the Green and Fifth Avenue at 90th Street. The festivities, including dancing and a costume contest, start at 10pm, and the fireworks explode at midnight.

### New Year's Eve Midnight Run

*Starts at Tavern on the Green, Central Park West at 67th St (212-423-2284; www.nyrrc.org). Subway: B, C to 72nd St; 1, 9 to 66th St–Lincoln Ctr. Dec 31.*
A four-mile jaunt through the park, the run also features a masquerade parade, a pre- and post-race live DJ, fireworks *(see above)*, prizes and a champagne toast at the run's halfway mark.

### New Year's Day Marathon Poetry Reading

*See* **The Poetry Project at St. Mark's Church**, *page 268 for listing.* *Jan 1.*
Big-name bohemians such as Patti Smith and Richard Hell traditionally grace the stage for this all-day spectacle of poetry, music, dance and performance art.

### Winter Antiques Show

*Seventh Regiment Armory, Park Ave at 67th St (718-665-5250; www.winterantiquesshow.com). Subway: 6 to 68th St–Hunter College. Mid-January.*
The city's most prestigious antiques fair offers items ranging from ancient works to Art Nouveau.

### Outsider Art Fair

*The Puck Building, 295 Lafayette St at Houston St (212-777-5218; www.sanfordsmith.com). Subway: F, V, S to Broadway–Lafayette St; 6 to Bleecker St. Late January.*
This three-day extravaganza draws buyers and browsers from all over the world. The fair's 35 dealers exhibit outsider, self-taught and visionary art in all media, at prices ranging from $500 to $350,000.

### Winter Restaurant Week

See **Summer Restaurant Week**, page 251. Late January.

### Chinese New Year

*Around Mott St, Chinatown (212-226-6280; www.nycvisit). Subway: J, M, Z, N, Q, R, W, 6 to Canal St. First day of the full moon between Jan 21 and Feb 19.*
The city's Chinese population celebrates the lunar new year in style, with dragon parades, performers and delicious food throughout Chinatown. Unfortunately, private fireworks were banned in 1995, so the celebrations don't have quite the bang they once did.

### Empire State Building Run-Up

*Empire State Building, 350 Fifth Ave at 34th St (212-860-4455; www.nyrrc.org). Subway: B, D, F, V, N, Q, R, W to 34th St–Herald Sq; 6 to 33rd St. Early February.*
This New York Road Runners race goes up the 1,576 steps from the lobby to the 86th floor, a distance of .3 kilometers.

### The Art Show

*Seventh Regiment Armory, Park Ave at 67th St (212-940-8590; www.artdealers.org). Subway: 6 to 68th St–Hunter College. Late February.*
This is one of New York's largest art fairs. Exhibitors offer paintings, prints and sculptures dating from the 17th century to the present. Proceeds go to the Henry Street Settlement, a Lower East Side arts and social-services agency.

### International Artexpo

*Jacob K. Javits Convention Center, Eleventh Ave between 34th and 39th Sts, entrance on 37th St (888-322-5226; www.artexpos.com). Subway: A, C, E to 34th St–Penn Station. Late February or early March.*
The Artexpo is the world's largest art exhibition and sale. It features original artwork, fine-art prints, limited-edition lithographs and more, by thousands of artists, from Picasso to photographer Monte Nagler.

### The Armory Show

*Piers 88 and 90, Twelfth Ave between 48th and 50th Sts (212-645-6440). Subway: C, E to 50th St. Early March.*
This international arts festival changed the course of art history in 1913, and is still one of the biggest on the avant-garde calendar. It showcases visual groundbreakers from galleries around the world.

**Handel, with care** Avery Fisher Hall is the site of an annual *Messiah* sing-along.

# Art Galleries

From Brooklyn to Harlem, New York's art scene is as vibrant and vital as ever

Like food lovers weighing the city's limitless dining possibilities, art connoisseurs in New York can find just about whatever they desire. For those who want visual comfort food, uptown's emporiums are filled with works by the old masters: Drop in to any of 57th Street's big-name galleries for a host of haute options. Chelsea is the white-hot center of the trendy and experimental. And the smaller wallet-friendly venues in Williamsburg, Brooklyn, are the equivalent of take-out: Stop in for a taste, or maybe grab something to go.

You can see art for free in almost every corner of the city. Galleries are popping up all over—in scruffy Long Island City, in the Meatpacking hinterland of the West Village, in revitalized Harlem—even on the Brooklyn waterfront in Dumbo (Down Under the Manhattan Bridge Overpass).

Gallerygoers should check the weekly listings and reviews in *Time Out New York* and the Friday and Sunday editions of *The New York Times*. For unopinionated (but more extensive) listings, pick up a monthly *Art Now Gallery Guide* (free for the asking at most galleries or $3 at museum bookstores).

Opening times listed are for September to May or June. Summer visitors should note that from late June to early September, most galleries are open only on weekdays, and some close for the month of August. Call before visiting.

## Soho

Soho was once Disneyland for art lovers; today, it's largely the province of high-end furniture and retail stores. But there are still quite a few notable galleries, including several important nonprofit outfits *(see page 264)*. What follows is a selection of must-sees.
*Subway: A, C, E, J, M, Z, Q, W, 1, 9 to Canal St; N, R, W to Prince St; 6 to Spring St.*

► For weekly reviews and listings, pick up a copy of ***Time Out New York***.
► If you want to view larger collections of art, see chapter **Museums**.
► For more cultural sights, see section **Sightseeing**.

### Deitch Projects

*18 Wooster St between Canal and Grand Sts (212-941-9475). Tue–Sat noon–6pm. Call for summer hours.*
Jeffrey Deitch is an art-world impresario whose Wooster Street gallery features live spectacles almost as often as it presents large-scale works by new artists in virtually all media, including sculpture, fashion, music and film. The Grand Street space focuses on elaborate, provocative multimedia installations from buzz-worthy artists, as well as new painting exhibits. The Williamsburg gallery is the most recent addition. **Other locations** ● *76 Grand St between Greene and Wooster Sts (212-343-7300). Subway: A, C, E to Canal St. Tue–Sun noon–6pm.* ● *110 North 1st St between Berry St and Wythe Ave, Williamsburg, Brooklyn (phone TBA). Subway: L to Bedford Ave. Thu–Sun 1–7pm.*

### Leo Koenig, Inc.

*249 Centre St between Broome and Grand Sts (212-334-9255). Tue–Fri 10am–6pm. August by appointment.*
A happening site on the eastern edge of Soho, Leo Koenig, Inc. made a splash when it opened three years ago with young painters such as Jeff Elrod, Erik Parker and Lisa Ruyter. It's been running at the front of the pack ever since.

### Nolan/Eckman

*560 Broadway at Prince St, sixth floor (212-925-6190). Sept–Jun Tue–Fri 10am–6pm; Sat 11am–6pm. Summer by appointment only.*
Small but serious Nolan/Eckman exudes a welcome warmth and primarily shows work on paper by major contemporaries like Carroll Dunham, Jim Nutt, Sigmar Polke and Peter Saul.

### Ronald Feldman Fine Arts

*31 Mercer St between Canal and Grand Sts (212-226-3232; www.feldmangallery.com). Sept–Jun Tue–Sat 10am–6pm. Jul, Aug Mon–Thu 10am–6pm; Fri 10am–3pm.*
This Soho pioneer has brought us landmark shows of legendary avant-gardists such as Eleanor Antin, Joseph Beuys, Leon Golub and Hannah Wilke. There are also current favorites, like painters Nancy Chunn and Carl Fudge.

## Chelsea

Chelsea has the city's greatest concentration of galleries. No fan of contemporary art should miss it. The neighborhood's distinctive architecture and amazing gallery spaces are fun

**Surreal estate** For elaborate, thought-provoking art, check out Soho's Deitch Projects.

for even the casual art lover. Several former warehouses—most notably those at 529 West 20th Street and 526 West 26th Street—hold multiple galleries, and there are many more on nearly every block between West 19th and West 29th Streets. Keep in mind that the subway takes you only as far as Eighth Avenue—you'll have to walk at least one long avenue farther to get to the galleries. Otherwise, take the M23 crosstown bus or catch a cab.
*Subway: A to 14th St; C, E to 23rd St; L to Eighth Ave; 1, 9 to 14th, 18th, 23rd Sts.*

### Andrea Rosen Gallery

*525 W 24th St between Tenth and Eleventh Aves (212-627-6000). Sept–Jun Tue–Sat 10am–6pm. Call for summer hours.*
This is the venue that shined a light on John Currin's unsettling romantics, Wolfgang Tillmans' uneasy fashion photos, and Andrea Zittel's compact model homes. Recent additions like Craig Kalpakjian and Matthew Ritchie make the future look brighter still.

### Andrew Kreps Gallery

*516A W 20th St between Tenth and Eleventh Aves (212-741-8849). Sept–Jul Tue–Sat 11am–6pm.*
Among the radicals in Kreps' adventurous stable are Ricci Albenda, Roe Ethridge, Robert Melee and Ruth Root.

### Anton Kern Gallery

*532 W 20th St between Tenth and Eleventh Aves (212-965-1706). Sept–Jul Tue–Sat 10am–6pm.*
The son of artist Georg Baselitz, Kern presents young American and European artists whose futuristic, sometimes melancholy installations have provided the New York art scene with some of its most visionary shows. Stop in for the unbounded likes of Kai Althoff, Jim Lambie, Sarah Jones, Michael Joo, and scary Monica Bonvicini.

### Casey Kaplan

*416 W 14th St between Ninth and Tenth Aves (212-645-7335). Sept–Jun Tue–Sat 10am–6pm. Jul Mon–Fri 10am–6pm. Closed August.*
One of the first to settle in the increasingly fashionable Meatpacking District, this gallery is one of the hot spots on the downtown map, introducing work by photographers Amy Adler and Anna Gaskell, and sculpture artists Liam Gillick and Carsten Holler, among others.

### Cheim & Read

*547 W 25th St between Tenth and Eleventh Aves (212-242-7727). Tue–Sat 10am–6pm. Summer Tue–Fri 10am–6pm.*
Louise Bourgeois and Jenny Holzer are examples of the high-profile artists that John Cheim and Howard Read showcase in their impressive new gallery. Look for a high concentration of photographers as well as

# THE STUDIO MUSEUM IN HARLEM

144 West 125th Street, New York City • 212.864.4500 • www.studiomuseum.org

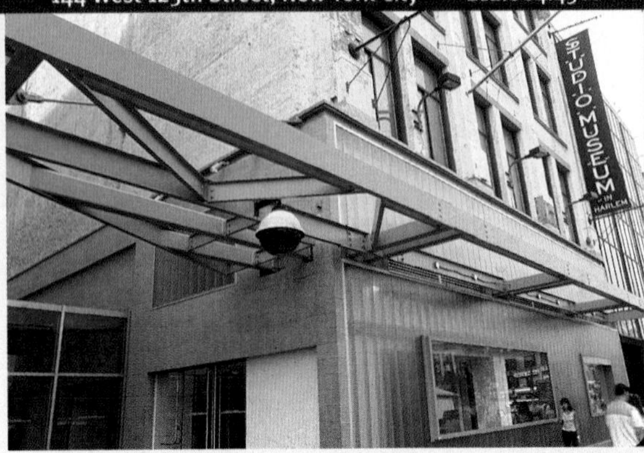


Photo: Adam Reich

# EXHIBITIONS

## Spring 2003: Apr 23–June 29

### Frederick J. Brown: Portraits in Jazz, Blues, and Other Icons

Over the past 30 years, Frederick J. Brown has been a driving force reclaiming figuration's importance after an epoch of minimalism and abstraction. His work celebrates individuals who have shaped and directed American cultural life, such as Stagger Lee, John Henry, Crazy Horse, Geronimo and Martin Luther King. This exhibition will draw together over 40 of Brown's most inimitable paintings, demonstrating his impact as one of our culture's most prominent and prolific portrait painters and creative geniuses. Curated by **LOWERY STOKES SIMS,** *Frederick J. Brown* is organized by the Kemper Museum of Contemporary Art, Kansas City, MO. Catalogue available.

## Summer 2003: July 16–Sept 28

### Harlem Envisioned

(working title)

Organized by **THELMA GOLDEN,** this exhibition will examine Harlem as a changing landscape. For over two centuries, the communities and histories of Harlem have evolved in a variety of ways. For *Harlem Envisioned*, The Studio Museum will invite several of today's most compelling African-American architects to present ideas and proposals for multiple sites around Harlem. These practitioners will contemplate Harlem as a cultural, architectural, territorial, psychological, historic, and economic site. The exhibition will include a presentation of these projects not only through traditional model and plan forms, but also through photography, video, digital media, and installation.

### From the Studio: Artists-in-Residence 2002-2003

This annual exhibition will feature the work of **LOUIS CAMERON, DEBORAH GRANT,** and **MICKALENE THOMAS.** Conceived at the formation of the Museum over 30 years ago, the A-I-R program and exhibition remain central to SMH's identity. Distinguished alumni include Chakaia Booker, David Hammons, Kerry James Marshall, Julie Mehretu and Nari Ward. Catalogue brochure available.

The Artist-in-Residence Program is made possible by major support from The Andrea Frank Foundation. Generous support was also provided by The Rockefeller Brothers Fund, The Peter Norton Family Foundation, The Greenwall Foundation, Dedalus Foundation, The Helena Rubinstein Foundation, Jerome Foundation, The R and B Feder Charitable Foundation for the Beaux Arts, and Sun Hill Foundation.

## Fall 2003: Oct 15-Jan 4, 2004

### Black Belt

Curated by **CHRISTINE Y. KIM,** *Black Belt* will feature 22 contemporary artists of diverse backgrounds reflecting on the intersection of Black and Asian American cultures through a shared and oftentimes conflicting fascination with Bruce Lee, Kung Fu and Eastern martial arts. Growing up in the 70s and 80s, the artists touch on the emergence of multicultural spaces that disrupted political ideologies of the 60s, and that preceded the discouses of critical race theory, multiculturalism and identity politics of the 90s. The exhibition will feature work in various media—sculpture, painting, drawing, photography and video—and includes site-specific installations. Catalogue available.

# Education & Public Programs

In conjunction with exhibitions on view, the SMH Department of Education & Public Programs offers a range of programs, activities and events that engages a cross section of artists, writers, scholars, and critics who share diverse perspectives.

**Where the wild things are** Anton Kern Gallery presents visionary young talents such as Michael Joo, who introduced art lovers to *The Pack* in 2002.

contemporary painters and sculptors like Pat Steir and Lynda Benglis.

### David Zwirner

*525 W 19th St between Tenth and Eleventh Aves (212-727-2070). Sept–May Tue–Sat 10am–6pm. Summer Mon–Fri 10am–6pm.*

This maverick German expatriate's shop recently moved to spiffy new quarters, taking its head-turning roster of international contemporaries with it, including Stan Douglas, Marcel Dzama, Toba Khedoori, Jockum Nordstrum, Raymond Pettibon, Diana Thater, Jason Rhoades and Thomas Ruff.

### Gagosian Gallery

*555 W 24th St between Tenth and Eleventh Aves (212-741-1111; www.gagosian.com). Sept–Jun Tue–Sat 10am–6pm. Call for summer hours.*

Larry Gagosian's mammoth (20,000-square-foot) contribution to 24th Street's row of top-level galleries (for the uptown location, *see page 262*) was launched in 1999 with a thrilling Richard Serra show. Follow-ups have featured exhibitions with works from Ellen Gallagher, Damien Hirst, Anselm Kiefer, Ed Ruscha, Julian Schnabel and Andy Warhol. The annual summer display of refreshing new video art is also a high point, but whatever is offered, expect something big and breathtaking.

### Gorney Bravin + Lee

*534 W 26th St between Tenth and Eleventh Aves (212-352-8372). Sept–Jun Tue–Sat 10am–6pm. Jul Tue–Fri 10am–6pm. August by appointment only.*

This friendly gallery's attention-getting stable of contemporary artists, especially strong in photography and sculpture, includes Sarah Charlesworth, Justine Kurland, Catherine Opie, James Siena, Jessica Stockholder, Gillian Wearing and James Welling.

### Greene/Naftali

*526 W 26th St between Tenth and Eleventh Aves, eighth floor (212-463-7770). Tue–Sat 10am–6pm. Call for summer hours.*

Wonderful light, a spectacular view and a history of rock 'em–sock 'em group shows of a Conceptualist nature characterize this gallery. Its international mixed-media roster includes Jacqueline Humphries, Daniel Pflumm, Blake Rayne and Daniela Rossell.

### James Cohan Gallery

*533 W 26th St between Tenth and Eleventh Aves (212-741-9500; www.jamescohan.com). Tue–Sat 10am–6pm. Jun, Jul Tue–Fri 10am–6pm. Closed August.*

Cohan recently moved his 57th Street operation into this onetime garage, where he's already a neighborhood standout with forward-looking artists such as Trenton Doyle Hancock, Richard Long, Roxy Paine, Fred Tomaselli and Bill Viola.

### Klemens Gasser & Tanja Grunert, Inc.

*524 W 19th St between Tenth and Eleventh Aves (212-807-9494). Tue–Sat 10am–6pm. Call for summer hours.*

Transplants from the vital Cologne art scene, Grunert and husband Grasser continue presenting contemporary American and European artists. The video works are among the best in town.

### Mary Boone Gallery

*541 W 24th St between Tenth and Eleventh Aves (212-752-2929; www.maryboonegallery.com). Tue–Fri 9am–6pm; Sat 10am–5pm.*

See page 261 for review.

### Matthew Marks Gallery

*523 W 24th St between Tenth and Eleventh Aves (212-243-0200; www.matthewmarks.com). Sept–May Tue–Sat 10am–6pm. Jun–Aug Mon–Fri 10am–6pm.*

The Matthew Marks Gallery was a driving force behind Chelsea's transformation into an art destination and it remains one of the neighborhood's biggest draws, with two major spaces: on 24th Street, a 9,000-square-foot, two-story locale; on 22nd Street, a beautifully lit, glass-faced converted garage. Both showcase some of the most influential artists in the Western world, including Lucian Freud, Nan Goldin, Andreas Gursky, Gary Hume, Ellsworth Kelly, Willem de Kooning, Brice Mardin, Ugo Rondinone and Weegee.
**Other location** • *522 W 22nd St between Tenth and Eleventh Aves (212-243-1650). Sept–May Tue–Sat 11am–6pm. Jun–Aug Mon–Fri 11am–6pm.*

### Murray Guy

*453 W 17th St between Ninth and Tenth Aves, second floor (212-463-7372; www.murrayguy.com). Tue–Sat 10am–6pm. August by appointment only.*
The dynamic Margaret Murray and Janice Guy mount elegant shows featuring artists such as Fiona Banner, Matthew Buckingham, Francis Cape, Munro Galloway and Beat Streuli. Painted wood floors, pleasant personalities and human-scale rooms offer a refreshing change from the gargantuan, impersonal spaces that are the norm in Chelsea.

### PaceWildenstein

*534 W 25th St between Tenth and Eleventh Aves (212-929-7000). Sept–May Tue–Fri 9:30am–6pm; Sat 10am–6pm. Jun, Jul Mon–Thu 10am–5pm; Fri 10am–4pm. Closed August.*
This welcoming downtown branch of the famous 57th Street gallery houses grand-scale installations by big-time contemporaries like Georg Baselitz, Chuck Close, Philip-Lorca DiCorcia, Alex Katz, Sol LeWitt, Elizabeth Murray and Kiki Smith, in a space designed by artist Robert Irwin. (For the 57th Street location, *see page 261.*)

### Paula Cooper Gallery

*534 W 21st St between Tenth and Eleventh Aves (212-255-1105). Sept–May Tue–Sat 10am–6pm. Jun–Aug Mon–Fri 10am–5pm.*
Cooper was the first to open a gallery in Soho, and as an early West Chelsea settler, built an impressive art temple. Now she's opened a second space across the street. Cooper is known for showing off Minimalist and Conceptual work. Artists whose careers have flourished on her watch include sculptors Tony Smith, Carl Andre, Donald Judd and Sherrie Levine, and photographers Zoe Leonard and Andres Serrano.
**Other location** • *521 W 21st St between Tenth and Eleventh Aves (212-255-5247). Sept–May Tue–Sat 11am–5pm. Jun–Aug Mon–Fri 10am–5pm.*

### Paul Morris Gallery

*465 W 23rd St between Ninth and Tenth Aves (212-727-2752; www.paulmorrisgallery.com). Sept–Jun Tue–Sat 11am–6pm. Jul, Aug Mon–Fri 11am–6pm.*
Paul Morris may have one of Chelsea's rare shoe-box galleries, but the talents on display are plenty large, especially photographers such as Esko Männikkö, Tracey Moffatt and Arnold Odermatt, and superior draftsmen Robert Crumb and Ewan Gibbs.

### Postmasters Gallery

*459 W 19th St between Ninth and Tenth Aves (212-727-3323; www.postmastersart.com). Sept–Jul Tue–Sat 11am–6pm.*
Postmasters is an intriguing international gallery run by Magdalena Sawon, who presents decidedly

**Live from New York...** Postmasters Gallery showcases multimedia creations from the likes of Wolfgang Staehle, whose *2001* included a real-time feed from lower Manhattan.

techno-savvy art, most of which has Conceptualist leanings, in sculpture, painting, new media and installation. Some of her brighter spots include Diana Cooper, Christian Schumann, Wolfgang Staehle and Claude Wampler.

### Robert Miller Gallery

*524 W 26th St between Tenth and Eleventh Aves (212-366-4774; www.robertmillergallery.com). Sept–May Tue–Sat 10am–6pm. Call for summer hours.*
This former 57th Street stalwart often shows work you might expect to see at a museum: Al Held, Lee Krasner, Joan Mitchell, Alice Neel and Philip Pearlstein, as well as photographers John Clarence Laughlin, Renee Cox and Bruce Weber.

### Sean Kelly

*528 W 29th St between Tenth and Eleventh Aves (212-239-1181; www.skny.com). Sept–Jun Tue–Sat 11am–6pm. Jul–mid-Aug Mon–Fri 10am–5pm.*
This Brit expat's project-oriented gallery offers exhibitions by established Conceptualists, including Marina Abramovic, Ann Hamilton and Lorna Simpson, as well as younger talents James Casebere and Frank Theil.

### Sonnabend Gallery

*536 W 22nd St between Tenth and Eleventh Aves (212-627-1018). Sept–Jul Tue–Sat 10am–6pm. August by appointment only.*
This elegant old standby in a museumlike space is a reliable retreat. Look for strong new work from John Baldessari, Ashley Bickerton, Gilbert & George, Candida Hofer, Jeff Koons, Haim Steinbach and Matthew Weinstein.

### 303 Gallery

*525 W 22nd St between Tenth and Eleventh Aves (212-255-1121; www.303gallery.com). Tue–Sat 10am–6pm. Call for summer hours.*
To experience essential contemporary art, one must visit 303, a space showcasing critically acclaimed artists who work in a variety of media—photographers Thomas Demand and Collier Schorr, sculptor Daniel Oates and painters Inka Essenhigh, Karen Kilimnik and Sue Williams, just to name a few.

## 57th Street

The home of Carnegie Hall, Tiffany & Co., Bergdorf Goodman and a number of art galleries, 57th Street is a beehive of cultural and commercial activity—expensive, lively and chic.
*Subway: E, V to Fifth Ave–53rd St; F, V to 57th St; N, R, W to Fifth Ave–59th St; 4, 5, 6 to 59th St.*

### Artemis Greenberg Van Doren Gallery

*730 Fifth Ave at 57th St, seventh floor (212-445-0444). Tue–Sat 10am–6pm. Summer Mon–Fri 10am–5:30pm.*
It may sound like a law firm, but this gallery shows established artists such as Jennifer Bartlett and David Hammons, plus younger talent like painters Benjamin Edwards and Lane Twichell and photographers Katy Grannan, Malerie Marder and Jessica Craig-Martin.

### Galeria Ramis Barquet

*41 E 57th St between Madison and Park Aves (212-644-9090; www.ramisbarquet.com) Mon–Fri 10am–6pm; Saturday by appointment. Summer Mon–Fri 10am–5:30pm.*
Located in a famous midtown gallery building, this operation shows prominent South American artists such as Marco Arce, Marta Maria Peréz Bravo, Ernesto Pujol and Betsabee Romero.

### Marian Goodman Gallery

*24 W 57th St between Fifth and Sixth Aves, fourth floor (212-977-7160; www.mariangoodmann.com). Mon–Sat 10am–6pm. Closed August.*
This is one of the finest galleries in town, offering a host of world-renowned names, including Christian Boltanski, Maurizio Cattelan, Gabriel Orozco, Gerhard Richter, Thomas Struth and Jeff Wall. You haven't truly experienced the New York art scene until you've visited Marian Goodman.

### Mary Boone

*745 Fifth Ave between 57th and 58th Sts, fourth floor (212-752-2929; www.maryboonegallery.com). Tue–Sat 10am–6pm.*
This onetime Soho celeb continues to produce hit shows on 57th, featuring young artists. But her prize possession is her newer gallery in Chelsea *(see page 259)*, where the list of star attractions includes established players like Ross Bleckner, Peter Halley, Barbara Kruger and hipster Damian Loeb.

### PaceWildenstein

*32 E 57th St between Madison and Park Aves (212-421-3292). Sept–May Tue–Fri 9:30am–6pm; Sat 10am–5:00pm. Call for summer hours.*
For some of the 20th century's most significant art stalwarts, head for this institution, where you'll find pieces by Chuck Close, Agnes Martin, Pablo Picasso, Ad Reinhardt, Mark Rothko and Lucas Samaras, along with Elizabeth Murray and Kiki Smith. Pace Prints and Primitives, at the same location, publishes works on paper—from old masters to big-name contemporaries—and keeps a fine collection of African art. (For the Chelsea branch, *see page 260.*)

## Upper East Side

Many galleries on the Upper East Side sell masterpieces to millionaires. Still, anyone can look for free; many pieces are treasures that could vanish from public view for years to come. Check the auction-house ads in *The New York Times,* the art monthlies or on the Web for viewing schedules of important private collections before they go on the block.
*Subway: 6 to 68th St–Hunter College or 77th St.*

### C & M Arts

*45 E 78th St at Madison Ave (212-861-0020; www.c-m-arts.com). Tue–Sat 10am–5:30pm. Summer Mon–Fri 10am–5:30pm.*

If you'd like to view or study the works of historic figures like Joseph Cornell, Willem de Kooning, Jackson Pollock, Mark Rothko and Andy Warhol, check out this major player in the secondary-art market.

### Gagosian Gallery

*980 Madison Ave at 76th St (212-744-2313; www.gagosian.com). Tue–Sat 10am–6pm. Summer Mon–Fri 10am–6pm.*

During the 1980s, Larry Gagosian was a force to be reckoned with in the world of contemporary art. Today, he's just as important to the scene. Francesco Clemente, Damien Hirst, Richard Serra and new stars Cecily Brown and Jenny Saville are all regularly featured artists. Gagosian has also succeeded in the resale market and maintains a premier exhibition space in Chelsea *(seepage 259).*

### Mitchell-Innes & Nash

*1018 Madison Ave between 77th and 78th Sts, fifth floor (212-744-7400; www.miandn.com). Tue–Sat 10am–5pm. Summer Mon–Fri 10am–5pm. Call for hours in August.*

This five-year-old gallery is run by two former Sotheby's specialists with an ambitious program in Impressionist, modern and contemporary works. Artists include Max Beckmann, Edgar Degas and Kojo Griffin. It's an interesting (and high-priced) collection.

### M. Knoedler & Co.

*19 E 70th St between Fifth and Madison Aves (212-794-0550). Sept–May Mon–Fri 9:30am–5:30pm; Sat 10am–5:30pm. Jun–Aug Mon–Sat 9:30am–5:30pm.*

The longest-running gallery in New York represents museum-quality Abstractionists and Pop artists, including Helen Frankenthaler, Nancy Graves, Frank Stella and Donald Sultan.

### Zwirner & Wirth

*32 E 69th St between Madison and Park Aves (212-517-4178; www.zwirnerandwirth.com). Tue–Sat 10am–6pm.*

After flourishing in Soho, gallerist David Zwirner opened this uptown space in 1999 with a Swiss partner and a list of blue-chip contemporary artists that includes Dan Flavin, Martin Kippenberger and Bruce Nauman.



## Curb your enthusiasm

**Explore the sidewalks of New York for quirky originals at a fair price**

Thelma Blitz Knitz's Technicolor sunglasses are speckled with glitter and decorated with lively figurines—cows, camels, hula dancers—and go for as little as $10. Ralph Turturro, cousin of actor John, commutes from upstate to hawk his abstract paintings, many inscribed with his own poetry, for about $300 each. Antonio Suarez recently netted a cool $2,000 for two impasto landscapes he sold to Donald Trump, who was just passing by. (Suarez keeps a copy of the check in his pocket as proof.)

As demonstrated by a weekend stroll down West Broadway between Prince and Spring Streets, some of New York's most soulful craftsmanship is found not in tony galleries but on the surrounding sidewalks, where you might pick up crocheted baby booties, hand-printed business cards or paintings à la Basquiat. Despite a drop in tourism, street artists are out in full force, offering buyers affordable alternatives to gallery pieces, which can cost more than a new Mercedes.

While making a buck is nice, many sidewalk artists insist they have a greater purpose. "I do this every weekend, even in winter," says Israeli artist Isack Kousnsky. "I wake up at 5am. I fight the rain. I fight the police. I fight for a space. But it's worth it to show my art. I have one motto: Keep working, no matter what."

Kousnsky, 51, relocated from Israel to the East Village in the 1980s, when New York's art scene teemed with talent and experimentation. As a veteran of solo and group shows, he's watched the gallery scene change. "I got tired of the 'How much can I get?' mentality. It hasn't been about the art or the artist in a long time. Like everything else, it's about money."

Galleries usually collect a 30 to 70- percent commission on works sold. Eight years ago, Kousnsky decided to cut out the middleman, taking to Soho's sidewalks to sell his mixed-media creations—photo transparencies on oil-slathered canvasses depicting scenes such as cityscapes, daffodils or ocean waves. "People touch my work," he said. "They ask questions. Sometimes they buy, but either way, I feel fulfilled."

Alas, fulfillment has a price. Throughout his first term as mayor, Rudolph Giuliani targeted street artists who peddled without permits,

## Harlem

### The Project

*427 W 126th St between Morningside Dr and Amsterdam Ave (212-662-8610). Subway: A, C, B, D, 1, 9 to 125th St. Wed–Sun noon–6pm.*

One of the funkiest galleries in New York is also one of the most exciting, and it's located in Harlem, one of the city's most architecturally distinctive neighborhoods. Just a few blocks from the Studio Museum *(see page 47)*, the Project has an award-winning roster unlike anyone else's.

## Brooklyn

Artists living and working in the old Italian and Polish neighborhoods of Brooklyn have created a thriving new gallery scene, especially in Williamsburg. Just a short subway ride from Manhattan, Billyburg has the quaint and convivial atmosphere of a provincial village. There's also an exciting scene along the cobblestoned waterfront between the Manhattan and Brooklyn Bridges. In summer and fall, area artists hold group exhibitions in their studios or at art fairs, usually on weekends. There are now more than 30 Brooklyn galleries; most are open on Sundays and Mondays, when Manhattan galleries are closed.

### Momenta

*72 Berry St between North 9th and North 10th Sts, Williamsburg (718-218-8058; www.momentaart.org). Subway: L to Bedford Ave. Mon–Fri noon–6pm.*

Momenta presents strong solo and group exhibitions from an exhilarating mix of emerging artists.

### Pierogi 2000

*177 North 9th St between Bedford and Driggs Aves, Williamsburg (718-599-2144; www.pierogi2000.com). Subway: L to Bedford Ave. Sept–Jul Mon–Fri noon–6pm and by appointment.*

One of Williamsburg's first art havens, this artist-run gallery remains an attraction. Under Joe Amrhein, its young, creative talents have begun to receive international recognition. You'll understand why if you stop in to see works by painter Yun-fei Ji, photographer Lisa Kereszi and sculptor Robert Lazzarini.

and many were arrested and fined. The artists claimed a First Amendment right to express themselves through their work, and in 1996, they won the right to vend without a license.

Now they may be in for a new fight. In August 2002, Mike Bloomberg, Giuliani's successor, introduced legislation that would require a permit to sell "visual" materials (including newspapers, books and artworks) on the streets or near parks.

But the artists remain committed to what is both a living and a way of life. "You mark your territory by 6am, or you won't get a spot," says portraitist Shelby Edgar. "Then you go get coffee, wait, and keep your fingers crossed."

**WHERE TO BUY**

Soho has the greatest concentration of street art. Take the N, R or W to Prince Street and walk west to West Broadway. If you're in the market for jewelry, try the corner of Houston and Thompson, where you can shop for bronze earrings or turquoise amulets. Sidewalks near the Metropolitan Museum of Art *(see page 44)* are great for finding reproductions of masters like Picasso and Dali, or to have your portrait sketched. Artists are scattered in and around Central Park, many setting up at the 79th and 82nd Street entrances. For photographs of the city, try the stands outside the Columbus Circle park entrance, where you can often spot both new and familiar prints. Sellers specializing in abstracts and collages tend to gather outside Chelsea's elite galleries—check Tenth and Eleventh Avenues between 24th and 26th Streets.

**Shady character** Thelma Blitz Knitz models her multicolored sunglasses, which she calls "wearable art."

### Roebling Hall

*390 Wythe Ave at South 4th St, Williamsburg (718-599-5352). Subway: J, M, Z to Marcy Ave. Mon, Fri–Sun noon–6pm.*

Directors Joel Beck and Christian Viveros-Fauné cook up provocative shows featuring up-and-coming artists at this Williamsburg treasure—a must on the Brooklyn circuit.

### Smack Mellon

*56 Water St between Dock and Main Sts, Dumbo (718-422-0989; www.smackmellon.org) Subway: A, C to High St; F to York St. Wed–Sun noon–6pm.*

This multidisciplinary nonprofit in Dumbo presents avant-garde shows in its drafty but accommodating space.

## Nonprofit spaces

### ApexArt Curatorial Program

*291 Church St between Walker and White Sts (212-431-5270; www.apexart.org). Subway: 1, 9 to Franklin St. Sept–Jul Tue–Sat 10am–6pm.*

At this unconventional gallery, the inspiration comes from independent critics, curators and artists who experiment with a variety of media in cleverly themed shows. The work rarely follows prevailing fashions; more often than not, it anticipates them.

### Art in General

*79 Walker St between Broadway and Lafayette St (212-219-0473; www.artingeneral.org). Subway: J, M, Z, N, Q, R, W, 6 to Canal St. Sept–Jun Tue–Sat noon–6pm.*

Now celebrating its 21st year, this Chinatown oddball has a vigorous exchange program, introducing newcomers—from New York, Europe, Cuba and elsewhere in Latin America—in a homey, almost familylike atmosphere.

### Dia Center for the Arts

*548 W 22nd St between Tenth and Eleventh Aves (212-989-5566; www.diacenter.org). Subway: C, E to 23rd St. Wed–Sun noon–6pm. Closed mid-Jun–Aug. $6, seniors and students $3, children under 10 and members free.*

Dia is the closest thing New York has to a European-style Kunsthalle. While it isn't a museum, the center offers each of its floors to an especially timely artist, or provocateurs (Alfred Jensen, Juan Muñoz, Jorge Pardo) who deserve closer looks.

### The Drawing Center

*35 Wooster St between Broome and Grand Sts (212-219-2166; www.drawingcenter.com). Subway: A, C, E, J, M, Z, N, Q, R, W, 6 to Canal St. Sept–Jul Tue– Fri 10am–6pm; Sat 11am–6pm.*

This 20-year-old stronghold of works on paper has assembled critically acclaimed programs of emerging art stars, as well as major shows exhibiting pieces by James Ensor and Rembrandt, along with Tacita Dean, Ellsworth Kelly, Henri Michaux and Rosemary Trockel.

**Film fest** Pace/MacGill Gallery features prints from such diverse artists as Walker Evans, Man Ray and William Wegman as well as portraits by Judith Joy Ross (shown above).

### Grey Art Gallery at New York University

*100 Washington Sq East between Washington and Waverly Pls (212-998-6780; www.nyu.edu/greyart). Subway: A, C, E, F, V, S to W 4th St; N, R, W to 8th St–NYU. Sept–mid-Jul Tue, Thu, Fri 11am–6pm; Wed 11am–8pm; Sat 11am–5pm. Suggested donation $2.50.*

NYU's museum-laboratory has a collection of nearly 6,000 works covering the entire range of visual art. Exhibition subjects run the gamut from fine art and cultural trends to offbeat personalities in the history of art.

### Participant Inc.

*95 Rivington St between Ludlow and Orchard Sts. (917-488-0185) Subway: F, V to Lower East Side–Second Ave. Call for hours.*

Participant Inc. is the latest addition to the nonprofit scene, and founder Lia Gangitano, a veteran curator, is certain to make it a Lower East Side hot spot. Expect freewheeling yet thoughtful exhibitions crossbreeding the visual and performing arts, literature and new media.

### Sculpture Center

*44-19 Purvis St at Jackson Ave, between 43rd and 44th Aves, Long Island City, Queens (718-361-1750). Subway: E, V to 23rd St–Ely Ave. Sept–mid-Jul Mon, Thu–Sun noon–6pm.*

Formerly located on the Upper East Side, the Sculpture Center is now an important stop on the Long Island City art loop, and it remains one of the best places to see work by emerging and mid-career sculptors. Its steel-and-brick digs, designed by architect Maya Lin, opened in December 2002 with an exhibition by the exuberant Jimbo Blachly.

## Photography

During the past decade, New York has seen a renewal of interest in art photography, along with notable strides in the medium. For an overview, look for the bimonthly directory *Photography in New York International* ($4).

### Edwynn Houk Gallery

*745 Fifth Ave between 57th and 58th Sts, fourth floor (212-750-7070). Subway: N, R, W to Fifth Ave–59th St. Sept–Jul Tue–Sat 11am–6pm. Call for summer hours.*

This respected specialist in vintage and contemporary photography shows such artists as Brassaï, Lynn Davis, Elliott Erwitt, Dorothea Lange, Annie Leibovitz, Danny Lyon, Sally Mann, Man Ray and Alfred Stieglitz, each commanding top dollar.

### Howard Greenberg & 292 Gallery

*120 Wooster St between Prince and Spring Sts, second floor (212-334-0010). Subway: C, E, 6 to Spring St; N, R, W to Prince St. Tue–Sat 10am–6pm. Call for summer hours.*

These connecting galleries exhibit the works of one accomplished 20th-century photographer after another, including Berenice Abbot, Diane Arbus, Imogen Cunningham, Robert Frank and William Klein.

### International Center of Photography

*1133 Sixth Ave at 43rd St (212-857-0000). Subway: B, D, F, V to 42nd St; 7 to Fifth Ave. Tue–Thu 10am–5pm; Fri 10am–8pm; Sat, Sun 10am–6pm. $9, seniors and students $6. Cash only.*

The ICP's galleries, once split between locations in midtown and uptown, are now consolidated in this redesigned building. There is also a school and library, with back issues of photography magazines and thousands of biographical and photographic files. Begun in the 1960s as the International Fund for Concerned Photography, ICP houses work by photojournalists Werner Bischof, Robert Capa, David Seymour and Dan Weiner, all of whom were killed on assignment; exhibitions are thus strong on news and documentary photography. Two floors of exhibition space are reserved for retrospectives devoted to single artists, such as Sebastião Salgado, Weegee and Garry Winogrand.

### Janet Borden

*560 Broadway at Prince St, sixth floor (212-431-0166; www.janetbordeninc.com). Subway: N, R, W to Prince St. Sept–Jul Tue–Sat 11am–5pm. Jul Tue–Fri 11am–5pm.*

No tour of contemporary photography is complete without a visit to this Soho stalwart, where the latest work by Tina Barney, Lee Friedlander, Jan Groover and Sandy Skoglund is regularly on view.

### Julie Saul Gallery

*535 W 22nd St between Tenth and Eleventh Aves (212-627-2410; www.saulgallery.com). Subway: C, E to 23rd St. Sept–Jun Tue–Sat 11am–6pm. Jul, Aug Tue–Fri 11am–6pm.*

Come to Julie Saul Gallery for well-conceived contemporary-photography shows, featuring stunning images from Sally Gall, John O'Reilly and Paul Shambroom and others.

### Pace/MacGill

*32 E 57th St between Madison and Park Aves, ninth floor (212-759-7999). Subway: N, R, W to Lexington Ave–59th St; 4, 5, 6 to 59th St. Sept–late Jun Tue–Fri 9:30am–5:30pm; Sat 10am–6pm. Late Jun–Aug Mon–Thu 9:30am–5:30pm; Fri 9am–4pm.*

This gallery never misses. Look for well-known names such as Walker Evans, Robert Frank, Irving Penn and Joel-Peter Witkin, in addition to groundbreaking contemporaries Philip-Lorca DiCorcia and Kiki Smith.

### Yossi Milo Gallery

*552 W 24th St between Tenth and Eleventh Aves, second and third floors (212-414-0370; www.yossimilogallery.com). Sept–Jul Tue–Sat 11am–6pm.*

This two-floor operation has top-notch photographers from all over the globe. Expect new shows by Michal Chelhin, David Goldes and Shelby Lee Adams.

# Books & Poetry

Feeling bookish? New York's literary scene offers top-shelf reading, rhyming and listening.

Budding chefs dream of Paris. Would-be actors ache for Hollywood. But if you want to be a writer, New York City is the place to dip your pen. Home to some of history's most legendary scribes (including Mark Twain and Edgar Allan Poe), the city remains an international breeding ground for today's promising literary talents.

"It's not the easiest place in which to pursue a creative writing career," says novelist Tracy Quan, author of the semi-autobiographical *Diary of a Manhattan Call Girl,* "but it feels like it's the only place." For many emerging writers, New York acts as both muse and publicist, offering mentorship through respected writing programs as well as access to some of the industry's biggest movers and shakers.

As much as New York is a writers' town, it's also a hot spot for readers. Whether you're looking to score a signed first edition of *To Kill a Mockingbird* or to hear Alan Furst read from his latest espionage thriller, there's no limit to the literary resources available at the city's myriad bookstores and performance spaces.

## Author readings

Events range from low- to highbrow: You're as likely to catch *Sopranos* star Jamie-Lynn Sigler pushing her memoir for young adults as you are Jeffrey Eugenides reading from his latest work. The following offer frequent author readings, signings and talks.

### Barnes & Noble

*See page 235 for listing.*

Event calendars for each branch are available in-store. Check the phone book or website for locations.

### Bluestockings

*See page 285 for listing.*

### Borders Books and Music

*See page 235 for listing.*

Event calendars for both Borders branches are available in-store and on the website.

► Check the Around Town and Books sections of ***Time Out New York*** for weekly listings and reviews.
► See chapters **Gay & Lesbian** and **Shopping & Services** for more bookstores.

### Corner Bookstore

*1313 Madison Ave at 93rd St (212-831-3554). Subway: 4, 5, 6 to 86th St. Mon–Thu 10am–8pm; Fri 10am–7pm; Sat 10am–5pm; Sun 11am–6pm.*

Pick up a calendar of upcoming readings.

### Partners & Crime

*44 Greenwich Ave at Charles St (212-243-0440). Subway: 1, 2, 3, 9 to 14th St. Mon–Thu noon–9pm; Fri, Sat noon–10pm; Sun noon–7pm.*

Mystery buffs can get their kicks at this independent bookseller.

### Rizzoli Bookstore

*31 W 57th St between Fifth and Sixth Aves (212-759-2424). Subway: F to 57th St. Mon–Fri 10am–7:30pm; Sat 10:30am–7pm; Sun 11am–7pm.*

This arty bookstore is a prime spot for catching artists, designers and photographers on book tours.

## Reading series

These venues host fiction and poetry readings; some also offer lectures.

### The Half King

*505 W 23rd St at Tenth Ave (212-462-4300). Subway: C, E to 23rd St. 9am–4am. AmEx, DC, MC, V.*

This bar-restaurant co-owned by Sebastian Junger offers popular—and free—Monday-night readings. Arrive about a half-hour early if you want to get a seat, or make a dinner reservation; the readings are at 7pm.

### Housing Works Used Books Cafe

*126 Crosby St between Houston and Prince Sts (212-334-3324; www.housingworks.org/usedbookcafe). Subway: F, V, S to Broadway–Lafayette St; N, R to Prince St. Call or visit website for schedule of events. Free.*

Check out the impressive lineup of writers at this organization dedicated to raising money for the HIV-positive homeless.

### KGB

*85 E 4th St between Second and Bowery (212-505-3360). Subway: F, V to Lower East Side–Second Ave; 6 to Astor Pl. Mon 7:30pm. Free.*

This Soviet-themed East Village bar puts on a weekly reading series. Many are must-hears. Some will have you reaching for the tomatoes.

### Makor

*See page 312 for listing.*

The mingling scene is marvy at this Jewish cultural center, though the events have nothing to do with

**Let's talk about sex, baby** Judith Levine discusses *Harmful to Minors* at Bluestockings.



dating per se. Makor's calendar includes poetry slams and book groups. Some events are free; some aren't.

### National Arts Club

*See page 83 for listing.*

This private club in an elegant landmark building opens its doors to members of the W.B. Yeats Society and to the public for free readings by contemporary writers.

### 92nd Street Y Unterberg Poetry Center

*1395 Lexington Ave at 92nd St (212-996-1100; www.92ndsty.org). Subway: 6 to 96th St. Call or visit website for schedule of events. Admission varies.*

The Academy of American Poets and the Y co-sponsor readings with such acclaimed scribes such as Edward Albee and Jonathan Franzen.

### Rocky Sullivan's

*Rocky Sullivan's Pub, 129 Lexington Ave between 28th and 29th Sts (212-725-3871). Subway: 6 to 28th St. Wed 8pm. Free.*

Every Wednesday evening, this Gramercy Park hangout transforms into a literary oasis as authors of Irish ancestry share newly published works. Scramble for a seat to hear the likes of Frank McCourt, Edna O'Brien or Jimmy Breslin.

### Selected Shorts: A Celebration of the Short Story

*Symphony Space, 2537 Broadway at 95th St (212-864-5400; www.symphonyspace.org). Subway: 1, 2, 3, 9 to 96th St. Mid-Jan–mid-Jun. Call or visit website for schedule of events. $21, seniors $20.*

Accomplished Broadway and Hollywood actors tackle short stories in this series, one of the longest-running programs at Symphony Space.

### Writer's Voice/West Side YMCA

*5 W 63rd St between Central Park West and Broadway (212-875-4124; www.ymcanyc.org). Subway: 1, 9 to 66th St–Lincoln Ctr. Call or visit website for schedule of events. Free–$5.*

Events include readings by playwrights, poets and novelists, as well as popular open-mike nights.

## Spoken word

### A Gathering of Tribes

*Tribes Gallery, 285 E 3rd St between Aves B and C (212-674-3778; www.tribes.org). Subway: F, V to Lower East Side–Second Ave. Sun 5–7pm. Free–$3.*

The gallery's well-known Gathering of Scribes open-mike series is held on Sunday evenings.

### A Little Bit Louder

*Thirteen, 35 E 13th St at University Pl (212-979-6677; www.bar13.com). Subway: L, N, Q, R, W, 4, 5, 6 to 14th St–Union Sq. Mon 7:30pm. $5, students $4.*

Every Monday, the mod lounge 13 hosts a stimulating poetry forum; two nights a month, it's dedicated to the slam game. The rest of the time, expect open-mike nights or theme readings.

### Bowery Poetry Club

*308 Bowery at Bleecker St (212-614-0505; www.bowerypoetry.com). Subway: F, V, S to Broadway–Lafayette St; 6 to Bleecker St. Call or visit website for schedule. Admission varies.*

The vibe at Bowery is definitely experimental; the weekly lineup features a unique mix of poetry-themed hip-hop, dance and theatrical events.

### Dixon Place

*Vineyard 26, 309 E 26th St between First and Second Aves (212-532-1546; www.dixonplace.org). Subway: 6*

*to 28th St. Call or visit website for schedule of events. Free–$12.*
Founder-director Ellie Covan offers an open-mike night on the first Wednesday of each month. *The New York Review of Science Fiction* reading series is held on the second Monday of each month.

### Knitting Factory

*See page 310 for listing.*
This legendary performance space hosts local and national poets in the cozy Alterknit Theatre.

### Nuyorican Poets Cafe

*236 E 3rd St between Aves B and C (212-505-8183; www.nuyorican.org). Subway: F, V to Lower East Side–Second Ave. Call or visit website for schedule of events. Admission varies.*
The 29-year-old Nuyorican goes beyond open mikes and slams with multimedia events, staged readings, hip-hop poetry, short films and more. Slams are held Friday nights and every Wednesday except the first one of each month.

### Poetry Project

*St. Mark's Church in-the-Bowery, 131 E 10th St at Second Ave (212-674-0910; www.poetryproject.com). Subway: L to Third Ave; 6 to Astor Pl. Call or visit website for schedule. $10, seniors and students $7.*
The legendary Poetry Project, whose hallowed walls have heard the likes of Allen Ginsberg and Anne Waldman, remains a thriving center for discovering the new and noteworthy. Living legends such as Jim Carroll and Patti Smith occasionally take the stage.

**Rhyme and reason** Poet and editor Joel Lewis reads at the famed Poetry Project.

## Talks & lectures

### The Brooklyn Public Library

*Grand Army Plaza, Prospect Heights, Brooklyn (718-230-2100; www.brooklynpubliclibrary.org). Subway: 2, 3 to Eastern Pkwy–Brooklyn Museum. Call or visit website for schedule of events. Free.*
Brooklyn's main library branch offers lectures and readings of impressive scope.

### New School University

*66 W 12th St between Fifth and Sixth Aves (212-229-5488; www.newschool.edu). Subway: F, V to 14th St; L to Sixth Ave. Call or visit website for schedule of events. Admission varies.*
The school holds lecture series, poetry nights, fiction forums and political discussions.

### New York Public Library, Celeste Bartos Forum

*Fifth Ave at 42nd St (212-930-0855; www.nypl.org). Subway: B, D, F, V to 42nd St; 7 to Fifth Ave. Call or visit website for schedule of events. Admission varies.*
Several lecture series feature renowned writers and thinkers in this wonderful vaulted room.

### 92nd Street Y

*See page 267 for listing.*
The Y offers regular lectures by and dialogues between top-notch speakers. The literary likes of Paul Auster and Wole Soyinka have spoken here.

## Walking tours

### Greenwich Village Literary Pub Crawl

*White Horse Tavern, 567 Hudson St at 11th St (212-613-5796). Subway: A, C, E, 1, 2, 3, 9 to 14th St; L to Eighth Ave. Sat 2pm. $15. Reservations recommended.*
This 2.3-mile crawl to four watering holes once frequented by legendary village writers is guided by actors from the New Ensemble Theatre Company Inc.

### Greenwich Village Past and Present

*Washington Square Park, Fifth Ave at Waverly Pl (212-969-8262; www.streetsmartsny.com). Subway: A, C, E, F, V, S to W 4th St. Call for schedule. $10.*
This two-hour walk by Street Smarts N.Y. meets at the Washington Square Arch. It takes you past the homes and hangouts of famed Village writers and artists.

### Mark Twain's New York

*Broadway at Spring St, southwest corner (212-873-1944; www.salwen.com/mtny). Subway: 6 to Spring St. Season varies. $15.*
This annual tour is led by Twainologist Peter Salwen. The walk ends at Twain's former home on West 10th Street.

# Cabaret & Comedy

After the sun goes down, torch singers and sparkling wits light up the night

## Cabaret

New York is the cabaret capital of the U.S. and, quite possibly, of the world. In what other city can you find a dozen different shows on any given night? The term *cabaret* covers both the venue and the art form. It's the club where songs are sung, generally by one person, but sometimes by a small ensemble; it is also the vocal interpretation of songs usually drawn from what's known as the Great American Songbook, a vast repertoire of the American musical theater, supplemented with the occasional new number by a contemporary composer. More than anything else, cabaret is an act of intimacy: The best singers are able to draw in the audience until each member feels he or she is being personally serenaded.

The Golden Age of cabaret in New York was the 1950s and early '60s. The advent of rock & roll lured away many performers, but plenty of singers and fans keep the classic sound alive. Mid-October marks the Cabaret Convention at the **Town Hall** *(see page 313)*, which attracts top performers for a weeklong showcase of the best in the genre. Today's venues fall into two groups: posh, expensive boîtes such as **Feinstein's**, the **Oak Room** and **Cafe Carlyle** (where you'll hear the likes of theater stars such as Betty Buckley and Christine Ebersole, as well as cabaret mainstays Andrea Marcovicci and Bobby Short) and less formal, less pricey neighborhood clubs such as **Danny's Skylight Room**, **Don't Tell Mama** and the **Duplex**, where up-and-coming singers and Broadway babies perform.

### Classic nightspots

#### Cafe Carlyle

*The Carlyle Hotel, 35 E 76th St at Madison Ave (212-744-1600, 800-227-5737). Subway: 6 to 77th St. Mid-Sept–Jun Mon 8:45pm; Tue–Sat 8:45, 10:45pm. Cover: $75. AmEx, DC, MC, V.*

This is the epitome of chic New York, especially when the legendary Bobby Short performs. (Woody Allen sometimes sits in as clarinetist with Eddie Davis and his New Orleans Jazz Band on early Monday night shows—call ahead to confirm.) Don't dress casual; the Carlyle is a place to plunk down your cash and live the high life. To drink in some atmosphere without spending as much, try Bemelmans Bar across the hall, which always features an excellent pianist *(Tue–Sat 9:45pm–12:45am; $15 cover).* The playful murals of Ludwig Bemelmans, creator of the lovable *Madeline,* adorn the walls.

► For an alternative cabaret experience, see **Fringe Scene**, page 31.

#### The Duplex

*61 Christopher St at Seventh Ave South (212-255-5438; www.theduplex.com). Subway: 1, 9 to Christopher St–Sheridan Sq. Show times vary. Piano bar 9pm–4am. Cover: $5–$25, two-drink minimum. Cash only.*

The Duplex doesn't have that classic glamour, but it's the city's oldest cabaret. Going strong for 50-plus years, the place sets the pace for campy, good-natured fun. A mix of regulars and tourists laugh and sing along with classy drag performers, comedians and rising stars.

#### Feinstein's

*The Regency, 540 Park Ave at 61st St (212-339-4095). Subway: N, R, W to Lexington Ave–59th St; 4, 5, 6 to 59th St. Tue–Thu 8:30pm; Fri, Sat 8:30, 11pm. Cover: $50–$75, $25–$50 food-and-drink minimum. AmEx, DC, MC, V.*

Cabaret's crown prince Michael Feinstein draws top-shelf talent to this swank room in the Regency Hotel, including elegant Ann Hampton Callaway, sexy singer-guitarist John Pizzarelli and his wife, the phenomenal singer Jessica Molaskey. Check *Time Out New York*'s weekly listings for bookings of wacky Hollywood footnotes such as Nell Carter, Tony Danza and Sally Kellerman.

#### The Oak Room

*Algonquin Hotel, 59 W 44th St between Fifth and Sixth Aves (212-840-6800). Subway: B, D, F, V to 42nd St; 7 to Fifth Ave. Tue–Thu 9pm; Fri, Sat 9, 11:30pm, $50 prix fixe compulsory at first Friday and Saturday shows. Cover: $50, $20 drink minimum. AmEx, DC, Disc, MC, V.*

This resonant banquette-lined room is the place to enjoy the best cabaret performers, among them Karen Akers and Andrea Marcovicci, plus ascendant stars Stacey Kent and Jane Monheit. And yes, all you Dorothy Parker fans, it's *that* Algonquin *(see page 151).*

### Standards

#### Danny's Skylight Room

*Grand Sea Palace, 346 W 46th St between Eighth and Ninth Aves (212-265-8133; www.dannysgsp.com).*

**With Love comes Payne** Darlene Love, left, and Freda Payne woo the room at Feinstein's.

*Subway: A, C, E to 42nd St–Port Authority. Show times and cover prices vary, $10 food-and-drink minimum. AmEx, DC, MC, V.*
A pastel nook in the Grand Sea Palace restaurant, "where Bangkok meets Broadway" on touristy Restaurant Row, Danny's usually features the smooth sounds of pop and standards. In addition to up-and-comers, a few mature cabaret and jazz standbys, such as Blossom Dearie, perform.

## Don't Tell Mama

*343 W 46th St between Eighth and Ninth Aves (212-757-0788; www.donttellmama.com). Subway: A, C, E to 42nd St–Port Authority. 4pm–4am, 4–8 shows per night. Cover: $10–$20 in cabaret room, two-drink minimum; no cover for piano bar, two-drink minimum (no food served). Cash only.*
Showbiz pros adore this Theater District venue. The acts range from strictly amateur to potential stars of tomorrow. The nightly lineup may include pop, jazz or Broadway singers, female impersonators, magicians, comedians or revues.

## Judy's Chelsea

*169 Eighth Ave between 18th and 19th Sts (212-929-5410; www.judyschelsea.com). Subway: C, E to 23rd St; 1, 9 to 18th St. Mon–Thu 8:30pm; Fri, Sat 8:30, 11pm; Sun 3, 5:30, 8:30pm. Cover: $12–$15, $12 food-and-drink minimum. AmEx, MC, V.*
The outré folksinger Go Mahan often performs in this space, and the geek-chic Lounge-O-Leers keep piano-bar patrons laughing with grooved-out versions of Top 40 hits. Co-owner–singer Judy Kreston and pianist David Lahm often perform on Saturdays.

## Triad

*158 W 72nd St between Columbus Ave and Broadway (212-799-4599). Subway: B, C, 1, 2, 3, 9 to 72nd St. Show times and cover prices vary, two-drink minimum. AmEx, Disc, MC, V ($10 minimum).*
This Upper West Side spot has been the launching pad for many revues over the years, several of which *(Forbidden Broadway, Forever Plaid)* later moved on to larger Off Broadway venues. Dinner is available, and there's an occasional singer or benefit show in the downstairs lounge, which opens at 4:30pm.

## Upstairs at Rose's Turn

*55 Grove St between Seventh Ave South and Bleecker St (212-366-5438). Subway: 1, 9 to Christopher St–Sheridan Sq. 4pm–4am. Show times vary. Cover $5–$15, two-drink minimum. Cash only.*
This dark room with zero atmosphere tends to emphasize comedy or one-act musicals such as *Our Lives & Times,* a hilarious spoof of current events, and *Indigo Rat,* a spin on life in wartime Berlin.

## Alternative venues

### Joe's Pub

*See page 309 for listing.*

This plush club and restaurant in the Public Theater is at once hip and elegant. Performers include chanteuses such as Lea DeLaria, Ute Lemper and Audra McDonald, and singing sensations as diverse as Aimee Mann and Mo'Guajiro. Show times and cover prices vary.

### Torch

*137 Ludlow St between Rivington and Stanton Sts (212-228-5151). Subway: F to Delancey St; J, M, Z to Delancey–Essex Sts. Sun–Thu 6pm–2am; Fri, Sat 6pm–4am. Show times vary. No cover. AmEx, DC, MC, V.*

This Lower East Side bar-restaurant features cabaret acts seven nights a week. Its tasteful interior was destroyed in a fire in February 2002. The refurbished club will reopen in early 2003.

# Comedy Venues

Live comedy used to mean a two-drink minimum of watered-down cocktails and a bunch of guys in front of a brick-wall background, delivering dopey observations that all begin with the phrase, "*Didja ever notice…*"

Well, that nightmare is over. You can still get your share of traditional stand-up in New York, and some of it is even good. But the real treasures lurk off the beaten path, outside the traditional club circuit—and they're usually more budget-friendly. New York's premier underground show is the Monday-night staple *Eating It* at **Luna Lounge**, mixing new acts with established performers such as David Cross, Janeane Garofalo and Sarah Silverman. You'll find a similar blend of innovation and entertainment at theaters like **Ars Nova** and **Upright Citizens Brigade**. So while the big rooms (**Carolines**, the **Comedy Cellar**, **Gotham Comedy Club**, etc.) are still lively, it's the less conventional venues that offer that only-in-New York flavor. And after all, isn't that why you came here in the first place?

### Ars Nova Theater

*511 W 54th St between Tenth and Eleventh Aves (SmartTix 212-206-1515, info 212-997-1700; www.arsnovanyc.com). Subway: A, B, D, 1, 9 to 59th St–Columbus Circle; C, E to 50th St; . Show times and cover prices vary. AmEx, Disc, MC, V.*

A rare joy in NYC's comedy machine, Ars Nova presents national and local acts in a beautiful, cozy environment (though the neighborhood is a bit dodgy). Best bet: the *Automatic Vaudeville* comedy-variety show, Tuesdays at 8pm for only $10.

### The Boston Comedy Club

*82 W 3rd St between Sullivan and Thompson Sts (212-477-1000; www.bostoncomedyclub.com). Subway: A, C, E, F, V, S to W 4th St. Mon 8, 10pm; Tue–Thu 9:30pm; Fri, Sat 8, 10pm, 12:15am; Sun 9pm. Cover: $7–$12, two-drink minimum. AmEx, MC, V.*

This is not the classiest joint in town, but it's in a great Village location, and the club gets its share of high-quality acts and rising stars.

### Carolines on Broadway

*1626 Broadway between 49th and 50th Sts (212-757-4100; www.carolines.com). Subway: N, R, W to 49th St; 1, 9 to 50th St. Mon–Wed 7:30, 9:30pm; Thu, Sun 8, 10pm; Fri, Sat 8, 10:30pm, 12:30am. Cover: $15–$35, two-drink minimum. AmEx, DC, MC, V.*

If you're nostalgic for the 1980s comedy boom, you can occasionally find guys like Bobcat Goldthwait, Gilbert Gottfried and Emo Philips here, mixed in with newer stars such as Dave Attell, Dave Chappelle and D.L. Hughley.

### Chicago City Limits Theatre

*1105 First Ave between 60th and 61st Sts (212-888-5233; www.chicagocitylimits.com). Subway: N, R, W to Lexington Ave–59th St; 4, 5, 6 to 59th St. Wed, Thu 8pm; Fri, Sat 8, 10:30pm. Cover: $20, discount with student ID. AmEx, MC, V.*

CCL, which moved here from Chicago in 1979, performs topical sketches, songs and audience-inspired improv. The troupe's students perform on Sundays.

### Comedy Cellar

*117 MacDougal St between Bleecker and W 3rd Sts (212-254-3480; www.comedycellar.com). Subway: A, C, E, F, V, S to W 4th St. Sun–Thu 9, 11pm; Fri 9, 10:45pm, 12:30am; Sat 7, 9, 10:45pm, 12:30am. Cover: $10–$15, two-drink minimum. AmEx, MC, V.*

If you like your comedy underground—literally more than figuratively—you can't go wrong at this subterranean stand-up spot. *Saturday Night Live* alum Colin Quinn and 7-Up pitchman Godfrey practically live here. *TONY* favorites, such as Todd Barry, Louis C.K. and Marc Maron, also appear frequently.

### The Comedy Garden

*Madison Square Garden, Seventh Ave at 32nd St (Ticketmaster 212-307-7171; www.comedygarden.com). Subway: A, C, E, 1, 2, 3, 9 to 34th St–Penn Station. Show times and cover prices vary. AmEx, Disc, MC, V.*

The Garden doesn't host as many shows as other clubs, but it attracts plenty of high-profile acts, such as Brett Butler, Steve Harvey and Richard Lewis.

### Comic Strip Live

*1568 Second Ave between 81st and 82nd Sts (212-861-9386; www.comicstriplive.com). Subway: 4, 5, 6 to 86th St. Mon–Thu 8:30pm; Fri 8:30, 10:30pm, 12:30am; Sat 8, 10:15pm, 12:30am; Sun 8pm. Cover $12–$15, two-drink minimum. AmEx, Disc, MC, V.*

Chris Rock, Adam Sandler and Jerry Seinfeld have performed on this stage—albeit years before you'd ever heard of them. Always on the lookout for future stars, the Comic Strip continues to showcase some of New York's most promising young acts.

### Dangerfield's

*1118 First Ave between 61st and 62nd Sts (212-593-1650; www.dangerfields.com). Subway: N, R, W to Lexington Ave–59th St; 4, 5, 6 to 59th St. Sun–Thu 8:45pm; Fri 8:30, 10:30pm; Sat 8, 10:30pm, 12:30am. Cover: $12–$20. AmEx, DC, MC, V.*

Opened by respect-starved comedian Rodney Dangerfield in 1969, this old-school lounge predates not only its competitors, but also many of its performers. The club offers food (with no drink minimum) and $4 parking—a bargain in NYC.

### Eating It

*Luna Lounge, 171 Ludlow St between Houston and Stanton Sts (212-260-2323; www.eatingit.net). Subway: F to Delancey St; J, M, Z to Delancey–Essex Sts. Mon 8pm. Cover: $7, includes one drink ticket. Cash only.*

This haven for experimental comedy places as much emphasis on the *experimental* as it does on the *comedy.* Expect to see acts that have been (or will soon be) on *Conan, Letterman* and *SNL.*

### The Gershwin Hotel

*7 E 27th St between Fifth and Madison Aves (212-545-8000; www.gershwinhotel.com). Subway: N, R, W, 6 to 28th St. Wed–Sat 10pm. Cover: $5. AmEx, MC, V.*

In a small room off the lobby, you can catch top local stand-up comics, plus occasional sketch and music acts on Thursdays and Saturdays. Always a bargain.

### Gotham City Improv

*158 W 23rd St between Sixth and Seventh Aves (212-367-8222; www.gothamcityimprov.com). Subway: F, V, 1, 9 to 23rd St. Show times vary. Cover: $5–$7. Cash only.*

GCI presents improv, both short-form (the kind seen on *Whose Line Is It Anyway?*) and long-form (the more experimental, theatrical style preferred by the comedy elite).

### Gotham Comedy Club

*34 W 22nd St between Fifth and Sixth Aves (212-367-9000; www.gothamcomedyclub.com). Subway: F, V, N, R, W to 23rd St. Sun–Thu 8:30pm; Fri, Sat 8:30, 10:30pm. Cover: $10–$15, two-drink minimum. AmEx, DC, MC, V.*

This elegant club books top comics such as irascible *Daily Show* commentator Lewis Black, and a certain Mr. Seinfeld has been known to drop in occasionally to try out new material (but don't hold your breath).

### Gramercy Comedy Club

*35 E 21st St between Broadway and Park Ave South (212-254-5709; www.gramercycomedyclub.com). Subway: F, V, N, R, W, 6 to 23rd St. Wed–Fri 8:30pm; Sat 10pm. Cover: $15, two-drink minimum.*

The city's newest comedy venue is a ritzy affair that prides itself on its menu as much as on its comics. Be sure to ask about a discount at the neighboring Ten's gentleman's club, if that's your thing.

### New York Comedy Club

*241 E 24th St between Second and Third Aves (212-696-5233). Subway: 6 to 23rd St. Sun–Thu 9pm; Fri 9, 10pm; Sat 8, 10pm, 12:30am. Cover: $7–$10, two-drink minimum. AmEx, MC, V.*

This gritty club has two separate rooms, each with a bargain cover price and a packed lineup, including shows dedicated to NYC's best black *(Fri, Sat 11pm)* and Latino *(Fri 8pm; Sat 9pm)* acts.

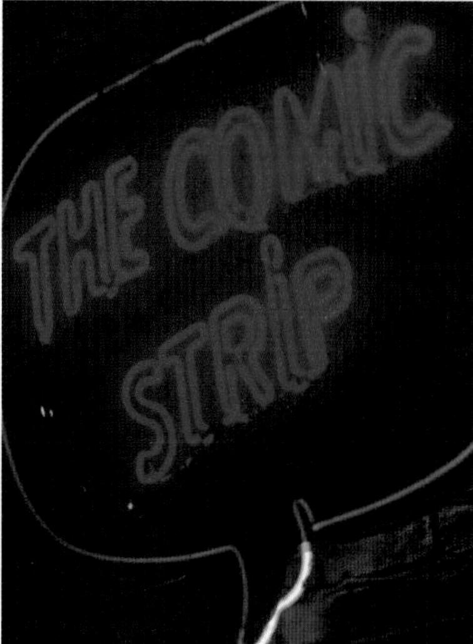


**Cartoon superheroes** The careers of many young stand-ups took off after performing at this Upper East Side club.

### PSNBC

*HERE, 145 Sixth Ave between Dominick and Spring Sts (212-647-0202; www.nbc.com/psnbc). Subway: C, E to Spring St. Mon–Thu 7:30pm. Free.*

Four nights a week, NBC uses this space to harvest the comedy stars of tomorrow, and all of its shows are free. For stand-up, come on Tuesdays.

### Stand-Up NY

*236 W 78th St at Broadway (212-595-0850; www.standupny.com). Subway: 1, 9 to 79th St. Sun–Wed 7, 9pm; Thu 6:30, 9pm; Fri, Sat 8, 10pm, 12:15am. Cover: $5–$12, two-item minimum. AmEx, MC, V.*

The Upper West Side's only stand-up club features a mix of circuit regulars and new acts in a cozy, traditional setting.

### Upright Citizens Brigade Theatre

*161 W 22nd St between Sixth and Seventh Aves (212-366-9176; www.ucbtheatre.com). Subway: F, V, 1, 9 to 23rd St. Show times vary. Cover: $5–$7. Cash only.*

Every night offers top-notch sketches and long-form improv—some of the most adventurous, mind-bending comedy in NYC. You might see folks from *SNL, Conan* and *The Daily Show,* in the audience or onstage (especially on Sundays).

Arts & Entertainment

# Clubs

Get your groove on at the city's most happening nightspots

New Yorkers are a cynical, hard-to-impress bunch. But despite their perennial been-there-done-that attitude, the city's club crawlers are proud of its nightlife. The birthplace of disco and hip-hop, New York also played a major role in the development of house music. These locally born sounds, along with drum 'n' bass, bleepy IDM, electroclash, Latin, R&B, reggae, techno, trip-hop and many other genres, can be found emanating from clubs and lounges every night of the week.

In the past, New York DJs offered a wide range of beats during the course of a night. But in recent years, dance floors have become more musically regimented. That may be a reason why so many venues are informally segregated by age, race or sexual orientation. There are plenty of exceptions to this trend; for example, a mixed crowd may be found at the long-running party **Shelter** *(see* **Safe haven**, *page 278).*

Cover prices for the following clubs vary according to the event and are usually cash only. It's generally of little use to arrive at any venue before midnight. When no closing time is noted, assume the place stays open until the party fizzles out. This chapter covers discos and lounges as well as live-music venues (*see also chapter* **Music**).

## Clubs

### Arc

*6 Hubert St at Hudson St (212-226-9212; www.arcspace.net). Subway: A, C, E, 1, 9 to Canal St. Fri midnight–10am; Sat 11pm–10am; Sun 4–11pm. Cover: $15–$25. Average non-alcoholic drink: $4.*

Even though it doesn't have a liquor license, Arc is still one of the city's premier nightspots. On Fridays, the great Danny Tenaglia throws his **Be Yourself** party with dark, tracky, house, minimal Basic Channel–type grooves and funked-up techno; Saturdays are given over to progressive-house sounds.

### Baktun

*418 W 14th St between Ninth Ave and Washington St (212-206-1590; www.baktun.com). Subway: A, C, E to 14th St; L to Eighth Ave. Mon, Wed–Sun 9pm–4am. Cover $3–$12. Average drink: $7.*

This former meat-processing plant is a welcome alternative to the upscale joints that have overtaken this

**Meat grinder** The percussive sounds of Filter 14 shake up the Meatpacking District.

gentrifying neighborhood. The small club offers an underground-heavy menu of art, performance, and deejayed and live (usually electronic) music events. On Mondays, techno party **Tronic** lures stars as well as local luminaries. The long-running drum 'n' bass **Direct Drive** waffles the woofers on Saturdays.

### Centro-Fly

*45 W 21st St between Fifth and Sixth Aves (212-627-7770; www.centro-fly.com). Subway: F, V, N, R, 6 to 23rd St. Thu–Sat 10pm–5:30am. Cover: $15–$25. Average drink: $7.*

Modeled and named after a late-1960s Italian disco, Centro-Fly is as groovy as its legendary predecessor. Op art, futuristic furniture and a sunken bar in the round set the mod mood. Two sound systems and a four-turntable DJ booth attract some of the best spinners. Notable nights include the disco-housey **GBH** on Fridays and the teched-up **Plant** affair on Saturdays *(see* **Plant Bar**, *page 173).*

### Club New York

*252 W 43rd St between Broadway and Seventh Ave (212-997-9510). Subway: A, C, E to 42nd St–Port Authority; N, Q, R, W, S, 1, 2, 3, 9, 7 to 42nd St–Times Sq. Thu–Sun 10pm–4am. Cover varies. Average drink: $6.*

Famous for the shooting that led to P. Diddy's brush with the law, Club New York is a mainstream Latin-music venue, where DJs spin merengue, salsa and Spanish rock and pop. Hip-hop, which had a night of its own until the Puffster incident, is now relegated to the small VIP room.

### Club Shelter

*20 W 39th St between Fifth and Sixth Aves (212-719-4479; www.clubshelter.com). Subway: B, D, F, V to 42nd St; 7 to Fifth Ave. Sat 11pm–noon. Cover: $10–$25. Average drink: $6.*

This four-room venue has an ever-shifting array of parties, but the club's raison d'être is Saturday night's **Shelter** event *(see* **Safe haven**, *page 278).*

### Exit2

*610 W 56th St between Eleventh and Twelfth Aves (212-582-8282; www.exit2nightclub.com). Subway: A, C, B, D, 1, 9 to 59th St–Columbus Circle. Fri 11pm–9am; Sat 11pm–3am. Cover: $30. Average drink: $8.*

Exit2 is largely the domain of liquored-up, overly aggressive knuckleheads. But on Saturdays, the famous Junior Vasquez takes over the amazing sound system to host the classic house party **Earth**, which attracts an appreciative crowd. Although the old fella is not quite what he used to be, dancing to his beats is the nightlife equivalent of visiting the American Museum of Natural History.

### Filter 14

*432 W 14th St at Washington St (212-366-5680). Subway: A, C, E, 1, 2, 3, 9 to 14th St; L to Eighth Ave. 10pm–4am. Cover: $5–$12. Average drink: $6–$10.*

Filter 14's no-attitude crowd matches its no-frills decor. It has a booming sound system that, depending on the night, blasts banging house beats or smooth-rolling drum 'n' bass.

### Lotus

*409 W 14th St between Ninth Ave and Washington St (212-242-9710). Subway: A, C, E, 1, 2, 3, 9 to 14th St; L to Eighth Ave. Hours vary with event. Cover: $10. Average drink: $7.*

Lotus was one of the first upscale clubs to invade the once-scuzzy Meatpacking District, and it immediately attracted legions of celebs, models and gawkers. Happily, the venue's patina of trendiness has faded a bit. Now Lotus can be appreciated as a well-furnished restaurant–lounge–dance club whose DJs spin a mainstream mix of sounds.

### Lunatarium

*10 Jay St at John St, Dumbo, Brooklyn (718-813-8404; www.lunatarium.com). Subway: A, C to High St; F to York St. Hours vary with event. Cover: $12–$17. Average drink: $4.*

Located near the waterfront, this loft space is gargantuan, with a beautifully eerie, postindustrial edge. Stars of underground techno or drum 'n' bass play on the weekends. Enjoy full-on slammage in the massive main area and subtler sounds in the smaller side room.

### Luxx

*256 Grand St between Driggs Ave and Roebling St, Williamsburg, Brooklyn (718-599-1000, www.clubluxx.net). Subway: L to Bedford Ave. 8pm–4am. Cover: $5–$9. Average drink: $4.*

Luxx is the only cabaret-licensed venue in Williamsburg. Currently, the ever-changing lineup includes Friday- and Saturday-night electroclash affairs, produced by longtime club eccentric Larry T.

### Nell's

*246 W 14th St between Seventh and Eighth Aves (212-675-1567; www.nells.com). Subway: A, C, E, 1, 2, 3, 9 to 14th St; L to Eighth Ave. 10pm–4am. Cover: $5–$15. Average drink: $8.*

Nell's spent its youth as a 1980s hot spot for champagne-swilling hipsters, young bankers and literary wild-children, but has gracefully aged into a nightlife institution. Upstairs, groove to laid-back jazz and funky soul (often with live bands). DJ-supplied hip-hop, funk, house, R&B, reggae and classics spin down below. The crowd is straight, multiracial, dressed up and ready to spend.

### Roxy

*515 W 18th St between Tenth and Eleventh Aves (212-645-5156; www.roxynyc.com). Subway: A, C, E to 14th St; L to Eighth Ave. Wed 8pm–2am*

► Get a close-up look at queer nightlife in chapter **Gay & Lesbian**.

► Turn to chapter **Bars** for additional club venues and DJ bars.

► For a listing of nightly club events, pick up a copy of ***Time Out New York***.

**Blue-light special** The Warehouse offers house music and a jam-packed dance floor.

*(roller skating only); Fri 10pm–4am; Sat 11pm–5am. Cover: $12–$25. Average drink: $7.*
The Roxy began life as a disco-era roller rink; on Wednesday, it's still possible to rent skates and go 'round and 'round. Other evenings, the mammoth space is a straight-up dance club. The spot generally hosts one-shot live-performance or DJ events, with primarily drum 'n' bass, house and techno sounds. Saturdays, Roxy features one of the city's biggest gay (but straight-friendly) dance parties, presenting many of the leading lights of the circuit-DJ scene.

### S.O.B.'s

*204 Varick St at Houston St (212-243-4940; www.sobs.com). Subway: 1, 9 to Houston St. Mon–Sat 6:30pm–4am. Cover: $10–$25. Average drink: $7.*
The venerable S.O.B.'s (Sounds of Brazil) opened in the mid-1980s as the worldbeat boom began. The club mounts concerts by African, Asian, Caribbean and Latin artists, in addition to discotheque-style events. Live Brazilian bands play on Saturday nights.

### Sound Factory

*618 W 46th St between Eleventh and Twelfth Aves (212-489-0001; www.soundfactorynyc.com). Subway: C, E to 50th St. Fri, Sat 11pm–6am. Cover: $20–$30. Average drink: $8.*
The legendary Sound Factory re-opened in 1997, and the sound system is much improved. However, DJ Junior Vasquez *(see* **Exit2**, *page 275)* no longer appears here, and for many fans of the original club, the current scene lacks authenticity. While the old Factory attracted a streetwise black and Latino gay audience, the new Factory crowd is mostly straight and suburban. Various jocks spin mainstream-leaning megaclub music on Fridays. Saturdays are ruled by DJ Jonathan Peters, who parlays his attack-mode brand of hard house.

### Spa

*76 E 13th St between Broadway and Fourth Ave (212-388-1062). Subway: L, N, Q, R, W, 4, 5, 6 to 14th St–Union Sq. Tue–Sat 10pm–4am. Cover varies. Average drink: $10.*
Spa no longer lures the limo-riding crowd, but it does have Thursday night's fabulous **Ülträ**, a party that harks back to the club-kid days of yore. On other nights, a suburban (though not bad-looking) crowd dances to hip-hop, house or good old-fashioned rock & roll.

### Thirteen

*35 E 13th St at University Pl (212-979-6677). Subway: L, N, Q, R, W, 4, 5, 6 to 14th St–Union Sq. Mon–Fri 4pm–4am; Sat, Sun 9pm–4am. Cover: $7–$10. Average drink: $5.*
This tiny spot offers the conventional hip-hop–R&B–classics mix, in addition to rock and house music. Parties come and go, but Sunday night's **Shout!** has survived them all; get down to Northern soul, 1960s psychedelic rock, freakbeat and various other mod genres.

## CRITICS' PICKS Clubs

These are the best nightspots to…

**…actually hear the music**
Halcyon *(see page 278)* blows away most big clubs in the sound-system department.

**…be overwhelmed**
Lunatarium *(see page 275)* is massive and has a stunning view of downtown Manhattan.

**…dance till dawn and beyond**
Shelter *(see* **Save haven**, *page 278)* revs up at 5am and often keeps going until mid-afternoon.

**…feel close to your neighbors**
Sapphire *(see page 279)* has the city's tiniest dance floor.

**…listen to the world's best DJ**
Arc *(see page 274)* welcomes the great Danny Tenaglia on a weekly basis.

**…relax and have a good time**
Filter 14 *(see page 275)* is the city's least pretentious nightspot.

**…take in a dose of '80s-fashion nostalgia**
Luxx's electroclash nights *(see page 275)* bring out the asymmetrical-haircut set.

### Void

*16 Mercer St at Howard St (212-941-6492). Subway: J, M, Z, N, Q, R, W, 6 to Canal St. 8pm–3am. No cover. Average drink: $5.*

Freethinking electronica jockeys, graphic designers, and experiemental musicians gather here for trip-hop, deep house and ambient groove. Void also provides digital video workshops and a supersharp projection screen that dominates the room.

### The Warehouse

*141 E 140th St between Grand Concourse and Walton Ave, Bronx (718-992-5974). Subway: 4, 5 to 138th St–Grand Concourse. 11:30pm–6:30am. Cover: $12–$15. Average drink: $6.*

The South Bronx remains one of New York City's most notorious neighborhoods, but it's also the proud home of the Warehouse nightclub. The mostly gay black crowd comes to hear house or Garage classics *(see* **Safe haven,** *page 278)* in the cavernous top level, and hip-hop or R&B on the smaller ground floor.

### Webster Hall

*125 E 11th St between Third and Fourth Aves (212-353-1600; www.webster-hall.com). Subway: L, N, Q, R, W, 4, 5, 6 to 14th St–Union Sq. Thu–Sat 10pm–5am. Cover: $20–$25. Average drink: $8.*

The crowd at this nightclub is primarily suburban, straight and sexually charged. Choose from various rooms blasting disco, hip-hop, soul, Latin, progressive house or today's pop hits; wherever you turn, you'll see energetic go-go dancers (male and female).

## Lounges & DJ bars

### APT

*419 W 13th St between Ninth and Tenth Aves (212-414-4245; www.aptwebsite.com). Subway: A, C, E to 14th St; L to Eighth Ave.Upstairs Sun–Wed 6pm–2am; Thu–Sat 6pm–4am. Downstairs Sun–Wed 9pm–2am; Thu–Sat 9pm–4am. Average drink: $9.*

APT used to be an ultrasecret snobatorium, but it has evolved into a nice, lushly appointed lounge with a sharp sound system and good DJs. At the monthly **Party Out of Bounds**, Metro Area (production whizzes Morgan Geist and Darshan Jesrani) proffers its peerless jazz–techno–disco–deep-house–boogie sound. Stop in on **Undressed Friday** to hear Ursula 1000 spin loungecore, sampledelica, samba and house.

### B Bar and Grill

*40 E 4th St at Bowery (212-475-2220). Subway: F, V, S to Broadway–Lafayette St; 6 to Bleecker St. Noon–4am. Average drink: $8.*

Once a watering hole for "celebutants" and models, B Bar now attracts mainly yuppies. The exception is Tuesday night's gay party, **Beige** *(see page 240)*, where DJs lay down a groovy just-this-side-of-camp soundtrack that includes everything from show tunes to 1980s electro-disco classics. Expect fashionistas, off-duty drag queens and plenty of attitude.

### Chateau

*133 Seventh Ave South between Charles and W 10th Sts (212-337-0777). Subway: 1, 9 to Christopher St–Sheridan Sq. Tue–Sat 7pm–3am. Average drink: $9.*

Rough wood beams, antique mirrors and a fireplace make for a ski-chalet feel at the spot formerly known as Moomba. Snackers can indulge in light tapas or dig into the specialty of the house, er, chalet: fondue.

### Halcyon

*227 Smith St between Butler and Douglass Sts, Carroll Gardens, Brooklyn (718-260-9299; www.halcyonline.com). Subway: F, G to Bergen St. Sun–Thu 11am–1am; Fri, Sat 11am–2am. Average drink: $5.*

**Fire down below** Warm yourself at the hearth in the Park's gorgeous lower-level lounge.

This mellow lounge–café–record store–knick-knack shop–music-lover hangout is one of the city's best places to hear high-quality underground beats. DJs spin house, techno, hip-hop and drum 'n' bass on an unparalleled sound system. Boozers beware: Halcyon doesn't serve the hard stuff, just beer and wine. The munchies menu more than compensates.

### Liquids

*266 E 10th St between First Ave and Ave A (212-677-1717). Subway: L to First Ave; 6 to Astor Pl. 8pm–4am. Average drink: $6.*

A working fireplace and cozy seating lend this East Village drink spot a ski-lodge feel. It's a good space to hear state-of-the-art musical musings from stellar local DJs. Check out the Tuesday night **Hooka Lounge** party, complete with a tent, water pipes and bubbling tech-house sounds from DJ Dots.

### Openair

*121 St. Marks Pl between First Ave and Ave A (212-979-1459; www.openairbar.com). Subway: L to First Ave; 6 to Astor Pl. Tue–Thu, Sun 7pm–4am; Fri, Sat 6pm–4am. Average drink: $6.*

This semisecret lounge is nearly invisible from the street; inside is one of the coolest high-tech venues in the city. House, hip-hop, techno, drum 'n' bass and ambient pump through an ace sound system.

### Plant Bar

See page 173.

### The Park

*118 Tenth Ave at 17th St (212-352-3313). Subway: A, C, E to 14th St; L to Eighth Ave. 11:30am–1am. Average drink: $10.*

A flash-with-cash crowd mingles in the gorgeous garden, two separate bars, dining room and "pri-

## Safe haven

**For years, Shelter bounced from space to space. Now NYC's preeminent underground party has finally found a place to call home.**

"Only on a Saturday / I feel like I can be as free as the spirit that lives in me." It's actually 8am on a Sunday, and we're a long way from church, but a religious awakening of sorts is occurring on a darkened nightclub floor in midtown. A fantastically diverse array of dancers—gay and straight, male and female, black, white, Latino, Asian—move to exquisitely soulful house music. The DJ orchestrating this harmonious hoedown is Timmy Regisford, a.k.a. "the Maestro," and the song he's playing is "Saturday" from Kevin Hedge and Josh Milan's production-songwriting team, Blaze. The lyrics are a celebration of the scene in progress: Shelter, Regisford and Hedge's underground party institution.

Shelter isn't a new soiree, but thanks to its relocation and a revamped sound system, the 11-year-old shindig is rocking Saturday-night-into-Sunday-morning harder than it has in years. Both longtime Shelterheads and fresh faces mix it up at the revitalized club, where regulars refer to each other as family members.

The event has retained an old-school clubbing environment that has nearly disappeared from the city's after-dark scene. As Shelter habitué Richard Alvarez puts it, "It doesn't matter if you can't afford the right sneakers. There's a real communal feeling at Shelter—it's the music that does it." Regisford spins old and new songs with "love and unity" lyrics and a gospel-tinged tone; it's a soundtrack that's rarely played in big clubs anymore. Inspirational tunes like "Optimistic" by Sounds of Blackness, "Pure" by Blue Six and anything by Blaze set the inviting party mood. "We get a crowd that listens to soulful music," says Regisford. "[They want] songs with lyrics that say something."

Hedge, 35, and Regisford, 38, have made this kind of music and clubbing their life's work. Hedge grew up in New Jersey on the postdisco, prehouse music that dominated underground clubs like Manhattan's Paradise Garage. Trinidad-born Regisford, who was spinning on the funk, soul and R&B station WBLS-FM in the early 1980s, was one of the sound's main proponents. When he heard Blaze's masterpiece "Whatcha Gonna Do," Regisford forged a friendship with the song's co-writer Hedge. "Timmy had always wanted to open a club," says Hedge. "He knew that Blaze had a lucrative publishing deal, and he [convinced me] to invest in this venture."

Shelter first opened in March 1991 on Hubert Street in Tribeca. In those early days, the club attracted a crowd similar to the one that frequented the Garage: largely gay people of color. Eventually, the club's demographic broadened, cutting across NYC's social and cultural strata to welcome

vate" Penthouse lounge of a lavishly remodelled former garage.

### Sapphire

*249 Eldridge St between Houston and Stanton Sts (212-777-5153; www.sapphirenyc.com). Subway: F, V to Lower East Side–Second Ave. 7pm–4am. Cover varies. Average drink: $5.*

One of the Lower East Side's first DJ bars, Sapphire schedules a fairly typical lineup: disco classics, hip-hop, reggae and R&B. However, deep- and tech-house parties (on Monday and Wednesday nights) often showcase superstar DJs such as Roger S.

## Roving parties

New York is home to a number of peripatetic ongoing soirees. Nights, locations and prices vary; telephone, e-mail or hit the websites for the latest updates.

### Drive By

*212-560-0951, or e-mail goldspot@hotmail.com for information.*

Two-step Garage has been popular in the U.K. for years, but this mishmash of house, breaks, drum 'n' bass and R&B has only recently made waves on this side of the pond; the **Drive By** party is largely responsible for the sound's burgeoning popularity here. Resident DJ Dinesh ropes in stars such as M.J. Cole and the Artful Dodger.

### Giant Step

*www.giantstep.net.*

Giant Step parties have featured Roni Size, Jazzanova, Saint Germain and King Britt. These high-quality wingdings, which roll out a range of underground

**Gimme Shelter** Avid fans won't let the famous Saturday-night party fade away.

anyone with an open-minded attitude. But as the party's spirit soared, Shelter began to encounter some turbulence. The club lost its lease in 1993, and spent the next five years moving around to various Manhattan locations—only to end up, in the summer of '98, back at the Hubert Street space. Although the party was still drawing crowds, a few of the faithful felt that some of the original mood had been lost. "Shelter started resting on its laurels," says Kip Britton, a longtime regular. "[Their attitude became,] 'We're all there is; if you want it, come to us.' "

Late in the summer of 2001, the management of the Hubert Street space decided to drop Shelter in favor of trendier (and potentially more profitable) progressive-house soirees. Hedge and Regisford prepared to close their party in style with one final blowout, scheduled for September 15. But September 11 disrupted that plan, and the event was canceled.

"We took the fact that we weren't able to say good-bye as an omen—that maybe it wasn't supposed to be over," Hedge says. In January 2002, the two announced that they were taking over a multiroom space on West 39th Street. "A lot of people wondered, 'How the hell did we get the money?' " Hedge says. "They don't know that Josh and I wrote several hits in the U.K. and Europe [for singers like De'Lacy and Amira]. We have about 14 gold and platinum records." The club officially reopened on March 30, 2002, with a packed-to-the-gills party that featured a performance from Shelter favorite Patti LaBelle, who had been slated to sing at the 2001 farewell affair.

The essence of Shelter—if it was ever gone—is definitely back. "The crowd, the vibe, everything just seems to be a lot better," says Hedge. "But we've always had people who are interested in music and dancing over glitz and glam. And the music at Shelter is the spirit that unites us all."

### Shelter

*See* **Club Shelter**, *page 275.*

Arts & Entertainment

**Making waves** Roving Turntables on the Hudson usually drops anchor near a river.

beats, have a loyal following of dedicated dancers. Highly recommended.

### Matter/:Form

*www.matter-form.com.*
Renowned for its booming boat parties, Matter/:Form occasionally commandeers a land-based dance floor. DJ Francis Harris spins deep house, tech-house and techno. Cool guests who recently manned the desks include U.K. acid-house stalwart Evil Eddie Richards and California-based deep-house dude Doc Martin.

### Motherfucker

*www.motherfuckernyc.com.*
The Motherfucker gang celebrates messy, omnisexual rock & roll hanky-panky. Michael T. and Justine D. play power pop, glam, new wave and disco, usually on those drunken nights before a big national holiday.

### Organic Grooves

*212-439-1147; www.codek.com.*
DJ Sasha Crnobrnja and his coterie of musicians conjure elements of funk, dub and disco for an off-kilter dance-floor–ready sound. The crowd is straight, comely and racially mixed.

### Tsunami

*212-439-8124; www.tsunami-trance.com.*
The Tsunami crew rides the psychedelic trance-wave into town on a semiregular basis, often setting up shop at retro-kitsch hot spot **Culture Club** *(179 Varick St between King and Charlton Sts, 212-243-1999)* or soulful-house center Club Shelter *(see page 275)*.

### Turntables on the Hudson

*212-560-5593; www.turntablesonthehudson.com.*
This ultrafunky affair pops up all over the place, as close to the water as possible. DJs Nickodemus, Mariano and guests do the dub-funky, worldbeaty thing using live percussionists. This is one of the city's best parties—the dance floor is packed all night long.

## Club rules

**Avoid run-ins with the law**
Bring a photo ID, leave weapons at home, and know that you may be searched at club entrances. If getting high is your cup of E, be careful—many clubs police their patrons' drug use.

**Dress to the beat**
Door policies can be brutal, so it's wise to look the part.

**Hang with the cool kids**
Many locals stick to mid-week clubbing to avoid the suburbanite crowds that overwhelm venues on the weekends.

**Phone ahead**
Parties can change lineup or location at a moment's notice. Before you leave, call the club, hit its website or check out www.timeoutny.com.

**Play it safe**
If you're out late, take a cab or a car service home (*see chapter* **Directory**).

**Straight guys shouldn't travel in packs**
Hetero-heavy venues often refuse entry to groups of men to maintain a desirable gender balance.

# Film & TV

In New York City, you can gaze at the stars on the silver screen or head to a television studio for your own close-up

## Film

New York has been the setting for countless famous films—*Annie Hall, Breakfast at Tiffany's, Do the Right Thing, On the Waterfront* and *Taxi Driver,* to name just a few. Not only is the city a great place for cinema because of the movies it "stars" in, but also because of the movies it shows. Revival, art and foreign films unspool at a variety of inviting places: large multiscreen venues devoted to independent cinema; historic, elegant theaters; and intimate 25-seat screening rooms. To catch a major Hollywood release, head to one of the plush multiplexes that were built during the heady financial times of the 1990s. There are so many theaters catering to different tastes that if you can't find a movie you like in New York, you probably don't like movies.

### Art & revival houses

New York screens more art films and old movies than any other city in the country. The following are the most popular venues.

#### Angelika Film Center

*18 W Houston St at Mercer St (212-995-2000; 777-FILM). Subway: F, V, S to Broadway–Lafayette St; N, R, W to Prince St; 6 to Bleecker St. $10, seniors and children $6. AmEx, MC, V.*

The six-screen Angelika features primarily new American independent and foreign films. You can hang out at the espresso-and-pastry café before the show. The complex is a zoo on weekends, so come extra early or buy your tickets by phone.

#### BAM Rose Cinemas

*See* **Brooklyn Academy of Music**, *page 318. For advance tickets, 777-FILM. $9; seniors, students and children $6. AmEx, MC, V.*

Brooklyn's premier art-house theater pulls double duty as a repertory house and a first-run multiplex for independent films.

#### Cinema Classics

*332 E 11th St between First and Second Aves (212-677-5368; www.cinemaclassics.com). Subway: L to First Ave; N, Q, R, W, 4, 5, 6 to 14th St–Union Sq. $3, plus one-drink minimum. Cash only.*

It may be shabby and cramped, but this is the place to go for screenings of classic Hollywood, foreign and indie films. The $5.50 double bills can't be beat.

#### Cinema Village

*22 E 12th St between Fifth Ave and University Pl (212-924-3363, box office 212-924-3364). Subway: L, N, Q, R, W, 4, 5, 6 to 14th St–Union Sq. $9, seniors and children $5.50, students $7. Cash only.*

Three-screen Cinema Village specializes in American indies and foreign films. The theater also runs midnight horror flicks on weekends.

#### Film Forum

*209 W Houston St between Sixth Ave and Varick St (212-727-8110; www.filmforum.com). Subway: 1, 9 to Houston St. $9.75, seniors and children under 12 $5. Cash only at the box office; AmEx, MC, V on website.*

If you have time to visit only one cinema in New York, go to the indispensible Film Forum. The art-house theater offers some of the best new films, documentaries and art movies around. Revival series, usually brilliantly curated, are also shown.

#### Landmark's Sunshine Cinema

*143 E Houston St between First and Second Aves, (212-358-7709; 777-FILM). Subway: F, V to Lower East Side–Second Ave. $10, seniors $6.50. AmEx, MC, V.*

This restored 1898 Yiddish theater is one of New York's newer art houses, presenting the best in independent cinema.

#### Lincoln Plaza Cinemas

*30 Lincoln Plaza, entrance on Broadway between 62nd and 63rd Sts (212-757-0359, tickets 212-757-2280; www.lincolnplazacinema.com). Subway: A, C, B, D, 1, 9 to 59th St–Columbus Circle. $9.50, seniors and children $6. Cash only at box office; AmEx, V over the phone or on website.*

Commercially successful European films can be seen at this cinema near Lincoln Center, along with American independent productions. All six theaters are

► For up-to-date movie reviews and showtimes, check out **www.timeoutny.com**, or pick up a copy of ***Time Out New York***.

► Museums and galleries other than those listed here often host special film series and experimental films. See also chapter **Museums**.

► Purchase tickets in advance at moviefone.com, or by calling 777-FILM or 1-800-535-TELL.

equipped with assisted-listening devices for the hearing-impaired and are wheelchair-accessible.

### Paris Theatre

*4 W 58th St between Fifth and Sixth Aves (212-688-3800; 777-FILM). Subway: F to 57th St; N, R, W to Fifth Ave–59th St. $10, seniors and children $6. Cash only at box office; AmEx, MC, V on website.*

This posh bijou is a de rigueur destination for cinéastes who love foreign-language films.

### Quad Cinema

*34 W 13th St between Fifth and Sixth Aves (212-255-8800; 777-FILM). Subway: F, V to 14th St; L to Sixth Ave. $9, seniors and children $6. Cash only at box office; AmEx, MC, V on website.*

Four small screens show a broad selection of foreign and American independent films, as well as documentaries—many dealing with sexual and political issues. Children under 5 are not admitted.

### Screening Room

*54 Varick St at Laight St (212-334-2100). Subway: A,C, E, 1, 9 to Canal St. $9.50, seniors and children $6.50. AmEx, MC, V.*

Attached to a swank bistro, this small theater is perfect for a dinner-and-movie date (it has love seats for two). It shows first-run films and revivals—and *Breakfast at Tiffany's* every Sunday afternoon.

### Symphony Space

*Leonard Nimoy Thalia, 2537 Broadway at 95th St (212-864-5400). Subway: 1, 2, 3, 9 to 96th St. $9, seniors $8, members $5. AmEx, MC, V ($15 minimum).*

The famed Thalia art house—featured prominently in Woody Allen's *Annie Hall*—was recently refurbished. It features well-selected programming of world cinema.

### Two Boots Pioneer Theater

*155 E 3rd St between Aves A and B (212-254-3300). Subway: F, V to Lower East Side–Second Ave; L to First Ave. $8.50; seniors, students and children $6. Cash only.*

The pizza chain Two Boots *(see* **The upper crust**, *page 191)* operates the East Village's only first-run alternative film center. The programming is a mix of new indies, revivals and themed festivals.

## Museums & societies

### American Museum of the Moving Image

*See page 57 for listing.*

The first U.S. museum devoted to moving pictures is in Queens. AMMI shows more than 700 films a year, covering everything from Hollywood classics and oddball industrial-safety films to series devoted to a single actor or director.

### Anthology Film Archives

*32 Second Ave at 2nd St (212-505-5181). Subway: F, V to Lower East Side–Second Ave. $8, seniors and students $5. Cash only.*

Anthology houses the world's largest collection of written material documenting the history of independent and experimental film and video.

**Save a rainy day** See a great indie film at Landmark's Sunshine Cinema.

### Brooklyn Museum of Art

*See* **Art and Soul**, *page 44, for listing.*

The museum's intelligent, eclectic roster concentrates primarily on foreign films.

### Film Society of Lincoln Center

*Walter Reade Theater, Lincoln Center, 165 W 65th St between Broadway and Amsterdam Ave, plaza level (212-875-5601, tickets 212-496-3809; www.filmlinc.com). Subway: 1, 9 to 66th St–Lincoln Ctr. $9.50, $5–12 children, $7 students. Cash only at box office; MC, V on website.*

The FSLC was founded in 1969 to promote contemporary film and video, and support filmmakers. It operates the Walter Reade Theater, a state-of-the-art showcase with the city's most comfortable theater seats. Programs are usually thematic, and often have an international perspective. Each autumn, the society hosts the **New York Film Festival** *(see page 282)* at Alice Tully Hall.

### Guggenheim Museum

*See* **Solomon R. Guggenheim Museum** *page 47 for listing.*

The Guggenheim's programs and series are insightful and provocative.

### IMAX Theater

*See* **American Museum of Natural History**, *page 41 for listing.*

The IMAX screen is four stories high, and daily programming explores the natural world.

### Metropolitan Museum of Art

*See page 44 for listing.*

The Met offers a full program of documentary films on art (many of which relate to current exhibitions) in the Uris Center Auditorium (near the 81st Street entrance).

### Museum of Modern Art

*Gramercy Theater, 127 E 23rd St between Park and Lexington Aves (212-777-4900; www.ticketweb.com). Subway: N, R, W, 6 to 23rd St. $12, seniors and students $8.50, children under 16 free, when accompanied by an adult. Fridays after 4pm pay what you wish. AmEx, MC, V.*

During the restoration of MoMA's main building, the museum has relocated its film program to the Gramercy Theater, where it has roughly 25 screenings each week; typically, they highlight a particular director's work, but they can also be based on other themes. Entry is free with MoMA QNS admission, within a 30-day period.

### The Museum of Television & Radio

*See page 57 for listing.*

The museum's collection includes thousands of TV programs that can be viewed at private consoles. Episodes are shown daily in the museum's two screening rooms and in its 200-seat MT&R Theater.

### Whitney Museum of American Art

*See page 48 for listing.*

In keeping with its aim of showing the best in contemporary American art, the Whitney runs a varied film-and-video schedule. Entry is free with museum admission.

## Foreign-language films

Many of the previous institutions screen films in languages other than English, but the following show only foreign-language films.

### Asia Society

*See page 54 for listing.*

You can see works from China, India and other Asian countries, as well as Asian-American productions.

### French Institute–Alliance Française

*See page 55 for listing.*

The institute shows movies from its homeland, in addition to well-made cinema from other countries. Films are usually subtitled and never dubbed.

### Goethe-Institut/ German Cultural Center

*See page 55 for listing.*

A cultural and educational organization, the Goethe-Institut shows German films in various locations around the city, as well as in its own opulent auditorium.

### Japan Society

*See page 56 for listing.*

The Japan Society Film Center organizes a full schedule of Japanese movies.

## Film festivals

Every September and October since 1963, the Film Society of Lincoln Center *(see page 281)* has hosted the prestigious **New York Film Festival**. The FSLC, with the Museum of Modern Art, also sponsors the highly regarded **New Directors/New Films** series each spring, to present works by on-the-cusp filmmakers from around the world. (Information on both may be found at www.filmline.com.) Smaller, equally anticipated festivals occur throughout the year. The **New York Independent Film and Video Festival** *(212-777-7100; www.nyfilmvideo.com)* lures cinéastes three times a year, in April, September and December. In May, Robert De Niro rolls out the **Tribeca Film Festival** *(www.tribecafilmfestival.org)*, a new but influential player on the scene. The popular **New York Lesbian & Gay Film Festival** screens in early June *(212-558-6855; www.newfestival.org)*. On summer Monday evenings, Bryant Park *(see page 252)* offers free classic flicks on a giant outdoor screen. January brings the annual **New York Jewish Film Festival** *(212-875-5600)*.

# Television

## Studio tapings

Tickets are available to several TV shows taped in New York City.

### *The Daily Show with Jon Stewart*

*513 W 54th St between Tenth and Eleventh Aves (212-586-2477). Subway: A, C, B, D, 1, 9 to 59th St–Columbus Circle. Mon–Thu 5:30pm.*

Reserve tickets three months ahead by phone, or call at 11:30am on the Friday before you'd like to attend to see if there are any unused tickets. You must be at least 18 and have a photo ID.

**Nuisance or news sense?** Jon Stewart's telling of the day's events usually gets a laugh.

### Late Night with Conan O'Brien

*212-664-3056; www.nbc.com/conan. Subway: B, D, F, V to 47–50th Sts–Rockefeller Ctr. Tue–Fri 5:30pm.*
Call three months in advance for tickets. A limited number of same-day standby tickets are distributed at 9am *(30 Rockefeller Plaza between 49th and 50th Sts, 49th St entrance)*; one ticket per person. You must be at least 16 and have a photo ID.

### Late Show with David Letterman

*Mailing address: Late Show Tickets, c/o Ed Sullivan Theater, 1697 Broadway, New York, NY 10019 (212-975-1003; www.cbs.com/latenight/lateshow). Subway: B, D, E to Seventh Ave. Mon–Wed 5:30pm; Thu 5:30, 8pm.*
Send a postcard (with your name, address and phone number) six to eight months in advance. You can also apply for tickets online. Standby tickets are available by calling 212-247-6497 at 11am on the day of taping. You must be at least 18 and have a photo ID.

### Saturday Night Live

*212-664-3056; www.nbc.com/snl. Subway: B, D, F, V to 47–50th Sts–Rockefeller Ctr. Dress rehearsals at 8pm, live show at 11:30pm.*
No advance tickets are available for spring 2003. Call or check website for fall and winter 2003 availability. Standby tickets for both the dress rehearsal and live show are distributed the day of taping; line up no later than 7am at 30 Rockefeller Plaza *(50th St between Rockefeller Plaza and Sixth Ave)*. You must be at least 16.

## Tours

Location tours often sell out. Reservations, via telephone or website, are required.

### Kramer's Reality Tour

*The Producers Club, 358 W 44th St between Eighth and Ninth Aves (800-KRAMERS; www.kennykramer.com). Subway: A, C, E to 42nd St–Port Authority. Sat, Sun 11:45am. $39.50. AmEx, Disc, MC, V.*
Kenny Kramer (yes, the real guy that Michael Richards' *Seinfeld* character is based on) takes you to many of the show's locations on a three-hour bus tour.

### Sex and the City Tour

*Pulitzer Fountain near Plaza Hotel, Fifth Ave between 58th and 59th Sts (212-239-1124; www.sceneontv.com/sexcity). Mon 11:30am; Thu 3pm; Sat 11:30am, 2:30pm. Subway: N, R, W to Fifth Ave–59th St. $30. AmEx, Disc, MC, V.*
Visit more than 40 sites where Carrie & Co. eat, drink, look for men, work out, gossip and shop.

### The Sopranos Tour

*Bryant Park fountain, Sixth Ave between 40th and 42nd Sts (212-239-1124, www.sceneontv.com/sopranostour). Subway: B, D, F, V to 42nd St. Sun 2pm; call for Saturday tours. $35. AmEx, Disc, MC, V.*
This tour stops at about 35 locations where filming takes place.

# Gay & Lesbian

New York's queer bars, restaurants, clubs and community make it the finest place to be out and about

San Francisco is often touted as the nation's gayest city, but if it's true that one out of every ten people is gay, then that means New York, with about 8 million inhabitants, is home to more homosexuals than the entire Bay Area population! And gay New Yorkers enjoy a thriving social scene, with hundreds of gay social and political organizations, as well as the opportunity for an enticing gay-friendly career. Is it any wonder that this city, with its huge queer populace, is the capital of fashion, beauty, theater, dance and design? But it's not only in the more glamorous fields that the rainbow contingent plays a vital role. From the New York Stock Exchange to the city council, openly gay men and women are pivotal in maintaining New York's world-class status.

As the site of the 1969 Stonewall riots and the birthplace of the American gay-rights movement, New York City is a homo haven. During the annual **Gay Pride** celebration, the Pride March (every June, typically the last Sunday), attracts up to a half-million spectators. The march is a great time to visit New York: You'll feel as if everyone is queer.

Arrive during the summer to sample lesbian and gay resort culture on **Fire Island** *(see page 348),* which is only a short trip from the center of town, and the stellar lineup of celluloid delights at the definitive **New York Lesbian & Gay Film Festival** *(see page 283).*

An essential stop for any gay or lesbian visitor to New York is the **Lesbian, Gay, Bisexual & Transgender Community Center** *(see page 286),* a downtown nexus of information and activity that serves as a meeting place for more than 300 groups and organizations. And don't miss *Time Out New York*'s lively Gay & Lesbian listings for the latest happenings around town.

Although the gay and lesbian population of New York is quite diverse, the club and bar scenes don't always reflect it; many places are gender-segregated, and tend to attract the single 35-and-under crowd. However, the alternatives are plentiful—among them, queer coffeebars, bookstores and restaurants, as well as dozens of gay-themed films and plays (*see chapters* **Cabaret & Comedy**, **Film & TV** *and* **Theater & Dance**).

**Flag-waver** The recently renovated Lesbian, Gay, Bisexual and Transgender Center is a community cornerstone.

## Books & media

### Bookshops

Many independent gay bookshops in NYC have closed over the past several years due to competition from online sellers and megastores. While most bookshops have gay sections (*see chapter* **Books & Poetry**), these remaining stalwarts cater especially to gays and lesbians.

#### Bluestockings

*172 Allen St at Stanton St (212-777-6028; www.bluestockings.com). Subway: F, V to Lower East Side–Second Ave. Tue–Sun 1–9pm. AmEx, Disc, MC, V.*
This funky Lower East Side bookstore devoted to

► For more on the Pride March and the Greenwich Village Halloween Parade, see chapter **By Season**.
► For strictly gay listings, see **Boys' Life**, page 287; for lesbian listings, see **Dyke Life**, page 294.

women's literature holds weekly readings and events. You'll find everything from dyke-hero comic books to feminist manifestos.

### Creative Visions

*548 Hudson St between Charles and Perry Sts (212-645-7573). Subway: A, C, E to 14th St; L to Eighth Ave. Mon–Thu noon–10pm; Fri, Sat noon–11pm; Sun noon–10pm. AmEx, Disc, MC, V.*
Only a short stroll from Christopher Street, this no-frills store stocks a nice selection of merchandise, including literature, travel guides, calendars and X-rated fare.

## Publications

New York's gay weekly magazines are *HX (Homo Xtra)* and *Next*—both of which include extensive information on bars, events, clubs, group meetings, restaurants...and loads of private sex parties. *HX* also devotes a couple of pages to lesbian listings. The newspaper *Gay City* provides feisty political coverage with an activist slant, while its arch rival, the *New York Blade News* (a sister publication of *The Washington Blade*) focuses on queer politics and news. The monthly *Go NYC*, "a cultural road map for the city girl" gives the lowdown on the local lesbian scene. All five are free and widely available. *MetroSource ($4.95)* is a quarterly glossy with a guppie slant, covering decorating, fashion and exotic travel.

Daniel Hurewitz's *Stepping Out ($16)*, which details nine walking tours of gay and lesbian NYC, is another fine resource.

## Television

New York has a hodgepodge of gay-related broadcasting, though much of it is amateurishly produced and appears on public-access cable channels. Programming varies by cable company, so you may not be able to watch these shows on a hotel TV. At night, Channel 35 (in most of Manhattan) runs sexually explicit programming that includes the infamous Robin Byrd's *Men for Men* soft-core strip shows. Manhattan Neighborhood Network (channels 34, 56, 57 and 67 on Manhattan cable) airs plenty of gay shows, ranging from zany drag queens milking their 15 minutes of fame to serious discussion programs. *HX* and *Next* provide the most current TV listings.

**Free press** Creative Visions is NYC's last independent bookstore for gays and lesbians.

## Centers & phone lines

### Gay & Lesbian Switchboard of New York Project

*212-989-0999; www.glnh.org. Mon–Fri 4pm–midnight; Sat noon–5pm.*
This phone service offers excellent peer counseling, legal referrals, details on gay and lesbian organizations, and information on bars, hotels and restaurants. Outside New York (but within the U.S.), callers can use the toll-free **Gay & Lesbian National Hotline**, at 888-THE-GLNH.

### Gay Men's Health Crisis

*119 W 24th St between Sixth and Seventh Aves (212-367-1000, AIDS advice hot line 212-807-6655; www.gmhc.org). Subway: 1, 9 to 23rd St. Advice hot line Mon–Fri 10am–9pm; Sat noon–3pm. Recorded information in English and Spanish at other times. Office Mon–Fri 9am–6pm.*
GMHC was the world's first organization dedicated to helping people with AIDS. It has a threefold mission: to push for better public policies; to help those who are sick by providing services and counseling to them and their families; and to educate the public to prevent the further spread of HIV. Support groups usually meet in the evenings.

### Lesbian, Gay, Bisexual & Transgender Community Center

*208 W 13th St between Seventh and Eighth Aves (212-620-7310; www.gaycenter.org). Subway: F, V, 1, 2, 3, 9 to 14th St; L to Eighth Ave. Mon–Fri 9am–10pm.*
This is where ACT UP and GLAAD got started. After being closed almost two years for major renovation, the center is up and running again, providing political, cultural, spiritual and emotional support to the 300-odd groups that meet here. The center also houses the **National Museum and Archive of Lesbian and Gay History**, and the **Vito Russo Lending Library**.

### Lesbian Herstory Archive

*P.O. Box 1258, New York, NY 10116 (718-768-3953; www.datalounge.net/lha). By appointment only.*
Located in Brooklyn's Park Slope area (known to

some as Dyke Slope for its large lesbian population), the Herstory Archive contains more than 10,000 books (theory, fiction, poetry, plays), 1,400 periodicals and assorted memorabilia. Donate a treasured possession and become part of Herstory.

### Michael Callen–Audre Lorde Community Health Center

*356 W 18th St between Eighth and Ninth Aves (212-271-7200; www.callen-lorde.org). Subway: A, C, E to 14th St; L to Eighth Ave. Mon 12:30–8pm; Tue, Thu, Fri 9am–4:30pm; Wed 2:30–8pm.*

This is the country's largest health center primarily serving the gay, lesbian, bisexual and transgender community. It offers comprehensive primary care, HIV treatment, STD screening and treatment, mental health services, peer counseling and free adolescent services (including the youth hot line **HOTT**: 212-271-7212).

### NYC Gay & Lesbian Anti-Violence Project

*240 W 35th St between Seventh and Eighth Aves, suite 200 (212-714-1184, 24-hour hot line 212-714-1141; www.avp.org). Subway: A, C, E, 1, 2, 3, 9 to 34th St–Penn Station. Mon–Thu 10am–8pm; Fri 10am–6pm.*

The project provides support to victims of antigay and antilesbian crimes. Working with the police department, volunteers offer advice on seeking police help. Long- and short-term counseling is available.

## Boys' Life

The Christopher Street area of the West Village has historical gay sites such as the **Stonewall** *(see page 290),* friendly show-tune piano cabarets and stores full of rainbow knickknacks and slogan T-shirts. But during the past decade, the gay epicenter has shifted to Chelsea and shows no sign of slowing down.

The neighborhood's main drag is Eighth Avenue between 16th and 23rd Streets, a strip lined with businesses catering to upwardly mobile gay men: gyms; sexy clothing and trendy home-furnishing stores; tanning and grooming salons; cafés, bars and restaurants. The cult of the body reigns in Chelsea, and it's a kick to watch the perfectly toned men strut down the avenue. True, some gym bunnies ignore the less muscle-bound, but the stereotype of Chelsea as a sea of supermen is exaggerated—queers of all types converge on the neighborhood.

Most of Manhattan's dance clubs are either in Chelsea or just a hop, skip and jump away from it; many feature a big gay house/techno night on weekends—bacchanals where sybarites can spin and twirl with hundreds of half-naked men until the wee hours (*see chapter* **Clubs**).

A more eclectic crowd thrives in the East Village's network of small, divey bars. You'll find the neighborhood's bohemian contingent—artists, drag queens, nightlife celebrities—as well as college students and the bourgeois set that has begun to gentrify the area. The scene is more mixed than Chelsea, both ethnically and sexually, though the crowd tends to be younger.

And you'd better believe that gays have helped change Brooklyn from Nowhereville to Fun City, U.S.A. Williamsburg is jam-packed with cute queers (most with adorable haircuts), as are other happening 'hoods, such as Cobble Hill and Carroll Gardens. Several queer spots have become popular, such as **Luxx** *(see page 292)* and **That Bar** *(see page 293).*

Men of all ages, shapes and sizes frequent the city's leather/fetish bars and clubs, such as **The Eagle** *(554 W 28th St between Tenth and Eleventh Aves, 646-473-1866)* in Chelsea and **The Lure** in the Meatpacking District *(see page 290).* If you're a devotee of the leather scene, check out the New York Mr. Leather Contest, which takes place in the autumn, or the Black Party at **Saint at Large** *(see page 292)*—a special all-night leather-and-S&M circuit party that attracts thousands every March.

For open-air cruising, try the **Ramble** in Central Park, between the 79th Street transverse and the Lake (but beware of police entrapment). Although the city has made every effort to clean up Times Square and turn it into Disney World, you can still find nude male burlesque at the **Gaiety Theatre** *(201 W 46th St between Broadway and Eighth Ave, 212-221-8868).* The

### CRITICS' PICKS Pssst...

Why follow the crowd? Seek out some of the city's unexpected queer pleasures:

**Best lesbian watering hole in midtown:**
Madison Square Garden, during WNBA basketball games featuring the New York Liberty *(see page 324).*

**Best place to imitate John Travolta:**
Spectrum *(802 64th St at Eighth Ave, 718-238-8213),* the Bay Ridge, Brooklyn, gay nightclub where *Saturday Night Fever* was filmed. The lit dance floor is still intact.

**Best place to see gay celebrities:**
Madame Tussaud's Wax Museum *(see page 88).* The queer cast includes RuPaul, Quentin Crisp, Billie Jean King and Elton John.

adjacent west-midtown area—nicknamed Hell's Kitchen but occasionally called by the less threatening moniker Clinton—is fast becoming the next hot homo zone. Take a stroll up Ninth Avenue between 42nd and 57th Streets to explore.

Don't worry if you're just an average T-shirt–and–jeans gay man. Not only will you feel comfortable in almost any gay space, you'll be surprised at how much cruising happens while you're simply walking around town, and how easy it is to turn a glance into a conversation.

## Accommodations

### Chelsea Mews Guest House

*344 W 15th St between Eighth and Ninth Aves (212-255-9174). Subway: A, C, E to 14th St; L to Eighth Ave. Singles and doubles $100–$200. Cash and traveler's checks only.*

Built in 1840, this guest house is exclusively for gay men. The rooms are comfortable, well-furnished and, in most cases, equipped with semiprivate bathrooms. Laundry and bicycle rental is included with your stay. Smoking is not allowed.

### Chelsea Pines Inn

*317 W 14th St between Eighth and Ninth Aves (212-929-1023; fax 212-620-5646; www.chelseapinesinn.com). Subway: A, C, E to 14th St; L to Eighth Ave. Doubles and triples $99–$139 (slightly higher during Gay Pride and holidays). AmEx, DC, Disc, MC, V.*

This centrally located inn near the West Village and Chelsea welcomes gay guests, both male and female. Vintage movie posters set the mood, and the 25 rooms are clean and comfortable; the majority have private bathrooms, and all include radios, televisions, phones, refrigerators and air conditioning.Continental breakfast is included with your stay.

### Colonial House Inn

*318 W 22nd St between Eighth and Ninth Aves (212-243-9669, 800-689-3779; www.colonialhouseinn.com). Subway: C, E to 23rd St. $80–$125 with shared bath; $125–$160 with private bath. Prices higher on weekends (15-percent discount Jan 2–Feb 28 with four-night minimum stay). MC, V.*

This beautifully renovated 1880s townhouse sits on a quiet street in the heart of Chelsea. Run by, and primarily for, gay men, Colonial House is a great



# Coming to terms

Let our gay glossary help you keep everyone…straight

**BABY BUTCHES**

Newly out young lesbians who are just getting comfortable embodying butchness. Telltale style elements: fully or partially shaved head, big jeans that hang low on the hips, an infantile sneer.

**Where to find them: Henrietta Hudson** *(see page 295)*; **Meow Mix** *(see page 295)* on Saturdays; Starlette Sundays at **Starlight** *(see page 290).*

**BEARS**

Burly men covered with facial and body hair, named for their resemblance to the furry forest creatures. Proud of protruding bellies and advanced hirsuteness, bears often mate within the species.

**Where to find them:** At **The Eagle** *(see page 287)* and **The Lure** *(see page 290)*; at **Metro Bears** gatherings *(www.metrobears.org).*

**BOIS**

Pronounced "boys," the term refers to those whose gender identity leans toward the male; it's used by various queer people but some don't like it. Use with caution.

**Where to find them:** Meow Mix; **Luxx** *(see page 292)*; roving drag-king parties; the East Village; and Williamsburg and Park Slope, Brooklyn.

**DYKE MIKES**

Men—gay or straight—who seek out the company of lesbians. While the term can have cachet for the straight guy, gay men may find the label cramps their cruising style.

**Where to find them:** Hanging with the girls in Henrietta Hudson, Meow Mix and Starlight; cheering wildly on the sidelines of the **Dyke March** during Gay Pride *(see page 251).*

**GUPPIES**

Gay yuppies, typically between the ages of 25 and 40, whose desire for expensive clothing and prime real estate matches that of their straight counterparts. Guppies slave at high-paying jobs, often in the finance and design industries.

**Where to find them:** The Beige party at **B Bar** *(see page 290)*; shopping at **Barneys** *(see page 209)*; summering in the **Hamptons** *(see page 350).*

**HIGH FEMMES**

Lesbians who take society's version of femininity to the extreme, indulging in makeup, fabulous hair, high heels, baubles and short skirts.

place to stay, even if some of the cheaper rooms are snug. Major bonuses: free continental breakfast and a rooftop deck (nude sunbathing allowed!).

### Incentra Village House

*32 Eighth Ave between Jane and 12th Sts (212-206-0007). Subway: A, C, E to 14th St; L to Eighth Ave. $119–$169, suites $149–$199. AmEx, MC, V.*

Two cute 1841 townhouses, perfectly situated in the West Village, comprise this guest house run by gay men. The intriguingly decorated rooms are spacious and come with private bathrooms and kitchenettes; some have working fireplaces. There's also a 1939 Steinway baby-grand piano in the parlor for show-tune enthusiasts.

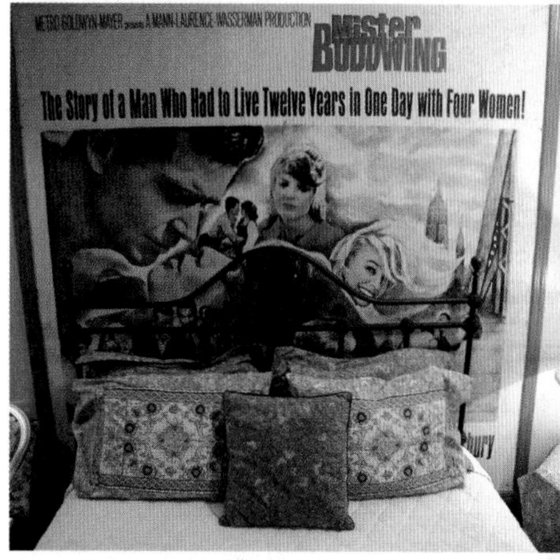


**Heterosexual agenda** Old posters at Chelsea Pines Inn help patrons count their blessings.

## Bars

Most bars in New York offer theme nights, drink specials and happy hours, and the gay establishments are no exception. Don't be shy, remember to tip the bartender and carry plenty of business cards. (*See also chapters* **Bars** *and* **Cabaret & Comedy**.)

**Where to find them:** Thursday's Gloss at Meow Mix; Starlette Sundays at Starlight; monthly **Shescape** events *(see page 295).*

**HOMO THUGS (ALSO HOMO THUGZ)**

Hip-hop heads who like kicking it with other guys, but who won't be waving no bitch-ass rainbow flags, know wh'amsayin'?

**Where to find them: The Warehouse** *(see page 277)* in the Bronx; the once-a-month party Papi-cock at **Club Shelter** *(see page 295).*

**MUSCLE MARYS**

Male gym fanatics who are obsessed with obtaining chiseled pumped-up bodies; especially prevalent in Chelsea.

**Where to find them:** Saturday nights at the **Roxy** *(see page 275);* the **David Barton** gym *(see page 293)* and **19th Street Gym** *(see page 294);* the Fire Island **Pines** *(see page 349).*

**PIER QUEENS**

Street-smart black and Latino youths named for the Christopher Street pier, a former queer stomping ground. In the style of *Paris Is Burning,* PQs are famed for their voguing skills and colorful slang ("She's a brick, Miss Honey!").

**Where to find them:** Strutting up and down Christopher Street (the pier is currently under renovation); hanging in Hudson River Park; outside the **Hetrick-Martin Institute**, a gay youth center *(2 Astor Pl between Broadway and Lafayette St, 212-674-2400).*

**SEX PIGS**

Relentlessly horny men who spend their time either (a) cruising for sex partners in bars and rest rooms, and on Internet sites, or (b) engaging in all sorts of sexual high jinks.

**Where to find them: J's Hangout** *(see page 292);* at Sperm, the Sunday-night party at the **Cock** *(see page 290).*

**TROLLS**

Older, unattractive gay males; considered to be lechers by younger, attractive gay males. The worst fear of a young gay person is to grow old and be offhandedly referred to as a troll.

**Where to find them:** In the audience at the **Gaiety** *(see page 287);* at happy hours in depressing bars; under bridges.

**TWINKIES**

Spirited young men who aren't old enough to get into clubs yet. They're full of energy, obsessed with fashion and pop music, and able to lip-synch all of Britney's hits.

**Where to find them:** Pop Rocks!, the Thursday-night party at **219 Flamingo** *(219 Second Ave between 13th and 14th Sts, 212-533-2860),* and the coffeehouse **Big Cup** *(see page 292).*

**A different stripe** Wonder Bar is relaxed, sexy and conversation-friendly.

## East Village

### B Bar and Grill

*See page 277 for listing.*

Amazingly, the Tuesday-night **Beige** party is going strong after a six-year run. By midnight, the sprawling restaurant-lounge is packed with toned, fashionable young men. Hang out with friends and check out the occasional celebrity—Calvin Klein, David LaChapelle, Monica Lewinsky, etc.

### The Cock

*188 Ave A at 12th St (212-946-1871). Subway: L to First Ave; N, Q, R, W, 4, 5, 6 to 14th St–Union Sq. Mon 9pm–4am; Tue–Sun 10pm–4am. Average drink: $6. Cash only.*

The Cock is location No. 1 for the hip, randy crowd, many of whom don't roll in until after 2am. Depending on the night, the music includes campy '80s standards and good old rock & roll.

### Starlight Bar and Lounge

*167 Ave A between 10th and 11th Sts (212-475-2172). Subway: L to First Ave; N, Q, R, W, 4, 5, 6 to 14th St–Union Sq. 9pm–3am. Average drink: $6. Cash only.*

On weekends, this bar is almost too popular for its own good. During the week, things are more manageable, and a nice bonus is that top-notch local entertainers often perform free shows in the comfy back lounge (usually around 10pm). Sunday night is the bar's popular lesbian party, **Starlette**, which attracts all sorts of hipsters.

### Urge

*33 Second Ave at 2nd St (212-533-5757). Subway: F, V to Lower East Side–Second Ave. 8pm–4am. Average drink: $6. Cash only.*

The neighborhood's newest bar features a small stage that's mostly inhabited by gyrating go-go boys—which provides the dimly lit joint with a naughty, sexually charged atmosphere. Video screens often feature hard-core porno, and DJs provide pounding beats.

► See chapters **Bars** and **Clubs** for more nightlife.

### Wonder Bar

*505 E 6th St between Aves A and B (212-777-9105). Subway: F, V to Lower East Side–Second Ave. 6pm–4am. Average drink: $6. Cash only.*

This smoky Euro-modern lounge is filled with sexy patrons, deep conversations and serious eyewear. The DJ's syncopated spinning defies you to not dance. Glam female bartenders keep spirits flowing as smart young drinkers grope their dates, or cruise for fresh action.

## West Village

### Bar d'O

*29 Bedford St at Downing St (212-627-1580). Subway: A, C, E, F, V, S to W 4th St; 1, 9 to Houston St. 7pm–3am. Average drink: $7. Cash only.*

At this cozy candlelit haunt, Tuesdays, Saturdays and Sundays feature intimate performances by the city's most talented drag queens. Catch Joey Arias, Raven O or Sade Pendavis—all of whom really sing, not lip-synch. On Mondays, the joint becomes a lesbian lounge called **Pleasure**.

### The Lure

*409 W 13th St between Ninth and Tenth Aves (212-741-3919). Subway: A, C, E to 14th St; L to Eighth Ave. Mon–Sat 6pm–4am; Sun 8pm–4am. Average drink: $4.50. Cash only.*

Now that the Meatpacking District has been taken over by French bistros and designer boutiques, the Lure is the neighborhood's last remaining outpost of kink. The newfangled fetish bar attracts a broad, energetic bunch, many of whom don leather, rubber or manly Levi's and army boots. **Pork**, a raunchy party for the young ones, is on Wednesdays.

### The Monster

*80 Grove St at Sheridan Sq (212-924-3558). Subway: 1, 9 to Christopher St–Sheridan Sq. Mon–Fri 4pm–4am; Sat, Sun 2pm–4am. Average drink: $6. Cash only.*

This bi-level landmark offers an old-school piano lounge upstairs, where the locals gather to sing show tunes. (And honey, you haven't lived till you've witnessed a bunch of tipsy queers belting out the best of Broadway.) The downstairs disco caters to a young outer-borough crowd just itchin' for fun.

### The Stonewall

*53 Christopher St between Sixth and Seventh Aves (212-463-0950). Subway: 1, 9 to Christopher St–Sheridan Sq. 3pm–4am. Average drink: $6. Cash only.*

This is another landmark, next door to the actual location of the 1969 gay rebellion against police harassment. For years the joint was a snore, but lately, it's had an infusion of sexy shenanigans, including go-go boys, guest appearances by various porn stars and strip contests. Wednesday is the packed-to-the-rafters Latin night called **Uncut**. Don't worry, circumcised guys are welcome too.

## Chelsea

### Barracuda

*275 W 22nd St between Seventh and Eighth Aves (212-645-8613). Subway: C, E to 23rd St. 4pm–4am. Average drink: $6. Cash only.*

This bar continues to draw hordes of boys. Friendlier and more comfortable than its neighborhood competition, the space is split in two, with a traditional bar up front and a frequently redecorated lounge in back. Drag-queen celebrities perform throughout the week, and there's never a cover.

### G

*225 W 19th St between Seventh and Eighth Aves (212-929-1085). Subway: 1, 9 to 18th St. 4pm–4am. Average drink: $6. Cash only.*

This lounge is one of the area's most popular destinations, especially for the well-scrubbed, fresh-faced set. Late in the evening, the space is often filled to capacity, while outside, a line of unfortunates waits to get in. Go early to stake your place.

### xl Chelsea

*357 W 16th St between Eighth and Ninth Aves (212-995-1400). Subway: A, C, E to 14th St; L to Eighth Ave. 4pm–4am. Average drink: $6. Cash only.*

This sleek tri-level bar is a study in style: witness the 30-foot aquarium in the bathroom. Fashion divas, muscle men, fag hags and a few trannies run amok under one roof. On Monday nights, there are free shows starring top-notch Broadway and cabaret performers.

## Midtown

### Chase

*255 W 55th St between Broadway and Eighth Ave (212-333-3400). Subway: A, C, B, D, 1, 9 to 59th St–Columbus Circle. 4pm–4am. Average drink: $6. AmEx, MC, V.*

Fans call it the G bar of Hell's Kitchen, and like that Chelsea spot, Chase draws a dapper, professional gay crowd. Later in the evening, the fashionistas arrive for cocktails and chic ambience. The main bar (designed with the aid of a feng shui expert) is a tiled confection of red, orange and yellow; it's as pleasing to the eye as the cute boys are to one another.

### Stella's

*266 W 47th St between Broadway and Eighth Ave (212-575-1680). Subway: N, Q, R, W, S, 1, 2, 3, 9, 7 to 42nd St–Times Sq. Noon–4am. Cover: $5 (Thu–Sun after 8pm). Average drink: $6. Cash only.*

One of the last gay vestiges of pre-Disney Times Square, Stella's offers go-go–boy floor shows starting around 11pm. Connoisseurs of Latin and African-American homeboys will be especially enthralled.

### The Townhouse

See page 293.

## Uptown

### The Works

*428 Columbus Ave between 80th and 81st Sts (212-799-7365). Subway: B, C to 81st St–Museum of Natural History; 1, 9 to 79th St. 2pm–4am. Average drink: $6. Cash only.*

This major hangout for young gay men on the Upper West Side draws an under-40 guppie crowd. On Sun-day evenings, there's a popular beer blast: Between 6pm and 1am, you pay only $5 for unlimited draft beer. Part of the proceeds benefit God's Love We Deliver, a meal-delivery service for homebound AIDS patients.

**G-force** Pick your poison at G, where hard stuff is served alongside juices and power drinks.

## Clubs

A number of New York clubs have gay nights; many of the following are one-nighters rather than permanent venues. For more clubs, the majority of which are gay-friendly, plus additional information about some of those listed below, see chapter **Clubs**.

### Dance clubs

#### Exit

*610 W 56th St between Eleventh and Twelfth Aves (212-582-8282). Subway: A, C, B, D, 1, 9 to 59th St–Columbus Circle. Sun 6am. Cover: $30. Average drink: $8. MC, V.*

Junior Vasquez, the undisputed champ of New York's DJs, doesn't start spinning the **Earth** party until 6am, late enough for the straight bridge-and-tunnel crowd to have departed. Thousands of damp, shirtless men pack the football field–size dance floor, and many don't leave till early Sunday evening.

#### La Nueva Escuelita

*301 W 39th St between Eighth and Ninth Aves (212-631-0588). Subway: A, C, E to 42nd St–Port Authority. Thu–Sat 10pm–4am; Sun 7pm–4am. Cover: $5–$15. Average drink $7. Cash only.*

Colombians, Dominicans, Puerto Ricans and other Spanish-speaking New Yorkers flock to this basement club, where the dance floor doubles as a stage for extravagant drag shows. The DJs play all sorts of music, but the revelers really come alive to the salsa and merengue tunes. Friday nights feature the lesbian party **Fever**; on Sundays, an African-American crowd cheers on hilarious emcee Harmonica Sunbeam.

#### Luxx

*See page 275 for listing. Cash only.*

How did the popular electronica dance party known as **Berliniamsburg** get its name? It seems promoter Larry Tee heard hot Christian Dior designer Hedi Slimane proclaim groovy Williamsburg the new Berlin. As Mr. Tee spins the sounds of Fisherspooner, Peaches and Chicks on Speed, the arty crowd dances, checks each other's outfits and absorbs the new-wave decor. (On Fridays, Tee also throws the **Mutants** party, with a similar format.)

#### Motherfucker

*Visit www.motherfuckernyc.com to get on the mailing list.*

If rock & roll is your style, you'll want to check out Motherfucker, the wildly popular, polysexual dance party that takes place about seven times a year, and almost always changes its location. The promoters insist that participants dress in some sort of rock gear. And why not, considering that the music is punk, new wave, glitter, Britpop, etc.?

#### Saint at Large

*To get on the mailing list, call 212-674-8541 or visit www.saintatlarge.com.*

The now-mythical Saint was one of the first venues where New York's gay men enjoyed dance-floor freedom. The club closed, but the clientele keeps its memory alive with four huge circuit parties each year. The **S&M Black Party**, the **White Party**, Halloween and New Year's Eve attract image-conscious men from around the U.S.

#### SBNY

*50 W 17th St between Fifth and Sixth Aves (212-691-0073; www.splashbar.com). Subway: F, V to 14th St; L to Sixth Ave; 1, 9 to 18th St. Sun–Thu 4pm–4am; Fri, Sat 4pm–5am. Cover varies after 9pm $5–$15. Average drink: $6. Cash only.*

The Chelsea institution formerly known as Splash is now officially referred to as SBNY (Splash Bar New York), though most folks still use the old name. Other changes include an expanded dance floor and a relocation of the famous onstage showers, where hunky go-go boys get wet and wild. And can it be that the supermuscular bartenders are bigger than ever? Locals and tourists alike dance away to music played by nationally known DJs.

### Bathhouses

Despite the city's crackdown on adult businesses, a few bathhouses for men still exist. Apart from the barlike **J's Hangout** *(675 Hudson St at 14th St, 212-242-9292)*—which is less blatantly sexual and more of an after-hours desperation cruise—there is the **West Side Club** bathhouse *(27 W 20th St between Fifth and Sixth Aves, 212-691-2700)* in Chelsea and its sister establishment, the **East Side Club** *(227 E 56th St at Second Ave; 212-753-2222, 212-888-1884)*. For up-to-the-minute details, consult *HX* magazine's Getting Off section.

## Restaurants & cafés

Few New York restaurants would bat an eye at a same-sex couple enjoying an intimate dinner. The neighborhoods mentioned above have hundreds of venues that are de facto gay restaurants, but here are a few of the most obvious gay places in town. For more dining options, see chapter **Restaurants**.

#### Big Cup

*228 Eighth Ave between 21st and 22nd Sts (212-206-0059). Subway: C, E to 23rd St. Mon–Fri 7am–1am; Sat, Sun 8am–2am. Average sandwich: $5.75. Caffe latte: $3.60. Cash only.*

Big Cup is as unmistakably Chelsea Boy as a pair of shiny polyester bikini briefs. The coffee is fine, as are the snacks—brownies, lemon bars and Rice Krispies Treats, plus sandwiches and soups. But no one pays much attention to those, because Big Cup is one of New York's classic gay meet markets. You don't put a disco ball in a coffeebar and expect patrons to lose themselves in Kierkegaard.

### Eighteenth & Eighth

*159 Eighth Ave at 18th St (212-242-5000). Subway: A, C, E to 14th St; L to Eighth Ave; 1, 9 to 18th St. Sun–Thu 9am–midnight; Fri, Sat 9am–12:30am. Average main course: $15. AmEx, MC, V.*

On warm summer evenings, the sidewalk in front of Eighteenth & Eighth is rife with clinking wine glasses, laughter and the bare legs of well-sculpted men, and the weekend brunch is one of the best in Chelsea. But even more than the winning menu, locals revel in the refined breeziness of it all.

### Elmo

*156 Seventh Ave between 19th and 20th Sts (212-337-8000). Subway: 1, 9 to 18th St. Mon–Thu 11am–1am; Fri, Sat 11am–2am; Sun 10am–1am. Average main course: $14. AmEx, MC, V.*

Hello, *Wallpaper* magazine, have we got a restaurant for you! This spacious, brightly decorated eatery has reasonably priced food that's good, not great, and if you're on a liquid diet, there's a bar that offers a view of the dining room, jammed with guys in clingy tank tops (regardless of the weather).

### Foodbar

*149 Eighth Ave between 17th and 18th Sts (212-243-2020). Subway: A, C, E to 14th St; L to Eighth Ave; 1, 9 to 18th St. 11am–4pm, 5pm–midnight. Average main course: $17. AmEx, MC, V.*

Foodbar's globally influenced American menu will get your mouth watering—if the customers haven't already. Balsamic-glazed roasted chicken, Moroccan salad and steak au poivre are entirely satisfying. Servers are efficient and flirty, not to mention impossibly good looking.

**Those lips, those eyes** That Bar shows Brooklyn's Smith Street a gay time.

### Lips

*2 Bank St at Greenwich Ave (212-675-7710). Subway: 1, 2, 3, 9 to 14th St. Mon–Thu 5:30pm–midnight; Fri, Sat 5:30pm–2am; Sun 11:30am–4pm, 5:30pm–midnight. Average main course: $17. AmEx, DC, MC, V.*

This restaurant certainly provides a festive atmosphere: The drag-queen waitstaff serves tasty meals and performs for very enthusiastic patrons. Weekdays, including Wednesday's **Bitchy Bingo**, tend to be a lot gayer than the weekends, when scores of shrieking women celebrate bridal showers.

### That Bar

*116 Smith St between Dean and Pacific Sts, Boerum Hill, Brooklyn (718-260-8900). Subway: F, G to Bergen St. Mon–Fri 4pm–4am; Sat 11:30am–4am; Sun 11:30am–2am. Average main course: $13. AmEx, MC, V.*

It was only a matter of time before a gay spot opened on Smith Street, Brooklyn's thriving restaurant and pub thoroughfare. Offering a full bar (two-for-one happy hour 4 to 8pm) and a tasty selection of American classics, the slickly designed hangout attracts lots of local queers, as well as venturesome Manhattanites. In the summer, patrons can lounge in the pretty backyard.

### The Townhouse

*206 E 58th St at Third Ave (212-826-6241). Subway: N, R, W to Lexington Ave–59th St; 4, 5, 6 to 59th St. Mon–Thu noon–3:30pm, 5–11pm; Fri, Sat noon–3:30pm, 5pm–midnight; Sun noon–4pm, 5–11pm. Average main course: $20. AmEx, DC, MC, V.*

If you're a reasonably attractive man under 40, you're likely to be greeted—or at least ogled—by one of the soused middle-aged regulars at this "gentlemen's" restaurant. In the dining room beyond the bar, you'll spot couples in various stages of courtship; the flirty service makes this a good place for solo diners as well.

## Gyms

For more fitness facilities, see page 328.

### David Barton

*552 Sixth Ave between 15th and 16th Sts (212-727-0004). Subway: F, V to 14th St; L to Sixth Ave. Mon–Fri 6am–midnight; Sat 9am–9pm; Sun 10am–11pm. $20 per day, weekly pass $100. AmEx, MC, V.*

David Barton mixes fitness with fashion and nightlife at this gym. Sleek locker rooms, artfully lit weight rooms and pumping music may make you feel as if you should have a cocktail instead of another set of reps. Besides free weights, Barton offers the three key Cs: classes, cardio equipment and cruising.

**Rita, Mae I?** Not to worry, you can come as you are to Rubyfruit Bar & Grill.

### 19th Street Gym

*22 W 19th St between Fifth and Sixth Aves (212-414-5800). Subway: F, V, N, R, W to 23rd St. Mon–Fri 5:30am–11pm; Sat, Sun 9am–9pm. $20 per day, weekly pass $75. AmEx, Disc, MC, V.*
Bulging muscles galore are on display at this popular Chelsea gym. Although it spans 16,000 square feet, the place is basically one huge room crammed with top-notch athletic equipment. Stretch and ab classes are available, as is personal instruction from staff trainers. After a workout, you can sip on something healthy at the juice bar and café.

# Dyke Life

The most exciting aspect of New York's lesbian scene is that the women you'll see defy stereotypes. While lesbian culture in New York is not as visible as that of gay men, it is also generally less segregated, and is far more welcoming.

If you're into community activism, you'll find plenty to spark your interest at the **Lesbian, Gay, Bisexual & Transgender Community Center** *(see page 286)*. And if you're a dyke who just wants to have some unbridled fun, New York City delivers.

The East Village lesbian bar **Meow Mix** *(see page 295)* is a popular gathering spot for alternadykes. And the unflappable promoter MegaBoy Kate throws large-scale dance parties including **Her/SheBar** at La Nueva Escuelita *(see page 292)* and **Lovergirl** *(see* **Club Shelter**, *page 295)*. Meanwhile, lesbian disco nights are getting progressively larger and are no longer held only in funky out-of-the-way dives (check *HX* or *Time Out New York* for the most current information). Some women's bars and clubs strive for an all-female environment—better check ahead if you're planning on bringing your male friends. And if drag-king shows are your thing, check out entertainer Murray Hill's website *(www.mrmurrayhill.com)*.

Outside Manhattan, the Park Slope neighborhood of Brooklyn remains a lesbian enclave, and is home to the Lesbian Herstory Archive *(see page 286)*. The area is lovely, and there is a number of relaxed coffeehouses, cafés and bars to choose from.

Whether in Brooklyn or Manhattan, if you're out late, consider taking a taxi rather than riding the subway alone. *(See* **Directory, Safety**, *page 372 or* **NYC Gay & Lesbian Anti-Violence Project**, *page 287.)*

## Accommodations

See also **Chelsea Pines Inn**, **Colonial House Inn** and **Incentra Village House**, pages 288–289.

### Markle Residence for Women

*123 W 13th St between Sixth and Seventh Aves (212-242-2400). Subway: F, V, 1, 2, 3, 9 to 14th St; L to Sixth Ave. $85 per night or $148–$240 per week, including two meals a day (one-month minimum). Disc, MC, V.*
Offering women-only Salvation Army accommodations in a pleasant Greenwich Village location, the Markle has clean, comfortable rooms, all of which have telephones and private bathrooms.

## Bars

See also Wonder Bar, page 290.

### Bar d'O

*See page 290 for listing.*
On Mondays, cozy Bar d'O transforms into **Pleasure**, the long-running lesbian lounge. The music (provided by DJ Sharee) is a mellow hip-hop groove, and the place is always full of rap and hip-hop enthusiasts who truly believe in "ladies first."

### Crazy Nanny's

*21 Seventh Ave South at Leroy St (212-366-6312). Subway: 1, 9 to Houston St. Mon–Fri 4pm–4am; Sat, Sun 3pm–4am. Cover varies. Average drink: $6. AmEx, Disc, MC, V.*

Catering primarily to women of color, Nanny's music runs from soul to Latin. Bone up on those Missy Elliott lyrics for karaoke on Wednesdays and Sundays. Happy hour is 4 to 7pm.

### Henrietta Hudson

*438 Hudson St at Morton St (212-924-3347). Subway: 1, 9 to Christopher St–Sheridan Sq. Mon–Fri 4pm–4am; Sat, Sun 1pm–4am. Average drink: $6. AmEx, Disc, MC, V.*

This bustling, casual lesbian watering hole is a magnet for women from all over the New York area, many of them quite frisky. Various DJs provide contemporary sounds.

### Meow Mix

*269 E Houston St at Suffolk St (212-254-0688). Subway: F, V to Lower East Side–Second Ave. Mon–Fri 5pm–4am; Sat, Sun 3pm–4am. Average drink: $5. Cash only.*

This lesbian lair hosts local live acts, mainly of the glam and garage varieties. DJs typically favor funk, disco, new wave, hip-hop, reggae and R&B. Thursday night is boisterous **Gloss**, which the promoters call the "glammest girly night around."

### Starlight Bar and Lounge

*See page 290 for listing.*

By 10pm on Sundays, the popular lesbian party **Starlette** is in full swing. It has a mix of glamour gals, tomboys, college students, etc., but a cool East Village style prevails. DJ Jolene spins lush house.

## Clubs

These are the current lesbian hot spots, but don't panic if they're not around in a few months' time—new events will have already blossomed. Check the lesbian listings in *HX* or *Time Out New York* for the latest info.

### Club Shelter

*20 W 39th St between Fifth and Sixth Aves (212-719-4479). Subway: S, 4, 5, 6, 7 to 42nd St–Grand Central. 10pm–noon. $17. Cash only.*

**Lovergirl**, the popular women's party at Club Shelter, offers a dynamite sound system and state-of-the-art lighting. The multiracial crowd enthusiastically shakes its groove thang to hip-hop, R&B, funk, reggae and Latin music, while ultrasexy go-go gals sport the latest in fashionable G-strings.

### La Nueva Escuelita

*See page 292 for listing.*

On Fridays, this Latin show palace hosts the mostly lesbian party **Fever**, complete with go-go dancers. DJs Steve "Chip Chop" Gonzalez and Francesca Magliano provide Latin-flavored tunes. Elaborate drag shows at 1:30am star the Escuelita "girls."

### Shescape

*To get on the mailing list, call 212-686-5665 or visit www.shescape.com.*

For 20 years now, Shescape has been offering lesbian get-togethers at nightclubs all over town. The crowd tends to be on the yuppie side—not the women you'd likely run into at a bar. The most popular parties are a mammoth Thanksgiving-eve bash and various events pegged to Gay Pride.

## Restaurants & cafés

### Cowgirl Hall of Fame

*519 Hudson St at 10th St (212-633-1133). Subway: 1, 9 to Christopher St–Sheridan Sq. 11:30am–4pm, 5–11:30pm. Bar Sun–Thu 5pm–1am; Fri, Sat 5pm–4am. Average main course: $13. AmEx, MC, V.*

Cheerful waitresses welcome girls and boys to this retro ranch-hand lounge, where the specialties are trailer-park originals like Fritos Chili Pie. Chase it with a margarita served in a mason jar.

### Rubyfruit Bar & Grill

*531 Hudson St between Charles and Washington Sts (212-929-3343). Subway: 1, 9 to Christopher St–Sheridan Sq. Mon–Thu 3pm–2am; Fri, Sat 3pm–4am; Sun 11:30am–2am. Average main course: $20. Average drink: $6. AmEx, DC, MC, V.*

A warm, energetic band of women patronizes Rubyfruit, the only dedicated lesbian restaurant and bar in town. Although the food is good, it's not the main selling point. Congenial customers, cabaret and an eclectic mix of music make this a great place for fun-loving old-school dykes.

**Starlight, star bright** You may just get the wish you wish at this East Village lounge.

# Kids' Stuff

Think Gotham is just for grownups? Having fun in New York is child's play.

When adults come to New York for the first time, many assume they're visiting a gritty, grown-up landscape, a preconception shaped by films like *Taxi Driver* and *Breakfast at Tiffany's.* But kids have their own frames of reference. Storybook New York includes the Metropolitan Museum of Art, where Claudia and Jamie took up residence after running away, in E.L. Konigsburg's *From the Mixed-Up Files of Mrs. Basil E. Frankweiler;* the palatial Plaza Hotel, where Kay Thompson's Eloise instituted a reign of playful terror (and where a real-life etiquette workshop for kids is held monthly); the Brooklyn of Maurice Sendak's *In the Night Kitchen* and *The Sign on Rosie's Door;* and the skyline of Faith Ringgold's *Tar Beach,* with its water towers, bridges and tiny dots of incandescent light. New York *is* its fictitious self, and for kids the illusion is real.

Much has been made of the new "family-friendly" Times Square, but don't limit yourself to midtown's tourist trappings. Explore the outer boroughs to give your kids a taste of New York's colorful grassroots pageantry: In summer, there's Brooklyn's **Mermaid Parade** *(see page 252)* and the **West Indian Day Carnival** *(see page 253),* which includes a children's parade.

If you're looking for free activities to fill an hour or two, pick up a copy of *Events for Children* from any branch of the New York Public Library; listings cover storytellings, puppet shows, films and workshops. The **Central Children's Room** in the Donnell Library *(see page 58)*, is the best place for events; it also houses the original Winnie the Pooh and other toys that belonged to Christopher "Robin" Milne.

## Amusement parks

### Astroland

*1000 Surf Ave at West 10th St, Coney Island, Brooklyn (718-372-0275). Subway: W to Stillwell Ave–Coney Island. Mid-Apr–late Oct Mon–Fri noon–midnight; Sat, Sun noon–10pm, weather permitting. $2 for single kiddie ride, $15 for ten kiddie rides. Mon–Fri $15 pay-one-price for major rides. Cash only.*

Don't postpone a trip to this well-aged (but still enjoyable) Coney Island amusement park—its appealing grunginess makes it a welcome alternative to certain mouse-themed parks. Older kids can take on the world-famous Cyclone roller coaster *($5);* the young ones will prefer the Tilt-a-Whirl, the Pirate Ship or one of the three carousels. In summer, look for future Mets stars at a Brooklyn Cyclones game in nearby KeySpan Park *(see page 324).*

### Nellie Bly Amusement Park

*1824 Shore Pkwy, Bensonhurst, Brooklyn (718-996-4002, 718-373-0828). Subway: M, W to Bay Pkwy, then B6 bus to Shore Pkwy. Apr–Jun, Sept, Oct Sat, Sun 11am–6pm. Jul, Aug 11am–11pm. 85¢ per ride ticket, $15 for 20, $26 for 40 (most rides require two or three tickets each). Unlimited-rides admission $9.50 during off-peak hours; call for details.*

Nellie Bly has none of the shriek-inducing excitement of Great Adventure—but it's accessible, inexpensive and totally New York. Local families bring their small children for a couple of hours of circular activity on Red Baron jets, hopping frogs and other rides. You'll also find bumper cars, a Ferris wheel, miniature golf and, of course, ice cream and cotton candy.

## Circuses

The Vegasy (and animal-free) **Cirque du Soleil** *(www.cirquedusoleil.com)* brings its big top to the metro area every spring. If you like a serving of social consciousness with your spectacle, look for free outdoor summer performances by Brooklyn's raucous alternative, **Circus Amok** *(www.circusamok.org).*

### Big Apple Circus

*Damrosch Park, Lincoln Center, 62nd St between Columbus and Amsterdam Aves (212-268-2500; www.bigapplecircus.org). Subway: 1, 9 to 66th St–Lincoln Ctr. Call or visit website for schedule and prices. AmEx, MC, V.*

New York's own traveling circus was founded 26 years ago as a traditional, intimate one-act-at-a-time answer to the Ringling Bros.' three-ring extravaganza. This nonprofit circus prides itself on being a family affair, with acts that feature the founder's equestrian wife and two teenage children. Clowns are the highlight, and the focus is on the company rather than star acts. The circus has a regular winter season (October through January) in Damrosch Park. Budget permitting, it travels to other city parks in early spring.

### Ringling Bros. and Barnum & Bailey Circus

*Madison Square Garden, Seventh Ave between 31st and 33rd Sts (212-465-6741; www.ringling.com). Subway: A, C, E, 1, 2, 3, 9 to 34th St–Penn Station. March or April. $25–$75. Call or visit website for schedule. AmEx, DC, Disc, MC, V.*

The most famous American circus has three rings, lots of glitz and a menagerie of animals big and

**Paint misbehavin'** Kids can show their true colors at the Brooklyn Museum of Art.

small (see page 250 for the midnight parade of animals through midtown). It's a hot ticket, so reserve well in advance. Arrive early for preshow in-the-ring activities for kids.

### UniverSoul Big Top Circus

*800-316-7439; www.universoulcircus.com. $15–$30. AmEx, DC, Disc, MC, V.*

This one-ring African-American circus has all the requisite clowns, animal acts and hoopla, with a twist: Instead of the familiar circus music, you get hip-hop, R&B and salsa. The show usually appears in Brooklyn's Prospect Park in the spring, but venues and performances change yearly. Call or visit the website for details.

## Film

The **Met** *(see* **Metropolitan Museum of Art,** *page 44)* and **MoMA** *(see* **Museum of Modern Art,** *page 282)* also offer seasonal film programs for kids.

### BAMkids Film Festival

*See page 318 for listing. March or April. $9, children $6.*

The Brooklyn Academy of Music's children's film festival screens features and short live-action and animated films from around the world. Young audience members select the winners by filling out ballots.

### International Children's Television Festival

*For listing, see* **Museum of Television & Radio,** *page 57. Nov Sat, Sun 1–4pm. Free with admission to museum.*

This annual monthlong celebration of the best children's television from around the world gives kids and their parents a glimpse of youngsters' lives in other countries. Each day includes a pair of thematic programs mixing animation, live-action and documentary.

### New York International Children's Film Festival

*Various venues (212-349-0330; www.gkids.com). February or March.*

This three-week festival is a must. Age-specific programs for tots through teens present an exciting mix of shorts and full-length features (many of them premieres) from indie filmmakers around the world—and not necessarily those who specialize in kids' flicks. Children determine the festival's winning films, which are then screened at an awards ceremony—it's a great party for all ages, with door prizes and a celebrity host. Reserve seats well in advance; the schedule is available in early January.

## Museums & exhibitions

Even museums not specifically devoted to children provide a wealth of activity for them. Kids will love exploring the Butterfly Conservatory (fall through spring) and the revamped dinosaur halls at the **American Museum of Natural History** *(see page 41).* The museum's much-hyped **Rose Center for Earth and Space** *(see page 41)* offers science exhibits and a multimedia space show within the largest suspended-glass cube in the U.S.

► For more ideas on where to take the kids, check out chapters **By Season** and **Sports & Fitness**.

► Need a baby-sitter? See page 361.

**Not-so-wild, but woolly** Kids make new furry friends at the Central Park Wildlife Center.



(almost an acre of glass panes). However, the hands-on displays are not very appealing to the under-10 set; the weekend astronomy workshops are more appropriate for younger children. Don't miss the Touch Tunnel at the **Liberty Science Center** *(see page 59)*. Also, the ***Intrepid*** **Sea-Air-Space Museum** *(see page 57)* houses a collection of military hardware on an aircraft carrier, as well as interactive battle-related exhibits. All of the major art museums offer family tours and workshops. Tours at the **Brooklyn Museum of Art** *(see* **Art and soul**, *page 44)*, the Met and **MoMA QNS** *(see* **Modern convenience**, *page 118)* include sketching in the galleries.

## ARTime

*718-797-1573. Oct–Jun first Saturday of the month 11am–12:30pm. $20 per parent-child pair, additional child $5.*

ARTime began introducing kids (ages 5 to 10) to contemporary art in Soho galleries in 1994. When the art world moved to Chelsea, ARTime followed; it has also recently ventured to Brooklyn's Dumbo and Williamsburg. Art historians with education backgrounds take children to three or four galleries showing cutting-edge art in various media. Kids must be accompanied by an adult.

## Brooklyn Children's Museum

*145 Brooklyn Ave at St. Mark's Ave, Crown Heights, Brooklyn (718-735-4400; www.brooklynkids.org). Subway: 1 to Kingston Ave. Sept 1–Jul 1 Wed–Fri 2–5pm; Sat, Sun 10am–5pm. Call or visit website for holiday hours. Suggested donation $4. Cash only.*

Founded in 1899 and redesigned in 1996, BCM was the world's first museum designed specifically for children. It has a fantastic collection of more than 27,000 artifacts from around the world, as well as small animals and hands-on exhibits. An animatronic dinosaur show opens Memorial Day 2003. In the music studio, children play synthesizers and instruments from around the globe, and dance on the keys of a walk-on piano. BCM's fabulous weekly world-music series runs Fridays in summer (6pm, free) in the rooftop theater. On weekends, a free shuttle bus *(see* **Borough haul**, *page 300)* runs from the Grand Army Plaza subway station to the museum.

## Children's Museum of the Arts

*182 Lafayette St between Broome and Grand Sts (212-274-0986; www.cmany.org). Subway: 6 to Spring St. Wed, Fri–Sun noon–5pm; Thu noon–6pm. $5, Thu 4–6pm voluntary donation. AmEx, MC, V.*

Kids under 7 love this low-key museum, with its floor-to-ceiling chalkboards, art computers and vast store of art supplies. Weekend and vacation workshops are also offered.

## Children's Museum of Manhattan

*212 W 83rd St between Amsterdam Ave and Broadway (212-721-1234; www.cmom.org). Subway: 1, 9 to 86th St. B, C to 81st St–Museum of Natural History. Wed–Sun 10am–5pm; call for summer and holiday hours. $6. AmEx, MC, V.*

This children's museum promotes several types of literacy through its playful interactive exhibitions. In fall 2002, it launched a five-year visual-arts initiative: Through September 2003, the groundbreaking "Art Inside Out" lets kids get acquainted with the work of artists Elizabeth Murray, William Wegman and Fred Wilson. Mainstays include "WordPlay," an exhibition designed to encourage verbal (and preverbal) interaction between babies and their caregivers, and various exhibits devoted to the work of kid-lit stars. In the Inventor Center, computer addicts can take any idea they dream up—a flying bike, a talking robot—and design it on screen using digital imaging. There's also a state-of-the-art media center where kids can produce their own TV shows. Workshops are offered on weekends and during school vacations.

### Lower East Side Tenement Museum

*See page 51 for listing.*

Housed in an old tenement building that was home to successive families of immigrants, this museum features a weekly interactive children's tour of the Sephardic Confino family's former home. The tour is led by 13-year-old Victoria Confino (actually a staff member playing her), who teaches visitors about New York in the early 1900s by dancing the fox-trot, playing games with them and forever answering the question "Where does everyone sleep?" Tours are recommended for ages 7 to 14 and are given on weekend afternoons at noon, 1, 2 and 3pm ($8, children $6).

### New York Hall of Science

*See page 59 for listing.*

This museum is located inside the onetime Space Pavilion of the 1964 New York World's Fair. Director Dr. Alan Friedman is nationally known for his enlightened approach to science education, which he bases on the premise that kids learn by asking questions. Perhaps his biggest contribution to the hall is the 30,000-square-foot outdoor Science Playground (spring through December, ages 6 and up), where children engage in whole-body science exploration, discovering principles of balance, gravity, energy and so on, while they play on a giant seesaw or turn a huge Archimedes screw to push water uphill. There's plenty to see indoors, too.

### Socrates Sculpture Park

*See page 121 for listing.*

Unlike most art exhibitions, this outdoor city-owned spread of large-scale contemporary sculpture is devoid of snarling guards and DON'T TOUCH signs. Children can climb on, run through and sit upon works that seem to have been plopped haphazardly on the grounds of this four-acre park. Call for information about summer art workshops and outdoor film series for kids. On weekends, the free Queens Artlink shuttle stops at Socrates *(see* **Borough haul**, *page 300).*

### Sony Wonder Technology Lab

*Sony Plaza, 550 Madison Ave between 55th and 56th Sts (212-833-8100). Subway: E, V to Fifth Ave–53rd St; 6 to 51st St. Tue, Wed, Fri, Sat 10am–6pm; Thu 10am–8pm; Sun noon–6pm. Free.*

This digital wonderland lets visitors (or "media trainees") use state-of-the art communication technology to play at designing video games, assisting in surgery, crisis-managing an earthquake, editing a TV show and operating robots. Kids 8 and older will probably get the most out of this place, but it's also a great playground for younger children who like pushing buttons and seeing their faces on giant monitors. Make a reservation one week in advance, especially during the spring and summer.

## Music

### Carnegie Hall Family Concerts

*See page 318 for listing.*

Even kids who profess to hate classical music are impressed by a visit to Carnegie Hall; one youngster wrote a postconcert thank-you letter to "Dear Mr. Hall." The Family Concert series featuring world-class performers usually appeals to children—and only costs $5. Preconcert activities include a workshop and storytelling. The concerts are held four or five times each season, fall through spring, and are recommended for ages 7 and up. For more children's activities, visit the website.

### Jazz for Young People

*For listing, see* **Alice Tully Hall**, *page 320. $15, under 18 $10.*

These participatory concerts help kids answer questions such as "What is jazz?" and "Who is Louis Armstrong?" Led by trumpeter and jazz great Wynton Marsalis, the program is modeled on the New York Philharmonic Young People's Concerts.

### Little Orchestra Society

*For listing, see* **Avery Fisher Hall**, *page 320. For schedule information, visit www.littleorchestra.org.*

The Little Orchestra Society, founded in 1947 and the first orchestra to present professional classical concerts for kids, offers the Lolli-Pops concert series for children ages 3 to 5—participatory orchestral concerts that combine classical music with dance, puppetry, theater and mime. Among the most popular productions are *Peter and the Wolf*, performed in the fall at Kaye Playhouse, and the spectacular *Amahl and the Night Visitors* (complete with live sheep), held in early December. Happy Concerts for Young People (ages 6 to 12) are staged at Avery Fisher Hall two or three times a year. Prices vary.

### New York Philharmonic Young People's Concerts

*For listing, see* **Avery Fisher Hall**, *page 320. $6–$23.*

Musicians address the audience directly during these legendary educational concerts, made popular by the late Leonard Bernstein. Each concert is preceded by the hour-long Kidzone Live, during which kids meet orchestra members and try out their instruments.

## Outdoor activities

For zoos, see page 303.

### Brooklyn Botanic Garden

*See page 112 for listing.*
The highlight is the 13,000-square-foot Discovery Garden, where children can play botanist, make toys out of natural materials, weave a wall, and in general, get their hands dirty.

### Nelson Rockefeller Park

*Hudson River at Chambers St (212-267-9700). Subway: A, C, 1, 2, 3, 9 to Chambers St. 10am–sunset. Free.*
Come summer's swelter, river breezes keep this park cooler than the rest of the city. Besides watching the boats (Saturday is a good day for ocean liners), kids can participate in art, sports or street-game activities, and enjoy one of New York's best playgrounds. Tom Otterness's quirky sculptural installation, *Real World,* is situated in the picnic area near the Chambers Street entrance. Call for times and locations.

### New York Botanical Garden

*See page 127 for listing. Combined "Passport" admission to tram and specialized gardens $10, seniors and students $7.50, children $1, under 2 free.*
The immense Everett Children's Adventure Garden is a whimsical museum of the natural world, with interactive "galleries," both indoors and out. In the Family Garden (early spring through late October), children can run under Munchy, a giant topiary; poke around in a touch tank; and plant, weed, water or harvest vegetables. If it's too cold to wander outside, ask for a kids' guide to the Enid A. Haupt Conservatory, the spectacular glass house where papyrus, cocoa and bananas grow all year long.

### Piers 25 and 26

*Hudson River Park, West Side Hwy at North Moore St (212-791-2530). Subway: 1, 9 to Franklin St.*
Pier 25 has the ramshackle feel of a kid-friendly seaside town, with a mini-golf course ($2), a snack shack with ever-smoking barbecue, a water-and-sand play area and a volleyball court. On Pier 26, the River Project *(212-941-5901)* admits children on weekends, when they can examine aquariums filled with fish from the Hudson River. Adventurous parents can rent a kayak from the Downtown Boathouse *(646-613-0375)* and take one or two tykes for a half-hour paddle between piers (weekends and holidays 10am to 5pm).

## Central Park

Manhattanites don't have yards—they have parks. The most popular, of course, is Central Park, which has numerous places and pro-

# Borough haul

Want the kids to see more than Manhattan? Then get on the bus!

Manhattan is loaded with kid-friendly activities, but the fun doesn't stop at the East River. While some parents may be intimidated by the thought of navigating the sprawling outer boroughs, three new shuttle buses make traversing Brooklyn and Queens a painless prospect.

### Brooklyn Children's Museum Trolley Express

*718-735-4400. Subway: 2, 3 to Grand Army Plaza. Sat, Sun, holidays 10:15am–4:15pm; departs on the hour from Grand Army Plaza station. Call for schedule.*
The Trolley Express has one true destination: the **Brooklyn Children's Museum**, the world's first museum designed just for kids *(see page 298)*. In addition to more than 20,000 artifacts, the attractions include Animal Out-post, where children can get close to snakes, lizards and tadpoles, and Totally Tots, an arts area for kids 5 and under. The trolley also stops at the **Brooklyn Museum of Art** *(see* **Art and soul**, *page 44)* where you can connect to the Heart of Brooklyn Trolley *(see below)*. The trip from Grand Army Plaza to the Children's Museum takes 15 minutes.

### Heart of Brooklyn Trolley

*Wollman Rink in Prospect Park, Parkside Ave at Ocean Ave (www.prospectpark.org). Subway: Q to Parkside Ave. Sat, Sun, holidays noon–6pm; trolley departs rink hourly. Visit website for schedule. Free.*
It may not get equal billing, but Prospect Park rivals Central Park as the people's playground—and the free Heart of Brooklyn Trolley takes you to hot spots in and around the park.

Kids can burn energy at **Wollman Rink** *(718-282-7789)*, pedal boating in summer *(Apr–Oct Sat, Sun, holidays 11am–6pm; $10 per hour)* or ice-skating in the winter *(Nov–Mar call for hours; $4, seniors and children under 14 $2; skate rental $4)*. Or jump off the trolley for a ride on the antique carousel *(Apr 6–mid-May Sat, Sun noon–5pm; mid-May–Labor Day Thu–Fri*

Arts & Entertainment

grams designed just for children. (Go to centralparknyc.org for a calendar of nature programs, art workshops and other events.) Don't miss the beautiful antique carousel ($1 a ride) and the lively Heckscher Playground (one of 20), with handball courts, horseshoe pitches, softball diamonds, a puppet theater and a wading pool (for more on the park, *see* **The secrets of Central Park**, *page 96*).

### Charles A. Dana Discovery Center

See page 94.

### Conservatory Water

*Central Park at 74th St, near Fifth Ave. Subway: 6 to 77th St. Jul, Aug Sun–Fri 11am–7pm; Sat 2–7pm, weather permitting.*

Stuart Little Pond, named after E.B. White's storybook mouse, is the city's mecca for model-yacht racing. When the boat master is around, rent one of the remote-controlled vessels ($10 per hour). Nearby, a large bronze *Alice in Wonderland* statue makes for great climbing.

### Henry Luce Nature Observatory

*See page 94 for listing.*

This children's hot spot in Central Park has telescopes, microscopes and simple hands-on exhibits that help teach kids about the plants and animals living (or hiding) in the surrounding area. Kids (with a parent's ID) can borrow a discovery kit—a backpack containing binoculars, a bird-watching guide and cool tools.

**Green giant** A colossal topiary caterpillar prowls the New York Botanical Garden.

### North Meadow Recreation Center

*Central Park at 79th St (212-348-4867). Subway: B, C to 81st St–Museum of Natural History. Mon–Fri 9am–7pm; Sat, Sun 10am–6pm. Free.*

This is the place to check out a fun-in-the-park kit: a Frisbee, hula hoop, Wiffle ball and bat, jump rope,



*noon–3pm, Sat, Sun, holidays noon–6pm; 50¢ a ride).* Other stops include **Lefferts Homestead Museum** *(Flatbush Ave at Empire Blvd, 718-965-6505)*, a historic farmhouse that shows kids what Brooklyn's colonial life was like, with weekend storytelling and gardening activities. There's also the **Prospect Park Wildlife Center** *(450 Flatbush Ave at Empire Blvd, 718-399-7339)*, where a baboon troupe's red butts elicit giggles.

At the Brooklyn Museum of Art, you can check out the museum's terrific African collection, impressive totem poles and engaging kid-friendly shows. There are two Saturday series offered—Arty Facts, a workshop for children ages 4 to 7 *(11am, 2pm)*, and storytelling in the galleries *(4pm)*.

The trolley continues to the **Brooklyn Botanic Garden** *(see* **Seasons in the sun,** *page 112)*, where the Discovery Center's "Plants and You" exhibit *(Tue–Sun 10am–4pm)* lets kids operate a cotton gin and play with lift-and-sniff panels.

**Queens Artlink**

*212-708-9750; www.moma.org. Sat, Sun 10am–5:30pm. Free.*

Since the **Museum of Modern Art** *(see page 46)* relocated to Long Island City, Queens, MoMA has launched the Queens Artlink shuttle. One bus travels between the MoMA construction area on West 53rd Street and the museum's new site. Another makes the rounds of Queens cultural centers, so you can stop at the MoMA to browse or attend a tour, then hop on the other shuttle to visit **P.S. 1 Contemporary Art Center** *(see page 46)*. Each summer, a new artist installation turns the P.S. 1 courtyard into an urban beach. Past exhibits have incorporated mammoth hammocks, wading streams, whirring fans, clouds of cool mist and kiddie pools. The next stop is **Socrates Sculpture Park** *(see page 121)*.

If the skies open, head for the **American Museum of the Moving Image** *(see page 57)*. "Behind the Screen," a hands-on introduction to the history and art of filmmaking, gives kids a chance to mess with *Jurassic Park* sound effects, make computer-generated flip books and experiment with moving-image technology. The "<Alt>DigitalMedia" exhibit lets future programmers get their digits on creative, probing and playful applications of digital moving-image technologies.

kickball and other toys. Children 8 and up can try scaling the climbing wall (call for times).

### NY Skateout

*Fifth Ave at 72nd St, classes meet at Central Park entrance (212-486-1919; www.nyskate.com). Subway: 6 to 68th St–Hunter College. Two-hour weekend skate lessons, $25. Reservations required. Kid Skateout Sat 3–4pm; call to confirm. Free.*

Classes are offered for beginners and more advanced skaters (ages 5 and up). On Saturdays, children who have the hang of it can join a Kid Skateout group for a social spin around the park's loop road. NY Skateout is dedicated to safety, so don't forget the protective gear: helmet, kneepads and wrist guards. Call for information on equipment rental.

### Stories at the Hans Christian Andersen Statue

*Central Park at Conservatory Water (212-929-6871, 212-340-0906). Subway: 6 to 77th St. Jun–Sept Sat 11am. Free.*

Children 5 and older have gathered for generations near the foot of the Hans Christian Andersen statue to hear expert tale-tellers from all over America—a real New York tradition that's not to be missed.

## Play spaces

### Chelsea Piers

*See page 328 for listing.*

A gymnasium, roller rink, driving range and skate park help older kids burn energy.

### Creatability

*500 E 88th St between York and East End Aves (212-535-4033). Subway: 4, 5, 6 to 86th St. Call for times and prices.*

This tiny storefront is bursting with crafts activities, offering everything from classes to birthday parties. During midday, evening and weekend hours, the space is open to walk-ins who want to spend an hour or two making a puppet, a comic strip, a floatable boat—just about anything. Kids must be accompanied by an adult. All ages.

### Playspace

*2473 Broadway at 92nd St (212-769-2300; www.playspaceny.com). Subway: 1, 2, 3, 9 to 96th St. 10am–5:30pm. $7.50. Cash only.*

Children from 6 months to 6 years can build in the immense sandbox, ride on toy trucks and climb on the jungle gym. Play is supervised, and parents can relax in a café off to the side. There are also drop-in games, art classes and story times. Tuesdays and Wednesdays at 3:30pm, local folk-rockers from the kiddie circuit perform. Admission is for all day: You can leave and come back.

► See **The secrets of Central Park**, page 96, for more about Central Park.

► Stores for children's clothing and toys are listed in chapter **Shopping & Services**.

## Theater

While some small theaters offer weekend-matinee family performances, many of these productions are of questionable value. (Check *Time Out New York* for reviews and details.) The following are the best of New York's family theaters and series.

### Arts in the Parks

*212-988-9093. Jun–Aug Mon–Fri 10:30am. Call for schedule.*

Arts in the Parks programs provide free performances of magic, mime, music, puppetry and storytelling in city parks. Most are geared to the under-10 crowd.

### Family Matters

*Dance Theater Workshop, 219 W 19th St between Seventh and Eighth Aves (212-924-0077; www.dtw.org). Subway: C, E to 23rd St; 1, 9 to 18th St. Call or visit website for schedule. $15, children $10. AmEx, MC, V.*

Curated by a pair of choreographer parents for ages 6 and up, Family Matters is designed to jump-start children's imaginations. The quirky variety-show format blends dance, music, theater and art.

### Joyce Theater

*See page 343 for listing.*

This is the home of Ballet Tech, which was founded by Eliot Feld (he played Baby John in *West Side Story*). Don't miss the *NoTCRACKER* (the last two weeks of December), a nutty alternative to the traditional tutued production. Tickets are $35 for evening performances; weekend matinees are $25, $15 for children.

### Kids 'n Comedy

*Gotham Comedy Club, 34 W 22nd St between Fifth and Sixth Aves (212-877-6115; www.kidsncomedy.com). Subway: N, R, W to 23rd St. Sept–May Sun 4pm. $15 plus one-drink minimum.*

Kids 'n Comedy has developed a stable of funny kids between the ages of 9 and 15 who know how to handle three minutes in front of a mike. The regulars deliver their own stand-up material (much of it in the homework-sucks vein) while audience members nosh from a light menu. Kids 'n Comedy also holds a monthly audition workshop for would-be comics.

### Los Kabayitos Children's Theater

*CSV Cultural Center, 107 Suffolk St between Delancey and Rivington Sts (212-260-4080, ext 14). Subway: F to Delancey St; J, M, Z to Delancey–Essex Sts. $10.50, children $8.50. Cash only. Call for reservations and show times.*

On weekends, New York's only Latino children's theater stages bilingual English-Spanish performances of traditional and new Latin American musical theater (the venue is dark during school vacations).

**String fling** Puppetworks' productions are based on classic stories and fairy tales.

### New Amsterdam Theater

*214 W 42nd St between Seventh and Eighth Aves (212-307-4100). Subway: A, C, E to 42nd St–Port Authority. Tue 8pm; Wed 2, 8pm; Thu, Fri 8pm; Sat 2, 8pm; Sun 3pm. $30–$100. AmEx, DC, Disc, MC, V.*

Disney laid claim to 42nd Street by renovating this splendid Art Deco masterpiece. Its inaugural and perpetually sold-out show, *The Lion King,* is directed by puppet mistress Julie Taymor.

### The New Victory Theater

*See page 339 for listing.*

New York's only year-round, full-scale young people's theater, the New Victory shows the very best in international theater and dance at junior prices.

### Puppetworks

*338 Sixth Ave at 4th St, Park Slope, Brooklyn (718-965-3391). Subway: F to Seventh Ave. Sat, Sun 12:30, 2:30pm. $7 adults, children 2–18 $6. Cash only.*

This company stages productions based on classic tales, such as *Beauty and the Beast.* The plays are usually performed with marionettes and are accompanied by classical music. Puppetworks also performs a holiday show at Macy's Herald Square *(see page 210)* from Thanksgiving to Christmas ($2.50).

### TADA! Youth Ensemble

*15 W 28th St between Fifth Ave and Broadway (212-252-1619). Subway: N, R, W to 28th St. 10am–6pm; call for schedule. $15, under 17 $6. AmEx, MC, V.*

This group presents musicals performed by and for children. The ensemble casts, ages 8 and up, are drawn from open auditions. The popular shows are well presented; reservations are advised. Call for details about weeklong musical-theater workshops.

## Zoos

### Bronx Zoo/Wildlife Conservation Society

*See page 127 for listing.*

Inside the Bronx Zoo is the Bronx Children's Zoo, geared to the very young with lots of domesticated animals to pet, plus exhibits that show the world from an animal's point of view. Camel and elephant rides are available from April through October. Don't miss the sea lion feeding (daily at 3pm).

### Central Park Wildlife Center

*Fifth Ave at 64th St (212-861-6030). Subway: N, R, W to Fifth Ave–59th St. Mon–Fri 10am–5pm; Sat, Sun 10:30am–5:30pm. $3.50, seniors $1.25, children 3–12 50¢, under 3 free. Cash only.*

This 130-species zoo is one of the highlights of the park. You can watch seals frolic above and below the waterline, crocodiles snap at swinging monkeys, and huge polar bears swim endless laps. Zookeepers interact with kids on July weekends. Penguins and other cool dudes are celebrated during the Summer Chill-Out party weekend in August.

### New York Aquarium for Wildlife Conservation

*Surf Ave at West 8th St, Coney Island, Brooklyn (718-265-3400, 718-265-3474). Travel: F to Ave X, then the F shuttle bus to the aquarium. Mon–Fri 10am–6pm; Sat, Sun, holidays 10am–7pm. $11, seniors and children 2–12 $7, under 2 free. Cash only.*

Like Coney Island itself, this aquarium is a little shabby, but kids enjoy seeing the famous beluga whale family and the scary sharks. They can also glimpse the kinds of fish brave enough to call the East River home, and take in a sea lion show.

# Music

New York has *all* genres covered—live and onstage now!

## Popular Music

New York is well known for bluster, so it's no surprise that the city's music scene has always been skilled at promoting itself. From punk and hip-hop to the downtown experimental scene, NYC has spawned some of the most significant music trends of the past 40 years. However, in the early 1990s, even the most ardent boosters had to admit that the mood had become lackluster. The buzz brought on by groups like Sonic Youth had died, and hip-hop's focus had moved to the West Coast and the South. In addition, the outlook of clubgoers had grown bleak: The Giuliani administration—obsessed with squelching late-night noise and other quality-of-life issues—had put a damper on club activities. Skyrocketing rents made it hard for artists to find rehearsal spaces.

But as the 21st century drew near, a radical shift occurred. Rents too high in Manhattan? Several clubs opened in Brooklyn. Inspiration lacking? Bands looked to the city's own glorious past for enlightenment. Fledgling groups recaptured the fusion of minimal funk and postpunk pioneered by Liquid Liquid and ESG (which made a stunning comeback). Guitar strummers subverted Greenwich Village's historic folk tradition by calling their new music "antifolk" and spiking it with arty attitude (for more on local bands, *see* **This *is* it**, *page 310*). Intimate recording studios thrived in Manhattan and Brooklyn, and the city's energy lured bands from all over the world. It's no wonder PJ Harvey recorded one of her finest albums, *Stories from the City, Stories from the Sea,* in NYC.

In order to navigate the scene, it's important to remember that many music spots offer a

**Lone star** Texan Rhett Miller, the charismatic frontman of twangy rockers Old '97s, performs passionate pop from his solo album at the Bowery Ballroom.

**Head-bangers' ball** Metal mavens act out their rock & roll fantasies at Arlene Grocery's heavy-metal karaoke on Monday nights. The rest of the week live bands perform.



different genre every night. The venues below are categorized according to their primary genre, and cross-referenced where necessary.

New York clubs are fairly rigid about checking ID (you must be 21 to drink, and often, to enter), but some people still try to concoct a winning lie to sway the bouncer. It hardly ever works. A driver's license or passport is always best—school IDs are an immediate red flag for door people.

Tickets are usually available from clubs both in advance and at the door. A few small and medium-size clubs also sell advance tickets through local record stores. For larger events, it's wise to buy through **Ticketmaster** *(see page 375)* on the web, over the phone or at one of the outlets located throughout the city. Tickets for some events are available through **www.ticketweb.com**. You can also buy online from websites of specific venues (web addresses are included in venue listings where available). For more ticket details, see page 374. And remember to call first for info and show times, which may change without notice.


▶ See chapter **By Season** for annual music festivals and events.
▶ For more live-music venues, see chapters **Cabaret & Comedy**, **Clubs** and **Gay & Lesbian**.

▶ Pick up a copy of ***Time Out New York***, which lists specific shows and previews upcoming concerts.

## Arenas

### Continental Airlines Arena

*East Rutherford, NJ (201-935-3900; www.meadowlands.com). Travel: NJ Transit Meadowlands Sports Complex bus from Port Authority Bus Terminal (212-564-8484), Eighth Ave at 42nd St, $3.25 each way. From $25. Cash only at box office.*

This arena is north Jersey's answer to Madison Square Garden. The CAA has recently played host to Britney Spears, Eminem and No Doubt. The arena is also the site of radio-sponsored pop and hip-hop extravaganzas.

### Madison Square Garden

*Seventh Ave at 32nd St (212-465-6741; www.thegarden.com). Subway: A, C, E, 1, 2, 3, 9 to 34th St–Penn Station. Box office: Mon–Sat noon–6pm. $25–$350. AmEx, DC, Disc, MC, V.*

Awright, Noo Yawk! Are you ready to rock & roll? The acoustics may be more suited to the crack of hockey and the slap of basketball, but MSG remains one of the most famous rock venues in the world. Cher, Bob Dylan and Madonna are but a few who've sold out the place. Be warned: The cost of a good seat is high—tickets for special occasions can sell for more than $1,000; regular shows can easily top $100.

### Nassau Veterans Memorial Coliseum

*1255 Hempstead Tpke, Uniondale, Long Island (516-794-9303; www.nassaucoliseum.com). Travel: From Penn Station, Seventh Ave at 32nd St, take LIRR (718-217-5477) to Hempstead, then N70, N71 or N72 bus. From $25. AmEx, Disc, MC, V.*

Many of the same performers that can be seen at CAA and MSG come here too, and the Coliseum is probably the quintessential place to hear piano man Billy Joel, Long Island's favorite son (sorry, Lou Reed).

## Rock, pop & soul

### Apollo Theater

*253 W 125th St between Adam Clayton Powell Jr. Blvd (Seventh Ave) and Frederick Douglass Blvd (Eighth Ave) (212-749-5838; www.apollotheater.com). Subway: A, C, B, D, 1, 9 to 125th St. Box office: Mon, Tue, Thu, Fri 10am–6pm; Wed 10am–8:30pm; Sat noon–6pm. $10–$35. AmEx, MC, V.*

It helped launch the careers of Ella Fitzgerald and Michael Jackson, it served as *the* hub for R&B music for years, and it continues to house the revamped *Showtime at the Apollo* television program. This recently renovated Harlem auditorium is smaller than it looks on TV, and most seats give you a good view of the hallowed stage. The weekly Wednesday **Amateur Night** endures.

### Arlene Grocery

*95 Stanton St between Ludlow and Orchard Sts (212-358-1633). Subway: F, V to Lower East Side–Second Ave. Free–$10. Cash only.*

Named for the actual Lower East Side bodega that it replaced, recently expanded Arlene Grocery runs as many as seven groups a night through its top-notch sound system. You can catch worthy local acts such as Sean Altman, Sam Bisbee or the Adam Roth Challenge. Heavy-metal karaoke on Monday night remains a popular draw.

### BAMcafé at Brooklyn Academy of Music

*See page 318 for listing.*

The Brooklyn Academy of Music used to save the funk, jazz and pop-based world music for the fall **Next Wave Festival**. Now the BAMcafé, a high-ceilinged lounge above the lobby, hosts weekly live-music events. The mix of genres includes folk, hip-hop, jazz, world music and spoken word. The **Sounds of Praise Sunday Gospel Brunch** offers a fine opportunity to hear gospel groups while feasting on a soul-food buffet.

### Beacon Theatre

*2124 Broadway at 74th St (212-496-7070). Subway: 1, 2, 3, 9 to 72nd St. Box office: Mon–Fri 11am–7pm; Sat noon–6pm. $15–$175. Cash only at box office.*

What can you say about the site of the Allman Brothers' annual two-week residency? The gilded interior and gigantic statues guarding the stage work perfectly for mature sounds—and that could mean the semi-ambient drones of Icelandic band Sigur Rós, the acerbic tones of Elvis Costello or the overwrought moans of Tori Amos.

### The Bitter End

*147 Bleecker St at Thompson St (212-673-7030; www.bitterend.com). Subway: A, C, E, F, V, S to W 4th St. $5–$10. AmEx, DC, Disc, MC, V.*

One of Bleecker Street's classic spots, the Bitter End hosts a selection of hopeful young singer-songwriters and the occasional folk or roots star, such as Ramblin' Jack Elliott (who's been playing here since the 1960s).

### The Bottom Line

*15 W 4th St at Mercer St (212-228-6300; www.bottomlinecabaret.com). Subway: N, R, W to 8th St–NYU. Box office: 10am–11pm. $15–$35. Cash only.*

This Greenwich Village cabaret is most famous for a run of 1970s Springsteen shows that catapulted the Boss to rock-star status, but this steadfast club remains the city's premier acoustic venue for young folkies and touring classic rockers. The Bottom Line hosts country and Americana acts (Loretta Lynn and Kathy Mattea played recently). Local acts such as the Magnetic Fields and the Harry Smiths stop by too. Word of warning: After all these years, the management still hasn't perfected the seating plan, so the sight lines can suck.

### Bowery Ballroom

*6 Delancey St between Bowery and Chrystie St (212-533-2111; www.boweryballroom.com). Subway: J, M to Bowery; 6 to Spring St. Box office is at Mercury Lounge (see page 312). $10–$25. AmEx, MC, V (bar only).*

In terms of size, comfort level and booking policy, Bowery Ballroom is one of the city's best venues. There's plenty of space, including a downstairs bar where you can escape the opening band that shouldn't have left the garage. The stage, sight lines and sound are solid, and you could catch acts like the Donnas, Lambchop and local stars such as the Yeah Yeah Yeahs. Note: Bands frequently run late, and the no re-entry policy can be a hassle.

### CBGB

*315 Bowery at Bleecker St (212-982-4052; www.cbgb.com). Subway: F, V, S to Broadway–Lafayette St; 6 to Bleecker St. $3–$12. Cash only.*

The progressive spirit and sense of diversity that helped launch Blondie, the Ramones and Talking Heads are all but gone; rote metal and punk bands have taken over the stage at CBGB. There are exceptions, such as the night when country superstar Alan Jackson played a raucous set, or the occasional **HomoCorps** events, which showcase queer-friendly acts. No matter who's playing, anyone interested in the history of rock should check out the venue.

### CB's 313 Gallery + CBGB's Downstairs Lounge

*313 Bowery at Bleecker St (212-677-0455; www.cbgb.com). Subway: F, V, S to Broadway–Lafayette St; 6 to Bleecker St. $6–$10. AmEx, MC, V.*

Located right next door, these two small venues are CBGB's more cultivated cousins (the Lounge is under

"Innovative and essential."

–*The New York Times*

"Fresh and provocative."

–*USA Today*

"World class casting."

–*Newsday*

For tickets to these or to any of the 12 other operas in the 2003-2004 season: visit www.nycopera.com, call Ticketmaster at (212) 307-4100, or visit the New York State Theater Box Office at Lincoln Center.

CITY OPERA

Fall Season: September 9 – November 23, 2003
Spring Season: March 5 – April 25, 2004

the Gallery). At the Gallery, acoustic fare and local singer-songwriters dominate. A similar lineup lulls the Lounge, except on Sunday, when it hosts the weekly series **Freestyle Avant Jazz and Other Musics**.

### Continental

*25 Third Ave at St. Marks Pl (212-529-6924). Subway: N, R, W to 8th St–NYU; 6 to Astor Pl. Free–$6. Cash only.*

These days, Continental may host more tributes to the Ramones than surprise gigs by Ramones members, but the boxy room's "legendary" status is reflected on its walls, which are lined with photos of past performers, including Iggy Pop. The booking is almost uniformly rock, metal and punk of the local variety; out-of-town acts have grown scarce recently.

### Don Hill's

*511 Greenwich St at Spring St (212-219-2850). Subway: C, E to Spring St; 1, 9 to Houston St. Free–$10. AmEx, DC, Disc, MC, V.*

Part live-music venue, part dance club, loud and divey Don Hill's sponsors events such as Wednesday's **Röck Cändy** party, which serves up glammy, punky bands.

### Elbow Room

*144 Bleecker St between La Guardia Pl and Thompson St (212-979-8434). Subway: A, C, E, F, V, S to W 4th St. $5–$10. Cash only.*

The Elbow Room achieved A-list status a few years ago when its Wednesday-night karaoke party drew celebrities such as Claire Danes and Courtney Love to the mike—and inspired a short-lived (thank God) VH1 series. Local music of all stripes rules every other night of the week.

### Fez

*Inside Time Cafe, 380 Lafayette St at Great Jones St (212-533-2680). Subway: F, V, S to Broadway–Lafayette St; 6 to Bleecker St. $5–$18, two-drink minimum. Cash only for cover charge. AmEx, MC, V for food and drink.*

Located downstairs from the restaurant Time Cafe, Fez is one of the city's finest venues for lounge acts and softer rock bands (Eleni Mandell, the Nields, Mia Doi Todd ). On Thursdays, the Mingus Big Band introduces a new generation of listeners to the robust, sanctified jazz of the late Charles Mingus. Perhaps best of all, this club has a sweet tooth for gender-bending entertainment by the likes of Jackie Beat and Hedda Lettuce. Fez's dinner theater–style seating leaves little standing room, so make reservations, arrive early and prepare for a strictly enforced two-drink minimum.

### Galapagos

*70 North 6th St between Kent and Wythe Aves, Williamsburg, Brooklyn (718-782-5188; www.galapagosartspace.com). Subway: L to Bedford Ave. $5–$12. Cash only.*

Galapagos's two rooms welcome live music and theatrical performance art. Its front room is a popular neighborhood hangout, with affordable drinks and

**The eclectic company** Elegant Joe's Pub draws a wide array of music stylists.

free music, some of it deejayed. The back room offers new-music composers (the string quartet Invert calls itself Galapagos's house band), experimental funk and electronica, mostly culled from Williamsburg's vibrant community of artists.

### Hammerstein Ballroom

*Manhattan Center, 311 W 34th St between Eighth and Ninth Aves (212-279-7740, 212-564-4882). Subway: A, C, E to 34th St–Penn Station. Box office: Mon–Sat noon–5pm. $10–$50. AmEx, MC, V.*

This mid-sized venue may not be the best place to see a show—security is a hassle and the sound is fairly crummy—but the management books top acts. Doves, Jay-Z, OutKast, Pet Shop Boys, PJ Harvey and the Chemical Brothers have tackled the mighty Ballroom. Try scoring a seat in the front of the first balcony.

### Irving Plaza

*17 Irving Pl at 15th St (212-777-6800; www.irvingplaza.com). Subway: L, N, Q, R, W, 4, 5, 6 to 14th St–Union Sq. Box office: Mon–Fri noon–6:30pm; Sat 1–4pm. $10–$30. Cash only.*

Irving Plaza, the city's original mid-size venue, pulls in an excellent roster of artists from around the globe. The room has recently welcomed reunion shows from postpunk bands Wire and Mission of Burma. In a given week, the Plaza might host Bright Eyes, Dolly Parton, Tortoise, or Marianne Faithfull. Generous elbowroom makes a full house more comfortable.

### Izzy Bar

*166 First Ave between 10th and 11th Sts (212-228-0444). Subway: L to First Ave; 6 to Astor Pl. $5–$10. AmEx, MC, V.*

Izzy Bar is one of NYC's better temples of groove. Smokin' nights geared toward lovers of house, drum 'n' bass, funk bands and jazz-tinged jam sessions keep the party going until 4am.

### Joe's Pub

*425 Lafayette St between Astor Pl and W 4th St (212-539-8770) Subway: N, R, W to 8th St–NYU; 6 to Astor Pl. Box office: 1–6pm. $12–$35. AmEx, MC, V.*

Named in honor of Public Theater founder Joseph Papp, Joe's Pub features some of the most eclectic entertainment in town (Julee Cruise, Eartha Kitt, Nick Lowe, the Trachtenburg Family Slideshow Players) in a lush cabaret setting. Beware: Seating is limited, and the door policy can be selectively enforced. *(See also page 271.)*

### Knitting Factory

*74 Leonard St between Broadway and Church St (212-219-3055; www.knittingfactory.com). Subway: A, C, E to Canal St; 1, 9 to Franklin St. Box office: Mon–Fri 10am–11pm; Sat, Sun 2–11pm. $5–$20. AmEx, MC, V ($15 minimum charge).*

On some nights, you can traverse entire galaxies of music just by moving from room to room. The main performance space hosts well-known stars (Lou Reed, Sonic Youth), indie stalwarts (Stereo Total, New Bomb Turks) and genre jumpers (Arto Lindsay, Sun City Girls). Come summer, when the main floor swelters, find a perch in the balcony. The Knitactive Sound Stage and Old Office showcase poetry performances, alternative cinema and jazz artists.

### Lakeside Lounge

*162 Ave B between 10th and 11th Sts (212-529-8463; www.lakesidelounge.com). Subway: L to First Ave; N, Q, R, W, 4, 5, 6 to 14th St–Union Sq. Shows are free. AmEx, MC, V.*

The Lakeside is a great downscale hangout that revels in its scruffiness. A killer jukebox, a photo booth

## This *is* it

**Thanks to a Strokes-stoked revival, the city's rock scene thrives once again**

For New York City, punk rock was a tough act to follow. That pierced, pissed-off movement produced some of the city's most recognizable names—Blondie, the Ramones, Talking Heads, Television—but after Pussy Galore and Sonic Youth sparked an indie surge in the mid-1980s, the NYC rock scene shriveled. Compared to Seattle, Chicago or even Olympia, Washington, the Big Apple was the Big Empty. The success of the Strokes in 2001 brought the scene back to life: Now there are electrifying local bands playing every night of the week.

Following the Strokes—who broke big with their CD *Is This It*—the Yeah Yeah Yeahs, a drums-guitar-vocal trio, caught the fancy of downtown clubgoers. Led by indomitable singer Karen O, the group built its reputation on stage, touring constantly and playing every dive in NYC (and once, a parking lot in Williamsburg, Brooklyn). It also prudently tested the waters by releasing two EPs before its full-length debut. At press time, Karen O was dating Angus Andrew, the lead singer from Liars, another high-profile local band. In a way, their pairing exemplifies the passing of the torch from one generation to another: O and Andrew have replaced the Blues Explosion's Jon Spencer and Boss Hog's Christina Martinez as NYC's sexpot rock couple.

The city is now thrumming with top-notch live bands that have embraced dance music. Some groups have successfully rejuvenated the spirit of the late 1970s and early '80s, when postpunk bands such as ESG, Gang of Four and Liquid Liquid blended rock, angular rhythms and cerebral funk. Out Hud, for instance, is a mostly instrumental group that starts with a deep, dub-influenced bass and then goes off on an unabashed disco tangent. The crew shares members with the like-minded !!! (pronounced "chik-chik-chik"), a large, boisterous collective that does not rest until every last person is on the dance floor.

Some time this year, New York label Death From Above (DFA) will release a new record from the Rapture. After a number of fairly straightforward rock EPs, the band switched gears and released *House of Jealous Lovers* and *Olio*, both on DFA (which also distributes material from local groups the Juan Maclean and LCD Soundsystem). These two records wink at the indie-rock constituency. But the DFA sound, like the NYC scene, is hard to pigeonhole. For example, the label's Black Dice has moved from cacophonous noise rock to a gentler form of aggression within two years. Its new sound creates a heavy ambience, with bright melodic tones (if not actual melodies), repetition and psychedelic touches. Black Dice's gigs can be as satisfying as they are loud, with fierce playing and unpolished experimentation.

Adventurous listeners should seek out the Animal Collective, which showcases electronicists Avey Tare, Panda Bear, Geologist and Deaken. No two Animal shows are alike; the group juggles monotone pastoral folk with chanted and chirped vocals. In the same vein, Onairlibrary, a trio that creates a glow of brightly colored psychedelic fuzz, uses loud, angelic melodies to produce dense, hazy sounds.

New York is also known for its electroclash sound, spearheaded by promoter Larry Tee. Tee

and rockabilly- and roots-loving singers and groups lend the bar an urban-roadhouse feel.

### L'Amour

*1545 63rd St between 15th and 16th Aves, Bay Ridge, Brooklyn (718-837-9506; www.lamourrocks.com). Subway: M, W to 62nd St; N to New Utrecht Ave. $10–$15. Cash only.*

L'Amour has brought hard rock back to Brooklyn by booking hair-metal rockers who played the club in the '80s and tribute bands such as Sack Blabbath. The likes of Dee Snider (of Twisted Sister) will take you back to the age of *Dynasty* and designer jeans, while today's rap and death-metal bands (Biohazard, Enthroned, Hate Eternal) befoul you and your eardrums.

### The Living Room

*84 Stanton St at Allen St (212-533-7235; www.livingroomny.com). Subway: F, V to Lower East Side–Second Ave; J, M, Z to Delancey–Essex Sts. One-drink minimum. Cash only.*

Befitting its name, the Living Room is a low-key, intimate lounge. Singer-songwriter guests play right up close and personal.

### Luna Lounge

*171 Ludlow St between Houston and Stanton Sts (212-260-2323; www.lunalounge.com). Subway: F, V to Lower East Side–Second Ave. Free. Cash only.*

This popular Lower East Side hangout's best feature is its reasonable cover charge: nothing. Therefore, the music can leave something to be desired. But some of

**Fuzzy Dice** The feedback-heavy sound of Black Dice isn't for all tastes, but fans love the band's experimental edge.

released highly regarded compilations on his label, Mogul Electro, organized an electroclash festival and launched the popular Berliniamsburg nights at **Luxx** *(see page 275)*. Local bands in the retro-electro scene include so-so offerings W.I.T. and Soviet and the Plantains, along with genuine originals such as My Robot Friend, a one-man band consisting of Howard Robot, who wears a costume powered with a 40-pound battery pack; neon and Christmas lights curl around his limbs and dot his helmet. MRF shows are hilarious affairs: He banters with the crowd in a Mr. Roboto–esque voice and sings over prerecorded tracks while also playing keyboards and guitar.

Another quirky group, the Moldy Peaches, evolved out of the East Village–based antifolk family. Famous for its potty-mouth lyrics, weird stage outfits and irresistible hooks, the duo went on hiatus last year after putting out a well-received self-titled album and touring incessantly for 18 months. But don't despair: Peaches Kimya Dawson and Adam Green now have solo careers, and have released *I'm Sorry that Sometimes I'm Mean* and *Garfield,* respectively.

There are a few oddball bands that don't fit in to any easily defined category. After relocating from Seattle in 2002, the Trachtenburg Family Slideshow Players instantly established themselves as one of NYC's most ingenious offerings. Starring piano man Jason Trachtenburg—who sings biting, satirical lyrics inspired by slides he digs up at estate sales—and his nine-year-old daughter Rachel (on drums, naturally), this family act offers agit-pop at its most subversive. The instrumental trio Big Lazy may be the city's most versatile band, sliding easily from polished twang and soft, romantic waltzes to haunting, tremolo-laden rockabilly.

Some say that the New York music scene is about to succumb to its own hype. But if hype means great homegrown records and a steady supply of sharp live bands, then bring it on!

the city's better underground pop and roots bands, such as the Pasties and 34 Satellite, frequent the stage, as do a few touring bands.

### Luxx

See page 275.

### Makor

*35 W 67th St between Central Park West and Columbus Ave (212-601-1000; www.makor.org). Subway: 1, 9 to 66th St–Lincoln Ctr. $5–$12. AmEx, MC, V.*

Makor, a Jewish cultural center on a fancy Upper West Side street, presents music shows in the basement. The programming emphasizes folk, blues, roots, world music and local singer-songwriters.

### Maxwell's

*1039 Washington St, Hoboken, NJ (201-798-0406; www.maxwellsnj.com). Travel: PATH train to Hoboken; NJ Transit bus #126 from Port Authority Bus Terminal. $6–$15. AmEx, MC, V.*

Maxwell's has been the most consistently forward-looking rock club in the metropolitan area for more than 20 years. Since it's in another state, many visiting acts play a date here as well as at the Bowery Ballroom, Knitting Factory, etc. It can get a little snug when a show sells out, but hey, it's a landmark. Music ranges from garage and punk to indie and roots.

### Meow Mix

See page 295.

### Mercury Lounge

*217 Houston St at Ave A (212-260-4700; www.mercuryloungenyc.com). Subway: F, V to Lower East Side–Second Ave. Box office: Mon–Fri noon–7pm. $8–$12. Cash only.*

The crowded bar that greets you is usually a tight squeeze, but beyond its mass of humanity, you'll find the brick-walled room in back that makes Mercury Lounge one of the city's better live-music spots. The sound is great, you can see from just about anywhere (so long as you're not too short), and the staff actually treats you nicely. The Mercury books plenty of locals and touring acts of all flavors. Within a span of two weeks, the room welcomed the Datsuns, Lali Puna and Steve Wynn.

### New Jersey Performing Arts Center

*See page 346 for listing*

NJPAC, the sixth-largest performing arts center in the U.S., has hosted everything from the Buena Vista Social Club to Jewel and Mandy Patinkin.

### 9C

*700 E 9th St at Ave C (212-358-0048). Subway: F, V to Lower East Side–Second Ave; L to First Ave; 6 to Astor Pl. Free–$5. Cash only.*

Deep in the heart of Alphabet City, this unassuming roadhouse bar hosts many of New York's smaller country-tinged acts, such as Oakley Hall & Company.

### 92nd Street Y

*See page 267 for listing.*

The Y's popular music schedule extends to gospel, indigenous folk styles and mainstream jazz. **Jazz in July** lures swingers young and old into the comfy surroundings, as does the **Lyrics & Lyricists** series, which celebrates the tunesmiths who wrote the American Songbook.

**Sweet jam** Winterville plays at cozy Pete's Candy Store, which has no bad seats.

### Northsix

*66 North 6th St between Kent and Wythe Aves, Williamsburg, Brooklyn (718-599-5103; www.northsix.com). Subway: L to Bedford Ave. Box office: 8pm–midnight. $8–$12. Cash only.*

This bare-bones, 400-capacity club is one of the city's top spots to hear burgeoning rock & roll. The club books an eclectic range of rock acts, including Brooklyn-based bands and international groups such as Tokyo's Ghost and Chicago's Shellac.

### Pete's Candy Store

*709 Lorimer St between Frost and Richardson Sts, Williamsburg, Brooklyn (718-302-3770; www.petescandystore.com). Subway: G to Metropolitan Ave; L to Lorimer St. Free.*

Pete's is perhaps the city's most charming venue. Shaped like an old railroad car, the tiny space feels as small as a living room, and performances assume the intimacy of a children's puppet show. The confines can seem too close for comfort when the singer sucks, but on a good night, this quirky space can be oh-so-sweet.

### Radio City Music Hall

*1260 Sixth Ave at 50th St (212-247-4777: www.radiocity.com). Subway: B, D, F, V to 47–50th Sts–Rockefeller Ctr. Box office: Mon–Sat 10am–8pm; Sun 11am–8pm. From $25. AmEx, MC, V.*

Walking through this awe-inspiring Art Deco hall is almost as exciting as watching the superstars who perform: 2003 headliners include Tori Amos, the Rolling Stones and India.Arie.

### Roseland

*239 W 52nd St between Broadway and Eighth Ave (212-245-5761, concert hot line 212-249-8870). Subway: B, D to Seventh Ave; C, E, 1, 9 to 50th St. Box office open only on the night of the show. From $15. Cash only.*

Oasis, Queens of the Stone Age and Wilco have recently graced the stage of this 1930s-era ballroom. Megastars (David Bowie and Madonna) also pop in from time to time.

### Roxy

See page 275.

### Sidewalk

*94 Ave A at 6th St (212-473-7373). Subway: F, V to Lower East Side–Second Ave; 6 to Astor Pl.Free.*

They call it "the Fort at Sidewalk," possibly because you have to wend your way through several rooms of diners and drinkers to reach the music space, way in back. The latest band to break out of Sidewalk's antifolk scene was goofy duo the Moldy Peaches, and both Kimya Dawson and Adam Green regularly stop in for solo sets. Open mikes and jam sessions occur frequently, in case you want to drop by with your acoustic guitar.

### S.O.B.'s

See page 276.

### Southpaw

*125 Fifth Ave between Sterling and St. John's Pls, Park Slope, Brooklyn (718-230-0236; www.spsounds.com). Subway: M, N, R, W to Pacific St; Q, 4, 5 to Atlantic Ave; 2, 3 to Bergen St. $7–$15. Cash only.*

One of the finest rock venues in New York is in Brooklyn—but it's not in the hipster haven of Williamsburg. Southpaw is in residential Park Slope. A spacious stage, top-notch sound system, two-tiered floor plan and excellent sight lines make this a great place to see a band. The club presents a good mix of acts, both local (Oneida, The Mendoza Line, Out Hud) and touring (Bis, Soledad Brothers).

### The Theater at Madison Square Garden

*Seventh Ave at 32nd St (212-465-6741; www.thegarden.com). Subway: A, C, E, 1, 2, 3, 9 to 34th St–Penn Station. Box office: Mon–Sat noon–6pm. Prices vary. AmEx, DC, Disc, MC, V.*

This is the smaller, classier extension of Madison Square Garden, and since it's not an arena, it also sounds better. The theater has hosted world-music celebrations, mainstream hip-hop shows, R&B extravaganzas, medium-size rock shows by James Taylor and Bonnie Raitt, and a bizarre event in which Elvis Presley's old backing band accompanied giant movie-screen images of the deceased singer.

### Tonic

*107 Norfolk St between Delancey and Rivington Sts (212-358-7503; www.tonic107.com). Subway: F to Delancey St; J, M, Z to Delancey–Essex Sts. Box office: 8–11pm. $8–$40. Cash only.*

Tonic, a former kosher winery on the Lower East Side, has become one of the world's leading venues for avant-garde, creative and experimental music, taking an inclusive view; rock, pop and electronic sounds frequently rub elbows with jazz and improvised pieces. You could catch one of guitar legend Derek Bailey's annual appearances, or see local band Calla turn up the late-night vibes.

### The Town Hall

*123 W 43rd St between Sixth and Seventh Aves (212-840-2824; www.the-townhall-nyc.org). Subway: B, D, F, V to 42nd St; N, Q, R, W, S, 1, 2, 3, 9, 7 to 42nd St–Times Sq. Box office: Mon–Sat noon–6pm. $15–$85. AmEx, MC, V ($2.50 surcharge for credit card orders).*

An 81-year-old theater with superb acoustics, the Town Hall was conceived as the "people's auditorium," and its democratic bookings keep that spirit alive. The summer is slow, but the fall season brings folk and traditional music artists from around the world (including many Persian and Indian talents), as well as a mix of pop artists ranging from Bruce Hornsby to Bob Geldof.

### Village Underground

*130 W 3rd St between MacDougal St and Sixth Ave (212-777-7745; www.thevillageunderground.com). Subway: A, C, E, F, V, S to W 4th St. Box office: 1–8pm. $8–$20. AmEx, MC, V (food and drink only).*

The Village Underground is a cozy basement nook where one can stand (albeit awkwardly) or sit (and eat fried food). Bookings lean toward adult-alternative and rootsy fare (Freedy Johnston, Amy Rigby), and has included some big stars for such a small room—you might get Sleater-Kinney or Ike Turner, depending on the night. The club has also hosted **Cavestomp!**, where you can catch a mix of veteran '60s garage rockers (? and the Mysterians, the Monks) and younger combos (the Dirtbombs, the Detroit Cobras).

### Warsaw at the Polish National Home

*261 Driggs Ave at Eckford St, Greenpoint, Brooklyn. (718-387-5252; www.polishnationalhome.com). Subway: G to Nassau Ave. Box office: 5pm. Cash only.*

The Polish National Home is a spacious, old-fashioned ballroom with a bar in front that serves affordable Polish beers and pierogi. The cavernous main room, run by the bookers of the Village Underground, offers a schedule of local draws with national appeal, such as Le Tigre and Blond Redhead, and touring artists like Phantom Planet, as well as the **Electroclash Festival**.

## Jazz & experimental

### Birdland

*315 W 44th St between Eighth and Ninth Aves (212-581-3080; www.birdlandjazz.com). Subway: A, C, E to 42nd St–Port Authority. $20–$35, $10 food-and-drink minimum. AmEx, MC, V.*

The flagship venue for midtown's recent jazz resurgence, Birdland hosts many of jazz's biggest names amid the neon scene of Times Square. Ron Carter and Dave Holland have made recent appearances, but Birdland is also notable for its roster of great bands in residence. Sundays belong to the Chico O'Farrill Afro-Cuban Jazz Orchestra. Mondays are reserved for the Toshiko Akiyoshi Jazz Orchestra, featuring Lew Tabackin. Swing tubaist David Ostwald pilots the Louis Armstrong Centennial Band in the early evening every Tuesday.

### Blue Note

*131 W 3rd St between MacDougal St and Sixth Ave (212-475-8592; www.bluenote.net). Subway: A, C, E, F, V, S to W 4th St. $10–$65, $5 food-and-drink minimum. AmEx, DC, MC, V.*

"The jazz capital of the world" is how this famous club describes itself, and the big names who play are often greeted like visiting heads of state. In recent years, it has become the premier place to commemorate birthdays and other milestones (Belgian harmonica virtuoso Toots Thielemans recently celebrated his 80th birthday with special guest Billy Joel, and the vocal group Manhattan Transfer celebrated 30 years in showbiz). All this glamour comes at a price: Dinner will cost you at least $25 a head.

### Carnegie Hall

*See page 318 for listing.*

Playing venerable Carnegie Hall remains synonymous with hitting the big time. Many of the venue's showcases are reminders that the hall's acoustics were designed for classical music—period. But that didn't stop Carnegie's honchos from launching an annual jazz program, directed by star trumpeter Jon Faddis. Other nights, expect performers such as jazz-congo madman Poncho Sanchez or the singers who appeared on the soundtrack for *O Brother, Where Art Thou?*

### Cornelia Street Cafe

*29 Cornelia St between Bleecker and W 4th Sts (212-989-9318; corneliastreetcafe.com). Subway: A, C, E, F, V, S to W 4th St. $5–$15, $6 one-drink minimum. AmEx, DC, MC, V.*

Much of the music at Cornelia Street Cafe is rather avant-garde, but don't let that scare you. Something about walking down the stairs of this Greenwich Village eatery brings out the calm in the scene's most adventurous players, such as Marty Ehrlich or Tony Malaby. The result is dinner music with a contemporary edge.

### Iridium

*1650 Broadway at 51st St (212-582-2121; www.iridiumjazzclub.com). Subway: 1, 9 to 66th St–Lincoln Ctr. $25–$30, $10 food-and-drink minimum. AmEx, DC, Disc, MC, V.*

Iridium's new location has placed it one step closer to Times Square, but that hasn't changed the club's attitude. It still lures upscale crowds with a lineup that's split between household names and those known only by the jazz-savvy. The sight lines and sound system are truly worthy of celebration. Monday nights belong to guitar hero Les Paul.

### Jazz Gallery

*290 Hudson St between Dominick and Spring Sts (212-242-1063; www.jazzgallery.org). Subway: C, E to Spring St; 1, 9 to Houston St. $12. Cash only.*

It's a tad snug, but the astonishing acoustics at this jazz haunt make it a prime place to get intimate with the music. No wonder top-shelf musicians such as Roy Hargrove often drop in for impromptu jams. Jazz Gallery's weekend showcases have also become a draw for newcomers like Orrin Evans and Vijay Iyer.

### Jazz Standard

*116 E 27th St between Park and Lexington Aves, (212-576-2232; www.jazzstandard.net). Subway: N, R, 6 to 28th St. $15–$25, $10 food-and-drink minimum. AmEx, DC, Disc, MC, V.*

Renovation was just what the doctor ordered for the jazz den below restaurateur Danny Meyer's **Blue Smoke** barbecue joint *(see page 195)*. Now the room's marvelous sound matches its already splendid sight lines. In keeping with the rib-sticking chow served upstairs, the jazz is of the groovy, hard-swinging variety (organist Dr. Lonnie Smith, Larry Goldings).

### Stanley H. Kaplan Penthouse at Lincoln Center

*165 W 65th St, Rose Building, tenth floor (212-875-5050; www.jazzatlincolncenter.org). Subway: B, D,*

**Urban legend** Harlem's refurbished Lenox Lounge is better than ever, offering all manner of live jams—hardbop, hip-hop, jazz, reggae and more.

*E to Seventh Ave; 1, 9 to 50th St. Tickets from Alice Tully Hall box office 11am–6pm. AmEx, DC, Disc, MC, V.*
If you thought Lincoln Center housed only grand concert halls, you should hear one of the jazz events at the Kaplan Penthouse. A 100-seat room with a terrace that offers a scenic view of the Hudson River, the Penthouse is the place for the Lincoln Center jazz program's duets and solo recitals. It's almost like having Andy Bey or Bill Charlap tickle the ivories in your living room.

## Knitting Factory

See page 310.

## Lenox Lounge

*See page 177 for listing.*
This is where a street hustler named Malcolm worked before he got religion and added *X* to his name. The hardbop outfits that jam at this classy Harlem institution proudly carry on an old tradition.

## Merkin Concert Hall

*See page 319 for listing.*
Just across the street from Lincoln Center, Merkin's polished digs provide an intimate setting for jazz and experimental acts (Matthew Shipp, Robert Ashley, Klezmatics trumpeter Frank London) that are not likely to appear at Avery Fisher Hall.

## Roulette

*228 West Broadway at White St (212-219-8242; www.roulette.org). Subway: C, E to Canal St; 1, 9 to Franklin St. $10. Cash only.*
The atmosphere at trombonist Jim Staley's 11-year-old salon is relaxed—until the music starts. The players, Staley's friends, represent an encyclopedia of world-famous music experimentalists, including computer-music pioneer Maxime de la Rochefocauld and avant-jazz cellist Okkyung Lee.

## Smalls

*183 W 10th St at Seventh Ave South (212-929-7565). Subway: 1, 9 to Christopher St–Sheridan Sq. $10. Cash only.*
Smalls books high-profile up-and-comers. You'll hear 13 hours of jazz on weekend nights, and pianist Jason Lindner's big band plays most Mondays. There's no liquor license, but you can bring your own booze or sample some of the juices and teas at the bar.

## Smoke

*2751 Broadway between 105th and 106th Sts (212-864-6662; www.smokejazz.com). Subway: 1, 9 to 103rd St. Sun–Thu free. Fri, Sat $10–$25. MC, V.*
Smoke is a classy little room that has figured out how to lure patrons uptown and downtown. Early in the week, evenings are themed: Sunday, Latin jazz; Tuesday, organ jazz; Wednesday, funk. On weekends, internationally renowned jazz locals hit the stage (George Coleman, Eddie Henderson, Cedar Walton), and seem to relish the opportunity to play informal gigs in their own backyard.

## St. Nick's Pub

*773 St. Nicholas Ave at 149th St (212-283-9728). Subway: A, C, B, D to 145th St. Free. Cash only.*
St. Nick's may be the closest thing to an old-fashioned juke joint you're likely to find in the city. Located in Harlem's Sugar Hill section, it has live music six nights a week, charmingly makeshift decor, a soul-food menu and mature Heineken-sipping patrons nurturing their hedonistic impulses. The music runs from bebop and vocal-driven to funk. Big names, such as James Carter, occasionally stop by for the Monday-night jam. A must-visit for any serious jazz fan.

**Swing 46**

*349 W 46th St between Eighth and Ninth Aves (212-262-9554; www.swing46.com). Subway: A, C, E to 42nd St–Port Authority. Box office: noon–4pm. $7 (Sun–Wed), $12 (Thu–Sat). MC, V.*

You don't have to throw on a zoot suit or a poodle skirt to make the scene at this midtown bastion of retro, but it certainly will enhance the mood. Seven nights' worth of bands that jump, jive and wail await you, so be sure to wear your most comfortable shoes. Live music starts at 10pm, and dancing is de rigueur.

**Tonic**

See page 313.

**Village Vanguard**

*178 Seventh Ave South at Perry St (212-255-4037; www.villagevanguard.net). Subway: A, C, E, 1, 2, 3, 9 to 14th St; L to Eighth Ave. Call to reserve tickets. $25–$30, $10 drink-minimum. Average drink $6. Cash only.*

After 66 years, this basement club is still blowing strong. Its stage—a small but mighty step-up—hosts the crème de la crème of mainstream jazz talent and has seen the likes of John Coltrane, Miles Davis and Bill Evans. The Monday-night regular is the 16-piece Vanguard Jazz Orchestra, which has held the same slot for more than 30 years.

## Reggae, world & Latin

**Babalu**

*327 W 44th St between Eighth and Ninth Aves (212-262-1111; www.babaluny.com). Subway: A, C, E to 42nd St–Port Authority; N, Q, R, W, S, 1, 2, 3, 9, 7 to 42nd St–Times Sq. Tue–Thu, Sat 5:30pm–1am; Fri 5:30pm–3am. $10–$12. AmEx, DC, Disc, MC, V.*

This 21st-century version of the Tropicana supper club from *I Love Lucy* showcases live salsa, merengue and Latin pop.

**Copacabana**

*560 W 34th St between Tenth and Eleventh Aves (212-239-2672). Subway: A, C, E to 34th St–Penn Station. $20, $30 at tables. AmEx, Disc, MC, V.*

Copacabana, long the city's most iconic destination for Latino music, has moved farther east into a sprawling three-floor space. It's still a prime stop for salsa, *cumbia* and merengue, but in addition to booking world-renowned stars (Ruben Blades, Tito Nieves and Conjunto Clasico, El Gran Combo), the Copa now has an alternative nook called the House Room, where dancers can spin to disco, house and Latin freestyle.

**S.O.B.'s**

See page 276.

**Zinc Bar**

*90 Houston St between La Guardia Pl and Thompson St (212-477-8337; www.zincbar.com). Subway: A, C, E, F, V, S to W 4th St. $5. Cash only.*

Located where Noho meets Soho, Zinc Bar is the place to hoot and holler with die-hard night owls. The after-hours feel starts well before midnight, and the atmosphere is enhanced by the cool mix of African, flamenco, jazz, Latin and samba bands. Cidinho Teixeira's **Brazilian Showfest** draws crowds on Sundays, guitarist Ron Affif holds down the fort on Mondays and African Blue Note, a mesmerizing Afropop cover band, delivers African funk on Fridays.

## Blues, country & folk

**B.B. King Blues Club & Grill**

*237 W 42nd St between Seventh and Eighth Aves (212-997-4144; bbkingblues.com). Subway: A, C, E to 42nd St–Port Authority; N, Q, R, W, S, 1, 2, 3, 9, 7 to 42nd St–Times Sq. Sun–Tue, Thu 11am–midnight; Wed 11am–5am; Fri, Sat 11am–3am. Cover varies. AmEx, DC, Disc, MC, V.*

Praise the Lord and pass the bacon—B.B. King's is shakin' to the beat of J.C., and we don't mean Jim Croce. At this well-appointed 42nd Street club, there is one dynamite, can't-miss event every week: **The Harlem Gospel Choir** buffet brunch on Sunday. The club also hosts stellar soul and blues performers such as James Brown, Buddy Guy and Etta James.

## CRITICS' PICKS Record stores

These are the best places…

**…to hear the next dance-music trend**

Throb *(47 Orchard St between Grand and Hester Sts, 212-925-6069)* was the first to spot the nu-electro/neo-wave/whatever thing.

**…to find that elusive Korean cast album of *Cats***

Footlight Records *(113 E 12th St between Third and Fourth Aves, 212-533-1572)* offers a huge musical-theater inventory, and the staff won't bat an eye when you request Ethel Merman's disco album.

**…to acquire French hip-hop and Cuban *son* on the same trip**

Tower Records *(see page 243)* stocks tunes from around the globe.

**…to overhear a conversation out of *High Fidelity***

Other Music *(see page 244)* shoppers and salespeople can discuss the difference between micro-house and minimal techno for hours on end.

**…to buy a kraut rock reissue on Christmas day**

Mondo Kim's *(see page 244)* is open until midnight 365 days a year.

**Afternoon delight** Summer means outdoor concerts in Brooklyn's Prospect Park.

### Kate Kearney's

*251 E 50th St between Second and Third Aves (212-935-2045). Subway: E, V to Lexington Ave–53rd St; 6 to 51st St. Free.*

The crowd at this small Irish pub is friendly and energetic. Thursdays, you can see an informal jam session (called a *seisiún*) with Don Meade and Patrick Ourceau, while other nights feature a variety of Irish-flavored country and folk.

### Paddy Reilly's Music Bar

*519 Second Ave at 29th St (212-686-1210; www.paddyreillys.com). Subway: 6 to 28th St. Fri, Sat $5–$10. AmEx, MC, V.*

The premier local bar for Irish rock hosts nightly music from groups such as Prodigals, with *seisiúns* thrown in as well.

### Rodeo Bar

*375 Third Ave at 27th St (212-683-6500). Subway: 6 to 28th St. Free.*

This sawdust-strewn joint books local roots outfits (Demolition String Band, Mary McBride) and visiting country acts. The club seems to have a particular connection to Austin, Texas; some of that city's finest acts (BR549, Rosie Flores, Hot Club of Cowtown, the Meat Purveyors) drop by regularly.

## Summer venues

### Castle Clinton

*Battery Park, Battery Pl at State St (212-835-2789). Subway: E to World Trade Ctr; N, R, W to Rector St; 2, 3 to Park Pl; 4, 5 to Bowling Green. Free.*

Space is limited at this historic fort in the heart of Battery Park. At the summer Thursday-night concert series, lucky music hounds get an unobstructed view of performers such as Neko Case and Rosanne Cash.

### Central Park SummerStage

*See page 252 for listing.*

On a humid summer weekend, SummerStage is one of New York's great treasures. The booking policy is delightfully ecumenical, from world music (Orchestra Baobab, Super Rail Band) and hip-hop (Common) to country (Lyle Lovett) and dance (Basement Jaxx). Show up early—many people had to be turned away from the Manu Chao show, to name just one instance.

### Giants Stadium

*See page 325 for listing.*

At Giants Stadium, you can catch biggies such as U2 and 'N Sync, while overhead, airplanes fly to and from Newark Airport. Band members look like ants, and you'll wait a long, long time for beer, but the hot dogs aren't that bad. Because it's outdoors, it's the only remaining venue in the Meadowlands complex where you can smoke.

### Lincoln Center Plaza

*See page 320 for listing.*

The home of Lincoln Center's **Midsummer Night Swing** *(see page 252)* and **Out-of-Doors** festivals, the Plaza hosts many of New York City's sundry cultural communities. In one week, it's possible to hear the world's hottest Latin and African bands (Papa Wemba, the Congolese fashion plate who helped invent the rumbalike *soukous* sound, recently dropped by) and a concert by tenor-saxophone god Sonny Rollins, or pianists Diane Schuur and Cyrus Chestnut.

### Prospect Park Bandshell

*See page 112 for listing.*

Prospect Park Bandshell is to Brooklynites what Central Park SummerStage is to Manhattan residents: *the* place to hear great music in the great outdoors. The programming for the summer festival **Celebrate Brooklyn** *(see page 252)* mirrors the borough's diversity; the music runs from Egyptian *sha'bi* (Hakim) and salsa (the Machito Orchestra) to Afropop (Rokia Traore) and hip-hop (Talib Kweli). Prospect Park also books indie-pop touring bands (Flaming Lips), excellent modern-dance troupes (Mark Morris) and a film series.

### The Tommy Hilfiger at Jones Beach Theater

*Jones Beach, Long Island (516-221-1000). Travel: LIRR from Penn Station, Seventh Ave at 32nd St, to Freeport, then Jones Beach bus. $18–$65. Cash only.*

Even though it's far away for the carless and the sound isn't that great, you can't beat the alfresco setting at this beachside amphitheater. From July to September, most of the big tours make a pit stop. Expect to catch acts like Aerosmith, Coldplay, Toby Keith, Alicia Keys, OutKast, Weezer and The Who.

# Classical Music

Every once in a while, you might catch a classical music lover longing for a bygone golden age. But judging from the wealth of musical presentations available in New York City, *these* are the good ol' days. The New York Philharmonic is playing better than ever under Lorin Maazel, a music director who can be brilliant or controversial, but never ever boring, and the Metropolitan Opera boasts one of the finest orchestras in the world to support the dazzling stars on its stage. Carnegie Hall plays host to outstanding orchestras and soloists, both homegrown and imported. In addition, the city's churches, museums and schools cater to every conceivable musical taste—from devotional medieval works to contemporary experimentalism.

## Tickets

You can buy tickets directly from most venues, either in-person or online. For some sites, you can also purchase tickets over the phone, though a surcharge is added. See page 374 for more ticket information.

### CarnegieCharge

*212-247-7800. 8am–8pm. AmEx, DC, Disc, MC, V. $4.75 surcharge per ticket.*

### Centercharge

*212-721-6500. Mon–Sat 10am–8pm; Sun noon–8pm. AmEx, Disc, MC, V. $5.50 surcharge per ticket.*
Centercharge sells tickets for events at Alice Tully Hall, Avery Fisher Hall and the **Lincoln Center Festival** *(see page 252)*.

### Metropolitan Opera

*212-362-6000. 10am–8pm. AmEx, MC, V. Surcharge $5.50 per ticket.*
The Met sells tickets for its own events and those of American Ballet Theatre.

## Backstage passes

It's possible to go behind the scenes at several of the city's major concert venues. **Backstage at the Met** *(212-769-7020)* shows you around the famous house during opera season (September to May); **Lincoln Center Tours** *(212-875-5350)* escorts you inside Avery Fisher and Alice Tully Halls, and the New York State Theater; **Carnegie Hall** *(212-247-7800)* ushers you through what is perhaps the world's most famous concert hall. You may also sit in on rehearsals of the **New York Philharmonic** *(212-875-5656)*, usually held on the Thursday before a concert, for a small fee.

## Concert halls

### Brooklyn Academy of Music

*30 Lafayette Ave between Ashland Pl and St. Felix St, Fort Greene, Brooklyn (718-636-4100; www.bam.org). Subway: G to Fulton St; M, N, R, W to Pacific St; Q, 2, 3, 4, 5 to Atlantic Ave. Prices vary. AmEx, MC, V.*
BAM's opera house is America's oldest academy for the performing arts. But the programming is more East Village than Upper West Side: BAM helped secure the reputations of Philip Glass (who still performs here regularly) and John Zorn. Current music director Robert Spano has carried the resident Brooklyn Philharmonic Orchestra to remarkable heights of creative achievement on a fraction of the budget its Manhattan counterpart enjoys. Every fall and winter, the **Next Wave Festival** provides an overview of established avant-garde music and theater, while the spring BAM Opera season brings innovative European productions to downtown Brooklyn.

### Carnegie Hall

*154 W 57th St at Seventh Ave (212-247-7800; www.carnegiehall.org). Subway: F, N, Q, R, W to 57th St; B, D, E to Seventh Ave. Prices vary. AmEx, DC, Disc, MC, V.*
A varied roster of American and international stars appears in two auditoriums: Carnegie Hall proper and the lovely, smaller Weill Recital Hall. This celebrated venue is undergoing a massive renovation; Zankel Hall, a vast subterranean performance space, is slated to open in September 2003.

### Colden Center for the Performing Arts

*LeFrak Concert Hall, Queens College, 65-30 Kissena Blvd at 65th Ave, Flushing, Queens (718-793-8080; www.coldencenter.org). Subway: 7 or LIRR to Flushing–Main Street, then Q17, Q25 or Q34 bus to Kissena Blvd. Box office: Mon 10am–4pm; Wed noon–8pm; Fri noon–4pm; Sat 10am–2pm. $10–$30. AmEx, Disc, MC, V.*
The home of the Queens Philharmonic, this multipurpose hall also stages concerts by international artists who are in town for Manhattan performances. Due to the Colden Center's remote location, concert tickets are often half the price of those at the city's other venues.

### Florence Gould Hall

*French Institute–Alliance Française, 55 E 59th St between Madison and Park Aves (212-355-6160; www.fiaf.org). Subway: N, R, W to Fifth Ave–59th St;*

> ▶ For information on concerts, times and locations, see ***Time Out New York***'s Classical & Opera listings.
> ▶ The Theatre Development Fund *(see page 334)* provides information on all music events via its **NYC/Onstage** service.

Arts & Entertainment

**It's lonely at the top** Every classical musician dreams of playing beautifully designed Carnegie Hall, arguably the world's most renowned concert venue.



*4, 5, 6 to 59th St. Box office: Tue–Fri 11am–7pm; Sat, Sun 11am–3pm. $10–$35. AmEx, MC, V.*
You don't need to brush up on your French to attend the recitals and chamber pieces performed at this space, but the programming does have a decidedly French tone, in both its artists and repertoire.

### Merkin Concert Hall

*Kaufman Center, 129 W 67th St between Broadway and Amsterdam Ave (212-501-3330; www.elainekaufmancenter.org). Subway: 1, 9 to 66th St–Lincoln Ctr. $10–$25. AmEx, MC, V (for advance purchases only).*
This theater has rather dry acoustics and is tucked away on a side street in the shadow of Lincoln Center. But its mix of early music and avant-garde programming (heavy on recitals and chamber concerts) can make it a rewarding stop.

### New Jersey Performing Arts Center

*See page 346 for listing.*
Designed by Los Angeles–based architect Barton Myers, the NJPAC complex is impressive, featuring the oval-shaped, wooden 2,750-seat Prudential Hall and the more institutional-looking 514-seat Victoria Theater. It may sound far away, but it takes only 15 to 20 minutes to get there from midtown. It's a good place to catch big-name acts that may be sold out at Manhattan venues.

### 92nd Street Y

*See page 267 for listing.*
The Y emphasizes traditional orchestral, solo and chamber masterworks, but also foments the careers of young musicians.

### The Town Hall

*See page 313 for listing.*
This small, bi-level space is true to its name; it has an intimate feel and excellent acoustics.

## Lincoln Center

This massive arts complex, built in the 1960s, is the nexus of Manhattan's performing-arts scene. Lincoln Center hosts lectures and symposia in the **Rose Building**, in addition to events in the main halls—**Alice Tully**, **Avery Fisher**, **Metropolitan Opera House**, **New York State Theater**, the **Vivian Beaumont** and **Mitzi E. Newhouse Theaters** *(see page 339)*. Also on the premises are **The Juilliard School** *(see page 323)* and the **Fiorello La Guardia High School of the Performing Arts** (yes, the one from *Fame*, but in a different location), which occasionally sponsors professional performances. The **Mostly Mozart Festival** in August (at Avery Fisher and Alice Tully Halls) is a highly anticipated summer event, but lately it's been upstaged by the larger, multidisciplinary Lincoln Center Festival, which takes place in

July. The big guys (Yo-Yo Ma, Daniel Barenboim, Anne-Sophie Mutter) perform here, but the Center has also been venturing into more adventurous programming in recent years.

### Lincoln Center

*65th St at Columbus Ave (212-LINCOLN; www.lincolncenter.org). Subway: 1, 9 to 66th St–Lincoln Ctr.*
This is the main entry point for Lincoln Center, but the venues that follow are spread out in the square from 62nd to 66th Streets, between Amsterdam and Columbus Avenues.

### Alice Tully Hall

*212-875-5050. Box office: Mon–Sat 11am–6pm; Sun noon–6pm; also open for 30 minutes after the start of performance. Free–$75. AmEx, Disc, MC, V.*
Built to house the **Chamber Music Society of Lincoln Center** *(212-875-5788; www.chambermusicsociety.org)*, Alice Tully Hall somehow makes its 1,096 seats feel cozy. It has no central aisle, and the rows have extra legroom. Its **Art of the Song** recital series is one of the most extensive in town.

### Avery Fisher Hall

*212-875-5030. Box office: Mon–Sat 10am–6pm; Sun noon–6pm. $20–$90. AmEx, Disc, MC, V.*
After several major renovations, this 2,700-seat auditorium is now handsome *and* comfortable, and the acoustics are much improved. This is the headquarters of the **New York Philharmonic** *(212-875-5656; www.nyphilharmonic.org)*, the country's oldest orchestra (founded in 1842) and one of the world's finest. It holds free concerts and regular open rehearsals. The hall also schedules concerts by top international ensembles as part of the **Great Performers** showcase. Every summer, fans flock to the famous **Mostly Mozart** series. *(see page 252).*

### Metropolitan Opera House

*212-362-6000; www.metopera.org. Box office: Mon–Sat 10am–8pm; Sun noon–6pm. $12–$250. AmEx, Disc, MC, V.*
Marc Chagall's enormous mystical paintings hang inside the five geometric arches of this space: The Met is the grandest of the Lincoln Center buildings, a spectacular place to see and hear opera. It's home to the **Metropolitan Opera** from September to May, and it's also where major visiting companies are most likely to appear. Met productions are lavish (though not always tasteful), and cast the most current stars. Under artistic director James Levine, the orchestra has become a true symphonic force. Although audiences are knowledgeable and fiercely partisan (subscriptions stay in families for generations), the Met has tried to be more inclusive in recent years; digital English-language subtitles appear on screens affixed to railings in front of each seat, allowing operagoers to laugh in all the right places. Tickets are expensive, and unless you can afford good seats, the view won't

**Topsy-turvy** At the New York City Opera, Richard Suart plays Ko-Ko in Jonathan Miller's production of Gilbert & Sullivan's beloved *The Mikado.*

be great. Standing-room-only tickets start at $12; you have to wait in line on Saturday mornings to buy them. In recent years, the Met has commissioned productions by the likes of Robert Wilson—to mixed reception from its conservative audiences. Over-the-top Franco Zeffirelli productions of the classics remain the Met's bread and butter.

### New York State Theater

*212-870-5570. Box office: Mon 10am–7:30pm; Tue–Sat 10am–8:30pm; Sun 11:30am–7:30pm. $25–$100 (Mon–Fri), $30–$110 (Sat, Sun). AmEx, Disc, MC, V.*

NYST houses the **New York City Ballet** *(www.nycballet.com)* and the **New York City Opera** *(www.nycopera.com)*—which has tried to overcome its second-best reputation by being defiantly popular and ambitious. The opera company hires a number of American singers, often imbues old favorites with an especially theatrical spin, and performs many works in English, bringing American musicals into the spotlight. City Opera also champions modern opera, resulting in a few great successes and some noble failures. City Opera is ultimately much cooler than its stodgier neighbor, and tickets are about half the price.

### Walter Reade Theater

*212-875-5600. Box office: 2–6pm. $12–$15.*

The Walter Reade Theater's acoustics are poor—but uniformly perfect sight lines are a consolation. The Chamber Music Society uses the space regularly, and the Sunday-morning **Great Performers** concert series is fueled by pastries and hot beverages sold in the lobby.

## Opera

The Metropolitan Opera and New York City Opera may loom mightily, but they're hardly the only arias in town. The following companies perform a varied repertoire—both warhorses and works-in-progress—from Verdi's *Aida* to Wargo's *Chekhov Trilogy*. Call the organizations or visit their websites for ticket prices, schedules and venue details. The music schools *(see page 323)* have opera programs, too.

### Amato Opera Theatre

*319 Bowery at 2nd St (212-228-8200; www.amato.org). Subway: F, V, S to Broadway–Lafayette St; 6 to Bleecker St. $25, seniors and children $20. MC, V.*

Presented in a theater only 20 feet wide, Anthony Amato's charming, fully staged productions make you feel like you're watching opera in a cozy living room. Casting can be inconsistent, but many well-known singers have performed here.

### American Opera Projects

*South Oxford Space 138 South Oxford St between Atlantic Ave and Hanson Pl, Ft. Greene, Brooklyn (718-398-4024). Subway: C to Lafayette St; M, N, R, W to Pacific St; Q, 2, 3, 4, 5 to Atlantic Ave. Prices vary. Cash only.*

AOP is not so much an opera company as a living, breathing workshop. Productions are often a way to follow a work-in-progress.

### Dicapo Opera Theater

*184 E 76th St between Lexington and Third Aves (212-288-9438; www.dicapo.com). Subway: 6 to 77th St. $40. MC, V.*

This top-notch chamber-opera troupe benefits from City Opera–quality singers performing on intelligently designed, small-scale sets in the basement of St. Jean Baptiste Church. It's a real treat.

### New York Gilbert & Sullivan Players

*See* **Symphony Space**, *page 322.*

Is Victorian camp your vice? This troupe presents a rotating schedule of the Big Three *(H.M.S. Pinafore, The Mikado* and *The Pirates of Penzance),* plus lesser-known G&S works.

## Other venues

### Bargemusic

*Fulton Ferry Landing, next to the Brooklyn Bridge, Brooklyn Heights, Brooklyn (718-624-4061; www.bargemusic.org). Subway: A, C to High St; F to York St. $20–$35. Cash only.*

This former coffee barge offers four chamber concerts a week—and a great view of the Manhattan skyline. It's a magical experience, but bundle up in winter. When the weather warms, you can enjoy a drink on the upper deck during intermission.

### CAMI Hall

*165 W 57th St between Sixth and Seventh Aves (212-397-6900; www.cami.com). Subway: F, N, Q, R, W to 57th St. Prices vary. Cash only.*

Located across the street from Carnegie Hall, this 200-seat recital hall is rented for individual events, mostly by classical artists.

### Frick Collection

*See page 43 for listing.*

Concerts in this museum's tiny, elegantly appointed concert hall are always a rare treat, featuring lesser-known but world-class performers in an intimate setting (for instance, the Festetics Quartet playing Haydn on period instruments). Tickets are free, but acquiring them can be a chore: Written requests must be submitted in advance, and tickets are often gone weeks or months in advance. A line for returned tickets forms one hour before each event.

### The Kaye Playhouse

*Hunter College, 68th St between Park and Lexington Aves (212-772-4448; www.kayeplayhouse.com). Subway: 6 to 68th St–Hunter College. Box office: Mon–Sat noon–6pm. Free–$70. AmEx, MC, V.*

Named after comedian Danny Kaye and his wife, this refurbished theater offers an eclectic program of professional music and dance, including regular presentations by the delightful **New York Festival of Song**.

### The Kitchen

*See page 341 for listing.*

Occupying a 19th-century icehouse, the Kitchen has been a meeting place for the avant-garde in music, dance and theater for almost 30 years. Shows range from free to $25.

### Kosciuszko Foundation

*15 E 65th St at Fifth Ave (212-734-2130; www.kosciuszkofoundation.org). Subway: F to Lexington Ave–63rd St; 6 to 68th St–Hunter College. $15–$25. MC, V.*

This East Side townhouse hosts a chamber-music series with a mission: Each program must feature at least one work by a Polish composer. That means you might be choking on Chopin, or you could hear some unexpected delights.

### Metropolitan Museum of Art

*See page 44 for listing.*

This is one of the city's best chamber-music venues, so concerts usually sell out quickly. Respected veterans like Beaux Arts Trio and the Guarneri Quartet appear regularly, and international stars such as Dmitri Hvorostovsky and Mikhail Pletnev have made recent appearances.

### Miller Theatre at Columbia University

*Broadway at 116th St (212-854-7799; www.millertheatre.com). Subway: 1, 9 to 116th St–Columbia Univ. Box office: Mon–Fri noon–6pm. Prices vary. AmEx, MC, V.*

Columbia's acoustically excellent space has become the city's most dependable source of contemporary concert music, devoting entire evenings to composers like James Dillon, György Ligeti, Iannis Xenakis and John Zorn, as well as enterprising surveys of early music and innovative, multidisciplinary events.

### New York Public Library for the Performing Arts

*See page 58 for listing. Free.*

The Bruno Walter Auditorium hosts recitals, solo performances and lectures.

### 180 Maiden Lane

*180 Maiden Ln at Front St (212-799-5000, ext 313). Subway: A, C to Broadway–Nassau St; J, M, Z, 2, 3, 4, 5 to Fulton St. Free.*

Formerly known as Continental Center, this space is home to the **Juilliard Artists in Concert** series. One highlight includes free lunchtime student recitals on Tuesdays; the schedule expands during the summer.

### Symphony Space

*See* **Selected Shorts**, *page 267, for listing.*

The programming at Symphony Space is eclectic; best bets are the annual **Wall to Wall** marathons, which offer a full day of music featuring a composer or theme, from Bach to Miles Davis. The marathons are free, resulting in lines around the block.

### Tishman Auditorium

*The New School, 66 W 12th St at Sixth Ave (212-229-5689). Subway: F, V, 1, 2, 3, 9 to 14th St; L to Sixth Ave. Free–$12. Cash only.*

The New School's modestly priced **Schneider** chamber-music series features up-and-coming young musi-

**Sound salvation** A choir performs at the Upper East Side's Church of Ignatius Loyola, which produces the yearly Sacred Music in a Sacred Place series.

cians, as well as established artists, who play here for a fraction of the prices charged elsewhere.

## Churches

From sacred to secular, an enticing variety of music is performed in New York's churches. Many resident choirs are out of this world, while superb acoustics and serene surroundings make churches particularly attractive venues. Bonus: Some concerts are free or very cheap.

### Cathedral of St. John the Divine

*See page 103 for listing. Box office: 10am–6pm. Prices vary. AmEx, MC, V.*
The 3,000-seat interior is an acoustical black hole, but the stunning neo-Gothic setting provides a heavenly atmosphere for the church's own choir and groups such as the Russian Chamber Chorus.

### Christ and St. Stephen's Church

*120 W 69th St between Columbus Ave and Broadway (212-787-2755; www.csschurch.org). Subway: 1, 2, 3, 9 to 72nd St. Prices vary. Cash only.*
This West Side church offers one of the most diverse concert rosters in the city.

### Church of the Ascension

*12 W 11th St between Fifth and Sixth Aves (212-254-8553; voicesofascension.org). Subway: N, R, W to 8th St–NYU. Free–$40. MC, V.*
This little Village church has a wonderful professional choir, the Voices of the Ascension. The singers periodically travel uptown to perform at Lincoln Center, but their home turf is much more aesthetically pleasing.

### Church of St. Ignatius Loyola

*980 Park Ave at 84th St (212-288-2520; www.saintignatiusloyola.com). Subway: 4, 5, 6 to 86th St. Call to reserve tickets or purchase the day of performance. $10–$35. MC, V.*
The **Sacred Music in a Sacred Space** series is a high point of Upper East Side music culture. In recent seasons, other arts organizations, such as Lincoln Center, have begun to sponsor their own choral-music concerts here.

### Corpus Christi Church

*529 W 121st St between Amsterdam Ave and Broadway (212-666-9350; varenne.tc.columbia.edu/corpus). Subway: 1, 9 to 125th St. Prices vary. MC, V.*
Early-music fans can get their fix from **Music Before 1800** *(212-666-9266; www.mb1800.org)*, a series that presents innovative international musical groups as well as resident ensembles.

### St. Bartholomew's Church

*109 E 50th St between Park and Lexington Aves (212-378-0248; www.stbarts.org). Subway: E, V to Lexington Ave–53rd St; 6 to 51st St. Prices vary. AmEx, MC, V.*
Large-scale choral music and occasional chapel recitals fill the magnificent dome behind the church's facade, designed by Stanford White.

### St. Thomas Church Fifth Avenue

*1 W 53rd St at Fifth Ave (212-757-7013; www.saintthomaschurch.org). Subway: E, V to Fifth Ave–53rd St. $15–$60. AmEx, MC, V.*
Some of the finest choral music in the city can be heard here, sung by the country's only fully accredited choir school for boys. The church's annual performance of Handel's *Messiah* is a must-see.

### Trinity Church/St. Paul's Chapel

*Broadway at Wall St (212-602-0747; www.trinitywallstreet.org). Subway: E to World Trade Ctr; N, R, W to Rector St; 2, 3, 4, 5 to Wall St. Noonday Concerts series $2 donation. Choir series $25. AmEx, MC, V.*
Historic Trinity, in the heart of the Financial District, schedules individual concerts and the **Noonday Concerts** series, which is held at 1pm on Mondays at St. Paul's Chapel *(Broadway at Fulton St)* and on Thursdays at Trinity Church.

## Schools

Juilliard and the Manhattan School of Music are renowned for their students, faculty and artists-in-residence, all of whom regularly perform for free or at low cost. Noteworthy music and innovative programming can be found at several other colleges and schools in the city.

### Brooklyn Center for the Performing Arts at Brooklyn College

*Campus Rd at Hillel Pl, one block west of the junction of Flatbush and Nostrand Aves, Flatbush, Brooklyn (718-951-4543; www.brooklyncenter.com). Subway: 2, 5 to Flatbush Ave–Brooklyn College. Box office: Tue–Sat 1–6pm. $20–$50. AmEx, MC, V.*
While it hosts concerts by mass-appeal pop performers, this hall is also a destination for traveling opera troupes and soloists of international acclaim.

### The Juilliard School

*60 Lincoln Center Plaza, Broadway at 65th St (212-769-7406; www.juilliard.edu). Subway: 1, 9 to 66th St–Lincoln Ctr. Mostly free.*
New York's premier conservatory stages weekly concerts by student soloists, orchestras and chamber ensembles, as well as student opera productions.

### Manhattan School of Music

*120 Claremont Ave at 122nd St (212-749-2802, ext 4428; www.msmnyc.edu). Subway: 1, 9 to 125th St. Mostly free.*
MSM offers master classes, recitals and off-site concerts by its students, faculty and visiting pros. The **Augustine Guitar Series**, featuring recitals by top soloists and performances by the American String Quartet (in residence since 1984), is one of the highlights of the school's calendar. The opera program is quite adventurous.

# Sports & Fitness

Bike trails, boxing matches, big-league baseball—New York is all fun and games

New York, New York is a helluva sports town. The Apple boasts more professional teams than any other city, a rabid press corps that chronicles an athlete's every move, and die-hard fans who are convinced of their superior knowledge. But you can do more than just watch—pedal a bike through Central Park, kayak up the Hudson or go ice-skating at Rockefeller Center. Not only are these activities good exercise, they're great ways to see the city.

## Spectator Sports

The local papers carry massive quantities of sports coverage and list the day's events and TV schedule. *The New York Times* has the most sophisticated reporting, but the tabloids—the *Daily News* and the *New York Post*—are best for stats and opinions. Local broadcasters offer their own takes—the Fox Sports and Madison Square Garden TV networks provide 24-hour programming, while radio listeners can tune in to ESPN Radio (AM 1050) or WFAN (AM 660) for nonstop talk.

### Baseball

Abner Doubleday is usually credited with inventing baseball, but the rules of the modern-day game were drawn up in 1845 by local ballplayer Alexander Cartwright. By the 1920s, Babe Ruth and the **Yankees**' "Murderer's Row" cemented the game's hold on the city and the nation. Today, with 26 World Series titles to their credit, the Bronx Bombers remain the team to beat. Meanwhile, the National League **Mets** have struggled since the Yankees vanquished them in the 2000 "Subway Series," but the Queens-based team still has a faithful following. Minor league excitement returned in 2001 when the Staten Island Yankees and Brooklyn Cyclones (the farm team for the Mets) opened new ballparks.

#### New York Mets

*Shea Stadium, 123-01 Roosevelt Ave at 126th St, Flushing, Queens (718-507-TIXX; www.mets.com). Subway: 7 to Willets Point–Shea Stadium. Box office Mon–Fri 9am–5:30pm. Apr–Oct. $12–$33. AmEx, Disc, MC, V.*

#### New York Yankees

*Yankee Stadium, River Ave at 161st St, Bronx (718-293-6000; www.yankees.com). Subway: B, D, 4 to 161st St–Yankee Stadium. Box office Mon–Fri 9am–5pm; Sat 10am–3pm and during games. $8–$65. Apr–Oct. AmEx, Disc, MC, V.*

#### Brooklyn Cyclones

*KeySpan Park, 1604 Surf Ave between W 17th St and W 19th St, Coney Island, Brooklyn (718-449-TIXS; www.brooklyncyclones.com). Subway: W to Coney Island–Stillwell Ave. Jun–Sept. $11. AmEx, MC, V.*

#### Staten Island Yankees

*Richmond County Bank Ballpark, 75 Richmond Terr at Bay St, St. George, Staten Island (718-720-YANK; www.siyanks.com). Travel: Staten Island Ferry to St. George Terminal. Jun–Sept. $8, $10. AmEx, Disc, MC, V.*

### Basketball

Two National Basketball Association teams, the **New York Knicks** and the **New Jersey Nets**, dominate the local roundball scene, with the Knicks reigning supreme in most New Yorkers' hearts—if not in the NBA standings. For years, the Knicks, who play at famed Madison Square Garden, have been the hot ticket. But the Nets are on the rise and made it to the finals in 2002. The ladies hold court, too, when the Women's National Basketball Association's **New York Liberty** plays during the summer.

#### New Jersey Nets

*Continental Airlines Arena, East Rutherford, NJ (arena box office 201-935-3900, direct line for Nets tickets 800-7NJ-NETS; www.nba.com/nets). Travel: NJ Transit Meadowlands Sports Complex bus from Port Authority Bus Terminal (212-564-8484), Eighth Ave at 42nd St, $3.25 each way. $10–$95. Oct–May. AmEx, Disc, MC, V.*

#### New York Knicks

*Madison Square Garden, Seventh Ave between 31st and 33rd Sts (box office 212-465-MSG1; www.nba.com/knicks). Subway: A, C, E, 1, 2, 3, 9 to 34th St–Penn Station. Box office Mon–Sat noon–6pm. $25–$100. Oct–May. AmEx, DC, Disc, MC, V.*

#### New York Liberty

*Madison Square Garden, Seventh Ave between 31st and 33rd Sts (box office 212-465-MSG1; www.wnba.com/liberty). Subway: A, C, E, 1, 2, 3, 9 to 34th St–Penn Station. Jun–Aug. Box office Mon–Sat noon–6pm. $8–$57.50. AmEx, DC, Disc, MC, V.*

## Boxing

### Church Street Boxing Gym

*25 Park Pl between Broadway and Church St (212-571-1333; www.nyboxinggym.com). Subway: 2, 3 to Park Pl; 4, 5, 6 to Brooklyn Bridge–City Hall. Fights: $20–$25. Cash only.*

Church Street is a workout gym and boxing venue housed in an atmospheric cellar. Amateur fights are staged year-round, as are professional kickboxing bouts. Evander Holyfield, Mike Tyson and other heavy hitters are known to spar here when in town.

### Madison Square Garden

*Seventh Ave between 31st and 33rd Sts (box office 212-465-MSG1; www.thegarden.com). Subway: A, C, E, 1, 2, 3, 9 to 34th St–Penn Station. Box office Mon–Sat noon–6pm. Prices vary. All advanced tickets must be purchased through Ticketmaster (212-307-7171; www.ticketmaster.com). AmEx, DC, Disc, MC, V.*

Long since replaced by Atlantic City and Las Vegas for title fights, the Garden still hosts several major bouts each year.

## Football

New York is the only city in America with two pro teams. Of course, they both play at Giants Stadium in New Jersey, but that's a technicality. From September through December—and often into the playoffs in January—New York fans are football-crazed.

The vast majority of seats to **Giants** games are snatched up by season-ticket holders, so single-game tickets are hard to find. While the box office places a scattering of tickets on sale before the season begins (usually in August), you'll probably have better luck paying a broker or searching eBay. **Jets** tickets are even harder to find. When you call, a recorded announcement explains that tickets have been "sold out since the 1979 season."

### New York Giants

*Giants Stadium, East Rutherford, NJ (box office 201-935-8222; www.giants.com). Travel: NJ Transit Meadowlands Sports Complex bus from Port Authority Bus Terminal (212-564-8484), Eighth Ave at 42nd St, $3.25 each way.*

### New York Jets

*Giants Stadium, East Rutherford, NJ (box office 516-560-8200; www.newyorkjets.com). Travel: NJ Transit Meadowlands Sports Complex bus from Port Authority Bus Terminal (212-564-8484), Eighth Ave at 42nd St, $3.25 each way.*

## Hockey

It's a high-speed game with the potential for grotesque violence—no wonder ice hockey is so popular here. The **New Jersey Devils** have surpassed their competitors, the **New York Islanders** and **Rangers**, but the Rangers remain the hometown favorite. Tickets are on sale throughout the season, which runs from October through April.

**Spar wars** Amateurs and professionals get punchy at the Church Street Boxing Gym.

### New Jersey Devils

*Continental Airlines Arena, East Rutherford, NJ (201-935-6050, box office 201-935-3900; www.newjerseydevils.com). Travel: NJ Transit Meadowlands Sports Complex bus from Port Authority Bus Terminal (212-564-8484), Eighth Ave at 42nd St, $3.25 each way. $20–$90. AmEx, MC, V.*

► ***Time Out New York*** lists upcoming games played by area teams.

► For details on major sporting events, contact **NYC & Company** *(212-484-1222; www.nycvisit.com).*

► Visit **www.nyc.gov/sports** for the latest news on all professional sports in the city.

► For ticketing information, see page 374.

**Ball buster** Hop on a bus to Giants Stadium and watch the MetroStars kick it.

### New York Islanders

*Nassau Veterans Memorial Coliseum, 1255 Hempstead Tpke, Uniondale, Long Island (516-501-6700; www.newyorkislanders.com). Travel: From Penn Station, Seventh Ave at 32nd St, take LIRR (718-217-5477) to Hempstead, then N70, N71 or N72 bus. Box office Mon–Fri 9am–5pm. $19–$120. AmEx, Disc, MC, V.*

### New York Rangers

*Madison Square Garden, Seventh Ave between 31st and 33rd Sts (box office 212-465-MSG1; www.newyorkrangers.com). Subway: A, C, E, 1, 2, 3, 9 to 34th St–Penn Station. Box office Mon–Sat noon–6:30pm. $25–$150. AmEx, DC, Disc, MC, V.*

## Horse racing

There are three major racetracks near Manhattan: Thoroughbreds run at **Aqueduct**, **Belmont** and the **Meadowlands**. If you don't want to trek to Queens or New Jersey, head for an Off-Track Betting (OTB) outpost to catch the action and (reliably seedy) atmosphere.

### Aqueduct Racetrack

*110th St at Rockaway Blvd, Ozone Park, Queens (718-641-4700). Subway: A to Aqueduct–North Conduit. Thoroughbred races Oct–May Wed–Sun. Admission: clubhouse $3, grandstand $1. Cash only.*

The Wood Memorial, held each April, is a test run for promising three-year-olds headed for the Kentucky Derby.

► Find more places to exert yourself in **A river runs near it**, page 72.

### Belmont Park

*2150 Hempstead Tpke, Elmont, Long Island (718-641-4700). Travel: From Penn Station, Seventh Ave at 32nd St, take LIRR to Belmont Park. Thoroughbred races May–Oct Wed–Sun. Admission: clubhouse $4, grandstand $2. Cash only.*

The 1.5-mile Belmont Stakes, the third leg of the Triple Crown, is usually held on the second Saturday in June. Every fall, the year's best horses run in the $1 million Jockey Gold Cup.

### Meadowlands Racetrack

*East Rutherford, NJ (201-935-8500; www.thebigm.com). Travel: NJ Transit Meadowlands Sports Complex bus from Port Authority Bus Terminal (212-564-8484), Eighth Ave at 42nd St, $3.25 each way. Harness races Nov–Aug; Thoroughbred races Sept–Nov; check website for days. Admission:clubhouse $3, grandstand $1. Cash only.*

Top harness racers compete for more than $1 million in the prestigious Hambletonian, held the first Saturday in August.

## Soccer

Soccer may never rival the popularity of baseball or football in New York, but its fan base is on the rise, thanks in part to the exciting New York/New Jersey MetroStars, who play at Giants Stadium.

### New York/New Jersey MetroStars

*Giants Stadium, East Rutherford, NJ (888-4-METRO-TIX; www.metrostars.com). Travel: NJ Transit Meadowlands Sports Complex bus from Port Authority Bus Terminal (212-564-8484), Eighth Ave at 42nd St, $3.25 each way. Apr–Sept. $18–$75. AmEx, MC, V.*

## Tennis

### U.S. Open

*USTA National Tennis Center, Flushing Meadows–Corona Park, Queens (718-760-6200, tickets 866-673-6849; www.usopen.org). Subway: 7 to Willets Point–Shea Stadium. Late Aug–early Sept. $22–$325. AmEx, MC, V.*

Tickets go on sale in June for this grand-slam thriller, which features the game's biggest names.

# Active Sports

New York offers plenty for those who define *sports* as something to do, not watch. Central Park *(see page 93)* is an oasis for everyone from skaters to cricket players. Gyms *(see page 328)* have largely replaced bars as pickup spots, and massive complexes such as Chelsea Piers have brought suburban-style recreational space to the city.

### New York Sports Online

*www.nysol.com.*
Visit this site for a comprehensive roundup of recreational sports options in the city. Call ahead in case there are last-minute changes.

## Bicycling

One of the best ways to see New York is by bike—it's faster than walking, and since you set your own pace and itinerary, it's more liberating than a tour bus.

About 120 miles of paths lead riders through Manhattan from top to bottom. Visitors can take a DIY trip using rental bikes and path maps, or go on organized rides. A word of caution: Cycling in the city is serious business. Riders must stay alert and abide by traffic laws, as drivers and pedestrians often don't. But if you keep your ears and eyes open—and wear a helmet—you'll enjoy an adrenaline-pumping ride.

### Bike-path maps

#### Department of City Planning Bookstore

*22 Reade St between Broadway and Centre St (212-720-3667). Subway: J, M, Z to Chambers St; N, R, W to City Hall; 4, 5, 6 to Brooklyn Bridge–City Hall. Mon–Fri 10am–4pm.*
The Department of City Planning oversees the bike-path system. The Bicycle Master Plan has almost 1,000 miles of cycling lanes.

#### Transportation Alternatives

*115 W 30th St between Sixth and Seventh Aves, suite 1207 (212-629-8080; www.transalt.org). Subway: B, D, F, V, N, Q, R, W to 34th St–Herald Sq; 1, 2, 3, 9 to 34th St–Penn Station. Mon–Fri 10am–5pm.*
This nonprofit citizens' group lobbies for more bike-friendly streets. You can pop into the office to get free maps, or download them from the website. •

### Bike rentals

#### Gotham Bike Shop

*112 West Broadway between Duane and Reade Sts (212-732-2453; www.gothambikes.com). Subway: A, C, 1, 2, 3, 9 to Chambers St. Mon–Sat 10:30am–6:30pm; Sun 10:30am–5pm. $30 for 24hrs, plus $5 helmet rental. AmEx, MC, V.*
Rent a sturdy set of wheels from this shop and ride the short distance to the Hudson River esplanade, which runs from Battery Park to 23rd Street.

#### Loeb Boathouse

*Central Park, entrance on Fifth Ave at 72nd St (212-517-2233). Subway: 6 to 68th St–Hunter College. Apr–Nov 10am–5pm (weather permitting). $10–$25 per hour (includes helmet). AmEx, MC, V.*
If you want to cruise through the park, this is th place; it has more than 100 bikes available. Large groups should make reservations.

**Love affair** Every summer, New Yorkers flock to the USTA tennis center for the U.S. Open.

**Fore play** If you want to swing in the city, check out the Golf Club at Chelsea Piers.

Arts & Entertainment

## Organized bike rides

### Fast and Fabulous

*212-567-7160; www.fastnfab.org.*
This "queer and queer-friendly" riding group leads tours throughout the year, usually meeting in Central Park and heading out of the city. Visit the website for a comprehensive ride calendar.

### Time's Up!

*212-802-8222; www.times-up.org.*
An alternative-transportation advocacy group, Time's Up! sponsors rides year-round, including "Critical Mass," in which hundreds of cyclists and skaters meet on the steps of Union Square Park at 7pm on the last Friday of every month, and then go tearing through Greenwich Village.

## Bowling

### AMF Chelsea Piers Lanes

*23rd St at West Side Hwy, between Piers 59 and 60 (212-835-BOWL; www.chelseapiers.com). Subway: C, E to 23rd St. Sun–Thu 9am–1am; Fri, Sat 9am–2am. $7 per person per game weekdays, $8 weekends, $8 disco bowling; $4.50 shoe rental. AmEx, Disc, MC, V.*
Enjoy 40 lanes, a huge arcade and bar, and glow-in-the-dark "disco" bowling on weekends at this mega-complex.

### Bowlmor Lanes

*110 University Pl between 12th and 13th Sts (212-255-8188; www.bowlmor.com). Subway: L, N, Q, R, W, 4, 5, 6 to 14th St–Union Sq. Mon 11am–3am; Tue, Wed, Sun 11am–1am; Thu 11am–2am; Fri, Sat 11am–4am. $5.95 per person per game weekdays before 5pm; $7.25 weekdays and weekends before 5pm; $7.95 weekends after 5pm; $4 shoe rental. Under 21 not admitted after 6pm. AmEx, MC, V.*
Renovation turned a seedy but historic Greenwich Village alley (Richard Nixon bowled here!) into a hip downtown nightclub. Monday night's "Night Strike" features glow-in-the-dark pins and a techno-spinning DJ, not to mention unlimited bowling from 10pm to 3am, for $20 per scenester.

## Golf

### Golf Club at Chelsea Piers

*Pier 59, 23rd St at West Side Hwy (212-336-6400; www.chelseapiers.com). Subway: C, E to 23rd St. Apr–Sept 6am–midnight; Oct–Mar 6:30am–11pm. $15 minimum. AmEx, Disc, MC, V.*
The four-story Golf Club has 52 heated and weather-protected driving stalls, an automatic ball-teeing system and a 200-yard artificial fairway extending along the pier. The Golf Academy *(212-336-6444)* offers lessons with certified instructors. Rates vary.

### Van Cortlandt Park Golf Course

*See* **Still Vanny after all these years,** *page 330.*

## Gyms

For travelers who can't bear to miss a workout, many gyms offer single-day memberships. Call for class details. *(See also page 293.)*

### Crunch

*623 Broadway between Bleecker and Houston Sts (212-420-0507; www.crunch.com). Subway: F, V, S to Broadway–Lafayette St; 6 to Bleecker St. Mon–Fri 6am–11pm; Sat 8am–8pm; Sun 9am–8pm. Day pass $24. AmEx, Disc, MC, V.*
For a downtown feel without the attitude, Crunch wins hands down. Most of the ten New York locations feature NetPulse cardio equipment, which lets

you surf the Web or watch a personal TV while you exercise. Check the website for other locations.

### New York Sports Club

*151 E 86th St between Lexington and Third Aves (212-860-8630; www.nysc.com). Subway: 4, 5, 6 to 86th St. Mon–Fri 5:30am–11pm; Sat, Sun 8am–10pm. Day membership: $25. AmEx, MC, V.*

A day membership at New York Sports Club includes access to the weight room, aerobics classes, squash courts, cardio machines, steam room and sauna. The 62nd Street branch features squash courts. Call or visit website for gym locations.

### The Printing House Racquet and Fitness Club

*421 Hudson St between Clarkson and Leroy Sts (212-243-7600). Subway: 1, 9 to Houston St. Mon–Fri 6–11pm; Sat, Sun 8–10pm. Day membership: $25. AmEx, MC, V.*

Not only can you sample the latest aerobic machines or take a yoga or boxing class, but this penthouse gym offers breathtaking views of midtown.

## Horseback riding

### Claremont Riding Academy

*175 W 89th St between Columbus and Amsterdam Aves (212-724-5100). Subway: 1, 9 to 86th St. Mon–Fri 6:30am–10pm; Sat, Sun 8am–5pm. Rental $50 per hour; lessons $60 per 30 minutes; introductory package: 3 lessons for $165. MC, V.*

The academy, in an Upper West Side townhouse, teaches English-style riding. Beginners use an indoor arena; experienced riders can go for an unguided canter along the six miles of trails in Central Park. Be prepared to prove your mounted mettle: Claremont interviews all riders to determine their level of experience.

### Kensington Stables

*51 Caton Pl, Windsor Terrace, Brooklyn (718-972-4588; www.kensingtonstables.com). Subway: F to Fort Hamilton Pkwy. 10am–sunset. Guided trail ride $25 per hour; lessons $45 per hour. AmEx, Disc, MC, V.*

The paddock is small, but there are miles of lovely trails in Prospect Park *(see* **Prospect Park**, *page 112)*, which was designed to be seen by horseback.

## Ice-skating

### Rockefeller Center Ice Rink

*1 Rockefeller Plaza, Fifth to Sixth Aves, between 49th and 50th Sts (recorded information 212-332-7654). Subway: B, D, F, V to 47–50th Sts–Rockefeller Ctr. Call for hours. Mon–Thu $11, children under 12 $7.50; Fri–Sun $11, children under 12 $7.50; $6 skate rental. Figure skates available in sizes baby 6 to men's 14. Cash only.*

Rockefeller Center's famous outdoor rink, under the giant statue of Prometheus, is perfect for atmosphere but bad for elbow room. The rink generally opens with an energetic ice show in mid-October, but attracts most of its visitors when the towering Christmas tree is lit.

### Sky Rink at Chelsea Piers

*Pier 61, 23rd St at West Side Hwy (212-336-6100; www.chelseapiers.com). Subway: C, E to 23rd St. Call rink for hours. $12.50, seniors and children $9; $5.75 skate rental; $3 helmet rental. AmEx, Disc, MC, V.*

This is Manhattan's only year-round indoor ice-skating rink. There are several general-skating, figure-skating and ice hockey programs, including lessons and performances.

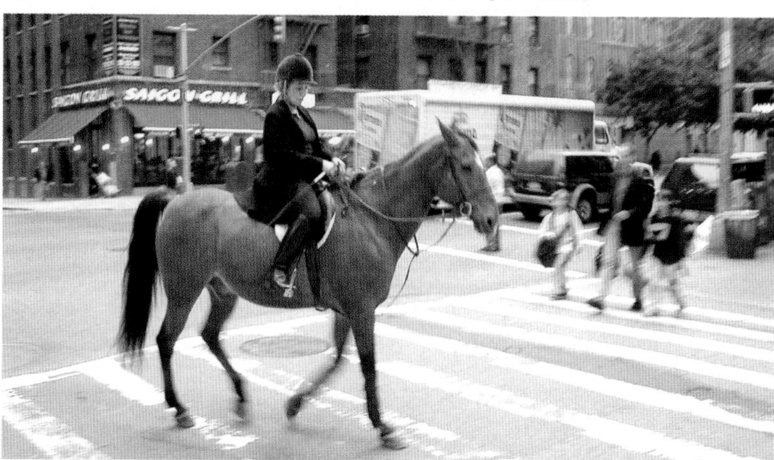


**Hot to trot?** The Claremont Riding Academy will teach you how to do it English-style.

## In-line skating

An estimated half-million in-line skaters, many of them hurtling toward oncoming traffic at 30 miles per hour, have made that hushed *skish-skish* a familiar sound on New York streets. A tamer crowd can be found whirling around Central Park, either on the Park Drive loop or near the Mall at 72nd Street. The "coneheads," or slalomers, strut their stuff near Central Park West at 67th Street, across from Tavern on the Green.

To give it a whirl, visit **Wollman Memorial Rink** April through mid-October *(Central Park, entrance on 59th St at Fifth or Sixth Aves, 212-439-6900)*. If you don't want to be restricted to the rink, rent skates there for $15 a day (plus a $100 deposit) and take off. Or try the nearby gear shop **Blades, Board and Skate** *(120 W 72nd St between Columbus and Amsterdam Aves, 212-787-3911)*.

Group skates—some mellow and social, others wild blitzkriegs on wheels—are a popular city pastime. Bring skates, a helmet and a sense of adventure.

### Empire Skate Club of New York

*P.O. Box 20070, London Terrace Station, New York, NY 10011 (212-774-1774; www.empireskate.org).* This club organizes frequent in-line and roller-skating events throughout the city, including island-hopping tours and nighttime rides, such as the Thursday Evening Roll. Skaters meet May through October at Columbus Circle *(59th St at Broadway, southwest corner of Central Park)* at 6:45pm.

**We can work it out** The Printing House Racquet Club is gonna make ya sweat.

## Kayaking

Kayak is a great way to explore New York Harbor and the Hudson River, but between tricky currents, the tide and the hairy river traffic, it's best to go on an organized excursion.

### Manhattan Kayak Company

*Pier 63 Maritime, 23rd St at West Side Hwy (212-924-1788; www.manhattankayak.com). Subway: C, E to 23rd St. Call or visit website for schedule and prices.*

# Still Vanny after all these years

Tee up at the oldest public golf course in America

On a typical morning at Van Cortlandt Park Golf Course in the Bronx, as the sun begins to illuminate the maples and oaks that line the rolling fairways, 64-year-old Kaspar Schroeter stands alone at the first tee. He swings, connects and, with a bag of clubs slung across his back, sprints after his shot, accompanied only by the sounds of birds and the morning traffic on the Mosholu Parkway and Major Deegan Expressway, both of which abut the course.

Schroeter is a starter at Vanny, as the course is affectionately called, and he doesn't like to dawdle. By the time he returns to the clubhouse, "the crew" of regulars has begun to drift in, sipping coffee and griping about their swings. They are doctors, lawyers, retirees, grocers and gardeners; even Wall Streeters squeeze in 18 before work. As one devotee put it, "We have people living from Social Security check to Social Security check, and we have CEOs of large corporations. It's like a little country club."

Well, the conditions aren't quite up to country-club standards, but Vanny—founded in 1895 and the nation's oldest municipal golf course—is better than ever. During the past three years, the city has poured more than $4 million into the track, money that's been spent reseeding once-rocky fairways, refurbishing greens and rebuilding sand bunkers and tee boxes.

Apart from the aforementioned highways, you wouldn't know you were golfing a mere ten miles north of Manhattan's urban canyons. Along the fairways, you might see swans, pheasants, the occasional deer, a couple of wild turkeys—even snapping turtles, which

Run by veteran kayaker Eric Stiller, who once paddled halfway around Australia, Manhattan Kayak Company offers beginner to advanced classes and tours. Paddle adventures include the Sushi Tour ($100 per person), in which the group paddles to Edgewater, New Jersey to dine at a sushi restaurant.

## Running

Join the joggers in Central and Riverside Parks or around Washington Square. Be alert and don't carry or wear anything that's obviously valuable.

### New York Road Runners

*9 E 89th St between Fifth and Madison Aves (212-860-4455; www.nyrrc.org). Subway: 4, 5, 6 to 86th St. Mon–Fri 10am–8pm; Sat 10am–5pm; Sun 10am–3pm. Annual membership $30. AmEx, Disc, MC, V.*

Hardly a weekend passes without some sort of run or race sponsored by the NYRR, which is responsible for the New York City Marathon. Most races take place in Central Park and are open to the public. The club also offers classes and clinics, and can help you find a running partner.

## Tennis

From April through November, the city maintains excellent municipal courts throughout the five boroughs. Single-play (one-hour) tickets cost $5. The Department of Parks *(212-360-8131)* also issues permits that are valid for unlimited play during the season *($50, senior citizens $20, under 17 $10)*. For a list of city courts, visit www.nyc.gov/parks.

## Yoga

While many gyms have yoga classes *(see* **Gyms**, *page 328)*, the city is brimming with dedicated yoga centers that teach a range of styles. See www.yogafinder.com for more.

### Integral Yoga Institute

*227 W 13th St between Seventh and Eighth Aves (212-929-0585; www.integralyogaofnewyork.org). Subway: A, C, E, 1, 2, 3, 9 to 14th St; L to Eighth Ave. Mon–Fri 9:45am–8:30pm; Sat 8:15am–6pm; Sun 10am–2pm. Call or visit website for schedule. $13–$60 per class; series $60–$150. AmEx, Disc, MC, V.*

Integral Yoga Institute offers a flexible schedule of classes for beginners and advanced students.

**Other location** • *200 W 72nd St at Broadway, fourth floor (212-721-4000). Subway: 1, 2, 3, 9 to 72nd St. Call for schedule. Cash only.*

### Om Yoga Center

*826 Broadway at 12th St, sixth floor (212-254-YOGA; www.omyoga.com). Subway: L, N, Q, R, W, 4, 5, 6 to 14th St–Union Sq. Mon–Fri 7am–9:45pm; Sat, Sun 9am–8:15pm. Call or visit website for schedule. $15 per class; series $27–$440. AmEx, MC, V.*

Director Cyndi Lee and her staff conduct vigorous, mindful *vinyasa* practice in a vast, airy new studio.

have been known to lay eggs in the sand traps. Observed one regular, "None of the other city courses compares."

Old timers also recall some crabgrass. The late 1980s and early '90s were difficult for Vanny, as they were for the rest of New York. In 1989, a horde of local delinquents attacked two greenkeepers, and one teen drove off with a cart. A few years later, a corrupt course manager was caught after he had facilitated the burial of some 500 truckloads of garbage next to the 17th hole. One morning in 1993, a player approaching the 14th green looked up to see a homeless man who'd hung himself from a tree.

But Vanny has its good days, too. Just ask club pro Paul Sliva. Judging by his stubble and cigarette-ravaged voice, he resembles a heavy-metal refugee more than a golf professional, and that's not far from the truth. In 1986, when he was the singer in a rock band, he visited Vanny with a few friends. The party had gotten a little rowdy when the golf-cart attendant, Artie Appel, arrived at the tenth hole to find Sliva standing on his cart, readying to tee off. Appel, who died in 1997, watched Sliva stripe the ball 200 yards down the fairway. "Instead of telling me to get the hell off his cart," Sliva remembers, "Artie said, 'Who taught you to *do* that?' " With Appel's encouragement, Sliva became a golf pro and has been at Vanny ever since.

A tall tale? Perhaps. But that's the kind of story you'll hear if you hang out in the 100-year-old clubhouse, munching on one of the best cheeseburgers in the city. True, the fairways aren't Pebble Beach lush, and the sound of cars whizzing by may be distracting, but the course is a good test (the brutal par-5 second hole stretches more than 600 yards). Besides, you come to Vanny for more than a walk in the park—you come for the people—and you leave knowing that if you can golf here, you can golf anywhere.

**Van Cortlandt Park Golf Course**

*Van Cortlandt Park South at Bailey Ave, Bronx (718-543-4595). Travel: 1, 9 to 242nd St–Van Cortlandt Park. Dawn to dusk. Mon–Fri $37; Sat, Sun $41; club rental $25. AmEx, DC, Disc, MC, V.*

# Theater & Dance

From Broadway to ballet, New York City will leave you stagestruck

## Theater

Gotham is the world leader in many arenas—commerce, publishing, shrieking car alarms. But perhaps no industry is more closely linked to New York than the theater. When it comes to the stage, the Big Apple is the big cheese. Even superstars line up for a chance to step into the Great White Way's red-hot spotlight. Big names who've recently braved the city's often unforgiving stages include Matthew Broderick, Anne Heche, Paul Newman and Billy Joel, whose hits provide the infectious score for *Movin' Out* (*see* **Broadway's jammin' oldies**, *page 334).*

Audiences eager to experience this art form pack the city's performance spaces, which range from midtown's landmark palaces to more intimate venues along 42nd Street's Theater Row and the mostly downtown nooks and crannies of Off Broadway and Off-Off Broadway. The performer-fan dynamic is more personal on the stage than on the screen. Not only can you watch your favorite actors perform just a few feet away, you can also request their autographs (politely) at the stage door, and maybe even grab a postshow meal at the same restaurant.

### BUYING TICKETS

If you have a major credit card, buying Broadway tickets requires little more than picking up a phone. Almost all Broadway and Off Broadway shows are served by one of the city's 24-hour booking agencies, which are

## CRITICS' PICKS The best bets on (and off) Broadway

### Broadway

***Hairspray***

*Neil Simon Theatre, 250 W 52nd St between Broadway and Eighth Ave (212-307-4100). Subway: C, E to 50th St.*

This musical is like a blown-up version of the original film—broader, more satirical and much funnier.

***The Producers***

*St. James Theatre, 246 W 44th St between Broadway and Eighth Ave (212-239-6200). Subway: N, Q, R, W, S, 1, 2, 3, 9, 7 to 42nd St–Times Sq.*

This ode to tastelessness mixes Broadway razzmatazz with borscht belt humor. It's not as good as you've heard—it's better.

***Thoroughly Modern Millie***

*Marquis Theatre, 211 W 45th St between Broadway and Eighth Ave (212-307-4100). Subway: N, Q, R, W, S, 1, 2, 3, 9, 7 to 42nd St–Times Sq.*

You can feel this musical click during a slick number that turns an office of stenographers into a freeway of racing tappers threatening to run over Broadway's new darling, spindly-legged Millie (Sutton Foster).

### Off Broadway

***De La Guarda***

*Daryl Roth Theatre, 20 Union Sq East at 15th St (212-239-6200). Subway: L, N, Q, R, W, 4, 5, 6 to 14th St–Union Sq.*

This athletic troupe puts on a sexy mix of carnival, rave, concert and dance, with performers flying through the air on bungee cords.

***The Donkey Show***

*Club El Flamingo, 547 W 21st St between Tenth and Eleventh Aves (212-307-4100). Subway: C, E to 23rd St.*

Bring your dancing shoes to this Midsummer Night's disco, where Shakespeare's comedy plays to a '70s soundtrack that includes such catchy tunes as "Car Wash" and "You Sexy Thing." This fusion of theater and nightlife shows no signs of slowing down.

***Monday Night Magic***

*McGinn/Cazale Theatre, 2162 Broadway at 76th St (212-307-4100). Subway: 1, 9 to 79th St. Mon 8pm.*

It's a mad array of swords through necks, vanishing fingers and levitations at New York's long-running magic show, featuring a cast of the city's best illusionists.

listed in the show's print advertisement or in the capsule reviews that run each week in *Time Out New York*. The venues' information lines can also refer you to ticket agents, sometimes merely by transferring your call (for additional ticketing info, *see page 374)*.

Some of the cheapest tickets on Broadway are rush tickets (purchased the day of a show at the theater's box office), which cost about $25—but not all theaters offer these, and many reserve them only for students. If a show is sold out, it's worth waiting for standby tickets just before show time. Tickets are slightly cheaper for matinees and previews (typically on Wednesdays, Saturdays or Sundays), and for students or groups of 20 or more. For discount seats, your best bet is **TKTS** *(see page 375)*, where you can get as much as 75 percent off the face value of some tickets on the day of the performance. Arrive early to avoid long lines. TKTS also sells matinee tickets the day before a show. (Beware scam artists selling tickets to those waiting in line; the tickets are often fake.) If you're interested in seeing more than one Off-Off Broadway theater or dance event, consider purchasing the **Theatre Development Fund**'s book of vouchers.

### Theatre Development Fund

*1501 Broadway between 43rd and 44th Sts (212-221-0013; www.tdf.org). Subway: N, Q, R, W, S, 1, 2, 3, 9, 7 to 42nd St–Times Sq. Check or money order only.*
TDF offers a book of four vouchers for $28, which can only be purchased at its office by visitors who bring

## Broadway's jammin' oldies

### These current musicals have a nice beat, and you can dance to them

Making a buck on Broadway isn't easy, so when someone finds a winning formula, followers look to capitalize on it. After the runaway success of **The Producers**, everyone began looking for cult films to reincarnate (hello, *Hairspray!*). When **Urinetown** took off, self-mocking musicals with offbeat subject matter soon became the show du jour.

**Mamma Mia!**, the international smash that weaves ABBA's greatest hits into a paper-thin narrative, also spawned a trend. Critics knocked the shallow characters and flimsy plot, but audiences (and not just ABBA fans) loved it, and the Winter Garden Theatre has been selling out since the show's 2001 debut.

The latest pop-influenced show to hit Broadway is a more ambitious affair. **Movin' Out**, a dance musical featuring songs from Long Island's favorite son, Billy Joel, is an unlikely marriage of Twyla Tharp's modern dance and Joel's Top 40 pop staples. There's almost no dialogue; the songs, sung by Billy Joel sound-alike Michael Cavanaugh, drive a narrative that centers on a young soldier losing his mind fighting in Vietnam.

And there's more to come. Boy George's risqué musical, **Taboo**, set in a 1980s nightclub, has garnered grudgingly good reviews across the pond ("bewitching," raved the London *Times*); and the show is expected to open on Broadway in April 2003, with Rosie O'Donnell producing. If it's a hit, don't be surprised if Queen's futuristic sci-fi musical *We Will Rock You*, also playing in London, soon finds its way to the Great White Way. And there's serious talk about a show set to Bruce Springsteen songs. Can *Livin' on a Prayer—The Musical* be far behind? While prefab productions make critics scoff, the shows benefit from a built-in audience that already knows all the words. But familiarity isn't enough. "We may have an advantage," says David Keeley, who plays Sam, the male lead in *Mamma Mia!* "But you've still gotta sell it. You need great songs and performances. These new shows must do more than just show up."

#### *Mamma Mia!*

*Winter Garden Theatre, 1634 Broadway at 50th St (212-239-6200). Subway: N, R, W to 49th St; 1, 9 to 50th St. $55–$99. Mon, Tue 8pm; Wed 2, 8pm; Thu, Fri 8pm; Sat 2, 8pm.*

#### *Movin' Out*

*Richard Rodgers Theatre, 226 W 46th St (212-307-4100). Subway: A, C, E to 42nd St–Port Authority; N, Q, R, W, S, 1, 2, 3, 9, 7 to 42nd St–Times Sq. $40–$95. Tue, Thu, Fri 8pm; Wed, Sat 2, 8pm; Sun 3pm.*

#### *Taboo*

At press time, *Taboo* was tentatively scheduled to open on Broadway in spring 2003, but a venue and date had not been set. For up-to-date information, pick up a current copy of *Time Out New York*.

**Sweatin' to the oldies** From left, Rod McCune, Mark Arvin, Elizabeth Parkinson and Scott Fowler trip the lite fantastic in *Movin' Out,* which fuses dance, drama and Billy Joel ditties.

their passport or out-of-state driver's license, or by students and residents on the TDF mailing list. Each voucher is good for one admission to an Off-Off Broadway theater, dance or music event, at venues such as the Atlantic Theater Company, the Joyce, the Kitchen, La MaMa, P.S. 122 and many more. TDF's **NYC/Onstage** service *(212-768-1818)* provides infor mation by phone on all theater, dance and music events in town.

### New York Shakespeare Festival at the Delacorte Theater

*A few minutes' walk inside Central Park. Enter the park from Central Park West at 81st St, then follow the signs (212-539-8750; www.publictheater.org). Subway: B, C to 81st St–Museum of Natural History.*

The Delacorte Theater in Central Park is the fair-weather sister of the **Public Theater** *(see page 339)*. When not producing Shakespeare, the Public offers the best of the Bard outdoors during the New York Shakespeare Festival (June through September). Tickets are free (two per person), and are distributed at 1pm on the day of the performance outside both theaters. Normally, 10am is a good time to begin waiting, but when shows feature box-office stars, the line starts as early as 6am.

## Broadway

Technically speaking, "Broadway" is the Theater District that surrounds Times Square on either side of Broadway (the avenue), mainly between 41st and 53rd Streets. This is where you'll find the grand theaters, most built between 1900 and 1930. Officially, 38 of them are designated as being part of Broadway, for which full-price tickets typically cost up to $100. The big shows are hard to ignore; new blockbusters, such as *Hairspray, Mamma Mia!* and the revival of *Into the Woods,* announce themselves from giant billboards. Still, there's more to Broadway than cartoon-based musicals and flashy pop spectacles. In recent years, provocative dramas like *Metamorphoses* and madcap comedies such as *Urinetown* have been remarkable successes, as have classics and British imports, including Michael Frayn's *Copenhagen* and his raucous farce *Noises Off.*

The charming **Roundabout Theatre Company** is the critically acclaimed home of classics featuring all-star casts (and the force behind *Cabaret*'s latest incarnation). Its deluxe Broadway space *(American Airlines Theatre, 227 W 42nd St between Seventh and Eighth Aves, 212-719-1300)* opened in 2000. You can subscribe to the Roundabout's full season or buy single tickets, if available.

### Broadway (Theater District)

*Subway: N, Q, R, W, S, 2, 3, 7 to 42nd St–Times Sq; C, E, 1, 9 to 50th St.*

**Masterpiece theater** Lincoln Center is the place to see big stars in classic productions.

## Off Broadway

Off Broadway theaters usually have fewer than 500 seats, and have been traditionally located in Greenwich Village. These days, however, they can be found on the Upper West and Upper East Sides, in midtown and lower Manhattan.

As Broadway increasingly becomes a place of spectacle and crowd-pleasing musicals, playwrights who would once have been granted a Broadway production now find themselves in the more risk-taking (and less financially demanding) Off Broadway houses, where audiences want a play with something to say.

So if it's brain food and adventure you're after, head Off Broadway. Below are some of the best theaters and repertory companies. Tickets typically run from \$20 to \$60.

### Atlantic Theater Company

*336 W 20th St between Eighth and Ninth Aves (212-645-8015; www.atlantictheater.org). Subway: C, E to 23rd St. AmEx, MC, V.*

Created in 1985 as an offshoot of the acting workshops taught by playwright David Mamet and actor William H. Macy, this dynamic little theater (in a former church sanctuary on a charming Chelsea street) has presented nearly 100 plays. Productions have included Mamet's *American Buffalo* (starring Macy) and the American premiere of Martin McDonagh's *The Beauty Queen of Leenane.*

### Brooklyn Academy of Music

*See page 318 for listing.*

Brooklyn's grand old opera house—along with the Harvey Theater, two blocks away at 651 Fulton Street—stages the famous multidisciplinary Next Wave Festival every October through December. The festival's 2002 theatrical events included an eye-popping music-theater collaboration between rocker Tom Waits and director Robert Wilson called *Woyzeck,* and Deborah Warner and Fiona Shaw's terrific *Medea.*

### Classic Stage Company

*136 E 13th St between Third and Fourth Aves (212-677-4210; www.classicstage.org). Subway: L, N, Q, R, W, 4, 5, 6 to 14th St–Union Sq. AmEx, MC, V.*

Under the tutelage of artistic director Barry Edelstein, the Classic Stage Company has become *the* place to see movie and TV stars perform the classics in daring new versions. Productions scheduled for 2003 include William Shakespeare's *The Winter's Tale* and Marguerite Duras's *Savannah Bay.*

### Irish Repertory Theatre

*132 W 22nd St between Sixth and Seventh Aves (212-727-2737; www.irishrepertorytheatre.com). Subway: F, V, 1, 9 to 23rd St. AmEx, MC, V.*

Dedicated to performing works by veteran and contemporary Irish playwrights, this Chelsea company has put on some compelling shows, including Frank McCourt's *The Irish and How They Got That Way* and Tom Murphy's *Bailegangaire.*

► To find out what's playing, see the listings and reviews in ***Time Out New York***.

► For plot synopses, show times and ticket info, call **NYC/Onstage** *(see page 335),* a service of the Theatre Development Fund *(see page 334).* You'll learn about shows on Broadway, Off Broadway and Off-Off Broadway, as well as classical music, dance and opera.

► If you know what you want to see, call the **Broadway Line** *(212-302-4111, outside New York 888-276-2392; www.ilovenytheater.com).*

### Lincoln Center

*See page 319 for listing.*

The majestic Lincoln Center complex includes two amphitheater-style drama venues: the 1,040-seat **Vivian Beaumont Theater** (considered a Broadway house) and the 290-seat **Mitzi E. Newhouse Theater** (considered Off Broadway). Expect polished productions of classic and new plays, with many a well-known actor. Recent productions range from Georges S. Kaufman and Edna Ferber's 1932 play *Dinner at Eight* to a touching musical adaptation of the movie *A Man of No Importance.*

### Manhattan Theatre Club

*City Center, 131 W 55th St between Sixth and Seventh Aves (212-581-1212; www.manhattantheatreclub.com). Subway: B, D, E to Seventh Ave. AmEx, MC, V.*

Manhattan Theatre Club has a reputation for sending young playwrights on to Broadway, as seen with such successes as David Auburn's *Proof* and Charles Busch's *The Tale of the Allergist's Wife.* The club's two theaters are located in the basement of City Center. The 299-seat **Mainstage Theater** offers four plays a year by new and established playwrights; the **Stage II Theater** serves as an outlet for works-in-progress, workshops and staged readings.

### The New Victory Theater

*209 W 42nd St between Seventh and Eighth Aves (646-223-3020; www.newvictory.org). Subway: A, C, E to 42nd St–Port Authority; N, Q, R, W, S, 1, 2, 3, 9, 7 to 42nd St–Times Sq. AmEx, DC, Disc, MC, V.*

The New Victory is a perfect symbol for the transformation of Times Square. Built in 1900 by Oscar Hammerstein, Manhattan's oldest theater became home to a strip club and XXX cinema in the '70s and '80s. Renovated by the city in 1995, the building now features a full season of family-friendly plays. It's a great place to see oddball international shows, such as *Thwack*, starring Australia's cartoonlike Umbilical Brothers. Updated classics are also scheduled, including *A Midsummer Night's Dream.*

**Sound investment** Second Stage Theatre, a haven for up-and-coming playwrights, keeps theatrical treasures in its vaults.

### The Pearl Theatre Company

*80 St. Marks Pl between First and Second Aves (212-598-9802; www.pearltheatre.org). Subway: L to First Ave; 6 to Astor Pl. AmEx, MC, V.*

Housed on the East Village's punk promenade, this troupe of resident players relies primarily on its actors' abilities to present the classics. Besides Shakespeare and the ancient Greeks, Pearl has brought to life the works of Eugene Ionesco, Jean Racine and George Bernard Shaw. Shows on tap for 2003 include Shaw's *Heartbreak House* and George Kelly's *Daisy Mayme.*

### Playwrights Horizons

*416 W 42nd St between Ninth and Tenth Aves (Ticket Central 212-279-4200; www.playwrightshorizons.org). Subway: A, C, E to 42nd St–Port Authority. $4 service charge per phone order. AmEx, MC, V.*

More than 300 important contemporary plays have premiered at this power-packed company, including dramas such as *Driving Miss Daisy* and *The Heidi Chronicles,* and musicals like James Joyce's *The Dead.* More recently, the works of Keith Bunin *(The World Over),* Kenneth Lonergan *(Lobby Hero)* and the brilliant Christopher Shinn *(What Didn't Happen)* have been staged.

### Public Theater

*425 Lafayette St between Astor Pl and E 4th St (212-539-8500; www.publictheater.org). Subway: N, R, W to 8th St–NYU; 6 to Astor Pl. AmEx, MC, V.*

This Astor Place landmark consistently delivers a rewarding theater experience. Founded by Joseph Papp (who bought the building from the city for $1), and dedicated to the work of new American playwrights and performers, the Public also presents the classics and new interpretations of Shakespeare *(see* **New York Shakespeare Festival**, *page 335).* The building houses five stages, a coffeebar and the cabaret space **Joe's Pub** *(see pages 271 and 309).* The theater is under the direction of George C. Wolfe, who directed Suzan-Lori Parks's *Topdog/Underdog* on Broadway and the historic New York premiere of Tony Kushner's *Angels in America.*

### Second Stage Theatre

*307 W 43rd St at Eighth Ave (212-246-4422; www.secondstagetheatre.com). Subway: A, C, E to 42nd St–Port Authority; N, Q, R, W, S, 1, 2, 3, 9, 7 to 42nd St–Times Sq. MC, V.*

Second Stage, housed in a former bank building, was created as a venue for American plays that didn't get the critical reception some thought they deserved; the theater now produces the works of new American playwrights. It staged the New York premieres of Mary Zimmerman's *Metamorphoses* and Ricky Jay's magic show *On the Stem.* Since 1999, the company has occupied a beautiful Rem Koolhaas–designed space, just off Times Square. Its lineup for 2003 is impressive, including Mary Zimmerman's cerebral entertainment *The Notebooks of Leonardo Da Vinci* and Craig Lucas's mysterious drama *Reckless.*

### Signature Theatre Company

*555 W 42nd St between Tenth and Eleventh Aves (212-244-7529; www.signaturetheatre.org). Subway: A, C, E to 42nd St–Port Authority. AmEx, MC, V.*

This award-winning company focuses on the works of a single playwright each season. From 2002 to 2003, it's Lanford Wilson; his *Burn This* became a star-studded production with Edward Norton and Catherine Keener. Signature has delved into the oeuvres of John Guare, Arthur Miller and Horton Foote, whose *The Young Man from Atlanta* originated here, and ultimately won the Pulitzer Prize.

### The Vineyard Theatre

*108 E 15th St at Union Sq East (212-353-3366; www.vineyardtheatre.org). Subway: L, N, Q, R, W, 4, 5, 6 to 14th St–Union Sq. AmEx, MC, V.*

This theater near Union Square produces excellent new plays and musicals, and also attempts to revive works that have failed in other arenas. The Vineyard is also home to such writers as Craig Lucas and the dark wit Doug Wright.

## Off-Off Broadway

The technical definition of Off-Off Broadway is a show presented at a theater with fewer than 100 seats, and created by artists who may not be card-carrying pros. It's where some of the most daring writers and performers experiment. Pieces often meld media, including music, dance, film, video and performance monologue—sometimes resulting in an all-too-indulgent marriage of theater and psychotherapy. The **New York International Fringe Festival** *(see page 252)* takes place every August, and it's a great way to catch the wacky side of theater. The **Target Margin Theater** group *(212-358-3657; www.targetmargin.org)* rents out different spaces to showcase avant-garde performances. But Off-Off Broadway—where tickets usually run $10 to $25—is not restricted to experimental or solo shows. You can also see classical works and more traditional plays staged by companies such as the **Mint Theater** *(311 W 43rd St between Eighth and Ninth Aves, fifth floor, 212-315-0231)* and at venues like **The Flea Theater**.

### The Flea Theater

*41 White St between Broadway and Church St (212-226-0051; www.theflea.org). Subway: A, C, E, N, Q, R, W, 6 to Canal St; 1, 9 to Franklin St. Cash only.*

This lovely Tribeca space is home to the **Bat Theater Company**, the brainchild of director Jim Simpson, playwright Mac Wellman and designer Kyle Chepulis. The company alternates experimental work (the rock-Kabuki epic *Benten Kozo*) with fresh takes on classic stories, such as an accessible play about Billy the Kid.

**What's cooking?** If you like experimental theater, see what the Kitchen is serving.

### The Kitchen

*512 W 19th St between Tenth and Eleventh Aves (212-255-5793; www.thekitchen.org). Subway: A, C, E to 14th St; L to Eighth Ave. AmEx, MC, V.*

Laurie Anderson, David Byrne and Cindy Sherman all got their start at this small experimental theater, founded in 1971. A reputable place to see avant-garde productions, the Kitchen presents an eclectic multimedia repertoire of theater, music, dance, video and performance art from September to May.

### LAByrinth Theater

*Center Stage/NY, 48 W 21st St between Fifth and Sixth Aves, fourth floor (212-929- 0900). Subway: F, V, N, R, W to 23rd St. AmEx, MC, V.*

Playwright Stephen Adly Guirgis and actor-director Philip Seymour Hoffman lead the hottest young theater group in the city. Plays like *Our Lady of 121st Street* and *In Arabia We'd All Be Kings* showcase the company's distinctively New York style: the fevered insanity and theatrical rage of a crazy person on the F train. Its ensembles are as good as any in the city.

### Performance Space 122

*150 First Ave at 9th St (212-477-5288; www.ps122.org). Subway: L to First Ave; F to Second Ave; 6 to Astor Pl. AmEx, MC, V.*

One of New York's most exciting venues, P.S. 122 (as it's casually known) is housed in a former school in the East Village. It's a nonprofit arts center for experimental works, with two theaters presenting dance, performance, music, film and video. Artists can develop, practice and present their projects here; P.S. 122 has provided a platform for Eric Bogosian, Whoopi Goldberg, Danny Hoch and John Leguizamo.

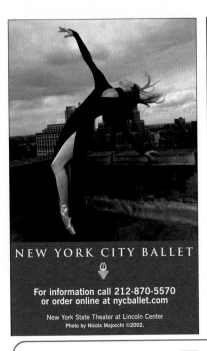

# Dance

The sheer diversity of choreographers and performers makes New York an incomparable setting for both classical and contemporary dance. Despite a lack of substantial government funding, the city has a vibrant community where national treasures like Trisha Brown, Merce Cunningham and Paul Taylor create work alongside experimental choreographers. European companies are often given the spotlight at the Brooklyn Academy of Music (though Cunningham's company will perform there in the fall of 2003 in conjunction with its 50th anniversary season). Of the two major seasons—October to December and March to June—the spring stretch is usually more enticing. Not only does Paul Taylor present his marvelous troupe each March, but the resident American Ballet Theatre and the New York City Ballet are onstage in full force.

If watching those beautiful bodies inspires you, some troupes offer classes. The **Mark Morris Dance Center** *(3 Lafayette Ave between Flatbush Ave and Fulton St, Fort Greene, Brooklyn, 718-624-8400)* and the **Martha Graham School** *(316 E 63rd St between First and Second Aves, 212-838-5886)* welcome walk-ins to beginner classes.

## Venues

### Brooklyn Academy of Music

*See page 318 for listing.*

BAM, which showcases superb local and out-of-town companies, is one of New York's most prominent cultural institutions. The **Howard Gilman Opera House**, with its Federal-style columns and carved marble, is one of the city's most beautiful dance venues. (The Mark Morris Dance Group performs each spring.) The 1904 **Harvey Theater** *(651 Fulton St between Ashland and Rockwell Pls)*, formerly called the Majestic, has hosted modern troupes such as Ballet Preljocaj and the John Jasperse Company. Each fall, BAM's Next Wave Festival welcomes to its stage experimental and established dance groups; in the spring, there is usually an assortment of ballet, hip-hop and modern dance.

### City Center Theater

*131 W 55th St between Sixth and Seventh Aves (212-581-7907). Subway: B, D, E to Seventh Ave; N, Q, R, W to 57th St. $25–$75. AmEx, MC, V. $4 per ticket surcharge.*

The City Center's lavish decor is golden, and so are the companies that pass through. You can count on superb performances all year long, including those of American Ballet Theatre in the fall, Alvin Ailey American Dance Theater in December and the Paul Taylor Dance Company in the spring.

### Joyce Theater

*175 Eighth Ave at 19th St (212-242-0800; www.joyce.org). Subway: A, C, E to 14th St; 1, 9 to 18th St. $20–$40. AmEx, DC, Disc, MC, V.*

Of the 472 seats at the Joyce, there's not a bad one in the house. The companies and choreographers who present work here, including Ballet Hispanico, David Parsons and Doug Varone, tend to be more traditional than experimental. In residence is Eliot Feld's Ballet Tech, which performs for two monthlong seasons (March and July) and for two weeks in December. The Joyce also hosts out-of-town crowd-pleasers like Pilobolus Dance Theatre (June), and the annual Altogether Different Festival (January), which offers audiences the opportunity to check out less established choreographers. During the summer, when many theaters are dark, the Joyce continues its pro-

**Living dolls** The Eliza Miller Dance Company performs at Danspace Project.

gramming. At the Joyce Soho, emerging companies present work nearly every weekend.
**Other location** • *Joyce Soho, 155 Mercer St between Houston and Prince Sts (212-431-9233). Subway: F, V, S to Broadway–Lafayette; N, R, W to Prince St; 6 to Bleecker St. $12–$15. Cash only.*

### Metropolitan Opera House

*See page 320 for listing.*
The Met hosts a range of international companies, from the Paris Opéra Ballet to the Kirov Ballet. Each spring, this majestic theater hosts American Ballet Theatre, which presents full-length story classics as well as works by contemporary choreographers like Mark Morris and Twyla Tharp. The acoustics are wonderful, but the theater is massive, so sit as close as you can afford.

### New York State Theater

*65th St at Columbus Ave (212-870-5570; www.nycballet.com). Subway: 1, 9 to 66th St–Lincoln Center. $16–$85. AmEx, MC, V.*
The neoclassical New York City Ballet headlines at this opulent theater, which Philip Johnson designed to resemble a jewel box. NYCB hosts two seasons: Winter begins just before Thanksgiving and features more than a month of performances of George Balanchine's magical *The Nutcracker,* and continues through January with the beginning of repertory performances. The eight-week spring season usually begins in April. The best seats are in the first ring, where the music comes through loud and clear and—even better—one can enjoy the dazzling patterns of the dancers. Choreography is by George Balanchine (the 89-by-58-foot stage was made to his specifications), Jerome Robbins, Peter Martins, the company's ballet master in chief, and Christopher Wheeldon, the resident choreographer *(see* **Orchestral maneuvers in the dark**, *below).* Cast lists are only available the week of performances.

## Alternative venues

### Aaron Davis Hall

*City College, 135th St at Convent Ave (212-650-7100). Subway: 1, 9 to 137th St–City College. AmEx, MC, V.*
Troupes at this venue often celebrate African-American life and culture. The companies that have



## Orchestral maneuvers in the dark

### NYCB resident choreographer Christopher Wheeldon lets the music lead

Ever since George Balanchine died in 1983, ballet has been in a state of limbo. Flickers of choreographic talent have appeared, and dancers at the city's world-class American Ballet Theatre and New York City Ballet continue to excel in artistry and technique. But now fans have a concrete reason to rejoice: Peter Martins, ballet master in chief of NYCB, has appointed Christopher Wheeldon as the company's resident choreographer. Wheeldon, who is British, will present his newest ballet at Lincoln Center in spring. Set to Saint-Saëns's *The Carnival of the Animals,* the work promises to be an extravaganza—delightful for kids, yet smart enough for adults.

This new piece, which premieres at the New York State Theater May 14, in conjunction with NYCB's spring gala performance, offers Wheeldon another opportunity to show off his flair for managing groups of dancers. It is hardly a risk; he has already proved his aptitude with two large-scale works—the elegant *Scènes de Ballet,* which he originally created for students at the School of American Ballet, and *Variations Sérieuses,* a comic look at life backstage.

NYCB's spring season, which runs April 29 through June 29, also includes Wheeldon's masterful *Morphoses,* a quartet set to the music of Romanian composer György Ligeti and originally created for Alexandra Ansanelli, Jock Soto, Wendy Whelan and Damian Woetzel. Set against a minimalist black background, the dancers, clad in orange leotards, perform stark and angular movements while vertical strips of continually changing color appear and disappear behind them. *Morphoses,* Wheeldon's third ballet set to the music of Ligeti (he has also created *Polyphonia* and *Continuum*), is both sophisticated and emotional, though never overrun by flashy pyrotechnics or vapid partnering. A gifted musical choreographer, Wheeldon infuses all of his ballets, no matter how austere, with a breathtaking command of theater. His work is not a hybrid of ballet and modern dance, but authentic ballet.

In the case of *Morphoses,* Wheeldon was inspired by Ligeti's String Quartet No. 1 ("Métamorphoses nocturnes"), composed in 1953–54. For the choreographer, the score conjures a surreal *Alice in Wonderland* environment. "I think it's very dark," he says. "Ligeti develops spongy musical phrases, so passages jump around from moments that sound like a house-of-horrors soundtrack to

performed in the modern, spacious theater include the Bill T. Jones/Arnie Zane Dance Company and the Alvin Ailey Repertory Ensemble.

### Dance Theater Workshop

*Bessie Schönberg Theater, 219 W 19th St between Seventh and Eighth Aves (212-691-6500, tickets 212-924-0077; www.dtw.org). Subway: A, C, E to 14th St; L to Eighth Ave; 1, 9 to 18th St. AmEx, MC, V.*

The recently renovated DTW is more impressive than ever: The space, which hosts work by contemporary choreographers, features a 192-seat theater, two dance studios and an artists' media lab. Choreographers on tap this spring include Lucy Guerin and John Jasperse.

### Danspace Project

*St. Mark's Church in-the-Bowery, Second Ave at 10th St (212-674-8194). Subway: L to Third Ave; 6 to Astor Pl. $12–$20. Cash only.*

This gorgeous, high-ceilinged sanctuary for downtown dance becomes even more otherworldly when the music is live. Choreographers are selected by the director, Laurie Uprichard, whose preference leans toward pure movement rather than technological experimentation. Semiregular choreographers include Douglas Dunn, Gina Gibney and David Gordon.

### The Kitchen

*See page 341 for listing.*

Best known as an avant-garde theater space, the Kitchen also offers experimental dance. Dance and performance curator Dean Moss, who is also a choreographer, presents artists who are inventive and, more often than not, provocative (tickets cost $8 to $25).

### Merce Cunningham Studio

*55 Bethune St between Washington and West Sts, 11th floor (212-691-9751; www.merce.org). Subway: A, C, E to 14th St; L to Eighth Ave. $10–$30. Cash only.*

Located in the Westbeth complex on the edge of the West Village, the Cunningham Studio is rented by independent self-producing choreographers. Performance quality ranges from horrid to surprisingly wonderful. Since the stage and seating area are in Cunningham's large studio, be prepared to take off your shoes. Arrive early too, or you'll have to sit on the floor. For more details, contact the Cunningham Dance Foundation *(212-255-8240).*

**Backward glance** Choreographer and former dancer Christopher Wheeldon recalls the joy of learning a new piece.

hazy and dreamy violin. It's quite melodic and danceable, but at the same time, it's totally schizophrenic."

Wheeldon fits in perfectly in New York City, which he now considers home. He was born in Yeovil, Somerset, where he began dancing at age seven at the East Coker Ballet School. At 11, he was accepted at the Royal Ballet School, and six years later, he joined the company. That same year, he won a gold medal at the Prix de Lausanne and was awarded the school's Ursula Moreton prize for choreography.

But Wheeldon felt antsy; in 1993, he moved to New York after Martins invited him to join NYCB's corps de ballet. A vivacious dancer with a graceful jump, Wheeldon was promoted to soloist in 1999, but he sensed that he wouldn't achieve the rank of principal. In 2000, he retired from the stage to devote himself to choreography.

Wheeldon sees himself as someone who makes up steps to music. This description may seem simple, but it's also revealing: For Wheeldon, satisfaction comes when all the pieces fit together. "My primary aim is to make work that's enjoyed by an audience," he says. "But I make my best work when I'm collaborating with dancers. As a dancer, I remember how it felt to have a ballet made for me. If it was a good ballet, it was the most important thing for me at that time in my career—in my *life*, really. So making a role for a dancer and having that dancer *love* the role stems into why I do it. That's why, in the end, it gives me pleasure, too."

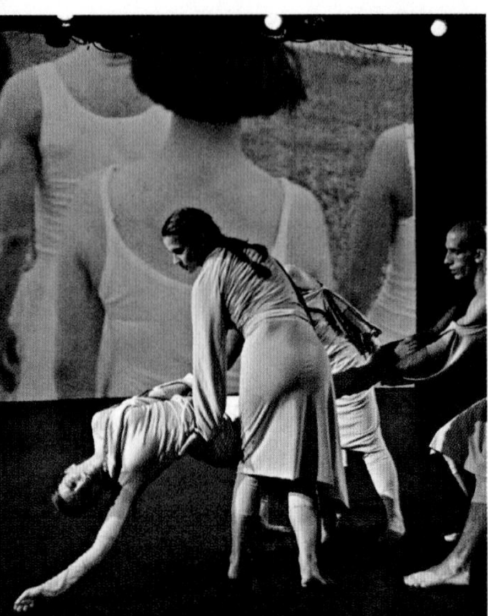

**Weight of the whirled** Troika Ranch attains liftoff at Williamsburg Art neXus.

### Movement Research at Judson Church

*55 Washington Sq South at Thompson St (212-598-0551; www.movementresearch.org). Subway: A, C, E, F, V, S to W 4th St. Free.*

Director Carla Peterson carries on the tradition of Monday-night performances at the Judson Church, which originally began in the groundbreaking '60s. At least two choreographers' works are shown each night, and the series runs from September to June.

### New Jersey Performing Arts Center

*1 Center St between Park Pl and Ronald H. Brown St at the waterfront, Newark, NJ (973-642-8989, box office 888-466-5722; www.njpac.org). Call for directions. $12–$64. AmEx, Disc, MC, V.*

The New Jersey Performing Arts Center serves as home base for the New Jersey Symphony Orchestra, and has hosted the Alvin Ailey American Dance Theater, the Miami City Ballet and Suzanne Farrell Ballet. Large open theaters make NJPAC a choice venue for dance. And it's not *that* far away.

▶ The Theater Development Fund's **NYC/Onstage** service *(see page 335)* offers information on dance events in town.
▶ For information on weekly dance performances, preview shows and classes, see ***Time Out New York***.
▶ See page 374 for ticket information.
▶ ***Dance Magazine*** gives information about performances far in advance.

### The New Victory Theater

*See page 339 for listing.*

Since opening in 1995, this intimate venue has offered exceptional dance programming. Much of it is geared toward children (there are plenty of early shows); recently, the theater hosted James Thiérrée's magical *Junebug Symphony.* Past artists have included Suzanne Farrell and Maguy Marin. Tickets are in the $8 to $25 range.

### 92nd Street Y Harkness Dance Project

*The Duke on 42nd Street Theater, 229 W 42nd St between Seventh and Eighth Aves (212-415-5500; www.92ndStY.org). Subway: N, Q, R, W, S, 1, 2, 3, 9, 7 to Times Sq–42nd St. $20. AmEx, MC, V.*

The 92nd Street Y presents its annual monthlong performance series at the Duke on 42nd Street. Past choreographers include Keely Garfield and Wil Swanson.

### Performance Space 122

*See page 341 for listing.*

An appealing range of up-and-coming choreographers (and the occasional established talent) present new and unconventional works *($9–$15).* Recent and upcoming performers include Stacy Dawson, Sarah Michelson, David Neumann and Yasuko Yokoshi.

### Symphony Space

*See page 322 for listing.*

The World Music Institute presents many international dance troupes, but there are also seasons with contemporary choreographers like Wally Cardona and Seán Curran. Tickets are between $10 and $20.

### Williamsburg Art neXus

*205 North 7th St between Driggs and Roebling Aves, Williamsburg, Brooklyn (718-599-7997; www.wax205.com). Subway: L to Bedford Ave. $10–$20. Cash only.*

This Brooklyn venue features dance by local choreographers in an intimate environment. So what if it's small? The sight lines are great, and the mix of artists is interesting.

## Summer performances

### Central Park SummerStage

*See page 252 for listing.*

This outdoor dance series runs on Fridays in July and the first two weeks in August. Temperatures can get steamy, but at least you're outside. Count on seeing contemporary dance, and arrive early to secure a seat close to the stage.

### Dances for Wave Hill

*See page 127 for listing.*

This is a lovely setting for outdoor dance. The series, sponsored by Dancing in the Streets, runs in July *($4, cash only).*

# Trips Out of Town



## Feature box



**Social climbing** Visit the Hudson Valley estate Kykuit to see how four generations of Rockefellers lived.

# Trips Out of Town

Sunny resorts and rustic getaways offer a different kind of New York adventure

You'd think there'd be plenty to keep New Yorkers busy 24/7, but come the weekend, they're scrambling to escape from the city, especially during warmer months. And no wonder—countless destinations, from celeb-infested beach towns to wooded regions with historic import, are within a few hours' reach. Wherever you go, one truism remains: Traffic is hell on Fridays and Sundays, so take advantage of your visitor status and plan your retreat for midweek or during off-peak times—or take public transportation.

**GENERAL INFORMATION**

**NYC & Company**, the New York visitors and convention bureau *(see page 375)*, has many brochures on upstate excursions. Look for special packages if you're planning to spend a few days away. *The New York Times* publishes a travel section every Sunday that carries advertisements for resorts and guest houses. *Time Out New York*'s annual Summer Getaways issue will point you in the right direction.

**GETTING THERE**

We've included information on how to reach all listed destinations from New York City. **Metro-North** and the **Long Island Rail Road** *(see page 357)* are the two main commuter rail systems. Both offer theme tours in the summer. Call the **Port Authority Bus Terminal** *(see page 356)* for information on all bus transportation from the city. For a more scenic route, travel by water. **NY Waterway** *(see page 132)* offers service to areas outside Manhattan. New York's car-rental rates are exorbitant; you can save up to 50 percent by taking public transportation out of the city, then renting a car at your destination. For more information on airports, buses, car rentals and trains, see chapter **Directory**.

## Beaches

Manhattan is surrounded by water, but we strongly advise against taking a dip in the Hudson River. Luckily, beachfront towns have no shortage of bracing Atlantic waters and fine sand. Of course, it's possible to reach the coast without even leaving city limits—the grungy waterside carnival known as Coney Island makes for a great day trip, as do the Rockaways. Yet many urban natives prefer the comparatively serene beaches of Long Island. From Memorial Day (late May) to Labor Day (early September), New Yorkers flock to summer rentals or day-trip destinations in the Hamptons and on Fire Island.

### Nearby

When the city heats up, shore relief is only 33 miles from Manhattan. **Jones Beach** *(516-785-1600; www.jonesbeach.org)* is good for picnicking and sunbathing. It's also the site of big summer music concerts *(see page 317)*. Closer still is **Long Beach** *(516-431-1000; www.longbeachny.org)*, easily accessible by the LIRR.

#### Getting there

**Jones Beach**

From mid-June through Labor Day, the LIRR offers an $11 package deal from Penn Station covering train-and-bus fare, plus entry to the beach. Take the Babylon line of the LIRR to Freeport, then board the JB62 bus to the beach. Trains leave Penn Station about every half hour.

**Long Beach**

As with Jones Beach, from mid-June through Labor Day, the LIRR has an $11 deal from Penn Station, including train fare and entry to the beach. Take the Long Beach line of the LIRR to its terminus; the beach is two blocks south of the station.

### Fire Island

Running parallel to the southern coast of Long Island, Fire Island is a 30-mile-long strip of land separating the Great South Bay from the Atlantic Ocean. Traffic-weary visitors can rejoice: Cars are barred from most of Fire Island, so expect to get a lot of sand in your shoes. Since there are no cars, there are no streets, and while many attractions don't have addresses, everything is fairly easy to find.

Many day-trippers head to **Robert Moses State Park** *(631-669-0449)*, on the island's western tip. Although it feels wild and isolated, it's only 90 minutes from Penn Station by train and bus. Parking is also available, so you

**Fire Island roast** Sun lovers get baked on the beach at Robert Moses State Park.

can drive instead. A long stretch of white sand fronts grassy dunes. Head east toward the lighthouse and let it all hang out at the fun, friendly nude beach.

To the east await Fire Island's various beach towns, such as Ocean Beach and the Pines. **Ocean Beach** is a sanctuary for sunbathing, Frisbee-flipping, volleyball-playing post-collegiates and families. The town has neither the frills nor the conveniences of the Hamptons, but nothing will stop an Ocean Beacher from enjoying a day in the sand—not even the beach's reputation as the "Land of No"; booze and food are verboten. You *can* drink at the dock in **Fair Harbor**; on Saturday evenings, sunset cocktails are a tradition. From Ocean Beach, follow the sand path known as the Burma Road to the dock, a 20-minute walk to the west. Don't forget to stick a bottle of wine or a six-pack in your beach bag—it's a BYO affair.

A magnet for Chelsea boy toys and other members of New York's gay community, the **Pines** is a world—and a half-hour water-taxi ride—away from Ocean Beach. Modern wood-and-glass houses line the community's carless streets. Pines residents keep a tight social schedule: sunning in the morning, working out in the afternoon and napping before cocktails at sunset. At 8pm, there's the "tea dance" (which involves neither tea nor dance) outside the **Pavilion** *(631-597-6131)* and partying until dawn.

## Where to stay, eat & drink

You can find burgers and bar food at **Albatross** *(Bayview at Dehnhoff Walks, Ocean Beach, 631-583-5697),* and anyone with a taste for buttercream-frosted cakes and gooey brownies should stop by **Rachel's Bakery** *(325 Bay Walk, 631-583-5953).* City slickers visiting Ocean Beach tend to share summer rentals with friends, sometimes cramming up to 25 people into a four-bedroom house. For roomier digs, try **Clegg's Hotel** *(478 Bayberry Walk, Ocean Beach, NY 11770, 631-583-5399)* or **Jerry's Accommodations** *(168 Cottage Walk, Ocean Beach, NY 11770, 631-583-8870).* In the Pines, guest rooms are available at **Botel** *(Harbor Walk, Fire Island Pines, NY 11782, 631-597-6500),* an unsightly concrete structure that houses the Pines' heavily used gym. Wherever you stay, make sure you have well-honed social skills…and plenty of sunblock.

## Getting there

### Ocean Beach

Take the Montauk line of the **LIRR** *($6.50–*

► ***Time Out New York*** publishes an annual summer-getaway issue with info on places to go near the city. Find past years' articles at www.timeoutny.com/archives.

*$9.50)* to Bay Shore, then walk or cab it to the ferry station. **Tommy's Taxi** *(631-665-4800; Mon–Sat $17 per person, Sundays and holidays $20 per person)* runs regular van service from various Manhattan locations; reservations are required. From Bay Shore, take the **Fire Island Ferry** *(99 Maple Ave near Aldrich Ct, Bay Shore, 631-665-3600, www.fireislandferries.com; round-trip $12.50, children $6).*

### The Pines

Take the Montauk line of the **LIRR** *($6.50–$9.50)* to Sayville, then walk or take a taxi to the ferry dock. From May to October, **Islanders Horizon Coach & Buses** *(212-228-7100, 631-654-2622; www.islanderstravel.com; one-way $20)* runs between Manhattan and the Sayville ferry station; there are Friday and Saturday departures, and Sunday and Monday return trips. From Sayville, take the **Sayville Ferry** *(41 River Rd at Willow St, 631-589-0810, www.sayvilleferry.com; round-trip $11, children under 12 $5).*

### Robert Moses State Park

From mid-June through Labor Day, the **LIRR** offers a $12 train-and-bus package from Penn Station. Take the Babylon line of the LIRR to Babylon and board the S47 bus. Buses run approximately every half hour on weekend days and hourly on weekdays.

## The Hamptons

The Hamptons, a series of small towns along the South Fork of Long Island, are the ultimate retreat for New York's rich and famous. Socialites, artists and hangers-on drift from benefit to benefit throughout the summer, while locals grin and bear the vainglorious invasion. The rest of us go for the beautiful sun-drenched beaches. For an up-to-date social calendar, pick up the free local rags *Dan's Paper* or *Hamptons Country Magazine,* available at area stores. The glossy *Hamptons Magazine* displays plenty of red-carpet pics of parties past. Check the *East Hampton Star* for local news.

After Memorial Day, the beaches attract celebs looking for rest and relaxation. At **Two Mile Hollow Beach** *(Two Mile Hollow Rd, East Hampton)* you might spot Calvin

# Inn coming!

An array of new Hamptons hotels provides more hospitality than ever

When it comes to lodging, the Hamptons have never offered a wealth of choices. Visitors faced an overpriced dump on the highway, a stuffy B-and-B, or a l-o-o-ong late-night drive back to the city. But in the past couple of years, hoteliers have noticed that there are many types of weekenders, and a range of inns has sprung up—good news if you don't know any locals with guest rooms. Below are several new hotels, catering to all, from low-key beachgoers to elite escapists. (All rates are per night, double occupancy.)

### Enclave Inn

*2668 Montauk Hwy, Bridgehampton, NY 11932 (631-537-0197; www.enclaveinn.com). $99–$349, three-night minimum Jun–Aug. AmEx, MC, V.*

The unpretentious Enclave has rapidly become a mini-empire. Two new branches, in Southampton and Wainscott, have joined the Bridgehampton flagship. Rooms are well lit, clean and furnished with raw-maple furniture. All the hotels have pools, well-maintained grounds and friendly staffers.

**Other locations** • *450 Country Rd, Southampton, NY 11968 (631-283-2548; www.enclaveinn.com). $99–$349, three-night minimum Jun–Aug. AmEx, MC, V.* • *380 Montauk Hwy, Wainscott, NY 11975 (631-537-9328; www.enclaveinn.com). $99–$349, three-night minimum Jun–Aug. AmEx, MC, V.*

### Hampton Inn Long Island/Brookhaven

*2000 North Ocean Ave, Farmingville, NY 11738 (631-732-7300; www.hamptoninn.com). $149–$279. AmEx, DC, Disc, MC, V.*

Have you ever neared the end of the expressway on a Friday night, after hours spent in hellish traffic, and wished you could rest? Now you can! This chain hotel, just off Exit 63, offers 161 rooms to crash in. Come morning, you're left with a mere 33-mile drive to Southampton.

### Hampton Resorts and Hospitality

*Atlantic, 1655 County Rd 39, Southampton, NY 11968 (631-283-6100; www.hrhresorts.com). $120–$550. AmEx, MC, V.*

*"Ce n'est pas un motel"* promises this hotel chain's sleek website, which boasts photos of boutique-style rooms and big beds with fluffy duvets and European linens. Truthfully, these former motor lodges *are* just motels—

Klein catching rays. Sagg Main *(Sagg Main St, Sagaponack)* has the ocean on one side and a pond on the other.

Keep your eyes peeled for Long Island's own Billy Joel enjoying a doughnut at **Dreesen's Excelsior Market** *(33 Newtown Ln near Rte 27, East Hampton, 631-324-0465)* or a baseball-capped Jerry Seinfeld strolling the town's tree-lined streets. If you want to shake your booty, **Jet East** *(1181 North Sea Rd between Lake Dr and North Sea Meacox Rd, Southampton, 631-283-0808)* and the **Southampton Tavern** *(125 Tuckahoe Ln at Rte 27, Southampton, 631-287-2125)* are beach-town versions of Manhattan's club scene, with VIP lounges, crowded dance floors and lots of pretty faces. The infamous club, **Conscience Point** *(1976 North Sea Rd at Old Field Rd, Southampton, 631-204-0600)* is where publicist Lizzie Grubman backed her SUV into several people (for which she served a bit of jail time).

**Montauk** is "a drinking town with a fishing problem," and while the seaside village is technically part of East Hampton, it has little in common with its neighbors; the locals like to keep their ruffian reputation intact. **Montauk Point Lighthouse** *(Montauk Pt, Rte 27, Montauk, 631-668-2544, 888-MTK-POINT; www.montauklighthouse.com)* is the oldest in New York State (built in 1795), and historic memorabilia are displayed inside. The lighthouse area is one of the most famous surf-fishing spots in the country; expect to see as many surf casters as there are rocks to stand on. Or take the day boat ***Lazybones*** *(Marlin's Dock, Montauk, 631-668-5671; $30)* for a fun half-day fishing excursion in summer or winter.

## Where to stay, eat & drink

Dining trends in the Hamptons change frequently, but standbys **Della Femina** *(99 N Main St at Cedar St, East Hampton, 631-329-6666)* and **Nick & Toni's** *(136 N Main St near Cedar St, East Hampton, 631-324-3550)* promise sophisticated food and at least one celebrity sighting per night. In the "fishing village," patrons frequent **Gosman's** *(Gosman's Dock, West Lake Dr near Soundview*

**The water's fine** Leap into the lovely pool at the affordable Enclave Inn in Bridgehampton.

refurnished with Ikea-type furniture, gray wall-to-wall carpeting and a big white bed tossed in to confuse you. Still, the locations are quiet and convenient, and the neon motel sign at the Atlantic is kitschy-cool.

**Other locations** • *Bentley, 161 Hill Station Rd, Southampton, NY 11968 (631-283-6100; www.hrhresorts.com). $130–$475. AmEx, MC, V.* • *Capri, 281 County Rd 39, Southampton, NY 11968 (631-283-6100; www.hrhresorts.com). $150–$500. AmEx, MC, V.*

**Montauk Yacht Club**

*32 Star Island Rd, Montauk, NY 11954 (631-668-3100, 888-MYC-8668; www.montaukyachtclub.com). $119–$429. AmEx, DC, Disc, MC, V.*

If your goal is to get away from it all, head to the far-east coast of New York and this high-class resort. It offers 84 recently renovated guest rooms, 23 separate waterfront villas and a surfeit of luxurious pampering. The fitness center, spa, tennis court and two restaurants on-site mean you need never leave the property.

**1770 House**

*143 Main St, East Hampton, NY 11937(631-324-1770). $100–$525; Jul, Aug three-night minimum on weekends, except Jul 4 and Labor Day (four-day minimum). AmEx, MC, V.*

This classic inn, just steps from a Jitney stop, reopened in 2002 following an extensive renovation. Designer Laura Maerov has combined traditional wallpaper, wood paneling and eclectic antiques to give each room special charm. As a bonus, 1770 House opened a much-anticipated restaurant with local star chef Kevin Penner in the kitchen.

*Dr, Montauk, 631-668-5330)* or **Dave's Grill** *(468 West Lake Dr, Montauk, 631-668-9190).* In town, indulge your craving for surf or turf at **Shagwong** *(774 Main St, Montauk, 631-668-3050).* Enjoy a beautiful sunset view over Fort Pond Bay at the **Montauket** *(88 Firestone Rd, Montauk, 631-668-5992).*

## Getting there

Take the Montauk line of the **LIRR** *($10.25–$15.25)* to Southampton, East Hampton or Montauk. The **Hampton Jitney** *(212-936-0440, 631-283-4600, 800-936-0440, www.hamptonjitney.com; one-way $25)* runs regular bus service between three locations in Manhattan and stops in all the towns in the Hamptons.

## Resources

### www.ihamptons.com

Launched by Hamptons maven Steven Gaines (who wrote the infamous tell-all *Philistines at the Hedgerow*), this website has real-estate sales and rental listings, services (cleaning, painting, etc.) and a live cam on the main street of every Hamptons community.

# The Hudson Valley

Just north of the city, the Hudson Valley is a quiet haven with breathtaking scenery, historic mansions and fine wineries. A trip to the valley and back can be made in a day. Metro-North frequently offers discounted rates; the Hudson Line follows the river nearly the entire way. NY Waterway, in conjunction with **Historic Hudson Valley** *(914-631-8200; www.hudsonvalley.org),* runs cruises from Manhattan and New Jersey to several of the grand houses.

## Historic homes

Magnificent houses (and their sprawling estates) dot the hills overlooking the Hudson River, including the summer residences of remarkable figures such as Franklin D. Roosevelt and Frederick Vanderbilt. The Historic Hudson Valley society maintains most of these sites, which are open to the public throughout much of the year.

### Boscobel Restoration

*1601 Rte 9D, Garrison, NY 10524 (845-265-3638; www.boscobel.org). Apr–Oct Mon, Wed–Sun 9:30am–5pm; Nov, Dec Wed–Sun 9:30am–4pm. $8, seniors $7, children 6–14 $5, children under 6 free. Disc, MC, V.*

Built in 1804 in Federal style by States Morris Dyckman, a wealthy British loyalist, the property hosts two plays per summer season for the Hudson Valley Shakespeare Festival.

### Kykuit

*Pocantico Hills, Tarrytown, NY 10591 (914-631-9491; www.hudsonvalley.org). Visitors' center at Philipsburg Manor, off Rte 9. Apr 27–Nov 3 Mon, Wed–Sun 9am–3pm. $20, seniors $19, children 10–17 $17. AmEx, MC, V.*

John D. Rockefeller Jr.'s Kykuit, pronounced "KYE-kut," was home to four generations of the Rockefeller family. Located on the banks above the Hudson, the house has a glorious view of the water. In addition to the house and gardens, there are carefully maintained antique carriages and automobiles in the coach barn. Tickets are sold on a first-come basis, so arrive early.

### Lyndhurst Castle

*635 South Broadway, Tarrytown, NY 10591 (914-631-4481; www.lyndhurst.org). Mid-Apr–Oct Tue–Sun, Monday holidays 10am–4:15pm; Nov–mid-Apr Sat, Sun, Monday holidays 10am–4pm. $10, seniors $9, students 12–17 $4, children under 12 free. Grounds fee: $4. AmEx, MC, V.*

Several notable figures have called this Gothic Revival mansion home, including former New York City mayor William Paulding and robber baron Jay Gould. From Grand Central, the estate is a scenic, 40-minute trip by Metro-North (Hudson Line to Tarrytown), and a five-minute taxi ride from the train station.

### Olana

*Rte 9G, Hudson, NY 12534 (518-828-0135; www.olana.org). Apr 1–Memorial Day, Oct 1–31 Wed–Sun 10am–5pm; Jun 1–Oct 1 Wed–Sun 10am–6pm; Nov Wed–Sun 10am–4pm; Dec–Mar call for hours. AmEx, MC, V.*

Hudson River School artist Frederic Church built his home here in the Catskills after seeing the views from this site. Influenced by his trips to the Middle East and Europe, Church incorporated Moorish touches and a rich, varied color palette into the design. Begun in 1870, the home took roughly 20 years to complete.

### Springwood

*4097 Albany Post Rd off Rte 9, Hyde Park, NY 12538 (845-229-9115; www.nps.gov/hofr). House 9am–5pm; grounds 8am–dusk. $10, under 17 free. MC, V.*

Hyde Park holds the definitive Hudson Valley estate: Springwood, Franklin D. Roosevelt's boyhood home. The house is filled with family photos and the former president's collections, including one of nautical instruments. In the nearby library and museum, you can examine items such as presidential documents and FDR's pony cart.

### Sunnyside

*West Sunnyside Lane, off Rte 9, Tarrytown, NY 10591 (914-591-8763, 914-631-8200). Mar–Dec Mon, Wed–Sun 10am–5pm. $9, seniors $8, children 5–17 $5. AmEx, Disc, MC, V.*

Washington Irving, the first American to make his

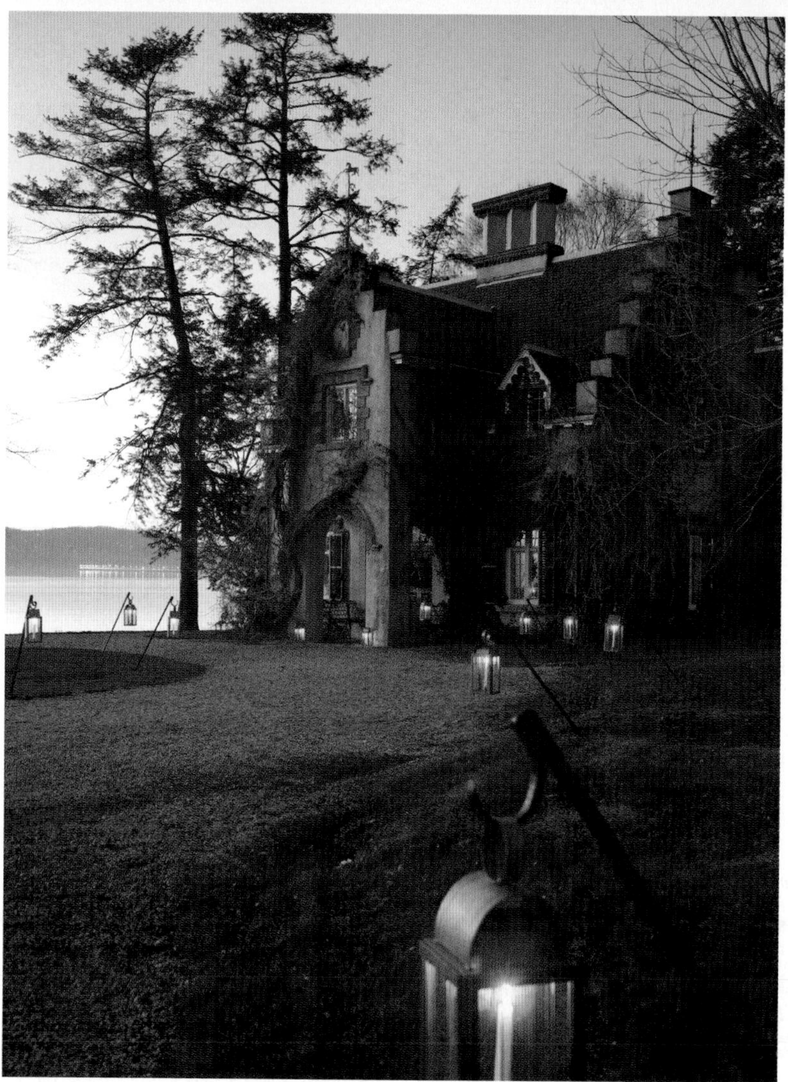

**Estate planning** By 1835, Washington Irving had earned more than enough money from his writing to buy a Dutch-colonial–era farm, called Sunnyside, overlooking the Hudson River.



living as a writer, renovated a charming 18th-century cottage on Sunnyside Farm. Located in tiny Tarrytown (which abuts Sleepy Hollow, the village Irving immortalized in print), you can walk to Sunnyside from adjacent Lyndhurst Castle via the Croton Aqueduct hiking trail (at West Sunnyside Lane, walk downhill toward the river).

## Vanderbilt

*519 Albany Post Rd, Hyde Park, NY 12538 (845-229-9115; www.nps.gov/vama). 9am–5pm. $8, under 17 free. AmEx, Disc, MC, V.*

Frederick Vanderbilt was the grandson of Cornelius "Commodore" Vanderbilt and the son of William Henry, both the wealthiest men in their respective generations. Compared to the opulent homes of his siblings, Frederick's "Hyde Park" is modest. Built on a bluff above the river, the Greek Revival structure and its grounds offer sweeping river views and winding walking trails.

## Wilderstein

*330 Morton Rd, Rhinebeck, NY 12572 (845-876-4818; www.wilderstein.org). May–Oct Thu–Sun*

*noon–4pm; Thanksgiving weekend–Dec Fri–Sun 1–4pm. $7, students $5, children under 12 free. Cash only.*
Beyond the reach of Metro-North, the charming town of Rhinebeck is cherished by history buffs. This 1852 Italianate villa was rebuilt in Queen Anne style in 1888.

## Where to stay, eat & drink

In Hyde Park, the **Culinary Institute of America** *(1946 Campus Dr, 845-471-6608; www.ciachef.edu)* boasts such illustrious alumni as celebrity chef Larry Forgione. Chefs-in-training prepare French, Italian, American contemporary and American regional cuisine in four different dining rooms. The **Apple Pie Bakery Café** is stocked with treats made by pastry majors. Rhinebeck's **Beekman Arms** inn may be historic, but the kitchen is nothing if not of-the-moment: Forgione is in charge of the **Beekman 1766 Tavern** *(845-871-1766)*. Show up in New Paltz with an appetite. **The Bakery** *(13A N Front St off Rte 32, 845-255-8840; www.ilovethebakery.com)* offers excellent baked goods, sandwiches and salads, all made in-house. There's also an excellent selection of teas and coffees.

In Putnam County, the 1832 **Hudson House** *(2 Main St, Cold Spring, NY 10516, 845-265-9355; www.hudsonhouseinn.com)* is a peaceful, convenient inn with an excellent American contemporary restaurant. A good place to rest in Hyde Park is **Fala Bed and Breakfast**, a private one-bedroom guest house with a pool—call ahead for reservations *(East Market St, Hyde Park, NY 12538, 845-229-5937)*. Rhinebeck boasts the nation's oldest continuously operating hotel, the **Beekman Arms** *(6387 Mill St, Rhinebeck, NY 12572, 845-876-7077, 800-361-6517; www.beekmanarms.com)*, in business for more than 300 years. **The Villa at Saugerties** *(159 Fawn Rd, Saugerties, NY 12477; www.thevillaatsaugerties.com)* is a bed-and-breakfast that offers stylish rooms in a rustic setting.

## Getting there

Ask about special package rates from NY Waterway *(see page 132)*. **Metro-North** *($7.75–$13)* runs trains daily to the Hudson Valley. The Hudson line ends at Poughkeepsie, a 20-minute taxi ride from Rhinebeck. Alternatively, you can take **Amtrak** *(see page 357)*, which is more expensive. **Short Line Buses** *(212-736-4700, 800-631-8405, www.shortlinebus.com; $25.75 round-trip)* runs regular bus service to Rhinebeck and Hyde Park.

## Wineries

Wine-tasting along the Shawangunk Wine Trail can be rewarding for the adventurous oenophile. Besides the scenic setting (the "trail" zigzags along a route that's roughly parallel to I-87, west of the Hudson River), there's the accessibility to the makers: You can sample the wine (for a small fee) and learn about how it is made. In addition, you might be able to taste peculiar potations, such as a ginseng-root blend. Plan your trip by visiting www.shawangunkwinetrail.com, which has directions to individual wineries.

### Adair Vineyards

*75 Allhusen Rd, New Paltz, NY 12561 (845-255-1377). Mar–Dec noon–6pm. AmEx, MC, V.*
Sample this 16-year-old vineyard's offerings in the tasting room, or take your drink by the stream.

### Applewood Winery

*82 Four Corners Rd, Warwick, NY 10990 (914-986-1684; www.applewoodorchardsandwinery.com). May–Nov Sat, Sun noon–5pm. MC, V.*
Fruit wines are the speciality at Applewood, a 120-acre farm that dates back to the 1700s.

### Brimstone Hill Vineyard

*61 Brimstone Hill Rd, Pine Bush, NY 12566 (845-744-2231). Jun–Aug Mon, Thu–Sun 11:30am–5:30pm. Sept–May Sat, Sun 11:30am– 5:30pm.*
Try the pinot noir at this cottage industry, operated out of a garage by two tweedy college professors.

### Brotherhood, America's Oldest Winery

*100 Brotherhood Plaza, Washingtonville, NY 10992 (845-496-9101; www.wines.com/brotherhood). May–Oct 11am–5pm; Nov–Apr Sat, Sun 11am–5pm. Guided tour $4, children 15–20 $2, under 15 free. AmEx, MC, V.*
Brotherhood's other claim to fame is that it skirted Prohibition by claiming that all of its wine was headed for the altar. Try the Rosario, a sangrialike red.

### Rivendell Winery

*714 Albany Post Rd, New Paltz, NY 12561 (845-255-2494; www.rivendellwine.com). 10am–6pm. Five tastings $3. AmEx, Disc, MC, V.*
Bob Ransom and his partner Susan Wine also run Manhattan's Vintage New York wine stores *(see page 240)*. Vino from around the state is sold at Rivendell and Vintage, along with a selection of cheeses. Picnics on the winery grounds are encouraged.

### Whitecliff Vineyard

*331 McKinstry Rd, Gardiner, NY 12525 (845-255-4613; www.whitecliffwine.com). Memorial Day–Oct Thu, Fri, Sun noon–5pm; Sat 11:30am–6pm. Nov, Dec Sat, Sun noon–5pm. AmEx, MC, V.*
The youngest of the region's wineries, Whitecliff opened in 1999 and was the first in the area to grow gamay noir grapes, which are used to create a wine similar to Beaujolais nouveau.

# Directory



## Feature boxes



**Top billing** Caps proclaiming city loyalty are worn by locals and tourists alike.

# Directory

Essential resources to help you navigate the city like a native

## Getting to and from NYC

### By air

There are three major airports servicing the New York City area, plus one in Long Island; for details, see page 358. Here are some sources for purchasing airline tickets.

#### Internet

A few sites to investigate for low fares are **www.airfare.com**, **www.cheaptickets.com**, **www.expedia.com**, **www.orbitz.com** and **www.travelocity.com**.

#### Newspapers

The best place to get an idea of available fares is the travel section of your local paper. If that's no help, get a Sunday ***New York Times***. It has plenty of advertisements for discounted fares.

#### Satellite Airlines Terminal

*125 Park Ave between 41st and 42nd Sts (212-986-0888). Subway: S, 4, 5, 6, 7 to 42nd St–Grand Central. Mon–Fri 8am–7pm; Sat 9am–5pm.*
This one-stop shop for travelers aggregates ticket counters of major international airlines. You can exchange frequent-flier mileage; process passports, birth certificates and driver's licenses; and arrange for transportation and city tours. Call the carriers individually or the information line above.
**Other locations** • *555 Seventh Ave between 39th and 40th Sts. Subway: N, Q, R, W, S, 1, 2, 3, 9, 7 to 42nd St–Times Sq.* • *1 E 59th St at Fifth Ave. Subway: N, R, W to Fifth Ave–59th St.* • *1843 Broadway at 60th St. Subway: A, C, B, D, 1, 9 to 59th St–Columbus Circle.*

#### Travel agents

Agents are specialized, so find one who suits your needs. Do you want luxury? Around the world? Student? *(See* **Students**, *page 373.)* Find an agent through word of mouth, newspapers, the Yellow Pages or the Internet. Knowledgeable travel agents can help you with far more than air tickets, and a good relationship with an agent can be invaluable, especially if you prefer not to deal with travel details.

### By bus

Buses are an inexpensive means of getting to and from New York City, though the ride is longer and sometimes uncomfortable. They are particularly useful if you want to leave in a hurry, since many bus companies don't require reservations. Most out-of-town buses come and go from the **Port Authority Bus Terminal**.

### Bus lines

#### Greyhound Trailways

*800-231-2222; www.greyhound.com. Buses depart 24hrs. AmEx, Disc, MC, V.*
Greyhound offers long-distance bus travel to destinations across North America.

#### New Jersey Transit

*973-762-5100; www.njtransit.com. AmEx, MC, V.*
NJT provides bus service to nearly everywhere in the Garden State; most buses run around the clock.

#### Peter Pan

*800-343-9999; www.peterpanbus.com. Buses depart 24hrs. AmEx, MC, V.*
Peter Pan runs extensive service to cities across the Northeast, and its tickets are also valid on Greyhound.

### Bus stations

#### George Washington Bridge Bus Station

*178th St between Broadway and Fort Washington Ave (800-221-9903). Subway: A to 175th St; 1, 9 to 181st St.*
A few bus lines that serve New Jersey and Rockland County, New York, use this station from 5am to 1am.

#### Port Authority Bus Terminal

*625 Eighth Ave between 40th and 42nd Sts (212-564-8484; www.panynj.gov). Subway: A, C, E to 42nd St–Port Authority.*
Many transportation companies serve New York City's commuter and long-distance bus travelers. Call for additional information.

### By car

Driving to and from the city can be scenic and fun. However, you may encounter restrictions at bridges and tunnels (check **www.nyc.gov** and **www.panynj.gov** before driving in). While you're on the road, tune in to **1010 WINS** on the AM dial for up-to-the-minute traffic reports. Expect delays of 15 minutes to 2 hours—plenty of time to get your money out for the toll (average is $5). Note that street parking in the city is very restricted, especially in the summer *(see* **Parking**, *pages 357 and 359)*.

### Car rental

If you're interested in heading out of town by auto, car rental is much cheaper on the city's outskirts and in New Jersey and Connecticut; reserve ahead for weekends. New York State honors valid foreign-issued driver's licenses. All car-rental companies listed below add sales tax. Companies located outside of New York State offer a "loss damage waiver" (LDW). This is expensive—almost as much as the rental itself—but without it, you are responsible for the cost of repairing even the slightest scratch. If you pay with an AmEx card or a gold Visa or MasterCard, the LDW may be covered by the credit-card company; it might also be covered by a reciprocal agreement with an automotive organization. Personal liability insurance is optional—and recommended (but see if your travel insurance or home policy already covers it). Rental companies in New York are required by law to insure their own cars, so the LDW is not a factor. Instead, the renter is responsible for the first $100 in damage to the vehicle, and the company is accountable for anything beyond that. You will need a credit card (or a large cash deposit) to rent a car, and you usually have to be at least age 25. If you know you want to rent a car before you travel, ask your travel agent or airline for any good deals.

### Avis

*800-331-1212; www.avis.com. 24hrs most locations. Rates from $70 a day, unlimited mileage. AmEx, DC, Disc, MC, V.*

### Budget Rent-a-Car

*800-527-0700; www.budget.com. In the city, call for hours; airport counters 5am–2am. Rates from $30 per weekday, $50 per day on weekends, unlimited mileage. AmEx, DC, Disc, MC, V.*

### Enterprise

*800-325-8007; www.enterprise.com. Mon–Fri 7:30am–6pm; Sat 9am–noon. Rates from $35 a day outside New York City; around $45 a day in New York City; unlimited mileage restricted to New York, New Jersey and Connecticut. AmEx, DC, Disc, MC, V.*
This inexpensive, reliable company has branches easily accessible from Manhattan. Try either the Hoboken, New Jersey, location (take the PATH train) or Greenwich, Connecticut (Metro-North from Grand Central). Agents will pick you up at the station. Call for locations within the five boroughs.

## Parking

If you drive to NYC, find a garage, park your car and leave it there. Parking on the street is subject to byzantine restrictions (for information on alternate-side-of-the-street parking, call 212-225-5368), ticketing is rampant (if you can't decipher the parking signs, find another spot), and car theft is common. Garages are plentiful but expensive. If you want to park for less than $15 a day, try a garage outside Manhattan and take public transportation in. Listed below are Manhattan's better deals. For other options—there are many—try the Yellow Pages. *(See also* **Driving**, *page 359.)*

### GMC Park Plaza

*407 E 61st St between First and York Aves (212-838-4158, main office 212-888-7400). 7am–2am.*
GMC has more than 70 locations in the city. At $22 overnight, including tax, this location is the least expensive.

### Kinney System Inc.

*212-502-5490.*
One of the city's largest parking companies, Kinney is accessible and reliable, though not the cheapest in town. Rates vary, so call for prices.

### Mayor Parking

*Pier 40, West St at Houston St. (800-494-7007). 24hrs.*
Mayor Parking offers indoor ($15 for 12 hours) and outdoor parking. Call for information.

## By train

Thanks to Americans' love affair with the automobile, passenger trains are not as common here as in other parts of the world. American rails are used primarily for cargo, and passenger trains from New York are used mostly by commuters. For longer hauls, call **Amtrak** (*see also chapter* **Trips Out of Town**).

## Train service

### Amtrak

*800-872-7245; www.amtrak.com.*
Amtrak provides all long-distance train service in North America. Traveling by Amtrak is more comfortable than by bus, but it's also more expensive (a sleeper costs more than flying) and less flexible. All trains depart from Penn Station.

### Long Island Rail Road

*718-217-5477; www.lirr.org.*
LIRR provides rail service to Long Island from Penn Station, Brooklyn and Queens.

### Metro-North

*212-532-4900, 800-638-7646; www.mnr.org.*
Commuter trains leave from Grand Central Terminal and service towns north of Manhattan.

### New Jersey Transit

See page 356.

### PATH Trains

*800-234-7284; www.pathrail.com.*
PATH (Port Authority Trans Hudson) trains run from five stations in Manhattan to various places across the Hudson River in New Jersey, including Hoboken, Jersey City and Newark. The system is fully automated and costs $1.50 per trip. You need change or crisp bills for the ticket machines, and trains run 24 hours a day. Manhattan PATH stations are marked on the subway map *(see page 409)*.

## Train stations

### Grand Central Terminal

*42nd–44th Sts between Vanderbilt and Lexington Aves. Subway: S, 4, 5, 6, 7 to 42nd St–Grand Central.*
Grand Central is home to Metro-North, which runs trains to more than 100 stations throughout New York State and Connecticut (*see chapter* **Trips Out of Town**).

### Penn Station

*31st–33rd Sts between Seventh and Eighth Aves. Subway: A, C, E, 1, 2, 3, 9 to 34th St–Penn Station.*
Amtrak, Long Island Rail Road and New Jersey Transit trains depart from this terminal.

## To and from the airport

For a list of transportation services between New York City and its three airports, call **800-AIR-RIDE** *(800-247-7433)*. Public transportation is the cheapest method, but often frustrating and time-consuming. Private bus services are usually the best bargain. Medallion (city-licensed) yellow cabs line up at designated locations. You may also reserve a car service in advance to pick you up or drop you off *(see* **Taxis & car services**, *page 360).* Although it is illegal, many car-service drivers and non-licensed "gypsy cabs" solicit riders around the baggage-claim areas. Avoid them.

## Airports

### John F. Kennedy International Airport

*718-244-4444; www.panynj.gov.*
There's a subway link from JFK (extremely cheap at $1.50), but it can take up to two hours to get to Manhattan. Wait for the yellow shuttle bus to the Howard Beach station and take the A train to Manhattan. (Currently, a light-rail system called AirTrain is under construction and will link all eight terminals with the subway and LIRR sometime in 2003.) Private bus services are often more pleasant and affordable *(see listings below).* A medallion yellow cab from JFK to Manhattan is a flat $35 fare, plus toll (varies by route, but usually $3.50) and tip (if service is fair, give at least $5). There is no set fare to JFK from Manhattan; depending on traffic, it can be as high as $45. Or try a car service for around $40.

### La Guardia Airport

*718-476-5000; www.panynj.gov.*
Seasoned New Yorkers take the **M60 bus** ($1.50), which runs between the airport and 106th Street at Broadway. The ride takes 20 to 40 minutes (depending on traffic) and runs from 5am to 1am. The route crosses Manhattan on 125th Street in Harlem; you can get off at Lexington Avenue for the 4, 5 and 6 trains; at Malcolm X Boulevard (Lenox Avenue) for the 2 and 3; or at St. Nicholas Avenue for the A, C, B and D trains. You can also disembark on Broadway at the 116th Street–Columbia University or 110th Street–Cathedral Parkway subway stations for the 1 and 9 trains. Other less time-consuming options: Private bus services cost around $14 *(see listings below);* taxis and car services charge about $25 plus toll and tip.

### Newark Liberty International Airport

*973-961-6000; www.newarkairport.com*
Although it's a bit far afield, Newark isn't difficult to get to and from. The best bet is a 40-minute trip by train and monorail *(www.airtrainnewark.com).* In the fall of 2001, the Port Authority completed a $415 million link that connects the airport's monorail, AirTrain Newark, to the New Jersey Transit and Amtrak train systems. For $11.55, you can ride to or from Penn Station *(see page 357).* Another economical way to the airport is by bus *(see listings below).* A car service will run about $40 and a taxi around $45, plus toll and tip.

### MacArthur Airport

*631-467-3210; www.macarthurairport.com.*
This airport is located in Islip on Long Island. Some flights into this airport may be cheaper than flying into those above. Getting to Manhattan, of course, will take longer and is more expensive. Colonial Transportation *(631-589-3500)* will take up to four people to Manhattan for $129.50, including tolls and tip. Visit the airport's website for other alternatives.

## Bus services

### New York Airport Service

*212-875-8200; www.nyairportservice.com.*
This service operates frequently to and from JFK ($13 one-way, $23 round-trip) and La Guardia ($10 one-way, $17 round-trip) from early morning to late at night, with stops near Grand Central *(Park Ave between 41st and 42nd Sts),* near Penn Station *(33rd St at Seventh Ave),* inside the Port Authority terminal *(see* **By bus**, *page 356)* and outside a number of midtown hotels (for an extra charge).

### Olympia Trails

*212-964-6233, 877-894-9155; www.olympiabus.com.*
Olympia operates between the following: Newark Airport, outside Penn Station *(34th St at Eighth Ave),* Grand Central *(41st St between Park and Lexington Aves)* and inside Port Authority *(see page 356).* The fare is $12 one-way ($19 round-trip) and buses leave every 15 to 20 minutes all day and night.

### SuperShuttle

*212-209-7000; www.supershuttle.com.*
Blue SuperShuttle vans offer 24-hour door-to-door service between NYC and the three major airports. Allow extra time when catching a flight, as vans will be picking up other passengers. The fare varies from $15 to $19, depending on pickup location and destination.

## Holidays

Most banks and government offices close on these major U.S. holidays (except Election Day), but stores, restaurants and some museums are usually open. If you will be in New York during or around a holiday, call ahead to the venues you want to visit to check for special hours.

**New Year's Day**
January 1

**Martin Luther King Jr. Day** third Monday in January

**Presidents' Day**
third Monday in February

**Memorial Day**
last Monday in May

**Independence Day**
July 4

**Labor Day**
first Monday in September

**Columbus Day**
second Monday in October

**Election Day**
first Tuesday after first Monday in November

**Veterans' Day**
November 11

**Thanksgiving Day**
fourth Thursday in November

**Christmas Day**
December 25

# Getting Around

Under normal circumstances, New York City is easy to navigate. However, subway changes can occur at the last minute, so pay attention to the posters on station walls and listen carefully to any announcements you may hear in trains and on subway platforms.

### Metropolitan Transportation Authority (MTA)

*Travel info 718-330-1234, hourly updates 718-243-7777; www.mta.info.* The MTA runs the subways and buses, as well as a number of the commuter services to points outside Manhattan. You can download the most current maps and news of service interruptions from its website.

## Buses

MTA buses are fine, but only if you aren't in a hurry. If your feet hurt from walking around, a bus is a good way to continue your sightseeing. They're white and blue with a route number (in Manhattan, look for the ones that begin with an M) and a digital destination sign. The fare is payable either with a token or **MetroCard** *(see* **Subways**, *below)*, or in exact change (silver coins only). Express buses usually head to the outer boroughs; these cost $3.

MetroCards allow automatic transfers from bus to bus and between buses and subways. If you use coins or a token, and you're traveling uptown or downtown and want to catch a crosstown bus (or vice versa), ask the driver for a transfer when you get on—you'll be given a ticket for use on the second leg of your journey. You can rely on other passengers for advice, but maps are posted on most buses and at all subway stations; they're also available from **NYC & Company** *(see page 375)*. The Manhattan Bus Map is reprinted in this guide, see page 408. Buses make only designated stops, but between 10pm and 5am you can ask the driver to stop anywhere along the route. All buses are equipped with wheelchair lifts. Contact the MTA *(see above)* for further information.

## Driving

Manhattan drivers are fearless, and taking to the streets is not for the faint of heart. If you're going to be tooling around the city, try to restrict your driving to evening hours, when traffic is lighter and there's more street parking available. Even then, keep your eyes on the road and stay alert. New York will honor all valid foreign driver's licenses.

### Parking

Make sure you read the parking signs and never park within 15 feet (5 meters) of a fire hydrant (to avoid getting a $105 ticket). Parking is off-limits on most streets for at least a few hours each day. Even where meters exist (either single-space or multi-space), daytime parking can be restricted. The **Department of Transportation** *(212-225-5368)* provides information on daily changes to parking regulations. If precautions fail, call 212-971-0770 for car towing and impoundment information *(see also* **Parking**, *page 357)*.

### Towing

#### Citywide Towing

*514 W 39th St between Tenth and Eleventh Aves (212-244-4420). 24hrs. Repairs 9am–6pm. AmEx, MC, V.* All types of repairs are made on foreign and domestic autos.

### 24-hour gas stations

#### Amoco

*610 Broadway at Houston St (212-473-5924). AmEx, DC, Disc, MC, V.* No repairs.

#### Hess

*502 W 45th St at Tenth Ave (212-245-6594). AmEx, Disc, MC, V.* No repairs.

#### Shell

*2420 Amsterdam Ave at 181st St (212-928-3100). AmEx, Disc, MC, V.* Repairs.

## Subways

Subways are the fastest way to get around town during the day, and they're cleaner and safer than they've been in 20 years. The city's system is one of the world's largest and cheapest—$1.50 will get you from the depths of Brooklyn to the northernmost reaches of the Bronx, and anywhere in between (the fare may increase to $1.75 or $2 in 2003). Trains run around the clock, but with sparse service and fewer riders at night, it's advisable (and usually quicker) to take a cab after 10pm.

Ongoing improvements have resulted in several changes. This guide has the most current subway map at press time *(see pages 409–411)* but you can also ask MTA workers in token booths for a free map.

To ensure safety, don't stand close to the edge of the platform, and board the train during nonrush hours from the off-peak waiting area, marked at the center of every platform (this area is safer because it's monitored by cameras; it's also where the conductor's car often stops). More advice: Hold your bag with the opening facing you, and don't wear flashy jewelry.

## MetroCards & tokens

Entry to the system requires a MetroCard or a token costing $1.50 (both also work on buses), which you can buy from a booth inside the station entrance. Many stations are equipped with brightly colored MetroCard vending machines that accept cash, debit cards and credit cards *(AmEx, Disc, MC, V)*.

If you're planning to use the subway or buses often, it's worth buying a MetroCard, which is also sold at some stores and hotels. Free transfers between subways and buses are available only with the MetroCard. There are two types: **pay-per-use cards** and **unlimited-ride cards**. Any number of passengers can use a pay-per-use card, which starts at $3 for two trips and runs as high as $80. A $15 card offers 11 trips for the price of 10. The unlimited-ride MetroCard (an incredible value for frequent users) is offered in three amounts: a 1-day **Fun Pass** ($4, available at station vending machines but not at booths), a **7-day pass** ($17) and a **30-day pass** ($63). These are good for unlimited rides on subways and buses, but can only be used once every 18 minutes (so just one person can use the card per trip).

## Subway lines

Trains are known by letters or numbers and are color-coded according to the line on which they run. Stations are named after the street at which they're located. Entrances are marked with a green globe or a red globe (which marks an entrance that is not always open). Many stations (and most of the local stops) have separate entrances to the uptown and downtown platforms—look before you pay *(see* **Walking**, *page 361,* for an explanation of the city's streets). Express trains run between major stops; local trains stop at every station. Check a subway map (posted in all stations; *see also pages 409–411*) before you board. Be sure to look for posted notices indicating temporary changes to a particular line.

# Taxis & car services

## Taxicabs

Yellow cabs are hardly ever in short supply—except in the rain and at around 4 or 5pm, when rush hour gets going and many cabbies—annoyingly—end their shifts. If the center light on top of the taxi is lit, it means the cab is available and should stop if you flag it down. Jump in and *then* tell the driver where you're going (New Yorkers give cross streets, not building numbers).

Taxis carry up to four people for the same price: $2 plus 30¢ per fifth of a mile, with an extra 50¢ charge after 8pm. This makes the average fare for a three-mile (4.5km) ride $5 to $7, depending on traffic and time of day. Cabbies rarely allow more than four passengers in a cab (it's illegal), though it may be worth asking. Smoking in cabs is prohibited, but not everyone obeys.

Some cabbies' knowledge of the farther reaches of the city is lamentably meager, so it helps if you know where you're going—and speak up. By law, taxis cannot refuse to take you anywhere inside the city limits (the five boroughs), so don't be duped by a cabbie who is too lazy to drive you to Brooklyn or the airport. In general, tip a buck; if the fare is high, 15 percent. If you have a problem, take down the medallion number and driver's number that are posted on the partition. Or ask for a receipt—there's a meter number on it. To complain or trace lost property, call the **Taxi and Limousine Commission** *(212-692-8294, Mon–Fri 9am–5pm)*.

Late at night, cabs stick to fast-flowing routes and reliably lucrative areas. Try the avenues and key streets (Canal, Houston, 14th, 23rd, 34th, 42nd, 57th, 72nd, 86th). Bridge and tunnel exits are also good for a steady flow returning from the airports, and passengerless cabbies will usually head for nightclubs and big hotels. Otherwise, try the following:

### Chinatown

Chatham Square, where Mott Street meets the Bowery, is an unofficial taxi stand. You can also try hailing a cab exiting the Manhattan Bridge at the Bowery and Canal Street.

### Lincoln Center

The crowd heads toward Columbus Circle for a cab; those in the know go to Amsterdam Avenue.

### Lower East Side

Katz's Deli *(Houston St at Ludlow St)* is a cabbies' hangout; otherwise, try Delancey Street, where cabs come in over the Williamsburg Bridge.

### Midtown

Penn Station and Grand Central Terminal attract cabs through the night, as does the Port Authority Bus Terminal.

### Soho

If you're on the west side, try Sixth Avenue; east side, the gas station on Houston Street at Broadway.

### Times Square

This busy area has 30 taxi stands—look for the yellow globes atop nine-foot poles.

### Tribeca

Cabs here (many arriving from the Holland Tunnel) head up Hudson Street. Canal Street is also a good bet.

## Car services

Car services are also regulated by the Taxi and Limousine Commission *(see above)*. What makes them different from a cab is that they aren't yellow and they can only offer prearranged pickups. Don't try to hail one and be wary of those that offer you a ride; they may not be licensed or insured and you might get ripped off. (If you see a black Lincoln Town Car, it's most likely a car service; to be certain, look for a license plate that begins with the letter T.)

The following companies will pick you up anywhere in the city, at any time of day or night, for a prearranged fare.

### Carmel
*212-666-6666*

### Sabra
*212-777-7171*

### Tel Aviv
*212-777-7777*

### Tri-State Limousine
*212-410-7600*

## Walking

One of the best ways to take in NYC is on foot. Most of the streets are part of a grid system and are relatively easy to navigate. Our maps *(see pages 394–401)* make it even easier. Manhattan is divided into three major sections: **downtown**, or all neighborhoods south of 14th Street; **midtown**, roughly the area from 14th to 59th Street; and **uptown**, or the rest of the island north of 59th Street.

Generally, avenues run along the length of Manhattan from south to north. They are parallel to one another and are logically numbered with a few exceptions (such as Broadway, Columbus and Lexington Avenues). Manhattan's center is Fifth Avenue, so all buildings located east of it will have "East" addresses, with numbers going higher toward the East River, and those west of it will have "West" numbers that go higher toward the Hudson River. Streets also run parallel to each other but they run east to west, or **crosstown**, and are numbered, beginning with 1st Street (a block north of East Houston Street), up to 220th Street. Almost all even-numbered streets run east and odd streets run west (the major crosstown streets, such as 42nd Street, are two-way).

The neighborhoods that define lower Manhattan—the **Financial District**, **Tribeca**, **Chinatown**, **Soho** and **Greenwich Village**—were settled prior to urban planning and can be confusing to walk through (but it's worth the effort, because they have some of the most scenic blocks). These streets lack logical organization, so it is best to use a map *(see pages 394–401)*, or ask a passerby for directions.

# Resources A to Z

## Age restrictions

In most cases, you must be at least 25 years old to rent a car in the U.S. You must be 18 to buy tobacco products and 21 to buy and be served alcohol. Some bars and clubs will allow admittance to patrons who are 18, but you will be removed from the establishment if you are caught drinking alcohol (carry a picture ID at all times). The age of consent for both heterosexuals and homosexuals is 17. You must be 18 to purchase pornography and other adult material, and also to play the lottery or gamble (where the law allows).

## Baby-sitting

### Avalon Nurse Registry & Child Service
*212-245-0250. Mon–Fri 8am–5:30pm; Sat, Sun 9am–8pm. AmEx, MC, V.*

Avalon provides baby nurses and sitters (four-hour minimum) for between $16 and $20 per hour, plus travel expenses.

### Babysitters' Guild
*212-682-0227; www.babysittersguild.com. 9am–9pm. Cash or traveler's checks.*

Long- or short-term multilingual babysitters cost $15 and up per hour (four-hour minimum). Sitters are available round the clock.

### Manhattan Tree House
*148 W 83rd St between Columbus and Amsterdam Aves (212-712-0113). Subway: B, C to 81st St–Museum of Natural History. 7:30am–9pm. AmEx, MC, V.*

Kids ages 6 months and up can have a night out at this drop-off center, which offers dinner and snacks, movies, face-painting and the like ($38 for three hours and $52 for five).

### Pinch Sitters
*212-260-6005. Mon–Fri 8am–5pm. Cash only.*

Charges are $14 per hour (four-hour minimum) plus travel fees after 9pm.

## Computers

There are hundreds of computer dealers in Manhattan. You might want to buy out of state to avoid the hefty sales tax. Many out-of-state dealers advertise in New York papers and magazines *(see also* **Cameras & electronics**, *page 236)*. Here are reliable places if you're just looking to rent:

### Fitch Graphics
*25 W 45th St between Fifth and Sixth Aves (212-840-3091). Subway: B, D, F, V to 42nd St; 7 to Fifth Ave. Mon–Fri 7:30am–2am. AmEx, MC, V.*

Fitch is a full-service desktop-publishing outfit, with color-laser output and prepress facilities. Fitch works on Mac and Windows platforms and has a bulletin board so customers can reach the shop online.

### Kinko's
*240 Central Park South at Broadway (212-258-3750, 800-2-KINKOS).*

*Subway: A, C, B, D, 1, 9 to 59th St–Columbus Circle. 24hrs. AmEx, Disc, MC, V.*
This is a very efficient, friendly place to use computers and copiers. Most branches have Windows and Macintosh workstations and design stations, plus all the major software. Color output is available, as are laptop hookups and Internet connections ($18 per hour, 49¢ per printed page). Check the phone book for other locations.

### USRental.com

*212-594-2222; www.usrental.com. Mon–Fri 8:30am–5pm. Call for appointment. AmEx, MC, V.*
Rent by the day, week, month or year. A range of computers, systems and networks, including IBM, Compaq, Macintosh and Hewlett-Packard, is on hand. Rush delivery service (within three hours) is also available.

## Consulates

Check the phone book for a complete list of consulates and embassies. *See also* **Travel advice**, *page 376.*

### Australia

*212-351-6500*

### Canada

*212-596-1700*

### Great Britain

*212-745-0200*

### Ireland

*212-319-2555*

### New Zealand

*212-832-4038*

## Consumer information

### Better Business Bureau

*212-533-6200; www.newyork.bbb.org*
The BBB offers advice on consumer-related complaints (shopping, services, etc.). Each phone inquiry costs $4.30 (including New York City tax) and must be charged to a credit card; the online version is free.

### New York City Department of Consumer Affairs

*42 Broadway between Beaver St and Exchange Pl (212-487-4444). Subway: 4, 5 to Bowling Green. Mon, Tue, Thu, Fri 9am–5pm; Wed 9am–5:30pm.*
This is where you go to file complaints on consumer-related matters.

## Customs & immigration

When planning your trip, check with a U.S. embassy or consulate to see if you need a visa to enter the country *(see* **Visas**, *page 376).* Standard immigration regulations apply to all visitors arriving from outside the United States, which means you may have to wait at least an hour in customs upon arrival. Due to tightened security at all American airports, expect even slower-moving lines. During your flight, you will be handed an immigration form and a customs-declaration form to be presented to an official when you land.

You may be expected to explain your visit, so be polite and prepared. You will usually be granted an entry permit to cover the length of your stay. Work permits are hard to get, and you are not permitted to work without one *(see* **Students**, *page 373).*

U.S. Customs allows foreigners to bring in $100 worth of gifts ($800 for Americans) before paying duty. One carton of 200 cigarettes (or 50 cigars) and one liter of liquor (spirits) are allowed. No plants, meat or fresh produce can be brought into the country. If you carry more than $10,000 in currency, you will have to fill out a report.

If you must bring prescription drugs into the U.S., make sure the container is clearly marked and that you bring your doctor's statement or a prescription. Marijuana, cocaine and most opiate derivatives, and other chemicals are not permitted. Possession of them is punishable by stiff fines and/or imprisonment. Check with the U.S. Customs Service *(www.customs.gov)* before you arrive if you have any questions about what you can bring. If you lose or need to renew your passport once inside the U.S., contact your country's embassy *(see* **Consulates**, *above).*

### Student immigration

Upon entering the U.S. as a student, you will need to show a passport, a special visa and proof of your plans to leave (such as a return airline ticket). Even if you have a student visa, you may be asked to show means of support during your stay (cash, credit cards, traveler's checks, etc.).

Before they can apply for a visa, nonnationals who want to study in the U.S. must obtain an I-20 Certificate of Eligibility from the school or university they plan to attend. If you are enrolling in an authorized visitor-exchange program, including a summer course or program, wait until you have been accepted by the course or program before worrying about immigration. You will be guided through the process by the school.

You are admitted as a student for the length of your course, in addition to a limited period for a year's worth of associated (and approved) practical training, plus a 60-day grace period. When your time is up, you must leave the country, or apply to change or extend your immigration status. Requests to extend »a visa must be submitted 15 to 60 days before the initial departure date. The rules are strict, and you risk deportation if you break them.

Information on these and all other immigration matters is available from the **U.S. Immigration and Naturalization Service (INS)**. The agency's 24-hour hot line *(800-375-5283)* is a vast menu of recorded information in English and Spanish; advisers are available from 8am to 6pm, Monday through Friday. You can visit the INS at its New York office located in the Jacob Javits Federal Building *(26 Federal Plaza, Broadway between Duane and Worth Sts, third floor).* The office is open 7:30am to 3:30pm, Monday through Friday, and cannot be reached directly by telephone.

The **U.S. Embassy** also offers guidance on obtaining student visas *(visa information in the U.S., 202-663-1225; in the U.K., 0-207-499-9000; www.travel.state.gov).* Or you can write to the Visa Branch of the Embassy of the United States of America, 5 Upper Grosvenor Street, London W1A 2J.

When you apply for your student visa, you'll be expected to prove your ability to support yourself financially (including the payment of school fees), without working, for at least the first full academic year of your studies. After those nine months, you may be eligible to work part-time, but you must have specific permission to do so.

If you are a student from the U.K. who wants to spend a summer vacation working in the States, contact **BUNAC** (British Universities North America Club) for help in arranging a temporary job and the requisite visa *(16 Bowling Green Lane, London EC1R 0QH; 0-20-7251-3472; www.bunac.org/uk).*

# Weather or not

## Rain or shine, New York City is mighty fine

Here are the average high and low temperatures, the number of days with precipitation, and the number of sunny days in NYC—but remember, there's always something to do indoors when it's too nasty to wander around outside.

| | Temperature | | Rain/Snow | Sun |
|---|---|---|---|---|
| | Hi ˚F/˚C | Low ˚F/˚C | Days | Days |
| Jan | 38/3 | 27/-4 | 11 | 8 |
| Feb | 40/4 | 28/-3 | 10 | 8 |
| Mar | 50/9 | 36/2 | 11 | 9 |
| Apr | 60/16 | 45/7 | 11 | 8 |
| May | 71/21 | 55/13 | 11 | 8 |
| Jun | 80/26 | 64/18 | 10 | 8 |
| Jul | 85/29 | 70/21 | 11 | 8 |
| Aug | 83/28 | 69/19 | 10 | 9 |
| Sept | 76/24 | 62/17 | 8 | 11 |
| Oct | 66/18 | 50/9 | 8 | 12 |
| Nov | 54/12 | 43/6 | 9 | 9 |
| Dec | 43/6 | 32/-1 | 10 | 9 |

**Source:** National Weather Service

## Disabled access

Under New York City law, all facilities constructed after 1987 must provide complete access to the disabled—rest rooms and entrances/exits included. In 1990, the Americans with Disabilities Act made the same requirement federal law. In the wake of this legislation, many owners of older buildings have voluntarily added disabled-access features. Due to widespread compliance with the law, we have not specifically noted the availability of disabled facilities in our listings. However, it's a good idea to call ahead and check.

Despite its best efforts, New York can be a challenging city for a disabled visitor, but support and guidance are readily available. One useful resource is the **Hospital Audiences Inc.**'s *(212-575-7660)* guide to New York's cultural institutions, *Access for All (www.hospaud.org).* The online guide tells how accessible each place really is, and includes information on the height of telephones and water fountains, hearing and visual aids, passenger-loading zones and alternative entrances. HAI also has a service for the visually impaired that provides descriptions of theater performances on audiocassettes.

All Broadway theaters are equipped with devices for the hearing impaired; call **Sound Associates** *(212-582-7678, 888-772-SOUND)* for more information. There are a number of other stage-related resources for the disabled. Call **Telecharge** *(212-239-6200)* to reserve tickets for wheelchair seating in Broadway and Off Broadway venues. **Theater Development Fund's Theater Access Project** (TAP) arranges sign language interpretation and captioning for Broadway and Off Broadway shows *(212-221-1103, 212-719-4537; www.tdf.org).* **Hands On** *(212-822-8550)* does the same.

In addition, the nonprofit organization **Big Apple Greeter** *(see page 133)* will help any person with disabilities enjoy New York City.

### Lighthouse International

*111 E 59th St between Park and Lexington Aves (212-821-9200, 800-829-0500). Subway: N, R, W to Lexington Ave–59th St; 4, 5, 6 to 59th St. Mon–Fri 10am–6pm; Sat 10am–5pm.*

In addition to running a store that

sells handy items for sight-impaired people, this organization provides the blind with info to help deal with living or vacationing in New York City.

### Mayor's Office for People with Disabilities

*100 Gold St between Frankfort and Spruce Sts, second floor (212-788-2830). Subway: J, M, Z to Chambers St; 4, 5, 6 to Brooklyn Bridge–City Hall. Mon–Fri 9am–5pm.*

This municipal office provides a broad range of services for disabled people.

### New York Society for the Deaf

*161 Williams St between Ann and Beekman Sts (212-777-3900). Subway: 4, 5 to Fulton St. Mon–Thu 9am–5pm; Fri 8am–4:30pm.*

The deaf and hearing-impaired come here for information and services.

### The Society for Accessible Travel and Hospitality

*347 Fifth Ave between 33rd and 34th Sts, suite 610 (212-447-7284; fax 212-725-8253; www.sath.org). Subway: B, D, F, V, N, Q, R, W to 34th St–Herald Sq.*

This nonprofit group was founded in 1976 to educate people about travel facilities for the disabled, and to promote travel for the disabled worldwide. Membership is $45 a year ($30 for seniors and students) and includes access to an information service and a quarterly travel magazine. No drop-ins; membership by mail only.

## Electricity

The U.S. uses 110–120V, 60-cycle AC current, rather than the 220–240V, 50-cycle AC used in Europe and elsewhere. With the exception of a dual-voltage, flat-pin plug shaver, any foreign-bought appliance will require an adapter. They're available at airport shops and some pharmacies and department stores.

## Emergencies

*See also* **Travel advice**, *page 376.*

### Ambulance

In an emergency only, dial **911** for an ambulance or call the operator (dial **0**). To complain about slow service or poor treatment, call the **Fire Dept. Complaint Hot Line** (718-999-2646).

### Fire

In an emergency only, dial **911**. See above for complaint line.

### Police

In an emergency only, dial **911**. For the location of the nearest police precinct, or for general information about police services, call 646-610-5000 or 718-610-5000.

## Health & medical facilities

The public health-care system is practically nonexistent in the United States, and the cost of private health care is exorbitant. If at all possible, make sure you have comprehensive medical insurance when you travel to New York.

### Clinics

Walk-in clinics offer treatment for minor ailments. Most require immediate payment, though some will send their bill directly to your insurance company. You will have to file a claim to recover the cost of prescription medication.

#### D•O•C•S

*55 E 34th St between Madison Ave and Park Ave South (212-252-6000). Subway: 6 to 33rd St. Walk-in Mon–Thu 8am–8pm; Fri 8am–7pm; Sat 9am–3pm; Sun 9am–2pm. Extended hours by appointment. Base fee $80–$290. AmEx, Disc, MC, V.*

These excellent primary-care facilities, affiliated with Beth Israel Medical Center, offer by-appointment and walk-in services. If you need X rays or lab tests, go as early as possible—no later than 6pm, Monday through Friday.

**Other locations** • *202 W 23rd St at Seventh Ave (212-352-2600). Subway: 1, 9 to 23rd St.* • *1555 Third Ave at 88th St (212-828-2300). Subway: 4, 5, 6 to 86th St.*

### Dentists

#### NYU College of Dentistry

*345 E 24th St between First and Second Aves (212-998-9872, off-hours emergency care 212-998-9828). Subway: 6 to 23rd St. Mon–Thu 8:30am–6:45pm; Fri 8:30am–4pm. Base fee $90. Disc, MC, V.*

If you need your teeth fixed on a budget, you can become a guinea pig for final-year students. They're slow but proficient, and an experienced dentist is always on hand to supervise. Go before 2pm to ensure a same-day visit.

### Emergency rooms

You will be billed for emergency treatment. Call your travel-insurance company's emergency number before seeking treatment to find out which hospitals accept your insurance. Emergency rooms are always open at:

#### Bellevue Hospital

*462 First Ave at 27th St (212-562-4141). Subway: 6 to 28th St.*

#### Cabrini Medical Center

*227 E 19th St between Second and Third Aves (212-995-6000). Subway: L, N, Q, R, W, 4, 5, 6 to 14th St–Union Sq.*

#### Mount Sinai Hospital

*Madison Ave at 100th St (212-241-7171). Subway: 6 to 103rd St.*

#### Roosevelt Hospital

*1000 Tenth Ave at 59th St (212-523-6800). Subway: A, C, B, D, 1, 9 to 59th St–Columbus Circle.*

#### St. Vincent's Hospital

*153 W 11th St at Seventh Ave (212-604-7998). Subway: F, V, L to Sixth Ave; 1, 2, 3, 9 to 14th St.*

### Gay & lesbian health

See chapter **Gay & Lesbian**.

### House calls

#### NY Hotel Urgent Medical Services

*3 E 76th St at Fifth Ave (212-737-1212; www.travelmd.com). Subway: 6 to 77th St. 24hrs. Weekday hotel-visit fee $200–$300; weekday office-visit fee $55–$155. Rates increase at night and on weekends.*

Dr. Ronald Primas and his partners provide medical attention right in your Manhattan hotel room or private residence. Whether you need a simple prescription or an internal examination, this service can provide a specialist. In-office appointments are also available (call for office hours).

## Pharmacies

See also **Pharmacists**, page 232.

### Duane Reade

*224 W 57th St at Broadway (212-541-9708). Subway: N, Q, R, W to 57th St. 24hrs. AmEx, MC, V.*

This chain operates all over the city, and some stores offer 24-hour service. Check the phone book for additional locations.

**Other 24-hour locations** ● *378 Sixth Ave at Waverly Pl (212-674-5357). Pharmacy 8am–9pm. Subway: A, C, E, F, V, S to W 4th St.* ● *1279 Third Ave at 74th St (212-744-2668). Subway: 6 to 77th St.* ● *2465 Broadway at 91st St (212-799-3172). Subway: 1, 2, 3, 9 to 96th St.*

### Rite Aid

*303 W 50th St at Eighth Ave (212-247-8736; www.riteaid.com). Subway: C, E to 50th St. 24hrs. AmEx, Disc, MC, V.*

Select locations have 24-hour pharmacies. Call 800-RITE-AID for a complete listing.

**Other 24-hour locations** ● *542 Second Ave at 31st St (212-213-9887). Subway: 6 to 33rd St. Pharmacy 8am–9pm.* ● *210 Amsterdam Ave between 69th and 70th Sts (212-873-7965). Subway: 1, 2, 3, 9 to 72nd St.* ● *144 E 86th St between Lexington and Third Aves (212-876-0600). Subway: 4, 5, 6 to 86th St.* ● *2833 Broadway at 110th St (212-663-8252). Subway: 1, 9 to 110th St–Cathedral Pkwy.*

## Women's health

### Liberty Women's Health Care of Queens

*37-01 Main St at 37th Ave, Flushing, Queens (718-888-0018). Subway: 7 to Flushing–Main St. By appointment only. AmEx, MC, V.*

This facility provides both surgical and nonsurgical abortions for up to 24 weeks of pregnancy. Unlike other clinics, Liberty uses abdominal ultrasound before, during and after the abortion to ensure safety.

### Park Med Eastern Women's Center

*44 E 30th St between Madison Ave and Park Ave South, fifth floor (212-686-6066). Subway: 6 to 28th St. By appointment only. AmEx, Disc, MC, V.*

Urine pregnancy tests are free. Abortion and counseling are also available.

### Planned Parenthood of New York City

*Margaret Sanger Center, 26 Bleecker St at Mott St (212-274-7200; www.ppnyc.org). Subway: F, V, S to Broadway–Lafayette St; 6 to Bleecker St. Mon 8am–5pm; Tue–Fri 8am–6pm; Sat 7:30am–5pm.*

This is the main branch of the best-known, most reasonably priced network of family planning clinics in the U.S. Counseling and treatment are available for a full range of gynecological needs, including abortion, treatment of STDs, HIV testing and contraception. Phone for an appointment or for more information on services. Call 212-965-7000 to make an appointment at any of three centers (the others are in the Bronx and Brooklyn). No walk-ins.

# Help lines

## Alcohol & drug abuse

### Alcoholics Anonymous

*212-647-1680. 9am–2am.*

### Cocaine Anonymous

*212-262-2463. 24-hour recorded info.*

### Drug Abuse Information Line

*800-522-5353. 8am–10pm.*

This program refers callers to recovery programs around the state.

### Pills Anonymous

*212-874-0700. 24-hour recorded info.*

You'll find information on drug-recovery programs for users of marijuana, cocaine, alcohol and other addictive substances, as well as referrals to Narcotics Anonymous meetings. You can also leave a message if you wish to have a counselor speak to you directly.

## Child abuse

### Childhelp USA's National Child Abuse Hotline

*800-422-4453. 24hrs.*

Counselors provide general crisis consultation, and can help in an emergency. Callers include abused children, runaways and parents having problems with children.

## Gay & Lesbian

See chapter **Gay & Lesbian**.

## Health

Visit the **Center for Disease Control** (CDC) website *(www.cdc.gov)* for up-to-date national health information or call one of its toll-free hot lines listed below.

### HIV & AIDS Hot Line

*800-342-2437. 24hrs.*

### STD Hot Line

*800-227-8922. 24hrs.*

### Travelers' Health

*877-FYI-TRIP. 24hrs.*

## Psychological services

### Center for Inner Resource Development

*212-734-5876. 24hrs.*

Therapists will talk to you day or night, and are trained to deal with all kinds of emotional problems, including those resulting from rape.

### Help Line

*212-532-2400. 24hrs.*

Trained volunteers will talk to anyone contemplating suicide, and will also help with other personal problems.

### The Samaritans

*212-673-3000. 24hrs.*

People thinking of committing suicide, or suffering from depression, grief, sexual anxiety or alcoholism, can call this organization for advice.

## Rape & sex crimes

### Safe Horizon Hotline

*212-577-7777. 24hrs.*

SHH offers telephone and one-on-one counseling for any victim of domestic violence, rape or other crime, as well as practical help with court procedures, compensation and legal aid.

### Special Victims Liaison Unit of the New York Police Department

*212-267-7272, rape hot line 212-267-7273. 24hrs.*

Reports of sex crimes are handled by a female detective from the Special Victims Liaison Unit. She will inform the appropriate precinct, send an ambulance if requested and provide counseling and medical referrals. Other issues handled: violence against gays and lesbians, child victimization and referrals for the families and friends of crime victims.

### St. Luke's/Roosevelt Hospital Crime Victims Treatment Center

*212-523-4728. Mon–Fri 9am–5pm, recorded referral message at other times.*

The Rape Crisis Center provides a trained volunteer who will accompany you through all aspects of reporting a rape and getting emergency treatment.

## Holidays

See **Holidays**, page 358.

## Insurance

If you are not an American, it's advisable to take out comprehensive insurance before arriving here; insurance for foreigners is almost impossible to arrange in the U.S. Make sure you have adequate health coverage, since medical costs are high. For a list of New York urgent-care facilities, see **Emergency rooms**, page 364.

## Internet & e-mail

### Cyber Café

*250 W 49th St between Broadway and Eighth Ave (212-333-4109). Subway: C, E to 50th St; N, R, W to 49th St. Mon–Fri 8am–11pm; Sat, Sun 11am–11pm. $6.40 per half hour, 50¢ per printed page.*

This is your standard Internet-connected café, though at least this one serves great coffee.

### Easy Everything

*234 W 42nd St between Seventh and Eighth Aves (212-398-0775). Subway: N, Q, R, W, S, 1, 2, 3, 9, 7 to 42nd St–Times Sq. 24hrs. $1.*

International travelers will recognize this giant Internet café. Its Times Square location has more than 700 PCs and costs $1, which will give you a minimum of 30 minutes and a maximum of four hours based on computer availability.

### Kinko's

See **Computers**, page 361.

### New York Public Library

*See* **Science, Industry and Business Library**, *page 59.*

The 85 branch libraries scattered throughout the five boroughs are a great place to e-mail and surf the Web for free. The few computer stations may make for a long wait, and once you're on, your user time is limited (this location has the longest duration). Check the phone book for the branch nearest you. See also **New York Public Library**, page 58.

### NYC Wireless

*nycwireless.net.*

This group has established 183 nodes in the city for free wireless access. (For example, most parks below 59th Street are covered.) Go to nyc.wireless.net for more information.

### Starbucks

*www.starbucks.com.*

Many branches of the coffeeshop are set up for paid wireless access (20¢ per minute or $29.99 per month).

## Laundry

See also **Wardrobe services**, page 376.

## Dry cleaners

### Madame Paulette Custom Couture Cleaners

*1255 Second Ave between 65th and 66th Sts (212-838-6827). Subway: 6 to 68th St–Hunter College. Mon–Fri 7:30am–7pm; Sat 8am–5pm. AmEx, MC, V.*

This 43-year-old luxury dry cleaners knows how to treat delicate garments. Take advantage of free pickup and delivery throughout Manhattan, and a worldwide shipping service.

### Meurice Garment Care

*31 University Pl between 8th and 9th Sts (212-475-2778). Subway: N, R, W to 8th St–NYU. Mon–Fri 7:30am–7pm; Sat 9am–6pm; Sun 9:30am–3pm. AmEx, MC, V.*

Laundry is serious business here. Meurice's roster of high-profile clients includes Armani and Prada, and the company handles all kinds of tricky stain removal and other repair jobs.

**Other location** • *245 E 57th St between Second and Third Aves (212-759-9057). Subway: N, R, W to Lexington Ave–59th St; 4, 5, 6 to 59th St. Mon–Fri 8am–6:30pm; Sat 9am–3pm. AmEx, MC, V.*

### Midnight Express Cleaners

*212-921-0111, 800-764-3648. Mon–Fri 9am–7pm; AmEx, MC, V.*

Midnight Express will pick up your dry cleaning anywhere below 96th Street at a mutually convenient time and return it to you the next day (that goes for bulk laundry too). It costs $6.95 for a man's suit to be cleaned, including pickup and delivery.

## Self-service laundry

Most neighborhoods have self-service laundries with coin-operated machines, but in New York, it doesn't cost much more to drop off your wash and let someone else do the work. Check the Yellow Pages for specific establishments.

### Ecowash

*72 W 69th St between Central Park West and Columbus Ave (212-787-3890). Subway: B, C to 72nd St; 1, 9 to 66th St–Lincoln Ctr. 7:30am–10pm. Cash only.*

For the green-minded, Ecowash uses only natural, nontoxic detergent. You can wash your own duds, starting at $1.75, or drop off up to seven pounds for $6.50 (each additional pound is 75¢).

## Legal assistance

If you are arrested for a minor violation (disorderly conduct, harassment, loitering, rowdy partying, etc.) and you're very polite to the officer during the arrest (and are carrying proper ID), you'll probably get fingerprinted and photographed at the station and be given a desk-appearance ticket with a date to show up at criminal court. Then you'll most likely get to go home.

Arguing with a police officer or engaging in something more serious (possession of a weapon, drunken driving, gambling or prostitution, for example) might get you processed, which means a 24- to 30-hour journey through the system.

If the courts are backed up (and they usually are), you'll be held temporarily at a precinct pen. You can make a phone call after you've been fingerprinted. When you get through central booking, you'll arrive at 100 Centre Street for arraignment. A judge will decide whether you should be released on bail and will set a court date. If you can't post bail, you'll be held at Rikers Island. The bottom line: Try not to get arrested, and if you are, don't act foolishly.

### Legal Aid Society

*212-577-3300. Mon–Fri 8am–5pm.* Legal Aid gives general information and referrals on legal matters.

### Sandback, Birnbaum & Michelen Criminal Law

*212-517-3200, 800-640-2000. 24hrs.* These are the numbers to have in your head when the cops read you your rights in the middle of the night. If no one at this firm can help you, they'll direct you to lawyers who can.

## Libraries

See **New York Public Library**, page 58, and **Internet & e-mail**, page 366.

## Locksmiths

The following emergency locksmiths are open 24 hours. Both require proof of residency or car ownership plus ID.

### Champion Locksmiths

*16 locations in Manhattan (212-362-7000). $15 service charge day or night, plus $35 minimum to fit a lock. AmEx, Disc, MC, V.*

### Elite Locksmiths

*470 Third Ave between 32nd and 33rd Sts (212-685-1472). Subway: 6 to 33rd St. $45 during the day; $75–$90 at night. Cash and checks only.*

## Lost property

For property lost in the street, contact the police. For lost credit cards or traveler's checks, see **Money** page 368.

### Buses & subways

*New York City Metropolitan Transit Authority, 34th St–Penn Station,*

# Toilet talk

Finding a rest room in the city isn't as easy as finding a hot dog vendor

Visitors to New York are always on the go. But in between all that go, go, go, sometimes you've really got to…go. Contrary to popular belief, the street is no place to drop trou. The real challenge lies in finding a legal public place to take care of your business. Although they don't exactly have an open-door policy, the numerous **McDonald's** restaurants, **Starbucks** coffeeshops and most of the **Barnes & Noble** bookstores contain (usually clean) rest rooms. If the door to the loo is locked, you may have to ask a cashier for the key. Don't announce that you're not a paying customer, and you should be all right. The same applies to most other fast-food joints (**Au Bon Pain**, **Wendy's**, etc.), major stores (**Barney's**, **Macy's**, **Toys R Us**; *see chapter* **Shopping**), and hotels and bars that don't have a host or maître d' at the door. Here are a few other options around town that can offer sweet relief (though you may have to hold your breath at some places).

## Downtown

### Battery Park

Castle Clinton. Subway: 1, 9 to South Ferry; 4, 5 to Bowling Green.

### Kmart

770 Broadway at Astor Pl. Subway: N, R, W to 8th St–NYU; 6 to Astor Pl.

### Tompkins Square Park

Ave A at 9th St. Subway: L to First Ave; 6 to Astor Pl.

### Washington Square Park

Thompson St at Washington Sq South. Subway: A, C, E, F, V, S to W 4th St.

## Midtown

### Grand Central Terminal

42nd St at Park Ave, Lower Concourse. Subway: S, 4, 5, 6, 7 to 42nd St–Grand Central.

### Penn Station

Seventh Ave between 30th and 32nd Sts. Subway: A, C, E, 1, 2, 3, 9 to 34th St–Penn Station.

### St. Clement's Church

423 W 46th St between Ninth and Tenth Aves. Subway: A, C, E to 42nd St–Port Authority.

### United Nations

First Ave between 42nd and 50th Sts. Subway: S, 4, 5, 6, 7 to 42nd St–Grand Central.

## Uptown

### Avery Fisher Hall at Lincoln Center

Broadway at 65th St. Subway: 1, 9 to 66th St–Lincoln Ctr.

### Delacorte Theater in Central Park

Mid-park at 81st St. Subway: B, C to 81st St–Museum of Natural History.

*near the A-train platform (212-712-4500). Mon–Wed, Fri 8am–noon; Thu 11am–6:30pm.*

### Grand Central Terminal

*212-340-2555. Mon–Fri 7am–7pm; Sat, Sun 9am–5pm.*
Call if you've left something on a Metro-North train.

### JFK Airport

*718-244-4444, or contact your airline.*

### La Guardia Airport

*718-533-3400, or contact your airline.*

### Newark Liberty International Airport

*973-961-6230, or contact your airline.*

### Penn Station

*212-630-7389. Mon–Fri 7:30am–4pm.*
Call for items left on Amtrak, New Jersey Transit or the Long Island Rail Road.

### Taxis

*212-692-8294; www.nyc.gov/taxi.*
Call this number if you leave anything in a cab.

## Messenger services

### A to Z Couriers

*105 Rivington St between Essex and Ludlow Sts (212-253-6500). Subway: F to Delancey St; J, M, Z to Delancey–Essex Sts. Mon–Fri 8am–7pm. AmEx, MC, V.*
These cheerful couriers will deliver to anywhere in the city (and Long Island, too).

### Breakaway

*335 W 35th St between Eighth and Ninth Aves (212-947-4455). Subway: A, C, E to 34th St–Penn Station. Mon–Fri 7am–9pm; Sat 9am–5pm; Sun noon–5pm. AmEx, MC, V.*
Breakaway is a highly recommended citywide delivery service that promises to pick up and deliver within the hour. The company employs 200 messengers, so you can take its statement seriously.

### Jefron Messenger Service

*141 Duane St between Church St and West Broadway (212-964-8441; www.jefron.com). Subway: 1, 2, 3, 9 to Chambers St. Mon–Fri 8am–5pm. Cash, checks, money orders only.*
Jefron specializes in transporting import/export documents.

## Money

Over the past few years, a lot of American currency has undergone a subtle face-lift—partly as a national celebration and partly to deter increasingly adept counterfeiters. However, the "old" money is still in circulation. One dollar ($) equals 100 cents (¢). Coins range from copper pennies (1¢) to silver nickels (5¢), dimes (10¢), quarters (25¢) and less common half-dollars (50¢).

In 1999, the U.S. Mint began issuing commemorative "state quarters." George Washington's profile still graces the front, but the reverse (or "tails") side is dedicated to one of the 50 states; each coin is stamped with a corresponding design symbolizing the state's history and achievements. These quarters are being issued in segments of five states per year in the order of state entry into the Union—by 2009 all 50 will be in circulation.

The year 2000 marked the introduction of the "golden dollar." The coin is about one inch in diameter and features a portrait of Sacagawea (the Native American woman who helped guide explorers Lewis and Clark on their journey across America). The new gold coin replaces the older Susan B. Anthony silver dollar, and satisfies a growing need for dollar coins in vending and mass-transit machines. You might still get a Susan B. on occasion—they're increasingly rare and worth holding on to. For more information on U.S. coins, call 800-USA-MINT or visit www.usmint.gov.

Paper money is all the same size and color, so make sure you fork over the right bill. It comes in denominations of $1, $2, $5, $10, $20, $50 and $100 (and higher—but you'll never see those). All denominations, except for the $1 and $2 bills, have recently been updated by the U.S. Treasury, which chose a larger portrait placed off-center with extra security features; the new bills also have a large numeral on the back to help the visually impaired identify the denomination. The $2 bills are quite rare and make a smart souvenir. Small shops will seldom break a $50 or $100 bill, so it is best to carry smaller denominations (and cab drivers aren't required to change bills larger than $20). For more information on paper currency, refer to the U.S. Treasury website at www.ustreas.gov.

### ATMs

New York City is full of automated teller machines (ATMs). Most accept American Express, MasterCard and Visa, among other cards, if they have been registered with a personal identification number (PIN). There is a usage fee, though the convenience (and the superior exchange rate) often makes ATMs worth the extra charge.

Call the following for ATM locations: **Cirrus** *(800-424-7787);* **Plus Systems** *(800-843-7587);* **Wells Fargo** *(800-869-3557).* Also, look for branch banks or delis, which often have mini ATMs by the front counter (the fees for these machines can be steep). If you've lost your number, or your card becomes demagnetized, most banks will give cash to cardholders with proper ID.

### Banks & currency exchange

Banks are generally open from 9am to 3pm Monday through Friday, though some have longer hours. You need photo identification, such as a passport, to cash traveler's checks. Many banks will not exchange foreign currency, and the *bureaux de change,* limited to tourist-trap areas, close between 6 and 7pm. It's best to arrive with a few dollars in cash but to pay mostly with credit cards or traveler's checks (accepted in most restaurants and larger stores, but ask first, and be prepared to show ID). In emergencies, most large hotels offer 24-hour exchange facilities; the catch is that they charge high commissions and don't give good rates.

### Chequepoint USA

*22 Central Park South between Fifth and Sixth Aves (212-750-2400). Subway: N, R, W to Fifth Ave–59th St. 8am–8pm.*

Foreign currency, traveler's checks and bank drafts are available here.

### People's Foreign Exchange

*575 Fifth Ave at 47th St, third floor (212-883-0550). Subway: E, V to Fifth Ave–53rd St; 7 to Fifth Ave. Mon–Fri 9am–6pm; Sat, Sun 10am–3pm.*

People's provides free foreign exchange on banknotes and traveler's checks of larger denominations; a nominal fee is applied to smaller amounts.

### Travelex

*29 Broadway at Morris St (212-363-6206). Subway: 4, 5 to Bowling Green. Mon–Fri 9am–5pm.*

A complete foreign-exchange service is offered.

**Other locations** ● *317 Madison Ave at 42nd St (212-883-0401). Subway: S, 4, 5, 6, 7 to 42nd St–Grand Central.* ● *1590 Broadway at 48th St (212-265-6063). Subway: N, R, W to 49th St; 1, 9 to 50th St.* ● *511 Madison Ave at 53rd St (212-753-2595). Subway: E, V to Fifth Ave–53rd St.*

## Credit cards

Bring plastic if you have it, or be prepared for a logistical nightmare. It's essential for necessities like renting cars and booking hotels, and handy for buying tickets over the phone and the Internet. The five major credit cards accepted in the U.S. are American Express, Diners Club, Discover, MasterCard and Visa. If cards are lost or stolen, contact:

### American Express

*800-528-2122*

### Diners Club

*800-234-6377*

### Discover

*800-347-2683*

### MasterCard

*800-826-2181*

### Visa

*800-336-8472*

## Traveler's checks

Before your trip, it is wise to buy checks in U.S. currency from a widely recognized company. Traveler's checks are routinely accepted at banks, stores and restaurants throughout the city. Bring your driver's license or passport for identification. If checks are lost or stolen, contact:

### American Express

*800-221-7282*

### Thomas Cook

*800-223-7373*

### Visa

*800-336-8472*

## Wire services

If you run out of cash, don't expect anyone at your embassy or consulate to lend you money—they won't, though they may be persuaded to repatriate you. In an emergency, you can have money wired from home.

### MoneyGram

*800-926-9400*

### Western Union

*800-325-6000*

# Newspapers & magazines

## Daily newspapers

### *Daily News*

The *News* has drifted politically from the Neanderthal right to a moderate but tough-minded stance under the ownership of real-estate mogul Mort Zuckerman. Labor-friendly pundit Juan Gonzalez has great street sense (and a Pulitzer).

### *New York Post*

Founded in 1801 by Alexander Hamilton, the *Post* is the nation's oldest daily newspaper. After many decades as a standard-bearer for political liberalism, the *Post* has swerved sharply to the right under current owner Rupert Murdoch. The *Post* includes more column inches of gossip than any other local paper, and its headlines are often as sassy as they are sensational.

### *The New York Times*

Olympian as ever after almost 150 years, the *Times* remains the city's (and the nation's) paper of record. It has the broadest and deepest coverage of world and national events—as the masthead proclaims, it delivers "All the News That's Fit to Print." The mammoth Sunday *Times* can weigh a full five pounds and typically contains hundreds of pages of newsprint, including a magazine and book-review, arts, finance, real-estate, sports and other sections.

### Other dailies

One of the nation's oldest black newspapers, ***Amsterdam News***, offers a trenchantly African-American viewpoint. New York also supports two Spanish-language dailies, ***El Diario*** and ***Noticias del Mundo***. ***Newsday*** is the Long Island–based daily with a tabloid format but a sober tone (it has a city edition). ***The Wall Street Journal*** views the world through a business lens.

## Weekly papers

Downtown journalism is a battlefield, pitting the scabrous neocons of the ***New York Press*** against the unreconstructed hippies of

***The Village Voice***. The *Press* uses an all-column format; it's full of youthful energy and irreverence as well as cynicism and self-absorption. *The Voice* is sometimes passionate and ironic, but just as often strident and predictable. Both papers are free. In contrast, ***The New York Observer*** focuses on the doings of the upper echelons of business, finance, media and politics. ***Our Town*** and ***Manhattan Spirit*** are on the sidelines; these free sister publications feature neighborhood news and local political gossip, and can be found in street-corner bins around town. In a world of it's own is the hilarious, satirical weekly, ***The Onion***.

## Weekly magazines

### New York

This magazine is part newsweekly, part lifestyle report and part listings.

### The New Yorker

Since the 1920s, *The New Yorker* has been known for its fine wit, elegant prose and sophisticated cartoons. In the postwar era, it established itself as a venue for serious long-form journalism. It usually makes for a lively, intelligent read.

### Time Out New York

Of course the best place to find out what's going on in town is *Time Out New York,* launched in 1995. Based on the tried-and-trusted format of its London parent, *TONY* is an indispensable guide to the life of the city (if we do say so ourselves).

## Magazines

### Black Book

Since its start in 1996, this quarterly covers New York high fashion and culture with intelligent bravado.

### Gotham

From the publisher of the glossy gab-rags *Hamptons* and Miami's *Ocean Drive, Gotham* unveiled its larger-than-life paparazzi-filled pages in 2001.

### Paper

*Paper* covers the city's trend-conscious set with plenty of insider buzz on bars, clubs, downtown boutiques and the people you'll find in them.

## Photocopying & printing

### Dependable Printing

*10 E 22nd St at Broadway (212-533-7560). Subway: N, R, W to 23rd St. Mon–Fri 8:30am–7pm; Sat 10am–4pm. AmEx, MC, V.*

Dependable provides offset and color printing, large-size Xerox copies, color laser printing, binding, rubber stamps, typing, forms, labels, brochures, flyers, newsletters, manuscripts, fax service, transparencies and more.

**Other location** ● *245 Fifth Ave between 27th and 28th Sts (212-689-2777). Subway: N, R, W to 28th St.*

### Fitch Graphics

See page 361.

### Kinko's

See page 361.

### Servco

*56 W 45th St between Fifth and Sixth Aves (212-575-0991). Subway: B, D, F, V to 42nd St; 7 to Fifth Ave. Mon–Fri 8:30am–6pm (open weekends by appointment).*

Photocopying, offset printing, blueprints and binding services are available.

## Postal services

See also **Messenger services**, page 368.

## U.S. Postal Service

Stamps are available at all post offices and from drugstore vending machines. It costs 37¢ to send a one-ounce (28g) letter within the U.S. Each additional ounce costs 23¢. Postcards mailed within the U.S. cost 23¢; for international postcards, it's 70¢. Airmail letters to anywhere overseas cost 80¢ for the first ounce and 80¢ for each additional ounce.

### General Post Office

*421 Eighth Ave at 33rd St (24-hour postal information 800-275-8777). Subway: A, C, E to 34th St–Penn Station. 24hrs.*

This is the city's main post office; call for the branch nearest you. There are 55 full-service post offices in Manhattan alone; lines are long, but stamps are also available from self-service vending machines. Branches are usually open 9am to 5pm, Monday through Friday; Saturday hours vary from office to office.

### Express Mail

*800-275-8777.*

You need to use special envelopes and fill out a form, which can be done either at a post office or by arranging a pickup. You are guaranteed mail delivery within 24 hours to major U.S. cities. International delivery takes two to three days, with no guarantee. Call for more information on various deadlines.

### General Delivery

*390 Ninth Ave at 30th St (212-330-3099). Subway: A, C, E to 34th St–Penn Station. Mon–Sat 10am–1pm.*

U.S. visitors without local addresses can receive their mail here; it should be addressed to recipient's name, General Delivery, New York, NY 10001. You will need to show some form of identification—a passport or ID card—when picking up letters.

### Poste Restante

*421 Eighth Ave at 33rd St, window 29 (212-330-2912). Subway: A, C, E to 34th St–Penn Station. Mon–Sat 8am–6pm.*

Foreign visitors without U.S. addresses can receive mail here; mail should be addressed to recipient's name, General Post Office, Poste Restante, 421 Eighth Avenue, attn: Window 29, New York, NY 10001. Be sure to bring some form of identification to claim your letters.

## Couriers

### DHL Worldwide Express

*Various locations throughout the city; call and give your zip code to find the office nearest you, or get pickup at your door (800-225-5345). AmEx, DC, Disc, MC, V.*

DHL will send a courier to pick up packages at any address in New York City, or you can deliver packages to its offices and drop-off points in person. No cash transactions.

### FedEx

*Various locations throughout the city; call and give your zip code to find the office nearest you, or get pickup at your door (800-247-4747; www.fedex.com). AmEx, DC, Disc, MC, V.*

FedEx rates (like those of its main

competitor, UPS) are based on the distance shipped, weight of the package and service chosen. A FedEx envelope to Los Angeles costs about $17; one to London, $30. Packages headed overseas should be dropped off by 6pm for International Priority delivery (depending on destination); by 9pm for packages to most destinations in the U.S. (some locations have a later time; call to check).

### UPS

*Various locations throughout the city; free pickup at your door (800-742-5877 for 24-hour service; www.ups.com). Hours vary by office; call for locations and times. AmEx, DC, MC, V.*
Like DHL and FedEx, UPS will send a courier to pick up parcels at any address in New York City, or you can deliver packages to its offices and drop-off points in person. UPS offers domestic and international service.

## Private mail services

### Mail Boxes Etc. USA

*1173A Second Ave between 61st and 62nd Sts (212-832-1390). Subway: F to Lexington Ave–63rd St; N, R, W to Lexington Ave–59th St; 4, 5, 6 to 59th St. Mon–Fri 9am–7pm; Sat 10am–5pm. AmEx, MC, V.*
Mailbox rental, mail forwarding, overnight delivery, packaging and shipping are available. Also on hand are a phone-message service, photocopying and faxing, typing service and business printing. There are more than 30 branches in Manhattan; check the phone book for locations.

## Telegrams

### Western Union Telegrams

*800-325-6000. 24hrs.*
Telegrams to addresses are taken over the phone at any time of day or night, and charges are added to your phone bill. Service is not available from pay phones.

## Radio

There are nearly 100 stations in the New York area. On the AM dial, you can find intriguing talk radio and phone-in shows that attract everyone from priests to sports nuts. Flip to FM for everything from free jazz to the latest Yeah Yeah Yeahs single. Radio highlights are printed weekly in *Time Out New York*, and daily in the *Daily News*.

### College radio

College radio is innovative and free of commercials. However, smaller transmitters mean that reception is often compromised by Manhattan's high-rise topography.

**WNYU-FM 89.1** and **WKCR-FM 89.9** *(see also* **Jazz**, *below)* are the stations of New York University and Columbia and offer programming that ranges across the musical spectrum.

**WFUV-FM 90.7**, Fordham University's station, plays mostly folk/Irish music, but also airs a variety of shows, including old-fashioned radio drama on *Classic Radio* every Monday at midnight.

### Dance & pop

American commercial radio is rigidly formatted, which makes most pop stations extremely tedious and repetitive during the day. Tune in on evenings and weekends for more interesting programming.

**WWRL-AM 1600** features R&B, Caribbean music and oldies.

**WPLJ-FM 95.5** and **WHTZ-FM 100.3** are Top 40 stations.

**WQHT-FM 97.1**, "Hot 97," is a commercial hip-hop station, with Star and Buc Wild cooking up a breakfast show for the homies; there's rap and R&B throughout the day.

**WRKS-FM 98.7**, "Kiss FM," has an "urban adult-contemporary" format, which translates into unremarkable American pop. But it does have the soul pioneer Isaac Hayes on weekday mornings (6–10am).

**WCBS-FM 101.1**'s playlist is strictly oldies.

**WKTU-FM 103.5** is the city's premier dance-music station.

**WWPR-FM 105.1**, "Power 105" plays top hip-hop, with some old-school hits.

**WLTW-FM 106.7**, "Lite FM," plays the kind of music you hear in elevators.

**WBLS-FM 107.5** plays classic and contemporary funk, soul and R&B. Highlights include Chuck Mitchell's house and R&B mix on Saturday afternoons, plus *Hal Jackson's Sunday Classics* (blues and soul).

### Jazz

**WCWP-FM 88.1** plays mostly jazz, plus hip-hop, gospel and world music.

**WBGO-FM 88.3** is strictly jazz. Branford Marsalis's weekly *JazzSet* program features many legendary artists, and there are also shows devoted to such categories as piano jazz.

**WKCR-FM 89.9**, the student-run radio station of Columbia University, is where you'll hear legendary jazz DJ Phil Schaap.

**WQCD-FM 101.9** is a soft-jazz station.

### Rock

**WSOU-FM 89.5**, a college station, focuses primarily on heavy metal.

**WFMU-FM 91.1** The term *free-form radio* still has some meaning at this Jersey-based station, which offers an eclectic mix of music and other aural oddities.

**WXRK-FM 92.3** and **WAXQ-FM 104.3** offer classic and alternative rock. FM 92.3 attracts the city's largest group of morning listeners, thanks to Howard Stern's 6–10am weekday sleaze fest.

**WLIR-FM 92.7** plays alternative (indie and Goth) sounds with a British bias.

### Other music

Wacky talk shows, sports games and music air on **WEVD-AM 1050**.

**WQEW-AM 1560**, "Radio Disney," has kids' programming.

On **WNYC-FM 93.9** and **WQXR-FM 96.3** you can hear a range of classical music; WNYC is more progressive and plays less strict classical.

Tune into **WYNY-FM 107.1** for Spanish and Latin music.

### News & talk

**WABC-AM 770**, **WCBS-AM 880**, **WINS-AM 1010** and **WBBR-AM 1130** offer news throughout the day, plus traffic and weather reports. WABC-AM 770 offers a morning show featuring the street-accented demagoguery of Guardian Angels founder Curtis Sliwa and radical attorney Ron Kuby (weekdays 5–10am). Right-winger Rush Limbaugh also airs his views here (noon–3pm).

**WNYC-AM 820/FM 93.9** and **WBAI-FM 99.5** are commercial-free public radio stations providing news and current affairs. Highlights include WNYC's popular *All Things Considered* (weekdays AM: 4–6pm, 7–8pm; FM: 4–6:30pm) and guest-driven talk shows, notably WNYC's *The Leonard Lopate Show* (weekdays noon–2pm) and WNYC-FM's *Fresh Air* (weekdays 7–8pm). WNYC also airs Garrison Keillor's *A Prairie Home Companion* and Ira Glass's *This American Life*. WBAI is a platform for left-wing politics.

**WLIB-AM 1190** is the voice of black New York, airing news and talk from an Afrocentric perspective, interspersed with Caribbean music. Former mayor David Dinkins has a show on Wednesdays (10–11am).

**WNEW-FM 102.7** is primarily talk, with an emphasis on the wacky.

### Sports

**WFAN-AM 660** airs Giants, Knicks, Mets and Rangers games. In the mornings, talk-radio fixture Don Imus offers his opinion on whatever's going on in the world (Tue–Fri 5:30–10am).

**WABC-AM 770** broadcasts the Devils, Jets and Yankees games.

**WEVD-AM 1050** is devoted to news and sports talk and is the home of the Islanders.

**WWRU-AM 1660**, "Radio Unica," covers MetroStars soccer games in Spanish.

## Religion

Here are just a few of the many places of worship in New York. Check the Yellow Pages for a more detailed listing.

### Baptist

#### Abyssinian Baptist Church

See page 106.

### Catholic

#### St. Francis of Assisi

*135 W 31st St between Sixth and Seventh Aves (212-736-8500; www.st.francis.org). Subway: B, D, F, V, N, Q, R, W to 34th St–Herald Sq; 1, 2, 3, 9 to 34th St–Penn Station. Services: Mon–Fri 6, 7, 7:30, 8, 8:30, 11, 11:45am, 12:15, 1:15, 4:30, 5:30pm; Sat 8, 10am, noon, 4, 4:15, 5:15 and 6:15pm; Sun 8, 9:30, 10 (Korean), 11am, 12:30, 5:15, 6:15pm.*

#### St. Patrick's Cathedral

See page 91.

### Episcopal

#### Cathedral of St. John the Divine

See page 103.

### Jewish

#### UJA-Federation Resource Line

*212-753-2288; www.youngleadership.org. 9am–5pm. 24-hour voice mail.*

This hot line provides referrals to other organizations, groups, temples and synagogues as well as advice on kosher food and restaurants.

### Methodist

#### St. Paul and St. Andrew United Methodist Church

*263 W 86th St between Broadway and West End Ave (212-362-3179). Subway: 1, 9 to 86th St. Services: Sun 11am.*

#### Salem United Methodist Church

*2190 Adam Clayton Powell Jr. Blvd (Seventh Ave) at 129th St (212-678-2700). Subway: A, C, B, D, 2, 3 to 125th St. Services: Sept–Jun Wed noon; Sun 11am. Jul, Aug Wed noon; Sun 10am.*

### Muslim

#### Islamic Cultural Center of New York

*1711 Third Ave between 96th and 97th Sts (212-722-5234). Subway: 6 to 96th St. 9am–5pm and for all prayers.*

### Presbyterian

#### Fifth Avenue Presbyterian Church

*7 W 55th St at Fifth Ave (212-247-0490; www.fapc.org). Subway: E, V to Fifth Ave–53rd St; 6 to 51st St. Services: Sun 9, 11am.*

## Rest rooms

See **Toilet talk**, page 367.

## Safety

New York's crime rate, particularly violent crime, has waned during the past decade. More than ever, most crime occurs late at night in low-income neighborhoods. Don't arrive thinking your safety is at risk wherever you go; it is unlikely that you will ever be bothered.

Still, a bit of common sense won't hurt. If you look comfortable rather than lost, you should deter troublemakers. Do not flaunt your money and valuables. Avoid desolate and poorly lit streets, and if necessary, walk facing the traffic so no one can drive up alongside you undetected. On deserted sidewalks, walk close to the street; muggers prefer to hang back in doorways and shadows. If the worst happens and you find yourself threatened, hand over your wallet or camera at once (your attacker will likely be as anxious to get it over with as you will be), then dial **911** as soon as you can (it's a free call).

Be extra alert to pickpockets and street hustlers—especially in crowded tourist areas like Times Square—and don't be seduced by cardsharps or other tricksters you may encounter. That shrink-wrapped camcorder you bought out of a car trunk for 50 bucks could turn out to be a couple of bricks when you open the box.

New York women are used to the brazenness with which they are stared at by men and usually develop a dismissive attitude toward it. If unwelcome admirers ever get verbal or start following you, ignoring them is better than responding. Walking into the nearest shop is your best bet to get rid of persistent offenders. If you've been seriously victimized, see **Emergencies**, page 364, or **Rape & sex crimes**, page 365, for assistance.

## Smoking

New Yorkers are the target of some of the strictest anti-smoking laws on the planet (well, except for California). The 1995 NYC Smoke-Free Air Act makes it illegal to smoke in virtually all public places, including subways and movie theaters. Recent legislation may ban smoking in restaurants *and* bars as early as March 2003. Fines start at $100, so be sure to ask before you light up. Now could be the time to quit.

## Students

Student life in NYC is unlike anywhere else in the world. An endless extracurricular education exists right outside the dorm room—the city is both teacher and playground. For further guidance, check the ***Time Out New York Student Guide***, available free on campuses in August and for $1.95 at Hudson News.

### Student identification

Foreign students should get an **International Student Identity Card** (ISIC) as proof of student status and to secure discounts. These can be bought from your local student travel agent (ask at your students' union). If you buy the card in New York, you will also get basic accident insurance—a bargain. The New York branch of the **Council on International Educational Exchange** can supply one on the spot. It's at 205 East 42nd Street between Second and Third Avenues *(212-822-2700; see* **Student travel**, *below)*. Note that a student identity card may not always be accepted as proof of age for drinking (you must be 21).

### Student travel

Most agents offer discount fares for those under 26; specialists in student deals include:

#### STA Travel

*205 E 42nd St between Second and Third Aves (212-822-2700; www.statravel.com). Subway: S, 4, 5, 6, 7 to 42nd St–Grand Central. Mon–Sat 10am–6pm. Call 800-777-0112 for other locations.*

## Telephones

New York, like most of the world's busy cities, is overrun with telephones, cellular phones, pagers and faxes. This increasing dependence on a dial tone accounts for the city's abundance of area codes. As a rule, you must dial 1 + area code before a number, even if the place you are calling is in the same area code. The area codes for Manhattan are 212 and 646; Brooklyn, Queens, Staten Island and the Bronx are 718 and 347; generally, 917 is reserved for cellular phones and pagers. The Long Island area codes are 516 and 631, and the codes for New Jersey are 201, 609, 732, 856, 908 and 973. Numbers preceded by 800, 877 and 888 are free of charge when dialed from anywhere in the United States. When numbers are listed as letters (e.g., 800-AIR-RIDE) for easy recall, dial the corresponding numbers on the telephone keypad.

Remember, if you carry a cellular phone, make sure you turn it off on trains and buses, and at restaurants, plays, movies, concerts and museums. New Yorkers are quick to show their annoyance at an ill-timed ring. Some establishments even post signs designating "cellular-free zones."

### General information

The Yellow Pages and white pages directories offer a wealth of useful information in the front, including theater-seating diagrams and maps; the blue pages in the center of the white pages directory list all government numbers and addresses. Hotels will have copies; otherwise, try libraries or Verizon (the local phone company) payment centers.

#### Collect calls & credit-card calls

Collect calls are also known as reverse charges. Dial 0 followed by the area code and number, or dial AT&T's 800-CALL-ATT, MCI's 800-COLLECT or Sprint's 800-ONE-DIME.

#### Directory assistance

Dial 411 (free from pay phones). For long-distance directory assistance, dial 1 + area code + 555-1212 (long-distance charges apply). Verizon also offers national 411 directory assistance, but the charges can be high.

#### Emergency

Dial **911**. All calls are free (including those made on pay and cell phones).

#### International calls

Dial 011 + country code (Australia 61; New Zealand 64; U.K. 44).

#### Operator assistance

Dial 0.

#### Toll-free directory

Dial 1 + 800 + 555-1212 (no charge).

### Pagers & cell phones

#### InTouch USA

*212-391-8323, 800-872-7626. Mon–Fri 8:30am–6pm. AmEx, DC, Disc, MC, V.*
InTouch, the city's largest cellular-phone rental company, leases equipment by the day, week or month.

### Public pay phones & phone cards

Public pay phones are easy to find. Some of them even work. Verizon's phones are the most dependable (those from other phone companies tend to be poorly maintained). Phones take any combination of silver coins: Local calls usually cost 25¢ for three minutes; some require 50¢, but allow unlimited time on the call. If you're not used to American phones, know that the ringing tone is long; the "engaged" tone, or busy signal, is short and higher pitched.

If you want to call long-distance or make an international call from a pay phone, you need to go through one of the long-distance companies. Most pay phones in New York automatically use AT&T, but phones in and around transportation hubs usually contract other long-distance carriers, whose charges can be outrageous. Look in the Yellow Pages under Telephone Companies. MCI and Sprint are respected brand names *(see* **Collect calls & credit card calls**, *above)*.

Make the call either by dialing 0 for an operator or by dialing direct (the latter is cheaper). To find out how much a call will cost, dial the number and a computerized voice will tell you how much money to deposit. You can pay for calls with your credit card.

The best way to make long-distance calls is with a **phone card**, available in various denominations from any post office branch or from chain stores like Duane Reade or Rite Aid *(see* **Pharmacies**, *page 365)*. Delis and kiosks sell phone cards, including the New York Exclusive, which has favorable international rates. Dialing instructions are on the card.

## Recorded information

For the exact time and temperature, plus lottery numbers and the weather forecast, call 212-976-2828—a free call 24 hours a day.

## Telephone answering service

### Messages Plus Inc.

*1317 Third Ave between 75th and 76th Sts (212-879-4144). Subway: 6 to 77th St. 24hrs. AmEx, MC, V.*
Messages Plus provides telephone-answering service, with specialized (medical, bilingual, etc.) receptionists if required, and plenty of ways to deliver your messages. It also offers telemarketing, voice mail and interactive website services.

## Television

A visit to New York often includes at least a small dose of cathode radiation. American TV can inflict culture shock, particularly for British and European visitors.

*Time Out New York* offers a rundown of weekly television highlights. For full TV schedules, save the Sunday *New York Times* TV section or buy a daily paper.

### The networks

Six major networks broadcast nationwide. All offer ratings-led variations on a theme.

**CBS** (Channel 2 in NYC) has the top investigative show, *60 Minutes,* on Sundays, and the network's overall programming is geared to a middle-aged demographic *(Judging Amy, Touched by an Angel)*. But check out *CSI* (Thursdays at 9pm) for fast-paced drama or *Everybody Loves Raymond* (Mondays at 9pm) and *The Late Show with David Letterman* (weeknights at 11:30pm) for solid humor.

**NBC** (4) is the home of the political-drama series *The West Wing,* the long-running sketch-comedy series *Saturday Night Live* (Saturdays at 11:30pm), and popular sitcoms such as *Will & Grace.*

**Fox-WNYW** (5) is popular with younger audiences for shows like *Malcolm in the Middle, The Simpsons* and *24*.

**ABC** (7) is the king of daytime soaps and family-friendly sitcoms *(The Drew Carey Show, Life with Bonnie)*.

**UPN-WWOR** (9) and **WB-WPIX** (11) don't attract huge audiences like other networks, but they feature some offbeat programming, including *Angel, Buffy the Vampire Slayer* and *Smallville.*

**WXTV** (41) and **WNJU** (47) are Spanish-language channels that offer game shows and racy Mexican dramas. They're also your best noncable bet for soccer.

### Public TV

Public TV is on channels 13, 21 and 25. Documentaries, arts shows and science series alternate with *Masterpiece Theatre* and reruns of British shows like *Inspector Morse*. Channel 21 broadcasts *BBC World News* daily at 6am, 7 and 11pm.

### Cable

All channel numbers listed are for Time Warner Cable in Manhattan. In other locations, or for other cable systems—such as Cablevision and RCN—check listings.

**NY1** (1), **CNN** (10), **MSNBC** (43) and **Fox News** (46) are where you'll find news all day, the first with a local focus.

**TNT** (3), **TBS** (8) and **USA Network** (40) stations show notable reruns *(ER)* and feature films.

**Nickelodeon** (6) presents programming suitable for kids and nostalgic fans of shows like *The Brady Bunch* and *Happy Days.*

**Lifetime** (12) is "television for women."

**A&E** (16) airs the shallow but popular *Biography* documentary series.

**The History Channel** (17), **Sci-Fi Channel** (44) and **Weather Channel** (72) are self-explanatory. **Discovery Channel** (18) and **Learning Channel** (52) feature nature and science programs.

**VH1** (19), MTV's more mature sibling, airs the popular *Behind the Music* series, which delves into the lives of artists like Vanilla Ice and the Partridge Family.

**MTV** (20) increasingly offers fewer music videos and more of its original programming *(Jackass, The Osbornes* and *The Real World)*.

**Court TV** (23) scores big ratings when there's a hot trial going on.

**E!** (24) is "Entertainment Television," a mix of celebrity and movie news. This is where you'll find tabloidy segments like the unmissable *E! True Hollywood Story,* which profiles the likes of Mr. T and the Brat Pack.

**Fox Sports** (26), **MSG** (Madison Square Garden, 27), **ESPN** (28) and **ESPN2** (29) are all-sports stations.

**Public Access TV** is on channels 34, 56 and 57—surefire sources of bizarre camcorder amusement.

**Channel 35** is where you'll find the fun, risqué *Robin Byrd Show*.

**Bravo** (38) shows arts programming such as *Inside the Actors Studio,* art-house films and classic series, such as *Twin Peaks.*

**Comedy Central** (45) is all comedy, airing the raunchy cartoon *South Park* (Wednesdays at 10pm), and *The Daily Show with Jon Stewart* (weekdays at 7 and 11pm).

**C-SPAN** (64) is a forum for governmental affairs programming.

**Cinemax**, **Disney Channel**, **HBO**, **The Movie Channel** and **Showtime** are premium channels often available for a fee in hotels. They show uninterrupted feature films, exclusive specials and acclaimed original series such as *The Sopranos* and *Sex and the City.*

## Tickets

It's always show time somewhere in New York. And depending on what you're after—music, sports, theater—scoring tickets can be a real hassle. Smaller productions often have their own box office that sells tickets. Large venues like Madison Square Garden have ticket agencies—and an equal number of devoted spectators. You may have to try more than one tactic to get into a popular show.

## Box-office tickets

### Moviefone

*212-777-FILM; www.moviefone.com. 24hrs. AmEx, Disc, MC, V. $1.50 surcharge ($1 charge if purchased online).*
Use this service to purchase advance movie tickets by credit card over the phone or online, and pick them up at an automated teller located in the theater lobby. This service is not available for every theater.

### Telecharge

*212-239-6200; www.telecharge.com. 24hrs. AmEx, DC, Disc, MC, V. Average $6 surcharge per Broadway and Off Broadway ticket.*
Broadway and Off Broadway shows are the ticket here.

### Ticket Central

*555 W 42nd St between Tenth and Eleventh Aves (212-279-4200; www.ticketcentral.org). Subway: N, Q, R, W, S, 1, 2, 3, 9, 7 to 42nd St–Times Sq. Box office and phone orders 1–8pm. AmEx, MC, V. $3 surcharge per order.*
Off and Off-Off Broadway tickets are available at the office or by phone.

### Ticketmaster

*212-307-4100; www.ticketmaster.com. 8am–10pm. AmEx, DC, Disc, MC, V. $3–$8 surcharge per ticket.*
This reliable service sells tickets to a variety of large-scale attractions including rock concerts, Broadway shows and sports events. You can buy tickets by phone, online or at outlets throughout the city—Tower Records, the Wiz, HMV, J&R Music World and Filene's Basement, to name a few.

### TKTS

*Duffy Square, 47th St at Broadway (212-221-0013; www.tdf.org). Subway: N, Q, R, W, S, 1, 2, 3, 9, 7 to 42nd St–Times Sq. Mon–Sat 3–8pm; Sun 11am–7pm. Matinee tickets Wed, Sat 10am–2pm; Sun 11am–2pm. $3 surcharge per ticket. Cash or traveler's checks only.*
TKTS has become a New York tradition. Broadway and Off Broadway tickets are sold at discounts of 25 and 50 percent (plus a $3 service charge per ticket) for same-day performances; tickets to other highbrow events are also offered. The line can be long, but it's often worth the wait.
**Other location** • *1 Bowling Green at State St. Subway: 4, 5 to Bowling Green. Mon–Fri 11am–5:30pm; Sat 11am–3:30pm.*

## Scalpers & standby tickets

You needn't relinquish all hope when a show sells out. There's always the risky scalper option (however, it is illegal and you might buy a forged ticket). Before you part with any cash, make sure the ticket has the correct details, and be discreet—the police have been cracking down on such trade in recent years.

Some venues also offer standby tickets right before show time, while others give reduced rates for tickets purchased on the same day as the performance. Those in the know line up hours beforehand.

## Ticket brokers

Ticket brokers function like scalpers, although their activities are more regulated. It's illegal in New York State to sell a ticket for more than its face value plus a service charge, so these companies operate by phone from other states. They can almost guarantee tickets, however costly, for sold-out events, and tend to deal only in better seats. Look under "Ticket Sales" in the Yellow Pages for brokers. Listed below are three of the more established outfits.

### Apex Tours

*800-CITY-TIX; www.tixx.com. Mon–Fri 9am–5pm. AmEx, MC, V.*

### Prestige Entertainment

*800-2GET-TIX; www.prestige entertainment.com. Mon–Fri 9am–6pm; Sat 9am–1pm. AmEx, MC, V.*

### TicketCity

*800-880-8886; www.ticketcity.com. Mon–Fri 8:30am–9pm; Sat 11am–6pm; Sun 11am–3pm. AmEx, Disc, MC, V.*

## Time & date

New York is on Eastern Standard Time, which extends from the Atlantic coast to the eastern shore of Lake Michigan and south to the Gulf of Mexico. This is five hours behind Greenwich Mean Time. Clocks are set forward one hour in early April and back one hour at the end of October. Going from east to west, Eastern Time is one hour ahead of Central Time, two hours ahead of Mountain Time and three hours ahead of Pacific Time. Call 212-976-2828 for the exact time of day.

In the U.S. the date is written in this order: month, day, year; so 2/5/03 is February 5, 2003.

## Tourist information

Hotels are usually full of maps, leaflets and free tourist magazines that give advice about entertainment and events. But be forewarned: Their advice is not always impartial. Plenty of local magazines (including *Time Out New York*) offer opinionated, yet reliable, info.

### New York City's Official Visitor Information Center

*810 Seventh Ave at 53rd St (212-484-1222; www.nycvisit.com). Subway: B, D, E to Seventh Ave; N, R, W to 49th St; 1, 9 to 50th St. Mon–Fri 8:30am–6pm; Sat, Sun 9am–5pm.*
This center, run by NYC & Company, gives out leaflets on tours, attractions, etc., plus free advice on accommodations and entertainment, discount coupons and free maps.

### NYC & Company

*800-NYC-VISIT, 212-397-8222; www.nycvisit.com.*
This is the city's official tourism marketing organization.
**Other location** • *33–34 Carnaby St, London, UK, W1V 1CA (0-207-437-8300).*

### Times Square Visitors Center

*1560 Broadway between 46th and 47th Sts (212-768-1560). Subway: N, Q, R, W, S, 1, 2, 3, 9, 7 to 42nd St–Times Sq. 8am–8pm.*
This center offers discount coupons for Broadway tickets, MetroCards, an Internet station and other useful goods and services.

## Translation & language services

### All Language Services

*545 Fifth Ave at 45th St (212-986-1688; fax 212-986-3396). Subway: S, 4, 5, 6, 7 to 42nd St–Grand Central. 24 hrs. AmEx, MC, V.*

ALS will type or translate documents in any of 59 languages and provide interpreters.

## Visas

Nearly 30 countries participate in the Visa Waiver Program. Citizens of Andorra, Australia, Austria, Belgium, Brunei, Denmark, Finland, France, Germany, Iceland, Ireland, Italy, Japan, Liechtenstein, Luxembourg, Monaco, the Netherlands, New Zealand, Norway, Portugal, San Marino, Singapore, Slovenia, Spain, Sweden, Switzerland, the United Kingdom and Uruguay do not need a visa for stays shorter than 90 days (business or pleasure), as long as they have a passport that is valid for the full 90-day period and a return ticket. An open standby ticket is acceptable.

Canadians and Mexicans don't need visas but must have legal proof of residency. All other travelers must have visas. You can obtain information and application forms from your nearest U.S. embassy or consulate. In general, submit your application at least three weeks before you plan to travel. To apply for a visa on shorter notice, contact your travel agent.

For information on student visas, *see page 362.*

### U.S. Embassy Visa Information

*In the U.S., 202-663-1225; travel.state.gov/visa_services.html. In the U.K., 09061-500-590.*

## Wardrobe services

*See also* **Laundry**, *page 366.*

### Clothing rental

#### One Night Out/Mom's Night Out

*147 E 72nd St between Lexington and Third Aves (212-988-1122). Subway: 6 to 68th St–Hunter College. Mon–Fri 11am–6pm; Sat 11am–5pm. AmEx, MC, V.*

One Night Out rents and sells brand-new evening wear to uptown socialites and downtown girls who are trying to pass for the same. Across the hall, Mom's Night Out provides the service to expectant mothers for $195 to $375.

#### Zeller Tuxedos

*1010 Third Ave at 60th St (212-355-0707). Subway: N, R, W to Lexington Ave–59th St; 4, 5, 6 to 59th St. Mon–Fri 9am–6:30pm; Sat 10am–5pm. AmEx, MC, V.*

Calvin Klein and Lubiam tuxes are available for those who didn't think to pack their own. Check the phone book for other locations.

### Clothing repair

#### Ramon's Tailor Shop

*306 Mott St between Bleecker and Houston Sts (212-226-0747). Subway: F, V, S to Broadway–Lafayette St; 6 to Bleecker St. Mon–Fri 7:30am–7:30pm; Sat 9am–6:30pm. Cash only.*

Ramon's can alter or repair "anything that can be worn on the body." There's also an emergency service, and pickup and delivery is free in much of Manhattan.

#### R&S Cleaners

*212-475-9412. Mon–Fri 9am–5pm. Cash only.*

This pickup-and-delivery service specializes in cleaning, repairing and tailoring theatrical costumes, as well as leather jackets. Prices start at $35, and cleaning takes about a week.

### Jewelry & watch repair

#### Zig Zag Jewelers

*1336A Third Ave between 76th and 77th Sts (212-794-3559). Subway: 6 to 77th St. Mon–Fri 11am–7:30pm; Sat 10am–6:30pm; Sun noon–6pm. AmEx, DC, Disc, MC, V.*

These experts won't touch costume jewelry, but they'll restring and reclasp your broken Bulgaris and Harry Winstons. Watch repairs are always trustworthy, and estimates are free.

**Other location** • *963 Madison Ave between 75th and 76th Sts (212-472-6373). Subway: 6 to 77th St. Mon–Sat 10am–6pm; Sun noon–5pm. AmEx, DC, Disc, MC, V.*

### Shoe repair

#### Andrade Shoe Repair

*103 University Pl between 12th and 13th Sts (212-529-3541). Subway: L, N, Q, R, W, 4, 5, 6 to 14th St–Union Sq. Mon–Fri 7:30am–7pm; Sat 9am–6:30pm. Cash only.*

Andrade is a basic—but reliable—shoe-repair chain around town. Check the phone book for other locations.

#### Shoe Service Plus

*15 W 55th St between Fifth and Sixth Aves (212-262-4823). Subway: E, V to Fifth Ave–53rd St. Mon–Fri 7am–7pm; Sat 10am–5pm. AmEx, DC, Disc, MC, V.*

This shop is bustling with customers, and no wonder: The staff will give just as much attention to your battle-weary combat boots as to your pricey Jimmy Choos.

## Travel advice

For up-to-date information for traveling to a specific country—including the latest news on safety and security, health issues, local laws and customs—contact your home country government's department of foreign affairs. Most have websites with useful advice for would-be travelers.

**Australia**
www.dfat.gov.au/travel

**Canada**
www.voyage.gc.ca

**Ireland**
www.irlgov.ie/iveagh

**New Zealand**
www.mft.govt.nz/travel

**United Kingdom**
www.fco.gov.uk/travel

**USA**
www.state.gov/travel

# Further Reference

## In-depth guides

**Edward Sibley Barnard:** *New York City Trees.* Find the best places to hug a tree.

**Edward F. Bergman:** *The Spiritual Traveler, New York City.* This is a guide to sacred and peaceful spaces.

**Eleanor Berman:** *Away for the Weekend: New York.* Trips within a 200-mile radius of New York City.

**Eleanor Berman:** *New York Neighborhoods.* Ethnic enclaves abound in this food lover's guide.

**Arthur S. Brown and Barbara Holmes:** *Vegetarian Dining in New York City.* Includes vegan places.

**Dina Clason and Jill Fairchild:** *Where to Wear:* A staple for shopaholics.

**William Corbett:** *New York Literary Lights.* An encyclopedic collection of info about NYC's literary past.

**David Frattini:** *The Underground Guide to New York City Subways.*

**Alfred Gingold and Helen Rogan:** *The New Ultra Cool Parents Guide to All of New York.*

***Guide to New York City Landmarks:*** Produced by the Landmarks Preservation Commission.

**Hagstrom:** *New York City 5 Borough Pocket Atlas.* You won't get lost with this thorough street map.

**Colleen Kane (ed.):** *Sexy New York City.* Discover erotica in the Naked City.

**Chuck Katz:** *Manhattan on Film 2.* A must for movie buffs who want to scope out the city on foot.

**Ruth Leon:** *Applause: New York's Guide to the Performing Arts.* Detailed directory of performance venues.

**Anne Matthews:** *Wild Nights: Nature Returns to the City.* The urban jungle has more than pigeons and people.

**Lyn Skreczko and Virginia Bell:** *The Manhattan Health Pages.* Everything from aerobics to Zen.

**Earl Steinbicker:** *Daytrips New York 2002.*

**Linda Tarrant-Reid:** *Discovering Black New York.* This guide presents important black museums and more.

***Time Out New York Eating & Drinking Guide:*** The annual comprehensive critics' guide to thousands of places to eat and drink in the five boroughs.

**Zagat Survey:** *New York City Restaurants.* The popular opinion survey.

## Architecture

**Richard Berenholtz:** *New York New York.* Double-spread panoramic images of the city through the seasons.

**Margot Gayle and Edmund V. Gillan Jr.:** *Cast-Iron Architecture in New York.*

**Stanley Greenberg:** *Invisible New York.* Photographic account of hidden architectural triumphs.

**Karl Sabbagh:** *Skyscraper.* How the tall ones are built.

**Robert A.M. Stern et al.:** *New York 1930.* A massive coffee-table slab with stunning pictures.

**Norval White and Elliot Willensky (ed.):** *AIA Guide to New York City.* A comprehensive directory of important buildings.

**Gerard R. Wolfe:** *New York: A Guide to the Metropolis.* Historical and architectural walking tours.

## Culture & recollections

**Candace Bushnell:** *Sex and the City.* Smart women, superficial New York.

**George Chauncey:** *Gay New York.* The evolution of New York gay culture from 1890 to 1940.

**William Cole (ed.):** *Quotable New York.*

**Martha Cooper and Henry Chalfant:** *Subway Art.*

**Josh Alan Friedman:** *Tales of Times Square.* Sleaze, scum, filth and degradation in Times Square.

**Nelson George:** *Hip-Hop America.* The history of hip-hop, from Grandmaster Flash to P. Diddy.

**Pat Hackett (ed.):** *The Andy Warhol Diaries.*

**Robert Hendrickson:** *New Yawk Tawk.* Dictionary of NYC slang.

**A.J. Liebling:** *Back Where I Came From.* Personal recollections from the famous *New Yorker* columnist.

**Legs McNeil and Gillian McCain (ed.):** *Please Kill Me.* Oral history of the city's 1970s punk scene.

**Joseph Mitchell:** *Up in the Old Hotel and Other Stories.* An anthology

## Websites

**www.timeoutny.com**
The *Time Out New York* website covers all the city has to offer. When you're planning your trip, check out the New York City Guide section for a variety of itineraries that you can use in conjunction with this guide.

**eatdrink.timeoutny.com**
Subscribe to *TONY* Eating & Drinking Online and instantly search thousands of reviews written by our critics.

**www.mta.info**
Subway and bus service changes are always posted here. Plus an interactive subway map points out sights near each stop.

**www.nyc.gov**
City Hall's "Official New York City Website" has lots of links.

**www.nycvisit.com**
This site is run by NYC & Company, the local convention and visitors bureau.

**www.ny1.com**
NY1 News' site covers local events, news and weather.

**www.nytimes.com**
"All the News That's Fit to Print" online from *The New York Times.*

**www.centralparknyc.org**
Find out the nitty-gritty on the city's favorite park.

**www.clubplanet.com**
Follow the city's nocturnal scene and buy advance tickets to big events.

**www.dailycandy.com**
Hot tips on shopping, beauty, restaurants and services.

**www.forgotten-ny.com**
Remember Old New York here.

**www.hipguide.com**
A short 'n' sweet site for those looking for what's considered hip.

**www.nycsubway.org**
For fans of the New York underground system.

**www.pagesix.com**
Catch up on all the celeb canoodling going on around town, courtesy of the *New York Post*'s gossip site.

**www.whitehouse.gov**
Your connection to the top dogs of the U.S. government.

of the late journalist's most colorful reporting.

**Frank O'Hara:** *The Collected Poems of Frank O'Hara.* The great NYC poet found inspiration in his hometown.

**Alice Powers et al.:** *The Brooklyn Reader: 30 Writers Celebrate America's Favorite Borough.*

**Andrés Torres:** *Between Melting Pot and Mosaic.* African-American and Puerto Rican life in the city.

**Heather Holland Wheaton:** *Eight Million Stories in a New York Minute.*

## Fiction

**Kurt Andersen:** *Turn of the Century.* Millennial Manhattan seen through the eyes of media players.

**Paul Auster:** *The New York Trilogy: City of Glass, Ghosts, the Locked Room.* A search for the madness behind the method of Manhattan's grid.

**Kevin Baker:** *Dreamland.* A poetic novel about Coney Island's glory days.

**James A. Baldwin:** *Another Country.* Racism under the bohemian veneer of the 1960s.

**Caleb Carr:** *The Alienist.* Hunting a serial killer in New York's turn-of-the-previous-century demimonde.

**Adam Davies:** *The Frog King.* A young man works an entry-level publishing job while trying to finish his novel and find love.

**Bret Easton Ellis:** *American Psycho.* A serial killer is loose among the young and fabulous in 1980s Manhattan.

**Ralph Ellison:** *Invisible Man.* Coming of age as a black man in 1950s New York.

**Larry Kramer:** *Faggots.* Hilarious gay New York.

**Jonathan Lethem:** *Motherless Brooklyn.* This cult fave is a rollicking whodunit romp through the borough.

**Phillip Lopate (ed.):** *Writing New York.* An excellent anthology of short stories, essays and poems set in New York.

**Emma McLaughlin and Nicola Kraus:** *The Nanny Dairies.* A funny, scathing portrayal of caring for the young of wealthy New York families.

**Toni Morrison:** *Jazz.* The music, glamour and grit of 1920s Harlem.

**Dawn Powell:** *The Locusts Have No King.* A stinging satire of New York's intelligentsia.

**David Schickler:** *Kissing in Manhattan.* Explores the lives of quirky tenants in a Manhattan apartment building.

**Hubert Selby Jr.:** *Last Exit to Brooklyn.* Brooklyn dockland degradation, circa 1950s.

***Time Out Book of New York Short Stories:*** Of course we like these original short stories by 23 American and British authors.

**Edith Wharton:** *Old New York.* Four novellas of 19th-century New York, by the author of *The Age of Innocence.*

**Tom Wolfe:** *The Bonfire of the Vanities.* Rich/poor, black/white. An unmatched slice of 1980s New York.

## History

**Irving Lewis Allen:** *The City in Slang.* How New York living has spawned hundreds of new words and phrases.

**Herbert Asbury:** *The Gangs of New York: An Informal History of the Underworld.* Asbury's racy journalistic portrait of the city at the turn of the last century has been reissued to coincide with the release of Martin Scorcese's film.

**Patrick Bunyan:** *All Around the Town.* A book about fun Manhattan facts and curiosities.

**Robert A. Caro:** *The Power Broker.* A biography of Robert Moses, the mid-20th-century master builder in New York, and his checkered legacy.

**Eric Darton:** *Divided We Stand.* A history of the World Trade Center.

**Federal Writers' Project:** *The WPA Guide to New York City.* A wonderful snapshot of 1930s New York by writers employed under FDR's New Deal.

**Sanna Feirstein:** *Naming New York.* An account of how Manhattan places got their names.

**Mitchell Fink and Lois Mathias:** *Never Forget: An Oral History of September 11, 2001.* A collection of first-person accounts.

**Alice Rose George (ed.):** *Here Is New York.* A collection of nearly 900 powerful amateur photos documents the aftermath of September 11.

**Clifton Hood:** *722 Miles: The Building of the Subways and How They Transformed New York.*

**Kenneth T. Jackson (ed.):** *The Encyclopedia of New York City.* An ambitious and useful reference guide.

**Rem Koolhaas:** *Delirious New York.* New York as a terminal city; Urbanism and the culture of congestion.

**David Levering Lewis:** *When Harlem Was in Vogue.* A study of the 1920s Harlem Renaissance.

**Shaun O'Connell:** *Remarkable, Unspeakable New York.* The history of New York as literary inspiration.

**Mitchell Pacelle:** *Empire: A Tale of Obsession.* The story of the fight for the Empire State Building.

**Jacob A. Riis:** *How the Other Half Lives.* A pioneering photojournalistic record of gruesome tenement life.

**Marie Salerno and Arthur Gelb:** *The New York Pop-Up Book:* Interactive historical account of NYC.

**Roy Rosenzweig and Elizabeth Blackmar:** *The Park and the People.* A lengthy history of Central Park.

**Luc Sante:** *Low Life.* Opium dens, brothels, tenements and suicide salons in New York from the 1840s to the 1920s.

**Jennifer Toth:** *The Mole People: Life in the Tunnels Beneath New York City.*

**Mike Wallace and Edwin G. Burrows:** *Gotham: A History of New York City to 1898.* The first volume in a planned mammoth history of NYC.

## A few favorite films

***After Hours*** (1985): Martin Scorsese has built a career out of New York stories; this film, about a mousey yuppie who gets sucked into the downtown art scene, is one of his best.

***Do the Right Thing*** (1989): The hottest day of the summer leads to a riot in Bedford-Stuyvesant. Racial tension portrayed with taut, clear-eyed brilliance.

***Manhattan*** (1979): Woody Allen's Gershwin-drenched b&w masterpiece is the ultimate love letter to a city.

***Six Degrees of Separation*** (1993): Fred Schepisi's film version of the 1990 John Guare play (from the real-life case of a black teen posing as Sidney Poitier's son) encapsulates the Upper East Side's status-conscious liberal politics.

# Index



Numbers in **bold** indicate key information on a topic; *italics* indicate photographs.

## C

## m

# Advertisers' Index

# Maps



**The roads most traveled** Signposts at Battery Park tell visitors where to go.

# Street Index

## MANHATTAN

## BROOKLYN

## QUEENS

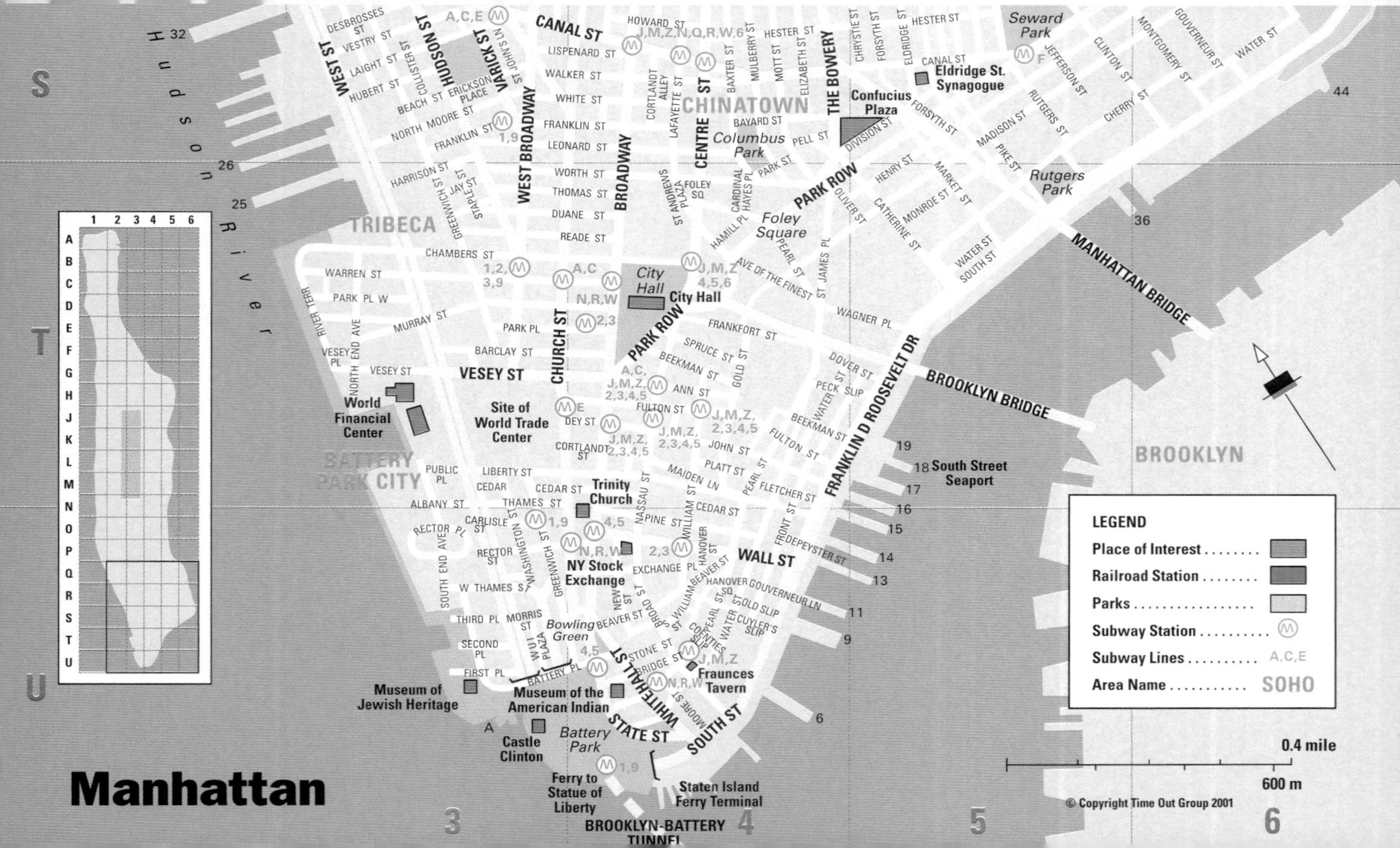
Manhattan
LEGEND
Place of Interest
Railroad Station
Parks
Subway Station
Subway Lines
A,C,E
Area Name
SOHO
0.4 mile
600 m
TRIBECA
CHINATOWN
BATTERY PARK CITY
BROOKLYN
Hudson River
CANAL ST
WEST ST
HUDSON ST
VARICK ST
WEST BROADWAY
BROADWAY
CHURCH ST
CENTRE ST
THE BOWERY
PARK ROW
VESEY ST
WALL ST
WHITEHALL ST
STATE ST
SOUTH ST
FRANKLIN D ROOSEVELT DR
BROOKLYN BRIDGE
MANHATTAN BRIDGE
BROOKLYN-BATTERY TUNNEL
World Financial Center
Site of World Trade Center
City Hall
Trinity Church
NY Stock Exchange
Museum of Jewish Heritage
Museum of the American Indian
Castle Clinton
Fraunces Tavern
Ferry to Statue of Liberty
Staten Island Ferry Terminal
South Street Seaport
Confucius Plaza
Eldridge St. Synagogue
Columbus Park
Foley Square
Seward Park
Rutgers Park
Battery Park
Bowling Green
© Copyright Time Out Group 2001

Dia Center for the Arts
CHELSEA
FLATIRON
GRAMERCY PARK
Madison Square
Flatiron Building
Joyce Theater
Gramercy Park
Union Sq
Stuyvesant Square
Peter Cooper Village
Stuyvesant Town
Manhattan Marina
East River
GREENWICH VILLAGE
Washington Square
New York University
Grace Church
St. Mark's in the Bowery
Tompkins Square
EAST VILLAGE
East River Park
SOHO
Guggenheim Soho
St Lukes
LITTLE ITALY
LOWER EAST SIDE
W 23RD ST
E 23RD ST
W 14TH ST
E 14TH ST
TENTH AVE
NINTH AVE
EIGHTH AVE
SEVENTH AVE
SIXTH AVE
FIFTH AVE
BROADWAY
PARK AVE SOUTH
LEXINGTON A
THIRD AVE
SECOND AVE
FIRST AVE
FRANKLIN D ROOSEVELT DR
WEST SIDE HWY (JOE DIMAGGIO HWY)
HUDSON ST
SEVENTH AVE S
W HOUSTON ST
E HOUSTON ST
LAGUARDIA PL
WEST BROADWAY
LAFAYETTE ST
FOURTH AVE
THE BOWERY
VARICK ST
CANAL ST
CENTRE ST
HOLLAND TUNNEL
WILLIAMSBURG BRIDGE
GRAND ST
EAST BROADWAY
2
3
4
5
6
Q
R
S

De Witt Clinton
CLINTON
THEATER DISTRICT
GARMENT DISTRICT
MIDTOWN
TWELFTH AVE
ELEVENTH AVE
TENTH AVE
NINTH AVE
EIGHTH AVE
SEVENTH AVE
BROADWAY
SIXTH AVE
FIFTH AVE
MADISON AVE
VANDERBILT AVE
PARK AVE
PARK AVE SOUTH
LEXINGTON AVE
THIRD AVE
SECOND AVE
FIRST AVE
FRANKLIN D ROOSEVELT DR
WEST SIDE HWY
LINCOLN TUNNEL
W 42ND ST
W 40TH ST
W 34TH ST
W 23RD ST
E 42ND ST
E 40TH ST
E 34TH ST
E 23RD ST
CARDINAL STEPINAC
GALVIN AVE
DYER AVE
ROCKEFELLER PLAZA
UN PLAZA
TUDOR CITY PL
MT CARMEL PL
ASSER LEVY PL
BEEKMAN PL
MITCHELL
SUTTON PL SOUTH
NY Visitors Bureau
Museum of Modern Art
Radio City Music Hall
St. Patrick's Cathedral
Rockefeller Center
Saks Fifth Ave
Helmsley Building
Grand Central Terminal
Chrysler Building
News Building
United Nations Headquarters
TKTS
Times Square
Port Authority Bus Terminal
Bryant Park
NY Public Library
Javits Center
Pierpont Morgan Library
Macy's
Herald Square
Empire State Building
Manhattan Mall
General Post Office
Madison Square Garden
Penn Station
Chelsea Park
Madison Square
Flatiron Building
Dia Center for the Arts
East River
Manhattan Marina

Carl Schurz Park
GRACIE
Great Lawn
Goethe House
UPPER EAST SIDE
Metropolitan Museum of Art
Delacorte Theater
Belvedere Castle
Rose Center
HENRY HUDSON PKWY
W 79TH ST
AMSTERDAM AVE
79TH ST TRANSVERSE RD
E 79TH ST
EAST END AVE
Central
American Museum of Natural History
John Jay Park
CHEROKEE PLACE
The Ramble
Loeb Boathouse
WEST DRIVE
The Bow Bridge
Conservatory Water
Whitney Museum of American Art
RIVERSIDE DR
The Dakota
Strawberry Fields
Bethesda Terrace
Naumburg Bandshell
W 72ND ST
E 72ND ST
FRANKLIN D ROOSEVELT DR
Frick Collection
EAST DRIVE
Sheep Meadow
Roosevelt Island
FREEDOM PL
BROADWAY
COLUMBUS AVE
CENTRAL PARK WEST
WEST END AVE
Tavern on the Green
Rockefeller University
65TH ST TRANSVERSE RD
Temple Emanu-El
FIFTH AVE
MADISON AVE
LEXINGTON AVE
THIRD AVE
SECOND AVE
FIRST AVE
Lincoln Center
Heckscher Playground
The Dairy
Zoo
PARK AVE
Wollman Memorial Rink
YORK AVE
WEST SIDE HWY
Bloomingdales
TRAMWAY
QUEENSBORO BRIDGE (59TH ST)
Columbus Circle
CENTRAL PARK SOUTH
Grand Army Plaza
SUTTON PLACE
W 57TH ST
Carnegie Hall
Trump Tower
ELEVENTH AVE
NINTH AVE
0.3 mile
400 m
© Copyright Time Out Group 2001

UPPER WEST SIDE
SPANISH HARLEM
YORKVILLE
Riverside Park
Morningside Park
Central
The
Harlem
Great Lawn
Jefferson Park
Carl Schurz Park
Cathedral of St. John the Divine
Cathedral Close
Verdi Square
Symphony Space
Soldiers' & Sailors' Monument
Conservatory Gardens
Metropolitan Museum of Art
El Museo del Barrio
Museum of the City of NY
Jewish Museum
Cooper-Hewitt National Design Museum
Guggenheim Museum
Goethe House
Gracie Mansion
HENRY HUDSON PKWY
RIVERSIDE DR
WEST END AVE
BROADWAY
AMSTERDAM AVE
COLUMBUS AVE
MANHATTAN AVE
CENTRAL PARK WEST
W 96TH ST
W 86TH ST
WEST DRIVE
EAST DRIVE
97TH ST TRANSVERSE RD
86TH ST TRANSVERSE RD
LENOX AVE
ST NICHOLAS AVE
MORNINGSIDE DR
CENTRAL PARK
CATHEDRAL
DUKE ELLINGTON
HENRY J BROWNE
FIFTH AVE
MADISON AVE
PARK AVE
LEXINGTON AVE
THIRD AVE
SECOND AVE
FIRST AVE
YORK AVE
EAST END AVE
FRANKLIN D ROOSEVELT DR
E 96TH ST
E 86TH ST
W 113TH
W 111TH
W 109TH
W 107TH
W 105TH
W 103RD
W 102ND
W 100TH
W 98TH
W 94TH
W 92ND
W 90TH
W 88TH
W 84TH
W 82ND
E 113TH
E 111TH
E 109TH
E 107TH
E 105TH
E 103RD
E 102ND
E 100TH
E 98TH
E 94TH
E 92ND
E 90TH
E 88TH
E 84TH
E 82ND
GRACIE
1,9
1,2, 3,9
B,C
2,3
6
4,5,6
1
2
3
4
5
J
K
L
0
0.3 mil
400 m
© Copyright Time Out Group 2001

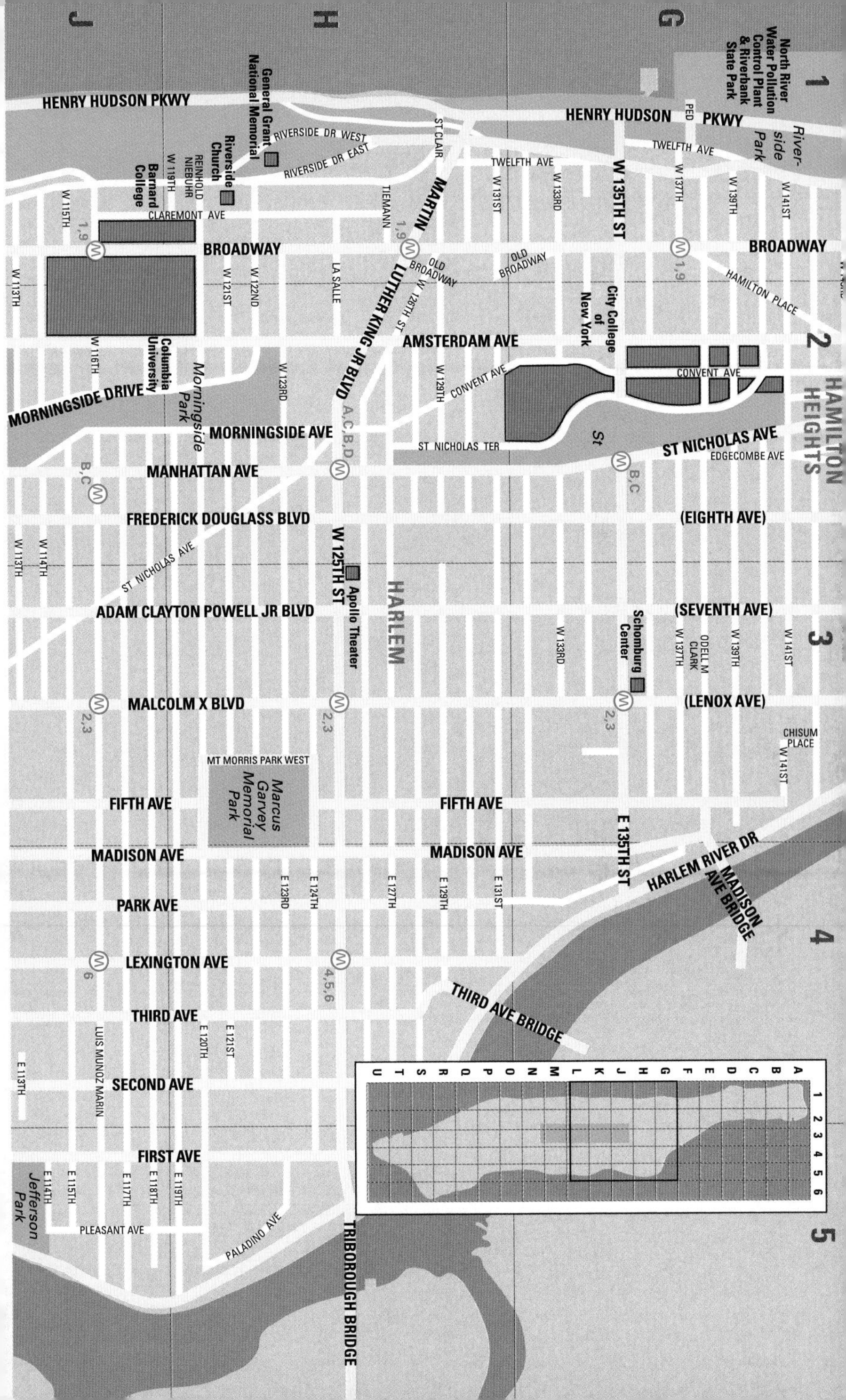

J
H
G
1
2
3
4
5
North River Water Pollution Control Plant & Riverbank State Park
Riverside Park
HENRY HUDSON PKWY
HENRY HUDSON
PED
PKWY
General Grant National Memorial
Riverside Church
Barnard College
RIVERSIDE DR WEST
RIVERSIDE DR EAST
TWELFTH AVE
ST CLAIR
W 115TH
W 119TH
REINHOLD NIEBUHR
TIEMANN
W 131ST
W 133RD
W 135TH ST
W 137TH
W 139TH
W 141ST
CLAREMONT AVE
BROADWAY
1,9
MARTIN LUTHER KING JR BLVD
OLD BROADWAY
W 126TH ST
HAMILTON PLACE
W 113TH
W 121ST
W 122ND
LA SALLE
City College of New York
AMSTERDAM AVE
W 116TH
Columbia University
Morningside Park
W 123RD
W 129TH
CONVENT AVE
HAMILTON HEIGHTS
MORNINGSIDE DRIVE
A,C,B,D
MORNINGSIDE AVE
ST NICHOLAS TER
St Nicholas Park
ST NICHOLAS AVE
EDGECOMBE AVE
MANHATTAN AVE
B,C
FREDERICK DOUGLASS BLVD
(EIGHTH AVE)
W 113TH
W 114TH
W 125TH ST
Apollo Theater
HARLEM
ADAM CLAYTON POWELL JR BLVD
(SEVENTH AVE)
Schomburg Center
W 133RD
W 137TH
ODELL M CLARK
W 139TH
W 141ST
MALCOLM X BLVD
(LENOX AVE)
2,3
CHISUM PLACE
W 141ST
MT MORRIS PARK WEST
Marcus Garvey Memorial Park
FIFTH AVE
FIFTH AVE
E 135TH ST
MADISON AVE
MADISON AVE
HARLEM RIVER DR
MADISON AVE BRIDGE
E 123RD
E 124TH
E 127TH
E 129TH
E 131ST
PARK AVE
LEXINGTON AVE
6
4,5,6
THIRD AVE BRIDGE
THIRD AVE
E 120TH
E 121ST
LUIS MUNOZ MARIN
E 113TH
SECOND AVE
FIRST AVE
E 114TH
E 115TH
E 117TH
E 118TH
E 119TH
Jefferson Park
PLEASANT AVE
PALADINO AVE
TRIBOROUGH BRIDGE
A B C D E F G H J K L M N O P Q R S T U
1 2 3 4 5 6

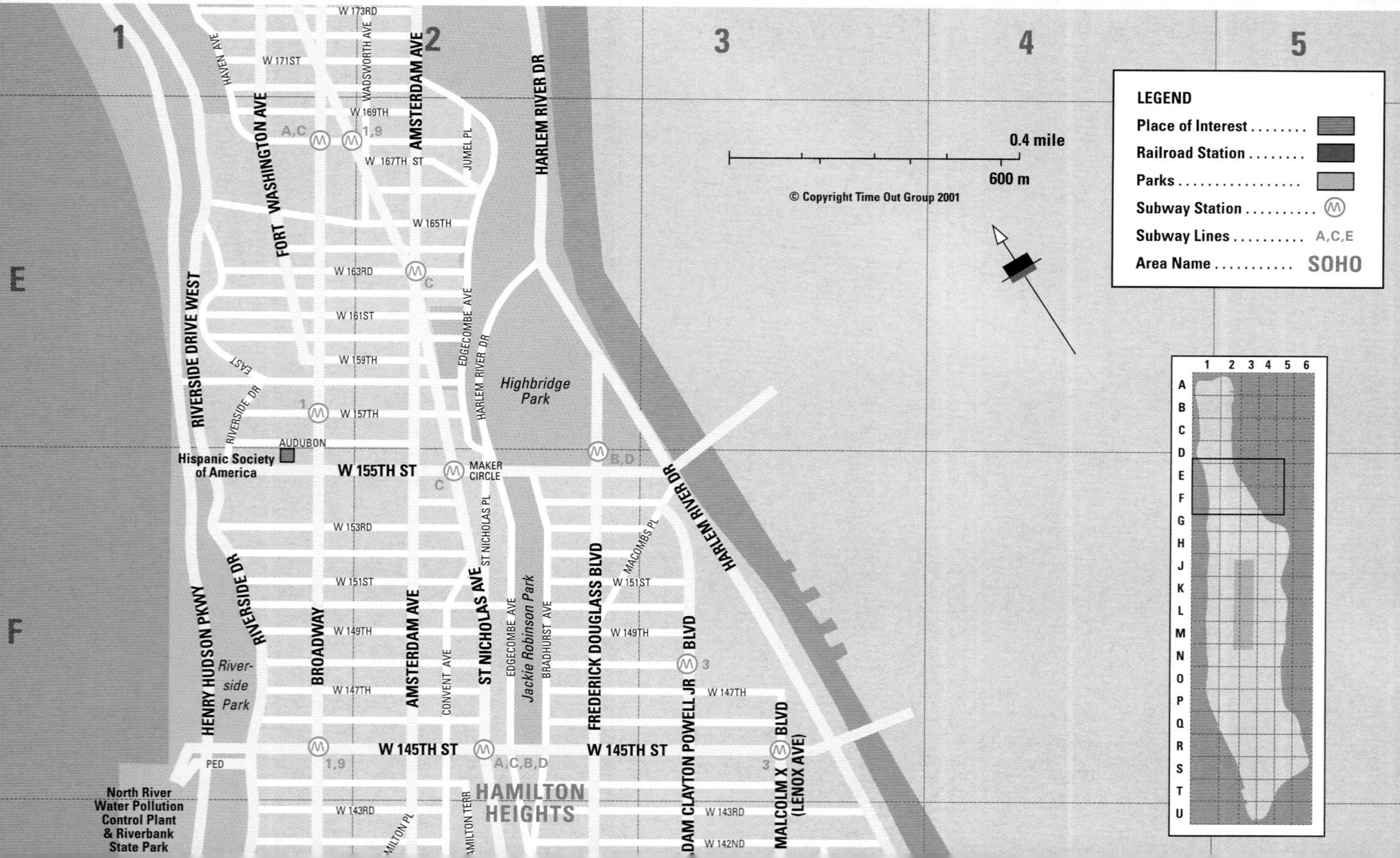

1
2
3
4
5
E
F
LEGEND
Place of Interest
Railroad Station
Parks
Subway Station
Subway Lines
A,C,E
Area Name
SOHO
0.4 mile
600 m
© Copyright Time Out Group 2001
RIVERSIDE DRIVE WEST
HENRY HUDSON PKWY
RIVERSIDE DR
RIVERSIDE DR EAST
River-side Park
Hispanic Society of America
AUDUBON
FORT WASHINGTON AVE
HAVEN AVE
BROADWAY
AMSTERDAM AVE
WADSWORTH AVE
JUMEL PL
EDGECOMBE AVE
HARLEM RIVER DR
Highbridge Park
MAKER CIRCLE
W 155TH ST
W 145TH ST
ST NICHOLAS AVE
ST NICHOLAS PL
CONVENT AVE
Jackie Robinson Park
BRADHURST AVE
FREDERICK DOUGLASS BLVD
MACOMBS PL
ADAM CLAYTON POWELL JR BLVD
MALCOLM X BLVD (LENOX AVE)
HAMILTON HEIGHTS
HAMILTON TERR
HAMILTON PL
PED
North River Water Pollution Control Plant & Riverbank State Park
W 173RD
W 171ST
W 169TH
W 167TH ST
W 165TH
W 163RD
W 161ST
W 159TH
W 157TH
W 153RD
W 151ST
W 149TH
W 147TH
W 143RD
W 142ND
A,C
1,9
C
1
B,D
A,C,B,D
3

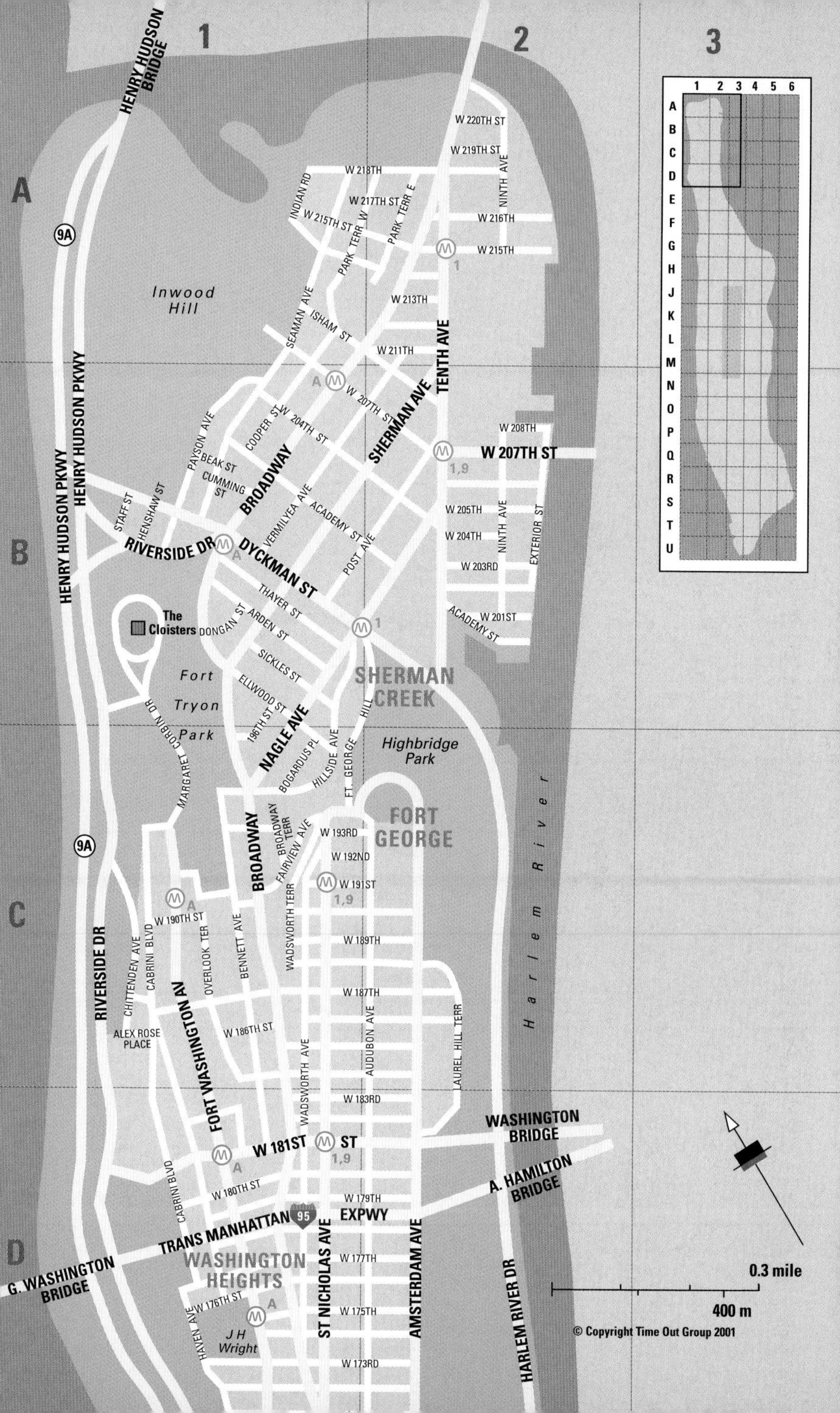

1
2
3
A
B
C
D
HENRY HUDSON BRIDGE
9A
Inwood Hill
HENRY HUDSON PKWY
W 220TH ST
W 219TH ST
W 218TH
INDIAN RD
W 217TH ST
PARK TERR W
PARK TERR E
W 215TH ST
W 216TH
NINTH AVE
W 215TH
W 213TH
SEAMAN AVE
ISHAM ST
W 211TH
TENTH AVE
W 207TH ST
SHERMAN AVE
PAYSON AVE
COOPER ST
W 204TH ST
BEAK ST
CUMMING ST
BROADWAY
W 208TH
W 207TH ST
STAFF ST
HENSHAW ST
VERMILYEA AVE
ACADEMY ST
W 205TH
W 204TH
W 203RD
RIVERSIDE DR
DYCKMAN ST
POST AVE
EXTERIOR ST
THAYER ST
W 201ST
ACADEMY ST
The Cloisters
DONGAN ST
ARDEN ST
SICKLES ST
SHERMAN CREEK
Fort Tryon Park
ELLWOOD ST
196TH ST
NAGLE AVE
HILL
Highbridge Park
CORBIN DR
MARGARET
BOGARDUS PL
HILLSIDE AVE
FT. GEORGE
BROADWAY TERR
FAIRVIEW AVE
W 193RD
FORT GEORGE
W 192ND
W 191ST
Harlem River
W 190TH ST
OVERLOOK TER
BENNETT AVE
WADSWORTH TERR
W 189TH
CHITTENDEN AVE
CABRINI BLVD
W 187TH
LAUREL HILL TERR
ALEX ROSE PLACE
W 186TH ST
FORT WASHINGTON AV
WADSWORTH AVE
AUDUBON AVE
W 183RD
WASHINGTON BRIDGE
W 181ST
ST
1,9
A
W 180TH ST
W 179TH
A. HAMILTON BRIDGE
95
TRANS MANHATTAN
EXPWY
G. WASHINGTON BRIDGE
WASHINGTON HEIGHTS
W 177TH
W 176TH ST
HAVEN AVE
W 175TH
J H Wright
ST NICHOLAS AVE
AMSTERDAM AVE
HARLEM RIVER DR
W 173RD
0.3 mile
400 m
1 2 3 4 5 6
A B C D E F G H J K L M N O P Q R S T U

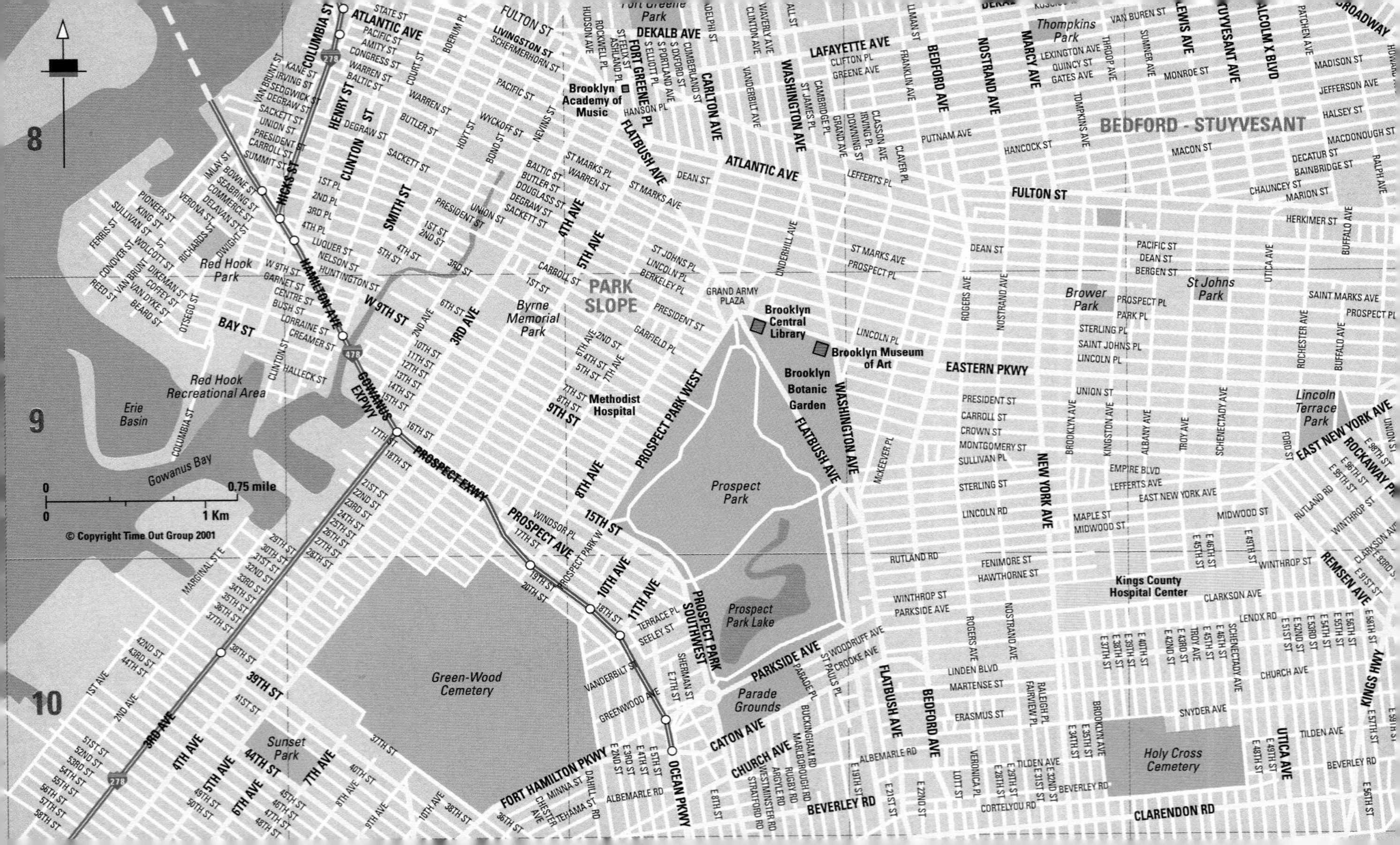
8
9
10
0
0.75 mile
0
1 Km
© Copyright Time Out Group 2001
Red Hook Park
Red Hook Recreational Area
Erie Basin
Gowanus Bay
PARK SLOPE
Byrne Memorial Park
Methodist Hospital
Brooklyn Academy of Music
Fort Greene Park
Grand Army Plaza
Brooklyn Central Library
Brooklyn Museum of Art
Brooklyn Botanic Garden
Prospect Park
Prospect Park Lake
Parade Grounds
Green-Wood Cemetery
Sunset Park
Kings County Hospital Center
Holy Cross Cemetery
Brower Park
St Johns Park
Lincoln Terrace Park
Thompkins Park
BEDFORD - STUYVESANT
ATLANTIC AVE
FULTON ST
FLATBUSH AVE
PROSPECT PARK WEST
PROSPECT PARK SOUTHWEST
EASTERN PKWY
PROSPECT EXWY
GOWANUS EXPWY
HAMILTON AVE
HICKS ST
COLUMBIA ST
HENRY ST
CLINTON ST
SMITH ST
4TH AVE
5TH AVE
3RD AVE
8TH AVE
9TH ST
15TH ST
10TH AVE
11TH AVE
PROSPECT AVE
FORT HAMILTON PKWY
OCEAN PKWY
CATON AVE
CHURCH AVE
PARKSIDE AVE
BEVERLEY RD
BEDFORD AVE
NOSTRAND AVE
NEW YORK AVE
WASHINGTON AVE
CARLTON AVE
DEKALB AVE
LAFAYETTE AVE
MARCY AVE
UTICA AVE
REMSEN AVE
CLARENDON RD
KINGS HWY
EAST NEW YORK AVE
ROCKAWAY PKWY
BROADWAY

Brooklyn
T
U
V
W
X
5
6
7
Hudson River
East River
Upper Bay
BATTERY PARK CITY
TRIBECA
SOHO
GREENWICH VILLAGE
FLATIRON
GRAMERCY PARK
LITTLE ITALY
CHINATOWN
LOWER EAST SIDE
EAST VILLAGE
BROOKLYN HEIGHTS
WILLIAMSBURG
BROOKLYN-BATTERY TUNNEL
WEST SIDE HWY
WHITEHALL ST
FRANKLIN D ROOSEVELT DR
HUDSON ST
WEST BROADWAY
CHURCH ST
BROADWAY
CENTRE ST
PARK ROW
VARICK ST
AVENUE OF THE AMERICAS
FIFTH AVE
PARK AVE SOUTH
THIRD AVE
SECOND AVE
E 23RD ST
E 14TH ST
W 14TH ST
W HOUSTON ST
E HOUSTON ST
LAFAYETTE
THE BOWERY
EAST BROADWAY
BROOKLYN BRIDGE
MANHATTAN BRIDGE
WILLIAMSBURG BRIDGE
Empire-Fulton Ferry State Park
Industrial Park
Wallabout Bay
Brooklyn Navy Yard
FURMAN ST
NASSAU ST
PARK AVE
LEE AVE
MARCY AVE
RODNEY ST
BROOKLYN-QUEENS EXWY
BEDFORD AVE
BERRY ST
DRIGGS AVE
KENT AVE
FLUSHING AVE
NOSTRAND AVE
UNION AVE
GRAND STREET EXT
BUSHWICK AVE
McCarren Park
McGolrick Park
Cooper Park
HUMBOLDT ST
NORMAN AVE
KINGSLAND AVE
GREENPOINT AVE
McGUINNESS BLVD
PULASKI BRIDGE
Newtown Creek
Dutch Kill
BORDEN AVE
VANDERVOORT AVE
METROPOLITAN AVE
GRAND ST
English Kills
KOSCIUSZKO BRIDGE
Calvary Cemetery
MYRTLE AVE
DEKALB AVE
LEWIS AVE
49TH AVE
51ST AVE
39TH ST
See Queens Map Page 403
See Manhattan Map Pages 394-5

Queens
W
X
Y
Z
1
2
3
4
5
6
7
East River
TRIBOROUGH BRIDGE
FIFTH AVE
PARK AVE
LEXINGTON AVE
THIRD AVE
SECOND AVE
FIRST AVE
Jefferson Park
Central Park
SPANISH HARLEM
0
0.75 mile
0
1 Km
© Copyright Time Out Group 2001
E 96TH ST
FD ROOSEVELT DR
YORKVILLE
E 86TH ST
UPPER EAST SIDE
EAST END AVE
Carl Schurz Park
E 79TH ST
John Jay Park
E 72ND ST
Roosevelt Island
QUEENSBORO BRIDGE
Queens Bridge Park
Hell Gate
Con Edison
Astoria Park
Bowery Bay
La Guardia Airport
RIKERS ISLAND BRIDGE
SHORE BLVD
DITMARS BLVD
ASTORIA BLVD
MAIN AVE
31ST ST
ASTORIA
St Michaels Cemetery
BROOKLYN QUEENS EXPY W
BROOKLYN QUEENS EXPY E
VERNON BLVD
21ST ST
34TH AVE
STEINWAY ST
31ST AVE
BROADWAY
CRESCENT ST
NEWTOWN RD
LONG ISLAND CITY
JACKSON HEIGHTS
NORTHERN BLVD
82ND ST
81ST ST
Sunnyside Yard
39TH ST
SKILLMAN AVE
43RD AVE
QUEENS BLVD
48TH ST
GREENPOINT AVE
Greenland Park
WOODSIDE
WOODSIDE AVE
ROOSEVELT AVE
BROADWAY
BAXTER AVE
45TH AVE
JACKSON AVE
THOMSON AVE
VAN DAM ST
SUNNYSIDE
See Brooklyn Map Pages 404-5
Dutch Kills
49TH AVE
QUEENS MIDTOWN TUNNEL
11TH ST
PULASKI BRIDGE
Newtown Creek
BORDEN AVE
New Calvary Cemetery
58TH ST
61ST ST
MIDDLE VILLAGE
Calvary Cemetery
Mount Zion Cemetery
MAURICE AVE
69TH ST
MCGUINNESS BLVD
GREENPOINT AVE
NORMAN AVE
HUMBOLDT ST
MASPETH
GRAND AVE
MASPETH AVE
61ST ST
LOMBARDY ST
KINGSLAND AVE
VANDERVOORT AVE
MANHATTAN AVE
McCarren Park
BERRY ST
BEDFORD AVE
DRIGGS AVE
English Kills
GRAND ST
FLUSHING AVE
FRESH POND RD
Mt Olivet Cemetery
ELIOT AVE
Juniper Valley Park
METROPOLITAN AVE
Linden Hill Cemetery
BUSHWICK AVE
UNION AVE
MARCY AVE
RODNEY ST
FLUSHING AVE
Lutheran Cemetery
Glen Ridge Park
CENTRAL AVE
278
495
25

Trips Out of Town
To Hunter Mtn, Ski Windham
Newburgh
To Poughkeepsie, Hyde Park & Rhinebeck
Beacon
Lake Candlewood
Cold Spring
Garrison
NEW YORK
CONNECTICUT
Danbury
New Haven
West Haven
New London
Westerly
New Croton Reservoir
Fishers Is
Bridgeport
Plum Is
Hudson River
Long Island Sound
Gardiners Is
Shelter Is
Stamford
Montauk
NEW JERSEY
Yonkers
New Rochelle
Great Peconic Bay
East Hampton
Long Island
Kings Park
Clifton
Southampton
See Manhattan Map Pages 394-401
La Guardia Airport
Newark
Jersey City
See Queens Map Page 403
Patchogue
Bay Shore
Newark Airport
New York
See Brooklyn Map Pages 404-5
Fire Is
Great South Bay
The Pines
Elizabeth
JFK Airport
Ocean Beach
Robert Moses State Park
Jones Beach State Park
Staten Is
Coney Is
Long Beach
ATLANTIC OCEAN
Raritan Bay
0
20 miles
0
30 km
87
95
9A
295
3
25
495
27
678
278

# Key Sights

Any trip to New York, New York, should include a stop at one of these fave places—maybe even all!

**American Museum of Natural History**
*Central Park West at 79th St (212-769-5000, recorded information 212-769-5100). Subway: B, C to 81st St; 1, 9 to 79th St.* *See page 41.*

**Apollo Theater**
*253 W 125th St between Adam Clayton Powell Jr. Blvd (Seventh Ave) and Frederick Douglass Blvd (Eighth Ave) (212-749-5838). Subway: A, C, B, D, 1, 9 to 125th St.* *See page 307.*

**Bronx Zoo/Wildlife Conservation Society**
*Bronx River Pkwy at Fordham Rd, Bronx (718-367-1010). Subway: 2, 5 to Bronx Park East.* *See page 127.*

**Brooklyn Botanic Garden**
*900 Washington Ave between Eastern Pkwy and Empire Blvd, Prospect Park, Brooklyn (718-623-7200). Subway: C to Franklin Ave, then S to Botanic Garden; 2, 3 to Eastern Pkwy–Brooklyn Museum.* *See page 112.*

**Brooklyn Bridge**
*Subway: J, M, Z to Chambers St; 4, 5, 6 to Brooklyn Bridge–City Hall.* *See page 109.*

**Central Park**
*From 59th to 110th Sts, between Fifth Ave and Central Park West. (212-360-3456).* *See page 96.*

**Chinatown**
*Subway: J, M, Z, N, Q, R, W, 6 to Canal St.* *See page 70.*

**Coney Island**
*Subway: W to Coney Island–Stillwell Ave.* *See page 115.*

**Empire State Building**
*350 Fifth Ave between 33rd and 34th Sts (212-736-3100). Subway: B, D, F, V, N, Q, R, W to 34th St–Herald Sq; 6 to 33rd St.* *See pages 25 and 88.*

**Ground Zero**
*World Trade Center Viewing Platform, Church St at Fulton St. Subway: E to World Trade Center; N, R, W to Cortlandt St.* *See page 64.*

**Metropolitan Museum of Art**
*1000 Fifth Ave at 82nd St (212-535-7710). Subway: 4, 5, 6 to 86th St.* *See page 44.*

**New York Public Library Center for the Humanities**
*Fifth Ave between 40th and 42nd Sts (212-930-0830). Subway: B, D, F, V to 42nd St; 7 to Fifth Ave.* *See page 58.*

**Reach for the sky** The Empire State Building, once again the tallest structure in New York, towers 1,250 feet above midtown.

**Rockefeller Center**
*48th to 51st Sts between Fifth and Sixth Aves (212-632-3975). Subway: B, D, F, V to 47–50th Sts–Rockefeller Ctr.* *See page 91.*

**Staten Island Ferry**
*South St at Whitehall St (718-727-2508). Subway: 1, 9 to South Ferry; 4, 5 to Bowling Green.* *See page 132.*

**Statue of Liberty and Ellis Island Immigration Museum**
*Liberty Island and Ellis Island (212-363-3200). Travel: N, R, W to Whitehall St; 4, 5 to Bowling Green, then ferry from Battery Park to Liberty Island and Ellis Island.* *See page 62.*

**Times Square/Theater District**
*Broadway at 42nd St. Subway: N, Q, R, W, S, 1, 2, 3, 9, 7 to 42nd St–Times Sq.* *See pages 85 and 335.*

Metropolitan Transportation Authority
MTA New York City Subway
with bus, railroad, and ferry connections
Key
MTA New York City Transit
Subway in four boroughs, buses in five boroughs, and the MTA Staten Island Railway
The subway operates 24 hours a day, seven days a week, but not all lines operate at all times. For detailed information, consult Passenger Information Centers in stations or call our Travel Information Center (24 hours) at 718-330-1234. Non-English-speaking customers call 718-330-4847 (7AM to 7PM).
visit www.mta.info
To show service more clearly, geography on this map has been modified.
© 2003 Metropolitan Transportation Authority
Design: Michael Hertz Associates, NYC
January 2003
Nights and weekends only
Station Name A·C
Full time service
Part time service
Local service only
All trains stop (local and express service)
Station served by one of two lines
Free subway transfer
Free out-of-system subway transfer (MetroCard only)
Normal service
Special rush hour or express service
Terminal
Commuter rail service
Hudson River
Harlem River
East River
Long Island Sound
MANHATTAN
THE BRONX
QUEENS
Van Cortlandt Park 242 St
238 St
231 St
Marble Hill 225 St
215 St
207 St
Inwood 207 St
Dyckman St
191 St
190 St
181 St
175 St
168 St-Washington Hts
Washington Hts 168 St
163 St Amsterdam Av
157 St
155 St
145 St
Harlem 148 St
137 St City College
135 St
125 St
116 St Columbia University
116 St
Cathedral Pkwy (110 St)
Central Park North (110 St)
103 St
96 St
86 St
81 St-Museum of Natural History
79 St
72 St
66 St Lincoln Center
59 St Columbus Circle
57 St
50 St
49 St
47-50 Sts/Rockefeller Ctr
42 St Port Authority Bus Terminal
Times Sq 42 St
Grand Central 42 St
5 Av/53 St
Lexington Av/53 St
5 Av/59 St
Lexington Av/59 St
Lexington Av/63 St
68 St Hunter College
77 St
110 St
125 St
Roosevelt Island
Woodlawn
Mosholu Pkwy
Bedford Pk Blvd Lehman College
Bedford Pk Blvd
Kingsbridge Rd
Fordham Rd
182-183 Sts
183 St
Burnside Av
Tremont Av
176 St
174-175 Sts
Mt Eden Av
170 St
167 St
161 St Yankee Stadium
149 St-Grand Concourse
138 St-Grand Concourse
3 Av-149 St
3 Av 138 St
Norwood 205 St
Wakefield 241 St
Nereid Av (238 St)
233 St
225 St
219 St
Gun Hill Rd
Burke Av
Allerton Av
Pelham Pkwy
Bronx Park East
West Farms Sq E Tremont Av
E 180 St
174 St
Freeman St
Simpson St
Intervale Av
Prospect Av
Jackson Av
Eastchester Dyre Av
Baychester Av
Morris Park
Pelham Bay Park
Buhre Av
Middletown Rd
Westchester Sq East Tremont Av
Zerega Av
Castle Hill Av
Parkchester-E 177 St
St Lawrence Av
Morrison-Sound View Avs
Elder Av
Whitlock Av
Hunts Point Av
Longwood Av
E 149 St
E 143 St St Mary's St
Cypress Av
Brook Av
Astoria Ditmars Blvd
Astoria Blvd
30 Av
Broadway
36 Av
39 Av
Queensboro Plaza
Queens Plaza
Court Sq
45 Rd Court House Sq
23 St-Ely Av
21 St
Hunters Point Av
Vernon Blvd-Jackson Av
21 St Queensbridge
Steinway St
46 St
Northern Blvd
65 St
33 St
40 St
46 St
52 St
61 St Woodside
69 St
74 St-Broadway
82 St-Jackson Hts
Jackson Hts Roosevelt Av
90 St-Elmhurst Av
Elmhurst Av
Junction Blvd
103 St-Corona Plaza
111 St
Willets Point-Shea Stadium
Flushing Main St
Grand Av Newtown
Woodhaven Blvd
63 Dr Rego Park
67 Av
Forest Hills, 71 Av
75 Av
Kew Gardens Union Tpke
Briarwood/Van Wyck Blvd
Sutphin Blvd
Parsons Blvd
169 St
Jamaica 179 St
Jamaica Van Wyck
Jamaica Center Parsons/Archer
Sutphin Blvd Archer Av
121 St
111 St
104 St
Woodhaven Blvd
Ozone Park Lefferts Blvd
Middle Village Metropolitan Av

STATEN ISLAND
BROOKLYN
Jamaica Bay
MTA Staten Island Railway
Stadium (game days only)
St. George
Tompkinsville
Stapleton
Clifton
Grasmere
Old Town
Dongan Hills
Jefferson Avenue
Grant City
New Dorp
Oakwood Heights
Bay Terrace
Great Kills
Eltingville
Annadale
South Ferry
Bowling Green
Whitehall St
Rector St
World Trade Center
Chambers St
Canal St
Houston St
Christopher St Sheridan Sq
14 St
23 St
34 St Penn Station
Times Sq 42 St
Grand Central 42 St
Port Authority Bus Terminal
Vernon Blvd–Jackson Av
Hunters Point Av
Borough Hall
Jay St Borough Hall
DeKalb Av
Atlantic Av
Prospect Park
Coney Island Stillwell Av
Brighton Beach
Sheepshead Bay
Broadway Junction
Howard Beach JFK Airport
Rockaway Park Beach 116 St
Far Rockaway Mott Av
W via Lower Manhattan late nights and weekends only until spring 2004

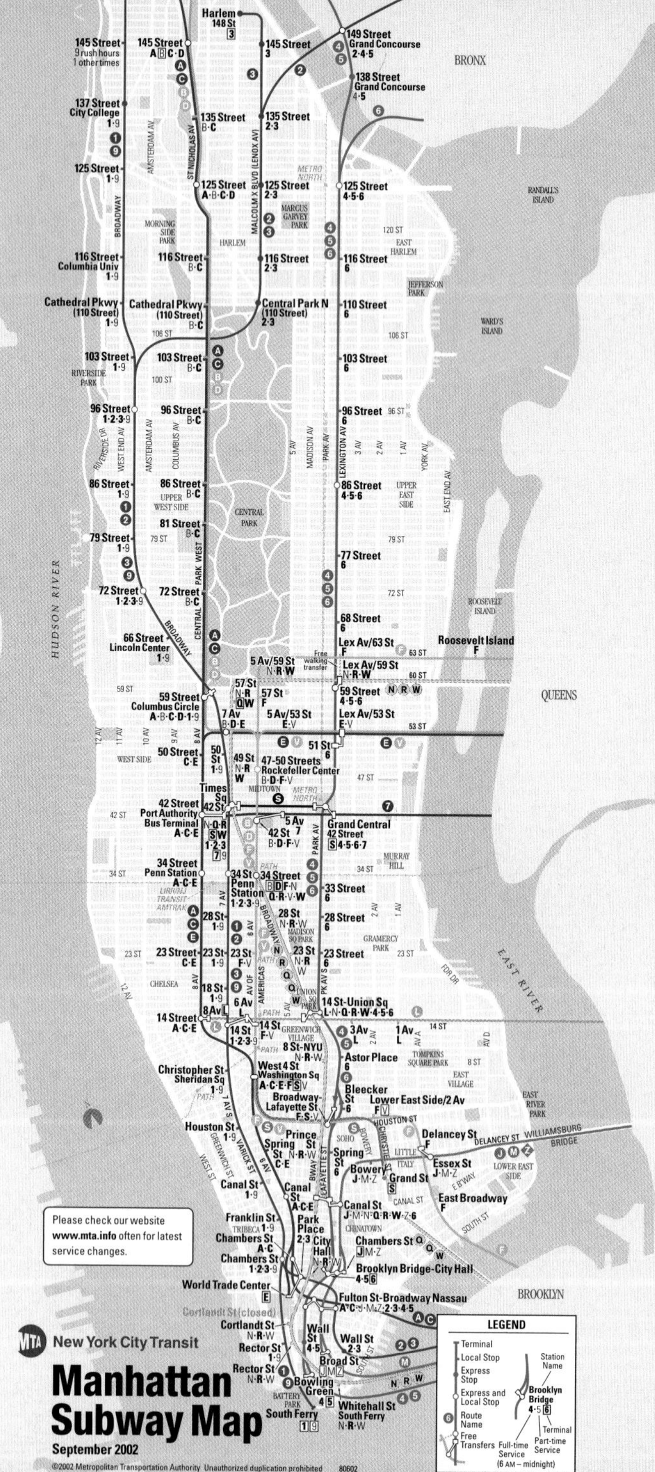

Harlem 148 St 3
145 Street 9 rush hours 1 other times
145 Street A B C D
145 Street 3
149 Street Grand Concourse 2·4·5
BRONX
138 Street Grand Concourse 4·5
137 Street City College 1·9
135 Street B·C
135 Street 2·3
125 Street 1·9
125 Street A·B·C·D
125 Street 2·3
125 Street 4·5·6
METRO NORTH
RANDALL'S ISLAND
MARCUS GARVEY PARK
MORNING SIDE PARK
HARLEM
EAST HARLEM
120 ST
116 Street Columbia Univ 1·9
116 Street B·C
116 Street 2·3
116 Street 6
JEFFERSON PARK
Cathedral Pkwy (110 Street) 1·9
Cathedral Pkwy (110 Street) B·C
Central Park N (110 Street) 2·3
110 Street 6
WARD'S ISLAND
106 ST
103 Street 1·9
103 Street B·C
103 Street 6
RIVERSIDE PARK
100 ST
96 Street 1·2·3·9
96 Street B·C
96 Street 6
96 ST
86 Street 1·9
86 Street B·C
86 Street 4·5·6
UPPER WEST SIDE
UPPER EAST SIDE
CENTRAL PARK
81 Street B·C
79 Street 1·9
79 ST
77 Street 6
HUDSON RIVER
72 Street 1·2·3·9
72 Street B·C
72 ST
68 Street 6
ROOSEVELT ISLAND
66 Street Lincoln Center 1·9
Lex Av/63 St F
63 ST
Roosevelt Island F
5 Av/59 St N·R·W
Free walking transfer
Lex Av/59 St N·R·W
60 ST
59 ST
57 St N·R Q W
57 St F
59 Street 4·5·6
QUEENS
59 Street Columbus Circle A·B·C·D·1·9
7 Av B·D·E
5 Av/53 St E·V
Lex Av/53 St E·V
53 ST
51 St 6
50 Street C·E
50 St 1·9
49 St N·R W
47-50 Streets Rockefeller Center B·D·F·V
WEST SIDE
47 ST
MIDTOWN
Times Sq 42 St N·Q·R S W 1·2·3 7 9
42 Street Port Authority Bus Terminal A·C·E
42 ST
5 Av 7
42 St B·D·F·V
Grand Central 42 Street S 4·5·6·7
MURRAY HILL
34 Street Penn Station A·C·E
34 St Penn Station 1·2·3·9
34 Street B D F·N Q·R·V·W
33 Street 6
34 ST
LIRR NJ TRANSIT AMTRAK
28 St 1·9
28 St N·R·W
28 Street 6
MADISON SQ PARK
GRAMERCY PARK
23 Street C·E
23 St 1·9
23 St F·V
23 St N·R W
23 Street 6
23 ST
CHELSEA
FDR DR
EAST RIVER
18 St 1·9
14 Street A·C·E
8 Av L
6 Av L
14 St 1·2·3·9
14 St F·V
14 St-Union Sq L·N·Q·R·W·4·5·6
UNION SQ PARK
GREENWICH VILLAGE
3 Av L
1 Av L
14 ST
8 St-NYU N·R·W
Astor Place 6
TOMPKINS SQUARE PARK
EAST VILLAGE
8 ST
Christopher St Sheridan Sq 1·9
West 4 St Washington Sq A·C·E·F S V
Broadway-Lafayette St F·S·V
Bleecker St 6
Lower East Side/2 Av F V
EAST RIVER PARK
HOUSTON ST
Houston St 1·9
Prince St N·R·W
Spring St C·E
Spring St 6
SOHO
LITTLE ITALY
Delancey St F
DELANCEY ST
WILLIAMSBURG BRIDGE
Essex St J·M·Z
LOWER EAST SIDE
Bowery J·M·Z
Grand St S
Canal St 1·9
Canal St A·C·E
Canal St J·M·N·Q·R·W·Z·6
CANAL ST
East Broadway F
Please check our website www.mta.info often for latest service changes.
Franklin St 1·9
TRIBECA
Chambers St A·C
Chambers St 1·2·3·9
Park Place 2·3
City Hall N·R·W
Chambers St J M·Z
CHINATOWN
Brooklyn Bridge-City Hall 4·5 6
World Trade Center E
Fulton St-Broadway Nassau A·C·J·M·Z·2·3·4·5
BROOKLYN
Cortlandt St (closed)
Cortlandt St N·R·W
Wall St 4·5
Wall St 2·3
Rector St 1·9
Rector St N·R·W
Broad St J M Z
Bowling Green 4 5
BATTERY PARK
South Ferry 1 9
Whitehall St South Ferry N·R·W
MTA New York City Transit
Manhattan Subway Map
September 2002
LEGEND
Terminal
Local Stop
Express Stop
Express and Local Stop
Route Name
Free Transfers
Station Name
Brooklyn Bridge 4·5 6
Terminal
Full-time Service
Part-time Service
(6 AM – midnight)
©2002 Metropolitan Transportation Authority Unauthorized duplication prohibited
80602

Please check our website
www.mta.info often for latest
service changes.
New York City Transit
Manhattan
Bus Map
September 2002
LEGEND
All Day Service (Every day 7AM - 10PM)
Part-time Service
Direction of Service (two-way service has no arrows)
Full-time Terminal
Part-time Terminal
BRONX
QUEENS
BROOKLYN
HUDSON RIVER
EAST RIVER
Bx19 to Botanical Gardens via Southern Blvd
Bx33 to Port Morris/Walnut Av -132 St
Bx15 from Fordham Plaza
Bx15 to Fordham Plaza via Third Av
60 to LaGuardia Airport
Q102 to Astoria Astoria Blvd - 8th St Operated by Queens Surface Corp
Q32 to Jackson Heights 81 St - Northern Blvd
Q60 to Jamaica 109 Av - 157 St; Operated by Green Bus Lines
Q101 to Astoria 19 Av - Hazen St; Operated by Queens Surface Corp
B39 to Washington Plaza, Williamsburg; connection with B24,B40,B44, B46, B60,B61, Q54, Q59
B51 to Fulton Mall, Downtown Brooklyn